THE OFFICIAL®
PRICE GUIDE TO

CIVIL WAR

COLLECTIBLES

THE OFFICIAL®
PRICE GUIDE TO

CIVIL WAR
COLLECTIBLES

RICHARD FRIZ

FIRST EDITION

House of Collectibles • New York

Important Notice. All of the information, including valuations, in this book has been compiled from the most reliable sources, and every effort has been made to eliminate errors and questionable data. Nevertheless, the possibility of error, in a work of such immense scope, always exists. The publisher will not be held responsible for losses that may occur in the purchase, sale, or other transaction of items because of information contained herein. Readers who feel they have discovered errors are invited to *write* and inform us, so they may be corrected in subsequent editions. Those seeking further information on the topics covered in this book are advised to refer to the complete line of *Official Price Guides* published by the House of Collectibles.

Published by: House of Collectibles
201 East 50th Street
New York, NY 10022

Distributed by Ballantine Books, a division of Random House, Inc., New York and simultaneously in Canada by Random House of Canada Limited, Toronto.

Manufactured in the United States of America

ISSN:1081-9444

ISBN: 0-876-37951-X

Text design by Holly Johnson
Cover design by Kristine Mills
Cover photo by George Kerrigan

First Edition: September 1995

10   9   8   7   6   5   4   3

Contents

THE OFFICIAL®
PRICE GUIDE TO

CIVIL WAR
COLLECTIBLES

INTRODUCTION

CIVIL WAR MEMORABILIA— A MARKET OVERVIEW

Such is the awesome range of Civil War memorabilia that prices have a yo-yo effect. One related category may be experiencing an all-time low (as coin expert Marc Hudgeons indicates is currently the case in the world of numismatics*), while conversely, a host of other collecting specialties go ballistic, commanding blockbusting prices.

Many observers attribute the kindling of a recent boom in Civil War collecting to Ken Burns' PBS documentary *The Civil War* that attracted 14 million viewers when first shown on the small screen in 1990. Several months after its debut, *U.S.A. Today* reported that a reawakening stirred by the documentary had helped inflate prices for Civil War items by some 25 percent.

The late Brian Riba, whose Wethersfield, Connecticut, auction house had hammered down any number of significant and record-setting Civil War documents, letters, and photographs over the past 10 years, felt that the upswing, or almost magnetic drawing power of such material has been more of a delayed action phenomena, perpetuated by a combination of influences.

There is, for instance, that other mini-series, the riveting *Roots* by Alex Haley, a docudrama that performed wonders in heightening awareness among African Americans of their origins, heritage, and culture.

Followers of the cult of Lincoln point to the 175th anniversary of the Great Emancipator's birth in 1984, which inspired federally funded traveling exhibits and any number of scholarly treatises and tomes.

The following Civil War collecting categories reflect intensive activity and ascendancy to almost beatific status among dealers and collectors alike at recent auctions, shows and exhibitions.

---

*See *The Official Blackbook Price Guide of United States Coins*, published by House of Collectibles.

Photographs—Almost an automatic choice when it comes to market acceptance, vitality, and stability. Only a few daguerreotypes of Lincoln are known. When a ¼ plate dag of a beardless (c. 1860) image presented by Lincoln himself to a Harriet Chapman (from the A. Conger Goodyear collection) came on the block at Riba's in March of 1984, it quickly shot up to $16,000. At the time this dag, the only known example in private hands, proved to be the second highest price dag ever sold at auction.

In October 1994, at Swann Gallery, New York City, over 600 lots of photographs yielded a number of Civil War gems. An Anthony Berger oval albumen 1864 portrait of Lincoln in the "Brady Chair" (basis for a cropped image that appeared on the $5 bill) sold at $6,000 as did an oval albumen Brady print of a seated Robert E. Lee, dated 1865. A leading museum purchased still another Brady image of Gen. Wm. T. Sherman and his generals, from the Andrew Burgess Collection, fiercely contested at $5,400.

Manuscripts including letters, diaries, official documents—Lincoln's birthday anniversary in 1984 saw a document auction record eclipsed as a signed Lincoln copy of the Emancipation Proclamation brought a stunning $297,000 at Sotheby's in New York with Malcolm Forbes the top bidder.

In November 1994 at Superior Gallery, a Society of Cincinnati certificate (an organization later active in the South during the Civil War) signed by George Washington in 1789, along with a Society medal, commanded $45,000. A 13th Amendment document proposing the abolition of slavery, dated February 1865 and signed by Hannibal Hamlin (vice president under Lincoln, but at the time a member of the U.S. Senate) and Secretary of State Forney and 104 members of the 38th Congress, tallied $26,000 (both entries were from the estate of the eclectic Paul Richards).

Last spring at Riba's a pair of presidential signed naval commissions, one by Lincoln in '64, the other by Andrew Johnson in '67, each brought $6,000. Also at Riba's, another gem—a mere scrap of paper, but printed in scrolled type at the top was "Headquarters Mosby's Battalion." The card attested that "Albert G. Lyon is an enrolled member of this command." Signed in cursive by Maj. John Singleton Mosby it proved the Grey Ghost lives on, at a memorable bid of $7,000. Finally, in what was to be Riba Auctions final sale in July 1994, a Jefferson Davis "reward" broadside, accusing him of having "incited and concerted the assassination of Lincoln and the attack on Mr. Seward" found favor at $14,000.

In November 1994 at Eldred's in East Dennis, Massachusetts, a Lincoln signed letter concerning the appointment of a hospital chaplain handily surpassed estimates at $8,000.

Prints and Broadsides—Among 7,000 or so images created by the prolific Messrs. Nathaniel Currier and James Ives, at least 100 prints relate to Civil War battles and leading generals, admirals, and statesmen, as well as offer sentimental, often treacly vignettes from the home front.

Currier and Ives prints in every category have doubled, even tripled, over the past few years. A large folio, *Life of a Hunter, A Tight Fix,* topped-off at a scintillating $57,500 in 1993 with noted dealer/collector Paul

Richards the winning bidder. Ironically, following Richards' untimely passing last year, 670 Currier and Ives prints from his collection were subsequently resold at Collector's Sales & Services in Enfield, Connecticut, in November 1994, and *Life of the Hunter* took an appreciable dip, closing at $40,000.

Rated among the consensus Top 50 (also among the top prices realized) are such vibrant Civil War favorites as the large folio *Splendid Naval Triumph on the Mississippi*; small folio *Terrific Combat Between the Monitor & Merrimac*; and *Hon. Abraham Lincoln*. A large folio, *Terrific Engagement Between "Monitor" 2 Guns, and "Merrimac" 10 Guns in Hampton Roads*, brought $1,000 at the Richards estate sale.

Print authority Frank Donegan, writing in *Americana Magazine*, has a solution for those who find that Currier and Ives prints have gone prohibitively expensive: "There are any number of far less banal and meritricious steel and copper plate engravings [that] invariably display a higher standard of printmaking." What Donegan alluded to are the superb Civil War poster and print renderings by such eminent period lithographers as Kurz & Allison, Chicago; Strobridge & Company, Cincinnati; A. Hoen, Baltimore; John H. Bufford, Washington, D.C.; Louis Prang & Co., Boston; and Wagner & McGuigan, Thomas Sinclair, and P.S. Duval & Son, all of Philadelphia.

Playing Cards, Games and Toys—*Prices of Civil War–era playing cards, games, toys, banks, and other playthings of the past are swirling ever upward in a wave of thematic cross-currents: military, black, political, folk art.* At Noel Barrett's recent sale of the Leonard Schneir collection of Playing Cards in New Hope, Pennsylvania, the sale's most manic bidding focused on a meticulously drawn, hand-painted Confederate playing card set, c. 1864, by William Aiken Walker. Validated as original works of art by the noted Southern artist, this set bore a marked resemblance to a Walker deck featured in the June 1967 *American Heritage Magazine*. At the time the article was written, the folk art–like playing cards were assumed to be unique. A French collector flew all the way from Paris to ante up $28,000 and win the deck. Also in the Schneir collection, a deck of *Monitor & Merrimac* cards by Andrew Daugherity, New York, in original wrapper, c. 1865, sold at $3,600; a pair of opposing sides decks by Mortimer Nelson, New York, c. 1863, fetched $2,000 for the set of Confederate generals and $1,700 for the Union general set. A later vintage deck, *National Cards*, by B.W. Hitchcock, New York, c. 1883, featuring both Abraham Lincoln and Chester A. Arthur as picture cards, far exceeded estimates at $3,100.

In the summer of 1992, Barrett sold the vintage game collection of Herb Siegel, arguably the finest of its kind ever assembled. Among the superb Civil War/black-related board games and educational toys, many were unlisted and unfamiliar to most of even the most advanced board gamers gathered at the preview.

Two lotted card games in the Siegel collection game sale at Barrett's brought $750 for the pair. The first, an 1859 *New Military Game* by G.W. Fisher of Rochester, featured hand-colored cards and a Union infantryman on the box cover; the second, *Commander of Our Forces* by E.C. Eastman, Concord, New Hampshire, c.1863, offered vignettes of Zouaves and the climactic battle between the *Monitor* and the *Merrimac*.

An unusual "Circular Coon" deck, c. 1900 by Hartley Bros., New York, entailed each card being lithographed on circular pieces of tin with cartoon imagery reflecting blatant racist stereotypes. Bidding intensity for this deck was a strong indicator as to the vigor of the black Americana market. It quickly transcended estimates on the way to $1,400.

Among the other highlights of the sale:

A c. 1891 *Game of Strategy* (a backgammon-type game) by McLoughlin Bros. with strong imagery on the lithographed box of a Union cavalry in full charge, rose to $500.

A c. 1891 McLoughlin chess-type game called *Skirmish at Harper's Ferry*, with colorful lithograph box depicting Union forces converging from opposite sides of a river, sold at $700.

A real "sleeper" c. 1870s by Oakley and Mason, *Parlour Monuments to Illustrious Dead*, consisted of lithographed paper on wood blocks with images of Washington and Lincoln (including a maudlin casket view) and text referring to Lincoln and the Emancipation Proclamation with words of praise in Negro dialect. This very early piece brought $550.

A Milton Bradley Historiscope, *Panorama of America #1*, with a hand-colored reel of Civil War images, one of the few "steals." The replaced knobs curtailed it at $350.

A Myriopticon *Historical Panorama of Rebellion*, also by Bradley, included scenes of the firing on Fort Sumter and Sherman's burning of Atlanta. It managed $475 despite replaced scrollers.

A vibrant litho paper on wood *Fort Sumter Target Game* by W.S. Reed, with a marble-firing cannon and a number of wood toy soldiers (not original to toy) went for an amazing $2,200.

MacLaughlin Bros.' *Game of the Watermelon Patch*, a variation of the classic fish pond game, with watermelons "fished" out of the patch, sold at $1,200.

Anglo Game Go. (under Parker Brothers license) *The Cakewalk Game*, a race track type board contest, showing black couples dancing in all their finery: $2,000.

The McLoughlin Bros.' *Bulls & Bears: The Great Wall St. Game* sold for a memorable $28,000.

Mechanical Banks—These, often commanding a king's ransom lately, are indisputedly the most recession-proof toy category (or any *other* antique or collectible category for that matter). Prices have escalated dramatically by at least 35–40 percent since the landmark Edwin Mosler sale in 1982, according to the bank folks, and are verified by auction figures.

Civil War–related and ethnic banks have performed at their peak in recent times. The *Octagonal Fort* far exceeded expectations at Christie's Seamens Bank Collection sale in New York, selling for $5,000. From that same sale, a frog-bodied *Gen. Butler* caricature still bank also tallied $5,000, and a unique brass mold for producing the *Tammany Bank* (lampooning Boss Tweed and corruption in U.S. Grant's administration) brought $9,200. The John Harper (Eng.) *Dinah* ethnic bank sold for $1,000

At Bertoia-Brady's Norman collection outing in Philadelphia late in '91, a mint example of the Tammany bank itself brought $5,500, while an Artillery Bank in its original box quadrupled estimates at a resounding $22,000. Kaiser & Rex *Mammy & Child* made $10,000 and the J.&E. Stevens *Darktown Battery* scored an individual high of $17,000. (No *Darktown* example had ever brought more than $5,200.)

The sale of the Norman collection boasted an astounding total of 29 mechanical banks hovering at or beyond the $20,000 mark. Time after time, new plateaus were achieved for banks of specific patent and manufacturer.

At the Joe Levy bank collection sale by Brady & Bertoia in December 1993, a mad scramble ensued for a *Jolly Nigger* bank (usually euphemistically referred to as the "N" bank) on pedestal, a virtually mint presentation piece from J.&E. Stevens foundry employees, engraved "To Mr. Stevens," the firm's president. Peaking at $8,500, it shows there are no holds barred for an item that unique and special (even though of questionable taste).

Painted Clockwork Tinplate Toys—The good news/bad news syndrome clearly applies to anything Civil War–related in this class. Rating right near the top as to quality, ingenuity, desirability—they're also among the priciest.

A real tongue-twister, the dashing Zouave Autoperitatetikos (or walking Zouave), c. 1862 by Enoch R. Morrison, is reputedly (along with a lady doll version) the first mechanical toy produced in America. Roller-type projections under the shoes enable the figure to lurch along. At the spring 1991 Tom Anderson collection sale at Noel Barrett's, a *Zouave*, including original box with instruction label, made $3,600. A trio of clockwork tinplate shuffling figures in cloth mufti produced in 1875 by Arthur E. Hotckiss also qualify as Civil War/black Americana–related. At the Anderson sale, a *Gen. Benj. Butler* brought $4,000 (an example in the 1990 Bernard Barenholtz sale reached $10,500); an elusive *Democratic Donkey* (supposedly modeled from the Thomas Nast caricature) sold for $20,000; and an *Old Black Joe* (a.k.a.*Uncle Tom*) went for $21,000. The *General Grant Smoking a Cigar* Ives (1876) clockwork toy—also classified as an automaton due to its intricate multiple action—is accorded the honor as centerpiece for even the most advanced collection. When wound the seated general raises an arm, puts a cigar in his mouth, then withdraws the cigar and exhales smoke rings. A real plus with the Anderson entry was its mahogany platform base with "Fort Henry 5¢ Segars" in gold stenciling on front, indicating it may have served as a tobacconist's trade stimulator. This example sold for $20,000, the exact amount another example brought in Acevedo's Bernard Barenholtz tag sale a few years earlier.

The only Civil War period Lincoln toy, to our knowledge, is a winner: an articulated lithographed paper on pasteboard with glass front sand toy, *Lincoln Hurdy-Gurdy*, c. 1862 by Gerrard Calgani. When activated, Lincoln cranks the music box while Gideon Welles, Lincoln's secretary of the navy with the body of a monkey, strums a fiddle and dances on a table to the delight of several youngsters. A restored example of this satirical classic brought $5,000 at Acevedo's Barenholtz sale.

Massachusetts dealer Rex Stark's summer 1994 fixed price catalog served up a C.S.A. novelty hand carved in bone that may well be a veteran's memento c. 1880s. The 6" x 6" x 3½" multicolor toy features a be-whiskered artilleryman in kepi seated atop a box marked "Artillery." The lid flips up to reveal a small bone cannon with spring plunger that fires clay marbles. Unique and whimsical, it was priced at $1,500.

To our knowledge, only one major collection of Afro-American memorabilia has come to auction—the 1,135 lot Edgar and Donna Orchard collection at Rick Opfer's in Timonium, Maryland, in February 1993. Among the engaging tin minstrel windups, the topper was *Jazzbo Jim Ham & Sam, the Minstral Team* by Ferdinand Strauss at $825, and the multi-action Louis Marx *Charlestown Trio* at $550. A late nineteenth-century cap bomb of a black man with caved-in stove pipe hat made a strong $350.

A highpoint for many in Bertoia-Brady's $1.7 million "Something for Everyone" auction in October 1993 was the black memorabilia toy collection of Glenn and Linda Smith. A pair of antebellum clockwork gems by Ives, *Women's Rights Advocate* (based on Civil War abolitionist Sojourner Truth) and *Political Stump Speaker,* sold at $9,500 and $6,000 respectively (a minor disappointment, but not bad, in lieu of a thin, if not anorexic market at the time). A pair of minstrels by Jerome Secor, *The Banjo Player* and *Tambourine Player,* sold to the tune of $23,000 and $35,000, new records for the elusive pair. (See "Toys and Games" section for prices realized of other premier examples from this auction.)

The "holy grail" of all toys and mechanical banks by almost every account is the *Freedman's Bank* manufactured by Jerome Secor and distributed by Ives, Blakeslee & Co., c. 1880. When a coin is fed into the toy, a black Freedman figure seated at a desk sweeps the penny into a slot with his left hand, and derisively thumbs his nose with his right. One of Lincoln's final acts in 1865 was to establish the Freedman's Bureau within the War Department to aid newly freed slaves. The Bureau was riddled with corruption and proved highly unpopular, particularly in the South. The exalted bank was pricey, even in its day, advertised for $4.50. Only a handful are known to collectors and the last example, offered at the Leon Pearlman Museum collection "Great Grab" of 1988 (Alex Acevedo's glorified tag sale), brought a stunning $250,000. Chances are, if a *Freedman's* becomes available, it will change hands privately. If offered at auction, most observers feel it would command at least a half million dollars. The late Andrew Emerine, a legend in the hobby, once ran a classified ad for the *Freedman's* in a hobby magazine. He enjoyed relating that a librarian in Mexico City responded to the ad, and Emerine purchased a superb specimen for all of $11.

Civil War Uniforms and Accouterments—Insatiable demand intensified by growing ranks of re-enactors has certainly hyped this category. At a November Auction of military goods at Paul Dias Auctions in Hanson,

Massachusetts, the day's high achiever, a bright green wool Berdan's Sharpshooter kepi out of a New Hampshire estate, went for an amazing $6,500. A Union 5th Cavalry Hardee hat, replete with eagle side emblem and feather plume, excelled at $2,100. Probably the most elusive of all military livery are C.S.A. navy and marine frock coats, with a price of $25,000 not considered outrageous.

Firearms—Indisputably, the most significant sale within recent memory of Civil War firearms, edged weapons, and accouterments took place on July 4, 1994, at Conestoga Auctions in Lancaster, Pennsylvania. Consigned from the estate of noted Texan William A. Bond, the collection entailed over 40 years of consummate selectivity. Through the years, Bond had acquired the vast majority of this veritable arsenal of over 700 entries from three legends in the hobby—Norm Flayderman, Bill Albaugh, and Red Jackson. The heaviest concentration was in the ever-elusive and highly coveted Confederate weaponry. A highlighting of the more desirable longarms at the two-day Contestoga outing follows (see "Weapons" section for more detailed listing):

A Palmetto Armory M 1842 C.S.A. musket . . . . *$5,750.*
A Cook & Bro., Athens, Georgia, dated 1863 C.S.A. two-band rifle . . . .
. . . . *$16,000* (over twice top estimate.)
Early type M 1855 C.S.A. Fayetteville two-band rifle. . . . . *$14,500.*
Tyler, Texas, two-band rifle, .54 cal., C.S.A. . . . . *$15,500.*
Bilharz, Hall rising breech carbine, C.S.A. . . . . *$16,000.*
Richmond, Virginia, Sharp's carbine, C.S.A. . . . . *$9,500.*

Butterfield & Butterfield's sale in San Francisco of the fabled Alan S. Kelley firearms collection last July set the hobby agog when an "E" Co. Colt No. 120 1847 Walker model percussion revolver—the finest military Walker known—realized $170,000. A world record was set at $18,000 for a box of .44 cal. Henry rifle cartridges (only one of four known).

Few of the major players at the Bond sale came prepared for the rapid fire salvo of bids for a trio of coveted revolvers that pushed prices beyond estimates.

A Cofer (Portsmouth, Virginia) Serial number 1 percussion revolver and a Columbus, Georgia, revolver each made . . . . *$77,750.*
Colt Walker Model 1847 percussion C Company No. 31 reached . . . . *$27,500.*
L.E. Tucker Navy revolver, .36 cal. with name of officer and date "1864" lightly inscribed on cylinder . . . . *$45,000.*
Colt Holster Model No. 5 Paterson with belt, holster, service records of C.S.A. Capt. (& Texas Ranger) Wm. M. Lowe . . . . *$70,000.*
Even a fake Schneider & Glassick iron-frame revolver "essentialy unlike the three known and accepted brass frame products of S&G" managed *$5,500*

Union Colt army and Navy revolvers exact higher prices—$1,500–2,500 in *good condition*. Other U.S. hand guns are more reasonable at $350–800. C.S.A. examples usually start at $2,000 or more, and can escalate rapidly in the $5,000–7,000 price bracket. C.S.A. rarities such as the Cofer Percussion

Model (Thos. Cofer, Portsmouth, Virginia; less than 10 survive) and the Schneider & Glassic (Memphis, Tennessee) Navy six-shooter (only three known) assuredly will bring outer orbit prices when offered on the market.

Most gunsmen rate an average Union issue longarm in the $750–1,500 range; C.S.A., $3,500–5,000.

Anyone fortunate to own a Symmes under-lever breech carbine with dropping block, however, could name his own price. This also holds true for a C.S.A. Tallassee, Alabama, carbine which may readily reach $50,000.*

Swords, Sabers, Cutlesses—Swords have straight blades; sabers are curved; cutlesses are short sabers. A few Bond sale high points:

Boyle & Gamble Presentation C.S.A. foot officer's sword with scabbard by W.T. Edge, Richmond, ". . . to Capt. J.S. Michard by Co. E., Aug. 1863". . . . . . *$24,400.*

Leech & Rigdon staff and field officer's sword with scabbard. *$13,000*

L. Haimin Presentation field officer's sword with scabbard, by L. Haiman, Columbus, Georgia. L.L. Gray over C.S.A. in panel. *$2,000*

Sharp & Hamilton (Nashville, Tennessee) Cavalry saber with scabbard. . . *$10,500.*

Union issues rate in the $350–1000 range; C.S.A. edged weapons are known to command three or four times that price, when they appear "correct." In fact, most C.S.A. blades hover in the $2,500–5,000 range. Swords with ornately engraved patriotic symbols and inscriptions and special scabbards and presented to officers (usually for devotion to duty or heroism under fire) often exceed six figures.

Flags—Last year, at Brian Riba Auctions in Connecticut, a swallowtail guidon (small pennantlike banner) of homespun wool with stitched crossed sabers, authenticated as young Union 3rd Cavalry officer George Armstrong Custer's first personal flag, went sky high at $40,000.

Upstaging even the gun lobby at the Conestoga Auction was a mounted and framed Army of Northern Virginia battle flag, from the Bill Albaugh collection. "Captured by 18 Mass. Regt. from 27 S.C. Regt. Aug 21, 1861" inked in on white border next to sleeve. It was catalogued as 95 percent intact, with colors bright and vivid, and handily shattered auction records at $67,000. The battle flag was acquired by a historic site foundation for a museum under development in Dinwiddie, Virginia.

A C.S.A. First National Pattern Flag with 11 applied stars, captured from a Confederate battery near Acquia Creek by the Union Navy in a night assault, provided a fitting coda to the Bond sale at $20,000.

Many post-war U.S. flags are being foisted on the collecting world as stemming from the 1860–65 period, so they should have *no more than 33 or 34 stars*. Many guides rate them at $150 to $500 but we've seen them sell for a lot higher recently. Union artillery guidons and company flags will run from $1,500–2,000; brigade, division, and other identifiable flags: $2,000–3,000; regimental battle colors: $4,000–6,000.

---

*Prior to the Macon Arsenal issuing the carbines to C.S.A. troops, it was captured by the Union, and most of the Tallassees were believed to be destroyed.

Just as with weaponry, C.S.A. flags are in far shorter supply and run commensurately higher than Union examples. C.S.A. swallowtail pennants normally run $1,500–2,000; Stars and Bars in any pattern: $1,500–3,500; Company colors: $4,000–5,000; and regimental battle colors: $6,000–12,000 (sometimes higher).

HISTORY OF CIVIL WAR MEMORABILIA COLLECTING

To historians, the American Civil War is the great watershed event from which all subsequent history flows. This fratricidal war was the first such conflagration to truly harness industrial technology for killing—a key step in the evolution of warfare from Napoleon to Patton. Today, 134 years from that momentous date when the South seceded from the Union, the Civil War continues to sustain a sense of immediacy and reality. Among scores of current magazines focusing on the Civil War, the masthead of *Blue & Gray* succinctly sums it up: "For Those Who Still Hear the Guns."

Collecting Civil War artifacts had its origins in the late 1860s, following Lincoln's assassination. The nation was gripped in morbid fascination, clamoring for photographs, prints, broadsides, stereo cards, newspapers, and other journals depicting deathbed scenes, the gut-wrenching cross-country funeral procession back to Springfield, and the pursuit, roundup, and punishment of Lincoln's assassins. Ironically, it was to be 34 years after Lincoln's death that a retrospective of Lincoln prints was first exhibited at New York City's Grolier Club, yet collector interest remains at fever pitch to this day.

There were few families across this land who weren't touched in some way by the events of the Civil War. Loved ones of those who fought in the war religiously saved letters, tintypes, daguerreotypes, ambrotypes, and cartes de visites depicting their heroes. As time went on, the stirring battlescene images of Mathew Brady, Alexander Gardner, George Bernard, Timothy O'Sullivan, and other front-line photographers who preserved for posterity these stirring, often devastating events, were especially coveted.

The U.S. Centennial Exposition in 1876 and the Columbian Exposition of 1893 served to rekindle interest in the country's rich patriotic heritage, including the Civil War. The Age of Chromolithography brought mass-produced decorative broadsides, post cards, trade cards, posters, framed prints, and wall hangings into millions of homes.

Over 250,000 Americans are self-described Civil War buffs or "hobbyists" and actively belong to one of the hundreds of Civil War round tables or societies. Union veterans who have convened at regional and national Grand Army of the Republic (GAR) encampments since its founding in 1866 engender a wealth of ribbons, medals, and other relics of their own. The GAR's counterparts, the United Confederate Veterans (UCV); the

Southern Historical Society, founded in 1869; as well as the Sons of Confederate Veterans, created in 1896, were established with the purpose of "preserving and defending the history and principles of The Old South."

Today, travel agencies and airlines offer package tours of Civil War battlefields. Historic battles are realistically staged and restaged, on site, by Civil War re-enactment societies, which have sprung up all over the country with memberships exceeding 40,000. These re-enactors spend hundreds of dollars a year each on replica or authentic uniforms, sabers, and muskets.

Because the Civil War Centennial in 1961 coincided with the most passionate years of the civil rights movement, it lacked the fanfare of the Tall Ships and fireworks of the nation's Bicentennial. Consequently, Americans have never had a chance to be bored by the anniversary.

The Civil War Trust of Washington, D.C., dedicated to the preservation of historic sites and battlegrounds, recently helped save an endangered Mill Springs battle site in Kentucky. There is also an Association for the Preservation of Civil War Sites headquartered in Fredericksburg, Virginia.

One of George Bush's last acts as president was to sign into law the Civil War Battlefield Commemorative Coin Act. It authorizes the U.S. Mint to strike three coins for sale to the public in 1995. Profits go to battlefield preservation.

In late 1994, when the Walt Disney Company announced their plans for a $650-million history theme park on historic land near Manassas National Battlefield Park in Virginia, Civil War historians and citizens groups raised a firestorm of opposition. Their objection: the theme park with its virtual-reality battles would not only desecrate Civil War sites, but trivialize and sanitize American history. Disney has abandoned the Manassas site and put the project on hold.

Dozens of Civil War–related magazines line newsstands. Over 50,000 separate books or pamphlets on the war have been published over the last century and a quarter, with new Civil War titles released by book publishers each year.

Fourteen million Americans viewed the stunning 11-hour TV documentary on PBS, *The Civil War*, in 1990. Reaction to the PBS film reflected a marked division of opinion, falling just where one would expect, on the Mason-Dixon line. Since the silent screen era of D.W. Griffith's *Birth of a Nation* and Buster Keaton's *The General*, movie and TV buffs have flocked to see Civil War–related epics such as *Roots, Glory, Gone With the Wind* (including the sequel), *Raintree County* with Elizabeth Taylor, *The Littlest Rebel* with Shirley Temple, *General Spanky*, an Our Gang one-reeler, ABC's *The Rose and the Jackal*, and *North & South*. The most recent TV event was a mini-series adaptation of Allan Gurganus' stirring best-seller, *Oldest Living Confederate Widow Tells All*. In Vicksburg, Mississippi, a dramatic film presentation titled *The Vanishing Glory* covering the 47-day siege and fall of that city, is shown year-round in a restored downtown theater.

On the technological front, computer software now exists to access regimental information on thousands of Union and C.S.A. Regiments, with officers' names, battle details, and graphic battle statistics. Selected Civil War photographs, normally visible only at the Library of Congress and other institutions, are now available in multimedia CD-ROM.

As for collecting Civil War memorabilia, intense cross-currents of interest are thematically and emotionally intertwined—blacks and slavery, abolitionists, the Ku Klux Klan, Reconstruction, suffrage, and political parties. Transcending the entire spectrum, however, is the cult of Lincoln. Once considered the nation's most unpopular and despised president, Abraham Lincoln has come full circle in popularity to become America's (and the entire globe's) most revered and popular folk hero and icon. Anniversaries of Lincoln's birth (the 100th in 1909 and the 175th in 1984) have helped propel prices of Lincoln prints, photographs, and other artifacts to beyond reality.

Collectors of Civil War memorabilia are known to interconnect topically. Various areas of collecting include autographs, photography, glassware, ceramics, weaponry, toys, dolls and games, statuary, philately, sheet music, currency, broadsides, postal envelopes, trade cards, and other ephemera. These various areas most often can be broadly categorized under the following headings:

1. Battlegrounds and Naval Engagements: Alphabetical listings of pivotal battles appear in many sections, including Prints and Photographs.

2. Blacks: Including slavery, abolitionism, suffrage, and other cause items. Underground Railway; Dred Scott Decision; black military units in the war; post-war Reconstruction; Freedman's Bureau items.

3. The Confederacy: a) Material related to nonmilitary aspects: cotton industry and other Southern socioeconomic influences affecting the war; the Secession itself; the setting up of a new government and monetary system under Jefferson Davis; **b)** Military leaders, items with cross-referencing to specific battles. Brief two- or three-line biography after each leader's name.

4. The G.A.R., Southern Historical Society and Sons of Confederate Veterans: Antebellum collectibles, souvenirs from hundreds of national encampments.

5. Ku Klux Klan, Copperhead, No-Nothing Collectibles: Divisive factions which opposed any progress relating to minorities.

6. Lincoln: In reality, a major collecting category in itself—so vast that it merits its own special section. Includes early Springfield law practice and senatorial material; Lincoln-Douglas Debate items as well as items from both 1860 and 1864 presidential campaigns; items relating to Nancy Hanks, Mary Todd Lincoln—the entire Lincoln family; assassination and memorial artifacts.

7. Political: Memorabilia covering political campaigns from 1855 to the antebellum 1870s—from presidents Buchanan through Benjamin Harrison—as they relate to the slavery question.

8. The Union: a) Nonmilitary aspects with items relating to funding, conscripting troops, and slavery issues confronting various Northern states, including border states; Emancipation Proclamation and its ramifications; **b**) Military leaders, with cross-referencing to specific battles; brief biography of each leader.

As an indication of how popular the Civil War era and its collectibles have become, Jeanette Carson, editor of *Black Ethnic Collectibles Magazine*, stated recently in *USA Today:* "Items depicting positive and historical images were prominent at the Black Memorabilia Collectibles Show in Washington, D.C., which drew more than 6,000." And James M. McPherson, Edwards Professor of American History at Princeton University, states: "For better or for worse, the flames of the Civil War forged the framework of modern America." And finally, recently retired editor of *American Heritage Magazine*, Byron Dobell, states: "There has never been a revival of interest in the Civil War, because it has never gone away."

GRADING CIVIL WAR MEMORABILIA

In this guide's panorama of Civil War collecting sub-strata ranging from Advertising to Uniforms, one common denominator profoundly affects the allure, quality, and value of each entry—and that is *condition*.

It has become increasingly obvious in recent auctions and shows that dealers and collectors alike are becoming more discriminating (almost obsessively so). Rigid standards are imposed by various collecting organizations.

To alert you to various defects that detract aesthetically and monetarily, we offer the following acceptability criteria by major collecting categories.

Badges and Other Pinbacks

Brass and tin pinbacks are vulnerable to deep scratches, surface bumps, structural damage, broken solder points, advanced oxidation. Celluloid and paper inserts may be flawed by staining, flaking, and the number one enemy, because it is irreversible—foxing. Items are graded by a system ranging from A+ to E.

With Grade A specimens, the less description the better. In each case, a judgment call was made that the visual impact of the specimen and its physical condition are of superior quality. No obvious marks or flaws are visible. Condition ranges from Essentially Perfect (A+) and Excellent (A) to Nearly Excellent (A-).

Grade B specimens have minor flaws that fall short of grade A condition, but not necessarily flaws that are immediately obvious superficially. Within a range of B+ to B-, these specimens may be regarded as Very Good.

Grade C specimens have more obvious flaws, but in some cases may yet achieve top price, if combined with rarity and desirability.

Grade D specimens would be relegated to a Poor Condition rating, for detractions noted. Collectors regard these items as fill-ins until such time as they can upgrade.

Grade E specimens fail to pass muster in acceptability and have little or no intrinsic value.

Glassware and Ceramics

Glassware and ceramic entries entail few of the grading pitfalls that relate to paper, textile or other fragile Civil War memorabilia. The biggest nemesis to glassware and ceramics is breakage, followed closely by chipping and hairline cracks, although some forms of pasteware will eventually suffer degradation if precautions are not taken. Chips and cracks significantly detract from value, particularly if they are highly visible on an object when displayed. Once again, skilled artisans and glass and ceramic restorers can work wonders in resurrecting a specimen to "as new" condition, with cost the only drawback.

Paper: Advertising, Maps, Prints, Broadsides, Letters, Documents

For convenience, prints, including Currier & Ives, carrry letter designations in four sizes, as follows:

V.S. (Very Small)—up to about 7" x 9"
S (Small)—approx. 8.8" x 12.8"
M (Medium)—approx. 9" x 14" to 14" x 20"
L (Large)—anything beyond 14" x 20"

Imperfections Alert

1. Any tear in the image area (plate, illustration) itself is a serious defect. Margin tears are acceptable. Do not allow three or four tiny margin nips to squelch acquiring any desirable image.

2. Moderate impairments include foxing or mildew staining, acid mat burn, excessive age toning, and brown lines caused by wood backing boards frequently found on old frames. Line creases from folding of letters and documents also may be deemed as not fatal. Although as a buyer, minor flaws may help you strike a better bargain, they should not squelch a possible sale. It should be noted that knockdown prices at auction on items in better preserved condition typically will command prices four times higher than those that were not so well preserved.

3. Major detractions include knothole stains (again from wood backing), silverfish (or other insect) damage, and worm holes. Pass on the item if this damage is extreme and in the image area itself.

4. Prints should not be tacked or glued, wet or dry mounted in any way. The one possible exception: an otherwise badly mutilated print of such rarity that this was a last resort. Otherwise, pass.

5. Paper items such as trade cards, postal covers, and cigar labels that have been glued or pasted into albums can usually be soaked off. If done

carefully, the obverse or image side of the specimen remains unsullied and displayable, although some value is lost due to residual stains on the reverse.

6. Poor centering and poor registration profoundly downgrade value. No recourse here.

7. Little can be done to compensate for lack of color freshness or vibrancy. Fading is due to exposure to the harmful ultraviolet rays of sunlight over the years.

8. With paper specimens that have been repaired with scotch tape, particularly in the image areas, damage is usually irreversible.

9. It *is* possible for a paper specimen to be upgraded as a result of successful, professional restoration. Remarkable wonders have been wrought in this area in recent years. Although the defect may be adroitly masked or ameliorated to present a more pleasing aesthetic effect, and on occasion, a step up in value, the defect remains inherent, and should be listed in any description.

10. Small folio posters or prints have a margin of approximately $^3/_4$". Medium folio: 1" or wider. Large folio: $1^1/_2$" or wider. Currier and Ives authority Robert L. Sargeant estimates that 95 percent of all these prints existing today have their border shaved or trimmed to some extent. In *Currier & Ives in America*, Colin Simkins notes, "Prints with margins trimmed to the illustration are almost worthless." Conversely, in *The World of Currier & Ives*, Roy King and Burke Davis write, "a print that has 'ample margins' has a rarity value of its own."

Many astute prints and documents specialists are wary and steer clear of specimens elaborately mounted and framed. Too often, upon closer scrutiny, the hapless purchaser finds the showcasing hides trimmed margins and images irretrievably wedded (glued) to wood, masonite, or pasteboard backing.

Small folio prints were produced on sheets of paper measuring up to approximately $13^1/_4$" x $17^1/_2$". Since they were not standard frame size, very little thought was given at the time to mat the print to fit. Thousands were summarily trimmed to conform to their more expensive frames. So many Currier and Ives prints exist that measure 10" x 14" that many collectors are under the illusion they have full margins.

Photographs: Daguerreotypes, Ambrotypes, Tintypes, Albumens, Cartes de Visites, Stereographs

These types of early photographs were offered in many sizes, but the standard sizes referred to by collectors and dealers are as follows. These are in terms of approximate plate size and *not* case size.

Whole Plate: $6^1/_2$" x $8^1/_2$"
Half Plate: $4^1/_2$" x $5^1/_2$"

Quarter Plate: 3$^{1}/_{2}$" x 4$^{1}/_{2}$"
Sixth Plate: 2$^{3}/_{4}$" x 3$^{1}/_{4}$"
Ninth Plate: 2" x 2$^{1}/_{2}$"
Sixteenth Plate: 1$^{5}/_{8}$" x 2$^{1}/_{8}$"

Daguerreotypes—Few dags have survived in perfect condition. A dag image is an amalgam of mercury and silver on a silver-coated copper plate. Minor deterioration is to be expected. Many dags on the market today, in fact, leave much to be desired as to condition. Years of neglect and overexposure to light (UV rays) have taken their toll in causing the image to become dark, obscure, spotted, and/or tarnished. Dags with these major flaws have little market value unless of momentous historical or social importance. Additionally, many dags are marred by small patches where image has been abraded away, usually a telltale sign that someone has made the mistake of trying to clean the plate with a cloth.

Dags should never be cleaned with a cloth, silver polish, or similar solution. The preferred method is to rinse both sides of plate in cold running water, gently rocking the image for up to half a minute in a mild solution of instant silver dip. Then re-rinse and immediately blow-dry the image. Do not wipe the plate dry. An excellent reference on cleaning and restoring photographs is *Caring for Photographs*, from the Time-Life Library of Photographs. This book describes how silver tarnish can be removed from a Civil War–era dag using a solution of thiourea and phosphoric acid, both available at chemical supply or photographic stores. You may want to opt to have this done professionally.

Cases. Dags, and often ambrotypes and tintypes as well, were often housed in miniature cases or frames of thermoplastic or gutta perca; a glass sheet covered the image to protect its delicate surface. Cases are often beautifully designed and enhanced with deep relief images of Greek and Roman deities, and floral and patriotic motifs. Those cases, when not cracked or chipped but in presentable condition, can add hundreds of dollars to the value of the plate itself. Casing adds value for two reasons: the preference for work as close as possible to its original state and the design of the case often provides the best clues as to dating the image.

Ironically, in the early twentieth century, dags were still so common that buyers were known to melt down the plates and resell the cases as cigarette or notions boxes.

Ambrotypes—Often referred to as "daguerreotypes on glass," are actually images made with a much different process. (See Photography section.)

By the advent of the Civil War, ambros had become the process in vogue, almost completely supplanting dags. Ambros are, in general, sturdier than dags, less expensive initially, and less valued today. Troublesome glare, typical of dags, was eliminated. Most important, if the back of an ambro appears to be flaking or peeling, the work can be rescued by scraping the shellac and substituting a black paper background.

Tintypes—The least expensive of the three processes, though not as aesthetically appealing or as coveted by collectors. Immensely popular for inexpensive portraiture, tintypes are the most commonly found specimens of Civil War imagery.

To have any value today, a tintype should be smooth and unbent with a clear, crisp image. If surface is overly dark, stained, badly cracked or faded, astute collectors prefer to pass.

Albumens—The combined wet plate/albumen print positive was in almost universal use by the late 1850s and remained the main system for printing positives for almost 40 years. Produced commercially, eliminating the need to prepare each print by hand, albumens quickly caught on. Availability, an advantage initially, poses a problem for collectors today as an unlimited number of prints could be made from a single negative. Albumens are subject to fading and tend to discolor easily, often around the outer edges of the image, creating a halolike effect. Albumen prints are often found cracked, the result of an excessive coating. High quality albumen prints were often toned with gold chloride, a process which imparted a distinctive pleasing warm brown tone—an amost certain sign that the work is a nineteenth-century print.

Carte de Visites (CDVs)—popular with the masses toward the end of the Civil War, CDVs were produced in a standard size 3½" x 2¼" photograph mounted on a 4" x 2½" card. In the United States, cartes focusing on Abraham Lincoln and the Civil War invariably commanded the highest prices. As to condition, most of the same criteria apply as with posters, prints, and other paper specimens. The most desirable cartes are those blessed with pictorial quality; a fine nineteeth-century image by an important photographer is valuable in any size print.

Stereographs—Many of the same condition flaws, lack of clarity, and fading inherent with albumens and CDVs are endemic in stereographs. There is also the added problem of brittleness and bending with torn corners and scratches due to frequent use in the stereoviewer. Evaluating and pricing is tricky with stereographs because of such variables as identity of photographer, the year it was taken (many popular images and sets have been reissued), and also type of photographic print (stereoscopic dags rate supreme in the pecking order).

The size and shape of a stereo card are important factors in determining approximate issue date. As a general rule, any card with square corners, regardless of publisher, probably dates to 1868 or earlier. These cards measure approximately 3½" x 7".

Stamps

Grades of issues most frequently traded are as follows:

Mint. The perfect stamp, unused, with superb centering, otherwise flawless, with original gum (if issued with gum).

Unused. The one drawback may be a hinge mark on reverse or loss of original gum.

Used. A normal stamp that has passed through U.S. or C.S.A. postal system and bears appropriate cancellation.

Cancelled to Order. Not passed through U.S.P.O. channels, but carefully cancelled by the government, chiefly for commemoration. Generally rated as less desirable by collectors.

Major detractions include perforations that cut into design of stamp; stamps that are off-centered with margins varying considerably; a badly separated stamp in which perforations are ragged or torn; and stamps that are heavily hinged, heavily cancelled (smeared and often unreadable), and lightly cancelled (wording and lines are too light to be legible).

Textiles: Ribbons, Banners, Flags

Originally made from silk, and later from cotton and other fabrics, ribbons, though proven more durable than paper, still comprise one of the more fragile of all Civil War–related categories. Designed as bookmarks and lapel devices, ribbons were cut in varying lengths from large bolts of material by hand. Lengths varied from 3" to 12". Length, therefore, is not as critical here, as long as there are adequate margins at top and bottom. Most early ribbons were printed from single black-on-white etched copper plate prints. They may actually be off-white, cream, or a number of other colors, depending on the supply of fabric at hand. Weave, dye fading, and state of preservation play a major role in grading.

The fragile nature of ribbons and banners and vulnerability to such perils as staining, tearing, rubbing, and fading make each specimen a special case. Certain varieties are practically unobtainable in any grade above "Good." The "unique" condition of each ribbon is thus predicated on a number of combination of factors. Ribbons, banners, and flags fall into six basic grades.

Mint. Clean and crisp with no perceptible defects interfering with content.

Excellent. Very few defects, extremely clean; an above-average specimen.

Good. Defects blend into image or don't materially detract from appearance.

Average. Defects noticeable and affect appearance.

Fair. Several serious highly visible defects.

Poor. Numerous defects, extremely low quality. Most collectors elect to pass on specimens in this state. If extremely rare and available at little monetary investment, it at least fills a void until you can upgrade.

Tokens and Medals

Political, patriotic, and commemorative medals and tokens are chiefly coinlike in nature. Grading criteria here complies with American Numismatic Association standards for coins.

Uncirculated. Specimens have no trace of wear but may display a number of contact marks; surface may be spotted or lack some luster.

About Uncirculated. Show traces of light wear on many of the high points. At least half of the mint luster is still present. Usually designated (AU) and not to be confused with the symbol for gold as an element.

Extremely Fine. Design is lightly worn throughout, but all features remain sharp and well defined.

Very Fine. Shows moderate wear on all high points of design; all major details clean.

Very Good. Well worn, with main features clear and bold, although rather flat.

Good. Evenly worn, with design visible but faint in areas. Many details are flat.

Poor. Numerous defects that substantially alter appearance of specimens.

DISPLAYING, STORING, AND PRESERVING YOUR CIVIL WAR MEMORABILIA COLLECTION

The style and method of displaying and housing a Civil War collection is strictly a matter of taste, personality, imagination, and creative flair.

We know of individuals who, as compulsive accumulators or "pack rats," will stash their treasures away in crates and boxes for an indeterminate "rainy day." At the opposite extreme, there is the Civil War enthusiast who "lives" his hobby, transforming his home or business into a veritable museum or shrine. Civil War memorabilia obviously lends itself to being displayed, admired, and examined at close hand periodically to evoke visions of epic battles and historic decisions that almost shook our nation to its very foundations.

Collectors should be mindful, however, that there are certain constraints to exposing a collection to daily scrutiny in open display areas. Excessive handling, dust, humidity, insects, pollutants, and direct sunlight can all take their toll. If not housed with protection in mind, your collection may depreciate in value or worse, fall victim to irreversible damage.

To avoid extended exposure to the above degrading elements, many Civil War collectors wisely rotate their artifacts, keeping those items not on display in special drawers, packing crates, and even temperature-controlled vaults. Be aware, however, that cardboard boxes emit a discernible amount of gases and peroxides that can cause fading and loss of detail. Storage boxes of heavy duty acid-free paper are recommended. When storing vertically, boxes should be packed fully, so the items will not curl. Peroxides found in most bleached and uncoated shelf boards can also prove invasive. Since photographs in particular are highly sensitive to new paint, allow at least a month before storing images in a newly painted room.

As to display items, it is generally advisable to avoid special knick-knack shelves, open armoires, and the like and rely instead on fully glass-enclosed bookcases, shelving units, custom built display cases or any of the plexiglass units available today.

To avoid the harmful glare of ultraviolet rays, most conservators and dealers recommend using low-wattage lights or some of the minishelf lights arranged in tandem. These lights show off your treasures to best advantage without distorting colors and tones. This also facilitates distinguishing variants. Fluorescent light would be a second choice, but it will give a slightly off-color cast. Treated plexiglass blocks out harmful UV rays that cause fading. It also is a good idea to locate your display in a part of the room where it will be in the shade during daytime hours.

Posters, prints, and other oversize flat objects, when not framed or hung on the walls, should be stored in the dark or under cover in wood or metal flat files (also known as map, plan, or artwork files), which are readily available from office supply and art supply houses. Remember, though, that a filing system is only as good as its retrieval system, and each print should be categorized, marked with a number or letter designation, and cross-referenced.

Oversize and bound paper collectibles are best stored flat, taking special care to refrain from stacking them so high as to incur damage when retrieving them from a drawer, file or case.

Transparent interleaves and folders made of Du Pont Mylar or a neutral polyester or polythalene also provide protection. Using Kraft paper envelopes, glassine sleeves, cellophane, or Saran Wrap is discouraged because they may interact to affect a lithographic image or, in the case of photographs, mar the emulsion or gradually affect the film's silver.

Philip Zea, a curator at Historic Deerfield in Deerfield, Massachusetts, suggests the following checklist for storing your prized possessions.

Define a specific area for each category.

Catalog each object, using an identifying number and a corresponding card with basic data including description, type of material, specifications, and sources. You may prefer to mark in archival ink or old-fashioned lead pencil. The latter can be easily removed with vinyl eraser, if you so desire. It pays to inventory your collection for a number of reasons, including insurance and appraisal purposes.

Make a seasonal cleaning schedule and stick to it.

Survey your collection at least once a year. Be on the alert for signs of trouble and take immediate steps to remedy the problem.

Be certain that more fragile objects, such as textiles and painted objects, remain in small heated rooms during the winter.

Minimize contact with acidic wood or paper.

Care of Specific Civil War–Related Artifacts

Paper—Noted archivists Tom Norris and Robert Knecht of the Kansas State Historical Society in Topeka offered these precautions concerning ephemera (printed or handwritten paper memorabilia): "Paper likes about

50 percent humidity, much as people do. Environmental control measures need not be extravagant—summer air conditioners and winter heating will generally provide a suitable atmosphere." Norris and Knecht added that dehumidifiers and humidifiers can help too.

Note that archival Civil War material, just as a vintage wine, does not like wild swings in temperature. You may want to invest in special humidity gauges, temperature monitors, alarms, and other devices to protect your valuables. These electronic gadgets are available through any number of catalog houses. Here are a few additional precautions:

Refrain from touching papers or any delicate artifacts as much as possible. Hands carry oil and dirt that can hastily cause deterioration.* Some purists insist on wearing white cotton or polyester gloves when it is necessary to handle materials, whether paper, cloth, or even metal.

Avoid folding paper, whether letters, documents, maps, or prints. It weakens the fibers and eventually fosters rips or tears across the creases.

Place stiff paper, pasteboard, or any material that resists flattening in a humid environment temporarily to help regain resiliency.

Always hold pamphlets, fliers, multiple-page letters, and documents with two hands—one to support, the other to lightly grasp the item and anchor it.

Never resort to paper clips, staples, or rubber bands. Metal fasteners can puncture or crease paper and leave ferrous oxide within paper or cloth fibers. We've seen examples where aged rubber bands have actually fused to the archival specimen.

Avoid using adhesive tape, either cellophane or Magic-Med, to repair or mount items. Enclosing in Saran Wrap invites a chemical breakdown when exposed to air, which leaves stains. Laying items flat in Mylar sleeves or Mylar corner holders are recommended for vertical display.

Never back paper items with high-acid cardboard, plywood, or composition stiffener, which attack delicate paper and textiles. When framing, the item should be mounted in acid-free mat to avoid direct contact with the glass.

Small documents and patches on larger ephemera can be cleaned with a vinyl eraser, rubbing lightly and in one direction only, while firmly anchoring paper with other hand to avoid sudden rips. Rubber erasers are known to implant tiny bits of sulphur which unite with moisture and form harmful sulfuric acid.

Glassware and Ceramics—These artifacts are relatively easy to care for, although one must exercise eternal vigilance against cracking and breakage.

When cleaning, use warm soapy water and a little vinegar. Use a plastic, not a metal dishpan. Avoid washing glassware that has enamel paint on its

---

*We were amused to note recently, in a fixed-price catalog, that a signed ambrotype of Stonewall Jackson, with an inky smudged fingerprint in the corner, was attributed to being that of the General himself, in this case, enhancing the value.

surface; we recommend professional conservators, should breakage or cracks occur. Attempting repairs yourself with miracle glues can prove disastrous. As a cautionary storage measure, try to display or store glass and ceramics in areas free from vibration, and allocate plenty of space for each item so that it's not in direct contact with another item. Try to keep handling at a minimum.

Textiles—Appearances are deceiving, but textiles are fragile and as vulnerable to attack as paper. Here again, clean gloves are recommended when handling delicate ribbons, banners, flags, samplers, etc. Avoid storing in plastic bags or in places where extreme temperatures exist. If you must fold a textile, insert acid-free tissues between folds. Flat textiles are best rolled on acid-free tubes for storage. When hanging textiles, always suspend them in the direction of the warp yarns, which are sturdier. A small hand-held vacuum cleaner may be used to clean dust and other matter from small textiles. Place a screen over the fabric and cover the vacuum nozzle with a cloth as you pass it over the fabric, being careful not to touch the screen. Hooked rugs and carpets should be vacuumed in the direction of the pile.

Metalware—Whether it's a cast-iron or tinplate toy, a fine saber, matchsafe, or firearm, here again handling with gloves is highly recommended. Surprisingly, an errant finger or thumb can readily etch an unsightly print on metal.

Cast or Wrought-Iron. When cleaning iron objects, 0000 grade steel wool and a light-grade mineral oil are recommended.

Copper, Brass. It is preferable to clean copper and copper alloys, including brass, with Ball & Ball's Golden Glow. Brasso is not as effective, as it has too much ammonia.

Pewter. It is best to clean pewter with Noxon. Dark, scaled areas will not polish up because the tin in pewter has oxidized, causing a blemish called "tin pest." Refrain from rubbing these areas any further.

Silver. Clean silver with Tarni-Shield and store in treated bags available from jewelry stores. Mothballs retard tarnishing in enclosed areas, but direct contact with silver should be avoided. Never store silver in regular plastic bags. Choose a silver polish with low ammonia content.

Rinse any polished metal, iron excepted, in warm water and Ivory soap to soften old polish residue before applying new polish. Afterward, rinse metalware in denatured alcohol and pat dry.

Avoid cleaning cast-iron toys, banks, and paperweights with soap detergent solutions. This is true even of painted items that remain perfectly bonded. Instead, use a clean cloth with a few drops of light machine oil, exerting very little pressure. Containers such as advertising and commemorative tins and bins, tin signs, tin toys, tin pinbacks, and all lithographed examples, can normally be cleaned safely with water and a mild detergent. Many recommend Murphy Oil, readily available at your nearest supermarket.

If a question arises as to advisabilty of using a specific cleaner on a lithograph tin, take a cotton swab dipped in the cleaner and test it in some hidden or inconspicuous place before tackling the entire tin. Murphy's has also proven effective in cleaning early lithographed game boxes and lithographed paper-on-wood toys. Here again, extreme caution is advised.

Leather—Leather saddles, boots, belts, sheaths, and leather-bound books stay well preserved and free from cracking by applying Lexol (potassium lactate) or Neet's foot oil on occasion. Apply to surface, wipe away excess, leave overnight and buff lightly the next day. When working with leather book bindings, insert barriers to prevent oil from having any contact with paper pages.

In the care, display and storage of Civil War artifacts, the best advice is the least interference the better. It is wiser to keep an object as close to its existing state as possible. Cosmetic touchup might make the object appear as new, but is often frowned upon by purists, and can actually depreciate its value.

Deerfield Museum Curator Philip Zea offers this salient conclusion: "Know what you *don't* know and ask for help. Professionals at regional conservation centers, large museums, and state historical societies are willing to give you the benefit of their experience."

Civil War Memorabilia Reproduction and Fantasy Detection Alert

In seventeenth-century England, the city of Birmingham became such a hotbed for counterfeit groats (or coins) that the term "brummingen" (a bastardization of "Birmingham") applies even today to define anything that is showy and cheaply contrived—a copy of the genuine article. At least since 1889, the centennial of George Washington's first inaugural, copies of reproductions have infiltrated the political and patriotic collecting hobby.

The pursuit of Civil War artifacts is addictive, and a veritable army of compulsive acquisitors add up to a multimillion dollar business. Today, in category after category, as collecting fever heats up and demand far exceeds supply, collectors and dealers are being taken to task over the onerous three R's: Reproductions, Repaints, and Replacements of parts, figures, and other trappings. These unfortunate incursions appear in a number of guises that merit clarification.

Reproduction—An item similar to, if not almost an exact clone of, the originally produced item, but issued subsequent to the period in which the artifact originated.

Authentic Reproduction—Pure doubletalk, often used in ads and promotions by so-called copycats, signifying nothing. If something is authentic in the legitimate sense, it is *not* a reproduction, and vice versa.

John Simon once stated in *Esquire*, "An authentic reproduction strikes me as not far removed from a genuine sham."

Fantasy—An original item, not a copy of a pre-existing artifact, giving every appearance of dating back to a specific year or era, but issued years later. Most fantasies rate as not being intentionally deceptive and are often commemorative in nature.

Rerun—An item completely reissued at a date subsequent to the original issue. Sole motive here seems based on exploiting the collector market.

Alteration—A recognized item, "doctored" or transformed into another incarnation or state, immediately bracketing it into a rarer classification. In the realm of coins, abnormalities arising from post-striking damage, intentional or accidental, and doctored into novelties are knows as phantoms.

Repainting and Retouching

Even when cleverly done, it is virtually impossible to perfectly match vintage paint with today's paint because of pigment variances. Many collectors feel cosmetic altering enhances the item aesthetically. It is when the item is resold that the ethical question arises. As a general rule-of-thumb, a repaint is valued about 50 percent less than an all-original.

A black light test easily differentiates: original red, for example, appears as olive green under the light; new paint will likely appear as bright orange. Areas of retouching become clearly apparent. The following *"Bogus Alert"* applies to a few known offenders and pretenders.

• Civil War newspapers. A number of bogus issues are known—particularly those dealing with pivotal battles, such as the 1st Battle of Bull Run, Antietam; momentous events, such as Lincoln's Gettysburg Address in 1862 and the inundation of editions announcing Lincoln's assassination in 1865.

Dealer Eric Caren of Caren Archives, Lincolndale, New York, cautions to watch for copies of the front page of the *New York Herald* that carried Lincoln's demise, reprinted for the 1892 Columbian Exposition as a promotional stunt. Sufficiently yellowed and aged, they often pass for the real thing. Watch particularly for spurious C.S.A. copies: a July 4, 1863 wallpaper edition of the *Vicksburg Daily Citizen* has been reproduced, as well as an August 9, 1862 *Chattanooga Rebel* edition. Reprinted in the early 1890s, they occasionally have fooled even the experts. Caren states that legitimate editions of Union newspapers can often still be found for under $10; the far rarer C.S.A. newspapers, however, start at a minimum of $75–100.

• Posters and broadsides. Currier and Ives reproductions exist from the 1940s and are easily detected by a pattern (known as moray, and easily seen under magnification) of multicolored geometric rings and dots, and a size (smaller) differential. In some cases, the title of the repro is inconsistent with the original.

• The telltale dots are also evident in a black-and-white "Workingman's Banner" campaign poster for U.S. Grant and Henry Wilson from the '72 race.

• A commemorative admission ticket to Andrew Johnson's impeachment proceedings on March 1, 1868, is marked "Reproduction 1974," in tiny letters just before the lower margin. If someone offers you a "trimmed" version, beware, as it's the reproduction, not the genuine article.

• Cast-iron mechanical banks have been reproduced, notably the *Artillery Bank* and its *Union and Confederate* variants. World Book Encyclopedia Bank repros, issued in the 1950s, have their logo cast on the base underside, and are slightly smaller than originals. Numerous bronzelike figural still banks have been issued featuring bust likenesses of Lincoln, Robert E. Lee, and Grant. All these specimens are actually painted slush-cast metal versions and hail from the nineteenth century (produced as late as the '60s) and *not of the period*. Recently we were called by a lady who had found an Uncle Sam Bank in her attic, and wanted to know if it was legitimate. When questioned further, she indicated that the word "Taiwan" was stamped in the back. Enough said!

• Cast-iron figural match safes featuring Horace Greeley and U.S. Grant have been "copied" in recent years. The bogus versions have the bust image wired to the back plate; originals are riveted. A grainy surface "feel" and the inscription "Lb 77/3" on the reverse also betray a bogus specimen.

• Badges and medals. Fortunately, Civil War-era badges have thus far escaped attempts at cloning (the cost to replicate would prove prohibitive). Watch for "doctoring," however. Look for signs of mismatched metal, new solder, replaced pins or other cosmetic tampering. An engaging fantasy badge, picturing John Fremont, is often mistakenly identified as "of the period." In reality, it was issued by the National Republican League in 1906 to commemorate the G.O.P.'s 50th anniversary, and was not intentionally deceptive.

• We frequently are asked to appraise political pinbacks or cels, and are amazed by the number of collectors who are fooled by imposters (and not very authentic looking copies at that!).

A good rule of thumb is that any celluloid or lithographed button picturing any president prior to William McKinley's campaign in 1896 is a repro or commemorative item produced at a much later date. These unintentional fakes were issued as election-year advertising premiums or giveaways by such firms as Boraxo, Kimberly Clark AMOCO, Procter & Gamble, Kiberty Mint, Crackerbarrel (a mail order firm), and General Motors, among others in the 1960s and '70s.

• As to medals, noted authority Edmund B. Sullivan, in his introduction to *American Badges and Medalets*, states, "Reproductions continue to be a serious concern. Washington 'inaugurals' are the artifacts most frequently copied. But collectors must also be on the alert for reproductions of early Jefferson and John Quicy Adams medals." Where repros are known to exist, Sullivan cites examples in the footnotes; there are several Lincoln and other Civil War–related medals that bear scrutiny.

• Photographs. Many Civil War paper photographs are copies, actually photographs of photographs. They lack clarity and contrast and are worth only about a third as much as an original. Fortunately, they are relatively easy to spot.

• Civil War textiles appear to be relatively immune to cloning, for obvious reasons. Chuck Lawless, however, points out in *The Civil War Sourcebook/A Traveler's Guide* to approach regimental battle flags (particularly the scarce C.S.A. specimens) with caution, "for there are many imitations around."

• Uniforms and weaponry. As might be expected, in lieu of the gathering hordes (recently estimated at over 40,000) of Civil War Battlefield re-enactors, there are simply not enough original uniforms and accoutrements to satisfy the demands. (Only 200 or so C.S.A. uniforms are known to exist in private collections.) Prices have escalated for any conceivable type of Civil War firearm or edged weapon. That's why you'll find sutlers (civilian provisioners to the military) at every major encampment or re-enactment hawking firearms, uniforms, and supplies.

The pages of countless Civil War publications abound with advertisements from firms catering exclusively to collector/re-enactors. Completely outfitting a re-enactor in recent-issue regalia entails an investment of $1,000 or more. We recently noted a Union officer's military coat copy advertised at $199. A reproduction cannon or field carriage will set you back $6,000–8,000. A Confederate D-guard bowie battle knife replica is available at $199. A limited edition (of 250) model hand-engraved, 24-carat-gold-plated Henry Rifle, originally presented to Abraham Lincoln, bears a price tag of $3,995. An Italian-made replica of the 1853 Enfield rifle costs in the $400 range. Another limited edition item (250 issued)—a rather macabre Civil War surgeon's amputation kit—is offered at $875.

• The traffic in swords and saber replicas is especially fast and furious, as well as spurious. Many well-crafted specimens of high-quality carbon steel blades and brass handguards look so authentic even the experts sometimes get taken.

The Ruckus over Firearms

There is no controversy quite so strong as that waged over the manufacture of replica Civil War firearms. Over the past 50 years, leading purveyors of replicas have included Navy Arms Co., Mars Equipment Co., Centennial Arms Corp., and Dixie Gun Works. A number of U.S. firms serve as sales outlets for Belgian and Italian fabricants. William B. Edwards, in *Civil War Guns*, relates how he came to found the Navy Arms Company. His rationale was that replicas fill those "high-priced, vacant gaps in many a collection, and for the modern shooter who wants to try out the old guns." Meanwhile, the collector fortunate to own the genuine article feels that the proliferation of replicas diminishes the value of the original.

The inundation of a veritable arsenal in war surplus weaponry in the late

1860s and '70s creates another dilemma for collectors—without written verification or provenance, it becomes almost impossible to verify a specific firearm or accessory as ever having seen action in the war itself. Leading purveyors, such as Marcellus Hartley (of Schuyler, Hartley & Graham) and Col. W. Stokes Kirk, peddled surplus equipment all over the globe before a committee to investigate sales of arms, headed by ex-vice-president Hannibal Hamlin in 1872, shut off the golden flood. Hamlin's charges that "sales in such large numbers seriously impaired the defense capacity of the country in time of war" led to Congress imposing drastic restrictions on arms trafficking. Well into the twentieth century, however, firms such as White Bros., New York City, and Francis Bannerman & Sons of Hudson, New York, were still selling surplus equipment to a fare-thee-well.

How to Avoid Fakes

Today, thanks to computer generated imagery and laser techniques, we need to be more vigilant than ever before. Getting stung is a blow to the ego, as well as the pocketbook. Do not be discouraged or dismayed by tales of intrigue and a tangled web of deception woven through the years. Fortunately, there are only a few simple rules to follow to avoid all that.

1. Watch Price. A "low-ball" price that appears incredibly out of line for an item you know to be uncommon may appeal to your baser instincts in taking advantage of a real bargain, but it's the first "red flag" that the item might not be authentic.

2. Assert yourself and don't hesitate to consult a dealer, auctioneer, or other seller about his or her knowledge of the item's provenance. A second opinion, especially from one whose reputation you trust implicitly, never hurts and may prove quite revealing.

3. Transact business only with dealers, auction houses, or fellow collectors who are known to be reputable and will back up any item they sell you. It is not uncommon these days to ask the seller to include a written guarantee of authenticity.

4. Many specialized publications in the trade regularly feature "Repro Alerts" as to recent incursions in the market. Follow these alerts religiously and clip articles for future reference.

5. Train yourself and your "third eye" to become almost instinctive in the appraisal and selection process. A high degree of perception can be attained through knowledge and experience. Meyric Rogers, an eminent antiques authority, was known to preface his antique buying forays by first taking a swing through the American wing of the Metropolitan Museum to get his eye accustomed or attuned to quality authentic pieces.

While you may not always have immediate access to a large collection of your specialty, there is invariably a treasure trove of books, early catalogs, flyers, newspaper and magazine clippings, and other reference material that one can consult. Area and national historical societies, libraries, G.A.R. and U.C.V. chapters, and collecting societies are other possible resources.

How to Use This Guide

All entries in this book are grouped alphabetically by category. Within each category are further subentries, also in ABC order. Material relating to battles, famous personages, and events is also alphabetized, as are the surnames of individuals.

When a group photo or print, cartoon, etc. is cataloged, we have attempted to alphabetize it under what we feel to be the most significant personage in that group, i.e., "General Robert E. *Lee* and General Staff on Eve of Gettysburg."

In instances where a personage's name does not appear in the title of the entry in question, the surname of that individual appears alphabetically, but in parentheses. For example, in the Advertising chapter, an entry under the subheading "Signs" might appear as: (*Lincoln*) "*Rail Splitter Cigars. The Great American Favorite. . . .*" This entry would be listed under "L," as opposed to "R."

In instances where memorabilia relates to a specific military unit, it would appear under the first letter of the actual numerical unit, i.e., *Co. "B" 54th Mass.* would appear under the letter "F" for "54th."

In a recent auction catalog of Civil War Weaponry, the brief description "Early Iron Mortar" appeared, which just goes to show what hapless collectors are often up against. If they missed the auction preview, they hadn't a clue as to what was being offered. A number of price guides we know of are just about as vague when it comes to description. It's all reminiscent of the classic Bob and Ray "Wally Ballou Sportscaster" skit, where Wally would rattle off Saturday's football scores, omitting the names of the teams. We want to give you the score and more, so forgive us if some descriptions run long. We feel that solid information gives you better insight and appreciation as to why certain items are valued higher than others. So think of this as being a Civil War "sourcebook" as well as a price guide.

The Prices in This Book

Try to imagine this vast sprawling field of Civil War collecting as one giant battlefield riddled with treasures as well as land mines. What strikes us as an appropriate objective here is taken from an idiom for the word "guide" from *Roget's Thesaurus*: "to set on one's way; to guide you safely through the mine fields."

The author does not subscribe to the old bromide, frequently disguised as a caveat in many price guides, that "the only true barometer of price is the price established between a willing seller and a willing buyer." To obtain prices for this guide, we've been observing and writing about various aspects of Civil War memorabilia for the past 15 years—observing firsthand the various trends and tremors. We've accumulated an extensive reference library of absentee and on-site auction catalogs and dealer price lists, and clipped countless dealer ads from the trade media. We've sought the advice and counsel of a number of leading authorities in their respective fields.

The gamut of citing condition factors in various guides runs from a single given value and no clue to a firearms catalog we noted recently that offers 12 different condition ratings—from 100 percent down to 10 percent. Unfortunately, most auction house listings are not very helpful as to condition—their point being, if you want the item badly enough, you should be on the premises to preview and judge it for yourself.

Consequently, our prices are arranged as follows: *$500–550*. The lower price reflects an entry in *average condition*. A higher value reflects an entry in *above average condition*. As often as we possibly could, we inserted a third value: the *price the entry achieved at auction or fixed price catalog*. Regarding the latter, however, there are still pitfalls since price may have been dictated by such variables as condition, rarity, the prestige of having come from a noted private collection or museum, or even the ego of the bidding participants. Further, no definitive formula exists that we know of to compensate for geographic and market variables. Coupled with price estimates based on condition, however, we think this will give you a clearer picture as to what the entry is worth.

Even so, folks, there has never been a field of collecting quite like Civil War Memorabilia in terms of vastness and complexity, where the value of an item is so open to interpretation.

ADVERTISING EPHEMERA

BOOKLETS

(Benjamin Butler) "Presidential Barn Door Reel/The Widow Takes the Cake." Ca. 1883. Adv.—A.P. Ordway, Boston, MA. Sulphur Bitters. Sepiatone cover illus. has Butler dressed in ladies' clothes dancing a jig while rivals Grant, Hancock, Tilden, and other hopefuls look on glumly. Back cover pictures black abolitionist Frederick Douglas and his wife in front of a pharmacy lined with boxes of bitters.
.... *$75–85*
"Freedman's Bank." 1879–early 1880s. Adv.—Jerome Secor, Bridgeport, CT. Dist. by Ives Blakeslee, NY. Introduces new clockwork-activated mechanical bank depicting black Freedman cashier, who deposits penny with act of defiance, thumbing his nose. Black on light magenta paper. Price, $4.50 each......... *$150–200*

POSTCARDS

Metamorphic cards (2). "Jefferson Davis after Fall of Ft. Sumter, 1861"; Second version same but with "1863" date. David Claypool, 1863. Pull tab to show Davis frowning/smiling; b&w; 4½" × 2¾".............................. *$500–600*

SIGNS

Curtin 5¢ Cigars. Ca. 1880s. Andrew Gregg Curtin bust portrait. Curtin, a Pennsylvania governor, was a staunch Lincoln supporter, raised Pennsylvania militia, provided pensions for veterans. Multicolor 7" × 10" two-side cardboard... *$50–65*
"Garfield Tea/Cures Constipation and Sick Headaches." Garfield Tea Co., Brooklyn, NY. 1880s. Paper poster; black, sepia, and flesh color. *$350–400*
   Garfield Co. also produced packets of Headache Powders ($5–10 ea.). Numerous giveaways were associated with product, including a Garfield Tea folding paper fan ($50–65).
" 'Goodbye, God Spare You' Soldier's Farewell." Ca. 1860s. Cincinnati, Hamilton & Dayton Railway. 17" × 11½" white against black oval background; embossed sign of departing soldier being embraced by sweetheart. Upper left inset of small map of railway. (A) $170. .... *$200–225*
(Benjamin Harrison) Champion Harvesting Machinery. 1880s. The Warder Bush-

nell & Glessner Co., Springfield and Chicago, IL. A formally dressed (in hat and suit) President Harrison sits rather uncomfortably on the seat of a horse-driven mower. A train rolls by in background. Multicolor litho on heavy pasteboard. *$750–800*

Hayes and Wheeler vs. Tilden and Hendricks. "The Republican & Democratic Candidates." 1876. Adv. for Boston Ink Co., Boston, MA. 13½" × 10¼", b&w pasteboard. *$85–100*

"Stonewall Jackson Cigars." Stand-up die-cut embossed tin sign, multicolor, 9½" × 11½". Shaped like a cigar box, with dimensional look; Jackson's portrait on lid as well as on sign with cigars (fake) displayed in the open box. *$350–400*

(Andrew Johnson) "A Big Thing! Great Rush to the Captain's Office." Ca. 1868. B&w 18" × 24" woodblock cartoon print cardboard poster of Johnson, with White House in background, seated by mountain of paper and large bottle of ink by Wells Petroleum Fluid, Philadelphia. He's besieged by Civil War vets and political hacks seeking handouts and appointments. *$1500–1700*

(Lincoln) "A Proclamation by Abraham Lincoln/75,000 Men Wanted. Enlist under One Captain." Ca. 1870s. Clever takeoff on recruiting broadside but actually advertising to men, women, and children to attend Massabesic House, a lake resort in Manchester, NH. 11" × 18", all type b&w. *$125–150*

(Lincoln) "Sangamo Insurance Co., Springfield, Ill./Capital $200,000." 1865. Vignettes depict rail splitting, Springfield home, tomb, Lincoln, Capitol in background. 9½" × 12½". Stark (A) $375. . . . . *$350–400*

(Lincoln) "Smoke the Rail Splitter Cigars." Ca. 1880. "The Great American Favorite" in ornate, flowing type. Heavy pasteboard in red, white, blue. U.S. Shield with multicolor label of Lincoln splitting rails; also oval bust portrait. . . . *$300–350*

TINS

All American Cigars. Washington, Franklin and Lincoln. 5" h.; 5¼" dia. Gold, black, white; oval bust portraits. *$75–85*

Ohio Boys Tobacco. Garfield, McKinley, and Benjamin Harrison. Multicolor paper label over tin with bust portraits of trio. 6" h., 4½" dia. *$300–350*

Old Abe Tobacco. 1870. 8¼" dia. × 2" deep. Browntone on tan. Bust of Lincoln with eagle, railsplitting and slavery vignettes. *$1200–1300*

Veteran Brand Coffee. Brewster Gordon Co., Rochester, NY. 4¼" × 5". Multicolor tin with bust portrait of gray-haired Union general. *$75–85*

TRADE CARDS

(Aesthetic Movement) "'Ceticism my bredren. It is something beautiful. Frintance I am light and airy—like de bean." Ca. 1885. Adv.—Clarence Brooks & Co., NYC Coach Varnishes. Highly satirical commentary on blacks' efforts to better their lot in life. Cartoon of simianlike black lecturer before black crowd espousing the latest fad, the Aesthetic Movement, widely promoted by Oscar Wilde. . . *$15–20*

"Auctioneer for Sale of Negroes." Adv.—S.R. Fondren, Richmond, VA. 1850s. All type. 3½" × 2½". (A) $330 . . . . *$250–350*

Blaine–Logan for President and Vice-President. 1892. Adv.—Muzzy Starch Co., oval portraits of Rep. hopefuls. *$10–15*

"Blaine–Logan Capaduras/The Best 5 ct. Segars." 1892. Blaine to Logan who wears his military regalia, White House in background: "We've got the nomination, but to get elected we must keep the boys supplied with Capaduras." Browntone on buff. *$25–35*

Benjamin Butler—Ayers Sasparilla. Ca. 1880. Gen. Butler as pitchman holds up packaged product. *$35–40*

Benjamin Butler—Durham Tobacco. Metamorphic trade card. 1870s. Ben Butler's bust portrait is interchangeable with Bismark and George Washington. *$25–35*

(Butler, Cleveland, Blaine, Logan) "We May Differ in Politics . . . But We All Agree That. . . ." 1884. Capadura Cigars. Depicts the 1884 hopefuls all drinking beer in tavern and having animated political discussion. Sepiatone on buff. *$25–35*

(Civil War) Rebel and Yank Exchange Pleasantries. 1870s. Love Tobacco Co., Richmond, VA. Rebel swaps tobacco with Yank for a cup of coffee. Multicolor. (See also chapter on Broadsides and Prints as poster) *$75–100*

(Civil War Cannoneers) Lowe's Metalic Paint Co. Ca. 1880s. Johns & Co., Cincinnati, litho. Large shield with Lowe legend. Father Time with scythe; cannoneers in vignette firing cannon. *$15–25*

"Jefferson Davis/The Glorious and Inglorious Career in Five Expressive Tableaus." Mechanical trade card. 1861. Highly satirical mix and match with different tops and bottoms. *$150–200*

Jefferson Davis. 1870s. Royal Glue adv. Litho bust portrait; red, white, blue, black, and gold. *$60–70*

(Adm. Farragut) Clark's Thread. Ca. 1894. Donaldson Bros., Five Points, NY. Three vignettes. Farragut, bust portrait; climbing mast rigging; his ship. . . . *$20–25*

"S.R. Fondren, Auctioneer for Sale of Negroes." Richmond, VA, 1850s. 3½" × 2½". (A) $330. . . . . *$250–350*

(Freedman's Bureau) Frank Miller's (Stove) Blacking. 1880s. Litho by Mayer, Merkel & Ottmann, NY. Uncle Sam seated, shaving in front of mirror. His foot rests on open drawer marked "Freedman's Bureau." Framed view of Miller factory on wall. Multicolor. *$50–65*

(Gen. Fremont) Best of the Cheapest—Corticelli (Cotton Thread). Litho by Chas. Shields & Sons. 1880s. Fremont with hat raised, atop Pike's Peak with three others. *$15–25*

(James Garfield) Generic. 1880. Die-cut of artist's pallette; bust portrait of Garfield. Multicolor. *$20–25*

(Garfield) Trade card puzzle. Four-card puzzle set. © 1880. Adv.—F.A. Pushee Wallpaper & Lamps, Racine, WI. Each of four cards shows a scenic vista horizontally but, when held vertically, the image of favorite candidate appears—Garfield, Arthur, Hancock, English. *$75–85*

(U.S. Grant) Cabinet trade card. 1886. Adv. for Moeller's Art Studio, Grand Island, NE. Photo of Grant. *$25–35*

(U.S. Grant) "The Boss Puzzle." 1872. Generic adv. Vexed political boss Roscoe Conkling agonizes over maneuvering numbered wooden game pieces represented by bust heads of various presidential candidates, including Gens. Grant, Sherman, and Butler, plus Blaine, Tilden, Train, Washburn, etc. Sepiatone on buff. . . . *$35–45*

(U.S. Grant) Puzzle trade card. The Campaign Puzzle/Find the Correct Likeness of Our Next President. 1872. Luther Jones Boots and Shoes, Ithaca, NY. Illus. of many styles of boots. Elongated shapes of Grant and Horace Greeley; card must be viewed almost flat at eye level to find hidden likeness. *$50–60*

"Grant as Bulldog." 1880. Adv. for John C. Stockwell, Stationers, NYC. Cartoon of Grant with cigar and bulldog's body. Bears pity slogans, "Diligence is the mistress of success," and "Discretion of speech is superior to eloquence." ... *$85–100*

Gen. Grant—Magnolia (Virginia Shallcross & Co.) Hams. Ca. 1880. Krebs Lithographic Co., Cincinnati. "That is a plump rat Chang Whang. But excuse me, I always carry Magnolia Hams." Several blacks carrying Magnolia Hams while bowing Chinaman offers a cigar-smoking, top-hatted Grant a dead rat on platter. Multicolor... *$50–65*

"Gen. Grant Stoves." U.S. 1890. Full color with cameo bust of Grant and large illus.. of cast-iron cook stove. Good Quality/Good Condition. (D) $30...........
.... *$25–35*

(Grant and Greeley) "What Are the Principles of the Democratic Party? Go West." 1872. Satirical cartoon of Grant on horseback questioning Greeley, who drags a Democratic "dead horse." Three disgruntled pols at right shout "Sold out." Generic adv. 5" × 7" b&w. In set with "I Must Have Colored Vote" below.......
.... *$75–100*

Horace Greeley, "I Must Have the Colored Vote." 1872. Generic adv. Satirical anti-Greeley shows black man being lifted up by the seat of his pants. The black mouths the words "Go West" as Greeley peers down his throat with telescope. B&w. One of a series. *$75–100*

Hancock Strutting Rooster. Metamorphic trade card. 1880. Generic adv. Anti-Dem showing Hancock turn from cock-of-the-walk into plucked chicken (by raising flap on card). Recto features poem about blacks and the South. *$100–125*

Benjamin Harrison Hat. Die-cut trade card. 1884. Large beaver-style hat die-cut (a type familiarly worn by Harrison) with inset bust image in circle of Harrison. Adv. for *Demorest Magazine* offer to buy copy of painting by Mrs. Harrison. .....
.... *$20–25*

Benjamin Harrison. New England Condensed Mince Meat, J.L. Daugherity, Brooklyn, NY. 1880s. High-office aspirants Benjamin Harrison, Brooks, Fisk, Thurmond, Morton, and Cleveland dine lavishly on mince meat.......... *$25–30*

(Benjamin Harrison) Metamorphic trade card. 1880. Electric Fives Cigars. Through proper folding of card, either Harrison or his opponents John Bidwell (Prohibitionist) and Grover Cleveland (Dem.) will appear in the presidential chair.
....

Benjamin Harrison and Grover Cleveland on Bicycle Race to White House. Optical trade card. 1888. Generic adv. Giving card a circular motion gives illusion of wheels actually turning.................................... *$50–65*

(Benjamin Harrison) "The Start"—Birdsell Mfg. Co., Carriages, Phaetons, Buggies, Farm Wagons and Clover Hullers. 1888. Harrison, Cleveland, Fisk, and Streeter as jockeys in horse race. Uncle Sam and Miss Liberty at finish line. White House and Birdsell factory in background. *$75–85*

(Benjamin Harrison/Whitlaw Reid) Republican Nominees. 1888. Adv.— Wright's Indian Vegetable Pills. Jugate portraits with flags, shield, White House. Black photo engraving. Red, white, and blue. Cleveland–Stevenson Dem. match.
.... *$20–25*

(R.B. Hayes) President and Mrs. Hayes Visit to Philadelphia. 1876. Adv.— Enterprise Mfg. Co., Cold Handle Sad Iron. Mrs. Hayes persuades husband to buy new iron at Centennial Expo. B&w illus.............................. *$35–50*

Gen. Edward Jones, Lt. Gov. of New Jersey. Adv.—*American Rural Home*. One of a series based on distinguished advertisers. He was president of Jones Scale Works. As a colonel commanding the 6th Massachusetts Regiment, he led the famous march to Baltimore and his was the first unit to arrive and save the nation's capital. Sepiatone. Oversize card, 6½" × 4"........................ *$10–12*

(Lincoln vs. McClellan) Cherokee Medicines. 1864. Bust portraits of two pres. candidates. "Guar. to cure universal lassitude, pain, weak nerves, etc." Sepiatone. 3" × 5". *$75–100*

(Lincoln) Honest Abe with Enterprise Faucet. © 1893. Lincoln turning on measuring faucet on molasses barrel. Four-line poem extolls its labor-saving virtues. Picture of Forestry Building at 1893 World's Columbian Exposition below. *$12–15*

(Gen. Logan) Six Strong American Candidates—for Public Favor—Belding Brothers (Thread). Litho by Gulger. 1894. Reps. Blaine and Logan vs. Dem. Cleveland Hendricks; Belding spool of thread and ball of yarn; cameos; furled flags. *$25–35*

(McKinley) (The) President Suspender Improved. 1896. "Who Gets It?" Miss Liberty proffers suspenders to William McKinley and Dem. rival William J. Bryan. Multicolor. *$25–35*

(McKinley) Lewis Cycle Co. Election Possibilities. Mechanical trade card. 1892. Double-sided with rotating wheel of heads. Dem. side: Cleveland, David Hill; Rep. side: McKinley, Benjamin Harrison, Whitlaw Reed. *$75–85*

Clipper Ship—Florence Nightingale. 1880. William T. Coleman & Co. "California Line for San Francisco": Nesbitt & Co., NY, Printers, E.W. Holmes Commander (of clipper ship). Unusual large format, 8¼" × 5½". Purple text printed on verso, signed by "Oliver Hazard Perry." Light border oxidation. (A) $2200 ......
.... *$2000–2200*

(Gen. Phil. Sheridan) Clark Threads. © 1894. Donaldson Bros., Five Points, NY. Three vignettes of Sheridan: bust portrait; streaking on famous ride; two horsemen with raised sabers. *$20–25*

"Stump Speaker" Bank. 1886. Adv.—Shepard Hardware Mfgr., Hamilton & Mathews Dist., Rochester, NY. Full-color picture of black carpetbagger with top hat as mechanical bank. *$300–400*

Uniforms of the Army of the United States Series. Trade card set. Civil War Era—1861–66 (also cards for 1841–51, 1872–80, 1883–93). Adv.—J.&P. Coats' Best Six Cord Spool Cotton. J.H. Buek Litho. Some of the cards precede or are post–Civil War. © by Brig. Gen. Samuel B. Holabird, Quartermaster of the Dept. of the Gulf from the 1860s; features regulation uniforms and accoutrements, 4" × 4¾". .... *$10–12 each*

MISCELLANEOUS

Fan. Flower City Tea Co., Rochester, NY. 1880s. Cardboard and wood; multicolor lithograph by Ellery & Wilson, NY. Union soldier marching in front of tent, Miss Liberty in foreground; cameos of Washington, Lincoln, and Grant below. (A) $165.
.... *$150–200*

Flyer. Artillery Bank. 1890. Adv.—Shepard Hardware, Buffalo, NY. Red ink on buff stock, line sketch of maker's latest mechanical bank; depicts Civil War soldier preparing to fire cannon at fortress. *$25–35*

Flyer. "If Lincoln will be elected or not. The people of South Carolina (whose rights have been trampled upon) . . . have the advantage of supplying themselves with clothing at the well known Carolina Clothing Depot." Ottolenguis, Willis & Barrett, Charleston. 1860. Slyly ambiguous adv. from *Charleston Courier*, with strong secessionist sentiment. Headings are interjected throughout adv. . . . *$75–85*

Foldout. (Gens. Sherman, Butler, McKinley) "(The) Two Political Parties Getting Strength by the Use of Anheuser Busch's Malt Nutrine. . . ." 1896. Cartoon by R. Frantz. © *Rollingpin Pub. Magazine.* A dozen candidates sipping from straws from huge bottles of Nutrine; Uncle Sam stands by with arm raised. *$300–350*

Tray. McKinley–Roosevelt. Household Ranges and Stoves. Serving tray. 1896. Oval tray with jugate portraits, eagle with flag and nation's capital. *$550–600*

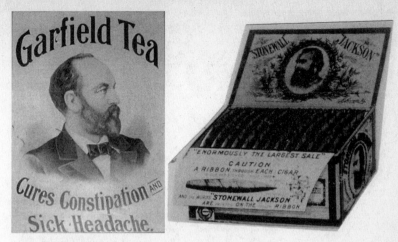

Left: *Garfield Tea Co., Brooklyn, NY. Paper poster, ca. 1880s, $350–$400.* Right: *Stonewall Jackson Cigars, advertising sign. Stand-up, die-cut, embossed tin sign, $350–$400.*

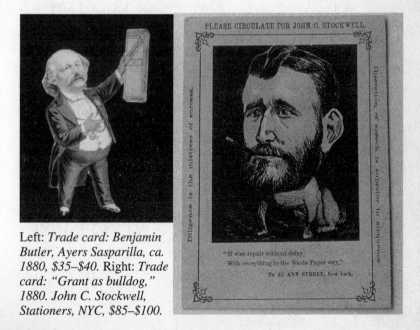

Left: *Trade card: Benjamin Butler, Ayers Sasparilla, ca. 1880, $35–$40.* Right: *Trade card: "Grant as bulldog," 1880. John C. Stockwell, Stationers, NYC, $85–$100.*

Trade card: General Grant pictured pitching Magnolia Hams, ca. 1880, $50–$65.

Left: *Trade cards: Uniforms of the Army of the United States, series (four in set). J. & P. Coates' Spool Cotton, $10–$15 each.* Right: *Advertising flyer, pre-war. Carolina Clothing Depot, $75–$85.*

AMMUNITION AND MISCELLANEOUS FIELD EQUIPMENT

AMMUNITION AND RELATED EQUIPMENT

References: *American Military Equipage 1851–1872*, Vol. II, by Todd. *Civil War Canteens, Civil War Collector's Encyclopedia*, by F. Lord; *A Directory of Military Goods, Dealers, and Makers, 1785–1885; Time-Life Echoes of Glory—The Confederacy; U.S. Military Holsters and Pistol Cartridge Boxes*, by E.S. Meadows.

Artillery Gauge. Confederate brass artillery gauge (436). Marked "For inspection of X inch Cartridges" on obverse; "CSNOW, Charlotte, NC, H.A.R." (Confederate States Naval Ordnance Works). One of set of four sold by Flayderman in '61 with correspondence. (A) '94, $3000. . . . . *$2700–3000*

Artillery Tar Bucket. Tar bucket with chain handle. (illus.) Complete. (A) Dias, Nov. '94, $425. . . . . *$425–450*

Bayonet Adaptor. Confederate; marked "BG&M, Richmond, Va. Pat. Sep. 2, 1861" (357). Good patina; missing securing screw. (A) '94, $500. . . . . . *$500–550*

Bullet Molds (2). Iron 2-cavity, .44 cal. marked "Colt's Patent." Also a brass 2-cavity .31 cal., scratched "Richmond, Va." on handle. Also miscellaneous pinfire and centerfire cartridges; iron mold poor; brass mold fair. (A) '94, $100. . . . . *$90–100*

Cannon Cleaning Brush. Artilleryman's cannon cleaning brush head. Wood with boar bristles. "J.N. Parker, 1861" stamped in wood. (A) Oct. '94, $125. . *$125–150*

Cannon Cleaning Head. Artilleryman's brush head. Wood with boar bristles; stamped "J.N. Parker, 1861." (illus.) Excellent condition. (A) Dias, Nov. '94, $300. . . . . *$300–325*

Cannon Powder Rammer. Leather-covered artillery rammer. Allegheny Arsenal, 1862, marked on top. (A) Dias, Nov. '94, $110. *$100–125*

Cannon Sponge Bag. Artillery woolen yarn bag. Designed to fit rammer head to sponge out cannon barrel after firing. (A) Dias, Nov. '94, $40. . . . . *$40–50*

Cannon Sponge Bucket. Artillery sponge bucket (complete). Large wrought-iron handle, lid. Dias, Nov. '94, $475. . . . . *$450–500*

Cannonball. Civil War cannonball without fuse. (A) Dias, Nov. '94, $160. *$150–175*

Cannonball Worm. Steel cannonball worm. Stamped "#12" in several places. (A) Dias, Nov. '94, $195. . . . . *$175–200*

Cap Box. Cap box with "U.S." in oval. Stamped "Woodbury Sub Inspector, U.S. Ordnance Dept." (A) Dias, Nov. '94, $170. . . . . *$175–185*

Cap Boxes (2). Leather cap boxes. One stamped "W. Kinsey, Newark," the other unmarked. (A) Dias, Nov. '94, $200. . . . . *$200–225*

Capper. Lt. D.C. Ellis, 7th NY Cavalry canteen. Brass, with copper spout. Name engraved in English script across body. Kidney-shaped. Stark, Dec. '93, $200. . . . . *$200–250*

.32 Long Rimfire Cartridge. .312" bullet dia., 975 fps. muzzle velocity. Manufactured 1861–1975. . . . . *$6–8*

.32 Short Rimfire Cartridge. .316" bullet dia., 700 fps. muzzle velocity. Manufactured 1861–1973. . . . . *$1–2*

.41 Short Rimfire Cartridge. .405" dia., 425 fps. muzzle velocity. Manufactured 1863–1942. . . . . *$3–4*

.44 Henry Flat Rimfire Cartridge. .446" dia., 1125 fps. muzzle velocity. Manufactured 1861–1934. . . . . *$7–8*

.44 Long Rimfire Cartridge. .451" dia., 825 fps. muzzle velocity. Manufactured 1862–1923. . . . . *$9–11*

.56–50 Spencer Rimfire Cartridge. .512" dia., 1250 fps. muzzle velocity. Manufactured 1864–1920. . . . . *$12–15*

.56–56 Spencer Rimfire Cartridge. 550" dia., 1200 fps. muzzle velocity. Manufactured 1862–1920. . . . . *$11–14*

Cartridge Belt. Belt for Spencer rifle cartridges. "U.S." buckle, bayonet, and scabbard. Covered cartridge holders all around belt, with early tag attached. Possibly experimental. (A) Oct. '94, $3000. . . . . *$3000–3200*

Cartridge Box. Cavalry leather cartridge box for percussion revolver. Manufactured by Davy & Co., Newark, NJ. With belt loops. (A) Oct. '94, $125. . *$150–175*

Cartridge Box. Chillingsworth's Alteration for Metallic Cartridges. With original tag marked by manufacturer and dated June 9, 1863. (A) Nov. '94, $187.50 . . . . *$175–200*

Cartridge Box. Confederate cartridge box for Enfield rifle musket. Imported from England. Unmarked but attributed to Issac Campbell (as below). Complete with straps. REF: Todd, *American Military Equipage 1851–1872*, Vol. II, p. 442. (A) Oct. '94, $410. . . . . *$400–450*

Cartridge Box. Confederate cartridge box for Enfield rifle musket. Imported from England and marked "Isaac Campbell & Co., 7 Jermyn St. London." With belt loops, buff leather closure loose inside. REF: *Time-Life Echoes of Glory—The Confederacy*, p. 266. (A) Oct. '94, $725. . . . . *$700–750*

Cartridge Box. Experimental U.S. army leather 40-round wood block cartridge box for Sharp's carbine. Manufactured by H. & C. Storms; with belt loops. REF: *A Directory of Military Goods, Dealers, and Makers, 1785–1885*, p. 82. (A) Oct. '94, $400. . . . . *$400–500*

Cartridge Box. Federal brass cartridge box plate. Oval. Marked "U.S." (A) Oct. '94, $100. . . . . *$75–100*

Cartridge Box. Federal carbine cartridge box. With U.S. brass plate; belt loops. (A) Oct. '94, $360. . . . . *$350–400*

Cartridge Box. .50 cal. Sharps leather cartridge box. Wood insert for 40 rounds; front cap pouches and belt loops. (A) Oct. '94, $400. . . . . *$400–450*

Cartridge Box. .58 cal. leather cartridge box. MVM (Massachusetts Volunteer Militia) emblem. Belt loops. Side stitching split. *$50–75*

Cartridge Box. Federal cavalry percussion revolver cartridge box, Model 1864. Marked Col. Mann's patent; reissued June 7, 1864/E. Gaylord Maker, Chicopee, MA. "U.S." in center; T.L. Shepard, Inspector. REF: E.S. Meadows, *U.S. Military Holsters and Pistol Cartridge Boxes*, p. 389. (A) Oct. '94, $300 . . . . *$300–350*

Cartridge Box. Model 1855 cartridge box. Ca. 1860. "U.S." in oval on front flap. "U.S. Ord. Dept." inspector's stamp in corner; Newark, NJ, manufacturer's stamp on left corner. (A) Dias, Nov. '94, $310. . . . . *$300–325*

Cartridge Box. National Guard .50 cal. cartridge box. Has white woven shoulder sling attached to box with two Civil War–period infantry buttons. (A) Oct. '94, $70.
. . . . *$75–100*

Cartridge Box. Navy pistol cartridge box. Embossed "USN" in oval on front. Stamped "U.S.N.Y., Boston" in oval on underflap. (A) Oct. '94, $200. . . *$200–250*

Cartridge Box. Navy pistol cartridge box. With unusual side opening lid; double belt loop. "USN" in oval embossed on top. *$150–175*

Cartridge Box. New York National Guard cartridge box. Ca. 1865–75. Brass-bound flap; "N.G." insignia; wood insert for 12 rounds. *$50–60*

Cartridge Box. Manufacturer J.I. Pittman rifle cartridge box. Leather with original tins, but main overflap cut off. (A) Oct. '94, $40. *$75–100*

Cartridge Box. Spenser Blakesley style for cavalry. 12¼" × 4"; six-sided box and holds ten tubes with cartridges to feed a rifle such as the Spencer. Complete with carrying strap. No identification marks. Minor scuffing. (A) Julia, Mar. '94, $330. *$325–350*

Cartridge Box. U.S. Army Model 1855 leather cartridge box. With belt loops. (A) Oct. '94, $135. . . . . *$150–175*

Cartridge Box. U.S. artillery pouch to carry cannon primers. Made by E. Gaylord & Co., Chicopee, MA. Crossed cannons in brass on outer flap. 6 ³⁄₈" × 1.5" deep.
. . . . *$75–100*

Cartridge Box Plate. Federal U.S. brass cartridge box plate. Eagle decoration. (A) Oct. '94, $60. . . . . *$50–75*

Cartridge Box Plate. U.S. oval cartridge box plate. (A) Oct. '94, $75. . . . . *$75–85*

Cartridge Loops. Model 1874 movable cartridge loops. Marked "U.S. Arsenal Bernicia." *$200–225*

Cartridge Pouch. Leather bullet pouch, U.S. issue. Complete with leather shoulder strap and eagle belt plate. "Watertown Arsenal, 1864, U.S." stamped in four lines on flap. Retains two thin cartridge boxes. Some crackling in leather but finish is 90%. (A) Julia, Mar. '94, $1100. . . . . *$1100–1200*

Cartridge Pouch. Leather bullet pouch. Marked inside with name "H.T. Stull." "U.S." oval leadback buckle, excellent, and retains straps and buckles. (A) Julia, Mar. '94, $302. . . . . *$300–325*

Cartridge Pouch. Pouch with "U.S." embossed in leather. Slightly larger version of above at 8" × 7". Incised in left corner of flap is stamp "White, U.S. Ordnance Insp." Some of original finish is missing from third paper pouch flap. (A) Julia, Mar. '94, $275. . . . . *$250–300*

Curb Bit. Artillery curb bit. With original ordnance tag and "U.S."-stamped brass emblems. (A) Dias, Nov. '94, $145. . . . . *$125–150*

Drover's Whip. Braided artillery drover's whip. 5' long with carrying loop and brass hook attachment. . . . .

Fuse Box. U.S. Navy fuse box. Stamped "Navy Yard, NY, 1864." With anchor insignias, belt loop. (A) Dias, Oct. '94, $150.. . . . . *$150–200*

Fuses. Union 20-sec. fuses. 1864. Original box. Frankford Arsenal. (A) Jenack, Oct. '94, $50. . . . . *$50–60*

Minié Balls. Ten rounds of .58 cal. Civil War Minié balls. Found on battlefield. . .
. . . . *$30–40*

Minié Balls. Ten rounds of .69 cal. Civil War Minié balls; as found, unfired. (A) Oct. '94, $35. . . . . *$25–50*

Paper Cartridges (2). Union paper cartridges. One for .544 cal. Enfield; other for .58 cal. rifle with Minié ball. (A) Oct. '94, $100. . . . . *$100–125*

Paper Wrapper. Confederate wrapper for buckshot cartridges. Label for cartridges fabricated at Fayetteville Arsenal. Unissued, detached from album. Includes correspondence. (A) '94, $850. . . . . *$850–900*

Pass Box. Federal naval 12-pound leather pass box. Used to carry cartridges to cannons during battle. Stenciled "12 PD" on lid. Complete with shoulder strap and pine sabot holder. (A) Oct. '94, $750. . . . . *$600–800*

Percussion Cap Tin and Ammo. 145–70/500 gr. U.S. Government cartridges by Winchester Repeating Arms Co. Includes three 20-cartridge boxes. Package of seven paper cartridges marked "D. 1862 for Rifle Musket/53/Bullet .55 dia. Waxpowder 2^1/$_2$ drs/wood plug.". *$275–325*

Pistol Box. Col. Mann's patented Model 1864 large size pistol box. Reissued June 7, 1864/E. Gaylord Maker, Chicopee, MA. "U.S." in center. "U.S. Ord. Dept." subinspector's stamp on obverse. Original strap, almost cut through. (A) Oct. '94, $75. . . . . *$75–1000*

Powder Flask. Batty U.S. military "Peace" flask. Copper body decorated with federal eagle; clasped hands surrounded by oval of 20 stars; panoply of arms with shield inscribed "U.S." Pat. brass adjustable charger stamped "Batty" with two suspension rings. *$350–400*

Powder Horn. Federal EM infantry horn (424). Unissued. Shoulder strap has wear on velvet center; very good spur. Includes single staff major's shoulder strap, plus single federal spur marked "Allegheny Arsenal." (A) '94, $200. . . . . *$150–200*

Powder Horn. Raised Confederate horn (565). Approx. 8^1/$_2$" overall. Marked "G.C. Clisby I. R. 6 ALA Reg Bull Run, Va. Jan. 1862." Includes correspondence. (A) July '94, $850. . . . . *$900–1000*

Powder Horn. Decorated Horn (463). Carved horn; approx. 6^1/$_2$" overall; depicts man on horse; hunter shooting at buck and inscribed "Eliot, Maine" and "E.W." Spin near spout. (A) $150. . . . . *$125–150*

Powder Horn (461). Carved steer horn; 8" overall; inscribed "G. Redding." Petal design around neck and base. *$80–100*

Powder Keg. Union-issue Dupont black powder keg. Pewter cap. Provenance attached. *$45–60*

BELTS AND HOLSTERS

Army Saddle Holsters. Pair of Colt 1860 holsters. Leather with full flap and brass bottoms. *$300–350*

Belt. Belt and pouch. Missing round eagle belt plate. Stencilled "GS" on strap. Inside paper pouch has 50% of finish gone. Excellent brass and leadback oval buckle on the front. (A) Julia, Mar. '94, $605. . . . . *$600–650*

Belt. Confederate belt with double serpent hooks. English import. Rated excellent. (A) Julia, Mar. '94, $181. . . . . *$175–200*

Belt and Holster. Handmade leather belt and holster, measures 39". Holds 32 cartridges 40/40 PR 45 Colt. Large brass buckle, complete with leather holster for Colt single-action revolver or one of comparable size. *$400–450*

Belt, Buckle, and Cap Box. Belt with retaining bar on end. *Ca. 1862.* Cap box and buckle not identified as to maker. Usual standard "U.S." on oval, brass. (A) Julia, Mar. '94, $330. . . . . *$300–325*

Belt, Buckle, and Cap Box. Oval Civil War buckle with arrow retainers. Belt measures 40"; is marked "F.A. Crossman Co., Newark, New Jersey." Cap box marked "F.A. Sniffen, U.S. Ordnance Dept., subinspector." Excellent. (A) Julia, Mar. '94, $605. . . . . *$550–600*

Belt, Buckle, and Cap Box. Wide waist belt. With Oval "U.S." embossed brass buckle. Attached cap box is marked "JJ-JE Cordiot, New York" in oval touch mark. (A) Julia, Mar. '94, $770. . . . . *$700–750*

Belt with Bullet Pouch. Leather pouch marked "Watertown, Oslo, 1864." Second flap has four lines including "U.S." Minimal cracking; nice even patina. (A) Julia, Mar. '94, $880. . . . . *$850–875*

Belts (3). Two U.S. Navy and one Rhode Island Militia. Early 1860s. R.I. cartridge belt for 45–70; blue web. Brass belt buckle has Mills patd. and "R.I." initials in oval. Naval officer's pistol belt and holster in blue web. Model 1852 buckle, not interlocking but held by latch. Eight-cartridge pouches on belt. Attached to belt is web holster with U.S. Navy button. Third item is U.S. Navy officer's belt with interlocking belt buckle (used from 1852–1870). (A) Julia, Mar. '94, $660. . . . . *$650–700*

Holster. Federal holster for small percussion revolver. (A) Oct. '94, $170. . . *$175–200*

Holster. Revolver holster and two patent saber hangers; stamped "R.I.A." (429). Holster minus leather tab and keeper; torn and repaired belt loop; saber hangers are flaking, but intact. (A) July '94, $780. . . . . *$900–1000*

CANTEENS

C.S.A. Square Tin Canteen. Measures 7" × 8" from bottom to top of spout. Has three flat tin rings; original linen shoulder sling. Similar to C.S.A. version illus. in Lord's *Civil War Collectibles Encyclopedia*, p. 74. . . . . *$350–400*

Civil War Pattern of 1858 Canteen. Khaki woolen cover; canvas strap with inspector's stamp. Catalogued as excellent. (A) Oct. '94, $275. . . . . *$250–300*

Confederate Canteen with Rattan Cover. Green-tinted bottle liner inside tight rattan cover; loops for carry cord. Missing stopper. *$40–50*

Confederate Cedar Wood Canteen. Initials "W.B.L.E. W 12" carved on obverse near top. Wood stopper; linen strap. Hank Ford Collection. *$2800–3000*

Confederate Copper Canteen. Round, 4²⁄₄" dia. Copper spout and 3" belt loop in back. Attached paper verifies it was displayed for many years in Civil War Museum in Laurey, VA. Badly dented. (A) Julia, Mar. '94, $275. . . . . *$300–350*

Confederate Filter-style Canteen. European, typically of those imported by C.S.A., since they had no access to filters from the North. REF: Lord, *Civil War Canteens*, pp. 150–155. (A) Oct. '94, $50. . . . . *$50–75*

Confederate Wood Canteen (422). Iron hoops. Neck missing and some shrinkage to wood. (A) '94, $800. . . . . *$700–800*

Trowbridge U.S. Army Cooking Canteen. Tin outer shell with bottle and cup inside; cork stopper. Thin rectangular shape; served as a broiler by filling hot water around glass. *$350–400*

Turpentine Canteen. Served to fill torches. REF: Todd, *American Military Equipage 1851–1874*, Vol. II, p. 400. (A) Oct. '94, $200. . . . . *$200–300*

Union Civil War Canteen. Ca. 1862. Signed "Jewet" with provenance. (A) Jenack, Oct. '94, $225. . . . . *$225–250*

Union Concentric Ring Canteen. Black cloth cover. "'J.H. Co. 1864" marked on spout. Stopper and chain appear original. (A) Julia, Mar. '94, $302. . . . . *$300–350*

Union Regulation U.S. Canteen. Ca. 1861. Original blue cover with white canvas strap. Dias, Nov. '94, $300. . . . . *$300–325*

Union Wooden Canteen. 9½" h. from feet to spot top. 7" dia. Footed with unknown wood; brown leather cross belts and string carrying device. REF: Lord, *Civil War Canteens*, p. 74. (A) Julia, Mar. '94, $385. . . . . *$350–400*

Water Purifying Union Issue Canteen. Center container is tin with narrow cylindrical compartment containing charcoal filters. Water is poured in right side; supposedly purified when drinking from left spout. Brass pat; wool covering. . . . *$400–450*

Wood Canteen with Iron Reinforcements. Cedar body with "S.N.Y" stenciled in gold. Eight-sided spout; three reinforcement straps. Excellent. (A) Julia, Mar. '94, $550. . . . . *$500–600*

Political and Patriotic

G.A.R. 33rd Encampment Glass Canteen. 1899. 4½" dia with multicolor label under glass. Pewter cap. *$250–275*

G.A.R. Encampment Canteen. Washington, D.C. 1892. 4½" nickel-plated flask with copper disc center. Embossed profiles of three Union generals including Grant and Logan. Chrome and cork stopper with eyelet. Stark FP Cat., Nov. '94, $185. . . . . *$150–175*

McKinley–T. Roosevelt "Our Candidates" Canteen. 1896. Political campaign glass canteen in sepiatone with red, white, blue shield; jugate paper portraits under glass. Shield and U.S. Capitol vignettes. *$450–500*

United Confederate Veteran Pewter Flask. 1896. Top half lifts off to reveal cap and spout. Engraved CSA battle flag. "U.C.V. Reunion . . . J.M. Curry, Peabody Education Fund, Richmond." Threaded cap engraved "We Remember." Stark FP Cat., Nov. '94, $950. . . . . *$850–900*

CAVALRY AND HORSEDRAWN INFANTRY GEAR

Bit. Horse bit with ring. Marked "W. & Co." with inspector's initials; "U.S." emblems. (A) Dias, Nov. '94, $200. . . . . *$200–250*

Carbine Boots. All-leather. Marked "Rock Island Arsenal" on reverse. Brass reinforcement pieces on front. Three straps. Looped to strap is carbine socket which is attached to saddle. *$300–350*

Carbine and Pistol Box. Mann's Cavalry box. Stamped "Col. Mann's patent, Dec. 8, 1863." C.S. Storms, NY, maker. "U.S." in oval, with percussion cap box on left side; with original tapering shoulder slings; brass hooks, insert block with 30 holes for .46 cal. metallic cartridges. (A) Dias, Nov. '94, $675. . . . . *$650–700*

Carbine Socket. Federal issue, complete with straps and "C.H.C." inspector's initials. (A) Oct. '94, $30. . . . . *$40–50*

Cavalry Clod. Civil War horse anchor. (A) Oct. '94, $100 . . . . *$100–125*

Cavalry Iron Picket Pin. U.S. Army; used by cavalrymen on the march. (A) Oct. '94, $110. . . . . *$100–125*

Cavalryman's Boots. Saddle leather cavalry boots. Horseshoe heels with spur insert holes, stamped "J.K. Smith/100 Rounds." English import; probably C.S.A. use. (A) Dias, Nov. '94, $300. . . . . *$300–325*

Curry Comb. Union cavalryman's horse curry comb. (A) Oct. '94, $100. . . . .
. . . . *$100–150*

Harness Emblems (2). U.S. Cavalry harness emblems. "U.S." in brass. . . . *$50–60*

Harness-Making Vise. Wooden harness maker's vise. (A) Oct. '94, $80. *$75–100*

Headstall. Horse headstall, wooden with Model 1863 artillery bit, watering bit, double reins with brass eagle rosettes. (A) Dias, Nov. '94, $120. . . . . *$125–150*

Holster Set. Cavalryman's set for Colt Model 1860 Army .44 cal. revolver. (A) Dias, Nov. '94, $375. . . . . *$375–400*

Horse Bit. Gilt, with applied silvered script "C" rosettes (434), 80% gilt overall; one rosette partially detached. (A) '94, $850. . . . . *$800–900*

Horse bit. U.S. Cavalry horse bit. Severe bit with mouth ring and high port; roller and curb chain; inspector's initials. Bright blue. (A) Oct. '94, $300. . . . . *$300–350*

Horse Brush. U.S. Cavalry leather horse brush. Stamped "U.S. Rock Island Arsenal." (A) Oct. '94, $130. . . . . *$125–150*

Horse Feed Bag. Union issue horse feed bag of canvas and leather. (A) Oct. '94, $140. . . . . *$125–150*

Horse Hobbles. Pair of leather cavalryman's horse hobbles with chain. "Watervliet Arsenal," inspector's initials, faintly stamped. (A) Oct. '94, $200. . . . . . . *$200–250*

Martingale. Cavalry officer's brass horse martingale 2nd U.S. Cavalry. Heart-shaped. (Martingale is a harness strap that connects girth to nose band to keep horse from throwing back head.) REF: Todd, *American Military Equipage*, Vol. II, p. 352. (A) Oct. '94, $150. . . . . *$150–200*

Picket Pin. Cavalryman picket pin, iron; used while on march. (A) Oct. '94, $110.
. . . . *$100–125*

Saddle. McClellan cavalry saddle. *1859.* Made by Whitman Saddle Co., NY. (A) Jenack, Oct. '94, $60. . . . . *$110–125*

Saddle. Union artillery saddle. Ca. 1863. Leather in good condition. (A) Jenack, Oct. '94, $80. . . . . *$100–125*

Saddlebags. Government issue leather saddlebags. 1860–65. Marked "U.S. Ordnance Dept.," subinspector oval stamp on one side. 18" l. × 8½" w. Flaps in excellent condition. Some scuffing on one flap. (A) Julia, Mar. '94, $412. . . . . *$450–500*

Spurs (3). Union Cavalry spurs with straps and chains. (A) Jenack, Oct. '94, $150.
. . . . *$150–200*

Stirrups. U.S. Artillery brass stirrups. Stamped "Watervliet Arsenal, NY," with P.V.H. inspector's initials. (A) Oct. '94, $295. . . . . *$275–325*

Stirrups. Pair of U.S. Cavalry stirrups. Stamped in brass. (A) Dias, Nov. '94, $350.
. . . . *$350–375*

Trace Springs. Pair of artillery trace springs. Has chain and hook for taking strain from surging team of horses. (A) Oct '94, $125. *$125–150*

Whip. Union Artillery driver's leather whip. Marked "W. Range, 7th Bat." with brass hook belt attachment. Carrying loop is loose. REF: Lord, *Civil War Collector's Encyclopedia*, p. 131. (A) Oct. '91, $275. . . . . *$275–300*

GROOMING ACCESSORIES: RAZORS

"Blaine & Logan." 1884. Straight razor with etched jugate portraits and names. . .
. . . . *$175–200*

"Henry Clay." 1850s. Straight razor by Rogers. Bust portrait etched on blade. . . .
. . . . *$350–375*

"U.S. Grant." Ca. 1862. Straight razor with bust portrait of Grant in Lt. Gen.'s uniform. Campaign memento. *$500–525*

"Winfield Scott Hancock." 1880. Straight razor with bust portrait, "Gen. Hancock." Campaign memento. *$400–450*

"Stonewall Jackson." Ca. 1862. By Wade & Butcher. Etched portrait. Large handle. *$900–950*

"William McKinley." 1896. Bone handle, straight razor with etched bust portrait of McKinley. *$125–150*

MESS EQUIPMENT

Coffee Boiler. Tin coffee boiler with bail. Neatly scratched with Wood's name and unit. Also includes leather-bound prayer book and discharge papers. Relating to Edwin R. Wood, Co. I, 21st Massachusetts Infantry, Dec. 31, 1863; another dated 1864 plus pension paper from 1881. (A) July '94, $295 . . . . *$250–300*

Coffeepot. Tin camp coffeepot. High domed lid. (A) Oct. '94, $30. . . . . . . *$25–50*

Coffeepot. Tin camp coffeepot. Side-pour style. (A) Dias, Nov. '94, $110. . . . .
. . . . *$110–125*

Coffeepot. Tin New Hampshire National Guard camp coffeepot. 1863. Old red paint with lettering in gold initials; two cups clip on at spout holder. Stark FP Cat., July '93, $385. . . . . *$325–350*

Coffee Roaster. Camp coffee roaster. Patented by E.J. Hyde, Feb. 1864. Mill Manufacturing Co., Philadelphia, with original wooden handle insert scoop. (A) Dias, Nov. '94, $175. . . . .*$175–200*

Cup, Camp. Tin camp cup with bail handle. (A) Dias, Nov. '94, $70. . . . . *$50–75*

Cup, Mess. Tin camp cup. For boiling water; bail handle. (A) Oct. '94, $115. . . . . .
. . . . *$100–125*

Cup, Tin. Union tin cup. Ca. 1860. Marked "U.S." (A) Jenack, Oct. '94, $25 . . . .
. . . . *$25–50*

Lantern (Folding). Late Civil War camp folding lantern. Minors patented, Jan. 24, 1865. (A) Dias, Nov. '94, $150. . . . . *$135–150*

Miscellaneous Utensils. Wooden handle camp utensils. Included with small iron cooking pot with lid and bail handle. (A) Oct. '94, $35. . . . . *$25–50*

Oil Lamp. Tin camp oil lamp with hanger. Pierced tin type with conical top. (A) Oct. '94, $50. . . . . *$50–75*

Utility Knife. Folding knife. Ca. 1860s. Bone-and-brass-handled. (A) Oct. '94, $80. . . . . *$75–100*

Utility Knife. Small utility knife. Horn handles and horn sheath. (A) Oct. '94, $25. . . . . *$25–50*

MILITARY BAND INSTRUMENTS AND ACCESSORIES

Sources: *A Pictorial History of Civil War Era Musical Instruments and Military Bands,* by Robert Garofalo and Mark Elrod; *U.S. Military Drums,* by Caba; *Arms and Equipment of the Union,* Time-Life Books, 1991.

Bugle. Keyed bugle in E-flat. Ca. late 1850s. Graves & Co., Boston, manufacturer. German silver with 12 keys mounted with footposts and screws. Telescopic turning shank in lead pipe to adjust overall pitch *$500–550*

Clarinet. Rosewood clarinet in E-flat. Ca. 1860s. Martin & Son, Paris, twelve nickel silver keys; two rings. *$375–400*

Cornet. Cornet in B-flat. Ca. 1862. Manufactured by Isaac Fiske, Worcester, MA. German silver; four side-action string rotary valves. *$375–400*

Cornet. German silver cornet in E-flat. Ca. 1862. Manufactured by W. Seefeldt, Philadelphia. Three string rotary valves. *$425–450*

Cornet. German silver cornet in E-flat. Ca. 1862. Manufactured by E.G. Wright, Boston. Three side-action string rotary valves. Used by Co. G, 24th Regt., Wisconsin Volunteer Infantry. *$475–500*

Cornet. Cornet in E-flat. Ca. 1861. Manufactured by C.A. Zorbisch & Sons, NYC. Brass with German silver trim; three string rotary valves. Includes coffinlike leather case. *$600–650*

Cymbals. Union 12" cymbals. Ca. 1861. Brass with leather carrying case and strap. *$250–275*

Drum. "Allie Turner Drum." 1862. Union Manufacturing Co., Baltimore. Drum was reputedly played by Allie Turner, one of Grant's youngest drummer boys. In this unusual drum, rope is fed through iron hooks as opposed to being laced through holes in loops. A drum with this type of attribution could well command five figures. REF: *Civil War Era Musical Instruments,* p. 39. . . . .

Drum. Artillery drum with eagle motif. Ca. 1860. Elias Howe, Boston, maker. Eagle with "E. Pluribus Unum" scroll in mouth against bright red field (red usually designates artillery), 13 gold stars emblazened across drum's face. Red, white, blue, gold. *$1800–2000*

Drum. Artillery drum, eagle with 32 stars. Late 1850s, early '60s. In red artillery background color with painted eagle and cannon extending from behind shield. Replaced snare cord and rope. (A) Riba, Oct. '90, $1700. . . . . *$1800–2000*

Drum. Confederate eagle drum, Co. D., regiment unknown. Eleven gold stars representing C.S.A. states surround eagle's head. Stars also appear on shield. Red and white banner with C.S.A. legend. *$5000–6000*

Drum. Eagle-design bass drum. Ca. late 1850s. William Horstman, Philadelphia; 28". Blue background. Eagle runs horizontally across drum face. Includes a beater. (A) Northeast Auctions, May '90, $4,000. . . . . *$4500–5000*

Drum. Eagle with breast-shield-decorated snare drum. Ca. 1860. Attributed to Boucher. Small, 17" h. Blue background. Northeast Auctions, May '90, $3000. . . . . *$3000–3500*

Drum. Eagle design Reg. U.S. Infantry drum. Marked "Ernst Vogt, Phila., Penn. Contract Dec. 29, 1864." Multicolor painted sides. Gilded eagle with star background and U.S. breast shield. Bright red rims. Arrows in left talon; laurel branch in right. *$2500–3000*

Drum. George Emmerson Company B, New Hampshire Volunteers snare drum. Ca. 1861. Probably handmade. Unit designation is stenciled in black over imitation wood grain color. Pictured in *Musical Instruments and Military Bands.* . . . .
. . . . *Value Indeterminate*

Drum. 5th Regiment Maryland National Guard. Ca. 1861. Five-star eagle drum. William Boucher, Jr., Baltimore. Multicolor. Five stars appear in gray-white cloud above eagle's wingspread. *$2000–2200*

Drum. Gettysburg eagle drum. Ca. 1861. Horstmann Bros., manufacturer. Served as model for 1870 oil painting "Battle of Gettysburg" by Peter Frederick Rosthermel. Drum was said to have been found at Gettysburg after the battle.. . . . .
. . . . *Value Indeterminate*

Drum. New Hampshire Militia bass drum. Ca. 1862. Probably handmade. No identifying marks but Dublin, NH, attribution. Circular brass tack pattern in drum face and straight line of tacks at seams where shell overlaps. *$1500–1700*

Drum. 9th Regiment New York Militia battle drum. Ca. 1860. Handprinted label inside shell: "Wm L. Tomkins & Sons, Makers, Yonkers, NY." Full-painted rendering of NY state seal against background of U.S. and regimental flags; cannon and stacked cannon balls; oak and laurel wreaths. Conceivably used at Spotsylvania and Wilderness campaigns. (A) Riba, Oct. '90, $4000. . . . . *$4500–5000*

Drum. 93rd Pennsylvania Infantry. Ca. 1861. William Boucher, Jr., Baltimore. Eagle with large shield in talons. Includes original transcript of 93rd with names of volunteers. New heads and replacement ropes; both rims repainted. Shell decoration original. (A) Riba, Oct. '90, $2000. . . . . *$2500–3000*

Drum. Pennsylvania snare drum. Ca. early 1860s. William Engt, Germantown, PA, maker. Unmarked as to unit but is similar to type used in battle of Gettysburg. Missing heads and ropes. REF: Caba's *U.S. Military Drums,* pp. 61, 62. (A) Riba, Oct. '90, $2500. . . . . *$2500–3000*

Drum. Reg. U.S. Infantry eagle drum. Ca. 1863. Horstmann Bros., Philadelphia. Multicolor with deep blue-green background. Heads, rope, braces, and snares all original. *$4000–4500*

Drum. Reg. U.S. Infantry as above. Ca. 1863. 14¼" × 16½". Same Horstman design as above. 9% paint; tension ropes probably replaced. (A) Conestoga, July '94, $3400. . . . . *$3800–4000*

Drum. 17th Michigan Infantry drum. Ca. 1861. Ernst Vogt, Philadelphia, manufacturer. Green, red, white plus walnut stain. *$2000–2200*

Drum. Union Artillery drummer (unit unidentified). Late 1850s. Unknown maker. Early-style metal rim hooks. Rampant eagle on tilted flagstaff with long billowing flag banner. (A) Riba, Oct. '90, $1500. . . . . *$1500–1750*

Drummer's Sling. Militia drummer's sling. White leather with name Joe England printed in ink on inside strap. (A) Dias, Nov. '94, $100. . . . . *$100–125*

Drum Major's Baton. Silver bulb-headed Union baton. Ca. 1863. Of Maine origin. Unmarked, 46" Rosewood with brass tips, gold braided worsted cord.
. . . . *$375–400*

Musician's Carpetbag. T.K. Jones Band—11th Maine Infantry. 1860s. Red, green, brown with musician's lyre symbol on flap. With copy of T.K. Jones of Portland service record, 13" w. Stark FP Cat., Nov. '94, $500. . . . . *$450–500*

Saxhorn. E-flat contrabass saxhorn of 1st Vermont Band. 1864. Played at battlefields of Wilderness and Petersburg. *$600–650*

Trumpet. Brass E-flat trumpet. Ca. 1850s. Manufactured by Graves & Co., Winchester, NH; brass with three Vienna twin-piston valves. *$450–500*

Trumpet. German silver B-flat. Ca. 1860. Granville Draper, Boston, manufacturer. Three string valves. *$500–525*

Trumpet. Brass B-flat trumpet. Ca 1861. B.F. Richardson, Boston. Three string rotary valves. Bell is positioned at bottom of instrument. *$525–550*

NAUTICAL EQUIPMENT

Axe Sheath. Boarding axe sheath, U.S. Navy. Stamped "U.S.N.Y., Boston" in oval. (A) Oct. '94, $250. . . . . *$250–300*

Boarding Pike. Naval boarding pike top. (A) Dias, Nov. '94, $50 . . . . *$50–75*

Boat Fenders. Pair of fenders to hang over boat rail for protection when mooring. Leather; cork filled. (A) Oct. '94, $25.. . . . . *$25–50*

Boat Fenders. Similar to above with "U.S. Navy" stamped on side. (A) Oct 94, $50. . . . . *$50–75*

Boat Fenders. Similar to above; cork-filled. Marked "U.S.N." with single star. (A) Dias, Nov. '94, $85. . . . . *$75–85*

Boat Pike. Union Navy boarding pike top. (A) Oct. '94, $60. . . . . *$50–75*

Cartridge Box. "U.S.N." pistol cartridge box. With interior tins, stamped "U.S.N.Y. Boston" in inner flap; missing closure tab. (A) Dias, Nov. '94, $125. . . . . *$125–150*

Document Box. "U.S.S. Benton, Commodore Porter's Iron Clad Flag Ship Bald Head." April 1863. 6" × 9" × 3½" wooden box. Legend in banner at top supported by eagles. Fort on hill at left. Multicolored painted scene. *$550–600*

Folding Knife. Navy-type folding knife with rosewood handle. (A) Oct. '94, $55. . . . . *$50–75*

Fuse Box. U.S. Navy fuse box. Stamped "Navy Yard, NY, 1864." Anchor design; belt loop. (A) Oct. '94, $150. . . . . *$150–200*

Leg Irons. U.S. Navy Towers patented leg irons. No key. (Pictured in Bannerman's 1907 catalog.) (A) Oct. '94, $50. . . . . *$50–75*

Sword. Naval wooden practice sword. Ca. 1862. Oak with leather guard. (A) Dias, Nov. '94, $50.. . . . . *$50–65*

Telescope. Navy four-draw telescope. Brass with leather wrap. (A) Oct. '94, $250. . . . . *$250–300*

Telescope. Navy single-draw telescope. Jones, London, Day or Night. (A) Oct '94, $170. . . . . *$150–175*

Telescope. Navy three-draw brass telescope. John Barker & Co., Ltd. With leather wraps. (A) Dias, Nov. '94, $275. . . . . *$250–300*

Warning Rattle. Naval battle warning rattle used aboard warships. Ratchet type. (A) Oct. '94, $175. . . . . *$150–200*

Warning Rattle. Similar to above but with double clapper. *$100–125*

Warning Rattle. Battle rattle from U.S.S. steam sloop *Pensacola*. Main mast wooden rattle with ship's name stencilled in black. 12½" × 71½" × 8" overall dimensions. Includes copies of *Pensacola*'s papers; originally purchased by Bannermans. (A) Dias, Nov. '94, $750. . . . . *$750–800*

Warning Rattle. Ship's masthead attached type. Missing clapper and crank handle. (A) Oct. '94, $125. . . . . *$125–150*

Water Bag. Naval canvas waterbag. Ropework binding and wooden plug. May well be handmade by federal sailor. *$75–100*

Surgeon's Equipment (Military)

Amputation Saw. Long surgeon's field amputation saw. Tapered with rounded end; pistol-grip handle. (A) Oct. '94, $150. . . . . *$150–175*

Bottle. Green glass medicine bottle. Marked "U.S.A. Hosp. Dept." (633). From site of Letterman Hospital near Gettysburg, PA, battleground. (A) July '94, $275. . . . .
. . . . *$250–300*

Crutch. Civil War wooden crutch. (A) Oct. '94, $30. . . . . *$25–30*

Mortice and Pestle. Doctor's porcelain units for grinding powders for poultices, etc. (A) Oct. '94, $25. . . . . *$25–35*

Scalpel. Surgeon's double scalpel. Ca. 1860s. Manufactured by Goldthwaite & Co. In tortoiseshell case. (A) Oct. '94, $50. . . . . *$50–75*

Tooth Extractor. Military dentist's extractor. Metal rosewood handle; rare adjustable extractor. (A) Oct '94, $250. . . . . *$250–300*

Trefoil. Trefoil or skull drilling saw. Has brass shaft and handle. Marked "P. McC & D., Chicago." (A) Oct. '94, $250. . . . . *$250–300*

Miscellaneous

Bracelet. Heavy slave bracelet from Ivory Coast, Africa. Twist and incise decoration. Chain and pin gone; good patina. (A) July '94, $10. . . . . *$25–35*

Camp Chair. Folding camp chair with carpet seat. (A) Dias, Nov. '94, $60. . . . *$60–75*

Cannonball Carrying Case. Leather case with heavy canvas lining. Heavy brown saddle leather exterior, 6¹/₂" dia.; 28" l. Leather handle. (A) Julia, Mar. '94, $605. .
. . . . *$550–600*

Field Glasses Case. Union issue field glasses case. Leather case; good condition. (A) Jenack, Oct. '94, $60. . . . . *$50–75*

Field Jug. Union field jug. Ca. 1860. Pottery. (A) Jenack, Oct. '94, $45. . . *$35–50*

Handcuffs. Pair of Civil War iron handcuffs with key. (A) Oct. 94, $125. . . *$125–150*

Saber Belt. U.S. black buff belt. Rectangular eagle plate and applied wreath of silver, with single hanger strap. Lon saber strap missing; leather dry but pliant. (A) '94, $400. . . . . *$300–400*

Shackles. Wrought-iron leg shackles. Manufactured in Fayetteville, NC. Light rust coating, but very good condition. (A) July '94, $300. . . . . *$300–400*

Spectacles. Pair of Civil War–period coin silver spectacles with extendable arms; made by Stone & Ball; in original tin case. (A) Oct. '94, $35. . . . . *$50–60*

Sword Belt. Militia officer's sword belt (430). Yellow leather with two applied black stripes. Rectangular belt plate with applied star within wreath. Leather is crackled and dry, but hangers still attached. (A) '94, $500. . . . . *$500–550*

Valise. Union Artillery leather valise. "U.S. Watervliet Arsenal" marked on each end; L.T. Prime inspector's stamp. Lined with original denim; all straps intact. REF: Lord, p. 124. (A) Oct. '94, $750. . . . . *$700–800*

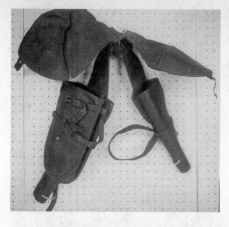

Saddle holsters: Complete, for Colt Dragoon and U.S. Model 1855 Springfield pistol, with shoulder stock, full strap, $1,200–$1,300. (Photo courtesy of Paul Dias Auctions)

George Armstrong Custer's campaign belt with brass eagle buckle, $18,000–$20,000. (Photo courtesy of Riba Auctions)

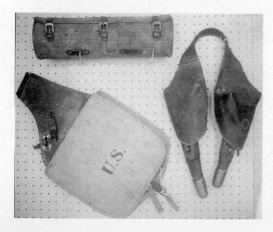

Top: *Post-war saddlebags, $250–$300.* Bottom left: *Saddle valise, $450–$500.* Right: *Cavalry holster set for Colt Model 1860 .44 calibre revolver, $350–$400.*

Top: *Leather drover's whip, $550–$600.* Center: *Cannon brush top, $50–$75; artillery cannon powder ramrod, $100–$125; 1867 carbine boot, $75–$100 (1887 model also pictured, but not priced); iron cannonball worm, $175-$200.* Bottom row: *Cannon sponge bucket, $455–$500; artillery tar bucket, $425–$450; swab bucket (not Civil War–era, not priced); cannon cleaning brush head, $300–$350; tin camp coffeepot, $100–$110. (Photo courtesy of Paul Dias Auctions)*

Left to right: *Folding camp chair, $50–$75; regulation U.S. canteen, blue cover, white strap, $300–$325; hide-covered, studded accessory trunk, $85–$100. (Photo courtesy of Paul Dias Auctions)*

Left: *C.S.A. cedarwood canteen with linen strap, $3,000–$3,200.* Top right: *New Hampshire regiment leather cartridge box, $2,000–$2,200. (Photo courtesy of Dublin NH Historical Society)* Bottom right: *C.S.A. eagle drum, regiment and maker unknown, ca. 1861, $10,000–$12,000.*

Left to right: *9th NY Militia drum, with painted state seal, $4,500–$5,000; 1820–1830 era infantry drum with tinned sheet-steel shell, $3,500–$4,000; 93rd Pennsylvania Infantry drum made by Wm. Boucher, Jr., Baltimore, $2,500–$3,000; snare drum made by Wm. Ent, Germantown, PA, saw service at Gettysburg, $3,000–$3,500.*

AUTOGRAPHS

The auction record for a Lincoln autograph or *any* Civil War–related autograph was set in 1984 at Sotheby's, NYC, when Malcolm Forbes purchased a signed copy of the Emancipation Proclamation for $297,000.

Abbreviations used in autograph collecting are as follows:

ADS: Autograph Document Signed. Identical to DS, except that body of document is also in the hand of the signer.

ALS: Autograph Letter Signed. A letter completely in the hand of the person listed and signed by that person.

ANS: Autographed Note Signed. Usually has no salutation or ending.

AQS: Autograph Quotation Signed. Same as QS except that quote is penned by signer.

CS: Card Signed.

DS: Document Signed. Any official document signed by the person listed.

FF: Free Frank. An envelope mailed by government official or other notable who has privilege of mailing correspondence at government expense. The signature is placed in lieu of postage and is often accompanied by word "free."

LS: Letter Signed. Body of letter is by a secretary or someone else other than the person listed as signer.

QS: Quotation Signed. Quotation itself may be typed, printed, or written in another hand.

SB: Signed Book.

SIG: Signature of person listed. Often found on a small card or as a "clipped signature" cut from a document or letter.

TLS: Typed Letter Signed.

TNS: Typed Note Signed.

CLIPPED SIGNATURES

Clipped signatures are signatures signed on album pages, notes, envelopes, and other scraps of paper.

C.S.A. Gen. Daniel W. Adams. He led Adams Louisiana Brigade; wounded and captured at Chickamauga. Exchanged, he later commanded the Dist. of Central Alabama. *$85–100*

C.S.A. Gen. William Wirt Allen. Commissioned Maj. 1st Alabama Cav. Made Brig. Gen. in '64 and led mounted brigade under Wheeler in Atlanta campaign. Later, opposed Sherman in the March to the Sea. *$100–125*

Union Gen. Benjamin Alvord. Maj. paymaster at war's onset. Promoted to Brig. Gen. in '62. Commanded Dist. of Oregon through most of war. *$20–25*

Union Gen. Jacob Ammen. Taught at U.S.M.A. Civil engineer when war began. Commissioned Capt. 12th Ohio in '61. Commanded the 10th Brigade in Army of the Ohio. Fought at Cheat Mt., Shiloh, and Corinth. *$20–25*

C.S. Gen. George Thomas "Tige" Anderson. Commissioned Col. 11th Georgia; fought in Seven Days' Battles, 2nd Bull Run (where he was wounded), and Antietam. In '62, appointed to Brig. Gen. after leading his brigade in Jones' Div. at Antietam. Seriously wounded at Devil's Den. Later, in Field's Div., he fought at Spotsylvania, Cold Harbor, Petersburg, and Appomattox. *$50–60*

Union Gen. Robert Anderson. "Hero of Ft. Sumter." Promoted to Brig. Gen. in May '61 and Dept. of Kentucky. Later in '61, led the Dept. of Cumberland. Retired for disabilities in '63. . . . . *$85–100*

C.S.A. Gen. Samuel Reed Anderson. Appointed Tennessee Maj. Gen. State Troops in May '61. Later in '61, as Brig. Gen., commanded a brigade under Loring in West Virginia. Fought in the Valley under T. Stonewall Jackson and on the Peninsula under Jeb Magruder. *$75–85*

21st President Chester A. Arthur. "Executive Mansion" printed in blue. Signed "Chester A. Arthur." Stained upper left corner. FP Cat., '93, $450. . . . . *$450–475*

C.S.A. Gen. Turner Ashby. Cavalry Gen. Led volunteer cavalry company in 1859 to Harpers Ferry. Jackson named him Comdr. of Point of Rocks area in Harpers Ferry Dist. As Col. he joined Jeb Stuart in disguising Johnston's link-up with Beauregard before 1st Bull Run. Jackson's Cavalry Comdr. in Oct. '61 as Col. 7th Virginia Cavalry; fought in Valley campaign. Already a legend in '62, he was killed in rear-guard action near Harrisburg. *$220–225*

Union Gen. Christopher Colin Auger. Ex–Mexican War infantry vet. In '62, as brigade Comdr., he was engaged in operations on the Rappahannock. Commanded force that captured Fredericksburg. Severely wounded at Cedar Mountain. Later served on military court investigating Mile's surrender at Harpers Ferry. *$20–25*

Union Gen. Romelyn Beck Ayres. Fought at Bull Run; Chief of Artillery for W.F. Smith's div. Took command of 1, 2, V Potomac in Aug. '63. Fought at Gettysburg, the Wilderness, through Cold Harbor. Wounded at Petersburg. Was breveted for Gettysburg. *$20–25*

Union Officer Orville E. Babcock. Was Banks A.D.C. until Aug. 61, building defenses around Washington; fought in Peninsular campaign attached to Eng. Bat. Served with IX Corps as Chief Eng. Breveted Brig. Gen. for war service, was Grant's A.D.C. until 1877. . . . . *$25–30*

Union Officer Adam Badeau. Staff of Gen. Sherman in '62; Lt. Col. Mil. Sec. to U.S. Grant. Author of *Military History of Ulysses Grant* and *Grant in Peace*. *$15–20*

Union Naval Officer Theodorus Bailey. Naval Comdr. in May '61 in blockade of Pensacola; 2nd in command under Farragut in attack on New Orleans, in gunboat *Cayuga*. Promoted Rear Adm. in '66. . . . . *$35–40*

C.S.A. Gen. Alpheus Baker. Col. 54th Alabama and captured at Island No. 10; exchanged in '62. Led regt. to Ft. Pemberton, Baker's Creek; wounded at Vicksburg. Commanded Brigade in Stuart's Div. under Hood in Atlanta campaign. In Jan. '65 went to Carolinas, fighting at Bentonville.. . . . . *$100–125*

Union Gen. Edward Dickinson Baker. English born, ex-Sen. from Oregon and leading San Francisco lawyer. Friend of Lincoln. Commissioned Col. 71st Pennsylvania in June '61 (called the "First California" in his honor). Comdr. Stones Div., Potomac. Killed at Balls Bluff late in '61. . . . . *$20–25*

Union Gen. Nathaniel Prentiss Banks. Noted ex-Cong., Gov. of MA; Pres. Illinois Central. Headed Dept. of Annapolis, then Dept. of Shenandoah. Defeated Stonewall Jackson at Kernstown. Was fall guy for ill-advised orders from Washington plus Jackson's strategy; he was reassigned to Pope's Army of Virginia; at Cedar Mt., Banks was again out-generaled by Jackson. Later succeeded Benjamin Butler in command of Dept. of Gulf. Heroic leader at Port Hudson, capturing it and removing the last obstacle to free navigation of the Mississippi River. Resigned in '64 after unsuccessful Red River campaign. Returned to civilian life and served in Congress up through late '80s. *$65–75*

C.S.A. Gen. William Barksdale. Ran pro-slavery newspaper in Tennessee prior to fighting in Mexican War. Was Cong. in '61 when he resigned to be named Q.M. Gen. of Mississippi; entered C.S.A. as Col. 13th Mississippi. Led regiment at 1st Bull Run. Appointed Brig. Gen. in '62; given a brigade under Longstreet; mortally wounded at Peach Orchard. *$400–450*

Union Gen. Francis Channing Barlow. Harvard grad., member of *NY Tribune* ed. staff. Commissioned Lt. Col. 61st New York Nov. '61. At siege of Yorktown, Fair Oaks, and promoted. Severely wounded at Antietam and at Gettysburg. There is story that C.S.A. Gen. John B. Gordon found him at Gettysburg, gave him water, and put him in building to save his life. He was breveted Maj. Gen. U.S.V. in Aug. '64 for Spotsylvania. As Att. Gen. after war, he led prosecution of "Boss" Tweed. *$20–25*

Union Gen. James Barnes. Taught at U.S.M.A. Commissioned Col. 18th Massachusetts in June '61; led regiment in Peninsular Campaign. Comdr. 1,1,V Potomac in Dec. '62. Fought Antietam, Chancellorsville, Fredericksburg. Wounded at Gettysburg. Breveted Brig. Gen. U.S.V. in Nov. '62 and Maj. Gen. U.S.V. (war service). *$50–60*

Union Gen. William Farquahar Barry. U.S.M.A. grad. Stationed at Leavenworth during "Bleeding Kansas" years. Helped Maj. Ringgold establish 1st light artillery battery in U.S. Army. As Maj. 5th U.S. Artillery in '61, he was in defense of Ft. Pickens, Florida. Fought at Bull Run as McDowell's Chief of Artillery during Peninsular Campaign; also for defenses of Washington. Became Sherman's Chief of Artillery in '64. Breveted Maj. Gen. for Atlanta, and J.E. Johnston's surrender. *$50–65*

C.S.A. Gen. P.G.T. Beauregard. *$130–150*

C.S.A. Gen. Bernard Elliott Bee. Appointed Brig. Gen. C.S.A. in June '61. Comdr. of brigade under Johnston at 1st Bull Run and immortalized T. Jackson with "Stonewall" allusion. Mortally wounded at Bull Run. *$200–225*

C.S.A. Cabinet Officer Judah Benjamin. U.S. Sen., lawyer. Served in C.S.A. as Sec. of War; later Sec. of State under Davis. Fled to England after war and became Queen's Consul in '72. . . . . *$125–135*

C.S.A. Gen. Henry Lewis "Rock" Benning. Jurist who handed down decision that Georgia Supreme Court was not bound by U.S. Supreme Court on constitutional questions. Commissioned Col. 17th Georgia in Aug. '61, Comdr. at Malvern Hill and 2nd Bull Run. Comdr. of Toomb's brigade at Antietam, Fredericksburg. Under

Hood at Gettysburg, Knoxville, and Chicamauga. Wounded at Wilderness. Impoverished by war, the part-Cherokee warrior rebuilt his lucrative law practice in Columbus, Georgia. *$110–125*

Union Officer F.W. Benteen. *$175–200*

C.S.A. Gen. Braxton Bragg *$250–275*

C.S.A. Lawrence O. Branch. A Dem. Cong. of North Carolina, he advocated moderacy, but when South seceded, he was named Q.M. and Paymaster Gen. of State troops; commissioned Col. 33rd North Carolina and in Nov. '61 Brig. Gen. C.S.A. of forces around New Bern. Fought at 2nd Bull Run, Cedar Run, Harpers Ferry. Killed at Antietam in Sept. '62. . . . . *$200–225*

Signed FF by 15th Pres. James Buchanan. Postmarked Aug. 10 but year not given. Signed franked envelope, "Free, James Buchanan" in bold ink. FP Cat., '93, $425. . . . . *$400–425*

C.S.A. Gen. Simon Bolivar Buckner. Kentuckian. Taught at West Point. Appointed Brig. Gen. C.S.A. Sept. '61. Surrendered to Grant at Ft. Donelson. Exchanged in Aug. '62. Promoted to Maj. Gen. and served under Bragg in N. Georgia and at Chickamauga. Given command of Dist. of Louisiana in '64. After war, became Dem. Gov. of Kentucky in 1887–92. Bolted party in '96 when they went for free silver platform. Ran as V.P. on Nat. Dem. ticket. Great friend of Grant and pallbearer at his funeral. Father of Gen. S.B. Buckner, Jr., who was killed in World War II at Okinawa in 1945. . . . . *$100–125*

Union Gen. Don Carlos Buell. Ohioan, who in Aug. '61 was given command of Army of Potomac; few months later succeded Sherman as C.G. of Dept. of Ohio. Stones River campaign, and a drawn battle at Perryville, led to public outpouring to have him replaced by Rosecrans. Mustered out of military service in May '64. Later Pres. of Green River Iron Co. Despite support from Grant, Buell was judged unequal to task of leading volunteer forces. *$30–40*

Union Gen. Ambrose Burnside. *$90–110*

Union Gen. Benjamin "Beast" Butler, a.k.a "Spoons." *$40–50*

C.S.A. Gen. Matthew Galbraith Butler. So. Carolinian. Commissioned Capt. in Hampton Legion and fought at 1st Bull Run. Lost right foot at Brandy Station in June '63. Returned to active duty as Brig. Gen. Sept. '63 and commanded brigade in fighting around Richmond. As Maj. Gen. in Sept. '64, joined Johnston in opposing Sherman in Carolinas. Later a Dem. Sen.; McKinley appointed him Maj. Gen. U.S.V. in 1898. . . . . *$50–75*

C.S.A. Gen. William Lewis Cabell. Virginia U.S.M.A. grad. Maj. in C.S.A. in '61; organized commissary and quartermaster depts. Chief Q.M. on Beauregard's staff during 1st Bull Run, then served under J.E. Johnston. Later given command of all troops in N.E. Arkansas. Captured leading Cav. Brig. at Marais Des Cygnes, Kansas, Oct. '64. Later four-time Mayor of Dallas. *$125–150*

Union Gen. Charles Thomas Campbell. Pennsylvania. Commissioned Capt. Btry. A. Pennsylvania Light Artillery May '61. Wounded three times at Fair Oaks; twice at Fredericksburg. Wounds kept him from further field service. Promoted to Brig. Gen. U.S.V. Nov. '62. . . . . *$30–35*

Union Gen. Edward Sprigg Canby. Kentucky. U.S.M.A. Col. U.S. Inf. May '61 in New Mexico. Held that terr. for Union and prevented C.S.A. invasion of California. Commanded troops in NYC after draft riots in '62. Severely wounded in W. Mississippi. Led assault on Mobile and accepted surrender of Taylor and Kirby Smith. Comdr. Dept. of the Gulf, June '65; breveted Brig. Gen. U.S. for Mobile. In 1866 Comdr. Dept. of Columbia and murdered by Modoc Indians while arranging peace treaty. *$40–50*

C.S.A. Gen. James Bonald Chalmers. Virginia lawyer. Commissioned Capt. C.S.A. Mar. '61; led 2nd Brigade, 3rd Div. II Corps at Shiloh. Wounded at Stones River. In '63 Comdr. of Dist. of Mississippi and E. Louisiana; Comdr. 1st Cav. Div. in '64. Was with N.B. Forest at Ft. Pillow. Post-war Dem. legislator and later sent to Congress. *$90–110*

Union Gen. Joshua Lawrence Chamberlain.. *$20–25*

C.S.A. Gen. Benjamin Franklin Cheatham. Tennessee. Promoted to Maj. in Tennessee Militia; Brig. Gen. of state forces May '61. In 1861–63 commanded div. in Polk's and later Hardee's corps as Maj. Gen. Surrendered with Johnston in No. Carolina. *$120–130*

Henry Clay, Abolitionist Statesman—Signed Free Frank Addressed to Capt. Leslie Combs. Undated, 1850s, with postmark "Washington City." Signed "Free/H. Clay." Minimum age toning. FP Cat., '93, $250. . . . . *$250–275*

Collection—Union Generals, Full Rank. Over 75 signatures in all from war date album. Includes Gens. Banks, Blair, Burnside, Butler, Davis, Dix, Foster, J.B. Fry, Hooker, Logan, McDowell, Meigs, Orr, Pope, Rosecrans, Sheridan, Sherman, Sickles, Thomas, J.H. Wilson. Also friends of Lincoln, i.e., W.W. Orme of Illinois, John P. Slough. Admirals include Farragut and Porter. Accompanied by complete biographical list. (A) Riba, Feb. '90, $2000. . . . . *$2200–2500*

C.S.A. Gen. Samuel Cooper. U.S.M.A. Highest ranking officer in C.S.A.; full Gen. from Virginia as of May '61. Served entire war in Richmond as Adj. and Insp. Gen. Helped Jefferson Davis organize War Dept. and army. Fled with Davis after Appomattox. Lived in Alexandria, Virginia, after parole. *$75–100*

ANS Gen. John Adams Dix. Sec. of Treasury under Lincoln. 10 Oct., 1863. Short note on Dept. of the East letterhead. Ft. Dix was named after the Gen. Harmer Rooke Absentee Auction, Oct. '94, $325. . . . . *$300–325*

Capt. Abner Doubleday A.C.S. Card Inscribed and Signed. 7 Aug. 1865. "Armed treason must be answered from the mouth of a cannon—Abner Doubleday, Capt. 1st U.S. Arty, Commanding Co. E. at Ft. Sumter, S.C." Incl. with C.D.V. of Doubleday signed "AHD." FP Cat., '93, $2,900. . . . . *$2500–2700*

C.S.A. Gen. Jubal Anderson "Old Jube" or "Jubilee" Early. Virginia U.S.M.A. Voted against Virginia secession, but followed state and commissioned Col. 24th Virginia. Va. Comdr. of Div. at 1st Bull Run; appointed Brig. Gen. C.S.A. July '61. Led brigade in Peninsular Campaign. Wounded at Williamsburg. . . *$140–150*

Ephriam Elmer Ellsworth of N.Y. Zouaves. $325–350

C.S.A. Gen. Richard Stoddard "Dick" Ewell. Washington, D.C. U.S.M.A. Appointed Brig. Gen. Comdr. 2nd Brigade at 1st Bull Run. Maj. Gen. in June '61. . . .

Union Adm. David Glascow Farragut.. . . . . *$85–100*

C.S.A. Gen. Samuel Wragg Ferguson. So. Carolina U.S.M.A. Brig. Gen. C.S.A. July '63 from Mississippi. Comdr. cav. brigade in Polk's Corps in Atlanta campaign. After war, he was lawyer and politician in Mississippi. *$100–125*

Nathan Bedford Forrest, Mounted Signature, Cut, Undated. Bold signature beneath copy of engraved Forrest portrait. Fine condition. FP Cat., '93, $895. . . . . *$800–850*

Nathan Bedford Forrest, ALS to Unnamed Autograph Seeker. 24 Oct., 1868. Half-page note: "Yours 5 June to hand and request complied with Yours Respectfully N.B., Forrest." In *Autographs of the Confederacy* Reese states that Forrest's is one of the most desirable of all C.S.A. autographs. FP Cat., '93, $1700. . . . . *$1500–1700*

Union Gen. John Gray Foster. New Hampshire. Taught Eng. at U.S.M.A. Supervised harbor installations and served under Anderson at Ft. Sumter. With Eng. Bureau, constructed forts along New Jersey coast. Comdr. 1st Brig. North Carolina Dec. '61–July '63. Also Dept. of Virginia and North Carolina. Injuries received from fall from horse forced sick leave, but later assigned command of Dept. of the South May '64–Feb. '65. Breveted Maj. Gen. for war service............ *$35–50*

Union Gen. John C. Fremont.................................. *$125–150*

C.S.A. Gen. Samuel Gibbs French. New Jersey. U.S.M.A. Named Chief of Ordnance when Mississippi seceded; commissioned Maj. Gen. C.S.A. artillery in Apr. '61. He led at Evansport, blocking the Potomac; took over at New Bern; then command of Dept. of Southern Virginia, North Carolina and appointed Maj. Gen. Oct. '62. Led div. under Johnston at Jackson, Mississippi, Atlanta campaign, and Hood's Franklin and Nashville campaigns. *$135–150*

Union Gen. William Henry French. Maryland U.S.M.A. Brig. U.S.V., Capt. 1st Artillery in '61. Comdr. of 3rd Brig., Sumner's Div., in defenses of Washington; led numerous units at Fair Oaks, Peach Orchard Station, Glendale, Malvern Hill. Led 3rd Div. II Corps at Antietam, Fredericksburg. Maj. Gen. in June '63 at Chancellorsville. Gen. Meade held him responsible for Mine Run failure, and he was replaced and saw no further field service after Comdr. of III Corps again. *$40–50*

C.S.A. Adley H. Gladden. So. Carolina. Brig. Gen. C.S.A. Sept. '61; led his brigade at Pensacola. Mortally wounded at Shiloh................... *$275–300*

C.S.A. Gen. Archibald Gracie, New York U.S.M.A. Capt. of Washington Light Inf. Co.; led troops that seized U.S. arsenal at Mt. Vernon. Commissioned Maj. 11th Alabama. Served under Kirby Smith in E. Tennessee as Col. 43rd Alabama. Commanded brigade under Preston at Chickamauga. Wounded at Bean's Station; fought in May '64 campaign around Wilderness and Spotsylvania. Killed by shell in siege of Petersburg. *$350–400*

Signature Card by 18th Pres. U.S. Grant and Wife Julia Dent Grant, possibly as Pres. and First Lady. Archivally framed in gold and silver frame. FP Cat., '93, $1250.. *$1100–1200*

C.S.A. Gen. Wade Hampton. So. Carolina. Opposed to slavery but raised Hampton Legion as Col. of Cav. and fought for C.S.A. at 1st Bull Run. Wounded in number of battles, including Southern Pines, Gettysburg. A brilliant horseman, he later taught his unit to fight on foot as mounts became scarce in Jan. '65. Elected Gov. of So. Carolina in 1876; U.S. Sen. until '91. Later, his conservative, predominantly "Old South" party was swept away............................. *$150–175*

C.S.A. Gen. Alexander Travis Hawthorne. Commissioned Lt. Col. 6th Arkansas in '61. Led regt. at Shiloh. Fought at Helena and Ft. Hindman under Holmes during Vicksburg campaign. Appointed Brig. Gen. C.S.A. Feb. '64. Led brigade at Jenkins' Ferry (Arkansas)... *$135–150*

C.S.A. Gen. Thomas Carmichael Hindman. Tennessee. Ex-Cong., ardent secessionist. Appointed Brig. Gen. from Arkansas Sept. '61. Commanded div. at Shiloh; then headed Trans-Mississippi Dept. Appointed Maj. Gen. in Apr. '62; fought at Chicamauga, Chattanooga, wounded in Atlanta campaign. After war, became involved in Reconstruction politics and was shot and killed in '68........ *$200–225*

C.S.N. Commodore George Nichols Hollins. Bolted the Fed. Navy, he was named C.D.R. of C.S.A. in June '61 and captured the *St. Nicholas* on the Potomac. Commanded Naval Station at New Orleans; defeated Union blockade on Mississippi River. Before New Orleans was captured, Hollins sat on Court of Inquiry on destruction of the *Virginia*..................................... *$225–250*

C.S.A. Gen. Thomas Jonathan "Stonewall" Jackson............. *$1200–1400*

Free Frank Signed by Andrew Johnson. Addressed from Pres. to Andrew Lord

of the Granite Bank in Boston. Very fine, but age-toned. FP Cat., '93, $1200.
. . . . *$1000–1100*

Union Gen. Phillip Kearny. New York. Military careerist. Lost left arm in Mexican War. Appointed Brig. Gen. U.S.V. in May '61, taking command of first New Jersey brigade to be formed. Distinguished himself at Williamsburg, Seven Pines, and 2nd Bull Run; appointed Maj. Gen. in July '62. Killed at Chantilly in Sept. '62 after accidentally riding into enemy lines and trying to fight his way out.
. . . . *$275–300*

C.S.A. Gen John Herbert Kelly. Alabama. Resigned as cadet at U.S.M.A. and commissioned 2nd Lt. C.S.A. With Hardee in Missouri, he was promoted to Asst. Adj. Gen. in '61. Led 8th Arkansas at Perryville and Stones River, where he was severely wounded. At 24, he was appointed Brig. Gen.; commanded cav. div. under Wheeler. Killed Aug. '64 near Franklin, Tennessee. *$375–400*

"R.E. Lee" Clipped Signature. Very fine, minimal fading. Matted and mounted in ebony frame with brass plate. FP Cat., $3150 . . . . *$1900–2000*

Free Frank Signed by Abraham Lincoln and Mary Todd Lincoln. Postmarked "Washington City, May 17, 1862." Perhaps *the* ultimate in presidential signed FFs. Addressed to James Sprigg in Montana. Lincoln's hand. Abraham Lincoln apparently noticed that "James" should be "John" and lined out the former, inserting "John" beneath it, then adding "A. Lincoln." Accompanied by C.D.V.'s of the couple. Very fine, with slight age-toning. FP Cat., '93, $22,500. . . . . . *$20,000–22,000*

"Thomas Nast, Dec. 22, 1881." Signed card by America's first true political cartoonist and a chronicler of Civil War in *Harpers Weekly, Leslies*, etc. FP Cat., '93, $189. . . . . *$175–200*

"P.H. Sheridan, General." Date unknown. Bold signature on calling card. Includes 4" × 7" b&w photo of Sheridan in uniform. Very fine, with minor age-toning. FP Cat., '93, $275. . . . . *$250–275*

"W.T. Sherman, General." Signed card mounted with dinner invitation dated 8 Feb. 1883, honoring Sherman's 63rd birthday. Matted, in walnut frame. FP Cat., '93, $550. . . . . *$400–500*

(John Slidell) Signed Clipped Free Frank. Ca. 1862. John Slidell was a Congr. Sen. and, in 1861, Commiss. of the C.S.A. to France. Slidell sucessfully obtained a large loan for the C.S.A. from France. He was captured by the U.S. Navy, along with James Mason, in the famous Trent Affair. Bold, clear signature. Fine condition with moderate age-toning. FP Cat., '93, $325. . . . . *$250–300*

DOCUMENTS

DS Oath of Office by Chester A. Arthur as Pres. 12 May 1875. Oath is for William C. Corbett as inspector of customs for Port of New York. Ex. Union Gen. Arthur was nominated as V.P. on Garfield ticket in 1880 and succeeded to presidency following Garfield's assassination. FP Cat., '93, $950. . . . . *$850–950*

Dispatch ALS by Gen. P.G.T. Beauregard. 14 April 1865. Written from Greensboro, N.C. to Gen. J.E. Johnson within hours of Lincoln's assassination. "Gen. Ferguson reports Yadkin Bridge not practicable river rising—He intends trying Franklin Ford Crossing." A week later Johnson and Beauregard both surrendered to Sherman at Durham Station, N.C. FP Cat., '93, $8500. . . . . *$7000–8000*

Engineering Report on Ft. St. Philip. ADS by P.G.T. Beauregard. For fiscal year ending June 30, 1861. Graphically points out repairs needed at Fort with projections for future costs. In ink on pale blue-lined paper and boldly signed "G.T. Beauregard." FP Cat., '93, $2250. . . . . *$1800–2000*

Gen. Beauregard ALS Proposal for Grand Strategy to End War. 26 May 1863. From Headquarters—Mil. Dis. Savannah, GA. Penned by Beauregard to his brother-in-law Cong. Charles Villere: "We must take the offensive, as you suggest . . . by a proper selection of the point of attack . . . let Lee act on the defensive and send Bragg 30,000 men . . . to take the offensive at once; let him . . . destroy or capture (as it is done in Europe) Rosecrans' army, then call on Indiana, Illinois & Missouri to throw off the accursed Yankee nation; then upon the whole Northwest to join in the movement, form a confederacy of their own and join us by treaty of alliance." (Beauregard is smarting over being removed from command of the Army of the West.) FP Cat., '93, $6500. . . . . *$5000–6000*

John Wilkes Booth Signed Conspiracy Check. 16 Dec. 1864. Check No. 1 in account of J.W. Booth, drawn on an account at "Jay Cooke & Co., Bankers in Washington, D.C. made out to M(Mathew) W. Canning," a friend and former manager of the actor. Only six additional checks were drawn from this account prior to the assassination. This is the only check of four known (2, 3, and 7) to survive that is not held by an institution. (The account ledger resides in the Chicago Historical Society.) According to James O. Hall, co-author of *Come Retribution: The Confederate Secret Service and the Assassination of Lincoln*, Booth established the account after a suspicious trip to Montreal a month earlier. FP Cat., $28,500. . . . *$23,000–25,000*

John Brown's Check. 12 Dec. 1848. For $200 at Cabot Bank, Cabotsville (no state named), accompanied by original envelope. Printed upper left corner: "Dist. Court Denver, Booth Malone Judge." Not much can be found relating to Brown, the "Father of Abolition." (A) Absentee, Harmer Rooke, Oct. '94, $2300. . . . *$2200–2300*

James Buchanan ALS, 1-Page Formal Letter. 30 July 1827. Written to a constituent, Thomas Elder from Lancaster, PA, while Buchanan was a member of the House of Rep. States his opposition to a suit filed by Elder against a man by the name of Bard. Almost 25 years later, Buchanan would strive to uphold the slavery compromise declaration of the 1850s. *$650–700*

Ship's Paper DS, James Buchanan as Pres. 20 Aug. 1859. In four languages, full-page folio for ship *Roman*. John C. Hamblin, Master; countersigned by John Appleton, Acting Sec. of State. U.S. Seal. For whaling voyage in South Pacific. *$600–700*

Jefferson Davis $300 Savings Bank of Memphis Check. Dated 7 Dec. 1861 and made out completely in Davis' hand. On left side of check is engraved image of female deity printed in red ink; holds shield anchor and word "Hope." FP Cat., '93, $1900. . . . . *$1500–1800*

Jefferson Davis DS Transmittal Letter to the C.S.A. Senate and House of Rep. 19 March 1862. Written from the Executive Dept. by Davis; concerns a report of Sec. of War Judah Benjamin. FP Cat., $2900. . . . . *$2200–2500*

Jefferson Davis SB *The Southern Review*, Vol. II, No. 3. 1867. Baltimore, Bledsoe & Browne. Ocatvio with full-printed wrappers. Full signature of Davis on title page. Contains book review of *Life & Campaigns of General Robert E. Lee* by James D. Macabe, Jr., Bellock & Co., New York, in which the author's unmitigated abuse of Davis is cited and deplored by the reviewer. FP Cat., $5500. . . . . *$5000–5200*

Jefferson Davis DS Voucher to C.S.A. Sec. of State P.J. Benjamin. 15 Feb. 1862. Signed "Jefferson Davis, Pres't of C.S.A." Issued for $1000 in gold for the Secret Service (provided for in Act of Feb. 15, 1864) and earmarked for a covert mission, possibly even the abduction of Lincoln. Quarto, 8" x 10". *$12,000–14,000*

Edward Everett Inscribed Pamphlet of Lecture Delivered to NY Historical So-

ciety. 1 June 1853. Thirty-two-page pamphlet on *The Discovery & Colonization of America & Immigration to the U.S.* Inscribed to "F. Sales, Esq. with the best respects of E. Everett." Moderate age-toning and small tear at upper left cover. FP Cat., '93, $75 . . . . *$75–85*

David Farragut LS (Mil. Order) on U.S.S. *Hartford* **stationery.** 2 March 1863. Orders an exchanged prisoner to repair north as soon as he has transferred the accounts of the *Queen of the West* and *Harriet Lane* to Paymaster Tarbell of the *Kensington.* Written in pencil. Includes framed C.D.V. of Farragut. FP Cat., '93, $1195. . . . . *$1500–1750*

Printed Circular, General Order No. 10, DS by Adm. David Farragut. 12 July 1864. Signed "D.G.F." Calling for vessels off Mobile Bay to prepare for combat. "The howitzers must keep a constant fire." (A) Riba, June '88, $2000. . . . . *$2500–3000*

Nathan Bedford Forrest DS Oath of Allegiance. 6 Aug. 1868. One-page quarto. Partly printed. A true copy of the oath pursuant to the proclamation of the president to the U.S. of 7 Sept. 1867. Forrest to Isaac Morrison, a Commiss. of the U.S. Circuit Court for Dist. West Tennessee, Shelby County. Also signed by Morrison. *$3000–4000*

Nathan Bedford Forrest Signed Railroad Bond. 1 Sept. 1869. Signed twice by Forrest as president of Selma, Marion & Memphis Railroad Co. Double-sheet folio with seal and $40 coupons. *$250–300*

James A. Garfield ANS. 13 July 187? (numeral not legible). "Written to Warren S. Young, Treasury Dept." and marked "For Government Business Only." Urges Young to call him later in the day at his (Garfield's) home. Includes steel engraving of Garfield. Very fine. FP Cat., '93, $795. . . . . *$750–800*

James Garfield LS on Mentor, Ohio Letterhead to W.H. Crowell. 6 Sept. 1880. Written by Garfield while he was campaigning for the presidency. Refers to a possible political appointment Garfield is trying to obtain for Crowell's brother through then-Pres. Hayes. FP Cat., '93, $750. . . . . *$700–750*

DS Franklin Gerhart Commutation Receipt. 19 Sept. 1863. Green on buff certificate acknowledging receipt of $300 at Norristown, PA, from Franklin Gerhart to buy himself out of the military draft; signed by David Newport, Receiver. Commutations such as these led to the '63 NY Draft Riots. (Among the more conspicuous buyouts—Grover Cleveland and Theodore Roosevelt, Sr.) (A) Absentee, Harmer Rooke, Oct. '94, $350. . . . . *$325–350*

Ships' Journals, Rear Admiral O.S. Glisson. 1863–64. Letter journals from both the steamer *Mohican* and the U.S.S. *Santiago de Cuba,* commanded by Glisson and engaged in naval blockade work for the the Union. *Mohican* journal is dated 29 Mar. '63–18 Apr. '64, many directed to Gideon Wells, Sec. of Navy. *Santiago* journal dated from 6 June '64–10 June '65, to Wells, Admiral Porter, etc. Mentions capturing Rebel blockade runners. Each journal approx. 120 pp. Also includes Glisson's 35-star naval flag, wooden painted trunk with his name; navy dress holster. (A) Riba, July '94, $4500. . . . . *$4500–5000*

Mentor Graham ADS, Appoint. for Peter Elmore to Constable. 2 Aug. 1874. Graham was a lifelong friend of Lincoln, taught Ann Rutledge, taught Lincoln surveying and grammar. Three signers besides Graham. Ex–Roy Crocker Collection. (A) Absentee, Harmer Rooke, Oct. '94, $85. . . . . *$75–85*

U.S. Grant First Battle Orders As a General. 7 Nov. 1861. Two-page written and signed letter from Headquarters Dist. S.E. Missouri onboard steamer *Memphis.* To Capt. Henry Walke, Commdr. of gunboat *Tyler.* Grant dictates sailing time when gunboats will advance, followed by 1st Brigade under Brig. Gen. McClernand; followed by 2nd Brigade under Col. Dougherity. "Latter will be landed at lowest point of Missouri shore." In what came to be known as the Battle of Belmont, this was the first instance where Grant led troops into battle. Rated fine. FP Cat., '93, $22,000. . . . . *$20,000–22,000*

Presidential Pardon DS by Grant as Pres. 8 Aug. 1873. For Greene B. Horne. *$500–600*

Presidential Pardon DS by Grant as Pres., Washington, D.C. 15 Jan. 1873. Warrant of the pardon of Joel Hughes. *$450–550*

Presidential Pardon DS by U.S. Grant. 13 Sept. 1876. Washington, D.C. partial. Countersigned by Sec. of State Hamilton Fish. Heavy browning but signatures very good. (A) Riba, July '94, $300. . . . . *$250–300*

Ship's Papers DS by Grant as Pres. 10 Aug. 1874. In four languages. One full-page folio, paper for the barque *Perry*, George W. Bassett, Master, countersigned by Hamilton Fish, Sec. of State. U.S. Seal. For whaling voyage to Atlantic Ocean.. . . . . *$800–1000*

U.S. Grant DS Soldier's Monument Association Certificate. Undated but post–Civil War and before Grant's presidency. The Assoc. sold certificates to fund erection of monument to Grant's hometown of Galena, IL. Grant signed as pres. of assoc. Engraved certificate features oval bust portrait of Lincoln with furled flags in background. Small cameos of Victory and other deities, American Flag, and Capitol dome. Framed with steel engraving of Grant. Very fine. FP Cat, '93, $1395. . . . . *$1000–1100*

Horace Greeley ALS Invitation. 23 Nov. 1860. Addressed to "Hon. E.R. Reynolds," apparently inviting him for a weekend visit to his home. Written on "Office of the *Tribune*" letterhead. Minimal age-toning. FP Cat., '93, $250. . . . . *$200–250*

Rutherford B. Hayes DS Presidential Pardon. 10 May 1878. Authorizing Sec. of State to pardon Edward D. Harper; signed "R.B. Hayes." Harper was possibly a C.S.A. soldier. Matted and framed in gold. Minimal age-toning. FP Cat., '93, $550. . . . . *$500–550*

ADS, William H. Herndon Concerning Bill of Chancery. 3 Dec. 1853. Herndon was Lincoln's third and last law partner and a close friend and pioneer biographer of Lincoln. Written during the partnership period. Three light folds. Ex–Roy Crocker Collection. (A) Absentee, Harmer Rooke, Oct. '94, $140. . . . . . *$125–150*

Andrew Johnson DS Land Title. 1 Dec. 1854. Two-page quarto signed by Johnson as Gov. grants James Ham 200 acres of land in Tennessee. Bold signature, apparent folds. FP Cat., '93, $1295.. . . . . *$1100–1200*

Andrew Johnson as Military Gov. of Tennessee, DS Military Commission. 1 Sept. 1862. Commission awarded Robert M. Thompson as Capt. 1st Tennessee Vols. With Tennessee state seal. Has engraved C.S.A. emblem in oval with furled flags at top. Apparent fold lines. FP Cat. '93, $1195. . . . . *$1200–1400*

Ship's Papers, DS Stamped Andrew Johnson. 16 July 1866. Partly printed one-page folio in four languages for barque *Sea Ranger*, William Lewis, Master. Countersigned by William Seward. U.S. Seal. For whaling voyage to South Pacific.. . . . . *$200–250*

Col. (later Gen.) Albert Sidney Johnston ALS Report on Condition of 2nd U.S. Cavalry. 13 Dec. 1855. Reports on good condition of his men and horses in preparation for march from Ft. Washita to Ft. Belknes. Written obviously before Johnson left the Union army and joined the C.S.A. staff. Very fine; fold lines visible. FP Cat., '93, $2150. . . . . *$1800–2000*

Robert E. Lee ADS Receipt. Ca. 1840s. Signed when Lee was superintending engineer for St. Louis harbor and the Upper Mississippi and Missouri Rivers. Asserts that the expenditure charged was necessary for improvements on the Mississippi above the mouth of the Ohio. FP Cat. Jefferson Rarities Coll., $4000.............. *$3000–3500*

LS Quarto "R.E. Lee/Maj. Gen. Comm." to Col. Philip St. George Cocke. 7 May 1861. Culpepper Court House, Headquarters Virginia Forces, Richmond. Lee designates authority to subordinate Cooke to position the C.S.A.'s first volunteer forces. Two days after this letter was written, Col. Cooke began concentrating his forces at Manassas Junction. Apparently a previously unpublished document. FP Cat., $39,500. .... *$30,000–35,000*

ANS Christmas Leave Endorsement by Lincoln as Pres. 23 Dec. 1863. Six lines plus signature and date of the integral blank of an ALS from Gen. John M. Schofield, Washington, D.C. Schofield deferentially requests permission from Lincoln to be absent from the Capitol, "pending the settlement of my affairs." On verso, Lincoln responds, with "toungue in cheek": "Not the slightest objection to Gen. Schofield's visiting West Point so that he be in call by Telegraph." Lincoln had removed the troublesome Schofield from his command in Missouri and had demoted him as Maj. Gen., then transferred and replaced by Rosecrans. FP Cat., '93, $12,500. .... *$11,000–12,000*

AES Endorsement by Lincoln of AES of Gen. Charles F. Smith. 10 Jan. 1862. Smith, writing from Paducah, Kentucky, contends that he's aware of a conspiracy to have him removed from his command and requests copies of allegations against him. In the interim, Gen. Smith led a charge against Ft. Donelson and was largely responsible for its subsequent surrender. Lincoln signed this letter "A.L" and writes "Sent for Gen. McClellan's perusal." A month later, Smith was promoted to rank of Maj. Gen. Rated very fine; very slight age-toning. FP Cat., '93, $5500...........
.... *$5500–6000*

Military Appointment DS by Lincoln. 13 April 1863. One-page folio, vellum. Appointing Hartman Buche as Col. of the Corps of Engineers. Countersigned by Sec. of War Stanton. Engraved eagle, flags, cannons.............. *$3000–3500*

Lincoln Military Commission DS as Pres. 20 April 1864. Washington, D.C. Vellum commission signed by Lincoln and Sec. of War Edwin Stanton appointing Frank L. Hays as "Additional Paymaster." Blue seal intact. Winged eagle at top. Engraving of flags and other military regalia below. FP Cat., '93, $5200. ....
.... *$4800–5000*

Lincoln DS Folio Naval Commission. 23 April 1862. Confers title of Chief Engineer of U.S.N. to Alexander Henderson. Eagle at top of document; Neptune riding waves in chariot with man-o-war. Official U.S. Navy seal affixed. Extra fine. FP Cat., '93, $6500... *$6000–6200*

Ratification of U.S. Treaty with Costa Rica, DS by Lincoln as Pres. 17 Nov. 1861. One of Lincoln's earliest official duties. Lincoln's signature is in the rare form "Abrahama Lincoln." Slight age-toning, still very fine, 25½" × 17½". FP Cat., '93, $15,500.. *$14,000–15,000*

Unsigned but Partially Written Manuscript by Abraham Lincoln and Judge Davis. March 1853. A land transaction document which Judge David Davis and Lincoln, while a Springfield lawyer, prepared. Over 300 words of testimony in Lincoln's hand. Davis, an 8th Circuit Judge and an intimate friend and political supporter of Lincoln, administered his estate after his assassination...... *$5000–6000*

Paymaster Appt., Abraham Lincoln DS. 23 Feb. 1864. Paymaster appointment of Egbert Smith, countersigned by Sec. of War Stanton. Seal present. Minor soiling, one pinhole. Bold signatures. (A) Riba, July '94, $5500. .... *$5500–6000*

Presidential Pardon, DS Partial, Abraham Lincoln. 25 Sept. 1863. Countersigned by Sec. of State Seward. Heavy browning, signatures clear. (A) Riba, July '94, $3500. . . . . *$3500–4000*

ALS Recommendation by Lincoln as Pres. to Sec. of Navy Gideon Wells. 9 January 1863. On Executive Mansion stationery, entirely in Lincoln's hand. Written to Gideon Wells concerning an officer, Charles S. Boggs of New Jersey, who had been nominated for promotion to captain a month earlier. "Give special attention to this case, and let me know the result. Yours truly, A. Lincoln." Very fine with minimal fold lines. FP Cat., '93, $25,750. . . . . *$23,000–24,000*

Ship's Paper DS by Lincoln and Seward. 18 May 1861. In four languages. Paper for the ship *"Contest,* Thos. Norton Master." Countersigned by Sec. of State William Seward. For whaling voyage to the Pacific. Official seal. *$7000–8000*

ALS by Gen. George Gordon Meade, Roster of Surviving Members of Army of the Potomac. 12 June 1872. On letterhead "Headquarters Military Division of the Atlantic, Philadelphia." Addressed to Henry B. Dawson, Moricania, NJ. Written the year of Meade's death. Very fine, with some age-toning. FP Cat., '93, $350. . . . . *350–375*

ADS Marriage Bond, by Zachariah Riney, Lincoln's First School Teacher. 12 Feb. 1824. Riney taught Lincoln in the famed one-room log-cabin school near Lincoln's home. 6" × 8"; some wear on folds. Ex–Roy Crocker Collection. (A) Absentee, Harmer Rooke, Oct. '94, $500. . . . . *$500–525*

ALS Invitation from Gen. Winfield Scott. 27 Nov. (no year). Written to C. King, Esq. Proffers a dinner invitation. Fine condition; minimal mounting traces on verso. FP Cat., '93, $350. . . . . *$300–325*

DS Jessee (sic) H. Stubbs Military Parole. 11 May 1865. Fredericksburg, Virginia. Issued from Office of Provost Marshal to C.S.A. soldier, swearing to uphold the Constitution, abide by the President's proclamations in reference to slaves. Fold and few other minor flaws. (A) Absentee, Harmer Rooke, Oct. '94, $160. . . . . *$150–175*

DS Maj. Gen. Joe Wheeler to Gen. Braxton Bragg Southern Tel. Co. Telegram (undated). Wheeler alerts Bragg that "12 miles north of Forsythe via Macon, enemy is still moving toward Macon by shortest direct road. Scouts report a force of enemy between Yellow and South Rivers." Partly printed and manuscript. *$350–400*

Robert E. Lee signed amnesty oath, dated October 2, 1865. From the Library of Congress.

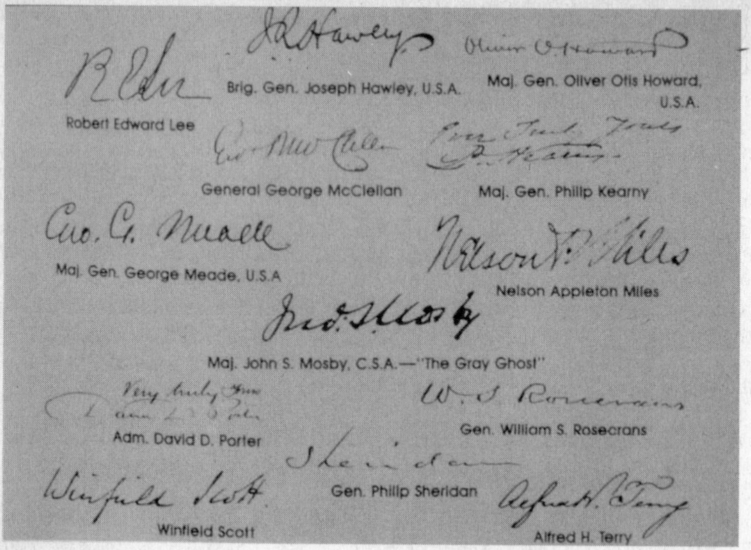

Brig. Gen. Joseph Hawley, U.S.A.

Maj. Gen. Oliver Otis Howard, U.S.A.

Robert Edward Lee

General George McClellan

Maj. Gen. Philip Kearny

Maj. Gen. George Meade, U.S.A

Nelson Appleton Miles

Maj. John S. Mosby, C.S.A.—"The Gray Ghost"

Adm. David D. Porter

Gen. William S. Rosecrans

Gen. Philip Sheridan

Winfield Scott

Alfred H. Terry

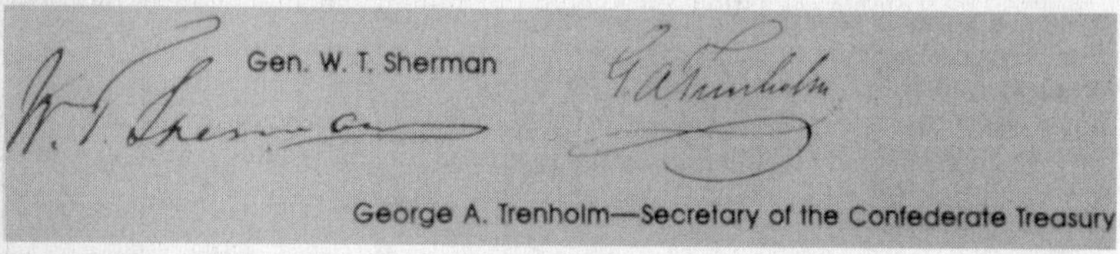

Gen. W. T. Sherman

George A. Trenholm—Secretary of the Confederate Treasury

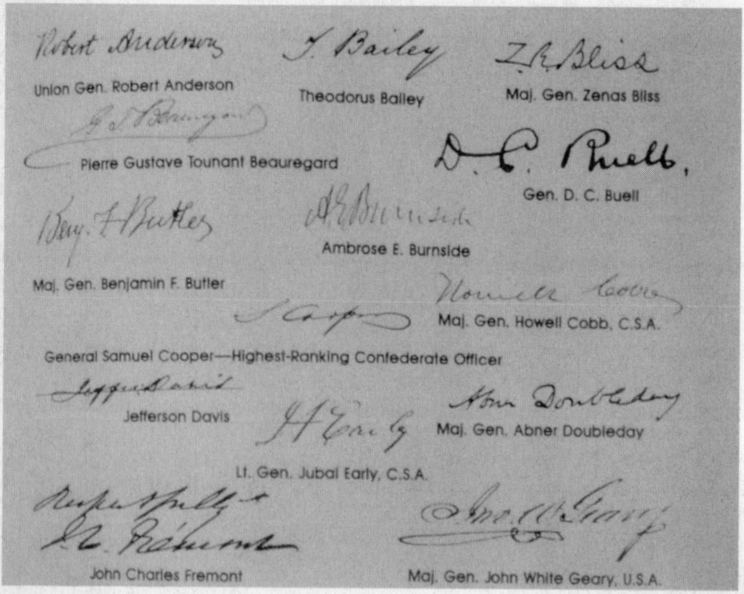

Union Gen. Robert Anderson

Theodorus Bailey

Maj. Gen. Zenas Bliss

Pierre Gustave Tounant Beauregard

Gen. D. C. Buell

Maj. Gen. Benjamin F. Butler

Ambrose E. Burnside

Maj. Gen. Howell Cobb, C.S.A.

General Samuel Cooper—Highest-Ranking Confederate Officer

Jefferson Davis

Maj. Gen. Abner Doubleday

Lt. Gen. Jubal Early, C.S.A.

John Charles Fremont

Maj. Gen. John White Geary, U.S.A.

On facing page: *Trimmed signature values. Brig. Gen. Joseph Hawley (USA), $35–$45; Maj. Gen. Oliver O. Howard (USA), $40–$50; Gen. Robert E. Lee (CSA), $1,900–$2,000; Gen. George McClellan (USA), $70–$80; Maj. Gen. Philip Kearny (USA), $275–$300; Maj. Gen. George Meade (USA), $60–$75; Gen. Nelson Appleton Miles (USA), $65–$75; Maj. John S. Mosby (CSA), $250–$275; Adm. David D. Porter (USA), $50–$65; Gen. William S. Rosencrans (USA), $125–$150; Gen. Philip Sheridan (USA), $100–$125; Gen. Winfield Scott (USA), $75–$85; Alfred H. Terry (USA), $35–$45; Gen. William T. Sherman (USA), $125–$150; George A. Trenholm (CSA), $000–$000; Gen. Robert Anderson (USA), $75–$100; Adm. Theodorus Bailey (USA), $35–$50; Maj. Gen. Zenas Bliss (USA), $25–$35; Gen P.T. Beauregard (CSA), $135–$150; Gen. Don Carlos Buell (CSA), $35–$45; Gen. Ambrose Burnside (USA), $85–$100; Maj. Gen. Benjamin F. Butler (USA), $40–$50; Maj. Gen. Howell Cobb (CSA), $85–$100; Gen. Samuel Cooper (CSA), $75–$100; Jefferson Davis (CSA), $325–$350; Maj. Gen. Abner Doubleday (USA), $225–$250; Lt. Gen. Jubal Early (CSA), $135–$145; Gen. John C. Fremont (USA), $125–$150; Maj. Gen. John W. Geary (USA), $30–$40.*

Grant to bounty land to Capt. Abraham Lincoln as a reward for service in the Black Hawk War, not priced. From the Library of Congress.

John Wilkes Booth signed conspiracy check. Drawn on Jay Cooke & Co.
Bankers. Only four checks from this account are known to have survived.
This is the only one not held by an institution, $23,000–$25,000.

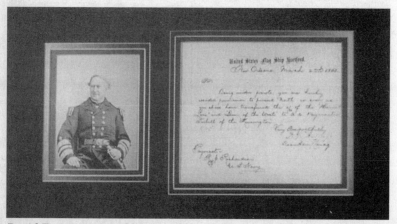

David Farragut, signed letter (military order), on U.S.S. Hartford
stationery, dated March 2, 1863, framed, $1,500–$1,750.

Abraham Lincoln, signed document. Military commission dated July 4, 1862; also signed by Secretary of War Stanton, $3,000–$3,500.

Badges, Medals, and Tokens

Badges, Shell

Antislavery "In Emancipation is National Unity." 1863. Solid silver pinback 2" × 1¾". Image of chained slave raising himself upward. Reverse inscribed "Women's LNL (Loyal National League), N.Y., 1863." Stark, Oct. '85, $1000. . . . . . . *$1000–1100*

"John Bell." 1860. 1" with brass rim; Edward Everett on reverse. Hole at top for ribbon. *$300–350*

"John Bell." 1860. 1" with brass rim; slightly different pose than above. Edward Everett on reverse. Hole at top for ribbon. *$300–350*

"John Bell/Constitution and Union." 1860. Brass shell stickpin. Shield with 13 stars at top, 20 stars below. On red, white, and blue sil rosette. *$175–200*

"Bell–Everett." 1860. Conjoined bust figs. Ferrotype with ropelike circular frame. Hake BE 3008. . . . . *$900–1000*

Hon. Montgomery Blair. 1860. Waist-up tintype of Postmaster Gen. under Lincoln; in brass frame. *$200–250*

"John C. Breckenridge." 1860. Southern Dem. Party; 1" with brass rim; "Jos. Lane" appears on reverse. *$400–450*

"John C. Breckenridge." 1860. Mini ferro ½"-shank clothing button. Name above bust portrait. *$250–300*

"Gen. Ambrose Burnside." Ca. 1862. Ferro bust profile of Burnside in ornate silver shield. Scales, Liberty, Constitution, swords, names of battles embossed. *$200–250*

Col. Cameron, New York Highlanders. Ca. 1862. 1⅝" × 1¾" tintype, Abbott & Co., NYC. Brass-framed bust portrait. Cameron served under Gen. William Sherman and was killed at Bull Run. *$125–150*

Hon. Salmon P. Chase. 1862. 1⅝" × 1¾" tintype by Abbott & Co., NYC. Bust portrait in rectangular brass frame. Lincoln's Sec. of Treasury; a '64 presidential hopeful; as Chief Justice, he presided over Johnson impeachment proceedings. *$300–350*

Cassius M. Clay. 1860. Bust portrait tintype in filigree brass frame. A prominent Rep. presidential hopeful in '60, this noted Kentucky abolitionist helped turn the nomination in Lincoln's favor. *$500–600*

Hon. John J. Crittenden. Ca. 1860. Tintype; bust portrait in rectangular brass frame. Kentucky Sen. who authored Missouri Compromise. Opposed secession. One son, George, became C.S.A. Gen. Another son, Thomas, and nephew, Thomas T., served as Union Gens. *$350–400*

Jefferson Davis/Gen. Beauregard. 1861. 1"-dia. braided border shell. Names under portraits. (Beauregard on reverse.). *$350–400*

Maj. Gen. John A. Dix. 1873. 1⅝" × 1¾" brass framed tintype from Abbott & Co., NYC; bust portrait of Gen. commanding the Dept. of Pennsylvania; later a Gov. of New York. *$150–175*

"Stephen A. Douglas." 1860. 1⅞" doughnut-style silvered brass rim. Bust portrait ferro of Douglas with name above head. Reverse portrait of Herschel Johnson as V.P. Dem. candidate. *$2500–3000*

"J.A. Garfield–C.A. Arthur." 1880. 1¼" × 1¾". Jugate bust portraits of pair; enclosed in shield with tassels; winged eagle on rod at top. Brass, with pine on reverse. *$1000–1100*

"Garfield." 1880. ⅝" dia. Profile bust portrait with name above. Stickpin reverse. .
. . . . *$250–275*

Gen. U.S. Grant. Date "1868" overprinted on Grant's chest; torso-up oval portrait. In filigree brass frame. 1" × 1¼". *$100–125*

(Grant). 1868. Sepia pasteboard oval bust photo in vertical draped flag design. Winged eagle atop. *$300–350*

(Grant) "The Boys in Blue." 1872. Grant ferro in silvered scroll shape with embossed corps badges; attached with figural anchor to blue ribbon suspended from large winged eagle clasp. Hake GR 3065. . . . . *$1100–1200*

U.S. Grant–Schuyler Colfax. 1868. Jugate conjoined ferrotype bust portraits with names appearing above heads. 1⅛" in scalloped oval brass shell. *$500–550*

"Grant–Colfax." 1868. Sepia cardboard bust portrait of Grant in uniform. 1" round brass shell. *$125–150*

"Grant–Colfax." 1868. Sepia cardboard conjoined bust portraits (Grant in uniform). Unusual horiz. rectangle format. *$300–350*

"Grant–Colfax." 1868. Ferro circular jugate portraits appearing under outspread eagle wings. Names above heads. Brass. Hake GR 3043. . . . . *$800–900*

(Grant) For President 1868/U.S. Grant. 1⅛" circular shell with bust ferro of Grant; Colfax on reverse. *$300–350*

(Grant) For President 1872/U.S. Grant. 1⅛" circular shell with bust ferro of Grant; Wilson on reverse. *$300–350*

"Grant." 1868. 1⅛" round doughnut shell with Grant bust ferro. Pin on reverse. . . .
. . . . *$200–225*

Grant Knapsack Badge. 1868. "U.S." and straps embossed on lid, which opens to reveal bust cardboard sepia Grant photo. Hake GR 3097. . . . . *$400–450*

Grant Star Badge. 1868. 1" × 1¼" ornately scrolled star-shaped shell badge with rope-designed circular inset. Bust ferro of Grant with name above; pin on reverse. .
. . . . *$500–550*

Grant Star Badge. 1868. Cardboard sepia bust photos of Grant and Colfax in 1¼" brass star. *$425–450*

Grant. 1868. 1" circular shell; Gen. in uniform bust ferro, fabric rim; pinback reverse. *$200–250*

Grant Deep Relief Portrait. 1872. Bust portrait in oval cameolike setting, framed by figural laurel leaves. Brass pinback. Hake GR 3146. . . . . *$150–200*

Grant–Wilson Jugate. 1872. Conjoined bust portrait ferro in brass oval with shell-like filligree top and bottom. *$1100–1200*

Grant–Wilson Jugate. 1872. Bust portrait ferrotypes; figural embossed flags, Liberty cap, laurel wreath. Unrecorded. Match to Greely 1872–73 . . . . *$3800–4000*

"Horace Greeley/Gratz Brown." 1872. 1³/₄" brass shell with circular jugates; winged eagle atop. *$1800–1850*

"Horace Greeley/Gratz Brown." 1872. Conjoined portraits, sepia oval ambro in brass frame. *$750–800*

"Horace Greeley." 1872. 1" × 1¹/₄" brass shell; Greeley bust portrait wearing black hat. Figural frame with eagle, laurel leaves. *$1000–1200*

"Horace Greeley." 1872. Maltese cross brass shell; Greeley bust portrait wearing black hat. Hake GR 3013. . . . . *$900–1000*

"Horace Greeley." 1872. Sepia paper bust portrait; Greeley under glass in donut rim. ³/₄" dia. with loop. *$400–500*

Horace Greeley—Quaker Hat. Hat suspended from clasped hands, tin shell pin. 1872. Hake GR 3050. . . . . *$200–250*

Greeley—"The Pen is Mightier Than the Sword." 1872. Large silvered brass quill pen with circular bust ferro of Greeley inset in middle. "Pen" motto extends length of quill and feather. Hake GR 3003. . . . . *$3500–4000*

Winfield Scott Hancock Strutting Rooster. 1880. Figural shell with rooster wearing belt and saber. Hake WSH 3012. . . . . *$125–150*

W.S. Hancock–William English. 1880. Jugate oval sepia pasteboard portraits in ornate brass shell; eagle hanger. Scarcest of all 19th-century jugate pasteboards. *$2500–3000*

W.S. Hancock. 1880. Nine-pointed star ferro with 1¹/₈" bust portrait set in raised brass shell. Minus eagle suspension clasp. *$550–600*

W.S. Hancock. 1880. Figural eagle at top with circular bust portrait set in shell of four die-cast flags. *$350–400*

Harrison and Morton "Our Champions." 1880. Multicolor jugate in brass-rimmed octagon shape as hanger from brass-winged eagle. "Protection for Home Industries" below. Hake H3200. . . . . *$1200–1400*

Lincoln–Hamlin Jugate Ferrotype. 1860. Names below portraits; beaded trim. *$3500–4000*

Lincoln–Hamlin Jugate Ferrotype. 1860. Unusual 1⁵/₈" donut size with elaborate floral border. *$1200–1300*

"For President Abraham Lincoln." 1864. Circular brass 1" ferro in shield—shaped opening A. Johnson ferro on reverse. *$1100–1200*

"For President/Hon. Abraham Lincoln." 1860. Gilded brass oval frame with braided border. 2¹/₂" h. Beardless Lincoln bust portrait. No lettering. Legend appears in yellow pasteboard insert on reverse plus "Manufactured by Geo. Clark Jr. and Co., Ambrotype Artists". *$1500–1700*

(Lincoln) "E. Pluribus Union." 1864. Ferro bust portrait to half left in raised oval shell; flying eagle figural above. Figural eagle clasp with red, white, blue ribbon suspended. King 136. 30 × 33 mm. . . . .

Abraham Lincoln. 1865. Oval bust portrait tintype in brass frame; 2" × 2¹/₂". . . *$600–650*

Lincoln and General Ambrose Burnside. 1861. Miniature brass book on hanger; opens like locket to four folding leaves; photos of beardless Lincoln and Burnside; two ladies. *$250–300*

"A. Lincoln—1864" Star. Circular bust ferro centered in five-point, raised-bordered brass on tin star. 48 mm. *$1000–1100*

(Lincoln) "Republican Invincibles." 1864. Silvered shield 22 × 24 mm. with embossed lettering. King 157. . . . . *$1200–1500*

(Lincoln) "Union Campaign Club." 1864. King 156. Silvered brass shield (same size as above). *$1200–1500*

John Logan. 1884. V.P. Dem. hopeful. Head portrait ferro of Logan in circle set in small star; hanger is black tin cartridge box, "Forty Rounds," gilt "U.S." emblem. The box was the badge of the 15th Corps. commanded by "Black Jack" Logan. . . .
. . . . *$250–300*

James M. Mason. Ca. 1861. 1⅝" × 1¾" tintype by Abbott & Co., NYC. Bust portrait in rectangular brass frame. Mason was the captured C.S.A. commissioner famous for the Trent Affair. *$250–275*

Gen. Geo. McClellan Ferrotype. 1862. Bust figure of McClellan in 1½" gilt shield. Embossed scales of justice, crossed sabers, Liberty, names of ten major battles from May–Sept. 1862, ending with Antietam stamped on beveled flange of shield. *$1100–1200*

Gen. Geo. McClellan Ferrotype. 1864. ¾" × 1" rectangular brass frame with blank reverse. *$300–350*

"G.B. McClellan." 1864. 1" dia. with brass rim; Pendleton bust port. on reverse; punched hole for string or ribbon. *$1000–1200*

"G.B. McClellan." 1864. 1" dia. doughnut with brass rim; Pendleton bust portrait on reverse. *$350–400*

Col. James H. Perry." Ca. 1862. 1⅝" × 1¾" tintype by Abbott & Co., Waterbury, CT. Bust portrait in rectangular brass frame. *$150–175*

Winfield Scott. 1860. First Gen.-in-Chief of Union Army. Figural bust profile in toga; silver shell with filled back. 2¾". Sullivan 1852–7. . . . . *$325–350*

Uniside Jugate Ferros (4) from 1860 Presidential Race. All ⅞" dia. Ornate brass pelletlike rim; names appear under conjoined bust portraits. (1) Abraham Lincoln and Hannibal Hamlin; (2) Stephen Douglas and Herschell Johnson; (3) John Breckenridge and Jos. Lane; (4) John Bell and Edward Everett. Rated near mint. (A) Dave Frend Mail Auction, March '91, $10,175. Sold as set. *$11,000–12,000*

Veterans Badge (Unidentified). 1870. Figural semidimensional crossed rifles, knapsack, and Kepi silvered brass shell pinback. *$25–35*

Hon. Gideon Wells. 1862. 1⅝" × 1¾" tintype by Abbott & Co., NYC. Bust portrait in rectangular brass frame. Wells was Lincoln's Sec. of Navy. *$250–275*

BADGES, MISCELLANEOUS

(Cello, Pinback) Gen. J.C. Breckenridge, CSA Reunion, Louisville, 1905. 1¾" dia. multicolor celluloid with bust portrait of Breckenridge; Kentucky state seal; Eagle and globe emblem—Case Threshing Machine Co. (MA). Stark, '92, $100. . . . . *$100–125*

(Belt Buckle, Shell) Stephen A. Douglas. 1860. Large oval ferrotype bust portrait of Douglas; brass; 1" × 1⅝". With ropelike brass border; loop for leather belt. . . . .
. . . . *$1500–1700*

(Badge) "Hancock Rifles." Aluminum pinback, penny-size. Crossed rifles. . *$25–35*

(Badge, Mech.) R.B. Hayes "National Sweepstakes." Figural hand above red, white, and blue shield holds jockey cap in place. Once pivoted, the cap reveals black transfer bust portrait of Benjamin Harrison, with legend "Harrison Will Win the Race." *$300–325*

(Badge, Stickpin) R.B. Hayes "Centennial Candidates For 1876." Shield with jugate portraits. *$650–700*

(Badge, Stickpin) R.B. Hayes "Our Boys in Blue We Go for Hayes." Litho under glass, 1876. Union veteran (G.A.R.) in uniform and wearing Hardee hat. Hake H3039.. *$2000–2200*

(Badge, Stickpin) Ku Klux Klan. Date unknown. 14-carat gold figural skull pin, enamel teeth, ruby eyes, and "KKK" lettering; crossed keys under skull.... *$150–175*

(Badge, Cello) Lincoln Thank Offering—Freedmans Aid Society. Ca. 1880. 1" dia., b&w. Organization formed to benefit former slaves. *$100–125*

(Badge) "Macon Volunteers." C.S.A. badge German silver, star suspended from bar; hand-engraved. "Constitution" atop three pillars (State Seal of Georgia). Reverse inscribed "Sgt. H.C. Lamar." *$200–250*

(Badge) Maryland Sixth Corps, "368th. AA Baltimore Md. C." Cross-shape T-bar pin, silver... *$125–150*

(Badge, Cello, William McKinley) Union Veterans Patriotic League—Our Comrade. 1896. ⅞", b&w. Bust photo of teenage McKinley in uniform as Civil War Pvt., COE, 23rd Ohio Volunteer. With brochure supporting his Rep. candidacy. ....

(Badge) "1862 *Merrimac* First Ironclad." Heart-shaped iron badge. Inscribed "Old Dominion, Va. The heart of a nation." *$35–45*

(Badge) 10th New Hampshire Veterans, Co. E. 18th Corps Badge. Foliated cross on obverse and inscribed "Sergt. J.K. Moultree" (and company designation). Reverse inscribed with lists of battles encircled: "Fredericksburg, Cold Harbor, Petersburg," etc... *$175–200*

(Badge) 2nd Corps, "Assoc. of the 93—NYSV (New York State Vols.) 2nd Brig. 3rd Div. 1861—Army of the Potomac 1865. Ca. 1870s. Three-leaf-clover-shaped with "93" in center, reunion badge, suspended from ornate bar..... *$75–85*

(Badge) "Seymour and Blair." 1868. Conjoined jugate waist-up cardboard oval portrait, with Seymour holding hand inside jacket. In small gilt brass frame........
.... *$275–300*

(Clothing Button, Slavery) "Am I Not a Man and a Brother?" 1850s. Brass embossed image of kneeling slave................................. *$600–650*

(Badge) William H. Seward. Ca. 1862 1⅝" × 1¾" tintype by Abbott & Co., NYC. Bust portrait in rectangular brass frame. Seward was Lincoln's Sec. of State. Other details on reverse....................................... *$250–300*

(Badge) "Sixth Army Corps—10th Mass. Vols." Ca. 1870s. Silvered brass cross-shaped reunion badge suspended from bar. Embossed (partly figural) crossed rifles with bayonets, canteen, and cartridge pouch.......................... *$75–85*

(Badges) United Confederate Veterans Badges (17). 1902–36. Seventeen medals, many with ribbons, from various encampments and conventions. From collection of R.W. Ferrule, Memphis, Tennessee. Some ribbons tattered or missing. (A) Conestoga, July '94, $3000. .... *$3000–3200*

MEDALS AND TOKENS

Antislavery "Am I Not a Man and a Brother." Ca. 1850s. 1¼" white metal. Kneeling slave praying. Reverse Golden Rule, "Whatsoever ye would...." *$75–100*

John Brown. Engraved by J. Wurden; 2¼" bronze; struck in Belgium. Bust portrait, "John Brown Born Torrington 9 May 1800/Assassinated Judicially at Charleston 2 Dec. 1859/Dedicated to those victims who died for their devotion to the liberty of the blacks" (in French). An example in gold was presented to Brown's widow. Choice uncirculated... *$1000–1100*

James Buchanan. 1856. The classic rebus medal of a deer (buck) and cannon; surrounded by star clusters. Hake BU 3017 . . . . *$700–750*

James Buchanan. Inaugural. 1857. Large bust portrait of 15th president. Hake BU 3016 . . . . *$600–650*

Cumberland Association Naval Vets., New Bedford, Baltimore, and Washington. 1892. With gold and white ribbon *$15–20*

Jefferson Davis. 1861. Brass. Anti-C.S.A. sentiment has man on gallows with slogan "Death to Traitors." *$75–85*

"11th Reg. Mass. V, Charleston, War of 1861." Pewter medal with profile bust of George Washington. Inscribed to "Wm. E. Wells." Hole pierced on right side . . . . .
. . . .

Gen. Fremont. 1864. 1½" bust. "The Coming Man." Lengthy list of Fremont's deeds, silvered brass. *$250–300*

Gen. Fremont. 1856. 1¾" brass. Bust on obverse. Surveying scene on reverse.
. . . . *$150–175*

(3) G.A.R. Medals and Ribbons. Including dedication at Fredericksburg, Humphrey's 1911, NY; G.A.R. Woman's Relief Corp. (A) Jenack, Oct. '94, $35. . . . . .
. . . . *$50–65*

(4) G.A.R. Encampment Medals and Ribbons. 1907, Saratoga, NY and 1912, California. (A) Jenack, Oct. '94, $45. . . . . *$50–65*

(G.A.R.) Comdr.-in-Chief Russell Alger, Staff Assn. Org. Boston. 1890. Bronze on ribbon with hanger. *$15–20*

(G.A.R.) 29th Convention, Louisville. *$20–25*

(G.A.R.) Numbered Medal M9280. Undated. Heavy blue/gilt enamel badge; T-bar; clasp of Sgts. chevrons. *$35–45*

(G.A.R.) 31st Encampment, Buffalo. 1897. Elaborate bronze with figural buffalo on ribbon clasp. *$15–20*

G.A.R. 32nd Encampment, Cincinnati. 1898. Brass with red, white, and blue enamel flags. *$15–20*

G.A.R. Representative, Dept. of Pennsylvania. Reading, 1905. Bronze medal with winged eagle with ribbon. *$20–25*

Silver Anniversary G.A.R., Detroit. 1891. Bust. of Gen. Sherman; bronze; ribbon and clasp. *$25–35*

James Garfield Inaugural Medal. Mar. 4, 1881. Struck by U.S. Mint in aluminum specifically for noted collector Virgil Brand. 3" dia. bust of Garfield. Reverse: Inaugural date stamped; no mention of assassination a few months later. Sold as part of the Jane Brand Allen estate by Bower & Merina, 1984. Uncirculated. Stark, Oct. '85, $450. . . . . *$450–500*

James Garfield The Great Republican Victory/Free Passage on Steamer Hancock/Capt. English/Salt River/Direct/Chinese Line." 1880. Copper, uncirculated. Boat is pictured (Salt River was symbol of political oblivion). *$75–100*

Gettysburg Memorial Medal. 1913. Bronze medal commemorating 50th anniversary of battle. Embossed busts of Gen. Meade and Gen. Lee. With ornate clasp marked "Souvenir." *$75–85*

Gettysburg Veterans Medal. 1893. Dedication of State Monuments, New York Day. Embossed bronze with image of deities surrounding NY State seal. Suspended on brass clasp with red, white, and blue ribbon background. *$75–100*

Gillmore Medal. 1863. Awarded to Pvt. Walcott Wetherell, 6th Connecticut Volunteers by Maj. Gen. Quincy Gillmore, Comdr. Dept. of the South. Round bronze medal had ruins of Ft. Sumter, and date "Aug 23d 1863" on observe; "For Gallant and Meritorious Conduct" on reverse. Clasp holding blue ribbon had engraved name of recipient..

Note: 400 Gillmore Medals were awarded to enlisted men who had distinguished themselves in operations around Charleston, SC, July–Sept. '63.

Grant "Commemorative of the 36 Ballots of the Old Guard for Ulysses S. Grant for President." Bronze bust profile portrait. G.O.P. Nat. Conv., Chicago. 1880. Hake GR 3010...................................... *$200–225*

Congressional Medal Issued to Gen. U.S. Grant. March 1865. Unique gold medal had bust profile of Grant on obverse; goddess astride some sheafs of laurel leaves on reverse. Said to weigh 3 pounds................. *Value Indeterminate*

Grant–Colfax. 1886. Overlapping profile bust portraits of Rep. candidates. 1½" brass medal suspended from figural eagle with crossed cannons clasp. Hake 3123. . *$75–100*

Grant "I Intend to Fight it Out." 1868. Bust left portrait. Slogan on reverse..... .... *$75–100*

Grant Peace Medal. 1871. Obverse: "Let Us Have Peace—Liberty, Justice, Equality" bust of Grant and peace pipe; reverse: bible, world globe, farm equipment. (312 were struck of this silver medal.) In exceptional condition. (A) Stark, Oct. '85, $2500.. *$2500–3000*

(Grant) "Surrender of Gen. Lee to Gen. Grant, April 9th, 1865." 1868. Bust by key facing left. "Lieut. Gen. U.S. Grant." Copper. *$75–85*

(Grant/Colfax) "The Nattick Cobbler/The Galena Tanner, 1872." Overlapping bust left profiles. Hake GR 3139................................. *$350–400*

"Grant/Colfax/Soldier Statesman, Patriots—Match 'em." 1868. Embossed bust portraits of candidates... *$65–75*

For President Horace Greeley (Gratz Brown on Reverse). 1872. 1⅜" brass shell with pierced hole. Names and eagle above embossed bust portraits. Hake HG 3006. .... *$900–1000*

Benjamin Harrison. 1888. Aluminum medal with pie-cut taken away to exemplify "your wages under free trade"; reverse has similar embossed message..... *$50–75*

Rutherford B. Hayes Inaugural Medal. Mar. 5, 1877. Struck by U.S. Mint in aluminum specifically for noted collector Virgil Brand. 3" dia. bust of Garfield. Reverse: inaugural date stamped; sold as part of the Jane Brand Allen estate by Bower & Merina, 1984. Uncirculated.................................... *$500–600*

"Maj. M. Hazard, Commanding 16th NY Cav." 1½" × 4" silver badge with applied gold swords, cannon, anchor. All hand-engraved. "Roanoke Island," "Newbern," "Fort Macon," Little Washington," "Antietam-South," "Mountain-Fredericksburg," "Gettysburg," etc. Includes photocopies of Hazard's service records, letters. FPC Stark, July '94, $2750. .... *$2200–2500*

"Maj. Gen. Joseph Hooker, Born 11/13, 1814." Pewter medal by Merriam. Obverse: profile bust of Hooker. Reverse: patriotic and military devices, "U.S. Army 1863—Liberty & Union." *$50–75*

The Kearney Cross. 1863. Brig. Gen. D.B. Birney, who succeeded Kearney, authorized a bronze cross of valor for enlisted men in his command. Simpler in design to Kearney Medal (below): a simple Maltese Cross with "Kearney Cross" inscribed in swirling banner. *$2000–2200*

The Kearney Medal. 1862. Capt. Abner W. Turner of 4th Maine Infantry. Latin inscription in circle over Maltese Cross: "Dulce et Decorum Est. Pro Patria More." "Kearney" appears in inner circle. Brass clasp holding maroon ribbon has figural laurel leaves.. *$1500–2000*

Note: In Nov. 1962, officers of 1st Div. III Corps, Army of the Potomac, adopted a gold medal to honor their late commander, Gen. Philip Kearney (killed in Battle of Chantilly). "Awarded to those who served honorably under Gen. Kearney and whose military record was without stain." During the war, 317 men were commended for the award for bravery.

Ku Klux Klan. Flags behind large burning cross. Inscribed "Onward Christian Soldiers." Round, nickel finish. *$75–85*

Lincoln Campaign Medal. Ca. 1860. Large white metal round silvered medal with bust of beardless Lincoln on obverse; split rails on reverse. *$150–175*

(Lincoln) "Abram (sic) Lincoln Free Land, Free Speech and Free Men." 1860–70. Legend surrounds beardless bust of Lincoln and eagle. Brass. The only 1860 Lincoln medal not showing Abe in profile. *$100–150*

Lincoln Memorial. 1865. 1¼" aluminum token. Beardless Lincoln bust, right facing. *$35–50*

(Lincoln) "Memorial in Aeterna." 1865. 2½" dia. bronze. Obverse: Lincoln bust profile. "Northwestern Sanitary Fair" on reverse with military camp, naval scene. Engraved by Paquet. Struck by U.S. Mint in June 1865. Uncirculated. . . *$300–350*

(Lincoln) "President's House." 1860. Bronze bust of Lincoln left with legend above view of White House. Matching pieces exist for other 1860 candidates. *$150–175*

Lincoln Wide Awake. 1860. Brass. Bust right profile Lincoln; "Wide Awake" on reverse. *$50–75*

Gen. Logan "Erie County Veteran Logan Region." 1880s. Heavy gilt pinback with embossed plumed knight (representing running mate Blaine); crossed rifles, inscribed "Forty Rounds," "U.S. Cartridge Case," and large anchor. Pinback. *$125–150*

(Gen. McClellan) "Geo. Gnau, Co. F. 195th Penn. Lancaster." Struck in pewter, with bust portrait of McClellan. *$150–175*

(Gen. McClellan) "Peninsular Campaign." Ca. 1862. ¾" dia. bronze; Obverse: bust profile. Reverse: blank. *$50–60*

(Gen. McClellan) "War of 1861." Brass. Bust portrait of McClellan, stamped "Frank J. Abbott, Co. B. 18th. Reg. Mass. V. Belgrade, Me." (a Maine soldier who joined a Mass. unit). *$175–185*

"Gen. McPherson Medal." 1864. Unique 2" engraved silver diamond-shaped medal with a separate cloth star ("Our Flag lost this Star") cut from the battle flag. In memory of James Birdseye McPherson and his comrades. He was killed at the Battle of Atlanta on July 22, 1864. Presented by Gen. Logan to James Goff 70th Ohio 2nd D15th. Corps in front of the Atlanta Grand Army unit. FPC Stark, July '94, $3650. . . . . *$3000–4000*

Medal of Honor. 1863. Five-pointed bronze medal with bas relief of Roman diety with spear. Awarded to Charles Hayes of the 27th Marine Volunteers. (D) $2000. . . . . *$2000–2500*

Note: Because no medal for valor existed at the war's outbreak, Congress authorized the Medal of Honor. It was awarded to some 2100 Union soldiers.

"Maj. Gen. Scott." 1852. Bust facing left. Aluminum/brass finish. "United We Stand/Divided We Fall." *$125–135*

Gen. Winfield Scott. 1852. Brass, bust left facing, 1¼"; slogans and patriotic vignettes. *$175–200*

Service Medal. 1860s. Brass medal with ribbon or bar loop; embossed bust portrait of Lincoln inscribed "With malice toward none. With charity for all." Unprefixed 1159. Rated extra fine. (A) Stark, '85, $175. . . . . *$150–175*

Silver Hero Cross of Ku Klux Klan. 1915. Silvered bronze medal with top loop; bust of C.S.A. Gen. Nathan Bedford Forrest; dates: "1866–1916." There is evidence that Forrest became a Grand Wizard of the KKK.. . . . . *$300–350*

Sharpshooter's Medal/12th NH USSS. Ca. 1863. 1½" brass star shape. FPC Stark, Dec. '94, $400.. . . . . *$300–350*

Gen. Philip Sheridan. Ca. 1862. 1½" white metal bust portrait in deep relief of Sheridan, "Souvenir" on reverse.. . . . . *$75–100*

Sumter Medal. 1861. 2½" bronze. Issued to Union officers and men who defended Ft. Sumter in April 1861. Obverse of round medal features bas relief bust profile of Gen. Robt. Anderson, the fort's commander. Reverse depicts soldier raising flag on fort's ramparts; "Chamber of Commerce New York Honors Defenders of Fort Sumter. First to Withstand Treason.". *$800–1000*

Left: *Lincoln-Hamlin ferrotype, 1860. Obverse and reverse in circular frame, $900–$1,000.* Right: *Horace Greeley and Gratz Brown. 1872, conjoined portraits, sepia oval ambrotype in brass frame, $750–$800.*

Gen. Nathan Bedford Forrest silver Ku Klux Klan "Hero Cross," $275–$300. (Photo courtesy of Rex Stark)

Gen. George H. Thomas medal "For Unflinching Valor & Patriotism." Silver presentation medal, 1865, given to Benj. Prentis. Includes CDV of Prentis, Company K, 9th Michigan, $6,000–$7,000. (Photo courtesy of Rex Stark)

Left: *Gen. Jas. McPherson medal. Dated July 22, 1864. Engraved silver medal with separate cloth star ("Our Flag Lost This Star" engraved on bottom of medal), $3,500–$4,000. (Photo courtesy of Rex Stark Auctions)* Right: *Silver medal engraved "Maj. M. Hazard, Commanding 16th NY Cav." Including Hazard papers, $2,200–$2,500.*

REVERSE

Unique medal presented by CSA President Jefferson Davis to Clay Stacker, who accompanied Davis as he attempted escape at the war's end, $4,000–$4,500. (Photo courtesy of Rex Stark)

Left: *Medal of Honor, 1863. Five-pointed bronze medal. Awarded to Charles Hayes of the 27th Main Volunteers. This medal was sold by a dealer for $2,000, and another example recently sold at auction for $4,000, $4,000–$4,500.* Right: *Two Lincoln campaign ferrotypes attached to black crepe rosettes and worn at Lincoln funeral rites, $650 each. (Photo courtesy of Harmer Rooke Galleries)*

BOOKS, PAMPHLETS, PORTFOLIOS: ANTIQUARIAN

CIVIL WAR TITLES

Books on the Civil War encompass over 50,000 related examples.

Abdill. *Civil War Railroads*. n.p. 1st Ed. 1951. Photos, 190 pp., dj *$18–20*

Alexander, Edward Porter. *Military Memoirs of a Confederate*. 1907. Charles Scribner's Sons, NY. *$45–55*

Alger, Horatio. *From Canal Boy to President*. 1st Ed. 1881. Biography of James Garfield, 334 pp., golden cloth binding. *$45–50*

Allan, William. *History of the Campaign of Gen. T.J. (Stonewall) Jackson in the Shenandoah of Virginia*. 1880. J.B. Lippincott, Philadelphia. Reprint: Morningside Bookshop, Dayton, OH, 1974. . . . . *$45–55*

Altsheler, Joseph. *Tree of Appomattox*. 1928. NY. *$35–45*

Anonymous. *Condensed History of 143rd. Regiment, NYVI*. 1909. (A) Jenack, Oct. '94, $80. . . . . *$80–90*

Anonymous. *Pinkerton/The Spy of the Rebellion*. 1883. (A) Jenack, Oct. 94, $45. . . . . *$50–75*

Avirett, James B. *The Memoirs of General Turner Ashby and His Compeers*. (Rev.) 1867. Selby & Dulaney, Baltimore. *$75–100*

Barton, W. *Paternity of Abraham Lincoln*. 1920. NY. *$35–45*

———. *The Women Lincoln Loved*. 1st Ed. 1927. . . . . *$45–55*

Bernard, George. *Photographic Views of the Sherman Campaign*. 1866. Contains 61 albumen prints. See chapter on Photography. (A) '70, $8500 . . *$20,000–25,000*

Bowman and Irwin. *Sherman and His Campaigns/A Military Biography*. 1st Ed. royal. 1865. 512 pp., cloth. (A) Jenack, Oct. '94, $30. . . . . *$35–45*

Brown, J. H. *The Soldiers in Our Civil War*. Vol. I. 1884. (A) Dias, Nov. '94, $85. . . . . *$75–100*

Butler, Benjamin F. *Autobiography and General Reminiscences*. 1st Ed. 1892. A.M. Thayers, Boston. *$45–55*

———. *Butler's Book*. 1st Ed. 1892. A.M. Thayers, Boston. Autobiography, 1154 pp., with maps. *$40–45*

Catton, Bruce. *Army of the Potomac.* 1952. Garden City, NY. 389 pp. *$12–15*

———. *Mr. Lincoln's Army.* 1951. Garden City, NY. 372 pp. *$10–12*

Coffin, Charles Carleton. *The Boys of '61.* 1862. Estes & Lauret, Boston. Full-color lith. cover by Armstrong & Co. An accounting of numerous battles early in the war. *$50–55*

Crane, Stephen. *Red Badge of Courage.* 1895. 1st Ed. Appleton. Novel. . . *$250–300*

Dabney, R.L. *Life and Campaigns of Lieut. Gen. Thomas J. Jackson.* (Rev.) 1865. Sterling & Albright, Richmond, VA. Reprinted by Sprinkle Pub., Harrisonville, VA, 1983. . . . . *$45–55*

Davis, Jefferson. *The Rise and Fall of the Confederate Government.* 1881. New York. Twelve field maps, 808 pp. *$50–75*

———. *The Rise and Fall of the Confederate Government.* 2nd Ed. 2 Vols. 1912. London. *$200–225*

Edmonds, S. Emma. *Nurse and Spy in the Union Army.* 1865. W.F. Wiliam & Co., Hartford. Originally published in 1864 as *Unsexed, or the Female Soldier.* . . . *$45–55*

Esposito, Col. Vincent J., Chief Ed. *The West Point Atlas of American Wars, Vol. 1, 1869–1900, U.S. Military Academy, West Point, Dept. of Military Art and Engineering.* Frederick Praeger, Pub., NY *$75–100*

Evans, Gen. Clement Anselm. *Confederate Military History: A Library of Confederate States History in 12 Vols., Written by Distinguished Men of the South.* 1st Ed. 1899. Confederate Pub., Atlanta, GA. Original cloth. *$650–675*

———. *Confederate Military History: A Library of Confederate States History in 12 Vols., Written by Distinguished Men of the South.* 1962. Thos. Yoseloff, Pub., NY *$250–300*

Foner, Eric. *Free Soil, Free Labor, Free Men: The Ideology of the Republican Party Before the Civil War.* 1970. Oxford Univ. Press. *$25–35*

Foote, Shelby. *Civil War: A Narrative.* 1st Ed. 1958, 1963, and 1974. Set. Random House, NY. *$750–800*

———. *Night Before Chancellorsville.* 1957. Signet Pub. *$50–75*

Freeman, Douglas Southall. *Lee's Lieutenants: A Study in Command. Manassas to Malvern Hill.* 1st Ed. 3 Vols. 1942. Charles Scribner's Sons, NY. *$325–350*

———. *Lee's Dispatches.* n.p. 1st Ed. 1957. 416 pp. *$14–16*

Gardner, Alexander. *Photographic Sketchbook of the War.* 2 Vols. 1866. . . . . *Value Indeterminate*

Gordon, John B. *Reminiscences of the Civil War.* *$45–55*

Grant, U.S. *Personal Memoirs of U.S. Grant.* 2 Vols. 1885. NY. *$100–150*

Irby, Richard, Capt. *Historical Sketch of the Nottoway Grays, Co. G. 18th Virginia, Garnett's Brigade.* Signed inscription from Irby to Rev. J.W. Jones, fighting parson of 13th VA. Tipped-in albumen photo of Robert E. Lee; also albumens of Irby and other officers. *$1000–1100*

Johnston, Joseph E. *Narrative of Military Operations During the Late War Between the States.* 1874. NY. *$55–65*

Kellog, Sanford C. *The Shenandoah Valley and Virginia, 1861–1865, A War Study.* 1903. Neale Pub., NY. *$65–75*

Lee, Robert E. *Recollections and Letters.* No date, no edition given. Seacaucus Pub. 472 pp. *$15–25*

Leslies Weekly, "Famous Leaders and Battle Scenes of the Civil War." 1896. (A) Jenack, Oct. '94, $80. . . . . *$85–100*

Thayer, William M. *From Log Cabin to White House/Life of James Garfield.* 1881.

James, H. Earle, Boston, MA. 478 pp., James, H. Earle "Log Cabin to the White House" Series. *$12–25*

————. *From Tannery to the White House.* (Grant biography.) James, H. Earl, Boston, MA. Same series as above. *$35–45*

LINCOLN TITLES

More books have been published on Abraham Lincoln than any other American.

Anonymous Booklet. *Lincoln Catechism—Guide to Presidential Election of 1864.* Negro caricature on cover. 48 pp. Anti-Lincoln with pro-McClellan questions and answers. *$75–100*

Anonymous Booklet. *Terrible Tragedy at Washington.* 1865. Barclay, Philadelphia. Paper cover has oval bust portrait of Lincoln. Illus. with assassination scene, map, portraits, funeral car, Booth's escape. 120 pp. *$175–200*

Anonymous Booklet. *Trial of Assassins and Conspirators.* 1865. Barclay, Philadelphia. Paper cover with portrait of Mrs. Surrat. Other members of plot pictured; maps; arrest scenes; Boston Corbett. *$200–225*

Arnold, Isaac N. *The Life of Abraham Lincoln.* 1906. McClurg, Chicago. . . *$50–60*

Basler, Roy P., Pratt, Marian Dolores, and Dunlap, Lloyd A. *The Collected Work of Abraham Lincoln.* 8 Vols. plus index; 1953–55. New Brunswick, NJ. Supplementary vol., 1974. . . . . *$75–100*

Bishop, Jim. *The Day Lincoln Was Shot.* 1984. Greenwich House. 304 pp. . . . . . .
. . . . *$10–15*

Carpenter, Francis Bicknell. *Six Months at the White House with Abraham Lincoln.* 1866. Hurd & Houghton, NY. *$65–75*

Chittendon, L.E. *Recollections of President Lincoln and His Administration.* 1891. Harper & Bros., NY. *$35–50*

Deddett, Tyler, Ed. *Lincoln and the Civil War in the Diaries and Letters of John Hay.* 1939. Dodd, Mead & Co. *$50–75*

Fehrenbacher, Don E. *Lincoln: A Documentary Portrait Through His Speeches and Writings.* 1964. NY. *$25–35*

Friedman, Russell. *Lincoln/A Photobiography.* 1987. Houghton Mifflin, NY. . . *$50–65*

Gunderson, Robert Gray. *The Log Cabin Campaign.* 1957. Univ. of Kentucky Press, Lexington, KY. *$20–25*

Hamilton, Charles, and Ostendorf, Lloyd. *Lincoln in Photographs/An Album of Every Known Pose.* 1963. Univ. of Oklahoma Press, Norman, OK. *$35–50*

Handlin, Oscar and Lillian. *Abraham Lincoln and the Union.* 1980. NY. . . *$20–25*

William Hanle. *Old Time Campaigning and the Story of the Lincoln Campaign Song.* April 20, 1920. Vol. XIII, Vol. XL1, Sept. 1948. Journal of the Illinois State Historical Society. *$45–55*

Hart, Charles Henry. *A Catalog of a Collection of Engraved and Other Portraits of Lincoln.* 1899. New York Grolier Club. *$125–150*

Hesseltine, William B., Ed. *Three Against Lincoln: Murat Halstead Reports the Causes of 1860.* 1960. Louisiana State Univ. Press. *$25–35*

Holland, Josiah G. *The Life of Abraham Lincoln.* 1866. Gurdon Bull, Springfield, MA. *$75–100*

Holzer, Harold, Boritt, George S., and Neely, Mark, Jr. *Changing the Lincoln Image.* 1985. Louis A. Warren Lincoln Library and Museum, Ft. Wayne, IN. *$15–20*

Kunhardt, Phillip B., Jr., Phillip III, and Kunhardt, Peter W. *Lincoln/An Illustrated Biography.* 1992. Alfred A. Knopf, NY. Companion vol. to ABC TV documentary. *$35–45*

Kunhardt, Dorothy and Phillip B., Jr. *Twenty Days.* 1965. NY *$12–15*

Lorant, Steven. *Lincoln: A Picture Story of His Life.* W.W. Norton. *$12–15*

McKee (1st name unknown). *Civil War Record of the 144th. Regiment NY Vol. Infantry.* 1902. (A) Jenack, Oct. '94, $70. . . . . *$75–85*

Randall, James G. *Lincoln the President.* 4 Vols. 1945–55. NY *$20–25*

Ransom, John (9th Mich. Cav.). *Andersonville Diary, Escape, List of the Dead.* 1881. Hardcover, minor wear to spine. *$175–200*

Sandberg, Carl. *Abraham Lincoln The Prarie Years.* 2 Vols. *Abraham Lincoln The War Years.* 4 Vols. 1939. NY. *$75–85*

Straudenraus, P.J., Ed. *Mr. Lincoln's Washington: The Civil War Diaries of Noah Brooks.* 1967. Thos. Yoseloff, S. Brunswick, NJ. *$15–20*

Thomas, Benjamin T. *Abraham Lincoln, A Biography.* 1952. NY. *$25–30*

Troutsdale, Winfield Porter. *Engraved and Lithographed Portraits of Abraham Lincoln.* 1933. Troutsdale Press, Champlain, NY. *$50–75*

Turner, Justin G., and Levett, Linda. *Mary Todd Lincoln: Her Life and Letters.* 1972. Alfred A. Knopf, NY. *$35–45*

Williams, T. Harry. *Lincoln and His Generals.* 1952. Alfred A. Knopf, NY. *$50–65*

MISCELLANEOUS TITLES

Longstreet, James. *From Manassas to Appomattox.* 1903. Philadelphia. . . . *$50–60*

Marvel, William. *Race of the Soil/The Ninth New Hampshire Regiment in the Civil War.* Broadfoot Pub., Washington, NC *$20–25*

McClellan, George B. *Army of the Potomac.* 1st Ed. 1864. Sheldon Pub., NY. 484 pp., original cloth, 1/250; inscribed, signed. *$400–450*

———. *McClellan's Own Story.* 1st Ed. 1887. New York. Memoirs. 1st edition royal 8vo. (9") edition, 678 pp. *$45–55*

Meade, G. Gordon. *Life and Letters of G. Gordon Meade.* 1913. NY. *$50–65*

Mitchell, Margaret. *Gone with the Wind.* 1st. Ed., 1st issue. Oct. 1936. Macmillan, NY. 1037 pp. *$1800–2000*

———. *Gone with the Wind.* Oct. 1936. Macmillan, NY. 1037 pp., gray cloth. *$35–50*

———. *Gone with the Wind.* 1975. Macmillan, NY. 1037 pp., Margaret Mitchell Anniversary Edition, boxed. *$50–65*

Phisterer, Frederick. *New York in the War of the Rebellion, in Six Volumes.* 1912. J.B. Lyon, Albany. *$250–300*

Prang, Louis. *Union Generals* (booklet). Ca. late 1860s. Portraits of 24 generals. Leather portfolio with b&w lithographs. Includes Gen. Daniel Butterfield and Brig. Gen. Kit Carson. *$200–250*

Pritzker, Barry. *Mathew Brady.* 1992. Crescent Books, NY and Avenel, NJ. . . *$15–20*

Scott, Gen. Winfield. *Autobiography of a Civil War General.* 1864. Sheld Co., NY. *$25–50*

Sears, Stephen W., Ed. *The Civil War/A Treasury of Art and Literature.* 1992. Hugh Lauter Levin Assoc., Inc. Distributed by Macmillan Pub. Co., NY. . . *$50–60*

Sheridan, Philip H. *Memoirs of P.H. Sheridan.* 1888. NY. *$50–60*

Sherman, William T. *Memoirs of W.T. Sherman.* 2 Vols. 1887. NY. *$50–60*

———. *Memoirs of W.T. Sherman.* 2 Vols. in one. 4th Ed. 1891 Ed. *$35–45*

Stephens (1st name unknown). *Pictorial History of the War of the Union.* Vol. I and II. 1864–66. (A) Jenack, Oct. '94, $45. . . . . *$50–75*

Stowe, Harriet Beecher. *Uncle Tom's Cabin, Or Life Among the Lowly.* 1st Ed./1st issue. 12 Vols. 1852. Boston. Original cloth. *$7000–7500*

———. *Uncle Tom's Cabin, Or Life Among the Lowly.* 1st Cruikshank illus. English Ed. 1852. London. Reviere binding. *$625–675*

———. *Uncle Tom's Cabin.* Ca. 1900. NY. 452 pp., gilt tan cloth. *$40–50*

Styron, William. *Confessions of Nat Turner.* 1st Ed. 1/500. 1967. Random House, NY. Signed, 428 pp., novel, red cloth with slipcase. *$250–275*

———. *Confessions of Nat Turner.* 1st trade Ed. 1967. Random House, NY. 428 pp., black cloth. *$40–50*

———. *Confessions of Nat Turner.* 1st English Ed. 1968. Cape Pub., London. 428 pp., brown boards. *$40–50*

Taylor, Richard. *Destruction and Reconstruction/Personal Experience of the Great War.* 1879. Memoirs. D. Appleton, NY. Considered the finest account of the war by a Confederate general. Reprinted in 1955. . . . . *$50–75*

Wallace, Lew. *Ben Hur; A Tale of Christ.* 1st Ed./1st Issue. 1880. NY. Presentation inscribed; slipcase. Novel. Lew Wallace was one of the Union's ablest generals. *$2700–2800*

Ward, Geoffrey; Burns, Ric; and Burns, Ken. *The Civil War/An Illustrated History.* 1990. Alfred Knopf, NY. Companion to PBS TV series. Still in print. Also in paperback. (See Bibliography.) *$45–50*

Warner, Ezra G. *Generals in Blue; Lives of the Union Commanders.* 1964. Louisiana Univ. Press, Baton Rouge, LA. *$45–55*

———. *Generals in Gray; Lives of the Confederate Commanders.* 1959. Louisiana Univ. Press, Baton Rouge, LA. *$45–55*

Warren, Robert Penn. *Jefferson Davis Gets His Citizenship Back.* 1st Ed. 1980. Lexington, KY. Inscribed and signed. *$100–125*

———. *John Brown, The Making of a Martyr.* 1st Ed. 1929. Payson Clarke. Author's first book, inscribed. *$1200–1350*

One of the numerous cards from Relics of the Southern Rebellion. *A sepiatone, promoting a "Union Volunteer Refreshment Saloon." If sold separately, the card would be valued in the $100–$125 range.*

Left: *Winslow Homer* Campaign Sketches. *Crayon sketches by Homer on the battlefront, set of six lithographs 11" × 14" in portfolio. Published by L. Prange, Boston, $500–$600.* Right: *Lithograph from* Campaign Sketches, *"The Letter Home."*

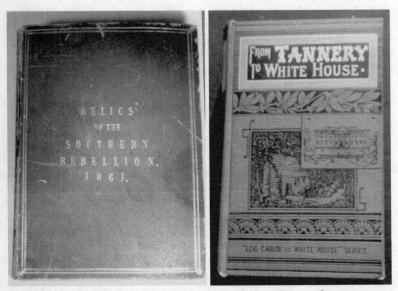

Left: *A Philadelphia lady went to great trouble to collect and preserve with great care Civil War mementos by having them leather bound as* Relics of the Southern Rebellion, 1861. *Value indeterminate.* Right: From Tannery to White House *by Wm. Thayer, about U.S. Grant, $35–$45.*

Left: Uncle Tom's Cabin, *1854. Children's picture book. Published by John Sewitt & Co., Boston, $200–$250.* Right: *Back cover illustration from* The Boys of '61, *by Charles Carlton Coffin, 1862, $50–$60.*

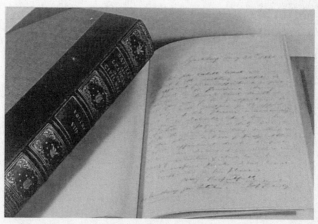

Battles and Leaders of the Civil War. *Contributions by Union and Confederate officers, including hundreds of portraits, maps, and prints of original photographs. Eight volumes bound in dark blue Moroccan leather, gilt backs. Also includes 110 original autographed letters and signature cuts of such Civil War figures as Grant, Lee, Sherman, Jefferson Davis, and Benjamin Butler. This brought $11,000 at Riba's Auctions in late 1991, $12,000–$14,000.*

Left: *24th National Encampment of the Grand Army of the Republic "Official Souvenir Program," 1890. Booklet came with roster, $50–$65.* Right: *Illustration from 1860s ABC Primer for Northern Youngsters, with patriotic motifs including soldier with the 34-star Civil War–era flag. Primer, $75–$100.*

BROADSIDES, PRINTS, POSTERS, AND MAPS

BROADSIDES

Lincoln Assassination/Martyrdom Related

"Constitution Extra." 1865. Cites "The Assassination of Lincoln"; "Booth Arrested" (untrue at time); death of Sec. Seward (also false). Reflects the hysteria of the nation at time of Lincoln's death. B&w, all type. *$600–700*

(Jefferson Davis Reward) "$360,000 Reward!" "Bureau of Military Justice has indubitable evidence that Jefferson Davis, Clement Clay . . . incited and concerted the assassination of Mr. Lincoln and the attack on Mr. Seward.—James Wilson Maj. General U.S. Army." May 8, 1865. Only known copy, 20" × 16". All type. Minor fold weaknesses and soiling. (A) Riba, July '94, $13,000. . . . . *$12,000–13,000*

"Extra Latest News/Death of a President." Sun. 15 Apr. 1865. "Death of the President. The last moments . . . Scene at deathbed/the murderer is still at large." Two cols. of text. (A) Riba, Oct. '92, $900.. . . . . *$1000–1100*

"Obsequies of President Lincoln/Order of Funeral Procession. May 4, 1865, Springfield, IL. Three-col. black-bordered broadside, 12" × 9". Lists order of Lincoln's cortege escort comprising military divisions, family members, fraternities, etc. Light soiling. (A) Riba, Nov. '91, $750. . . . . *$800–850*

$100,000 Reward/War Dept. April 20, 1865. "The murderer of our late beloved President, Abraham Lincoln is still at large." Edwin M. Stanton, Sec. of War. Gives descriptions of Booth, Surrat, and Herold. Variant, without three ambros of assassins. Mounted on linen. A few stains. Fold lines mended. (A) Riba, Oct. '88, $8500. . . . . *$9000–10,000*

"A Proclamation to Assemble at City Hall to Pay Respects to President." April 15, 1865. Rochester, NY. Issued by D.D.T. Moore, Mayor. Bold, all type, b&w. Broadside 19" × 13½". (A) $450. . . . . *$500–600*

Union League—Remember Lincoln—The Martyr in the Cause of Liberty. June 1, 1865. City Hall, Providence, RI. Announces eulogies to be delivered by William Lloyd Garrison and Hon. Thomas Davis. B&w, all type. *$400–450*

War Department, Washington, D.C., April 20, 1865/$100,000 Reward! The

Murderer of Our Late Beloved President, Abraham Lincoln. 24" × 12" with three mounted albumen photos of the accused assassins: (J.W.) "Booth," (John) "Surrat" (sic), and (Davy) "Herold." Signed in print by Edwin Stanton, Sec. of War. Arguably the most famous of all Lincoln and Civil War–related broadsides. Minor tape stains and fold lines. (A) Riba, Oct. '85, $7000. . . . . *$9000–10,000*
Same "Reward" version as above. In better condition (rated fine), but with blanks where albumen photos should be; was auctioned three years later. (A) Riba, Oct. '88, $8500. . . . . *$8000–9000*

Recruiting, Rallies, and Proclamations

"A Great Rush, To Join the 36th Regiment, New York Volunteers, Commanded by Col. W.H./Brown." "Nine Months. Don't Wait to be Drafted. Cost What it May, The nation must be saved." Multicolor vignettes of civilian with plowshare and store in background while soldier at right is blowing bugle; cannon, anchor, and flag. *$2000–2200*
"Another Chance! To Avoid the Draft. Enlist in the 7th Indiana Cavalry." "$100 bounty to all inexperienced recruits." P.C. Shanks. Indianapolis poster. B&w, large eagle with legend in talons reading "400 dollars bounty" (apparently those who had already served nine months received only a $400 bounty). *$1200–1400*
"Attention! Indian Fighters; U.S. Vol. Cavalry!" © 1864; pub. in Central City, CA; authorization by Gov. promises volunteers "all horses and other plunder taken from the Indians." *$2000–2500*
"Attention Recruits—By Order of His Excellence John A. Andrews." 24 July 1861. A call to arms at Gen. Recrit. Station and barracks, Boston, by MA Gov. Andrews. Large 29" × 43", in red, white, blue, and purple. Star border; array of ten furled U.S. and regimental flags. Stark FP Cat. D, Dec. '94, $2200 . . . *$2000–2200*
(Gen.) Pierre Beauregard. Broadside signed as Comdr. Gen. of Confederate Army in Corinth, MS, 1862. Addressed to soldiers of Shiloh and Elkhorn, preparing them for battle. *$100–125*
(Gen. P.G.T. Beauregard) General Orders "To the Soldiers of Shiloh and Elkhorn." Signed by Beauregard as Comdr. Gen. of the Forces of the C.S.A., Corinth, MI, 2 May 1862. Prepares men for impending battle at Corinth. "We are to decide whether we're freemen or vile slaves . . . We shall recover more than we have lately lost." Side margin trimmed. Signed by Gen. in bold ink. (A) Oct. '92, $4200. . . . . *$4500–5000*
Gen. Butler, "Proclamation, Headquarters, Dept. of the Gulf, New Orleans, May 1, 1862." By command of George C. Strong, A.A. Gen. Chief of Staff. Butler claims marital law and lists over 20 new laws as he assumes command of New Orleans. Woodcut eagle tops proclamation. Butler's dictatorial rule (hangings and outrageous injustices) prompted Lincoln to recall him. (A) Riba-Mobley, June '84, $550. . . . . *$800–1000*
California Recruiting. Ca. 1863–64. "Men Wanted For 1st Cav. California Volunteers For Active Service in Lower Cal. and Arizona." Lists pay scale for non-commissioned officers and enlisted men. "Apply . . . 1st Lt. L.F. Sanburn." 23" × 17", minor tape stain top margin. (A) Riba, June '88, $1100. . . . . *$1200–1300*
California Recruiting. Ca. 1863–64. "$100 Bounty! 50 Men Wanted for Company L., 1st. Cavalry, Cal. Vols!/For Active Service In Texas/Apply at . . . James, Gorman, Capt. *Stockton Daily Independent* Job Office Print." Large woodcut eagle illus. and black border, 23" × 16¹/₂". (A) Riba, June '88, $1600. . . . . *$1800–2000*
Charleston Mercury **Extra/"Union is Dissolved/Passed Unanimously at 1:15**

o'clock P.M. Dec. 20, 1860." Ordinance to dissolve union between So. Carolina and other states under the compact, "The Constitution on the U.S. of America." Extremely rare first C.S.A. imprint. Re: Hummel 2434. Minor staining; small hole lower right, not affecting text. (A) Riba, Oct. '92, $9000. . . . . *$9000–10,000*

"Chronicle—Extra Important News—The President's Emancipation Proclamation." 1 Jan. 1863. *NY Chronicle.* Small folio. Includes entire text of Proclamation. 12" × 10"; three cols. (A) Riba, Nov. '91, $900. . . . . *$1000–1500*

Co. "B" Ironsides Regiment Battle Scene. U.S., 1863; light blue ink. (A) $4180.
. . . . *$4000–$5000*

George Armstrong Custer, Congratulatory Order, Appomattox. April 9, 1865. Issued by Custer congratulating and praising the 3rd Cavalry. 5" × 12", all type.
. . . . : . . . *$1100–1200*

(Jefferson Davis) President's Message to the Senate and House of Rep. of C.S.A. May 2, 1864. Five-page printed pamphlet, 9" × 6". Updates progress of war. All type. *$100–150*

Open Letter to Mr. Jefferson Davis by John Brodhead, Candidate for City Treasurer. Philadelphia, March 1860. Vitriolic jibe at Jefferson Davis that Brodhead would like "to open up Nicaragua to civilization and niggers/I am tired of being a white slave at the North, and long for a home in the sunny South." (Ironically, five years later, Lincoln would express his own desire for using Nicaragua as haven for newly freed slaves of the South.) Small holes and a few minor tears. (A) Riba, June '88, $200. . . . . *$250–300*

Jefferson Davis on Prohibition. 1890. 8½" × 11" flyer with Davis' discourse on evils of alcohol. Davis opposed Prohibition, though, as an infringement on individual freedom and state sovereignty; also unenforceable. Stark FP Cat., Dec. '94, $85.
. . . . *$75–100*

W.H. Emery Proclamation. April 1863. "All U.S. Troops Commanded to shoot down at sight . . . all such bands of robbers and thieves." Order handed down by Emery, Head Qt. U.S. Forces, Opelousas, LA, following looting and plundering of captured property. Framed. (A) Riba, $380. . . . . *$450–500*

"Epitaph . . . Mutilated and Disjointed Remains of U.S.A. . . . Born July 4 1776. 6 Nov. 1860 Dissolved. Free White Race. Govt. of White Men." Quotes from Adams, Clay, Webster, Patrick Henry on integrity and patriotism of South. On reverse Boston pub. notes this had been sent North via C.S.A. soldier. Explains how C.S.A. has been grossly wronged. *$600–750*

"Fall in Men! Fall in promptly! To the Rescue of the State! Fill the Ranks of the Gray Reserves." Thomas Starks, Recrt. Officer, offers $10 bounty for each recruit. Large woodcut at top of men with muskets drawn charging into battle. Illus. signed "Bonfield." Professionally cleaned, linen mounted. 31¾" × 22¼". (A) Oct. '92, $4200. . . . . *$4500–5000*

Adm. Daniel G. Farragut. "General Order No. 10, U.S. Flagship Hartford Off Mobile Bay, July 12, 1864." Signed by Farragut "D.G.F." "Strip your vessels and prepare for the conflict . . . The vessels will run past the forts in couples, lashed side by side. . . ." Relates to Battle of Mobile Bay and Farragut's memorable command "Damn the torpedos: Full Speed Ahead." (A) Riba, June '88, $2000. . *$2500–3000*

"For the War—Gloucester (Mass.) Volunteers; By Special Order, No. 558." Ca. 1861. "His Excellency Gov. Andrew, to raise a company of infantry for three years or during the war." Printed by *Telegraph Press* in Gloucester. 38" × 25" (A) $200. . . . . *$350–400*

"Captain Printner's Company of Penn. Zouaves. Col. Gosline's Regiment is Now Receiving Recruits." Ca. 1860s. Philadelphia Grays Armory. $100 bounty.

12" × 18", b&w. Large eagle with shield and legend. Stark FP Cat., Dec. '94, $325.
. . . . *$325–350*

Gen. U.S. Grant–Henry Wilson. Rally broadside. "Rights are Invaded/Up with People/Down with Demogogues./10,000 Freemen to Rally at Oak Grove on Your Own Free Soil/Support National Republican Candidates." 1872 campaign. All type, b&w. *$350–400*

Recruiting Broadside for Gen. Hancock's 1st Army Corps of Veterans. Feb. 1865. Issued by Benjamin Franklin, Police Chief, Philadelphia. Long text of orders, bounties; vignettes. Re-enlisted vets to form Birney Brigade in memory of fallen Gen. *$550–600*

(Gen. W.S. Hancock) "Largest Bounties ($650/$750) Recruits Wanted for the Pennsylvania Volunteers/Hancock's Gallant Second Corps. . . ." King & Baird Printers, Philadelphia. Blue and red type with illus. of eagle; "L. Johnson & Co." signed in plate, 31½" × 23¾". Minor soiling and wrinkling, tiny corner missing. (A) Riba, Oct. '82, $3800. . . . . *$4000–4500*

(Gen. W.S. Hancock) "Look Out for Another Draft./Fortunes Made by Volunteering!" 9 Dec. 1864. Southbridge, MA. "Gen Hancock's Veteran Corps., 20,000 veterans wanted." Thirteen additional lines, 37" × 17½", framed and possibly laid down. Tears, some staining. (A) Riba, March '91. . . . . *$400–500*

Robert E. Lee Order. Signed in type. "Notice to all military officers . . . positively forbidden to interfere with officers . . . employees of any Railroads—Com. in Chief, Head Quarters, Richmond 26th April, 1861."(A) $880. . . . . *$800–900*

Maj. Gen. Loring, Chief of Staff. Charleston, Va., Sept. 14, 1862. "To the People of Western Virginia, The Army of the Confederate States has come among you to expel the enemy, to rescue the people from . . . Northern Bayonets." 13" × 6½". (A) Riba, June '85, $250. . . . . *$300–350*

(McClellan) "The Beginning. Election of McClellan. Pendleton. Vallandigham. Armistice. Fall of Wages. No market For Produce. Penn. A Border State. Invasion. Civil War Anarchy/Depotism. The End." 1864. 22" × 28" framed anti-McClellan broadside. All type. *$1400–1500*

"Men of the Keystone State Rally for Its Defense!" 1862. King and Baird Printers, Philadelphia. Probably post-Battle of Gettysburg. "The soil of Pennsylvania, where Liberty was first proclaimed 'throughout the land . . . must not be polluted by footsteps of traitors." 1st Regt. of Washington Guard, Col. William F. Small. 31½" × 22"; framed. Fold lines, some ink loss (A) Riba, $440 . . . . *$400–500*

"Gen. Morgan and Judge Hurd Will Address the People at Mt. Vernon." Oct. 10th, 1863. Gen. George Washington Morgan resigned in '63 after a disagreement with Gen. Sherman. He was against the use of Negro troops. Served as Dem. Cong. after the war. Eagle on masthead with "The Union Forever" banner in beak. *$700–800*

"Mulligan's Brigade! Last Chance to Avoid the Draft. $402 Bounty to Veterans.—Capt. J.J. Fitzgerald of the Irish Brigade." 1863. 23rd Reg. Illinois Volunteers. Printed in Chicago. All type b&w. *$1200–1500*

Navy Dept. General Order—Rendezvous in Boston. Dec. 23, 1861. Printed and engraved by F.A. Searle, Boston. Folio b&w woodcut illus. of three-masted ship. 44" × 29½". Written by Sec. of Navy Gideon Wells; lists military pay, benefits, cost of uniforms and bedding. Some water staining, age browning. (A) Riba, Oct. '85, $4200. . . . . *$5000–6000*

"$100 Bounty! Volunteers Wanted." "To complete Co. B. attached to Col. E.M. Gregory's Regt. now at Camp Chase, Capt. A.H. Bowman (Recruiting Officer)." King & Baird Printers, Philadelphia. Large illus. at top of American heroes waving to Liberty; two battle scenes. 31⅛" × 22". B&w, minor edge roughness, a few tears. (A) Oct. '92, $3000. . . . . *$3500–4000*

Ordinance of Secession. Dec. 20, 1860. "To Dissolve the Union Between the State of South Carolina and the other states . . ." Fold lines and age spots. One of the first C.S.A. imprints. (A) Riba, June '88, $600. . . . . *$700–750*

(Pennsylvania Volunteers) "Largest Bounties! Recruits Wanted For...." Ca. 1861; King & Baird Printers, Philadelphia; blue and red lettering with illus. of eagle; litho signed in plate (L. Johnson & Co.); 31½" × 23¾". (A) $4180. . . *$4500–5000*

(Philadelphia Recruiting) "To Arms! To Arms! Volunteers Wanted For the War." 1861. "Recruiting Officers are now open at Western Hotel and Butler House. Turn Out. Volunteers!" Eagle and flag vignettes. Substantial paper loss. (A) Conestoga, Manheim, PA, July '94, $850.. *$800–900*

"Rally for the Union/Down with Traitors! Gum Tree Inn." (PA). Sept. 1864. "Meeting will be Addressed by Buckeye Blacksmith, Comm. of Vigilence." Printed in West Chester, PA. Black on yellow paper. *$800–900*

"Recruits Wanted! Halleck Guard!" "Your country calls you to duty—From $13 to $23 per Month—Col. Elias Peissner." Red, black colors on bright yellow background. Goodwin Printers, NYC. *$2500–3000*

"Sharpshooters Last Chance. Bounty. 1865. Capt. Elsegood, 2nd Regiment Bucktain Rifle Brigade." Ca. 1862. An appeal to "first class men. R.S. Stones, 2d Lt." Recruiting Officer. 8" × 10", all type. *$750–800*

(To The) Sharp Shooters of Windham County. 1861. Bellows Falls, VT. "Capt. Weston has been authorized to raise a Company of Green Mountain Boys for Col. Berdan's Regiment of Sharp Shooters./You are invited to Bring Your Rifles/F.F. Streeter, Supt. of Trial." *$8000–9000*

Gen. James Shield Irish Brigade Recruiting. Ca. 1861–62. "2nd. Regt. to Be Raised in Philadelphia/Now is the time for Irishmen to get arms in their hands . . . a chance to use them against their inveterate foe, the Govt. of England. Recruits Enrolled Here." Both Shields and his aide, Col. Robert E. Patterson, were Irish-born. Illus. of soldiers parading. (A) Riba, June '88, $2200. . . . . *$2500–3000*

"Soldier's Attention, Read! Read!" 11" × 18", black yellow. U.S. Capitol pictured. Seeks attorney who works on soldier's pensions. *$125–150*

Spinola's Brigade Thurlow Weed Guard Recruiting. Zouave soldier standing over fallen Rebel; handcolored. (A) $1430 Pictured.. . . . . *$1200–1500*

Sprague Light Cavalry! "Now is the Time to Join the Best Corps in the Field!" Adds that "highest bounties paid promptly; Men allowed to furnish their own horses; All recruits uniformed immediately." Dramatic multicolor shows cavalry unit attacking C.S.A. forces. Clairy & Reilly Printers, NYC. *$3500–4000*

Stereoptican Show for Civil War and Crimean War. 1862. 9" × 24". Large type reads: "Rebellions. Battles. Cavalry Charges. Bombardments." Three b&w views. *$175–200*

"To Arms! To Arms! Volunteers Wanted for the War/Turn Out Volunteers." 1861. Western Hotel on Market Street is indicated as place to sign up (possibly Philadelphia). 19½" × 12½". Corners missing, other marginal paper loss. (A) Conestoga, July '94, $850. . . . . *$850–900*

"Volunteers Wanted!" Ingalls, Brockway & Berbe, Watertown, NY, printers. 1861. Illus. Eagle with banner in beak, "1776–1861." "An attack on Washington Anticipated/the Country to the Rescue." Signed William C. Browne, Col. commanding 36th Regiment, Watertown, Jefferson County, NY. B&w.. . . . . *$800–900*

"Wanted Immediately/Twelve Cannoneers for the 11 Independent Havelock

Battery at Present Stationed at Camp Pope Va." Ca. 1861. Printed on cloth; large woodcut eagle atop. (A) Riba, $450. . . . . *$500–600*

"War Meeting! In Kingsville at Town Hall." 1862. Signed by A.S. Hall, Cpl., 105 Ohio Regiment, and L.S. Sherman, Esq. B&w, eagle with banner in talons: "On To The Rescue!" Discusses the raising of additional troops in Ohio. . . . .
. . . . *$3500–4000*

"(The) Watchman." Salisbury, NC. Wed., Apr. 12, 1865. ". . . One last appeal, fight on, fight ever, we leave you for some spot on earth where Yankees cannot come." Said to be printed by Union troops but content is decidedly pro-South. . . *$500–600*

Slavery/African-American Related

Amalgamation Whig Ticket. Ca. 1843. Black dude in top hat dancing with demure white lady. "An Appeal to the White Whig Nigger of Rochester. Enter." Bitterly satirical text lambasts William Seward as candidate "for de Gubenor" and Luther Brandish "for de Lt. Gobernor." This anti-Whig flyer helped send Seward and Brandish down to defeat in New York state. (A) Riba, Feb. '90, $5000. . . . . . .
. . . . *$5000–6000*

(Anti-KKK) "The Most Exciting Story of the Century Will be Printed in the Saturday *Globe.***—White Caps/The Mounted Masqueraders Graphically Depicted."** 1899. Illus. of hooded Klansman. Cites disregard of law by KKK in Indiana, Ohio, and Kentucky, 18" × 24.". *$225–250*

"Anti-Slavery Meetings! To Be Addressed by Agents of the Anti-Slavery Society. Turn out!" 10½" × 6". Pub. in Salem, OH. "Union with Freemen—No Union with Slaveholders. Emancipation or Dissolution and a Free Northern Republic." All type, b&w. *$1500–1600*

"Caesar's Epitaph." 1852. 3½" circular with 8-line poem: "Here lies the best of slaves, all moldering into dust . . . and the blood of Jesus Christ was changed from black to white." (A daguerreotype of Caesar, plus biography, appears in book *Facing the Light*.) *$250–300*

Certificate for Liquor License, Decator County, Ga. 1850s. Contains oath not to sell to slaves or free persons of color without written consent of owners/guardians.
. . . . *$250–300*

Circular. Dated April 24, 1863. New Iberia, LA. Notifies that the Parish (St. Martin) is not subject to the Emancipation Proclamation and the slaves are not free. Forbids interference by U.S. Army officers "to use force in the restoration of slaves to masters." Threatens arrest to any master who uses force in abducting runaway slaves or inhumanely punishing or whipping them. Signed by A.B. Long, Capt. and Provost Marshal, Commanding Post. *$300–400*

"Caution!! Colored People of Boston One and All. . . ." April 21, 1851. Written by abolitionist Theodore Parker to warn Negroes to beware of the city police and watchmen, who under Fugitive Slave Act received fees for returning runaway slaves. (Later, some northern states threatened to punish those police who detained Negroes.) *$800–850*

"Colored Soldiers! Equal States Rights/And Monthly Pay with White Men!! Freedom to Over Three Millions of Slaves." Issued January 1, 1863 (as result of Emancipation Proclamation); as General Order No. 233 from President Lincoln. An addendum from Sec. of War Stanton threatens retaliation to Rebels who capture and sell into slavery any Union soldier because of his color. All type. . . . *$400–500*

C.S.A. Documents (50). In printed and manuscript form. 1862–64. Mostly from

No. Carolina. Claims for slaves used by C.S.A. in the war effort; includes names of slaves and owners. (Many slaves served menial duty at coastal forts.) Lotted with other slavery documents, including bills of sale, household inventory from Tennessee, Kentucky, So. Carolina. (A) $700. .... *$800–850*

"Daniel O'Connell, Democracy!" 1863. 11" × 29". Speech first made by Irish orator O'Connell in 1843 reprinted to generate Irish vote in NYC. Cites slavery as the enemy of free labor and democracy. *$325–350*

"Dreadful Riot on Negro Hill." Ca. 1816. Early satirical broadside in form of letter from "Bosson" (Boston). Whites trying to destroy black housing as related in black dialect. B&w woodcut of black woman with broom, black man on crutches being attacked by whites. Red-tinted clothes and blood............... *$400–450*

Regulations to Govern Hands. 1864. By order of W.W. Cozzens, Supt. of Plantations for leased plantations from Louisiana parishes. Deprives black servants of ownership of animals, numerous other rights, b&w, all type........... *$150–200*

PRINTS, POSTERS, AND MAPS

African-American (Colored) Heroes and Regiments

Assault by the 54th Mass. (Colored) Infantry on Ft. Wagner, South Carolina, July 18, 1863. Print. Anonymous. Depicts colored troops going up to ramparts in hand-to-hand combat with Rebels................................ *$450–500*

Henry "Box" Brown. Print. Ca. 1850s. Pictures runaway slave Brown who got his nickname "Box" by having friends nail him in a crate from Richmond and ship him north to Philadelphia and freedom. When uncrated, Brown's famous lines to his benefactors was "How do you do gentlemen?" B&w lithograph of Brown emerging from crate. *$75–100*

John Brown, Leader of the Harpers Ferry Insurrection. Print. Currier & Ives, NY, 1870 (3255). Portrait with vignettes. Handcolored............... *$100–125*

John Brown Meeting the Slave Mother and Her Child on the Steps of Charleston (sic) Jail on the Way to Execution. Print. Currier & Ives, NY, 1863. After oil painting by Louis L. Ransom (3253). Brown pauses before slave family, as stern-looking guard in Rebel uniform looks on. Handcolored. (S)..... *$200–250*

John Brown the Martyr. Print. Currier & Ives, NY, 1870 (3254). Handcolored; approx. 12" × 9". (S)... *$100–150*

(The) Colored Volunteer Marching into Dixie. 1862. Print. 1863. Currier & Ives, NY (1208). Three-quarter-length standing portrait of soldier. (S)....... *$100–125*

(The) Colored Volunteer. 1863. Currier & Ives, NY (1207). Young boy marching, using broom for musket in oval vignette. (M). *$125–150*

Come Join Us Brother. Print. Ca. 1863–65. 13¾" × 17⅞" chromolith. Pub. in Philadelphia by Supervisory Comm. for Recruiting Colored Regts. by Pierre S. Duval. An all-colored regt., including drummer boy led by white officer at left, lined up in front of tent..... .... *$800–900*

Frederick Douglas. Print. Ca. 1860. B&w engraving; 20" × 23", framed.. *$100–125*

Fifteenth Amendment. Print. 1870. Handcolored stone lithograph by Thomas Kelley. Central vignette—blacks celebrating right to vote on May 19, 1870. Numerous vignettes depict new Negro rights—education, marriage, electing reps., buying farms. Portraits of Grant–Colfax at top; Lincoln, Brown, Douglas, et al. *$1100–1200*

Gallant Charge of the 54th Mass. (Colored) Regt. July 18/1873. Print. 1865. Currier & Ives, NY (2210). (Adapted from relief works at Ft. Wagner, Morris Island, outside Charleston). ". . . and death of Col. Robert Shaw"; featured in movie *Glory.* (S). *$350–350*

A Hero's Welcome for Returning Black Veterans. Print. 1865. Litho from pencil drawing by A.R. Waud. A Lt. in foreground sweeps up his wife in an embrace. *$300–350*

Insignia from Flag of the 3rd U.S. Colored Infantry. Print. "I'd Rather Die a Freeman Than Live to be a Slave." Bareheaded black officer holds the U.S. flag at staff as Miss Liberty looks on. *$200–250*

Marriage Ceremony of Black Soldier and Freedwoman at Vicksburg, Mississippi. Print. *Harper's Weekly,* June 30, 1866. . . . . *$50–75*

"Miscegenation Ball." Cartoon print. Anonymous, 1864. "Political Caricature No. 4." Satirical view of Lincoln Inaugural Ball showing blacks and whites dancing together. Multicolored litho., 19" $\times$ $^3/_4$" $\times$ 23". *$600–750*

(From the) Reconstructed Constitution of the State of Louisiana. Print. 1868. Large oval portrait of O.J. Dunn, Lt. Gov. of Louisiana, plus cameos of 30 other black legislators, including Pickney Pinchback, later an acting Gov., highest state post held by a Negro in postwar South. Also flags, rifles, palm fronds. . . *$475–500*

Hon. H.R. Revels. Print. 1870. Artist unknown. From painting by Theodore Kaufman. Printed by Louis Prang, Boston. Bust portrait of noted clergyman and chaplain to black regiment in Mississippi. First black to be elected to U.S. Senate. 14" $\times$ 11$^1/_2$" chromolithograph. *$600–700*

Former Slaves Follow Gen. Sherman Troops Across Georgia. March 18, 1865. Print. *Frank Leslie's Illus. Newspaper.* *$50–75*

Fugitive Slaves Coming into Union Lines near Culpepper Court House, Virginia, Nov. 8, 1863. Print from pencil drawing by Edwin Forbes. *$200–250*

Slaves Seeking Admittance to Fortress Monroe, Virginia, Weeks after Onset of Civil War. Print. *Frank Leslie's Illus. Newspaper,* June 8, 1861. . . . . *$50–75*

Slaves from Plantation of Confederate President Jefferson Davis Arrive at Chickasaw Bayou, Mississippi. Print. *Frank Leslie's Illus. Newspaper,* Aug. 8, 1863. . . . . *$50–75*

"Slave Holder's Parody." Print. Ca. 1830s. Woodcut illus. of cleric whipping slave who holds a bible. Poem is all about clerics who preach salvation and sin but mistreat their own slaves. 6" $\times$ 9" b&w, minor foxing. Stark FP Cat., Dec. '90, $600. . . . . *$500–600*

(Colored) Soldiers of the 1st Louisiana Native Guard Standing Picket. Print from *Frank Leslie's Illus. Newspaper,* March 7, 1863. One sentry stands with musket and bayonet at ready; several sit around fire. Louisiana bayou in background. *$50–75*

Storming Fort Wagner. Print. 1890. Chromolith by Kurz & Allison, Chicago. 22" $\times$ 28". Col. Robert Shaw leads 54th Mass. colored troops to top of fort. Depicts Shaw being shot and mortally wounded (almost as it happened in the movie *Glory*). *$900–1000*

"Topsy's Recreation." Ca. 1880s. Two-sheet theater poster for *Uncle Tom's Cabin*; Topsy dances; small bust cameos of two other cast members in each top corner; full color; published by Erie Litho, Erie, PA. (A) $440. . . . . *$500–600*

Note: Eight posters in all comprised *Uncle Tom's Cabin* set: Other seven titles: "Uncle Tom & Eva," "They Turn on Him," "Ophelia and the Deacon," "Legree Whipping Uncle Tom," "Fight on the Rocky Pass," "Eliza's Escape," and "Uncle Tom Bidding His Children Farewell." . . . . *$500–$600* (each)

Twentieth U.S. Colored Infantry/Presentation of Colors, Col. Bartram, at Union League, NY, Mar. 5, 1864. Print. Handcolored woodcut. Probably *Harpers.*
.... *$75–100*

Vicksburg Contraband Ball. Print. Ca. 1863. Full-color woodcut. Negroes dancing at huge ball. Text below cites evils of slavery and miscegenation; stresses refinement of Negro culture; 16" × 20". Probably by *Harpers*........... *$125–150*

Battle Scenes, Military Leaders, Political Recruiting, Statesmen
CARRIER'S ADDRESSES

Carrier's or newsboys' addresses—an English carryover—was later popularized in the United States from the 1850s–'80s. Printed as a newspaper supplement, they contained single-sheet greetings, poems, commentaries on the times, and a plea for gratuities for the newsboys to supplement their meager wages.

Carrier's Union 1877. Roster of past presidents (newspaper not listed). Depicts eagle, shield, bust portraits of all presidents through Lincoln, Johnson, and Grant. Blue-tone on buff. *$100–125*

(Grant) *New York Herald.* **Jan. 1, 1874.** Central. 24-stanza poem about the war.
.... *$300–350*

(Lincoln) *Rochester NY Evening News.* 1864. Four cols. and 22 verses re: Lincoln, Stonewall Jackson, Battles of Gettysburg, Richmond, Chancellorsville, Wide Awakes, Copperheads.. *$300–350*

CIVIL WAR BATTLES—PRINTS
(See also special listing of Currier & Ives folios.)

A Group of 18 Chromolithographs. Prints. Ca. 1880. Louis Prang, Boston. Civil War battles, incl. "Capture of New Orleans, Battle of Mobile Bay," "Port Hudson," "Antietam." Most are signed by the artist, Thure deThulstrop. (A) $1500.........
.... *$2000–2500*

Alabama and Kearsarge. Print. 1887. Louis Prang, Boston. Chromolith. After painting by Juilen Oliver Davidson. The Battle of Cherbourg as seen from deck of the *Kearsarge*, with cannoneers cheering after a direct hit on the C.S.A. vessel. The artist had relied on the *Harper's Weekly* cover from July 1864. 15" × 22". *$300–350*

Maj. Robert Anderson/The Hero of Ft. Sumter. Print. 1861. Currier & Ives, NYC (3940). Vignette. (S). *$100–125*

Army of the Potomac/Roll of Honor. Print. Multicolored certification of service record with vignettes of Gen. William Rosecrans who led the Chattanooga Campaign for the Union; eagle flags and battle scenes with homilies, i.e., "Honor to the brave"; "For God & My Country." *$125–150*

Atlanta Occupied/View of Public Square. 1864. Print litho by Henry C. Eno, NYC. Union troops occupying city. 13" × 21", full color. (A) $450..... *$500–600*

Col. Edward D. Baker. Print. "U.S. Senator from Oregon Commanding the First California Regiment/Killed while fighting in Defense of the Union at Ball's Bluff near/Leesburg, Va. Oct. 21st, 1861. Currier & Ives (1187). Three-quarter-length vignette of Baker. (S). *$150–200*

Maj. Gen. Nathaniel Banks. Print. 1863. Currier & Ives, NYC (3924). Upright on horseback. Leader of Red River Campaign. (S)...................... *$125–150*

Confederate Camp. Print. Ca. 1865. M. & N. Hanhart chromolithograph, 10⅝" × 15¼", after oil painting by Conrad Wise Chapman. *$450–500*

(The) Battle of Gettysburg. Print. 1872. John Sartain, sculptor. P.F. Rothermel Pinx engraver, 21" × 36", hand-tinted. *$300–325*

Battle of Lookout Mountain. Print. Possibly by Louis Kurz; printed by Kurz & Allison, Chicago, 1889; full color; 22⅛" × 28". (D) $3500. .... *$2500–$3000*

Battle of the Weldon Railroad. Print. Aug. 21, 1864. Drawn by R. Holland; litho by J.H. Bufford, Boston. Hand-tinted. In fine condition. (A) $250. ..... *$350–400*

CURRIER & IVES, BATTLE RELATED

Over 40 prints, including variants, were issued by Currier & Ives, NY, in the 1860s commemorating major battles of the Civil War, all with the following preface:

The Battle at or **of:**

Antietam, MD. Sept. 17, 1862. (384) Three-line caption. (S)......... *$175–200*

Baton Rouge, LA. Aug. 4, 1862. (385) Shows battleships; four-line caption. (S). *$200–250*

Bentonville, NC. March 19, 1865. (386) (S). *$150–175*

Bull Run, VA. July 21, 1861. (391) (S)........................... *$200–225*

Cedar Creek, VA. Oct. 19, 1864. (392) (S) *$150–175*

Cedar Mountain. Aug. 9, 1862. (380) Two-line caption describes Army of Virginia, under Gens. Banks and Pope vs. C.S.A. Gens. Ewell and Stonewall Jackson. (S)... *$175–200*

(381) Variation of above. With same title with line "The Charge of Crawford's Brigade on the right ..." (S) ....

Champion Hills, MS. May 16, 1863. (394) (S) *$150–175*

Chancellorsville, VA. May 3, 1863. (395) (S) *$175–200*

Chattanooga, TN. Nov. 24–25, 1863. (396) (S)................... *$175–200*

Chickamauga, GA. (397) (S) *$175–200*

Coal Harbor, VA. June 1, 1864. (400) (S)....................... *$150–175*

Corinth, MS. Oct. 4, 1862. (401) Three-line caption. (S)............. *$125–150*

Fair Oaks, VA. May 31, 1862. (403) Five-line caption; depicts observation balloon—a first in U.S. warfare. (S) *$200–225*

(403) Size variation. With three additional lines; Gen. Sumner and staff keyed. (L) *$750–800*

Five Forks, VA. April 1, 1862. (382) Four-line caption. (S) *$150–175*

Fredericksburg, VA. Dec. 13, 1862. (405) Five-line caption. (S)...... *$175–200*

Gettysburg, PA. July 3, 1863. (406) Four-line caption. (L)........... *$800–850*

  (407) Size variation of above. Five-line caption. (S) *$200–225*

Jonesboro, GA. Sept. 1, 1864. (408) Six-line caption. (S)............ *$200–225*

Lexington, KY. 1861. (409) (S) *$175–200*

Malvern Hill, VA. July 1, 1862. (410) Terrific bayonet charge of federal troops and final repulse of Rebels. (S) *$175–200*

Mill Spring, KY. Jan. 19. (412) Terrific bayonet charge. (S).......... *$175–200*

(413) Entirely different scene, but same title as above. Union Gens. Thomas and Schoepff lead total rout of rebels. (S) *$150–175*

Missionary Ridge, GA. 1862. (383) (S) *$150–175*

Murfreesboro, TN. Dec. 31, 1862. (415) (L) *$800–900*

Newburn, NC. March 14, 1862. (419) Gen. Burnside's brilliant Union victory, total Rebel rout. (S) *$200–250*

Pea Ridge, AR. March 8, 1862. (420) Several additional lines. (S) *$200–250*

Pea Ridge, AR. March 8, 1862. (421) F. Crow on stone. (L) *$750–800*

Petersburg, TN. April 2, 1862. (422) Three additional lines. (S) *$200–250*

Pittsburg, TN. April 7. (423) Three additional lines, Union forces at right. (S) . . .
. . . . *$200–250*

Pittsburg, TN. April 7. (424) Union forces *now* appear at left. *$200–250*

Pittsburg, TN. April 7. (425) Two additional lines. Keyed are Gens. Crittendon, Wallace, Buell, Sherman, and Grant. (L) *$800–900*

Sharpsburg, MD. Sept. 16, 1862. (429) Lee, Stonewall Jackson, Hill, and Longstreet vs. McClellan. Three lines of description. (S) *$200–250*

Spotsylvania, VA. May 12, 1864. (430) Three additional lines. (S). *$200–250*

Wilderness, VA. May 5–6, 1864. (436) (S) *$225–275*

Wilderness, VA. May 5–6, 1864. (435) Three additional lines. (L). . . . .

MISCELLANEOUS

Col. Frank Blair, Jr. Print. "Death of 1st Regt. Missouri Vols." 1861. (1191) Three-quarter-length fig. of Blair. (S) *$75–100*

(The) Bombardment and Capture of Ft. Fisher, NC, Jan. 15, 1865. Print. Currier & Ives, NY. (589) Mounted; 8" × 12". $125 (D) *$350–400*

Gen. John C. Breckinridge. Print. 1862. Currier & Ives, NY. (2283) Upright portrait. (S). *$100–125*

Brilliant Naval Victory on the Mississippi River near Ft. Wright, May 10, 1862. Print. Currier & Ives, NY. (692) Key of ships and river ports: Mallory, Louisiana, Ram, Cincinnati, Benton, Cairo, Carondolet, St. Louis, Conestoga. Two additional lines. (S) *$350–400*

Burnside and Gens. of 9th Army Corps. 1861–1886. Print. 1886. 16" × 21". 25th reunion, b&w. *$125–150*

Maj. Gen. Ambrose E. Burnside, Commander in Chief of the Army of the Potomac. Print. 1862. Currier & Ives, NY. (3901) Full-length portrait on horseback. (S). *$150–200*

Maj. Gen. Ambrose E. Burnside at the Battle of Fredericksburg, VA, Dec. 13, 1862. Print. Currier & Ives, NY. (3902) Burnside on horseback. Upright. (S) . . . . .
. . . . *$150–200*

Maj. Gen. Benjamin F. Butler of Mass. Print. 1862. Currier & Ives, NY. (3903) Vignette portrait in uniform. (S) *$100–125*

C.S.A. Cartoon Etchings. Print portfolio. By Adelbert Volck, Philadelphia. Ca. 1880. Twenty-nine plates, images average 5" × 8". The original issue may have been suppressed by the author as caricatures bordered on treason. Volck was decidedly anti-Lincoln. Index page complete, missing cover. (A) $450. . . . . . . *$600–650*

Camp of the 148th Regt. NY Vols. near Portsmouth, VA. Print. Lang & Cooper, NY; J.S. Laidlaw, DE, 1862; litho., 10" × 6" framed. $150–250. . . . . . . *$300–400*

Champions of the Union. Print. 1861. Currier & Ives, NY. (993) Gens. Winfield Scott, George McClellan and 22 others. Round top vignette. (M). *$225–250*

Confederacy—The Secession Movement. Print. 1861. Currier & Ives, NY. (1236) (S). *$200–250*

Confederate Courage. Contemporary. Print. By Bruce Marshall. Ltd. edit., signed, triple matted and framed, 27" × 31". (A) Conestoga, July '95, $125. . . . . *$100–125*

Confederate States of America Circular Format. Print. "Inscribed 22 Feb. 1862." Multicolor stone litho by Andrew Graham, Washington, D.C. George Washington (a Virginian, remember) on horseback; encircled by laurel sprigs with crossed C.S.A. flags below. Latin inscription: "Deo Vindice." *$600–700*

Col. Michael Corcoran at the Battle of Bull Run, VA. Print. "July 21, 1861/The desperate and Bloody charge of the Gallant Sixty Ninth on the rebel batteries." Currier & Ives, NY. (1199) (S) *$250–300*

Col. Michael Corcoran/Commanding the 69th Irish Regiment/Erin Go Bragh. Print. 1861. Currier & Ives, NY. (1200) Three-quarter-length portrait. (S) *$100–125*

Council of War. Print. 1985. By Don Stivers, Ltd. edit. 581/650. Framed, matted, 27" × 30". (A) Conestoga, July '94, $525. . . . . *$475–500*

(Jefferson Davis) Lost Cause. Print. 1865. Large C.S.A. shield as focal point; cameos of Gens. R.E. Lee, Stonewall Jackson, President Jefferson Davis. Confederate bills serve as novel border, b&w. *$400–450*

Jefferson Davis and His Generals. Print. Ca. 1861. Pub. by Goupil et Cie, Paris, and Michael Knoedler, NYC. Handcolored lithograph of Davis surrounded by Gens. Beauregard, Albert Syden Johnson, Breckinridge, others, with troop movement in background. *$700–800*

Jefferson Davis—"Only Let Us Alone." Print. 1861. *Harper's Weekly.* Identified as the "Jeff Davis Target." Shows him in uniform with bullet holes sprayed all over his tunic, and words appear in cartoon balloon coming out of mouth. *$75–85*

The Domestic Blockade. Print. Currier & Ives, NY. (1598) Mother wields broom as daughter carries flag; son in Zouave costume has toy gun. Tables, chairs, etc. serve as barricade in mock warfare. (L). *$300–350*

11th Mass. Light Artillery Soldier's Memorial. Print. 1862. Currier & Ives, NY. Vignettes of Capitol Building, Union Camp, Standing Artilleryman (at center). Cameos of Lincoln, Winfield Scott, and McClellan. Multicolor, 16" × 20", framed. Stark FP Cat., July '94, $150. . . . . *$150–175*

Col. Elmer Elsworth/1st Regt. NY Zouaves/Assassinated at Capture of Alexandria. Print. 1861. (1188) Quotation with two additional lines. (S) *$100–150*

Col. Elmer Elsworth/1st Regt. NY Zouaves. Print. Variant of above, vignetted, with changes in composition. (1189). *$100–150*

Death of Col. Elsworth. Print. 1861. Currier & Ives, NY. (1476) Full-color litho. of Col. Elsworth of the Zouaves, treading on a C.S.A. flag and being mortally wounded by a civilian Rebel who, in turn, is killed by Elsworth's aide. (S). . . . .
. . . . *$125–150*

(The) Excavation of Richmond, Va., by the Gov. of the Confederacy on the Night of April, 2, 1865. Print. ¹/₂" top margin; lower edge punch holes. (A) $176 .
. . . . *$250–300*

(The) Fall of Richmond, Va., on the Night of April 2, 1865. Print. Currier & Ives, NY. (1821) (L). *$700–750*

   Same as above but (S). (1822) Small folio. *$200–250*

   Variant. (1823) With changes in pedestrians, carriages, etc. crossing bridge. (S)
. . . . *$200–250*

Comdr. David Farragut's Fleet Passing Forts on the Mississippi, Apr. 24th, 1862. Print. Currier & Ives, NY. (1214) U.S. Frigate *Mississippi* defeating Rebel ram *Manassas.* Key on Ft. St. Phillip, Ft. Jackson. (S) *$350–400*

(Farragut) "Great Naval Victory in Mobile Bay/Aug. 5, 1864." Print. (2633)

Adm. Farragut with four monitors and 14 wooden ships attacks C.S.A. ironclad ram *Tennessee* under Adm. Buchanan. (S) *$350–400*

(Adm. Farragut) "Splendid Naval Triumph on the Mississippi, Apr. 24, 1862." "The Destruction of the Rebel Gunboats, Rams and Iron Clad Batteries by the Union Fleet under Flag Officer Farragut." Print. 1862. Currier & Ives, NY. (5659) Three added lines and 15 indent. keys. (L) (Chosen by jury of emminent C&I collectors and dealers as one of the best 50 large folio prints.)...................... *$1200–1400*

Federal Generals. Print. 1862. Handcolored litho, 15" × 28". Gens. Butler, Hancock, McClellan, McDowell, Burnside—all on horseback............. *$100–125*

The 5th Regiment—Company E., New York Volunteer Artillery. Print. 1862. Currier & Ives, NY. (5603) (M)................................... *$200–225*

Bombardment of Ft. Fisher, Jan. 15, 1865. Print. Handcolored. Published by Endicott & Co., NYC. Sheet size 27³/₄" × 40¹/₂".................... *$1000–1200*

Com. Andrew H. Foote/The Hero of Ft. Henry 1862. Print. Currier & Ives. (1213) Three-quarter-length portrait of Foote in uniform. (S).......... *$100–125*

G.A.R. Grand Patriotic Celebration of Bunker Hill Day on Monday June 18th, 1883. Poster. Pub. by Forbes, Boston. Signed by Gen. Lander, Post 5, G.A.R., Lynn, MA. Promotes "Grand Sham Fight of the Great Battle of Roanoke Island." Includes re-enactment of bombardment of Richmond by gunboats and the burning of the city... *$150–200*

"Gallant Charge of the 69th on the Rebel Batteries at the Battle of Bull Run, Va., July 21st, 1861." Print. Currier & Ives, NY. (2213) (S).......... *$200–250*

Battle of Gettysburg. Print. Full-color litho by Donaldson from painting for State of Pennsylvania, 14" × 20"...................................... *$100–125*

Battle of Gettysburg. Print. Ca. 1860s. B&w litho by Kurz & Allison, 19" × 16". *$150–175*

(Union) Maj. Gen. Q.A. Gillmore/U.S. Army. Print. 1863. Currier & Ives, NY. (3927) Engineer specialist who supervised harbor fortification construction. Commanded the X Troops in the Dept. of the South. Vignette portrait. (S) ... *$100–125*

Gen. U.S. Grant/1884. Print. Currier & Ives, NY. (2312) (S) *$100–125*

Gen. U.S. Grant/1885. Print. Currier & Ives, NY. (2313) Half-length portrait. (S) *$100–125*

Gen. U.S. Grant/1885. Print. Currier & Ives, NY. (2314) Bust portrait. (S) *$100–125*

Gen. U.S. Grant/General-in-Chief of the Armies of the U.S. Print. 1862. Currier & Ives, NY. (2315) (S).. *$100–125*

Gen. Grant at Chattanooga. Print. Ca. 1880s. 19" × 25", multicolor battlefield portrait with Grant picking up fallen banner. His horse is in background. Dedicated to G.A.R. *$100–125*

Maj. Gen. U.S. Grant at the Siege of Vicksburg, July 4, 1863. Print. Currier & Ives, NY. (3928) Grant on horseback. (S) *$100–125*

Grant and His Generals/Distinguished Commanders in the Campaign against Richmond. 1865. Print. Currier & Ives. (2553). Vignette of Grant with ten other Union Gens. including Hancock, Meade, Warren, Humphrey. (M) *$250–300*

Grant and Lee Meeting Near Appomattox Court House, Va., Apr. 10, 1865. Print. Currier & Ives, NY, 1868. (2554) From original painting by Lt. Col. Otto Botticher. (S) *$200–250*

Grant in the Wilderness. Print by H.A. Ogden. By Knight & Brown Co., 1897; framed. (D) $115.. *$100–125*

(Grant) To the Grand Army of the Republic/This Print of Our Old Commander General is Respectfully Dedicated. Print. 1885. Currier & Ives, NY. (6068)

Grant on horseback; full length. (L)............................ *$450–500*

Great Fight at Charleston, S.C., April 7, 1863. Print. Currier & Ives. (2611) Five keys of naval battle. (S) *$350–400*

Great Victory in the Shenandoah Valley, Va., Sept. 19, 1864. Print. Currier & Ives, NY. (2653) Gen. Sherman's Cavalry charging Rebel horsemen. (S)....... *$200–250*

Maj. General Henry W. Halleck/General in Chief of the Armies of the U.S., July 1862. Print. 1863. Currier & Ives, NY. (3913) Halleck on horseback. (M) ...
.... *$125–150*

Maj. Gen. Winfield Scott Hancock at the Battle of Spotsylvania Court House, Va., May 12, 1864. Print. Currier & Ives, NY. (3936) Scott astride white horse. (S)
.... *$150–175*

In the Hands of the Enemy after Gettysburg. Print. 1889. Etching by Hovenden. B&w of wounded Rebel roped up beneath a Lincoln portrait and a U.S. flag, being treated by a Union family after the battle. Wounded Union troopers are also depicted in background.. *$100–150*

"Hardee's Tactics/Musket and Bayonet," 1861. Print by Chas. Magnus, NYC. Sixteen depictions of railways, waterways, military movements. Handcolored.....
.... *$300–350*

(The) High Water Mark, Gettysburg, July 3, 1863. 1988. Ltd edit. print by Mort Kunstler, signed and numbered 251/750. Framed and matted, 25" × 38". (A) Conestoga, July '94, $850....................................... *$750–800*

Maj. Gen. Joseph Hooker. Print. 1862. Currier & Ives, NY. (3921) Upright equestrian image. (A) *$150–200*

Maj. Gen. Joseph Hooker (Fighting Joe) at the Battle of Antietam, 1862. Print. Currier & Ives, NY. (3923) Full-length on horseback. (S) *$200–250*

Maj. Gen. Joseph Hooker. Commander in Chief of the Army of the Potomac. Print. 1862. (3922). (S).. *$150–200*

Lt. T.J. (Stonewall) Jackson. 1861. Print. Currier & Ives, NY. (6065) (S).......
.... *$125–150*

(C.S.A.) Gen. Joseph Johnston, 1861. Print. Currier & Ives, NY. (2285) Portrait. (S).. *$100–125*

(Gen. Joe Johnston, C.S.A.) Surrender of Joe Johnston Near Greensboro, NC. April 26, 1865. Print. Currier & Ives, NY. (5908) Gens. Johnston and Sherman keyed. (S).. *$250–300*

Lee and His Generals. Print. 1907. By G.B. Matthews. Litho by A.B. Graham, Washington, D.C., 18" × 29¼". (A) Conestoga, July '94, $225. .... *$150–220*

Lee at the Grave of Stonewall Jackson. 1872. Print. Currier & Ives NY. (3474) (S).. *$100–125*

Lee at the Grave of Stonewall Jackson. Print. 1872. Currier & Ives, NY. (2292) (S).. *$125–150*

The Lees of Virginia/C.S.A. Gens. 1861–1865. Prints. B&w etching of Robert E. Lee and four other Lees including Fitzhugh, a nephew, George Washington Custis Lee, R.E. Lee's eldest son, and William Henry Fitzhugh "Rooney" Lee, his second eldest. Family crest at top. Lee estate at bottom.................... *$250–300*

Note: See also Currier & Ives depicting Gen. Lee under Cat. No.'s 429, 1484, 1534, 2291–2, 2254, 3962, 4551, 5909–11.

(Lee) Death of Gen. Robert. E. Lee at Lexington, Va., Oct. 12, 1870. Print. Currier & Ives, NY. (1484) Age 62 mos., 6 days; two additional lines. (S) *$100–125*

(Lee) Decoration of the Casket of Gen. Lee. Print. Currier & Ives, NY. 1870. (1534) (S)... *$75–100*

Gen. Robert E. Lee. Print. 1861. Currier & Ives, NY. (2291) Vignette and facsimile sign. (S) *$100–125*

Lee Bust Portrait. Contemporary print. Printed by Tulsa Chapter, United Daughters of the Confederacy. Oval bust profile of Lee in uniform. (A) Conestoga, July '94, $250. . . . . *$200–250*

Lee Bust Portrait. Print. Date unknown. Kurz and Allison, Chicago. Three-quarter bust of Lee in uniform, 27" × 22". (A) Conestoga, July '94, $175. . . . . . . *$150–200*

Lee's Texans. Print. 1984 by Don Troiani. Artist's proof, ltd. edition, AP 27/50. Lee on horseback urging on his troops; 28" × 35", matted, framed. (A) Conestoga, July '94, $900. . . . . *$800–900*

(Lee/Grant) Old Bulldog on the Right Track. Print. Currier & Ives, NY. 1864. (4551) Cartoon vignette of Lincoln, Lee, Grant, Beauregard, McClellan. (M) *$300–350*

(Lee) Surrender of Lee at Appomattox Court House, Va. Print. 1865. Currier & Ives, NY. (5909) Upright, seated at table. Lee keyed above title. (S) *$200–250*

(Lee) Surrender of Lee at Appomattox Court House, Va. Print. 1868. Currier & Ives, NY. (5910) Variant. (S) *$200–250*

Life Studies of the Great Army. Print. © 1876; litho. by Edwin Forbes; portfolio containing 40 plates illustrating Union Army, 1862–65. . . . . *$1200–1500*

President Lincoln at Gen./Grant's Headquarters at City Point, Va./March 1865. Print. Currier & Ives, NY. (4881) Lincoln, Gens. Sherman, Sheridan, Grant. Rounded top corners. (S) *$250–300*

"Death of Gen. Lyon at Head of His Troops," 1861. Print. (A) $275 (lotted with Battle of Pea Ridge folio), $200–$300. . . . . *$300–400*

(McClellan) Gen. George B. McClellan and Staff/At the Battle of Williamsburg, Va., May 5th, 1862. Print. Currier & Ives, NY. (2259) (S) *$125–150*

(McClellan) Gen. George B. McClellan and Staff Before Yorktown, Va. April 1862. Print. Vertical. Gen. on horseback. *$250–300*

Maj. Gen. George G. Meade at the Battle of Gettysburg. July 3, 1863. Print. Currier & Ives, NY. (3911) On horseback with sword extended. Slightly rounded top corners. (S) *$200–250*

Maj. Gen. George G. Meade/Commander in Chief of the Army of the Potomac. July 3rd, 1863. Print. Currier & Ives, NY. (3912) Bust portrait in uniform, right-facing. (S) *$125–150*

Gen. Meagher at the Batle of Fair Oaks, Va., June 1, 1862. Print. Currier & Ives, NY. (2289) Three added lines. (S) *$200–225*

Gen. Thomas Francis Meagher at the Battle of Fredericksburg, Va., Dec. 13, 1862. Print. Currier & Ives, NY. (2301) Gen. on white horse, Irish flag. (S) *$200–225*

"Moving Day at Richmond." Print-cartoon. May 1, 1865. Pub. by H&W Voight. Sheriff's auction at C.S.A. headquarters as bonds and treasury notes are loaded into dog cart. Robert E. Lee carries out weapons. Negroes look on. *$150–175*

Col. James A. Mulligan of the Ill. Irish Brigade. 1862. Print. Currier & Ives, NY. (1197) Three-quarter standing portrait; telescope in left hand. (S) *$75–85*

State of New Jersey "Honoring Country's Brave Defenders." Print (certificate). Ca. 1864. Signed by NJ Gov. Marcus Ward and awarded to James L. Talmadge, Co. B, 27th Infantry of NJ. Vignettes of battlegrounds, battle between *Monitor* and *Merrimac*; soldiers leaving loved ones for battle and returning from war, cannons, anchors, female Roman deities. Black on buff engraving. *$200–250*

(The) Night after the Battle. Print. 1862. Currier & Ives, NY (4470) Soldier holding torch, while nurse and another soldier support wounded man. (S) . . . *$150–175*

Night Before the Battle/The Patriot's Dream. Print. 1861. Currier & Ives, NY. (4471) (M) *$200–250*

Off for the War. Print. 1861. Currier & Ives, NY. (4538) Officer with mustache; upright. (S) *$125–150*

Off for the War. Print. 1861. Currier & Ives, NY. (4538) Bearded officer, soldier with flag in background, upright. (S) *$125–150*

Off for the War/The Soldier's Adieu. Print. 1861. Currier & Ives, NY. (4539) Companion to No. 2858 "Home From the War" (S) *$135–165*

Ohio 137th—U.S. Military Record and Muster. Print. 19" × 24" litho. Lincoln portrait and other cameos. Blue, white, pink, brown. *$85–100*

One Hundred Fifty Miles Around Richmond. Map print. Ca. 1863. Charles Magnus map; large circular map in red, white, and blue. With cameos of Grant and Lee. Vignettes of battle scenes, 21" × 28". *$200–225*

Part of the Battle of Shiloh. Print. 1862. Currier & Ives, NY. (4709) (S) *$200–250*

Maj. Gen. John Pope/Commanding U.S. Army of Va. Print. 1862. Currier & Ives, NY. (3919). *$75–100*

Maj. Gen. John Pope/The Hero of New Madrid, Miss. Print. 1862. Currier & Ives, NY. (3920) Vignette. (S) *$100–125*

Prang's Naval Expedition Maps. Maps. 1862. Printed by Louis Prang, Boston. Eight different maps showing major ports used heavily during war. With flags of all maritime nations in full color; maps in light tones. (A) $250. .... *$300–350*

Rebel Yell. Contemporary print. Ltd. edit. by Bruce Marshall, signed and numbered 40/1865. Framed, matted with brass plate, 25" × 35". (A) Conestoga, July '94, $175. .... *$150–200*

Rebel Yell. Contemporary print. By Don Troiani. Ltd. edit. AP 15/50. 31" × 27", framed and matted. (A) Conestoga, July '94, $850. .... *$750–800*

Re-Union on the Secash–Democratic Plan. Print. 1862. Currier & Ives, NY. (5132) Southerner offers to surrender if Uncle Sam, burdened with $650 million C.S.A. debt and federal debts of $1 billion 500 million and slaves, will pay all expenses for war. Vignette. (S) *$300–350*

Maj. Gen. William S. Rosecrans at the Battle of Murfreesboro, Jan. 2, 1863. Print. Currier & Ives, NY. (3929) (S) *$150–175*

Maj. Gen. William S. Rosecrans, U.S. Army. Print. 1863. Currier & Ives, NY. (3930) (S) *$75–100*

(The) Secession Movement. Print. 1861. Currier & Ives, NY. (5451) Vignette of figures representing various Southern states riding pigs, mules, horses, and chasing butterfly to edge of cliff, of which they're oblivious. (S) *$400–500*

Second Battle of Bull Run/Fought Aug. 29th, 1862. Print. Currier & Ives, NY. (5452) Union army under Gen. John Pope at left and C.S.A. under Gens. Lee and Jackson; 2" + margins; minor staining 2" into image. (A) $330; lotted with "Battle of Fredericksburg," $175. (D) *$200–250*

Selling Out Cheap! Print. 1870. Currier & Ives, NY. (5460) Vignette of suffragist Charles Sumner with anti-Grant speeches piled on desk, telling Devil that he may have the country if he (Sumner) may gain revenge. (S). *$200–250*

Sharpshooter on Picket Duty, Army of the Potomac. Print. Nov. 16, 1862, by Winslow Homer. Full-page wood engraving from *Harper's Weekly*, 9" × 14", full borders. *$100–150*

Sheridan's Cavalry at the Battle of Fisher's Hill. Print. 1862. Currier & Ives, NY. (5489) (S) *$200–250*

Maj. Gen. Philip H. Sheridan. "Rallying his troops at battle of Cedar Creek, Va., after his famous ride from Washington, Oct. 19, 1864." Print. Currier & Ives, NY. (3925). Upright view; Gen. on prancing horse with sabre raised. (S) *$150–200*

Maj. Gen. Philip H. Sheridan/U.S. Army. Print. 1864. Currier & Ives, NY. (3926) Facsimile signature. Vignette. (S) *$125–150*

Sherman and His Generals/Distinguished Commanders in the Atlantic and Georgia Campaigns. Print. 1865. Currier & Ives NY. (5490) Incl. Gens. McPherson, Slocum, Blair, Thomas, Williams, Howard, Geary, Schoenfeld, Davis, Hazen, Lilpatrick, Logan as well as Sherman. (M) *$200–250*

Sherman's March to the Sea. Print. 1868. By F.O.C. Darley, A.M. Richie, engraver. Both pencil signed proof, before title; entered Congress by L. Stebbens. Handtinted, large folio, 25" × 40". *$600–700*

Maj. Gen. William T. Sherman, U.S. Army. Print. 1863. Currier & Ives, NY. (3932) Vignette and facsimile signature. (S) *$100–125*

Maj. Gen. William T. Sherman, U.S. Army. Print. 1863. Currier & Ives, NY. (2327) Variant of above. (S) *$75–100*

Maj. Gen. William T. Sherman on His Victorious March through Georgia and North Carolina. Print. 1863. Currier & Ives, NY. (3931) Sherman on horseback. (S). *$150–200*

Gen. W.T. Sherman, U.S.A. Commanding the Union Forces at the Taking of Port Royal, Nov. 7th, 1861. Print. Currier & Ives, NY. (678). Three-quarter length vignette. (S) *$125–150*

Gen. (James) Shields at the Battle of Winchester, Va., 1862. Print. Currier & Ives, NY. (2294) Three added lines. (S) *$200–250*

Maj. Gen. Franz Sigel, The Hero of the West. Print. 1863. Currier & Ives, NY. (3895) (S). *$125–150*

Maj. Gen. Franz Sigel, The Hero of the West. Print. 1863. Currier & Ives, NY. (3904) Variant of above. (S) *$125–150*

"(The) Siege of Charleston." Print. Currier & Ives, NY. (5508) Bombardment of Ft. Sumter, and Batteries Wagner, Gregg, under Gen. Gillmore command. Aug. 1863. One-inch margins. (S) (D) $175. . . . . *$200–250*

(The) Soldier Boy/Off Duty. Print. 1864. Currier & Ives, NY. (5588) Full-length camp scene in background, slightly rounded corners. (S) *$100–125*

(The) Soldier Boy/On Duty. Print. 1864. Currier & Ives, NY. (5589) Full-length of soldier; cannon in background. (S) *$100–125*

(The) Soldier Boy/The Last Defense. Print. 1864. Currier & Ives, NY. (5590) (S) *$100–125*

(The) Soldier Boy's Adieu. Print. 1864. Currier & Ives, NY. (5592) (S). . . *$125–150*

Variant of above with interior view. (5592) Another variant of above with horse seen through window. (5593). *$125–150*

"(The) Soldier's Dream of Home." Print. 1862. Currier & Ives, NY. (5595) Oval in rectangular border; two cols., four lines of verse. (S) Companion to No. 5599; some image stain. (A) $275.. . . . . *$100–150*

"(The) Soldier's Dream of Honor." Print. 1862. Currier & Ives, NY. (5596) (S) *$100–125*

"(The) Soldier's Grave." Print. 1862. Currier & Ives, NY. (5597) (S) . . *$100–125*

"(The) Soldier's Grave." Print. 1862. Currier & Ives, NY. (5598) Woman at tomb, weeping willow. "In Memory of—" on tombstone. Soldiers in rear, marching. (S) *$75–100*

"(The) Soldier's Home. The Vision." Print. 1862. Currier & Ives, NY. (5599)

Tape stain and repair on verso. Woman asleep dreaming her husband is leading troops. (S) (A) $275 . . . . *$100–150*

"(The) Soldier's Memorial/In Memory of—." Print. 1863. Currier & Ives, NY. (5600) Tombstone with woman mourner at left; troops marching in rear. Top rounded corners. (M) *$150–175*

"(The) Soldier's Memorial, The 126th Regiment. Company H—New York Volunteers." Print. 1862. Currier & Ives, NY. (5601) View of Washington, bombing of Ft. Sumter; three cols. listing personnel. (M) *$175–200*

"(The) Soldier's Memorial, The 3rd Regiment, Company B, Delaware Volunteers." Print. 1862. Currier & Ives, NY. (5602) Portraits of Washington, Lincoln, Gens. McClellan and Scott. (M). *$175–200*

"(The) Soldier's Record/The 150th Regiment/Co. G., New York State Vols". Print. 1862. Currier & Ives, NY. (5604) Nation's capitol and bombardment of Ft. Sumter. (M) *$175–200*

"(The) Soldier's Record/The 18th Regiment, Co. C., Conn. Volunteers." Print. 1862. Currier & Ives, NY. (5605) (M) *$175–200*

Soldier's Saloon/Cooper Shop Volunteer Refreshment Saloon/Philadelphia. Print. 1862. Litho by M.H. Traubel, Philadelphia. Two large folio chromo views on one sheet, 29" × 20". Top view of soldiers lined up outside with identified committee members greeting them. (First opened; lower view is interior of saloon.) (A) $300. . . . *$400–500*

South Carolina's "Ultimatum." Print. 1861. Gov. Pickins standing in front of mouth of cannon marked "Peace Maker" reaching to light; saying he'll fire if Lincoln doesn't surrender Ft. Sumter. (Shown in background) Buchanan begs Pickins not to fire until he gets out of office. (M). *$300–350*

Startling Announcement. Print. 1861. Currier & Ives, NY. (5712) Jefferson Davis is told by black boy that "Fort Donelson has been taken by "cinkum Bobolishunists." Davis refuses to believe it. (S) *$200–250*

Steamship of War *Regent.* Print. 1863, Shearman & Hart. Handcolored with tint stones; 24³⁄₄" × 35³⁄₄". Two-inch margins. *$800–900*

Gen. (George) Stoneman's Great Cavalry Raid, May 1863. Print. Currier & Ives, NY. (2295) Three additional lines. (S) *$200–250*

"(The) Storming of Ft. Donelson, Tenn., Feb. 15, 1862." Print. Currier & Ives, NY. (5824) Gens. Grant, Smith, McClernand. Good margins, slightly dark; 8" × 12" (D) $125. . . . . *$150–225*

(The) Truce. Print. 1983. By Don Stivers. Ltd. edit. print, 289/650; Rebels tending to wounded in lull of battle. Matted and framed, 25" × 31". (A) Conestoga, July '94, $450. . . . . *$350–400*

(The) 21st Regt. Wisconsin Vol./Crossing Pontoon Bridge at Cincinnati/Sept. 13, 1862. Print. By Middleton, Strobridge & Co., Cincinnati, OH. Full-color view of paddlewheelers near shore, 13" × 20¹⁄₂" with legend. Outside margins replaced. (A) $450. . . . . *$500–600*

(The) Union Discharge Certificate. Print. 1865. Currier & Ives, NY. (6287) Portraits of Sherman, Grant, Sheridan, and Lincoln. (S) *$100–125*

U.S. Screw Sloop *Nyack.* Print. 1863. Ward Stillman & Co., Pub. Handcolored with tint stones; 24³⁄₄" × 35³⁄₄". *$800–900*

U.S. Sloop of War *Kearsarge,* **7 guns.** "Sinking the Pirate Alabama, 8 guns, off Cherbourg, France, Sun. June 19th. 1864." Print. Currier & Ives, NY. (6338) Two added lines of description. (S) *$550–650*

U.S. Sloop of War *Kearsarge,* **7 guns.** "Sinking the Pirate Alabama, 8 guns, off Cherbourg, France, Sun. June 19th. 1864." Print. Currier & Ives, NY. (6339)

Kearsage in foreground flying two U.S. flags. Completely different view from (6338) above. (S) *$550–600*

U.S. Steam Frigate *Roanoke*. Print. 1862. Endicott & Co., NYC. Handcolored with tint stones; 24³/₄" × 35³/₄". *$800–900*

U.S. Steam Gunboat *Ottowa*. Print. 1863. Sherman & Hart, Pub. Handcolored with tint stones; 24³/₄" × 35³/₄". *$800–900*

View of the Philadelphia Volunteer Refreshment Saloons. Print. 1861. James Queen, artist; Thomas Sinclair, printer, Philadelphia. Four vignettes framed by draped U.S. flags; troops passing in review in front of saloon; a closeup view of saloon front; two interior views. Full color. *$450–500*

(The) Volunteers/in Defense of the Government against Usurpation. Print. 1861. Artist, James Queen. Printed by P.S. Duval & Son, Philadelphia, 1861. Printed in oil colors. Three men in foreground gesturing toward the Union banner. Troops on horseback in background.. *$650–700*

Washington/McClellan and W. Scott. Print. 1864. Currier & Ives, NY (6543). Three separate views; Washington remains intact; Scott and McClellan are pasted back to back, cut in strips, and placed over Washington's portrait at right angles. When mounted in deep rabbited frame, the viewer gets 3D effect. One of a number of Currier novelty pictures. (M)................................. *$600–650*

Washington, Sherman and Grant. Print. 1864. Same type as above (6544). (M) *$600–650*

Maj. Gen. John Wool/U.S. Army. Print. 1862. Currier & Ives, NY (3917). (M).. .... *$100–125*

Maj. Gen. John Wool/U.S. Army. Print. 1862. Currier & Ives, NY (3918). three-quarter length in uniform. Vignette. (S) *$75–100*

NAVAL PRINTS RELATED TO *MONITOR/MERRIMAC* AND OTHER IRONCLADS

Destruction of the Rebel Monster *Merrimac* off Craney Island, May 11, 1862. Print. Currier & Ives, NY. (1573) (S) *$400–500*

Destruction of the Rebel Ram *Arkansas* by the U.S. Gunboat *Essex* on the Mississippi R. near Baton Rouge, August 4, 1862. Print. Currier & Ives, NY. (1573) Both ships keyed... *$375–450*

Maps of the *Monitor* and *Merrimac* Fight, and the Course of the *Monitor* from Brooklyn to Hampton Roads. Map print. 1862. Anonymous. *$75–100*

(The) *Merrimac*, From a Sketch Made the Day Before the Fight. Print. 1862. Engraving after sketch by "Lt. B.L. Blackford, Del. March 7, 1862." Pub. in *Battles and Leaders of the Civil War.* *$700–800*

***(Monitor/Merrimac)* Great Fight Between the *Merrimac* and the *Monitor*/ The First Battle Between Iron Ships of War.** Print. 1862. Currier & Ives, NY (2612) From sketch by F. Newman, Norfolk, VA, of *Merrimac* in foreground. (S)... *$500–600*

John Jones/Ordinary Seaman, U.S.S. *Rhode Island*/Born in Bridgeport, Conn. Print. 1907. Pub. by Perrien-Keydel Co., Detroit. Circular bust image of Jones with vignette of U.S.S. *Monitor* sinking below. Jones, landsman, U.S.N., serving aboard the *Rhode Island*, was awarded the Cong. Medal of Honor for heroism in rescuing the *Monitor* crew when that ship sank in 1862....................... *$50–75*

John L. Lenhart, Chaplain, U.S.N. Print. First Navy chaplain to be killed in action while aboard U.S.S. *Cumberland*. From painting by Clayton Braun, b&w... *$75–100*

U.S. Ironclad Ram *Dicter*; U.S. Harbor and River Monitor *Tippecanoe Class*;

U.S. Harbor and River Monitor *Manhattan*. Three prints. 1863. Endicott & Co., Pub. Handcolored set with tint stones of three, sized 22½" × 36" each, identified in matrix. . . . . *$800–1000 (each)*

(The) *Monitor*. Print. 1862. *Leslie's Illus.* Cover lithograph of two cameo portraits of "Jeffers" and "Stimers" (Lt. William Jeffers took command of *Monitor* after March battle). Eight vignettes incl. view of wheelhouse, turret machinery, engine room, Captain's cabin; berth deck; interior of tower; wardroom and exterior of *Monitor* "Ready for Action." *$100–125*

Monitor **Montage.** Print. Constructed by Alan Dickerman, Esq., Oct. 1861 and Dec. 1862. Signed by Thomas Fitch Rowland. Three vignettes, including view of *Monitor* ship house at Green Point, NY; U.S.S. *Puritan* on the ways; plus view of action between U.S.S. *Monitor* and C.S.S. *Virginia*; b&w. *$400–500*

Naval Conflict in Hampton Roads—Action Between the *Monitor* and *Merrimac*. Print. 1868. From original painting by Chappel. *$300–400*

The Naval Engagement Between the *Merrimac* and the *Monitor* at Hampton Roads on the 9th of March 1862. Print. "On the spec. of Chas. Warren." Pub. by C. Bohn, Washington, D.C. Panoramic view of harbor with keyed legend to ships— sinking of *Cumberland* and burning of *Congress*; *Yorktown, Jamestown, Monitor*, and *Merrimac* also depicted. *$500–600*

Terrific Combat Between the *Monitor*, 2 Guns and *Merrimac*, 10 Guns. "The first Fight Between Ironclad ships of War which the *Merrimac* was crippled and the whole Rebel Fleet driven back to Norfolk. Print. Currier & Ives, NY. 1862 (5998) Handcolored. (L.). *$1200–1500*

Union Iron-clad Monitor *Montauk*/The Destroying of the Rebel Ship *Nashville* on the Ogeechee River near Savannah, Ga., Feb. 27th 1863. Print. Currier & Ives, NY. (6284) (S). *$400–500*

Williamsburg, VA, Terrific Combat Between the *Monitor*, 2 Guns and *Merrimac*, 10 Guns/In Hampton Roads, March 9, 1862. "The first fight between Iron Clad Ships of War." Print. Currier & Ives, NY. 1862 (5997) Handcolored. (S) (Rated among best 50 of C.&I. small folio prints by panel of eminent collectors and dealers.) *$500–600*

    Variants of Above with Changed Captions to "*Merrimac* with 11 Guns." Currier & Ives, NY. (5995 and 5996) Both (S) . . . . *$500–600 (each)*

Lincoln
ASSASSINATION/MARTYRDOM RELATED

Apothesis. "In Memory of Abraham Lincoln/The Reward of the Just." Print. 1865. . . . . *$75–100*

Abraham Lincoln, The Martyr Victorious. Print. By John Sartain after a design by W.H. Hermans. Pub. by W.H. Hermans, Pen Yan, NY, 1865. B&w engraving, 13⅞" × 18½". *$350–400*

(The) Assassination of President Lincoln at Ford's Theater, Washington, on the Night of Friday, April 14, 1865. Print. Printmaker unknown; Ca. 1865; Booth with dagger in hand leaps on stage from balcony as Lincoln (standing) has been hit; litho., 11¾" × 7¾". *$500–600*

Columbia's Noblest Lions. Print. By Kimmel & Forster. © Henry & Wm. Vought, pub. by Manson Lang, NY, 1865. Oval portraits of Washington and Lincoln flank full portrait of Liberty with foot on lion; small vignettes picture incidents from their lives; 19¼" × 13½". *$650–700*

Note: An identical print depicts Lincoln and Grant, and Liberty appears partially undraped.

Death Bed of Abraham Lincoln/Died April 15, 1865. Print. By John Magee, Philadelphia, 1865. Known for bizarre inaccuracies, i.e., Stanton looks like a dwarf, Catholic priest is pictured administering last rights (Lincoln was a Protestant); litho. 14" × 9¼". *$450–500*

Diogenes His Lantern Needs No More/An Honest Man is Found! Print. Pub. by N.P. Beers, NY, 1865. Diogenes holds lantern above oval portrait of Lincoln; White House in background; engraving, 12⅛" × 15¾". (See also Horace Greeley variant.). *$600–700*

(The) Home of Our Martyred President. Print. Printmaker unknown, 1865. Handcolored litho of house is not Lincoln's, but Ashland, Henry Clay's brick plantation, and even includes slaves and slave cabins; handcolored lithograph, 19½" × 13¾". *$200–250*

(The) Last Moments of Abraham Lincoln/President of the United States. Print. Engraving by Max Rosenthal after a design by Joseph Hoover; printed by Rosenthal, pub. by Hoover, 1865. Host of angels appear above bed. Handcolored litho, 23" × 17⅞". *$500–600*

(The) Last Offer of Reconciliation/In Remembrance of Pres. A. Lincoln/The Door is Open to All. Print. Pub. by Henry & Wm. Vought, NY, 1865. Liberty is seated in background as Lincoln and Jeff Davis prepare to shake hands; Gens. Grant and Lee also shown; vine borders; theme of forgiveness and reconciliation contrasts sharply with post-Lincoln assassination sentiment; litho. 24½" × 16⅞". *$650–700*

Lincoln and His Family. Print. By William Sartain after a Thomas Bell painting; pub. by Bradley & Co., Philadelphia, 1866. Mezzotint, 24¾" × 17¾". Later republished as a carte-de-visite. *$350–400*

Lincoln and His Family. Print. By D. Wiest after an A. Biegemann rendering; pub. by William Smith, Philadelphia, ca. 1865. Tinted litho, 24¼" × 18⅛" . . . *$300–350*

(The) Lincoln Family. Print. By John Chester Buttre after a Francis B. Carpenter oil painting on canvas, pub. by Buttre, NY, 1867. Family seated around dining room table. Mezzotint, 24¼" × 17¾". *$250–300*

(The) Lincoln Family. Print. Pub. by Haskell & Allen, Boston, ca. 1865. Expansion of Brady photo, adding Robert and Mary in family circle; b&w litho, 12¾" × 8¼". *$250–300*

Lincoln and Tad. Print. Pub. by John Smith, Philadelphia, ca. 1865. Printmaker unknown. After the 1864 Brady photo; handcolored litho, 18½" × 24". *$300–350*

The Nation's Martyr. Same as above, large folio *(L)*. *$250–300*

(The) Martyr of Liberty. Print. Artist unknown; ca. 1865. Both firing at Lincoln in lodge as Mary looks on; includes profound allusion by Shakespeare; litho. 8¼" × 9⅞". Mr. Lincoln, Residence and Horse by Louis Kurz; pub. by Alfred Storey, Chicago, 1865; Lincoln tips hat on horseback in front of Springfield, IL, home; litho, 20¾" × 15½". *$450–500*

In Memory of Abraham Lincoln—The Reward of the Just. Print. D.T. Weist, artist (almost identical to the John James Barralet Apothesis of Washington, pub. in 1802), pub. by William Smith, Philadelphia, 1865; stipple engraving, 18⅜" × 24". *$650–700*

The Nation's Martyr/Assassinated/April 14, 1865. Print. Pub. by Golden & Sammons, Chicago. Currier & Ives. (27) Bust of Lincoln, upright image. (S). *$150–175*

Our Fallen Heroes. Print. 1865. Large bust portrait of Lincoln surrounded by cameos of Col. Elsworth and fallen Union Gens. Vignette of Lincoln's tomb, 28" × 34"... *$200–250*

President Lincoln and His Family/Respectfully Dedicated to the People of the United States. Print. Pub. by Joseph Hoover, Philadelphia, 1865. Based loosely on A. Gardner photo; comically misproportioned figs.; handcolored litho, 24³/₈" × 17¹/₂".. *$300–350*

(The) Tomb of Lincoln, Springfield, Illinois. Print. 1865. Currier & Ives, NY. (6105) (S)... *$200–250*

Washington and Lincoln/The Father and the Savior of Our Country. Print. Currier & Ives, NY, 1865. (6510) Lincoln portrait based on Brady Studio photo; pair is shaking hands standing before Liberty pedestal with flame burning; 11" × 14⁷/₈". (M)... *$150–200*

BATTLEFIELD AND SECESSION RELATED

Lincoln Surrounded by Loyal Unionists. Print. Printmaker unknown. Second state of original Henry Sadd engraving after Matteson painting, NY, 1861........ .... *$450–500*

Loyal Americans. Print. C.D. Andrews after drawing by A.K. Kipps; pub. by Benjamin B. Russell, Boston, ca. 1861. Lincoln medallion bust portrait (based on 1858 Christopher S. German photo), encircled by cameos of cabinet members and leading Union officers. Litho, 8¹/₈" × 9³/₄". *$500–550*

(The) Outbreak of the Rebellion in the United States, 1861. Print. Kimmel & Forster, NY, 1865. One of publisher's series of allegorical history prints. Pictured in epic crowd scene are Lincoln, Liberty, Goddess of War, Jefferson Davis, Alexander Stevens, James Buchanan (shown asleep), a member of his cabinet, John Floyd, accused of financial corruption; litho, 24¹/₂" × 16⁷/₈". *$600–700*

EMANCIPATION RELATED

Abraham Lincoln/16th President of the United States. Print. By John Sartain after a painting by Edw. Dalton Marchant; pub. by Bradley & Co., Philadelphia, 1864; Lincoln seated at desk, with Proclamation under arm, pen in right hand; base of Liberty statue in upper right. Lincoln appears dapper in white bow tie. Engraving, 10" × 13".. *$300–350*

Abraham Lincoln/Emancipation Proclamation. Print. Multicolor poster with the entire Proclamation in type. Lincoln oval portrait and crossed flags and eagle at top. Female deities in columns flanking the Proclamation.................. *$250–300*

Abraham Lincoln Writing the Proclamation of Freedom/January 1st 1863. Print. By Peter E. Ehrgott and Adolphus Forbinger & Co., after painting by David Gilmour Blythe. Pub. by M. Dupuy, Pittsburgh, 1864. Unusual touches include bust statue of James Buchanan with noose around neck; masonic emblem hangs from bookcase (painter Blythe was a Mason). Chromolithograph, 18¹/₄" × 14¹/₂"......... *$400–450*

Allegorical Portrait of Abraham Lincoln. Print. By Peter S. Duval & Son, after drawing by R. Morris Swander. Pub. by Art Publishing Association of Philadelphia, Swander Bishop & Co., 1865. Calligraphic portrait formed by words of Proclamation. Lithographic vignettes in each corner. Litho, 15⁷/₈" × 21". *$350–400*

Emancipation/Freedom for All, Both Black and White. Print. J.L. Magee, Philadelphia, 1865. Lincoln holds Proclamation; one arm upraised; he's surrounded by poor whites as well as freed slaves. Schoolhouse in background: "Education to All Classes." In small vignette at right, a group of returning soldiers try to restrain whiteman from whipping naked slave girl. *$400–450*

Emancipation of the Slaves/Proclaimed on the 22nd September, 1862, by Abraham Lincoln President of the United States of North America. Print. J. Waeschle, Chicago, 1862. Almost identical scene to the Currier & Ives version. Evidence supports this being the original version, later pirated by Currier & Ives.. . . . . . $400–450

Emancipation Proclamation/Issued January 1st 1863. Print. By Peter S. Duval & Son; pub. by Gilman R. Russell, Philadelphia, 1865. Based on M. Brady photo. Lincoln stands at table with copy of Proclamation in script penmanship by Russell as part of shield background. Colored litho, 17¼" × 25½". $500–600

(The) First Reading of the Emancipation Proclamation of President Lincoln. By Alexander Hay Ritchie after a painting by Francis B. Carpenter; pub. by Derby and Miller, NY, 1864. Lincoln seated at table with cabinet members Seward, Stanton, Chase, etc. Engraving, 32⅜" × 20¾". $400–450

Freedom to the Slaves/Proclaimed January 1st 1863 by Abraham Lincoln, President of the United States (also quote from Lev. XXV, 10). Print. Currier & Ives, NY, 1865. (3137) Male slave kisses Lincoln's hand; mother with two children is in background; litho, 8¾" × 11¾". (S) $350–400

President Lincoln and His Cabinet in Council, Sept. 22, 1862, Adopting the Emancipation/Proclamation/Issued Jan. 1st 1863. Print. 1876. Currier & Ives, NY. (4879) Keyed with names of cabinet including Gideon Wells, Navy; William Seward, State; Edwin Stanton, War. U.S. Centennial item. (S). $200–250

President Lincoln and His Cabinet/Reading of the Emancipation Proclamation. Print. By Edward Herline; pub. by D. Hensel & Co., and Goff & Bros., Philadelphia, 1866. A piracy of Richie's engraving (see above); Lincoln is in profile—a mirror-image of Brady's 1864 photo of Lincoln and Tad. Litho, 29½" × 23⅝". $300–350

President Lincoln and Secretary Seward Signing the Proclamation of Freedom, January 1st, 1863. Currier & Ives, NY. (4880) Lincoln signing Proclamation at desk with Seward at right. Handcolored litho, 9¾" × 12". (S) $200–250

POLITICAL CAMPAIGN RELATED

A. Lincoln. Print. By Samuel Sartain after John Henry Brown miniature; pub. by James Irwin, Philadelphia, 1860. Bust of beardless Lincoln; facsimile signature. Litho, 4" × 5⅝". $200–250

A. Lincoln. Print. By C.H. Brainard after Thomas M. Johnston portrait and Christopher German photo, Boston, 1860. Oval bust with facsimile sig. Litho, 10¾" × 13⅞". $200–250

Abraham Lincoln. Print. Pub. by American Banknote Co., 1861. Bust portrait. Lincoln apparently signed three known proof copies of this print while enroute from Springfield to Washington for the inauguration. Engraving, 6" × 9". $900–1000

Abraham Lincoln. Print. By Louis Prang, Boston, ca. 1861. After A.K. Kipps drawing. Bust of beardless Lincoln in profile, based on familiar 1857 Hessler photo. Litho, 6" × 7⅞". $150–200

Abraham Lincoln/Andrew Johnson/President and Vice-President. Print. Edmund Burke and Elijah Chapman Kellogg, Hartford, CT and NY; co-pub. by F.P. Whiting; late 1864; ovals of Lincoln and Johnson; vignettes of Miss Liberty with scales of Justice, flanked by cornucopias; eagle, shield and crossed flags; railroads and shipbuilding; handcolored litho, 9" × 12⅛". $300–350

Abraham Lincoln Post Inaugural. Print. 1861. Beardless Lincoln surrounded by cameos of all previous presidents. Brief biography. Handcolored, 18" × 24".
. . . . $1100–1200

(Lincoln) Abraham's Dream/"Coming Events Cast Their Shadows Before." Print. 1864. Currier & Ives, NY. (29) Vignette of Lincoln dreaming he's being driven to White House while opponent George McClellan enters. (S) . . . *$250–300*

Grand National Union Banner for 1864/Liberty Union and Victory. Print. 1864. Currier & Ives, NY. (2510) Ovals of Lincoln and V.A. Johnson; cameos of winged eagle, crossed flags, Miss Columbia; man plowing field. Handcolored litho, 12" × 8³/₁₆". (S) *$400–500*

Hon. Abraham Lincoln "Our Next President." Print. Currier & Ives, NY, 1860. (2892) Based on 1858 photo; handcolored litho, 9¹/₄" × 13¹/₈". Match to "Our Next President" litho for John Bell. (S) *$350–400*

Hon. Abraham Lincoln/Republican Candidate for Sixteenth President of the United States. Print. Currier & Ives, NY, 1860. (2895) Beardless portrait after M. Brady "Cooper Institute" photo. Litho, 14" × 18³/₄". Rated among the Currier & Ives "top 50." (S) *$300–400*

Hon. Abraham Lincoln/Sixteenth President of the United States. Print. Currier & Ives, NY, 1861. (2896) Update shows full-bearded Lincoln and revised caption, deleting "Republican candidate for." Litho, 14" × 18³/₄". (M) *$300–400*

(The) Irrepressible Conflict. Cartoon print. 1860. Currier & Ives, NY. (3134) Lincoln at helm. Group of ten in sinking lifeboat. Negro wearing "Discord's Patent Life Preserver." Greeley throws Seward overboard. Jeff Davis stands on shore. (M) *$350–400*

"Letting the Cat Out of the Bag." Cartoon print. Lincoln/Greeley, 1860. Currier & Ives, NY. (3479) Horace Greeley and Lincoln asking abolitionist Sen. Charles Sumner not to let the cat "Spirit of Discord" out of bag. (M) *$400–450*

Lincoln as Flatboatman on the Mississippi River. Print. Ca. 1850s. From an engraving by H. Brown. *$500–600*

Lincoln, From a Photograph by Hesler. Print. E.M. Brown, Chicago; 1860. Oval portrait of beardless Lincoln, based on 1857 photo; issued for '60 Rep. Convention; woodcut engraving, 6" × 8". *$400–450*

Lincoln, Hamlin and Curtin! Print. 1860. B&w woodcut; announcement of Wide Awake Club's torchlight procession; (A) $550. . . . . *$500–600*

Lincoln, Hamlin/The Republican Banner for 1860. Print. Currier & Ives, NY. (513A) Multicolor. (S) *$500–600*

Lincoln–A. Johnson Grand Republican Banner 1864. Print. Currier & Ives, NY. (2510) Multicolor. Vertical tear in bottom. (S) *$500–550*

Lincoln–Johnson Inaugural Invitation, 4 March 1865. Print. Engraved invitation with jugate portraits of Lincoln and Johnson, separated by Liberty cap on pole. Eagles with legends at top of Roman columns at each side. List of managers and notables, including Civil War Gens. and Adms., b&w. (A) Riba, Nov. '91, $750. . . . . *$750–800*

Lincoln Recevant Les Indiens Comanches. Print. Pub. by C. Chardon the elder, Paris, 1863. Pictures March 1863 reception in White House with Lincoln welcoming Indian chief delegation. Rare handcolored engraving, 6⁵/₈" × 4³/₄". . . . *$700–750*

Lincoln Three-in-One Picture. Print. Ca. 1861. Currier & Ives, NY. (3549) Gens. Grant (right) and Sherman (left) are pasted back to back, and flank Lincoln portrait. (S) *$550–650*

Same as Above. Except Grant is at left and Sheridan replaces Sherman at right. Currier & Ives, NY. (3550) (S) *$550–650*

Little Game of Bagatelle Between Old Abe the Railsplitter and Little Mac, the gunboat General. Cartoon print. 1864. Currier & Ives, NY. (3634) (S) . *$300–350*

(The) National Game/Three "Outs" and One "Run"/Abraham Winning the Ball. Cartoon print. 1860. Currier & Ives, NY. (4388) Vignette of Lincoln with rail for bat marked "Equal Rights and Free Territory." Bell with bat labeled "Fushion"; Douglas bat, "Non-Intervention"; Breckinridge's "Slavery Extension." (M) *$450–500*

National Political Chart. Print. H.H. Lloyd, NY, 1861. Same format as below features Lincoln with military and cabinet officers. Litho, 25³/₄" × 34". *$550–600*

National Republican Chart/Presidential Campaign, 1860. Print. By H.H. Lloyd, NY, 1860. Depicts Lincoln with Vice-Pres. Hannibal Hamlin, map of U.S., portraits in border of 15 previous presidents. Wood-engraved broadside with type, 25³/₄" × 34". (Lloyd issued a Non-Partisan plus a Democratic match to broadside.) *$600–650*

National Union Republican Banner/1860. Print. Currier & Ives, NY. (4389) Jugate portraits of Lincoln and Hannibal Hamlin, upright. (S) *$300–350*

(The) Nigger in the Woodpile./The Young America. Cartoon print. 1860. Currier & Ives, NY. (4464) Lincoln and Horace Greeley seated in woodpile labeled "Republican Platform." Negro is hiding under woodpile. (M) *$350–450*

(The) Old Bulldog on the Right Track. Cartoon print. 1864. Currier & Ives, NY. (4551) Lincoln, Union Gens. Grant, McClellan plus C.S.A.'s Jefferson Davis, Gens. Lee and Beauregard. (M) *$350–450*

Political "Blondins" Crossing Salt River. Cartoon print. 1860. Currier & Ives, NY. (4820) Lincoln, Douglas, Buchanan, Breckinridge, Bell, Everett & Greeley vignette. (M) (Blondin means acrobat. A famed French daredevil by that name once crossed Niagara Falls on a tight wire.) *$300–400*

Political Gymnasium. Cartoon print. 1860. Currier & Ives, NY. (4823) Pres. candidates in gymnasium. Lincoln is straddling rail marked "President." Douglas and Breckinridge spar with each other; Everett steadying Bell seated on dumbbell; Greeley on horiz. bar. (M) *$300–400*

Progressive Democracy—Prospect of a Smashup. Cartoon print. 1860. Currier & Ives, NY. (4960) Cart labeled "Democratic Platform" with team and driver at each end and team pulling in opposite direction. A squatter drives Douglas and Johnson to left. "Old Buck" Buchanan at right drives Breckinridge and Lane. Cart is stalled on RR track, while locomotive labeled "Equal Rights," with Lincoln and Hamlin at controls, is about to bump off the cart. (M) *$400–500*

Rail Candidate. Cartoon print. 1860. Currier & Ives, NY. (5052) Lincoln is straddling rail marked "Republican Platform," held up by Horace Greeley and a Negro. (M) *$350–400*

(The) Rail Splitter at Work Repairing the Union. Cartoon print. 1862. Currier & Ives, NY. (S). *$300–400*

Republican Party Going to the Right House. Cartoon print. 1860. Currier & Ives, NY. Greeley carrying Lincoln on rail to building labeled "Lunatic Asylum." (M). *$400–450*

Running the "Machine." Cartoon print. 1864. Currier & Ives, NY. (5258) Union Gen. Francis Fessenden (son of Sec. of Treasury) turning wheel—"Chase Patent Greenback Wheel." Lincoln with Cabinet members Stanton, Seward, and Wells shown. (M). *$400–500*

Storming the Castle/Old Abe on Guard. Cartoon print. 1860. Currier & Ives, NY. (5828) Lincoln, Bell, Douglas trying to unlock door with keys marked "Regular Nom./Non-intervention, Nebraska Bill." Lincoln with lantern and rail. (M) *$300–350*

(The) True Issue or "What's the Matter." Cartoon print. 1864. Currier & Ives,

NY. (6236) Lincoln and Jefferson Davis ripping up map of the U.S. while Gen. Mc-
Clellan tries to get them to make peace. (S)........................ *$350–400*

Uncle Sam Making New Arrangements. Cartoon print. 1860. Currier & Ives, NY.
(6279) Uncle Sam stands on White House steps holding up "Wanted" sign plus a
document reading "This is to certify that I have hired A. Lincoln for four years. . . ."
Lincoln holds satchel and axe; Buchanan slinks away with satchel marked "Dirty
Linen." Bell, Breckinridge, and Douglas all apply for the job. (S)....... *$300–350*

Your Plan or Mine. Cartoon print. 1864. Currier & Ives, NY. (6873) Vignette of
Lincoln, Gen. McClellan, and Jeff Davis portraits. (S)............... *$300–350*

Yours Truly, A. Lincoln. Print. By Joseph Baker after Charles A. Barry life portrait; facsimile sig.; pub. by John H. Bufford, Boston, 1860. Stylized print of tous-
sle-haired beardless Lincoln; litho; appears in numerous pirated editions, 20¼" ×
27⅝"... *$300–350*

Yours Truly, A. Lincoln. Print. By Leopold Grozelier after Thomas Hicks life
portrait; pub. by W. Schaus, NY, 1860. Slightly in profile (vs. Baker version). This
pose subsequently inspired several photographic versions............. *$350–400*

Miscellaneous Political

(Bell) Grand National Republican Union Banner/1860. "Hon. John Bell of
Tenn. and Edw. Everett of Mass." Print. Currier & Ives, NY. (2509) Both rest
hands on scroll, "The Constitution of the U.S." (S)...........................

John C. Breckinridge/Vice President. Print. Currier & Ives, NY, 1856. (3258)
Half-length portrait seated. Handcolored. (S) *$100–135*

James Buchanan–John Breckinridge Grand National Democratic Banner.
Print. Currier & Ives, NY, 1856. (2495) (L) *$650–750*

(Buchanan) Great American Buck Hunt of 1856. Print. N. Currier. (2564) Stag
with head of Buchanan running toward White House. Millard Fillmore on rock
aiming rifle at "Buck" Fremont with exploded gun. (M).............. *$300–350*

**(Butler) Gen. Benjamin Butler/Greenback Party Candidate for the Presidency
of the U.S.** Print. 1884. (2242) (S)............................... *$100–125*

(The) Cabinet of Franklin Pierce, March, 1853. Print. Anonymous, *Gleason's
Pictorial.* June 1863. Pictures Franklin Pierce and Sec. of War Jefferson Davis,
among five other Cabinet Secs. *$250–300*

John C. Calhoun and Compromise of 1850 Consensus. Print. Henry Sadd after
Tompkins Harrison Matteson painting. William Pate, pub., 1852. Depicts Calhoun
with Henry Clay, Daniel Webster, Gen. Winfield Scott, William King, Howell
Cobb, John Bell, et al. Mezzotint engraving, 29⅜" × 22¼". *$400–500*

**(Davis) Prominent Candidates for the Democratic Nomination at Charleston,
S.C.** Print. 1861. *Harper's* centerfold featuring 11 cameo Brady portraits of leading
C.S.A. candidates including Jeff Davis, Breckinridge, Franklin Pierce, Sam Hous-
ton, etc.; 21" × 14"... *$150–175*

(Douglas) "Hon. Stephen A. Douglas." Print. 1860. Currier & Ives, NY. (2920)
(S)... *$100–150*

(Douglas) "Hon. Stephen A. Douglas From a Photograph." Print. 1860. (2921)
Bust portrait and vignette. (L) *$150–200*

(Douglas) "Hon. Stephen A. Douglas of Ill." Print. 1860. (2922) (S) .. *$100–125*

(Douglas) Stephen Finding His Mother. Print. 1860. Currier & Ives, NY. (5812)
Miss Columbia whipping Douglas with switch labeled "Maine Law." Uncle Sam
stands by. (M)... *$300–350*

Variant (5813) of above. But switch is marked "News From Maine." (M). . . . .
. . . . *$300–350*

Freemont and Dayton. Print. 1856. Woodblock. Winged eagle with legend in
talons; 6" × 13". *$200–250*

**John C. Fremont/Republican Candidate or/Fifteenth President of the United
States.** Print. 1856. Currier & Ives, NY. (3260) Portrait from a Brady photograph.
(S). *$150–175*

John C. Fremont's Last Grand Exploring Expedition in 1856. N. Currier.
(1192) Cartoon of Fremont riding Abolition Nag with head of Greeley, led by Seward. Border ruffians decry "Abolition Soup" and "Wooly Head" stew at White
House. (S). *$200–250*

**(Fremont) Grand National Republican Banner/Free Labor/Free Speech/Free
Territory.** "John C. Fremont and William L. Dayton." Print. 1856. N. Currier,
1856. (2502) (S) . . . .

(Fremont) Great Rep. Reform Party/Calling on Their Candidates. Print. 1856.
Currier & Ives, NY. (2647) Vignette: Freemont addressing callers. (S) . . *$200–250*

"James A. Garfield." 1880 Campaign. Print. Pub. by J.A. Ryder. James & Co.,
Cleveland litho; b&w images of Garfield as a boy, as Union Gen. and Statesman;
U.S. flag, log cabin, and White House in background. *$500–600*

James A. Garfield's Escutcheon. Print. 1880. "For President . . . James A.
Garfield." Pub. by J.P. Reynolds, Prop. of Reynolds Escutcheons of Military and
Naval Service. Printed by Forbes, Boston. Topped by eagle. Shows Maj. Gen.
Garfield's Civil War military record; b&w; 28" × 22". *$200–225*

(Garfield) Grand National Republican Banner/1880 Garfield and Arthur.
Print. Currier & Ives, NY. (2505) (S) *$500–600*

**Grand National Republican Banner/1880 James Garfield of Ohio and Chester A.
Arthur of NY.** Print. Currier & Ives, NY. (2506) Jugate portraits surmounted by
winged eagle. (L). *$500–600*

Grant at Home. Print. 1869. E. Blinner on stone. Currier & Ives, NY. (2556)
Capitol view through window, 7 keys. (L) *$500–550*

    Same image as above, but (2555). (S) *$75–100*

Grant at Peace. Print. 1869. Currier & Ives, NY. (2557) (S). *$75–100*

(Grant) Great American Tanner/The Great Sachem of Tamany. Print. 1868.
J.M. Ives, NYC. (2565) Thomas Worth sketch; J. Cameron on stone. Grant has
"tanned" Gens. R.E. Lee, Pemberton, and Buckner. Sachem is lining up other for
same treatment. *$350–400*

(Grant) Grand National Rep. Banner for 1872. U.S. Grant–Horace Greeley.
Currier & Ives, NY. (2503) (S) *$450–550*

**(Grant/Lee) Man of Words/The Man of Deeds/Which Do You Think the
Country Needs?** Print. Currier & Ives, NY. (3962) J. Cameron on stone. 1868.
Vignette of H. Seymour, surrounded by mob; Negro being hanged on lamppost.
Colored orphan asylum in flames; children jump from windows. At right, Grant
(the man of deeds) accepts Lee's sword, while his foot rests on a dragon. (S). .
. . . . *$200–225*

Gen. U.S. Grant–Schuyler Colfax National Union Republican Nomination.
Print. 1868. Currier & Ives, NY. Grant was seen second only to Lincoln as savior of
the Union. *$700–800*

(U.S. Grant) National Union Republican Banner. Print. 1868. Currier & Ives,
NY. (4390) Grant and Colfax portraits, upright. (M). *$250–400*

U.S. Grant on Horseback. Print. Pub. 1864. Pub. by Lloyd, NYC. Handcolored woodblock scene. Around perimeter a lengthy bio. of Grant plus letter from Lincoln praising him for capture of Vicksburg. Announces his commission as Lt. Gen. Framed. Probably campaign related. *$800–900*

"The Nation's Choice/Ulysses S. Grant." Print. 1872. National Republican Chart, pub. by H.H. Lloyd & Co. Shows presidents up to A. Johnson; 28" × 37", multicolor.. . . . . *$600–650*

Grant Republican Campaign Chart. Print. 1868. Pub. by Naughton, NYC. Portraits of Grant and Colfax, with bios. of candidates below. *$300–400*

(The) Working Man's Banner/For President/For Vice-President, Ulysses S. Grant "The Galena Tanner," Henry Wilson "The Natick Shoemaker." Print. 1872. Currier & Ives, NY. (6782) Upright, full-length figs. (S) *$200–250*

(Greeley) Greeley and Sumner. Print. 1860s. Greeley, Sumner, Whittier, and Seward. *$200–250*

(Greeley) Diogenes His Lantern Needs No More/An Honest Man is Found! Print. Pub. by N.P. Beers, NY, 1872. Diogenes holds lantern above oval portrait of Greeley (face mounted over that of Lincoln); White House in background; engraving, 12⅛" × 15¾". (Variant of Lincoln version issued in 1865, then withdrawn following Lincoln's assassination.) *$350–400*

Horace Greeley. Print. 1872. Facsimile sig. Currier & Ives, NY. (2936) (M). . . . .
. . . . *$125–150*

Horace Greeley–Gratz Brown 1872 Campaign. Print. Printer unknown. Liberal Rep. and Dem. slate. Cameos of the two plus Lincoln and Washington. Slogans: "Liberty, Equality, Fraternity"; "The Pen Is Mightier Than the Sword"; "In the Beginning was the Word. Then followed the War. Yet We shall Seal the Peace." Vignettes of soldiers and the masses, Miss Liberty. *$450–500*

(Greeley) "New Fountains of Democracy. Swill Milk for Hungry Suckers." Print. 1872. Currier & Ives, NY. (4423) By J. Cameron on stone. Vignette with stream labeled "Secession, Pro-Slaver, Tammany and Corruption." Greeley's head is attached to cow's body. The "Suckers" are Democrats, shade of Jackson says. Shades of Jefferson: "Have the Dem. Party sunk as low as that?" *Tribune* stables at left; building in background, "Cincinnati Slop Shop." (S) *$250–300*

Horace Greeley, Our Next President 1872. Print. Currier & Ives, NY. (2936) (A)
. . . . *$125–150*

(Greeley) Pap, Soup and Chowder. Print. J.L. Magee on stone. 1852. N. Currier, NYC. (4694) Greeley of *Tribune* carrying Gen. Winfield Scott piggyback. Scott is spilling his soup down Greeley's neck. Webster eating while sitting on shoulders of Webb of *Courrier & Enquirer*. (S) *$350–400*

(Greeley) Red Hot Republicans on the Democratic Gridiron/The San Domingo War Dance. Print. 1872. Currier & Ives, NY. (5095) Schurz, Sumner, Butler, and Greeley vignette. (S) *$250–275*

(Greeley) Splitting the Party/The Entering Wedge. Print. 1872. J. Cameron on stone. Currier & Ives, NY. (5664) Greeley standing in cleft rock, "Rep. party" holding paper in hands "Free Trade" and "Protection." Schurz with upraised mallet labeled "Cincinnati Nomination." Grant watches at left. Other politicos crouch, awaiting outcome. (S) *$250–300*

(Benjamin Harrison) Wooly Head! vs. Copper head! Ho For Salt River! Print. 1892. Harrison and Reid vs. Cleveland and Stevenson pictured in jugates topped by winged eagles. Anti-Harrison broadside issued by Dems.. . . . . *$350–400*

Gov. Rutherford B. Hayes of Ohio—Nat. Rep. Candidate for Pres. Print. 1876. Currier & Ives, NY. Head and shoulders portrait, b&w, 12½" × 16½".. . *$200–250*

(Hayes) Grand National Rep. Banner (Liberty and Union). "Gen. Rutherford B.

Hayes for Pres. Hon. Wm. Wheeler for V.P." Currier & Ives, NY, 1876. (2504) (S)
.... *$500–600*

John Jay. Print. From Jenkins *History of Political Parties in the State of New York.* Currier & Ives, NY, 1876. (3269) *$50–75*

(A. Johnson) (The) Smelling Committee. Print. 1868. J. Cameron on stone. Currier & Ives, NY. Vignette of Logan, Williams, Boutwell, Butler holding noses. Dark horse labeled "Impeachment," Johnson brings forward "Wooley Friend" labeled "30,000." (S)... *$200–250*

"Andrew Johnson." Print. 1865. B&w, Currier & Ives. Some age specks, framed. (A) Frent, '88, $225... *$225–250*

(George McClellan) (The) Beginning. The Election of McClellan! Armistice! Fall of Wages. No Market For Produce. Civil War! Anarchy. Print. 1864 campaign. Anti-McClellan Pennsylvania broadside. All type, 22" × 28". *$1200–1400*

McClellan! Pendleton National Dem. Banner 1864. Currier & Ives, NY. 10½" × 14". Handcolored... *$450–500*

(McClellan) Siamese Twins/The Offspring of Chicago Miscegination. Cartoon print. 1864. Currier & Ives, NY (4824). McClellan and George Pendleton joined, as fellow Dems. Vallandingham and Seymour approve of presidential slate. (M) ....
.... *$350–400*

Carl Schurz—Biggest Carpet Bagger of All. 1870s cartoon by Thomas Nast in *Harpers Weekly.* Shows former Union Gen. Schurz, who angered the radicals by attacking carpetbaggers. But since Schurz had moved to Missouri and was elected to Sen., Nast shows him with his *own* big carpet bag over his shoulder, "The one behind him, filled with his own faults, he never sees." b&w. *$75–85*

(Scott) Grand National Whig Banner. Gen. Winfield Scott, William A. Graham. N. Currier, NY, 1852 (2515) (S) *$250–300*

(Seward) Prominent Candidates for the Republican Nomination—1860. Cameo portraits of 11 hopefuls with William Seward in large oval at center. Includes Fremont, Lincoln, Salmon Chase, John Bell, Cameron, Cassius Clay, McLean. Vignette of Washington, D.C. skyline. From photographs by Brady; b&w, *Harpers Weekly*... *$150–200*

Hon. Horatio Seymour–Gen. Frank Blair National Democratic Banner of Victory, 1868. Currier & Ives. Vignettes of hands on plow and arm wielding sledge hammer. "Peace, Union & Constitutional Govt." Handcolored, multicolored......
.... *$250–300*

Taking the Stump or Stephen in Search of His Mother. Print. 1860. Currier & Ives, NY. (5962) Bell, Gov. Wise of VA, Douglas with peg leg. Buchanan, Breckinridge, Lincoln. (M) *$300–400*

Left: *Broadside, "$100,000 Reward" for Lincoln's assassin, with three mounted albumens of Booth, Surrat, and Harold. Red, black, and white. Sold at Riba's Auctions in October 1985 for $7,000. Current value, $9,000–$10,000.* Right: *Map of Forts Sumter, Pickins, Monroe, and McHenry. Published by Louis Prange & Co., 1862, $500–$600.*

Left: *Broadside, "To the Sharp Shooters of Windham County," $8,000– $9,000.* Right: *Broadside, "War Meeting in Kingsville," $3,500–$4,000.*

Left: *Broadside, "Ironsides Regiment," light-blue ink, $4,000–$4,500.*
Right: *Broadside, "Spinola's Empire Brigade," $1,200–$1,500.*

*Print, Currier and Ives, "Gallant Charge of Jonesboro, Sept. 1st, 1864,"
small folio, $200–$250.*

Poster, "The Lost Cause" uses CSA currency to frame portraits of Confederate leaders, $300–$350.

Print, Currier and Ives, "Storming of Ft. Donelson, Tenn., Feb. 15, 1862," large folio, $800–$850.

Broadside, "Carrier's New Year's Address," centennial edition, $750–$800.

Poster, "Union Volunteer Refreshment Saloon and Hospital," $1,000–$1,200. (Kit Barry Collection)

Left: *Print, Currier and Ives, Lincoln-Hamlin National Union Republican banner, 1860, small folio, $350–$450.* Right: *Broadside, "Amalgamation Whig Ticket," ca. 1843. A satirical broadside of a black man dancing with a white lady. Sold for $5,000 at Riba Auctions in 1993, $6,000–$7,000.*

Chromolith, "Alabama & Kearsarge," Louis Prange & Co., after Julian Oliver Davidson painting, $2,500–$3,000.

Top: *Chromolith, "Sheridan's Ride," Louis Prange & Co., 1885, after painting by Thure de Thurstrup: $2,000–$2,500.* Bottom right: *Chromolith, "Gen. Phil Sheridan," Shober & Carqueville, Chicago, 1891, $2,500–$3,000.* Bottom left: *Print, Currier and Ives, "Domestic Blockade," large folio, $450–$500.*

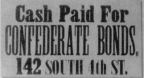

Left: *Print, lithographer unknown, U.S. Grant multicolor print with vignettes from his life, ca. 1880, $500–$600.* Right: *Broadside, CSA, "Cash Paid for Confederate Bonds," no city indicated, 6 ¹/₂" by 11 ¹/₂", $250–$300.*

Poster, promoting Broadway play version of Uncle Tom's Cabin, *with small portraits of Lincoln and Harriet Beecher Stowe, multicolor, $300–$350.*

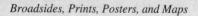

Print, Currier and Ives, Lincoln and Johnson Grand National Union banner, 1864, multicolor, large folio, $800–$900.

Poster, National Republican Chart, 1860, Lincoln and Hamlin,
$450–$500.

Lithographs, black-and-white souvenir cards, early 1860s: (top) 4" × 2 ¹/₄" cards of Henry Van Rensellair, Inspector General, and Col. H.L. Riggs, 10th Massachusetts, both by J.H. Buford, Boston, $20–$25 each; (bottom) 5" × 3 ¹/₄" cards of Hon. John Cochrane, Col., 1st U.S. Chasseurs, and Col. E.E. Elsworth of the 11th New York Zouaves, both by Louis Prange, Boston, $25–$30 each.

Lithograph, black-and-white souvenir cards, by Louis Prange, ca. 1860s, 4" × 2 ¹/₄", Mrs. Lincoln, Mrs. McClellan, Lt. Gen. U.S. Grant, and Mrs. Grant, $20–$25 each.

Print, "Am I Not a Man and a Brother?" black-and-white anti-slavery print, ca. 1850s, publisher unknown. This design was used in numerous pinbacks, plates, and novelties, $200–$250.

CANES

The Civil War yielded a rich bounty of parade and walking canes. Many elaborate and imaginatively created folk art varieties were carved from wood and bone by Union and Rebel soldiers, often while recovering from wounds or languishing in prison camps. After the war, a number of parade and encampment canes were popularized and sold as souvenirs.

Commemorative and political campaign canes exist in brass, pewter, lead, cast iron, and wood. Many have white metal, figural bust effigy cane heads depicting Lincoln, U.S. Grant, James Garfield, Rutherford Hayes, Winfield Scott Hancock, William McKinley, John Logan (founder of the G.A.R.), and other ex–Civil War generals.

Battle of Antietam. 1880s; carved commemorative cane depicting Grant and William H. Howard and other Gens. Inscribed "April 17, 1862"; 34" l.

Battle of Devil's Den/Gettysburg. "May 28, 1895"; figural officer with glass eyes, painted body; battlefield reunion; 37" l.

Battle of Gettysburg. 1880s; bizarre cane carved from human leg bone found in battlefield; 37" l.

Battle of Gettysburg. Inscribed "F.L.T./July 1,2,3, 1863/Designed by D.B. Foyle"; portraits of Lee, Meade, Lincoln. 35" l.

Battle of Seven Pines. 1880s; handcarved wood cane cut from pine tree at battle site; 35" l.

Blue & Gray. Confederate cane; 1913 Gettysburg Reunion; "In Memory '61–'65" and "C.S." carved in wood; 37" l. *$250–300*

Confederate Fig. Head Cane. Late 1860s; bearded figure in Kewpie cap with brass eyelet; 34" l.

G.A.R. 1865 "Libby Prison" Cane. 1860s; handcarved wood; relief figs. of G.A.R. medal, soldier, sailor; exotic South Seas lady, bust of Gen., dancers and baseball player; signed "John Tracy, '76" and "Libby Prison"; lower cover tip missing. (A) Riba, '94, $800. . . . . *$850–1000*

G.A.R. Bearded Union Soldier Bust Cane. 1866; carved wood with black finish; 33¼" l.

G.A.R. Crossed Cannons. Ca. 1880s; white metal, extended curved handle; G.A.R. and inscription.. . . . . *$25–35*

G.A.R. Flag Gadget Cane. 1880s; "G.A.R." on collar; cloth flag pops up; metal handle; 34" l.

G.A.R. Flag Gadget Cane. Dated "March 15, 1934"; silver-plated knob; cork plug holds cloth flag in place; 35" l.

G.A.R. "Grant" Cane. Dated 1892; round white metal top; bass relief bust of Grant on end; on sides—eagle, crossed cannons, and star G.A.R. symbol; "26th Annual Encampment, Washington, D.C." *$75–100*

U.S. Grant. 1868; cast-iron bust; brown finish; wood shaft; 35" l *$350–450*

Benjamin Harrison. 1888; white metal (silverlike) finish. *$250–300*

Rutherford B. Hayes. 1876; white metal effigy bust; wooden shaft *$300–350*

Abraham Lincoln. Ca. 1860; "L"-handled ivory cane with scrimshaw design of bearded Lincoln and Civil War symbols; "Our Honest Abe/With Charity to All, and Malice to None"; (A) $1210 . . . . *$1000–1500*

Abraham Lincoln. Ca. 1870; folk art; ebony cane with bearded effigy Lincoln profile carved just below the crook. (A) $1200. . . . . *$1500–2000*

William McKinley. 1896; white metal; "Protection and Prosperity" facsimile sig. on base; 3" pewter bust of McKinley effigy image *$75–125*

William McKinley. 1896; white metal; same as above without the legend. *$75–100*

William McKinley. 1896; flag cane; hollow bamboo cane with 15" pole insert with glazed muslin flag, 9" × 16", which pulls out when tip is removed. Flag is stars and stripes with "McKinley-Hobart" running vertically; red, white, blue lettering; 38" l. overall. *$350–400*

William McKinley. 1900; McKinley–Teddy Roosevelt bas relief portraits on opposite sides of round cane head; approx. 2½", white metal. *$150–200*

William McKinley. 1896; "Noisemaker" cane; "Patriotism, Prosperity, Protection," unpainted tin noisemaker horn runs horiz. at top to serve as handle. *$100–125*

William McKinley. 1896; torchlight cane; portrait litho paper on tin; round knob at top of cane unscrews to reveal wick and fuel reservoir; red, blue, black. . *$200–225*

William McKinley–Hobart. 1896; paper enameled cane with bluetone candidate's portraits appearing vertically with red, white, blue stripes; knob top in red. *$100–125*

16th NY Co. "C". Wraparound snake cane; ca. 1862; handcarved; snake winds around upper shaft and head appears at top of crook. (A) $450. . . . . *$400–450*

Pennsylvania Battery. Presentation cane to "T.H. Nevin Esq. of Nevin's Battery, 1862." Wood shaft; gold handle; small dent in handle. (A) Riba, '94, $1000. . . . . . .
. . . . *$800–900*

Horatio Seymour. 1868; losing Dem. presidential nominee; cast-iron figural bust head; brown patina; match to previous Grant example; 35" hickory shaft. *$350–400*

Slave Cane. Late 1880s; black male effigy top; possibly in ebony with spiral shaft; 39" l. *$500–550*

22nd Connecticut Vols. Battlefield of Seven Pines. 1864; sterling silver handle inscribed "E.K. Hubbard from F.A. Mitchell"; with musket ball; plus bronze G.A.R. medal Post 58, Mansfield, CT. (A) Riba, '94, $400 . . . . *$400–450*

Union Cane. 1880s; carved figural eagle's head on polychromed wood; inscribed "1861–65"; 34¾" l. *$500–550*

Union Canes. 1880s; pair of carved stick canes by same artist (unsigned); first has ivory knob top with eagle and regimental symbols; second has large carved eagle with wings fully spread; 34" l. each. *$600–700*

Union Soldier Figural Cane. 1860s; carved full body fig. crouched on cane's handle; bone collar; brass sword and epaulet insets on uniform; 35" l *$550–600*

Union Veteran's Cane. "T.W. Ridgeville Reunion /1900"; wood carved with leaves, laurels, flags, and camera; 37" l. *$400–450*

An array of canes celebrating noted Civil War leaders who ran for the presidency, including Benjamin Harrison, abolitionist Henry Clay, Wm. McKinley, General U.S. Grant (and the 1892 GAR Encampment), and R.B. Hayes.

Left: *U.S. Grant effigy cane head, cast iron, 2 1/2", brown paint, 1868, $250–$300.*
Right: *Carved elk antler figural cane belonged to a New Hampshire Medal of Honor winner, $150–$200. (Photo courtesy of Divine Auctions)*

CERAMICS

Coffee Maker. Jefferson Davis. White china and brass figural in shape of train with "President Jefferson Davis" monogrammed in gold................ *$2000–3000*

Cup. Stephen A. Douglas, 20th century. Handleless cup; transfer shows Douglas birthplace in Brandon, VT; 2¼" h................................... *$50–75*

Cups/Saucers. Confederate Mourning (pair), 1865. Porcelain portrait cups by R.T. Lux, New Orleans; multicolor portrait of Confederate widow; other image is of young girl holding bouquet............................... *$1200–1400 (pair)*

Figurine. Lincoln on Horseback, ca. 1880s. Staffordshire-type fig., probably German; "Abraham Lincoln" in raised letters (similar version featured Napoleon). *$1200–1300*

Figurine. "Uncle Tom and Little Eva," 1880s. Wedgwood multicolored painted bisque of *Uncle Tom's Cabin* characters........................... *$350–400*

Figurine. Sojourner Truth, 1880s. Bisque 6" h. black activist carrying banner "Votes For Women" and club, wearing corset in parade. *$500–600*

Flask. "G.A.R.—Our Martyred Heroes," ca. 1902. Polychrome portraits of Lincoln, McKinley, and Garfield; G.A.R. medal decoration on reverse. (Also see G.A.R. "Wall Hanging.").. *$65–75*

Flask. "G.A.R." (John Logan), 1870. "We Drank from the same canteen"; ceramic. Logan was a V.P. candidate in 1884; founded the G.A.R. and many canteens, including those of metal, bear his name and portrait................... *$100–150*

Gravy Boat. "Lincoln Delivering Gettysburg Address," early 1900s? Part of Homer Laughlin Co. Historical Set; red transfer print of Lincoln before large crowd; 8½" × 3⅜" h. (Also see "Serving Bowl.") *$50–75*

Jug. Abraham Lincoln; 1880s. Redware pottery with heavy colored overglaze. The body of the jug is fully rounded with a narrow neck. High relief green laurel leaf framing brown bust of Lincoln; handle........................... *$700–800*

Medallions. Slave in Chains; 1786 or '87. Cameos in b&w jasper, designed by William Hackwood for Wedgwood. Enclosed in gilt oval frames and used in jewelry and atop jewelry boxes. (Also see "Plate" example.) ..... *$1000–1200 (each)*

Mug. "For Gold and Our Country's Honor/McKinley Inaugural, March, 1897." Stoneware; design of large spread eagle and shield. *$125–150*

Mug. "Maj. Gen. Ulysses S. Grant," ca. 1872. Transfer of Grant on obverse; Maj. Gen. Quincy Adams Gillmore; bordered by blue bands............... *$300–325*

Mug. "(Benjamin) Harrison," ca. 1880s. Ironstone with black transfer portrait; 4¾" h... *$100–125*

Mug. "Benjamin Harrison/1889"—Harrison's inauguration; medallion bust of Harrison; matched by Washington bust on reverse...................... *$125–150*

Mug. "The Hayes and Wheeler Mug," ca. 1876. Campaign; incised lettering in red-ware with dark brown glaze from 1876 campaign (Hayes was a Civil War Union Gen.; served under Fremont in the Valley and was wounded at South Mountain in Antietam campaign.) *$300–350*

Mug. "Hayes and Wheeler/The Spirit of '76," 1876. Campaign; incised lettering on red earthenware. *$250–300*

Mug. Lincoln, ca. 1862. Black transfer of three-quarter bust of "President Abraham Lincoln"; 3¼" h. *$500–550*

Mug. Lincoln's Assassination, ca. early 20th century. Commemorative; black transfer of derringer used by John Wilkes Booth to assassinate Lincoln; background scene shows Booth leaping onto stage at Ford Theater. *$25–35*

Mug. William McKinley, ca. 1896. Double-handled stoneware mug with black transfer bust portrait; Bray match. *$75–100*

Mug. Zouave with rifle and bugle, ca. 1861. Small 3" h. blue transfer ceramic mug. *$150–200*

Mug (Toby). (Grant and Lee) The Antagonists; 1982. Royal Doulton double-sided toby. Gen. Grant profile on obverse; Gen. Lee on reverse. *$250–300*

Mug (Toby). Lincoln/Gettysburg, 1982. Royal Doulton. Lincoln in deep relief with Gettysburg Address on reverse. *$150–175*

Pin Tray. William McKinley, 1896; free-form campaign tray, with bust portrait and name and year enclosed in banner below. Hobart and Bryan matches. . *$50–75*

Pin Tray. William McKinley, possibly 1896 campaign item. Small oblong scalloped china tray; black transfer bust portrait with view of McKinley's birthplace in Canton, OH. *$25–35*

Pitcher. Anti-slavery: Memorial to Abolitionist, Elijah Lovejoy, 1840s. Staffordshire; blue and white pitcher, 5½" h. Negro kneels before Liberty, next to printing press. "The Tyrant's Foe—The People's Friend." On the reverse: 12-line text on Constitution and Bill of Rights. Lovejoy, editor of the *St. Louis Observer*, was killed by a pro-slavery mob in 1837. . . . . *$600–700*

Pitcher. Frederick Douglas Memorial, 1895. Handmade redware; high bust relief; in raised lettering: "Frederick Douglas/Born 1817. Died Feb. 20 1985/Slave/Orator/U.S. Marshall Recorder of Deeds D.C./Diplomat." Chain around neck of pitcher. *$2000–2200*

Pitcher. "I Wish I was in Dixay Landio," early 1870s. Black minstrel pitcher. Earthenware with transfer decoration in full color of nine seated musicians, each with instrument, tambourine, bones, fiddle. Small firing crack at handle base. (A) Riba, June '85, $650. . . . . *$750–800*

Pitcher. (Elsworth, Brownell, Jackson) "The Traitor." White ceramic. Francis Brownell was Union soldier who killed Rebel sympathizer James T. Jackson, Elsworth's assassin. Relief molded scene of eagle attacking snake. C.S.A. flag is upside down; 7½" h. Small crack (which is common with this example). *$550–600*

Pitcher. "Little Eva," ca. 1860s. English ceramic, 8½" h. Shows slave sale on one side; Little Eva on other; Rockingham-type glaze (base chip). (A) $605.. *$600–700*

Pitcher. James Garfield, 1881. Wedgewood Etruria creamware inauguration pitcher; "Born 1831; President 1881"; bust portrait surrounded by laurel leaves; reverse shows crossed flags, shield, and eagle; sepiatone, green, red. *$500–600*

Pitcher. James Garfield Memorial, ca. 1881. Stoneware with white glaze and flecked gold; relief bust of Garfield on both sides; handle and spout are shaped as eagle's head and neck; 8" h. *$400–500*

Pitcher. James Garfield Memorial, 1881. Stoneware glazed in rich brown; raised bust portraits, name on both sides; available in two sizes:..................
9":... $250–300
11":... $350–500

Pitcher. James Garfield Acrostic Memorial, 1881. English; crossed U.S. and British flags with portrait of Prince Albert on one side, Garfield on the other; saccharine acrostic eulogy to both deceased heroes in which the first letters of each line spell "G-a-r-f-i-e-l-d." $150–200

Pitcher. James Garfield, 1881. Pink luster with oval framed profile bust of Garfield; elaborate handles and gold trim; 9" h. $1000–1200

Pitcher. "J.A. Garfield," 1881. Bennington type with embossed profile bust, ornate laurel and filligree borders and on handle; dark brown; 7½" h. $300–400

Pitcher. U.S. Grant, 1864. Quarter-view painted images, with Adm. David Farragut on reverse; multicolor porcelain pitcher. (A) Skinners, $23,100............
.... $20,000–22,000

Pitcher. "Benjamin Harrison and Levi Morton," 1888. Pink glaze background with sepiatone transfers; white trim with filligree border.................. $200–250

Pitcher. Benjamin Harrison and Whitlaw Reid, 1892 campaign. Dresden china; with transfer images both sides; 6½" h. (Also see matching plate.) $200–250

Pitcher. "William McKinley," 1896. White porcelain with gilded rim and handle; polychrome transfer bust portrait; American flag on reverse............ $75–100

Pitcher. "William McKinley," 1896. Stoneware with black transfer bust portraits of McKinley and Republican running mate Garrett Hobart; elaborately shaped handle, base; 10" h. $300–350

Pitcher (Toby). William McKinley, 1896. Multicolored. Full-length figural caricature. Probably produced by one or more New Jersey potteries. Large Napoleon-type hat serves as brim of pitcher. Larger version may bear the inscription "American Napoleon Jug" or "The McKinley Jug." 5½" size (known in multi, brown, or green glazes): $250–300
9½" size:... $350–400

Pitcher (Toby). William McKinley, 1896. Unusual campaign-related figural caricature with McKinley seated in chair. Contains "Protection/Prosperity" and other slogans... $2000–3000

Plaque. Ku Klux Klan. Undated. Majolica plaque 11" dia. Red, white, blue, green; burning cross, flag, shield; "KKK" all in deep relief. $650–700

Plate. "Am I not a Man and a Brother?" Possibly 1820s. Bone china plate by Wedgwood with William Hackwood "Slave in Chains" black silhouette design on blue transfer bearing legend beneath slave image. Gilded floral border and scalloped rim. $500–600

Plate. Anti-slavery: Memorial to Abolitionist, Elijah Lovejoy, 1840s. Negro kneels before Liberty, next to printing press. "The Tyrant's Foe—the People's Friend." (Also see a pitcher and plate variation.)......................... $250–300

Plate. James Buchanan Inaugural, late 1890. By Sarreguemines, France; "1857–61"; one of series in cream glaze of commemorative plates; features black transfer of every president from Washington to McKinley. Surrounding eagle and flag design in reddish brown.................................... $100–125

Plate. Three Confederate Flags, 1860s. Multicolored china; gold border, "D'Arcy's Hand Painted" with curled tail serpent; 9¼" dia.; minor surface abrasions. (A) $125
.... $100–150

Plate. First Amendment Plate (a.k.a. Antislavery Plate), ca. 1837. Staffordshire.

Light purplish blue; four cartouches: "The tyrant's foe, the people's friend"; "We hold that all Men are Created Equal"; "Of one blood are all nation." Words from 1st Amendment are overprinted over sunburst in center of plate. American eagle and stars; slave in chains, Liberty beside printing press in border. (Prompted by killing of abolitionist editor, Elijah Lovejoy.) *$900–1000*

Note: Beware of reproductions, which are considerably thicker than original.

Plate. "Flowers That Never Fade" Anti-Slavery Theme, 1850s. English child's plate. "While God regards the wise and fair. The Noble and the brave. He listens to the beggar's prayer and the poor Negro slave." Transfer image of black slave woman holding out a plate for alms, entreating a white woman and small child. Multifloral border, 7". *$350–400*

Plate. James Garfield, 1880. Red with gray stripes; rectangle of white with black transfer bust print of Garfield in profile; signature below *$300–350*

Plate. James Garfield, 1880. Burford, East Liverpool, OH; 10" blue spatterware with raised bust profile. *$125–150*

Plate. James Garfield, ca. 1880. New Jersey Pottery; red clay with ancient Grecian pattern; bust of Garfield with facsimile signature *$75–100*

Plate. "Maj. Gen. U.S. Grant Alphabet," 1868. Campaign item; Staffordshire; black transfer on milkglass. *$350–400*

Plate. "Hon. Hannibal Hamlin," 1860. Lincoln's Rep. running mate; black transfer on white ceramic with filigree and small holes decorating rim *$75–100*

Plate. "For President/Benjamin Harrison," 1888. Black transfer bust portrait; name in large flowing script. Match for Rep. V.P. running mate, Levi Morton, opponent G. Cleveland. *$100–125*

Plate (or Pin Tray). (Harrison) "He's All Right," ca. 1892. Figural heads of a dog and two cats; 6¼". *$75–100*

Plate. Benjamin Harrison, ca. 1888. Glazed plate in beige with dark brown transfer of Harrison bust; facsimile sig.; brown leaf design on rim; 8" dia. *$50–75*

Plate. Benjamin Harrison, ca. 1888. Ironstone with black transfer bust portrait; no signature; gold trim on inner and outer borders; 8" dia. *$50–75*

Plate. Harrison–Cleveland, 1888. Matched pair of ironstone bread plates with brown portrait transfers of Dem. and Rep. candidates; "Give Us This Day Our Daily Bread" around rim . . . . *$125–150 (pair)*

Plate. "Benjamin Harrison and Whitlaw Reid," 1892. Campaign plate; transfer images of slate with furled flags below; match features Dem. slate, William J. Bryan and Sewell. *$100–125*

Plate. "Andrew Johnson," date unknown. Souvenir plate in blue and white earthenware; shows Johnson's home in Greenville, TN, with small cameo portraits of Johnson and wife Elisa. *$50–75*

Plate. K.K.K., "God Give Us Men," date unknown. Red, green, blue, white; 6" ceramic. *$65–75*

Plate. K.K.K. "God Give Us Women," date unknown. Red, green, blue, white; 6" ceramic. *$65–75*

Plate. Lincoln, ca. 1860s. Bust polychrome portrait; black stripe at rim . . . *$200–250*

Plate. Mary Todd Lincoln, ca. 1910. 6" octagon; back marked "Imperial China" and a "remarkable remembrance from Zunder-Pfeffer Co."; polychrome bust portrait with gold background; one of a commemorative series. *$20–25*

Plate. Lincoln, Sherman, and Grant, ca. 1863. Handpainted milk glass; full color; bust portraits of three with eagle and shield in center; clusters of flowers; purple, gold border. *$250–300*

Plate. Lincoln Alphabet Plate, ca. early 1860s. Milk glass with "President Abraham Lincoln" transfer in black. *$200–250*

Plate. Lincoln Alphabet Plate, ca. 1869. Blue transfer of Lincoln; embossed ABC's. *$300–350*

Plate. Lincoln's Tomb, Springfield, Illinois, 20th century. Transfer in orange with floral border. *$20–25*

Plate. Lincoln, with House in Springfield, ca. early 20th century. Blue transfer encircled by floral wreath; memorial plate with birth and death dates. *$25–30*

Plate. (Lincoln) "With Firmness in the Right/With Malice Toward None," 1909. Commemorative plate in naive style by unknown artist. Black on white. Celebrates 100th anniversary of Lincoln's birth. *$25–35*

Plate. John Logan, 1884 campaign. Rep. V.P. candidate, Gen. Logan; 8" ironstone; Logan founder of Memorial Day; one of four-piece set including Grover Cleveland, Thomas Hendricks, and James G. Blaine. *$75–100*

Plate. Arrival of Gen. McClellan, 1864. Child's soft paste alphabet plate; 6" dia.; black transfer on white. *$100–150*

Plate. William McKinley, 1896. Scalloped bonbon dish with black transfer bust of McKinley. *$50–75*

Plate. William McKinley, 1896. Campaign plate; bust portrait and signature in reddish brown; scroll pattern in gold along border. *$35–50*

Plate. William McKinley/Garret Hobart, ca. 1896. Jugate portraits in black transfer; facsimile signatures. *$75–100*

Plate. William McKinley Memorial, ca. 1901. Black transfer bust; five-line memorial tribute. *$25–35*

Plate. McKinley–T. Roosevelt, ca. 1900. Campaign jugate plate in reddish brown transfer on white; rim is green; holed border in circle and heart patterns; 5¾" dia. . . . *$50–75*

Plate. George McClellan, ABC Ceramic-Union Gen. U.S. 1865. Entering Frederick, MD, on horseback; 8" dia.; black transfer. Better quality/good condition. (D) $1500 . . . . *$1500–2000*

Plate. "Our Martyred Heroes," ca. 1900. Polychrome of Lincoln, Garfield, McKinley with small flags against gold circle; plate overall is white with royal blue strip near rim. *$25–50*

Plate. Gen. Windfield (sic) Scott, A.B.C., early 1860s. Transfer portrait of Scott; 5" dia.; note misspelled first name. (Match to Lincoln example.) *$200–250*

Plate. Gen. Winfield Scott for President, 1860 Dem. campaign. Black transfer bust on bone-colored background; black pinstripe around rim. *$125–150*

Platter. Abraham Lincoln and Theodore Roosevelt, 1890s. Oval portraits on scallop-edged oval platter. *$75–100*

Serving Bowl. Abraham Lincoln's Gettysburg Address, date unknown (possibly Lincoln Centennial item). Made by Homer Loughlin Co., Historical China Set; red transfer on both sides; crowd scene and floral border; 9½" × 7". (Also see Gravy Boat match.) *$35–50*

Tile. John Bell, 1860 campaign. Bell ran against Lincoln as Constitutional candidate for pres.; oblong; dark brown intaglio with ornate scrolled border in sepia. *$250–300*

Tile. U.S. Grant, ca. 1868. Bust portrait; 6" square; found in dark brown or vibrant blue. *$100–125*

Tile. Benjamin Harrison Portrait, ca. 1888. By C. Pardee Works, Perth Amboy, NJ; 6" square; purplish brown. *$100–125*

Tile. Slightly different Harrison pose than above, and in black. *$125–150*

Tile. Same as above, but in rust red. *$125–150*

Tile. Abraham Lincoln, 1909. Mosaic Tile Co., Zanesville, OH; Lincoln Centennial; hexangular; wedgwood blue and white. *$25–35*

Tile. Abraham Lincoln, 1909. Allen Tiling Co., Chicago; 3" h.; white on blue. *$25–35*

Tile. William McKinley, 1896. Encaustic Tile Co., Zanesville, OH; 3" tile in teal blue with McKinley portrait; part of four-tile set; other candidates: Hobart, Dems. Bryan and Sewall. *$40–50*

Tile. William McKinley, ca. 1896 campaign. "Our Next President" circular; 3½" dia; blue; profile bust. *$50–75*

Tile. William McKinley, ca. 1896. Square ceramic tile with polychrome bust portrait; no identification. *$35–50*

Trinket Box. U.S. Grant, ca. 1868. Ceramic white figural with bust of Grant; bas relief of eagle and shield; 5½" h. *$400–500*

Trinket/Match Box. Benjamin Butler, ca. 1874. Lightly glazed white china with bas relief Butler heads on each side. A Civil War kepi serves as a handle to lid. "Contraband of War/Set them to work" (Butler's response after the war as what to do with freed slaves in Union-occupied territory) appears on lid surface; "A Match For Anyone" incised around rim. Probably a Butler congressional campaign item. *$300–400*

Vase. U.S. Grant, ca. 1880s. Victorian-style flare vase with relief bust portrait of Grant; flowered edges. *$275–300*

Vase. Andrew Johnson, ca. 1865. Souvenir of Lincoln–Johnson inaugural; white china with sepia portrait of Lincoln and Johnson. *$200–250*

Vase. Abraham Lincoln, ca. 1880s. Match to the Grant vase above with relief bust of Lincoln. *$275–300*

Vase. Abraham Lincoln, ca. 1860s. Fenton Pottery, Bennington VT; oval with bas relief of Lincoln bust against bright blue background; filligree grape leaves and scalloping around oval. *$350–400*

Vase. Abraham Lincoln, 1860s. Brown glazed redware with embossed profile bust of Lincoln; encircled by solid black coloring on laurel wreath with eagle at top. *$600–700*

Wall Hanging. G.A.R. "Presidential Martyrs," 1901. Multicolor rounded enameled porcelain oval medallion, 5½" w. × 8" h. Pictures assassinated presidents Lincoln, Garfield, and McKinley plus G.A.R. star medal with ribbon. *$300–450*

Figurines. Left: *"Little Eva and Uncle Tom," salt and pepper shakers (white, pink, brown, black), $350–$400.* Right: *Staffordshire, rare image of Lincoln on horseback (white with red, black, and flesh tones). This was a variation of a Napoleon figurine made by Staffordshire that was altered for U.S. export, $1,200–$1,300.*

Top: *Plate, "Winfield S. Hancock," 1880, black transfer on white:* $75–$100. Bottom: *Plate, "James Garfield" signature, ca. 1880, New Jersey Pottery, black transfer on red ceramic,* $75–$100.

Pitcher, "The Traitor," white ceramic (Ellsworth, Brownell, Jackson), $550–$600 (Photo courtesy of Rex Stark)

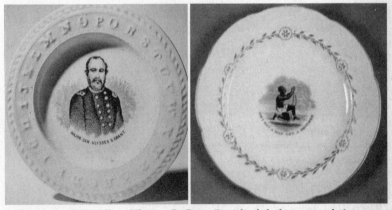

Left: *Plate, "Maj. Gen. Ulysses S. Grant" with alphabet around rim, Staffordshire, 1868, black transfer on white milkglass, $350–$400.* Right: *Plate, "Am I Not a Man and a Brother?" ca. 1820s. Bone china plate by Wedgwood with William Hackwood "slave in chains" black silhouette design on blue transfer, with gilded floral border, $500–$600.*

Currency

This chapter on currency concerns coins, paper money, and bank notes, including Confederate currency.

Coinage

Most coins soon went out of circulation at the war's onset. Due to lack of metal the New Orleans Mint failed. This threw the burden on the Philadelphia and San Francisco mints. Here, too, metal was a problem in the North although some coins were still minted. The only coins struck there for the C.S.A. were the cent and the half-dollar, both experimental—and now ultra rare. The Dahlonaga and Charlotte mints were closed for good. The following comprise some of the more widely used coins. Note also that throughout this chapter ABP=Average Buying Price, VF=Very Fine, and VG=Very Good.

Bronze Two-Cent Pieces: 1864–1865
(Actually Issued thru 1873)

The bronze two-cent piece was a short-lived denomination produced because small change was growing increasingly scarce during the Civil War. It was the first coin to bear the motto "In God We Trust."

1864 Small Motto. Shield, eagle, and laurel sprig.. . . . . . Good *$50,* Ex. Fine *$220*
1864 Large Motto. Shield, eagle, and laurel sprig. . . . . Good *$5,* Ex. Fine *$30*
1865 Large Motto. Shield, eagle, and laurel sprig. . . . . Good *$5,* Ex. Fine *$30*

Three-Cent Silver: 1860–1865
(Actually Issued thru 1873)

1860 Star with Shield in Center. "O" is in reverse on right of III. . . . .
. . . . ABP *$4,* Ex. Fine *$52*
1861 Star with Shield in Center. "O" is in reverse on right of III. . . . .
. . . . ABP *$4,* Ex. Fine *$52*

1862 Star with Shield in Center. "O" is in reverse on right of III. . . . .
. . . . ABP *$4*, Ex. Fine *$52*
1862 (2 over 1) Star with Shield in Center. "O" is in reverse on right of III. . . . .
. . . . ABP *$4*, Ex. Fine *$70*
1863 Star with Shield in Center. "O" is in reverse on right of III. . . . .
. . . . ABP *$250*, Ex. Fine *(no listing)*
1863 (3 over 2) Star with Shield in Center. "O" is in reverse on right of III. . . . .
. . . . ABP *$250*, Ex. Fine *(no listing)*
1864 Star with Shield in Center. "O" is in reverse on right of III. . . . .
. . . . ABP *$250*, Ex. Fine *(no listing)*
1865 Star with Shield in Center. "O" is in reverse on right of III. . . . .
. . . . ABP *$250*, Ex. Fine *(no listing)*

Half Dimes, Liberty Seated: 1860–1873

"United States of America" is on reverse. Mint marks are under wreath or within wreath on reverse.

1860. Legend.. . . . . ABP *$2.50*, Ex. Fine *$32*
1860 . . . . ABP *$2.50*, Ex. Fine *$35*
1861 . . . . ABP *$2.50*, Ex. Fine *$28*
1862 . . . . ABP *$2.50*, Ex. Fine *$30*
1863 . . . . ABP *$46*, Ex. Fine *$365*
1863S . . . . ABP *$7*, Ex. Fine *$115*
1864 . . . . ABP *$100*, Ex. Fine *$610*
1865 . . . . ABP *$80*, Ex. Fine *$500*

Dimes, Liberty Seated: 1860–1891

"United States of America" is on obverse. Mint marks are under wreath or within wreath on reverse.

1860 . . . . ABP *$3*, Ex. Fine *$32*
1860-O . . . . ABP *$80*, Ex. Fine *$2100*
1861 . . . . ABP *$2*, Ex. Fine *$29*
1861S . . . . ABP *$7*, Ex. Fine *$200*
1862 . . . . ABP *$2*, Ex. Fine *$30*
1862S . . . . ABP *$8*, Ex. Fine *$170*
1863 . . . . ABP *$75*, Ex. Fine *$510*
1863S . . . . ABP *$8*, Ex. Fine *$165*
1864 . . . . ABP *$80*, Ex. Fine *$550*
1864S . . . . ABP *$7*, Ex. Fine *$130*
1865 . . . . ABP *$115*, Ex. Fine *$600*
1865S . . . . ABP *$7*, Ex. Fine *$160*

Quarters, Liberty Seated: 1838–1865

No motto above eagle. Mint mark is below eagle on reverse.

1860 . . . . ABP *$4*, Ex. Fine *$60*

1860-O . . . . ABP *$6*, Ex. Fine *$85*
1861 . . . . ABP *$4.50*, Ex. Fine *$65*
1861S . . . . ABP *$15*, Ex. Fine *$290*
1862 . . . . ABP *$5*, Ex. Fine *$70*
1862S . . . . ABP *$21*, Ex. Fine *$325*
1863 . . . . ABP *$10*, Ex. Fine *$115*
1864 . . . . ABP *$21*, Ex. Fine *$190*
1864S . . . . ABP *$55*, Ex. Fine *$1100*
1865 . . . . ABP *$24*, Ex. Fine *$230*
1865S . . . . ABP *$26*, Ex. Fine *$340*

Half Dollar, Liberty Seated: 1839–1866

No motto above eagle. Mint mark is below eagle.

1860 . . . . ABP *$8*, Ex. Fine *$86*
1860-O . . . . ABP *$7*, Ex. Fine *$70*
1860-S . . . . ABP *$10*, Ex. Fine *$78*
1861 . . . . ABP *$7*, Ex. Fine *$55*
1861-O . . . . ABP *$7*, Ex. Fine *$60*
1861S . . . . ABP *$7*, Ex. Fine *$70*
1862 . . . . ABP *$10*, Ex. Fine *$95*
1862S . . . . ABP *$7*, Ex. Fine *$65*
1863 . . . . ABP *$9*, Ex. Fine *$75*
1863S . . . . ABP *$7*, Ex. Fine *$65*
1864 . . . . ABP *$7*, Ex. Fine *$75*
1864S . . . . ABP *$7*, Ex. Fine *$70*
1865 . . . . ABP *$6.50*, Ex. Fine *$82*
1865S . . . . ABP *$6.50*, Ex. Fine *$70*

Silver Dollars, Liberty Seated: 1840–1865

No motto over eagle. Mint mark is below eagle on reverse.

1860 . . . . ABP *$90*, VF *$1000*
1860-O . . . . ABP *$50*, Ex. Fine *$30*
1861 . . . . ABP *$100*, Ex. Fine *$960*
1862 . . . . ABP *$100*, Ex. Fine *$900*
1863 . . . . ABP *$80*, Ex. Fine *$600*
1864 . . . . ABP *$80*, Ex. Fine *$510*
1865 . . . . ABP *$80*, Ex. Fine *$600*

Gold Dollars: 1856–1889

Large Liberty head, feathered headdress large size. Mint mark is below laurel wreath on reverse.

1860 . . . . ABP *$75*, Ex. Fine *$150*
1860-D . . . . ABP *$1500*, Ex. Fine *$4500*

1860-S	ABP *$140*, Ex. Fine *$425*
1861	ABP *$90*, Ex. Fine *$145*
1861-D	ABP *$3000*, Ex. Fine *$11,000*
1862	ABP *$75*, Ex. Fine *$150*
1863	ABP *$200*, Ex. Fine *$725*
1864	ABP *$200*, Ex. Fine *$485*
1865	ABP *$200*, Ex. Fine *$575*

Quarter Eagles, $2.50, Gold Pieces: 1840–1907

Liberty head with coronet. Mint mark is below eagle on reverse.

1860	ABP *$90*, Ex. Fine *$220*
1860-C	ABP *$140*, Ex. Fine *$1300*
1860-S	ABP *$95*, Ex. Fine *$575*
1861	ABP *$85*, Ex. Fine *$165*
1861S	ABP *$100*, Ex. Fine *$1100*
1862	ABP *$90*, Ex. Fine *$240*
1862S	ABP *$110*, Ex. Fine *$1900*
1863	—30 proofs only—
1863S	ABP *$115*, Ex. Fine *$1200*
1864	ABP *$600*, Ex. Fine *$7000*
1865	ABP *$450*, Ex. Fine *$6200*
1865S	ABP *$110*, Ex. Fine *$600*

Three-Dollar Gold Pieces: 1854–1889

Liberty head with feather headdress. Mint mark is below wreath on reverse.

1860	ABP *$325*, Ex. Fine *$880*
1860-S	ABP *$325*, Ex. Fine *$1125*
1861	ABP *$260*, Ex. Fine *$925*
1862	ABP *$275*, Ex. Fine *$925*
1863	ABP *$275*, Ex. Fine *$925*
1864	ABP *$300*, Ex. Fine *$950*
1865	ABP *$325*, Ex. Fine *$1400*

Half Eagles, $5 Gold Pieces: 1839–1908

Liberty head with coronet. Eagle without motto.

1860	ABP *$100*, Ex. Fine *$500*
1860-C	ABP *$180*, Ex. Fine *$1400*
1860-D	ABP *$180*, Ex. Fine *$1400*
1860-S	ABP *$190*, Ex. Fine *$1600*
1861	ABP *$85*, Ex. Fine *$190*
1861-C	ABP *$600*, Ex. Fine *$2200*
1861S	ABP *$180*, Ex. Fine *$1600*

1862	ABP *$200*, Ex. Fine *$1750*
1862S	ABP *$370*, Ex. Fine *$2850*
1863	ABP *$325*, Ex. Fine *$2100*
1863S	ABP *$200*, Ex. Fine *$1900*
1864	ABP *$150*, Ex. Fine *$1700*
1864S	ABP *$70*, Ex. Fine *$4800*
1865	ABP *$450*, Ex. Fine *$2800*
1865S	ABP *$450*, Ex. Fine *$2400*

Eagles, $10 Gold Pieces: 1838–1907

Liberty head with coronet. No motto. Mint mark is below eagle on reverse.

1860	ABP *$140*, Ex. Fine *$800*
1860-O	ABP *$180*, Ex. Fine *$900*
1860-S	ABP *$700*, Ex. Fine *$4000*
1861	ABP *$125*, Ex. Fine *$300*
1861-S	ABP *$500*, Ex. Fine *$2100*
1862	ABP *$150*, Ex. Fine *$1000*
1862S	ABP *$500*, Ex. Fine *$2850*
1863	ABP *$1400*, Ex. Fine *$8000*
1863S	ABP *$450*, Ex. Fine *$2400*
1864	ABP *$450*, Ex. Fine *$2700*
1864S	ABP *$1600*, Ex. Fine *$7000*
1865	ABP *$400*, Ex. Fine *$2800*
1865S	ABP *$1200*, Ex. Fine *$4000*

Double Eagles, $20 Gold Pieces: 1849–1866

Liberty head. Mint mark is below eagle on reverse.

1860	ABP *$200*, Ex. Fine *$500*
1860-O	ABP *$1200*, Ex. Fine *$4600*
1860-S	ABP *$225*, Ex. Fine *$525*
1861	ABP *$200*, Ex. Fine *$450*
1861-O	ABP *$500*, Ex. Fine *$2900*
1861-S	ABP *$200*, Ex. Fine *$600*
1862	ABP *$200*, Ex. Fine *$900*
1862S	ABP *$190*, Ex. Fine *$650*
1863	ABP *$200*, Ex. Fine *$650*
1863S	ABP *$200*, Ex. Fine *$500*
1864	ABP *$200*, Ex. Fine *$725*
1864S	ABP *$200*, Ex. Fine *$600*
1865	ABP *$200*, Ex. Fine *$525*
1865S	ABP *$200*, Ex. Fine *$525*

CONFEDERATE COINAGE
Confederate Half Dollar: 1862

C.S.A. Secretary of Treasury C.G. Memminger used traditional half dollar but changed reverse to depict a Liberty cap, a stalk of sugar cane, and cotton, plus "Confederate States of America Half Dol."

1861 . . . . —Only 4 minted, Ultra Rare—
1861 (Restrike) . . . . ABP *$600,* Ex. Fine *$1000*
1861 Scott Token (C.S.A. reverse) . . . . ABP *$200,* Ex. Fine *$185*

> *Note:* Scott, an enterprising chap, somehow obtained original reverse die and struck off 500 specimens of his own to peddle to souvenir hunters. He used his own obverse with wording and no portraiture.

Confederate Cent: 1861

Liberty head, laurel wreath on reverse. Designed by Robert Lovett, Philadelphia.

One Cent (Original). . . . . MS-60 Unc. *$8500,* MS-65 Unc. *$15,000*
One Cent (Restrike-Silver), Proof. . . . . . MS-60 Unc. *$3600,* MS-65 Unc. *$4200*
One Cent (Restrike-Copper), Proof . . . . MS-60 Unc. *$3800,* MS-65 Unc. *$4800*

CONFEDERATE PAPER CURRENCY

Confederate paper currency came about as a result of an acute coinage shortage. Each side, in fact, resorted to printing of notes in lieu of bullion or real money. All told, the C.S.A. produced seven issues from 1861–64 totaling approximately $1½ billion in paper currency, which quickly became worthless at war's end, as the Federal government refused to redeem them.

The old song lyric "save your Confederate money, the South shall rise again" proved prophetic—these notes have seen a steady rise in value since the 1940s. Even so, many examples still appear as undervalued. Three types of cancels help determine value: the *cc or cut cancel,* in which knife or other sharp instrument has been used to pierce a design or pattern; the *coc or cut out cancel,* which leaves gaps in design and detracts by at least 25%; and the *pc or pen cancels,* which are least objectionable unless ink is heavy or smeary. A few rarities exist, among them the Alabama $1000 and $500 notes, which are worth more than their face value. A majority, particularly the later issues, have little worth.

REF: *Official 1995 Blackbook Price Guide to U.S. Paper Money,* House of Collectibles, NY. *1995 American Guide to U.S. Coins,* Charles French; *Collecting Paper Money for Pleasure and Profit,* Barry Krause, © 1992. *Confederate States Paper Money,* Slabaugh. *Confederate and Southern States Currency,* Cresswell (catalog nos. are used in this guide).

1861 Issue: National Bank Note Co., NY

Criswell-1: T-1, $1,000 Authorized by March 9th. Face design: Calhoun left; Jackson right. 607 issued...............................ABP *$1500,* Good *$2600*

Criswell-2. T-2, $500. Face design: green and black. Shows train and cattle crossing brook. 607 issued. ....ABP *$1500,* Good *$2600*

Criswell-3. T-3, $100. Minerva (milkmaid) at left. Railway train center. Engr. by J.T. Patterson, Columbia, SC. ....ABP *$800,* Good *$1000*

Criswell-4. T-4, $50. Negroes hoeing cotton. "$50" in discs. "Interest Half A Cent A Day." ....ABP *$600,* Good *$1200*

1861 Issue: American Bank Note Co., NY (though to appease C.S.A., listed as Southern Bank Note Co.)

Criswell-5. T-5, $100. Green and black; red fiber paper. Justice (left), Minerva (right), train (center)..................................ABP *$75,* Good *$190*

Criswell-6. T-6, $50. Green, black; red fiber paper. Pallas and Ceres seated on bale of cotton. George Washington oval at right...............ABP *$65,* Good *$140*

1861 Issue: Confederate States of America ($20,000 Authorized by "Act of May 16, 1861," Hoyer & Ludwig, Richmond, VA)

Criswell-7-13. T-7, $100. Ceres and Proserpina flying (center). Washington oval (left). ....ABP *$85,* Good *$165*

Criswell-14-22. T-8, $50. Washington oval (center), Tellus (lower left). ....
....ABP *$25,* Good *$40*

Criswell-21. $20. Counterfeit issue, printer unknown. Deity at center. Indian seated (lower right). Known in variety of colors...................ABP *$25,* Good *$40*

Criswell-23-33. T-9, $20. Large sailing schooner (center); large "20" left........
....ABP *$15,* Good *$35*

Criswell 34-40. T-10, $10. Liberty seated by eagle. Shield and flag. (42 minor variants of this note exist).................................ABP *$20,* Good *$72*

Criswell-42-44. T-11, $5. Liberty seated by eagle. Sailor (lower left). ....
....ABP *$100,* Good *$750*

1861 Issue: Confederate States of America ("J. Manouvrier, New Orleans," Date Written: "July 25, 1861")

Criswell-46-49. T-12, $5. Flowing legend "Confederate States of America" in blue on blue reverse....................................ABP *$200,* Good *$1600*

Criswell-50-58. T-13, $100. Negroes loading cotton (center). Man in top hat (lower left)..ABP *$15,* Good *$25*

Criswell-59-78. T-14, $50. Moneta seated by treasure chests (center), sailor (lower left)..ABP *$10,* Good *$20*

1861 Issue: "Southern Bank Note Co., New Orleans"

Criswell-79. T-15, $50. Train (center), Hope with anchor (lower left), Justice (right). Black and red on red fibre paper. .... ABP *$200,* Good *$500*

1861 Issue: "Keatinge & Ball, Richmond, Va."

Criswell-80-94. T-16, $50. Black, green; red fibre paper. Bust portrait of Jefferson Davis (center). .... ABP *$20,* Good *$50*

Criswell-99-100. T-17, $20. Black with green design; plain paper; Ceres seated between Commerce and Navigation (center); Liberty (left). .... ABP *$45,* Good *$90*

Miscellaneous

Criswell-101-136. T-18, $20. Hoyer & Ludwig, Richmond, VA. Large schooner; sailor at capstan (left). .... ABP *$6,* Good *$12*

Criswell-137. T-19, $20. Southern Bank Note Co., New Orleans. Black and red on red fibre paper. Navigator with charts (center), Minerva (left), blacksmith (right). .
.... ABP *$110,* Good *$500*

Criswell-139-140. T-20, $20. B. Duncan, Columbia, SC. Industry seated between beehive and Cupid (center); bust of Alexander Stevens (left)... ABP *$6,* Good *$15*

Criswell-141-143. T-20, $20. B. Duncan, Richmond, VA. .... ABP *$6,* Good *$15*

Criswell-144. T-21, $20. Keatinge & Ball, Columbia, SC. Portrait of Alexander Stevens (center), yellow green design. .... ABP *$15,* Good *$45*

Criswell-145-149. T-21, $20. Keatinge & Ball, Columbia, SC. Dark green design.
.... ABP *$15,* Good *$45*

Criswell-150-152. T-22, $10. Southern Bank Note Co., New Orleans. Black, red. Red fibre paper. Pair of Indians (center); Thetis (left); maiden with numeral X (right). .... ABP *$65,* Good *$15*

Criswell-153-155. T-23, $10. Leggett, Keatinge & Ball, Richmond, VA. Black, orange red. Wagon load of cotton (center); harvesting sugar cane (right); John E. Ward (left). .... ABP *$80,* Good *$160*

Criswell-156-160. T-23, $10. Leggett, Keatinge & Ball, Richmond, VA. Black, orange, red. R.M.T. Hunter (left); small child (right). .... ABP *$15,* Good *$40*

Criswell-161-167. T-24. Keatinge & Ball, Richmond, VA. (Same as above.).....
.... ABP *$15,* Good *$40*

Criswell-168-171. T-25, $10. Keatinge & Ball, Richmond, VA. Hope with anchor (center); R.M.T. Hunter (left); C.G. Memminger (right)...... ABP *$15,* Good *$25*

Criswell-173-178. T-26, $10. Keatinge & Ball, Richmond VA. Hope with anchor (center); R.M.T. Hunter (left); C.G. Memminger (right). With solid red "X" overprint.. .... ABP *$18,* Good *$45*

Criswell-189-210. T-210, $10. Same design as above but coarse lace "X" red overprint.. .... ABP *$15,* Good *$30*

Criswell-211-220. T-26. Same design. Fine lace "X" red overprint. ....
.... ABP *$15,* Good *$25*

Criswell-221-229. T-27, $10. Liberty seated by eagle and shield (upper left)......
.... ABP *$500,* Good *$2100*

Criswell-230-234. T-28, $10. Hoyer & Ludwig, Richmond, VA. Ceres and Commerce with urn (upper left). .... ABP *$8,* Good *$20*

Criswell-235-236. T-28, $10. J.T. Patterson, Columbia, SC. Same design as above.
.... ABP *$8,* Good *$20*

Criswell-237. T-29, $10. Negro picking cotton (center)....... ABP *$15,* Good *$35*

Criswell-238. T-30, $10. B. Duncan, Columbia, SC. Gen. Francis Marion's Sweet Potato Dinner (center); R.M. Hunter (left); Minerva (right). ... ABP *$8,* Good *$18*

Criswell-239-241. T-30, $10. No engraver identified. Same design as above.......
.... ABP *$7,* Good *$16*

Criswell-243-245. T-31, $5. Southern Bank Note Co., New Orleans. Black, red on red fibre paper. Minerva (left); Agriculture, Commerce, Industry, Justice, and Liberty seated (center). Statue of George Washington (right)..... ABP *$42,* Good *$85*

Criswell-246-249. T-32, $5. Leggett, Keatinge & Ball, Richmond, VA. Black and orange red. Blacksmith with hammer (right); small boy in oval (lower left).......
.... ABP *$70,* Good *$160*

Criswell-250-253. T-33, $5. Leggett, Keatinge & Ball, Richmond, VA. B&w note with blue-green ornamentation. C.G. Memminger (center); Minerva (right).......
.... ABP *$8,* Good *$22*

Criswell-254-257. T-33, $5. Keatinge & Ball. Same design as above...........
.... ABP *$10,* Good *$27*

Criswell-258-261: T-33, $5. No engineer identified. Same design as above.......
.... ABP *$8,* Good *$23*

Criswell-262-270. T-34, $5. Keatinge & Ball, Richmond, VA. C.G. Memminger (center); Minerva (right)............................. ABP *$15,* Good *$30*

Criswell-271. T-35, $5. Hoyer & Ludwig, Richmond, VA. Loading cotton at pier (left); Indian princess (right)........................ ABP *$850,* Good *$2100*

Criswell-272. T-36, $5. Hoyer & Ludwig, Richmond, VA. Ceres seated on bale of cotton (center); sailor (left)............................. ABP *$7,* Good *$17*

Criswell-274. T-36, $5. J.T. Patterson & Co., Columbia, SC. Same design as above.. ABP *$7,* Good *$14*

Criswell-276-282. T-36, $5. Same engraver as above......... ABP *$7,* Good *$15*

Criswell-284. T-37, $5. B. Duncan, Richmond, VA. Sailor seated beside cotton bales (center); C.G. Memminger (left); Justice and Ceres (right)...... ABP *$10,* Good *$22*

Criswell-285. T-37, $5. B. Duncan, Columbia, SC. Same as above.............
.... ABP *$8,* Good *$16*

Criswell-286. T-38, $2. Personification of South striking down Union. Dated "September 2, 1861" through error. The C.S.A. did not issue a $5 note in that year.....
.... ABP *$75,* Good *$290*

1864 Issue

7th Issue. $10. Central vignette of "Field Artillery" (a.k.a. "Horses Pulling Cannon"). Memminger portrait (lower right). Over 9 million issued; most common genuine C.S.A. note...................................... ABP *$3,* Good *$5*

7th Issue. $20. Capitol Building at Nashville (center); Alexander Stevens portrait (lower right). Keatinge & Ball, Columbia, SC................ ABP *$5,* Good *$7*

7th Issue. $100. Lucy Pickins, wife of Gov. F.W. Pickins of So. Carolina (center); George Randolph, C.S.A. Sec. of War in 1862 oval portrait (lower right). 896,644 printed. Keatinge & Ball, Columbia, SC. .... ABP *$6,* Good *$8*

U.S. Tender Notes (a.k.a. Legal Tender Notes), Note No. 1, Large Size

One Dollar Notes, 1862

These notes were engraved by Chittendon & Spinner. There is a portrait of Salmon Chase, Sec. of Treasury under Lincoln, on obverse.

Type I. National Bank Note, American Bank Note minus monogram; red seal. . . . . ABP *$50,* VF *$250*

Type II. National Bank Note, American Bank Note minus monogram ABNCO; red seal. . . . . ABP *$45,* VF *$200*

Type III. National Bank Note, American Bank Note minus monogram; red seal. . . . . ABP *$30,* VF *$180*

Type IV. National Bank Note, American Bank Note minus monogram with monogram ABNCO; red seal. . . . . ABP *$35,* VF *$210*

One Dollar Notes, 1863–1875

These notes are First Charter Period (large size). Face design: Name of national bank at top center; deities at altar below. Back design: Landing of Pilgrims at center with state seal of issuing bank.

Original Colby-Spinner. Red, white seal. . . . . ABP *$40,* VF *$190*

Original Jeffries-Spinner. Red, white seal. . . . . ABP *$120,* VF *$1200*

Original Allison-Spinner. Red, white seal. . . . . ABP *$30,* VF *$190*

1875 Allison-New. Red, white seal. . . . . ABP *$30,* VF *$190*

1875 Allison-Wyman. Red, white seal. ABP *$30,* VF *$190*

1875 Allison-Gilfillan. Red, white seal. . . . . ABP *$30,* VF *$195*

1875 Schofield-Gilfillan. Red, white seal. . . . . ABP *$30,* VF *$195*

Two Dollar Notes, 1862

These notes are United States notes, No. 19, large size. Front design: Alexander Hamilton. Back design: $2 in each corner.

1862 Chittenden-Spinner. Type I: American Banknote Co. vertical in left border; red seal. . . . . ABP *$70,* VF *$450*

1862 Chittenden-Spinner. Type II: American Banknote Co. vertical in left border; red seal. . . . . ABP *$70,* VF *$400*

Five Dollar Demand Notes, 1862

These notes are notes No. 32, large size. Face design: (left) Statue of Liberty, by Crawford, atop U.S. Capitol, numeral 5 appears large in green at center; (right) portrait of Alexander Hamilton. Back design: Number of small fives in ovals, no treasure seal. Signatures are by Treasury Dept. personnel who signed for officials. The following entires are listed by issuing city.

Boston (I) . . . . ABP *$250*, VG *$2200*
New York (I) . . . . ABP *$250*, VG *$2200*
Philadelphia (I) . . . . ABP *$250*, VG *$2200*
Cincinnati (I) . . . . ABP *$500*, VG *$15,000*
St. Louis (I) . . . . ABP *$500*, VG *$15,000*
Boston (II) . . . . ABP *$275*, VG *$900*
New York (II) . . . . ABP *$275*, VG *$900*
Philadelphia (II) . . . . ABP *$275*, VG *$900*
Cincinnati (II) . . . . ABP *$300*, VG *$1000*
St. Louis (II) . . . . ABP *$300*, VG *$1000*

Ten Dollar Demand Notes, 1861

These notes have no Treasury seal and are notes No. 60, large size. Face design: Bust portrait of Pres. Lincoln left. Female deity with sword and shield. Back design: Ornate representation of number ten, including Roman numeral X, with "United States of America" across design. The following entries are listed by issuing city.

Boston (I) . . . . ABP *$350*, VG *$7200*
New York (I) . . . . ABP *$350*, VG *$7200*
Philadelphia (I) . . . . ABP *$350*, VG *$7200*
Cincinnati (I) . . . . ABP *$500*, VG *$15,000*
St. Louis (I) . . . . ABP *$500*, VG *$15,000*
Boston (II) . . . . ABP *$275*, VG *$900*
New York (II) . . . . ABP *$275*, VG *$900*
Philadelphia (II) . . . . ABP *$275*, VG *$900*
Cincinnati (II) . . . . ABP *$300*, VG *$1000*
St. Louis (II) . . . . ABP *$300*, VG *$1000*

Ten Dollar Demand Notes, 1862–63

These are notes No. 61, large size. Face design: Similar to previous note. Back design: Roman Numeral X appears on both sides of oval. Very ornate pattern behind.

1862 Chittendon-Spinner. Red seal. . . . . ABP *$70*, VG *$500*
1862 Chittendon-Spinner. Red seal. . . . . ABP *$70*, VG *$500*
1863 Chittendon-Spinner. Red seal. . . . . ABP *$70*, VG *$500*

Twenty Dollar Demand Notes, 1861

Front design: Liberty with sword and shield. Back design: Number "20" in stylized shield with dense pattern background. No treasury seal.

Boston (I) . . . . ABP *Rare*, VG *Rare*
New York (I) . . . . ABP *$1600*, VG *$9000*
Philadelphia (I) . . . . ABP *$1600*, VG *$9000*
Cincinnati (I) . . . . ABP *Rare*, VG *Rare*

St. Louis (I) .... (Unknown in any collection)
Boston (II) .... ABP *Rare,* VG *Rare*
New York (II) .... ABP *$1600,* VG *$9000*
Philadelphia (II) .... ABP *$1600,* VG *$9000*
Cincinnati (II) .... ABP *Rare,* VG *Rare*
St. Louis (II) .... (Unknown in any collection)

Twenty Dollar Notes, 1862–1863

These are notes No. 86A, large size. Similar designs as above.

1862 Chittendon-Spinner. Red seal. .... ABP *$95,* VG *$1000*
1862 Chittendon-Spinner. Red seal. .... ABP *$95,* VG *$1000*
1863 Chittendon-Spinner. Red seal. .... ABP *$95,* VG *$900*
1862 Chittendon Spinner. Red seal. .... ABP *$95,* VG *$1000*
1862 Chittendon-Spinner. Red seal. .... ABP *$95,* VG *$1000*
1863 Chittendon-Spinner. Red seal. .... ABP *$95,* VG *$900*

Fifty Dollar Notes, 1862–1863

These are notes No. 104, large size. Front design: Alexander Hamilton to left. Back Design: Legend in large circle against dense pattern background.

1862 Chittendon-Spinner. Red seal. .... ABP *$1300,* VG *$9000*
1862 Chittendon-Spinner. Red seal. .... ABP *$1300,* VG *$9000*
1863 Chittendon-Spinner. Red seal. .... ABP *$1300,* VG *$8500*

One Hundred Dollar Notes, 1862–1863

These are notes No. 118, large size. Front Design: Large spread-wing eagle far left. Three disks with numbers "$100." Back design: Legend inside circle as above; two variations of word "obligation"; dense pattern background; green, red seal.

Chittendon-Spinner. Red seal. .... ABP *$1000,* VG *$7500*
1862 Chittendon-Spinner. Red seal. .... ABP *$1000,* VG *$7500*
1863 Chittendon-Spinner. Red seal. .... ABP *$1000,* VG *$7500*

MISCELLANEOUS STATE PAPER CURRENCY

State Currency

Civil War–era notes are lotted as follows. Georgia $1 bills: one sheet of three on Merchants & Planter's Bank, numbered, signed, and dated "Savannah, June 1, 1859; (12) three sheets of So. Carolina Revenue Bond scrips, four notes each in denominations of $1, $2, $5, $10, $20, and $50, some with "cotton picking" vignettes. Also sheet of one, on Bank of State of So. Carolina issued under Act of Feb. 1863, signed by Johnson. Plus, sheet of $1, $2, and $3 bills of Franklin Silk

Co., Franklin, OH. Additional sheet from Franklin Silk of three $5 and a $10. New England Commercial Bank, Newport, RI: pair of $1, one $2, and $3. Also sheet of one $10 and three $5s from same bank. (A) Riba, $320. . . . . *$325–350*

Fractional Currency

Fractional currency (a.k.a. Postal Currency) was issued at the onset of the Civil War as a small series of small paper notes, to be the equivalent of coinage denominations. They carried designs adapted from the current postage stamps of the period. There were five separate issues, three of which were introduced during the war, the last as late as 1874. As this is a highly esoteric area, we refer you to *The Official Black Book of United States Paper Money* (House of Collectibles, NY) for numerous nuances, variations, and prices.

Tokens, Civil War

Civil War tokens were store cards issued by various Union states and used in exchange for goods.

Connecticut 560A-1a. R-4. Payable in Postage Currency. EF-45. . . . . *$45–55*
Kentucky 150C-1a. R-4+, red and blue, unc. 60, 40% red. *$125–150*
Michigan 25A-1a. R-3, red and blue, unc. 60, 30% red. *$18–20*
Michigan 40B-2b. R-7, BU-60, full luster. *$75–85*
New Jersey 885A-1b. R-3, EF-40. . . . . *$8–10*
New York 10A-2a. R-2, VF-30. . . . . *$6–8*
New York 10F-1a. R-3, VF-discolored. *$5–6*
New York 10G-1a. R-3, Unc. 60, full subdued red. *$9–11*
New York 630B-1a. EF-45, traces of red. *$9–11*
New York 630AQ-4b. R-7, BU, nearly full luster. *$80–85*
New York 630BK-1b. R-7, full luster, small chip. *$45–50*
New York 630BOK-2a. R-1, BU-60, virtually full red. *$35–40*
New York 630M-13a. R-3, red and blue, AU 55, 30% red. *$10–15*
New York 630M-13b. R-4, BU, nearly full luster. *$10–15*
New York 630P-1a. R-2, CH, AU 55, 20% red. *$10–12*
New York 630AG-3a. R2, red and blue, Unc. 60, 40% red. *$15–20*
New York 630AK-2a. R-3, Ch, AU, traces of red. *$14–16*
New York 630AM-1a. R-1, CH, AU, traces of red. *$10–12*
New York 630AN-1a. R-3. AU, retoning. *$8–10*
New York 630AQ-1a. R-1. CH, AU, traces of red. *$10–12*
New York 630BK-1b. R-7, BU, full luster, small chip. *$50–60*
New York 630CH-3a. R-7, EF-40. . . . . *$13–15*
New York 630CI-4a. R-7, EF-40. . . . . *$14–16*
New York 905C-1a. R-3, red and blue, Unc. 60, 30% red. *$18–20*
Ohio 74A-1a. R-9, EF-40, retoning. *$16–18*
Ohio 165O-9a. R-7, BU, nearly full red, sheaf of wheat pictured. *$70–75*
Ohio 165W-6a. R-7, red and blue, Unc. 60, 20% red, Tr. token. *$80–85*
Ohio 165GL-8a. R-6, red and blue, Unc. 60, 10% red. *$35–40*

Ohio 165GO-4a. R-7, EF-45, Jefferson Saloon........................ *$35–40*
Ohio 165GR-1a. R-2, Unc. with 20% red, mottled toning. *$7–10*
Ohio 165GS-13a. R-7, EF-45.................................... *$25–30*
Ohio 230D-1a. R-5, CH, AU-55, 20% red........................... *$35–40*
Ohio 310A-1a. R-6, EF-40....................................... *$45–50*
Ohio 535A-4a. R-4, EF-40 .... *$13–15*
Ohio 995A-1a. R-2, Unc., obverse in full red, reverse light-toned brown... *$14–16*
Pennsylvania 750L-1fp. CH, AU, with most light silver wash intact...... *$15–20*
Pennsylvania 750M-1a. R-2, red and blue, Unc. 60, 30% red. *$15–20*
Pennsylvania 765P-13a. R-4, VF, uneven color...................... *$9–11*
Pennsylvania 750V-1a. R-4, VF-30................................ *$18–20*
Rhode Island 700A-4a. R-3, VF-30. .... *$9–11*
Wisconsin 510A-1a. R-8, AU, minor spot on obverse center. *$25–30*
Wisconsin 510U-1a. R-3, red and blue, Unc. 60, 20% red. *$28–30*
Wisconsin 510V-1a. Red and blue, Unc. 60, 10% red................. *$50–55*
Wisconsin 510W-1a. R-4, red and blue, Unc. 60, 10% red............. *$25–30*
Wisconsin 620G-1a. R-8, VF, dark. *$45–50*
Wisconsin 700C-3a. R-6, EF-45. .... *$25–30*
Wisconsin 700D-2a. R-5, red and blue, Unc. 60, 40% red. *$25–30*
Wisconsin 700G-1a. R-6, EF-40. .... *$65–70*

Confederate currency. Five, ten, twenty, and fifty dollar notes are pictured here. The most common note is the $10 note in the center, depicting horses pulling caissons; 9 million were issued by the CSA. Value of original notes varies, $15–$20.

DIARIES, LETTERS, AND DOCUMENTS

DIARIES AND JOURNALS

The following are all diaries unless otherwise stated in parentheses at beginning of entry.

John E. Albert's Naval Diary of Events Aboard U.S.S. *Genesee*. Sept. 1862–July 1865. Ninety-six-page handwritten account of naval engagement starting "South of Ft. Monroe." Albert writes of blockade runners, orders to Mobile blockade, capturing C.S.A. trade ships, battle against Rebel fleet inside Mobile Bay involving four ironclads and 14 wooden vessels. Ends with news of Lincoln's assassination. In leather-bound booklet, incl. milk glass photo of John Albert in uniform. (A) Riba, Oct. '85, $900. .... *$1200–1500*

(Journal) Sgt. Henry Brown, Co. G. 15th New Hampshire Vols. in La. 202-pp. journal. 1862–68. Principal incidents attending a nine-month campaign in Louisiana includes two small sketches by Brown. Talks of a review—"the finest military dispay ever seen . . . with regts. in line incl. 6th. Mich., 15th. NH, 128th. NY and Zouaves. Generals Dow and Sherman were present . . . Sgt. Swain and Co. D shot an alligator seven feet long." Describes the taking of Ft. Hudson and of Gen. Dow being captured at Springfield. Last few pages describe time in a military hospital plus listing of fellow officers and privates with their hometowns. (A) Riba, March '94, $1100. .... *$1200–1300*

W.H. Brown Diaries. 1863–65. By a Sgt. from Co. B of the 92nd Illinois, attached to Rosencrans' army. Regiment saw service in Kentucky, Tennessee, and later, the Atlanta Campaign until '64. Timely reports on major battles. Includes two military vols. on tactics and Brown's G.A.R. documents, ribbons, pins. Also C.D.V. album of major dignitaries of the war. (A) Riba, Feb. '89, $1000.. .... *$1200–1300*

J.W. Egleston, Union Officer. Nov. 1862–May 1863. Egleston never identifies his unit; obviously has inside knowledge of troop activity and recounts numerous battles in detail. In pencil; pages are often loose, damaged, or faded. (A) Riba, Oct. '88, $300. .... *$300–350*

Elisha W. Ellis, Co. A., 4th Marine Prison Diary. 1863. Ellis, a native of Monroe, ME, was a private during the 1st Battle of Bull Run. Shortly thereafter he was captured and spent ten months in three Rebel prisons. This diary, written from Jan. 1 to Dec., covers his time in the infamous Libby Prison. Cover and several pages at the end missing. (A) Andrews & Andrews, Belfast, ME, Oct. '94, $2000. . . . . *$1800–2000*

Capt. Warren F. Griffin, Co. B., 2nd Maine Volunteers Prison, Diary. July 21, 1861–May 29, 1862. Griffin, of Stockton Springs, ME, was a fellow prisoner of Ellis (see above). His diary, in two morocco-bound vols., reads: "A Journal of Prison Life in Richmond, Va., Tuscaloosa, Ala. and Salisbury, N.C. by Prisoner of war taken by the Confederates at the Battle of Bull Run, July 21, 1861. . . ." Griffin was wounded at Bull Run and narrowly missed being killed *after* being taken prisoner. "The next instance a Company of what was called the Black Horse Cavalry . . . was upon us, commanding us to lay down our arms. A Sgt. cocked his carbine and aimed directly at my head." (Just in time, a Reb Gen. appears.) Griffin speaks up, "Gen., I hope that we shall not be shot down like dogs." (The Gen. ordered his men to stop firing.) (A) Andrews & Andrews, Oct. '94, $4800. . . . . *$4500–5000*

Elmer Howell of Bergen County, NY, Diary. 1862. Leather-bound; ink and pencil entries. Howell was a band member, serving in Col. Peter A. Porter's Regt., 8th NY Artillery. Reports that "Lee is acros (sic) the river and all of Meads artilery and cavelery are camping around her." Many entries discuss activities of the band. . . . .
. . . . *$350–400*

Gen. James Rowan O'Beine, Provost Marshall, Dist. of Columbia. April 1865. First-hand account of O'Beine's pursuit of Lincoln assassins Booth and Herold. He implicates Dr. Samuel Mudd (who set Booth's leg) as "a wild rabid man . . . a black hearted man and possibly a conspirator see after him." He describes another named assassin, Geo. Atzerodt—"looks like a German, a smiling man, ordinary." Later, O'Beine "learns from a colored man at White Point, Va. that two men with black whiskers had landed a boat and left it hastily." His final entry concludes that "Booth and Herald have made a circuit . . . in which they are and were not 5 miles distant." Eight vols. written in ink and pencil. Housed in leather with cloth slipcase. (A) Riba, Oct. '88, $5000. . . . . *$6000–7000*

DOCUMENTS AND MANUSCRIPTS

The following are all documents unless otherwise stated in parentheses at beginning of entry.

(Manuscript) Battlefield Dispatch from Confederate Gen. Pierre G. Beauregard. April 14, 1865; ALS (Autographed Letter Signed) octavo; written within hours of Lincoln's assassination; with copy of portrait, matted and framed. (D) $8500. . . . . *$6500–7500*

Collection of Letters, Military Papers of Lt. Charles W. Glaser, 17th NY Volunteer Infantry. 130 items; vivid descriptions of battles of Antietam and Fredericksburg. (A) $1400. . . . . *$1500–1700*

U.S. Grant Presidential Inaugural Invitation to "Mr. & Mrs. Mathew Brady." 1869. Engraved invitation in script addressed to the noted Civil War photographer and wife and signed by Grant. (A) Winter, March '86, $400. . . . . *$500–600*

Enrollment Card Signed by "Gray Ghost" Maj. John Singleton Mosby. Nov. 2, 1863. In black type—"Headquarters Mosby's Battallion (attesting that) Albert G. Lyon is an enrolled member of this command." Signed in cursive "Maj. John Singleton Mosby." (A) Riba, March '94, $7000. *$7500–8000*

President Franklin Pierce Signed Commission for Capt. David Farragut. 1842. Vignette of winged eagle at top and deities just above seal at bottom. (A) Winter, Oct. '84, $2300. . . . . *$2500–2600*

Union Capt. Christian Schurr's Account of Escape from Rebel Prison. Jan. 1865. Ten pages detailing Schurr's escape from a Macon, GA, prison for ten weeks. With the help of Negro slaves (they provide him with a Rebel uniform and he passes unnoticed through enemy lines), he makes his escape to Augusta and joins up with Gen. John Hatch's Coast Div. Includes Schurr's discharge papers. (A) Riba, Nov. '87, $900. . . . . *$1000–1100*

LETTERS

The following abbreviations may appear in the listings below: (LS/DS) Letter Signed or Document Signed; (AES) Autographed Enclosure or Endorsement Signed; (ALS) Autographed Letter Signed.

C.S.A. Gen. William W. Adams to Jefferson Davis. Jackson, MI, June 26, 1864. ALS, 2¼". Adams, who organized the 1st Mississippi Regt. in '61, sent this letter marked "Private" concerning Union troop movement and possible C.S.A. counterploys, including ferrying troops across the Mississippi River "in hopes that it may assist you in the great labor and responsibilities of your position—Wirt Adams." Fold lines and minor fading; last page shows evidence of mounting. (A) Riba, Oct. '88, $280. . . . . *$350–400*

C.S.A. P.G.T. Beauregard to Col. Jno. M. Huger. Mobile, AL, August 2, 1862. ALS, 2 pp. Beauregard letter from Bladon, AL, makes light of Huger's proposition "to lead to victory or to death the gallant sons of my own native Louisiana." The Gen. cites ill health as preventing it; plus "so long as the Union has command of the River with gunboats, the recovery of New Orleans must depend on our taking St. Louis, Louisville, Cincinnati, Washington and Baltimore." He concludes, " 'Nil Desperandi' is my motto and I feel confident that ere long, the glorius sun of Southern Liberty will appear more radiant than ever." Signed and with corrections in Beauregard's hand. (A) Riba, Oct. '88, $2500. . . . . *$3000–3500*

Miscellaneous Letters and Telegram, P.G.T. Beauregard to Gen. Johnson. Greensboro, April 18, 1865. ALS, 1 p., 8 v.o. signed "G.T.B." in pencil, relates to final surrender of Rebel troops as Johnson was in negotiation with Sherman. *$700–800*

C.S.A. Gen. Braxton Bragg to Maj. Gen. D.H. Maury. Jan. 2, 1985. Official *copy* of letter, 1 p., 4 total. Informs Maury that Pres. Davis desires Gen. Hood to concentrate Rodney's cavalry brigade at Opelika and, a.s.a.p., put in motion for the Dist. of No. Alabama. Copy is signed "J.T. Parrish Asst. Adjt. Gen." Minor tears and some ink fading. *$100–125*

C.S.A. Gen. Braxton Bragg to Col. J.C. Ives. Richmond, VA, July 5, 1862. LS, 3½ pp. Headquarters Dept. No. 2, Tupelo, MI. Bragg responds to Ives' note referring to an Alabama member of the C.S.A. Congress, criticizing his performance and describing his troops as mutinous. Bragg refutes these allegations in strong language, and relates circumstances and obstacles he's faced serving under his superior officers. He closes with, "when it comes to pervert facts, assert falsehood and engender discord and mutiny, it becomes my duty to ask for his (the accuser's) name that the evil may be provided against." Fold lines, one soiled running through Bragg's signature; minor staining. (A) Riba, Oct. '88, $2000. . . . . *$2500–3000*

Four Illustrated Letters from John Beidler Brobst. 1863. Brobst was from Buck County, PA, and decorated his letters to nephew with Penn. Dutch–style roosters, birds, and sheep (one in five colors). One letter states, "drawn and painted with a stick by your dearest uncle . . . in the bloody war of 1863." Brobst's rank and unit are unknown, but one letter was sent from the Lincoln Gen. Hospital, Washington, D.C., with sketches of the hospital buildings. (A) $900 . . . . *$1300–1500*

(Signed "Yours in Truth") John Brown to Friends. Sept. 3, 1857. AL, 1 p., 8 vo. The famous abolitionist writes from Tabor, IA, after a fundraising convention in the East. He requests a personal interview with friends from Kansas. It was in this period that Brown began to enlist recruits for an attack on Harpers Ferry, to come two years later. (A) Riba, Feb. '87, $850 . . . . *$1000–1200*

C.S.A. Gen. William H. Browne to Jefferson Davis. Jan. 2, 1865, in camp near Adams, SC. ALS, 2¹/₂ pp. Browne sharply criticizes Jeff Davis for making Augusta, GA, a military sub-dist. and assigning Gustavus Woodson Smith to command it (suggesting Gen. Thomas R. Cobb in his place). Browne calls Smith "a very low politician, utterly unscrupulous . . . Atlanta is too important to give up to Smith to surrender, fight he never will." A prophetic letter, as Smith surrendered at Macon in April '65. (A) Riba, Oct. '88, $400 . . . . *$500–600*

Signed Endorsement on Verso of ALS by C.S.A. Gens. Simon Buckner and Bushrod R. Johnson from Lt. Col. R. Dudley to Camp 37th Regt. Tennessee Vols. Nov. 8, 1862. Letter, originally directed to Lt. Cross Frayser, complains, "I have been under arrest now for eight days and have been shown no charges against me" (the only charges had been forwarded to Buckner). Buckner and Johnson sign statement that they have received charges. (A) Riba, Oct. '88, $190 . . . . . *$250–300*

Gen. Benjamin Butler Letters. Early 1860–1870. One from 1862 addressed to his mother. Most post-war and includes Butler family photos. Twenty letters. (A) Brookline, Nov. '92 . . . . *$1200–1400*

C.S.A. Gen. Benjamin Franklin Cheatham to Gen. Gideon Johnson Pillow. Sept. 16, 1861, Fulton State Line. ALS, 1¹/₂ pp. Cheatham informs Pillow that he is forced to move his troops from Mayfield to "this place" because no water could be found. Cheatham was a friend of U.S. Grant. Minor fold lines and a few ink smears. (A) Riba, Oct. '88, $150. . . . . *$200–250*

C.S.A. Gen. Clement C. Clay, Jr., from Ft. Monroe to His Wife. Aug. 21, 1865. Clay was elected to 1st C.S.A. Congress and a close friend of Jeff Davis. He surrendered when hearing that the Federal authorities suspected him of being a part of the Lincoln assassination plot. He writes of "good treatment given him by the soldiers and officers . . . with as much tenderness as their orders permitted." Clay, broken in health, was released after a year in prison and never officially charged. *$1800–2000*

C.S.A. Gen. Howell Cobb, HQ. Georgia Reserve, Macon, Ga., to Brig. Gen. A.W. Reynolds. ALS, 1¹/₃ pp. Cobb orders that a Col. Young report to him immediately so he may move to reinforce Gen. William Hardee at Jonesboro. Written a few days after Sherman moved into Atlanta. Pre-war Cobb was a former Speaker of the House, Gov. of Georgia, and Sec. of Treasury. In 1864, he was credited with the defeat of Gen. George Stoneman at Macon. (A) Riba, Oct. 88, $200. . . . *$250–300*

Gen. Samuel Cooper to Adj. and Insp. Gen's. Office, Richmond, Va. Jan. 25, 1864. LS, 1p. Cooper, the C.S.A.'s highest ranking officer, relays Jeff Davis' request for an investigation of "shameful outrages committed by troops under the command of Generals (Jos.) Shelby and (Jno.) Marmaduke in Missouri. . . . take such stringent measures as will prevent recurrance of similar acts." Docketed on verso: "Refd. to Maj. Gen. Magruder." Signed "W.R. Boggs, Brig. Genl." Fold lines, signature a bit light. (A) Riba, Oct. '88, $550 . . . . *$600–700*

C.S.A. Officer J. Lucius Cross Letters (17). 1861–1865. Florida native fought in Virginia during the Valley Campaign. Writes of receiving appointment by Gov. as Capt. of Artillery. His letter from Mt. View in March 1862: "God forbid that the vile foot of an invading foe like that of the North shall ever pollute our land by their unhallowed feet. I shall never cease hoping for success as long as we hold territory." In 1864 he writes of reassignment to duty as A.A.G. of Maj. Gen. Robert Hoke's Division, Gen. Lee's Army. "If I only lose a limb, I shall be perfectly satisfied." Toward the war's end he voices concern of "waiting until there's money in the state treasury to get any for my bonds.". *$800–900*

Confederate President Jefferson Davis to Col. Crafts Wright. 1865. ALS, 7 pp., 8 v.o. (Ex–Oliver Barrett collection; see Parke Bernet Sale Lot #777.) Expresses sadness over Lincoln's death, disavowing any part in the conspiracy, adding that (Andrew Johnson) "was a malignant man . . . without the power and generosity, which I believe Lincoln possessed. Davis adds, "Though several attempts were made to assassinate me during the war . . . neither I, or those associated with me, believed Mr. Lincoln to be particeps criminis." Signed "Jefferson Davis." (A) Riba, Oct. '88, $15,000. . . . . *$17,000–18,000*

Jefferson Davis. May 13, 1864. AE, 8-line initialed of an ALS. From Maj. Gen. J.G. Walker, Hdq. Div. near Alexandria, LA. Walker refutes charges made by Brig. Gen. Thomas Waul to Davis that at the fall of Vicksburg, Gen. Gustavus Smith might have attempted to rescue the Rebel garrison there, had not (Walker) interfered. Davis ordered a copy to be forwarded to Waul, requesting him to furnish "copy of *his* report on my conversation with him." Soiled fold line on verso, tipped onto large sheet. (A) Riba, Oct. '88, $850. . . . . *$900–1000*

From C.S.A. Gens. Bragg and J.C. Pemberton to Jefferson Davis. Boydton, VA, March 9, 1864. Two initialed dockets on an ALS, 1 p. Pemberton asks to be reassigned service in the field: "There is much less prejudice against me now than there was." Pemberton is alluding to the subject of his surrender at Vicksburg, the subject of a court of inquiry, and is seeking a vote of confidence from Davis. Davis, in pencil, instructs a secretary to make a copy of his (vague) reply to Pemberton. Pemberton was a northern-born C.S.A. Gen. and many felt him guilty of treason after the Vicksburg defeat. He resigned a few months after this letter and served the rest of war as Col. and Insp. of Artillery. (A) Riba, Oct. '88, $700. . . . . . *$800–900*

"Edw. Stanley Derby to Lord Lyndhurst on the Trent Affair." 1861. ALS, 10 pp., 8 v.o. Derby states that "war between England and the U.S. is inevitable." Tension had built up when the officers of Union warship *San Jacinto* had removed two C.S.A. commissioners, James Mason and John Slidel (who were en route to secure diplomatic recognition from France), from the British mail steamer *Trent* and held them as prisoners. The incident provoked British sympathy for the South. Derby goes into a long discourse over the U.S. contention that the two commissioners were ambassadors and thus considered "contraband of war." (A) $200.. . *$300–350*

C.S.A. Gen. Jubal Early to Col. A.S. Pendleton. April 26, 1864. ALS, 1 p. Pendleton was A.A. Gen. 2nd Corps., A.N. Virginia. Gen. Early has been arrested by Gen. R.S. Ewell following a curious and obscure incident, which somehow implicated Mrs. Ewell. (REF: *Lee's Lieutenants*, by Douglas Southall Freeman, Vol. III, p. 333.) Gen. Early desires to know the limits of his confinement. Less than a month after this letter, Gen. Early was reinstated and ironically succeeded Ewell in command of the 2nd Corps. (A) Riba, Oct. '88, $1000. . . . . *$1100–1200*

C.S.A. Gen. Richard S. Ewell to Col. Jordon, A.A.G. 1861. ALS, 1 p. oblong, 8 v.o. Ewell relays news of an express arriving from Springfield with news that 2000 Union troops were marching on that place. He adds that he's sending mounted parties on the roads in that direction, "and hold my command in readiness to see what is going on. I shall notify Gen. Early." On verso is endorsed "Gen'l Beauregard or Gen. Longstreet." Light folds; glue stain at top margin. (A) Riba, Oct. '88, $1200.. . . . . *$1500–1700*

Ex-President Millard Fillmore to Lincoln. May 16, 1863. ALS. (Endorsed by

Lincoln) interceding in behalf of nephew, Lt. George Fillmore, dismissed from his company for "alleged intemperance and inefficiency." (A) $22,000. . . . .
. . . . *$18,000–$20,000*

Millard Fillmore from Rome to Former Law Partner Solomon G. Haven. ALS, 4 pp. Talks of an audience with the Pope and declares that the countries he's visited "seem wholly unfit for a Republican form of government." Extraordinary content with deep insight into Fillmore's opinions and the political and religious climate of the pre–Civil War era. (A) Riba, June '88, $5500. . . . . *$6000–7000*

Nathan Bedford Forrest to Maj. Gen. Earl Van Dorn. March 30, 1864, Columbia, TN. ALS, 1 p. Reports complaints from around Columbia as to the conduct of the C.S.A. corps—"doing more harm than the Enemy would if they were here in person." He advises that "the entire command be moved forward to join their respective regiments . . . as they have succeeded in getting . . . men who won't fight and are worthless at home." Less than two months after this letter, Van Dorn was shot to death by a local doctor. Forrest was shot by an angry junior officer, but survived to lead his feared cavalry unit. After the war, he founded the notorious Ku Klux Klan. (A) Riba, Oct. '88, $3500. . . . . *$4500–5000*

C.S.A. Capt. Geo. Washington Gordon Letters (8). Written from Camp Chase Prison, and Johnsons Island, OH. March–Aug. 1862. Later, Gordon was released in a prison exchange and rose to rank of Gen. After the war he became Comdr.-in-Chief of United Confederate Veterans. He writes, "We are treated pretty well here and ought not to complain." Letters to young daughter indicate that some of his letters out "have been burned or cast aside as trash. We are daily expecting orders concerning Exchange. Tell the negroes howdy . . . I thank God I have no compunctions of conscience for my past course or for my present." (A) Riba, Nov. '87, $850. . . .
. . . . *$1000–1100*

U.S. Grant to E.M. Stanton, Sec. of War. May 26, 1865. ALS, 1 p. Re: appointment of Brig. Gen. Hugh Ewing to Maj. Gen.: "I think his recognition due." (A) Riba, June '88, $1000. . . . . *$1500–2000*

C.S.A. Gen. W.J. Hardee to Jefferson Davis. Dec. 1, 1863. ALS, 3 pp. Hardee asks to be relieved of his command because he feels unequal to the task and asks that new men be sent in because of "the demoralization among the troops caused by the late disaster" (Battle of Chicamauga). Hardee's request was granted, but in Oct. 1864 he was placed in Command of Dept. of So. Carolina, Georgia, and Florida. Historians rate him one of the C.S.A.'s ablest commanders. (A) Oct. '88, $2800. . .
. . . . *$3000–3500*

Lincoln's Secretaries' Letters (2). ALSs. (1) John Hay to James Redpath, (2) John Nicholay to Col. J. Tarbell. John Hay's letter of May 3, 1871, to James Redpath, the founder of the Boston Lyceum Bureau, states his willingness to lecture. (Hay had left the diplomatic corps in 1870 and was, at the time, editorial writer for the *NY Tribune*.) (A) Riba, Oct. '88, $380. Nicholay's letter of Dec. 22, 1862, responds to Tarbell's request for reinstatement following court martial: "the President will not entertain the application unless the applicant brings the governor's written declaration.". *$450–500*

William H. Herndon to Mr. Morris. Springfield, IL, Dec. 15, 1866. ALS, 4 pp. "I rec'd copy of a letter from Mr. L. to yourself; It is Lincoln all over, is it not? Enclosed is the slip of paper you sent . . . as *interpretation*. The letter is plain and does not need a slip to explain." Herndon was Lincoln's law partner in 1844 and remained his close friend until the President's death. (A) Oct. '88, $450. . . *$500–600*

Levi Hines, Vermont Union Volunteer Letters (75). 1862–64. Writes mostly to sister, but a few to brother and parents. In 1862: "You did have quite a piece of news, when you told me of Charley's marriage, but either you felt so bad or something else you forgot to tell me *who* he married. I hope it was not the one I was intending to have but I warrent it was. . . ." In Aug. 1863 he gets a pass to see Lincoln in Washington: "There was no austentatious (sic) display about our President or his escort, he rode a plain dappled gray horse which any country farmer might possess." Description of being fired upon near Cold Harbor, VA: "Since I commenced the last sentence a shell has come hissing over from the Rebel guns and burst in the air, but a short distance away." His last letter describes crossing pontoon bridge near Petersberg, VA, on June 18, 1864. There he was captured and sent to Andersonville Prison and died in the prison hospital less than a month later.. *$2000–2200*

Gen. "Fighting Joe Hooker" to Sen. Ira Harris. May 12, 1862. ALS. Hooker writes from a camp near West Point and is scathingly critical of Gen. McClellan's dispatches detailing the Battle of Williamsburg which slights Hooker's contribution to the victory: "Whether it arises from his ignorance of soldiership of unwillingness to appreciate it in any but his favorites." (A) Riba, March '89, $1500. . . . .
. . . . *$2000–2500*

Mass. Vol. Edmund L. Hyland Letters (20). 1863–65. To sisters, parents; three from sister to Hyland, who is hospitalized for unknown injury. Hyland writes, "I have got to get back to soldiering again . . . I sit on the ground and write on the bottom of my tin plate." *$250–300*

From Laura Keene, Forwarding a Letter Plus Small Scrap of Paper with Sentiment, Signed. Jan. 4, 1883. ALS, 1 p., 8 v.o. Laura Keene was an actress in the play *An American Cousin* on the night Lincoln was assassinated. (This was penned almost 20 years later, losing its timeliness.) Includes a CDV of Ms. Keene. . . . . . .
. . . . *$75–100*

Letters (20) of Capt. John Kelley of the Union Rifles of the 14th Indiana Vol. to his Wife, Mary. 1861–62. ALS. Describes numerous battles and includes his officer's commission and tintypes, including Rich Mountain and raiding a secessionist camp. His commanding officer, Gen. Landers, dies of a brain inflammation and is succeeded by Gen. James Shields. Kelley receives a mortal wound at the battle of Winchester a few weeks later. The last few letters are written by Mary Kelley who visits her husband in the Army hospital: "We are right here amid the groans of the wounded and dying. There are some of the finest ladies here, mostly Quaker . . . This is the noisiest place every anybody was in. The nurses that Mrs. Dix brought in from Washington the other day to take care of the wounded. They are a perfect nusance. Their cleanliness is more troublesome than the dirt." (A) March '94, $2500.
. . . . *$2500–3000*

C.S.A. Gen. Fitzhugh Lee Letters (3). Feb. 22, 1893. ALS. From Glasgow, VA: "I will adopt a phrase said to have been uttered by Gen. R.E. Lee, 'Duty is the sublimest word in the English language'." A TTS, from Lee to Gen. S.S. Carroll regarding a saber and sword belt being returned to Carroll. Also a CDV of Fitzhugh Lee in his C.S.A. uniform. Anthony photo. Ink identification below image. (A) Riba, March '89, $250.. . . . . *$250–300*

Mary Custis Lee (Widow of R.E. Lee) to Col. Charles Marshall. No date given, ca. 1870s. ALS. Mary Lee writes to Marshall, Lee's wartime aide and biographer, embittered by the attacks in Congress on her husband's memory. She details R.E. Lee's conflict with Gen. Winfield Scott and others, the confiscation of his belongings and other actions that made his entry into the C.S.A. inevitable. She tells of her husband's offer by Lincoln to become Supreme Comdr. of the Army. Lee remonstrated, "How can I take up arms against my state, my family, all I hold dear." Gen. Scott later told Lee it was the biggest mistake he ever made in his life. (A) Riba, Feb. '90, $3000.. . . . . *$3500–4000*

Gen. Robert E. Lee Amnesty Letter. Richmond, June 13, 1865. ALS, 1¼ pp., 8 v.o. To Gen. Ord, enclosing an application for amnesty, to be presented to Gen. Grant "provided it is not the inclination of the Govt. to prosecute me." An historic document. (A) Riba–Mobley, Feb. '87, $16,000. . . . . *$17,000–18,000*

Confederate Gen. Robert E. Lee. 1865. Retained letter signed by Lee (probably penned by aide); proposed using blacks as soldiers; offering emancipation to all who enlist. (A) $2200. . . . . *$2500–3000*

Gen. R.E. Lee to Maj. Earl Van Dorn, U.S., 1857. ALS. Both later resigned commissions and joined Confederate. (A) $4500. *$5000–6000*

Robert E. Lee to Gen. S. Cooper, Adj. Insp. Gen. Aug. 20, 1863. ALS. Lee recommends offering a position to Capt. William H. Rogers, who had been serving in Longstreet's corps as a vol. while seeking permanent duty. (A) Riba, March '89, $1800. . . . . *$2000–2500*

A. Lincoln—"Let this Man Polk Walters Take the Oath of Feb. 28, 1865 and be Discharged." AES. Written on the remaining portion of integral leaf of ALS from Gen. Thomas Wood to Gen. Ambrose Burnside, penned Feb. 15, introducing a Mr. Murray who apparently initiated Walters' discharge. Fold lines and age-toning to endorsement. (A) Riba, Oct. '88, $2500. . . . . *$3000–3500*

Abraham Lincoln to W.W. Danahower. ALS. Apologizing for canceling an interview; reflects that "time is a matter of life and death with me." Fine quality/Fine condition. (A) $7000. . . . . *$8000–9000*

To A. Lincoln from Gen. James McMillan. July 18, 1864. Lincoln autograph, 1 p., 7 lines. Endorsement signed on verso. While visiting White House, Gen. McMillan asked Lincoln to approve a recommendation for appointment of a Brigade Quartermaster. Lincoln requests that he put it in writing, and the Gen. accedes. Lincoln writes several lines on verso in pen, and signs, approving request for appointment. (A) Riba, March '88, $2500. . . . . *$3000–3500*

(Lincoln) Union Defense Council, NY. Request for Promotion of Col. Francis L. Vinton to Brig. Gen. 1862. Lincoln autograph, endorsement signed, 2 pp. Signed by a council of seven men, including John Jacob Astor, Jr. Lincoln notes on verso: "If Gen. Halleck recommends this appointment, I will make it not otherwise.—A. Lincoln, Sept. 10, 1862." (A) Riba, March '88, $2500. . . . . *$3000–3500*

Letter (Mary Todd Lincoln) to Quartermaster Capt. Thomas. Jan. 15, 1864. ALS, 1 p., 8 v.o. "Please give Capt. Stackpole and his friends transportation . . . to Norfolk and return. Mrs. Lincoln." Fold lines, some weakness, few light age spots. (A) Riba, March '88, $2000. . . . . *$2000–2100*

Letters (57) from John Moore, Medical Dir. of Army of the Potomac, and Brother Robert to Sister Mary. 1862. Vividly describes Battles of Fredericksburg, Vicksburg, and the Atlanta and Savannah Campaigns. He reports of partaking of crackers and cheese with "Old Abe" who happened to visit 5th corps headquarters. He later writes that 27,000 Rebel prisoners were immediately paroled after Vicksburg, because of the expense of feeding and transporting them, "plus requiring 6 or 8,000 of our own men as guard." (A) March '94, $8000. . . . . *$8000–9000*

Letters (63) to Robert and Cynthia More of Schoharie, NY, from Four Union Soldier Relatives. Nov. 27, 1861–June 20, 1865. ALS. Grouped as follows:

William Gallager: Boasts of wanting to "kill Jef (sic) Davis and bring them one of the gold buttons of his coat." Describes shells bursting from ramparts of Ft. Taylor. Displays blatant bigotry by portraying certain Pensacola (FL) residents as "miserable Niggars, and a race of mongerals (sic) called Dagoes (sic) . . . a meaner, abominal treacherous and thieving lot never cursed the bosom of mother earth."

Michael Hubbard, of the 134th Regt. of NY Vol., writing from a camp near Fredericksberg: "We are sick of war, we can stand on picket and talk with the Rebs . . . we let them have coffee for tobacco . . . Our Captain is dead." Hubbard also describes his part in the battle of Lookout Mt. His last letter: "Johnson (Gen. Joseph E. Johnson) has surrendered his whole army to Sherman and tomorrow we start for home . . . we got to march to Richmond . . . but the war is over."

Alpheus Haner, member of Army of the Cumberland, at camp at Lookout Valley, TN, Jan. 9, 1864: "War is about to end, old Jeff has called for 60 days to come to some settlement . . . the rebs are about played out anyway, we have made a finish of old Longstreet, he is dead and old Bragg can't fight anymore." Later, in a Nashville military hospital, "I would like to see this cruel war end for it has gone far enough and there has been enough blood shed."

Peter More, describing Lee's surrender to Grant: "I wish you could have been there . . . cannons were fired . . . we took 2,000 prisoners (relates parade to City Point) . . . We had a live rooster and a pig strapped fast to the mule's back." (A) Riba, Oct. '88, $2000. . . . . *$2200–2300*

Letters (3 CDVs, over 41 ALSs) of (Union) Col. Samuel C. Pierce. 1862–63. Relates news of Rebel Gen. Longstreet at Swift Creek, with a large force; also of Gen. Bragg and Johnson; the Union's relations with France on the Mexico question; cites British involvement. In a letter to his sister from Harpers Ferry, after visiting the battleground the following day: "the rebels lay pild (sic) up 3 and 4 deep. We have been whipping the Rebels like fur." Description of Rebel prisoners taken: "About half of them had no shoes." Collection includes letters from a Lt. Vaughan with Gen. Nathaniel Bank's expedition. (A) Riba, Feb. '89, $700. . . . . *$800–900*

Gen. Fitz-John Porter to Col. Wright. ALS, 1^1/2 p., 8 v.o. Letter (with copies directed to Nicholay, Hay, and Gen. Burnside) was part of a 24-year crusade by Porter to clear himself of court-martial charges that he'd disobeyed orders at 2nd Battle of Bull Run. He refers to "lies in book by Secretaries Hay and Nicholay." (REF: Nicholay letter and also *Abraham Lincoln* biography in Bibliography.) *Note*: Many scholars subscribe to view that Gen. Porter's offense was not poor combat leadership at 2nd Bull Run, but indiscretion in criticizing a superior—he did nothing to conceal his low opinion of Gen. John Pope. (A) Riba, Oct. '88, $350. . . . . *$500–600*

Col. Putnam from the 7th NH Reg. 1855–1863s. Putnam was later killed at Ft. Wagner. Included are a number of letters while a cadet at West Point (one describes Col. Robert E. Lee getting his commission in the Mexican War); several letters while serving as military commander at St. Augustine, FL; also while he was a topographical engineer in the late 1850s. Includes letter describing doing survey duty with Capts. Meade and Turnbil; letters to prisoners of war; 5 letters to C.S.A. Gen. Weis of VA; one from Nathaniel Tyler, editor of the *Richmond Enquirer*, calling for Gen. Braxton Bragg's removal. A letter from home from Putnam's grandson relating that he killed a Negro and some Yankees. (A) Brookline, NH, Nov. '92, $1500. . . . . *$2000–2500*

Letters (58 total) of Michael Quinan, Hudson Co., NY Union Soldier. Written to sisters and friends. Relates encounters with Rebel forces while serving with Gen. Bank's Div.; describes battles of Fort Hudson and Pontchatoula; capturing of prisoners, including 20 Indians. A C.S.A. officer offers $1800 bribe to be freed. Seeing remnants of the *Monitor-Merrimac* sea battle while aboard steamship *Asarego*; also the harassment of Negro regiments by the Zouaves. Also 25 miscellaneous letters to Quinan from Irish relatives. (A) Feb. '87, $1500. . . . . *$1800–2000*

Jared Richards Letter Describing Battle of *Monitor* and *Merrimac*. March 1862. Vivid, detailed account of famed ironclads battle by a young Union midshipman. (A) Winter, March '86, $400. . . . . *$600–700*

Letters (16) of Newton and George Smith, Both of the 24th NYS Vols. 1861–64.
Written to their younger brother Asa. Note with letter states that George was killed
at Battle of Bull Run. July 1861: "Last night we hurd cannon adin off towards Richman and they all think that McLellan is in Richman now." Oct. 1861 at Arlington
Heights: "They was some men went up in a baloon yesterday and they got shot at
with two cannon balls and they came about five rods from them . . . tell the folks . . .
we are camped in Gen. Lee's land. He is the southern general you have read about."
Feb. 1861, Upton's Hill: "Gen. McLellan said . . . he shall advance on Manassas
and he says he shant go there without he takes a lot of artillery. He has got eighty
six thirty two pounders rifle cannons over one hundred batteries." Feb. 1864 at
Camp Parole: Newton writes of sending money home and the possibility of re-
enlisting for 3 more years. *$450–600*

Edwin Stanton and Horace Greeley. 1865. ALS. Two copies of telegraph mes-
sages from Sec. Stanton to Edw. Pierrepont of NY. Stanton pushes for a military
trial for the accused conspirators in Lincoln assassination, where rules would be
less restricting and punishment would be meted out swiftly. Horace Greeley sharply
criticized Stanton's harsh measures. Stanton talks of prosecuting Greeley crimi-
nally and also by civil suit. The suit never materialized but enmity between the two
continued for years. (A) Riba-Mobley, May '86, $3000. . . . . *$3500–4000*

Charles Sumner. ALS. By abolitionist, January 9, 1855, to clerk of Senate: "I have
the honor to acknowledge receipt of the Senate and House Journals. . . ." . *$75–100*

Union-C.S.A., Van Valkenburgh—A Family Divided. 1861–65. Several ALS
from Robert B. Van Valkenburgh, who fought for the 107th Regt. of NY; one from
1865, after being appointed Acting Commission of Indian Affairs by Pres. A. Johnson. A brother, David H., also with the Union, is shot and killed while in command
of the 1st Artillery at Fair Oaks and there are a number of letters written by him to
his mother. Still another brother, Gerit S. (referred to as Gerry), fought for the Confederacy: a 4-p. ALS from 1861. Reports on the convention of the Gulf Confederacy in 1861 and describes how Louisiana has joined the C.S.A. Arkansas is ready to
break from the Union. Later, Gerit is captured by the North and sends a number of
letters from prison on Johnson's Island. In a poignant letter to his mother in 1865,
he begs forgiveness for causing a rift in the family. Thirty-five items, including a
lifesize gilded plaster bust of Robert. (A) Riba, July '91, 1900. . . . . . . *$2000–2500*

Timothy Vedder, 14th Regt. NY. 1861–63, 43 ALS. In May 1861, when Vedder
describes barracks life at Camp Douglas near Philadelphia; then on to Arlington
Hgts., VA; describes retreating soldiers from battlefields: ". . . from Bull Run . . .
some with arms broken and taken off and limping on one leg." Vedder is a brother to
the man that killed Elmer Ellsworth, the First Union soldier to be killed in the war.
Relates storming of Munson Hill; burning of Union houses and barns by the Rebs;
guarding Carlingcourt's reconnaissance ballroom; McClellan's review of 70,000
troops; combat with Lee's army between Harrison's Landing and Richmond; battles
of Antietam and Fredericksburg. (A) Riba, March '89, $1000. . . . . *$1100–1200*

James White, Unionville, CT. 1862–64, 12 ALS. Talks of his cavalry unit skirmishing near the Rapidan; capturing a Rebel working party of 150 who were building a bridge. Gen. Reno and Capt. Woodruff come to his unit's aid in helping them
ford river. Later, White fights at Chancellorsville; is captured and taken to Ft.
Bernard, VA. After becoming ill in prison, he is furloughed. Tells of rumors of
joining Burnside. Final letter is one of condolence, following White's death in Atlanta in 1864, written by one of his comrades. Some ALS include covers. (A) Riba,
March '89, $500. . . . . *$600–700*

Dr. Henry Wirz, Commandant of Infamous Andersonville Prison. ALS. Written 12 days prior to his hanging, protesting his innocence. *$2500–3000*

Diary, prison diary of Captain Warren F. Griffen, Co. B, 2nd Maine Volunteers, July 21, 1861–May 29, 1862. Sold for $2,000 at Andrews & Andrews Auction in October 1994, $1,800–$2,000. (Photo courtesy of Mark Sisco)

Furniture and
Decorative Accessories

Box (Decorative). Anti-slavery box. 1840s. William Hackwood "Am I not a man and a brother" slave in chains design. Black silhouette on enameled oval box. (See also Ceramics section, i.e., jewelry rosettes and ceramic plates.) *$2000–2500*

Box (Decorative). Eagle with crossed cannons. 1864. Inlaid mahogany box with numerals "18" and "64" flanking winged eagle and patriotic shield. Small stars; furled U.S. flags; $3^{1}/_{2}$" h. × $9^{1}/_{4}$" w. × 12". Possibly for papers or jewelry. (A) Oct '92, $1800. . . . . *$1800–2000*

Chair. Gen. James Longstreet. Ca.1862. Morovian-style carved oak chair. Relief portrait bust of Longsteet carved into high scalloped back. Flat plant seat; pegged back. *$1200–1300*

Chair. Folding camp chair with carpet seat. (A) Dias, Nov. '94, $60. . . . . . *$50–75*

Collar Box. Chester A. Arthur. 1880. Brown gutta percha lid with bas relief bust likeness of vice-presidential running mate to Garfield (see below). *$200–225*

Collar Box. William H. English. 1880. Brown gutta percha hinged lid with bas relief bust likeness of English. Wood bottom. Democrat match to Garfield and Arthur variants. *$200–225*

Collar Box. James Garfield. 1880. Brown gutta percha lid with bas relief bust likeness of Garfield. Wood bottom. License stamp of "The Standard Colar Co." appears on bottom; 5" × 5" × 3" d. Originally licensed under 1872 patent. *$225–250*

Collar Box. Rutherford Hayes and William Wheeler Inaugural. "Our President and Vice-President, 1877." Jugate portraits. Shows girl on ladder picking cherries from tree. "Cherry Ripe Collar Co." Oval tin, $4^{3}/_{4}$" × 3" d. with wire handle. . *$200–250*

Desk. Appomattox Courthouse desk. 1865. Mahagony with two shelves and turned legs; on casters. One of three used at official signing of surrender papers by C.S.A.'s Gen. Lee to U.S. Grant. Described by Maj. Thomas Gideon Welles, an eyewitness to signing. Includes notarized letter and bill of sale from descendent Thomas Welles Brainard. Has original finish. (A) Riba, Feb. '86, $15,000. . . . .
. . . . *$15,000–17,000*

Document Box. Civil War vintage, leather covered. Brass studs; paper-lined interior, stamped "B. Goss." (A) Dias, Nov. '94, $75. *$75–85*

Doorstop. "G.A.R." 1880s. Standing Union trooper wearing cape, leaning on musket. 9" h., cast iron, black finish. *$200–250*

Doorstop. "U.S. Grant." Early 1900s. Match to Lee doorstop following with identical hatless pose. Three-dimensional painted cast iron, $7^{1}/_{2}$" h. *$100–125*

Doorstop. "Infantryman." Late 19th century. Painted cast iron, deep relief figural of Union soldier with musket standing at attention.. . . . . *$35–50*

Doorstop. "Robert E. Lee." Early 1900s. Cast-iron, three-dimensional painted fig. Lee wears gauntlets; stands with hat in one hand, the other rests on sword hilt, 7¹/₂" h.. . . . . *$75–100*

Doorstop. "McKinley Memorial." 1901. Cast iron, three dimensional; bust of McKinley at top; birth and death dates at base of bust. Soldier and sailor flank bas relief portrait of Liberty. Bas relief Liberty bust; inscribed below: "His Last words were, 'Thy Will be done'." 12¹/₂" h., black finish. *$250–275*

Doorstop. "Gen. McClellan on Horseback." Early 1900s; bareheaded equestrian in deep relief cast iron. Figural painted white with black stand. Pose similar to bronze shelf plaque. (See Statues and Statuettes chapter.) *$75–100*

Doorstop. "Rhett." 1930s. Popularity of doorstop is enhanced by assumption that "Rhett" is Rhett Butler of Margaret Mitchell's Civil War novel *Gone with the Wind*. Rhett has top hat, sideburns, and natty bow tie; 8" × 5¹/₂"; bronze finish. . . . .
. . . . *$300–325*

Gun Rack. Civil War–vintage musket rack. Has brass cannon fittings. Holds 50 muskets. Made by Anc. & Hon. Artillery Co., Boston. (A) Dias, Nov. '94, $550. . .
. . . . *$500–550*

Knick-knack Shelf. U.S. Grant. 1870s. Carved walnut bas relief bust image of U.S. Grant; stars and stripes shield above, eagle on globe below bust. (A) $440. . . .
. . . . *$450–500*

Sewing Bird "Zouave." Cast-iron figure with flag, cannon. High relief; 5" h; red, green paint. Table clamp and hinged tension weight for thread. *$850–950*

Trunk. Civil War–vintage leather accessory trunk. Brass bail handle. Hide-covered, studded with marbled paper interior, 15" × 9" × 7". (A) Dias, Nov. '94, $95. . . . . *$100–125*

Trunk. Civil War–vintage leather. Western-style, small dome-top trunk. (A) Dias, Nov. '94, $75. . . . . *$75–85*

Umbrella Stand. Union Gens., Grant, Meade, and Sherman. 1865. 3¹/₂" h. Pictorials of officers; on glass-covered panels encased in six-sided walnut frame, base. (A) $400. . . . . *$450–500*

Window, Stained Glass. James Garfield. Ca. 1870s. Ruby-colored frosted window with portrait of Garfield, 28" × 18". Border is frosted white with dragon head and scepter design. Name appears in ornate border at base of window. Possibly issued for barber shops or pharmacies. *$250–300*

Window, Stained Glass. U.S. Grant. Ca. 1870s. Match to above. Ruby-colored frosted window with Grant's portrait, 28" × 18". *$250–300*

Window, Stained Glass. Abraham Lincoln. 1870s. Match to above. Ruby-colored frosted window with Lincoln's portrait. *$300–350*

Window, Stained Glass. Abraham Lincoln. 1870s. Lincoln portrait with various shades of stained glass vs. rub glass. *$650–700*

Window, Stained Glass. "Columbia." 1870s. Image of Lady Liberty holds furled U.S. flag and patriotic shield is at her feet. Issued in conjunction with above windows, 28" × 18". (A) Riba, Feb. '86, $150. . . . . *$200–225*

Wood Stove. Lewis Cass. 1870. Cast-iron Franklin-type stove with bas relief portrait of Cass. Matte black finish. Has Zachery Taylor match. *$1200–1500*

Box, decorative, "Eagle with crossed cannons," 1864. Inlaid mahogany box, 9 ½" × 12". Sold for $1,900 at Skinner Auctions in October 1992, $1,800–$2,000.

Left: *Appomattox Courthouse desk, 1865. Mahogany with two shelves and turned legs, on casters. One of the three used at official signing of surrender papers. Sold for $15,000 at Riba Auctions in February 1986, $15,000–$17,000.* Right: *Chair, ca. 1862. Morovian-style carved oak chair with relief portrait bust of Gen. James Longstreet on back, $1,200–$1,300.*

Doorstops. Left: *"Robert E. Lee," early 1900s, cast-iron, 7 ½" high, $75–$100.* Right: *"U.S. Grant," early 1900s, cast iron, 7 ½" high, $100–$125.*

GLASSWARE

Bottle. William H. English. 1880. Figural blown bust image. Opening in head; possibly cologne or tonic, 11" h. Ardent opponent of secession; nominated for V.P. on Dem. slate with Hancock. Image is often attributed to be that of Robert E. Lee. . . .
. . . . *$400–500*

Bottle. U.S. Grant tomb bottle. Early 1900s. Opaque white; possibly sold at tomb dedication ceremonies. Opening appears on roof of tomb. *$35–50*

Bottle (Tonic). George McClellan. 1864. Figural pedestal bust, mold blown glass. Jet black, 6" h. Match to Scott bottle below. *$500–600*

Bottle (Tonic). Winfield Scott. 1864. Figural pedestal bust, mold blown glass. Jet black; 6" h. with opening in top of head for tonic. *$500–600*

Compote. Old Abe Battle Eagle. Covered compote in clear glass with frosted figural image of famous Battle Eagle as lid handle. Old Abe was mascot of 8th Wisconsin Co. C. Regt. (known as the "Eagle Regiment" in war) surviving 36 battles and skirmishes; was once wounded in wing. Appeared in numerous parades and at Grant's inaugural. Design also featured in four-piece table set, plus sauce dish and salt dish. *$300–350*

Cup. Benjamin Harrison. 1888. Large medallion bust portrait of Harrison. Light amber. Pattern also exists in clear glass. *$75–125*

Flask. Blaine–Logan. 1884. Clear crystal pink flask with medallion portrait with names below; Blaine on obverse; Logan on reverse. *$75–100*

Flask. McKinley–Roosevelt "Our Candidates." 1900. Partially clear glass, in center obverse is painted jugate bust images, plus eagle shield and White House; ¹/₂ pint. Metal loops at sides from red, white, blue cord. Metal screw cap. *$350–400*

Goblet. U.S. Grant. 1872. Bust medallion embossed portraits of Grant and running mate Henry Wilson, 6¹/₄", handblown. *$500–600*

Goblet. Horace Greeley. 1872. Bust medallion embossed portraits of Greeley and running mate B. Gratz Brown, 6¹/₄" h. Match to Grant goblet above. *$600–650*

Inkstand. Little Eva and Uncle Tom. 1860s. Staffordshire-type figural of named characters. Attached sander and inkwell (top missing). (A) $130. . . . . . . *$150–200*

Knick-knack Shelf. Carved walnut bas relief bust image of U.S. Grant. 1870s. Stars and stripes shield above, eagle on globe below bust. Fine Quality, Fine Condition. (A) $440. . . . . *$450–500*

Mug. "Union Forever." 1870s. U.S. (possibly Centennial); clasped hands motif. (D) $225 . . . . *$200–300*

Mug (Shaving). James Garfield. 1880. White milk glass with bas relief portrait of Garfield head and leaf motif. Separate compartment on handle to hold shaving brush. Garfield's wife Lucretia appears on reverse. *$800–900*

Plate. John Logan. 1884. Classic 11" circular pattern clear glass with frosted bust portrait of Rep. V.P. candidate. Set includes Logan's running mate James Blaine; also Dems. Cleveland and Hendricks. *$200–250*

Plate. John Logan. 1884. Similar to above but in 11½" size within rectangular frame and stippled ivy leaves. Handle on each side. Part of paired set with James Blaine. . . . . *$175–200 (each)*

Plate. McKinley. 1896 campaign. Designed by David Baker, Canton Glass Co.; milk glass ribbon plate with interlaced gold ribbon in gothic border and bas relief bust likeness in gold to symbolize his favoring the Gold Standard. *$150–175*

Plate. McKinley. 1896 campaign. Black amethyst ribbon plate with gold bas relief bust of McKinley; gold silk ribbon interlaced in gothic border; match of Bryan, except in silver. *$250–275*

Plate "McKinley." Ca. 1900 campaign. Lacy milk glass; with oval bust photo of McKinley under layer of clear glass; framed by blue paint; outer rim in gold; 8¼". *$125–150*

Sugar. William McKinley. 1894. Heisey cut glass, clear with bas relief bust image; fanciful filligree swirls. Domed top (often found missing). Bryan match. *$75–100*

Tray. Blaine–Logan. 1884. Crystal glass with leaf border and bust portraits of Rep. slate in frosted square. Double-handled. Cleveland–Hendricks match. . . . *$125–150*

Tumbler. Civil War ordinance decoration, U.S. 1860s. Cannon with grape, American flag with 34 stars. (D) $350 . . . . *$400–500*

Wall Plaque. James Garfield. 1878. Milk glass. High relief bust of Garfield; possibly a memorial piece. Ridged reverse with hole for looping. *$125–150*

Wall Plaque. Benjamin Harrison. 1888. Milk glass. Very similar to above. *$75–100*

Wall Plaque. Abraham Lincoln. 1864. Milk glass. High relief bust of Lincoln centered in oval shaped with latticed pattern of split rails. White with textured surface. (Sometimes found with traces of brown paint.) *$450–500*

Wall Plaque. William McKinley. 1901. Milk glass memorial item; similar to above. *$50–75*

LIGHTING DEVICES

OIL LAMPS

Gens. Grant, Sherman, Sheridan. Lamp with iron base, brass font; frosted glass chimney with black transfer bust images of three Gens.; Gilt arches over portraits. Has been electrified. *$600–650*

"Harrison 1892." Pink Bristol glass base with handpainted legend and floral above and reverse. Base is 4½" h. Plain glass chimney on brass holder. (A) Riba, Feb. '86, $300 . . . . *$350–400*

Benjamin Harrison, 1888. Bust portrait of Harrison and flags in sepia on frosted glass chimney background. Cleveland match. *$175–200*

Lincoln and Washington Double-Globed Centennial Lamp. Ca. 1876. Two 10" glass globes (similar to milk glass, but lighter weight) surround fluted chimney; bust images of Lincoln–Washington molded in high relief. Globes painted cranberry/turquoise. Heavy metal base. Electrified. *$1200–1400*

(Lincoln) Ft. Monroe Conference Lamp. 1865. Historic brass lamp, 8" h. with original glass globe; used in Lincoln's bedroom on night of secret conference between Lincoln, Stanton, and Charles Sumner, with Gens. Grant and Wool. From collection of Capt. Samuel C. Wright, a relative of Wool and obtained from the family. Wright himself was a Medal of Honor winner for his heroism at Antietam. Photocopies of documentation papers and notarized letter from Norman Flyderman attesting authenticity. (A) Riba, Nov. '87, $2800. . . . . *$3000–3500*

McKinley and Hobart. 1892. Etched glass chimney, jugate portraits in white. Crossed flags and G.O.P. shield. *$225–250*

PARADE LANTERNS

John Bell Salem Lantern. 1860. Glass. Rebus image (large Bell) and "Salem" (MA). Four-sided glass, with black over cobalt blue colors. Bell was pro-slavery as well as pro-Union. Ran as pres. under Constitutional Union Party. *$2000–2500*

Henry Clay. 1844. Tin. High domed with top loop for carrying, punched hole design throughout to emit light. "Clay" letters pierced into door. *$500–600*

Fillmore–Donelson. 1844. Tin. Political campaign lantern as above, for pro-slavery slate. *$600–700*

Garfield–Arthur. 1880. Paper. Red, white, and blue accordian paper lantern; lettering of candidates and stars. *$225–250*

U.S. Grant. 1872. Paper. Bust portrait in circle with geometric and floral design. Other panels feature bucolic vignettes from Grant's life. Six-paneled, expandable paper shell by Sprague & French Mfg., Norwalk, OH. Reds, green, and brown. Hanging wire, candle holder, 23" h............................ *$300–450*

"Indiana for Grant and Colfax." 1868. Glass. Transparent glass panels; four-sided, with above motto plus "The People's Choice; United States Grant/I am For Peace/Taxpayers Want Peace; Democracy Sold Out Cheap/Gone Down With Rebel Colors Flying. Seymour and Blair Uniform/Aristocracy/Blair Rebel Champion.".. .... *$2000–2500*

Grant–Wilson. 1872. Paper. Accordian-pleated style with candidates names and stars appearing in dark blue and light purple, 12" h. × 7¹/₂" dia.......... *$300–350*

Greeley–Brown. 1872. Accordian-pleated paper and cardboard with letter and pair of clasped hands (above candidate's names) in fuschia and blue over beige, 12" h. × 7¹/₂" dia. *$300–350*

(Harrison) "Protection/We Will Support the Interests of America. Tippecanoe and Morton Too/1850/1888." 1888. Paper. Vignettes on panels of log cabin, Capitol building, cider barrel, and a host of Benjamin Harrison's grandfather, William Harrison's symbols from 1840 race. Six-paneled expandable paper, multicolored. *$300–350*

Rutherford B. Hayes and William Wheeler. 1876. Paper. Mfgr. by F. Morandi, Boston. "Toppans Pat. Waterproof" under tin lip. Accordian-pleated with tin candle socket attached to cardboard bottom disk. Blue, black, red, or brown ink. Stars and bust portraits of Rep. candidates, 9¹/₂" h. Tilden and Hendricks match..... *$250–300*

A. Lincoln. 1865. Paper. Accordian-type wire bail handle lantern. Tin candle holder. Sides: Lincoln bust portrait, "Union Freedom," "1776—George Washington" on verso with portrait. Possibly a memorial or commemorative item. (A) $200. .... *$200–250*

Lincoln and Johnson. 1864. Glass. Three-sided opaque glass-paneled tin lantern with Alexander Gardner image of Lincoln. Third panel is glass. *$2000–2500*

(Lincoln) "Liberty and Union." 1860. Glass. Three-sided opaque glass. Crude lettering, black painted on white glass. *$1500–2000*

(Lincoln) "22nd Ward Wide Awakes." 1860. Glass. Railroad-type lantern; globe with "Cleat" pattern, made by Sandwich Glass. Lettering with remnants of old blue paint and gilt lettering. Tin flared base with large ring handle........ *$1000–1100*

(McClellan) "The Union It Was." 1864. Paper. Four-sided paper lantern. Bust portrait of McClellan with above slogan plus "Equity and Justice" and "Trial By Jury," 8" h. × 8¹/₂" w.. *$450–500*

McClellan. 1864. Glass. Three-sided opaque glass-paneled tin lantern with litho bust portrait and slogan "Union & the Constitution" panels.......... *$1200–1500*

Seymour–Blair. 1868. Accordian-pleated 7¹/₂" dia × 12" h. cardboard and paper. Beige background with purple and dark blue stars and tasseled ribbon design. *$300–325*

PARADE TORCHES

Ballot Box Torch. 1880. Probably Garfield–Arthur Rep. slate. (Some variants have ptd. title and "Garfield & Arthur" painted on glass.) Ptd. by J.M. Adams, Chicago,

4" × 10" overall, red, white paint. Glass canister globe contained with upper and lower metal supports, with vertical posts at each corner.. . . . . *$200–250*

(Harrison) Beaver Top Hat. 1888. Tin figural hat with brass wick holder extending from top. Black finish, 10¹/₂" h., 6¹/₂" w., 6¹/₂" l. *$200–250*

(Harrison) Log Cabin. 1888. Old black paint. Figural with pierced pattern on sides. 6¹/₂" × 5". (A) Riba, Oct. '86, $200. . . . . *$250–300*

Harrison and Morton Swivel Canister Torch. 1888. Back-to-back b&w bust portraits of candidates.. . . . . *$300–325*

Hartford Wide Awake Double-Swivel Torch. 1860. Identified by the shorter, more squat contours of the canister and its ability to swivel in two directions.. . . . . .
. . . . *$200–250*

(Lincoln) Eagle. 1860. Two-sided gilt figural copper eagle with double burners, one in each wing. Similar to Eagle Torchiere carried by Roman Legions. Ex– Bernard Barenholtz collection, 12" h. × 9" w. × 2¹/₂" d. (A) Riba, 1987, $2800. . . .
. . . . *$3500–4000*

Hurrah for Lincoln Axe Torch. 1860. Figural tin ax canister torch with wick at top of axe butt. Flat gray or black. *$350–400*

Hurrah for Lincoln. 1860. Double-swivel canister torch with red letters and trim over buff, 15¹/₂" h. *$750–800*

(McKinley–T. Roosevelt) "Four More Years of the Full Dinner Pail." 1900. Figural dinner pail of slogan pierced in side to emit light, 9", Hake 3016. Other versions carried "Four More Years of Same Dinner Pail" slogan. (A) Riba, Oct. '86, $500. . . . . *$550–600*

Rifle Torch. 1860. Wood-carved rifle with swivel canister at end of barrel. Used by paraders in manual of arms performances. Unless precisely identified with candidate's name from 1860s, an example could stem from the 1880s when they were more popularly used. *$250–300*

Figural Rooster Torch. 1856. Probably for Buchanan candidacy. Painted red, white figural.. . . . . *$350–400*

Six-Sided Star Figural. 1860 and 1864. Painted tin in red, white, blue. Most often found unmarked as to party preference. Possibly used at Lincoln rallies and parades. *$200–225*

Left: *"Wide Awake" cleat pattern sandwich glass and tin lantern, with "22nd Ward Wide Awake" gilded on the globe, $700–$800.* Right: *Lincoln's personal brass oil lamp, used at a secret conference at Fortress Monroe between President Lincoln and Generals Grant and Wool. From the Samuel Wright collection. Sold for $2,800 at Riba Auctions in March 1988, $3,000–$3,500.*

NEWSPAPERS AND
NEWSWEEKLIES

"Acts of Bravery." Newspaper, April 10, 1985. *The Banner of Freedom* military newspaper, Sumter, SC; pub. by E.H. Smith, Co. D. 56th NYV. News of Union acts of bravery; notice to local citizenry informing them they have been defeated. Official announcement that Richmond, Petersburg, Mobile, and Selma have been taken. Printed on one side only. *$250–300*

"*Alabama* Sinks Off Cherbourg." Newsweekly, *Harper's Weekly*, July 23, 1864. Full-cover lithograph of dramatic sinking of notorious Rebel warship. Union rescue boats from U.S.S. *Kearsarge* attempt to pick up survivors. Portraits and biographies of Capt. John Winslow of the *Kearsarge* and Pirate Capt. Raphael Semmes of the *Alabama*. Full-page map of Rebel invasion in Maryland. Panoramic two-pager of Grant's Petersburg Campaign; Brady photos of Gens. Meade and Burnside with staff. *$75–100*

Antietam—Sept. 20, 1862—"The Great Victory." Bloodiest Battle in American History. Newspaper, *New York Times*. Turning point of Civil War. Victory gave Lincoln enough breathing room to enact his Emancipation Proclamation. Bold headlines proclaim "Battle of Antietam Creek . . . full particulars from our special correspondant. The Most stupendous battle of modern times. Vividly detailed accounts." *$125–150*

Antietam—"Movements of Our Army in Maryland." Newspaper, *Richmond Enquirer,* Sept. 23, 1862. Makes counterclaim of victory for C.S.A., "Intelligence was received last evening of the recent Confederate victory at Sharpsburg. The spirits of the troops, flushed with victory, high and warm." *Enquirer* adds acidly that "reports in the Northern Newspapers prove to have been sheer and shameless fabrications.".
. . . . *$150–175*

Fall of Atlanta. Newspaper, Sept. 19, 1864, *New York Daily Tribune,* 8 pp. Announces complete Union victory. Front-page map, "Flanking of Gen. Hood's Army & Capture of Atlanta." Also article of how news of McClellan's presidential aspirations elated the Rebels. *$175–200*

Battle at Crooked Run. Newspaper, Aug. 25, 1864, *New York Times*. Reportage of Gen. G.A. Custer's cavalry at Crooked Run, Nathan Forest's bold raid, and an attack on Memphis. Mosby's Rangers daring attack at Snicker's Gap Road. Feature on treatment of Federal prisoners in the South. *$75–100*

Battle of the Ironclads, Hampton Roads, VA. Newspaper, March 15, 1862, *New York Tribune,* 8 pp. Describes battle of *Monitor* vs. *Merrimac* on March 9. Heralds beginning of modern warfare on the seas. New Madrid, MO, is captured by Union after heavy cannonading by Gen. John Pope. Rebels fled to Island No. 10. A map shows positions at New Madrid. *$175–200*

Battle of Lookout Mountain Plus Grant and Hooker's Front Line Dispatches. Newspaper, Dec. 7, 1863, *The Oregonian Statesman.* Many other battles cited, including siege of Knoxville. Reports on Lincoln's advice to Gen. Joseph Hooker: "In passing through Kentucky, beware of Bourbon county." An article on Rebel terms for peace. In addition, colorful local coverage of Old West mining, murder, and mayhem. Only known copy of this issue. *$150–175*

Battle of Pea Ridge (AR). Newspaper, March 14, 1862, *New York Semi-Weekly Tribune.* Incisive coverage of the most pivotal battle in the Trans-Mississippi West. Reports death of C.S.A. Gen. Ben McCulloch by sharpshooters, with 1000 prisoners taken; official report of Gen. Curtis. Also good coverage of Battles of Bull Run and Manassas, capture of Cockpit Point, Winchester, VA, skirmishes. *$65–75*

C.S.A. Election Notices. Newspaper, Vol. 11, No. 18, April 4, 1863, *Opelousas (LA) Courier.* Printed on wallpaper (pattern shows through from reverse). 13" × 19 ½". Lengthy address by Cong. Lucius Dupre. Notice of livestock auctions and military recruiting, runaway slaves. Because of shortage of newsprint in the South, news was often printed on "necessity paper" including wallpaper, wrapping paper, even corn husks. . . . . :. *$250–300*

(C.S.A.) Fall of New Orleans. Newspaper, Oct. 17, 1861, *New Orleans Daily Delta.* Fascinating details about how the capture of the city and blockade of the Mississippi River was accomplished; also need for law and order and reference to John Brown in Virginia. *$1100–1200*

(C.S.A.) Gen. John G. Walker Battles Heroicly in Red River Campaign. Newspaper, *Houston Daily Telegraph*, May 19, 1864. Battles of Mansfield (LA) and Pleasant Hill are vividly recounted. Led by "chivalrous Col. Overton Young, the men of the 8th Texas dashed to the front and through storm of shells, fought their way through Yankee infantry." Gen. Lee is reported victor over Gen. Meade in Virginia. Brig. Gen. Elkanah Greer gets orders "to recruit men 17 years of age for Confederacy." Another ad calls for 200 boys, girls, and ladies to make cartridges for small arms. *$550–600*

C.S.A. (Mostly) Newspapers Highlight Major Battles (45 total). Majority of newspapers are Nashville-based, i.e., *Republican Banner*; *The Daily Press*; *Daily Union*; incl. South's reaction to Emancipation Proclamation. *Daily Times* and *True Union*: Incl. Sherman's move on Macon; Lincoln's assassination; *Dispatch*: Incl. McClellan declaring for presidency; *Daily Press* and *Times*; *Weekly Union*; also *Louisville Daily Journal*; from the North—*N.Y. Times*; *Hickman Weekly Courier*; *Cincinnati Daily Gazette. N.Y. Times*: incl. coverage of impeachment trial of Andrew Johnson. Rated very good to excellent. (A) Riba, July '94, $700. . . *$800–900*

Casualties Counted Among C.S.A. Officers and Men. Newspaper, *Opelousas (LA) Courier*, Aug. 1, 1863. List of exchanged officers as prisoners, and casualties. Runaway slave ads; plantations for sale. Printed in French and English. . . . .
. . . . *$900–1000*

"499th Day of Siege of Charleston." Newspaper, *Charleston Daily Courier*, Nov. 19, 1864. Includes front-page criticism of Jefferson Davis' message to Confederate Congress claiming govt.'s right to purchase and emancipate slaves to fill army's ranks. "C.S.A. govt. threatens to put upon us all the evils we threw off the domination of Yankee enemies to avoid." Old tape mend, light copy. (D) $275. . . . . *$300–350*

***Chattanooga Gazette* Extra. Death of President Lincoln Seward Badly Wounded.** Newspaper, April 15, 1865. Two cols. Black border. Lists accounts of assassination from various cities, including Washington, D.C. Reports swear-

ing in of A. Johnson as pres. "at 11 AM this morning." (A) Riba, Oct. '85, $200.
. . . . *$225–250*

Corruption in the Union Navy Dept. Newspaper, Feb. 1, 1865, *Rochester Daily Union & Advertiser.* Proposition is presented to appoint a standing committee to investigate outrageous frauds in the Navy Dept. Cites massacre of 25 Federal soldiers by Tennessee guerillas: "15 outlaws . . . one a black scoundrel, who boasted he had killed three." The Senate discusses retaliation for poor treatment of Federal prisoners. Sherman is reported as en route to Charleston. *$35–50*

(Gen.) Custer Leads Cavalry Charge! Newsweekly, *Harper's Weekly*, March 19, 1864. Full-cover etching of Brig. Gen. George A. Custer on horseback with saber raised high, troops behind him. Also a full-page portrait of Gen. Judson "Kill Cavalry" Kilpatrick, "whose late raid in the rear of Lee's army is the most successful of the war." Also, full-page map of U.S. "with dissolving view of Rebellion, representing the proportions to which it has diminished since Oct. 1861." Also, a picture of the 20th U.S. Colored Troops being honored at Union Square, March 5, 1864. . .
. . . . *$100–125*

President Jefferson Davis Arrives in Richmond. Newspaper, June 6, 1861, *Southern Enterprise,* Greenville, SC. Four war steamers, led by U.S.S. *Minnesota,* leave Ft. Monroe to blockade Charleston. One thousand So. Carolina troops head for Manassas Gap. Account of Battle of Fairfax (VA) Courthouse; Ocquia Creek naval skirmish. Reports on latest deeds of the C.S.A. Gens. R.E. Lee, P. Beauregard, David Twiggs (who resigned after turning over all of the Union forces and supplies in Texas to Ben McCullach and his Texas Rangers). Decries Lincoln's proclamation that those sailing under C.S.A. banner be treated as pirates. Only copy know to exist. *$800–900*

Death of Rebel Guerrila Leader John Morgan. Newsweekly, *Harper's Weekly*, Sept. 24, 1864. Lithograph of fallen leader and details of ambush by Federal troops while trying to escape in E. Tennessee. Stunning two-pager by Thomas Nast with emotional renderings of "The Blessings of Victory" as portrayed by two classic female deities. Article on Grant's campaign: "The Trenches Before Petersburg." . . .
. . . . *$100–125*

"Devil-daring, God-fearing Men Wanted." Newspaper, *Columbia (SC) Guardian,* Jan. 26, 1864. Urgent appeal from 50-year veteran (see headline) who also "will ever hold inviolate the purity of women." Reports on "Prince John" Magruder's line of battle. Also announced launching of new C.S.A. cruiser *Rappahonick.* An open letter to Yankee Gen. Wilde from Col. Joel Griffin on alleged outrages committed by Griffin. *$500–550*

Farragut Attacks C.S.A. Positions at Mobile Bay. Newspaper, July 29, 1864, *Galveston (TX) Tri-Weekly News*, 2 pp. Direct report from Mobile Bay of Adm. David Farragut's naval engagements. Also includes remarkable document outlining C.S.A.'s "dispositions, principles and purposes." Report on Indian raid on W. Texas town. Rebel soldier in Georgia describes exciting artillery raid, raking down a ravine with but one piece of artillery. *$450–500*

54th Massachusetts Colored Infantry—Its Much Lauded Attack on Fort Wagner. Newsweekly, *Harper's Weekly*, Aug. 15, 1863. Portrait of Col. Robert G. Shaw and his heroic 1000 men who were killed at this battle at Morris Island, SC, and immortalized in the movie *Glory.* Includes birds-eye view of Charleston Harbor; five other scenes of nearby Sea Islands. A.R. Waud engravings, "Reminiscences of the Maryland Campaign." Cover illus. portrays "Morgan's raid-entry of Morgan's Freebooters into Washington, Ohio." *$100–125*

Folly of Union Compromise with the South. Newsweekly, *Harper's Weekly,* Sept. 3, 1864. Thomas Nast's powerful rendering makes editorial statement against compromise. Two-page engraving depicts Adm. David Farragut's fleet entering Mobile Bay; Gen. Sherman, in council with war staff, prophesizes, "I intend to place this Army southwest of Atlanta." *$75–100*

Fort Pillow Massacre. Newspaper, April 16, 1864, *New York Herald.* Chilling account of "indiscriminate butchery of whites and blacks" by C.S.A. Gen. N.B. Forrest, even after Maj. Gen. Bradford had surrendered the fort. Two maps accompany military history of Ft. Pillow and its position on the Mississippi. Cites attack on Paducah, KY, "with unconditional surrender," dispatches from C.S.A. Gen. Abraham Buford to William H. Lawrence. News from Army of the Potomac covering Mosby's dash near Bristoe Station. *$75–85*

Bombardment of Fredericksburg. Newsweekly, *Harper's Weekly*, Dec. 28, 1862. Account of Lee and Jackson's forces repelling Burnside's relentless charges, as witnessed by a reserve. Exciting engravings illus. the great slaughter in the Battle of the 13th and Burnside withdraws to the north side of Rappahannock. *$75–100*

Gettysburg Cemetery Dedicated. Newspaper, Nov. 21, 1863, *Hartford Evening Press.* Orator Edward Everett's two-hour speech is given all the ink in this edition, while Lincoln's short Gettysburg Address is completely passed over. Accounts of fighting around Knoxville are reported by Gen. Ambrose Burnside. A special notice offers one month's pay plus bonus of $402 in advance for new recruits to fill old regiments. *$50–75*

Gettysburg—Horrible Realities of War Graphically Depicted in Brady Photographs. Newsweekly. *Harper's Weekly*, August 22, 1863. Moving scenes brought to readers a month after epic battle. Also pictured: Army of Potomac crossing the Rappahannock; Federal troops drawing rations; portrait of Gen. George Stoneman. *$100–125*

Henry W. Halleck Relieved of Command as General in Chief of Army. Newspaper, March 16, 1864, *New York Herald.* Halleck resigns at his own request (his field commanders felt handicapped by his lack of strategic sense); Grant assumes command. Negroes vote on reorganization of LA. Lincoln calls for 200,000 more troops. *$65–75*

Hazlett's Battery Highlighted at Cemetery Hill. Newsweekly, *Harper's Weekly*, July 25, 1863. Three famed Civil War artists—A.R. Waud, Theodore Davis, and Thomas Nast—vividly depict major battles. Waud covers Gettysburg and Hazlett's charging battery at Cemetery Hill with 2-page spread; Nast's full-page engraving shows Rebs shelling NY Militia on Main St., Carlisle, PA; David offers six detailed views of Vicksburg operations plus front-cover image of Gen. Grant. . . . *$150–200*

Stonewall Jackson Wounded at Chancellorsville. Newspaper, *Houston Tri-Weekly Telegraph*, June 3, 1863. Jackson, who had earlier lost his arm in battle, had already died from other wounds on May 10, by the time this edition appeared. Also reported is Battle of Fredericksburg and the death of C.S.A. Gen. A.P. Hill. Federal Gen. McClellan is mentioned in article as losing ground by failing to take advantage of opportunities at Manassas, Williamsburg, Antietam, the Peninsula. Ironically, all three—Jackson, Hill, and McClellan—were classmates at West Point. Also, report of Robert E. Lee, Jr., a Pvt. in the Rockbridge, VA, artillery. Texas C.S.A. papers are very scarce. *$550–600*

Assassination of Lincoln (2 Versions). Newspapers, copies of 1st Editions, April 15, 1865—*Rochester Evening Express*, black bordered; *Rochester Daily Union & Adv.*, "Appalling National Calamity." Plus Rochester proclamation broadside by Mayor D.D.T. Moore to close all businesses that day ". . . to assemble and pay respects to late President." (A) Riba–Mobley, Oct. '85, $480. *$600–700*

Lincoln's Assassination. Newspaper, April 22, 1865, *National Police Gazette*. Front page features "The Assassins Carnival" with six lithographed scenes of attack on Lincoln, Seward; image of John Wilkes Booth. Story is inside. . . . . .
. . . . *$125–150*

Lincoln Assassination Report. Newspaper, April 17, 1865, *Philadelphia Inquirer*, 8 pp. All pages bordered in black. Large picture of John Wilkes Booth on cover with diagram of his escape route. *$100–125*

Lincoln's Death Premonition. Newspaper, Feb. 1, 1864, *Rochester Daily Union & Advertiser*. Over 13½ months prior to his assassination, Lincoln is reported as noting to a visitor, "Which ever way it (the war) ends, I have the impression that I shan't last long after it is over." Shows fine engraved Lincoln portrait with signature facsimile. Accompanies article about unusually high demand for his autograph. Also, a signed Lincoln order calling for draft of half a million men for three years. Plus report on Rebel proposition to lay down their arms. *$175–200*

(Lincoln) Extra. Death of President Lincoln, Seward Badly Wounded. Newspaper, April 15, 1865, *Chattanooga Gazette*, two cols., black border. Lists accounts of assassination from various cities, including Washington, D.C. Reports swearing in of A. Johnson as president "at 11 AM this morning." (A) Riba, Oct. '85, $200. . . .
. . . . *$300–400*

(Lincoln) The Funeral of the President. Newsweekly, *Harper's Weekly*, May 6, 1865. The second edition to appear following the assassination. Stunning two-page array of engravings incl. the President at home; scene at the deathbed; Lincoln's funeral procession; funeral service at the White House. Report on attempted assassination of William Seward. *$500–600*

Lee's Surrender; Lincoln's Funeral Cortege Moves to Springfield; Death of Lincoln's Assassin, John Wilkes Booth. Newsweekly, *Harper's Weekly*, May 20, 1865. Signing of peace treaty is correlated with religious celebration of Palm Sunday. End of war review shows graphic engravings of burning of Rebel ram *Webb* below New Orleans; explosion of steamer *Sultana*. *$125–150*

President Lincoln Shot! Newspaper, April 15, 1865, *New York Daily Tribune*. Hour-by-hour countdown on events surrounding the assassination. Cites Seward's being attacked in his home; siege of Mobile; inauguration of Andrew Johnson. Also included: letters from Virginia citizens appealing to Gov. William Smith not to abandon Richmond. *$1300–1500*

Morris Island Evacuated by Rebels. Newspaper, Sept. 10, 1863, *New York Herald*, triple sheet. Nearly a half-page-size map showing Charleston Harbor, "Morris Island Ours." "Gillmore's Splendid Success"—Ft. Wagner, "Gregg Abandoned by Beauregard," and "Charleston at Mercy of Gillmore's (Gen. Quincy Gillmore) Guns." Excellent naval coverage including Adm. John Dahgrens demand of surrender of Fort Sumter. *$35–50*

Mourning Editions of Civil War and Political Leaders. Newspapers, approx. 70. Newspapers from all over U.S. announce deaths of Lincoln, Jefferson Davis, James Garfield, countless others, citing Civil War battles, 1860s–1915. Range from poor to excellent. (A) Riba-Mobley, Oct. '85, $350. . . . . *$600–650*

"Positioning and Skirmishing at Murfreesboro—A Great Battle Imminent!" Newspaper, Dec. 30, 1862, *The Charleston Mercury,* A scathing appraisal of Gen. Butler's control of New Orleans. Front-page letter from C.S.A. officer who witnessed Union troops under flag of truce, reclaiming their dead at bloody Fredericksburg. Notable quote from Stonewall Jackson to a brigadier at Cedar Run: "Never say anything good about your enemies." *$250–300*

(Union's) Capture of New Orleans. Newspaper, May 8, 1862, *New York Herald*.

Coverage of siege and capture of undefended New Orleans by Adm. David Farragut. Details of bombardment of Ft. Jackson and Ft. St. Philip and passage of Union gunboats up the Mississippi. News of Battle of Williamsburg with evacuation of Rebels and withdrawal up the peninsula. Affairs in Ft. Macon (GA).......
.... *$175–200*

New York Riots. Two Rioters Killed; Colored Orphanage Burned, Stores Sacked. Newsweekly, August 1, 1863, *Harper's Weekly.* Chilling account of weeklong disturbances vividly portrayed in ten engravings on two-page spread. "Vicksburg Captured" account. Theodore Davis engravings of Grant and Gen. John Pemberton (who prematurely surrendered to Grant) and was accused of treason by the C.S.A... *$75–100*

Second Battle of Bull Run. Newspaper, Sept. 1, 1862, *New York Herald.* Shows full-page map of battlefields in Virginia. 2nd Bull Run skirmish detailed with names of many of those killed or wounded. Details of Gen. John Pope's recent battles with Gen. Stonewall Jackson. Pope falls back to Centreville. Proclamation of Gov. Charles Robinson of Kansas, who organized most of his state's regiments. . .
.... *$75–100*

Gen. Sherman Marches to the Sea! Newspaper, *Army & Navy Messenger* (for the Trans-Miss. Dept.), Shreveport, LA, Dec. 22, 1864. Scouts report on Sherman's position moving toward Davien, GA, headed for the sea. Other important articles include "Adoption of Church of the Army"; an account by Col. L.M. Lewis of "barbarities of our enemies, citing "deplorable conditions and treatment of Reb prisoners in Alton, Ill." According to Gregory's "Union List of Newspapers," only one copy of this date and title exists............................. *$900–1000*

Sherman Takes Savannah. Newspaper, Dec. 27, 1864, *Newark Daily Advertiser.* Sherman's famous dispatch to Lincoln: "I beg to present you a Christmas gift, the City of Savannah, with 150 heavy guns." Critical article on Jefferson Davis' request for pay raise. Contends that C.S.A. Quartermaster Gen. and Quartermaster have so dutifully taken care of Davis' needs that "let's hope those two officers will send the remainder, if there be any, to the trenches of Richmond." Fascinating ad offers advice on how to "Avoid the Draft."........................... *$50–75*

Gen. Richard Taylor Takes 2,500 Fed. Prisoners at Mansfield. Newspaper, May 18, 1864, *Galveston (TX) Tri-Weekly News,* 2 pp. Blow-by-blow account of battle, with Union forces routed. In possibly C.S.A.-slanted account, Grant is reportedly in retreat, with Lee in hot pursuit; Gen. Lucius Polk has recaptured Vicksburg but the enemy has burned the city; destruction of Union gunboats on Red River.............. *$450–500*

Texas Rangers and Gen. James Chalmers Storm and Capture Union Fortress at Green River. Newspaper, *Houston Tri-Weekly Telegraph,* Nov. 21, 1862. Also talks of recognition being forthcoming from England and France, based on Southern successes in the West and in Virginia. Account of 1st Battle of Manassas is related by a Lt. Ben Baker, who was injured in battle. Capt. Curley writes of troop movement around Helena...................................... *$850–900*

The War Begins! Newsweekly, April 27, 1861, *Harper's Weekly.* Reports of bombardment of Fort Sumter by Rebs fill this keystone issue. Detailed map of Charleston Harbor, plus full-figure portrait of Gen. P.G.T. Beauregard who fired first shots at Federal forces. Also includes fine Brady photograph of Abraham Lincoln, plus issue of his proclamation calling forth "the Militia to the aggregate number of 75,000 in order to supress said combinations."................. *$100–125*

"War Maps and Diagrams." Newspaper. July 13, 1861, *New York Herald.* (A) Janeck, Oct. '94, $45. .... *$50–60*

War Years Collection. Seventeen southern newspapers from nine southern states.

Covers span from July 11, 1861 to Feb. 15, 1865. Range from: *North Alabamian* (Tuscombia, AL) coverage of Jeff Davis' election; *Daily Mississippian* (Jackson, MS) which gives Acts and Resolutions of Congress of C.S.A. states; *Charleston Mercury*, a Ft. Sumter Report; *Charleston Tri-Weekly Courier*, arrival of Pres. Davis in Richmond. All papers are four pages and most are complete. Some soiling and oil spots. (A) Riba-Mobley, Oct. '85, $500. . . . . *$700–800*

Wounding and Death of Gen. Stonewall Jackson. Newspaper, May 18, 1863, *Rochester (NY) Daily Union & Advertising*. Riveting account of the mortal wounding by friendly fire of beloved C.S.A. Gen. at Battle of Chancellorsville, extracted from *Richmond Whig* and *Richmond Enquirer*. "All my wounds are by my own men," Jackson quote. His last words reveal the courage of Lee's ablest general. Further news of capture of Alexandria, LA, fighting in MS; proposed disposition of Negro troops and their officers. Mentions Gens. Van Dorn, Hooker, Beauregard, McClellan, and Butler *$65–85*

Year-end Civil War Overview in 1863. Newspaper, *London Times*, Dec. 31, 1863. Pro-South British point to Rebels being victorious in two great-pitched battles, despite "superior resources of its adversary . . . Nor has its (C.S.A.'s) ablest commander ceased to threaten the Federal Capital . . . It is perhaps unfortunate that an artificial prosperity has thus far protected them from suffering the ordinary evils of war." Includes Gen. Jackson's dispatches from the front. *$25–35*

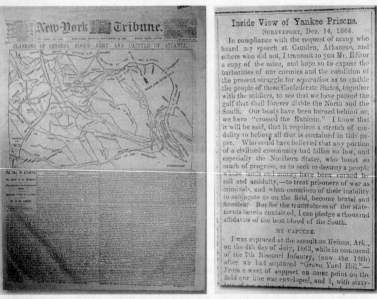

Left: New York Daily Tribune, *September 19, 1864, capture of Atlanta, with map of the city and environs, $175–$200.* Right: Army & Navy Messenger *(for CSA's Trans-Mississippi Department), "Inside View of Yankee Prisons," December 14, 1864, $900–$950.*

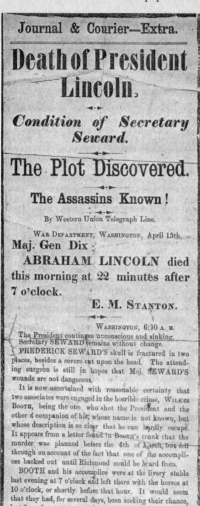

Left: New York Journal &
Courier—Extra, *April 15,
1865. Sold for $850 at Riba
Auctions in June 1990,
$900–$1,000.* Right: Bugle
Call Extra. *Special
newspaper insert printed by
the Great National Sanitary
Fair, ca. 1863, $75–$85.*

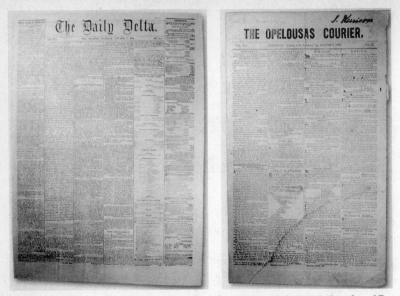

Left: The Daily Delta, *New Orleans, "Fall of New Orleans," October 17, 1861: $1,100–$1,200.* Right: The Opelousas Courier, *Opelousas, Louisiana, August 1, 1863, $900–$1,000.*

Top to bottom: New York Times *article proclaiming victory for the North at Antietam, September 19, 1862, $100–$125;* Richmond Enquirer *report claiming victory for the South at Antietam (Sharpsburg), September 23, 1862, $150–$200.*

NOVELTIES

GENERAL ITEMS

Bicycle Decorations. Ku Klux Klan figural burning cross. Ca. 1920s. Red painted and silver metal; burning cross with K.K.K. letters. Clamps to handlebars near grips... *$75–100*

Collar. Grant–Colfax cloth detachable collar. 1868. Black transfer images of U.S. Grant and Schuyler Colfax on each side of winged collar. Worn by party faithful. *$75–100*

Disk. Bone disk, "13th Kentucky D Co." In red and black, incised letters; separated by chevron. Small holes at sides. Probably once attached to C.S.A. kepi or Bummers cap. Stark FP Cat., Oct. '93, $275. .... *$200–225*

Mine/Inkwell. Union mine converted to souvenir inkwell. Ca. 1862. Conversion from 4" wood and bottle mine. Stark PF Cat., Summer '93, $200....... *$200–225*

Money Clip. (K.K.K.) Klansman with flag and fiery cross money clip. 1920s. Brass.. *$35–45*

Neckerchief Slide. Man with saber and flag. Ca. 1863. Carved bone, possibly in prison camp. Rev. NWW, Co. A., MCC. (Mail A) Stark, Summer '93, $175...... .... *$175–200*

Plaque. Anti-slavery kneeling slave. Ca. 1850s. Famed slave-in-chains-pleading-for-mercy figure in 3" × 3¹/₂" cut-out, openwork, tortoiseshell plaque. Stark FP Cat., $1000 .... *$900–1000*

PRESENTATION ITEMS

Coffee Pot. Hannibal Hamlin silver coffee pourer. 1860s. Handchased 10" h. coin silver coffeepot engraved "Presented to the Hon. Hannibal Hamlin by Ray Tompkins in consideration for his generous support of his father Daniel D. Thomkins." The latter served as Gov. of NY and V.P. under Monroe. Stark F.P. Cat., Dec. '94, $2850.. *$2600–2800*

Goblet. United States Revenue Marines presentation goblet. 1865. 6¹/₂" h., silvered, elaborate cartouche with ornate scrolled monogram and "Capt. Alvan A. Fenger commissioned by President Lincoln in 1865" engraved around top. Stark FP Cat., July '94, $700. .... *$600–700*

Hardtack. G.A.R. simulated hardtack. 1887. 4" diamond shape composition hardtack suspended from red, white, and blue ribbon with black transfer bust of Gen. Henry W. Slocum; Reunion of Slocum Post G.A.R., Providence, MA. *$35–45*

Macerated Currency. Profile figural bust of Lincoln. Ca. 1860s. Old paper currency pulp was macerated then mixed with paste solution and molded into patriotic shapes. Other examples known for Grant and Harrison. *$75–100*

Pinholder. "Keep the Old Ship Afloat! (Rev. anchor) Cast It In Union Harbor." 2½" multicolor silk pinholder with flag and anchor motif. Star border. Stark FP Cat., July '94, $150. . . . . *$125–150*

Scales. Anti-slavery brass scales. Handheld brass scales, with chain and shackles. "Am I not a man and a Brother" inscription, 5" black and gold painted tin case. . . .
. . . . *$500–550*

Scrimshaw. Grant scrimshaw turtle shell. Ca. 1880. Carved bust of U.S. Grant on entire turtle shell. *$350–400*

Seal. Carved ivory Lincoln figural wax sealer. 1860s. 3½" finely carved ivory and brass seal with Lincoln's bust fig. Stark FP Cat., Dec. '94, $475. . . . . *$450–475*

Sign. Lynch die-cut folk art sign. Date unknown. Rather macabre rebus sign of black man being hanged (ergo "Lynch"). Wrought iron, painted black. Stark FP Cat., Summer '93, $900. . . . . *$900–950*

Sled. Gen. Howard Sled. Ca. 1870. 39" painted wood sled, with name gilded in center, old red paint filligree border. Gen. Oliver Otis Howard was awarded the Medal of Honor for Fair Oaks. After the war he was a commissioner for the Freedman's Bureau and founded Howard University. Stark FP Cat., July '94, $300. . . . .
. . . . *300–325*

Spoon. Commemorative Gen. George Meade silver spoon. Bust of Meade with Gettysburg scenes. Bowl has battlescene, "Hancock Wounded," falling from horse.
. . . . *$50–75*

Stencil. "God Bless the Soldiers and confound the Copperheads." Union printing stencil. Ca. 1860. 4" × 19", brass. Made by C. Sumner. Stark FP Cat., Dec. '94, $500. . . . . *$400–450*

Commemorative, cast-iron trivet, "CSA, Richmond, VA, 1922," $200–$250.

A

B

Lincoln memorial fan, with cameos of Union generals and portrait of Lincoln on the front (A) and vignettes of the "ironclads" Monitor and Merrimac, and the events surrounding Lincoln's assassination on the reverse (B). French. Silk fan with ivory ribs and gilt decoration, $1,200–$1,500.

Left: *A rather bizarre Horace Greeley cardboard fan with a series of cartoons on the reverse. Face area is browntone with white whisker hair. By McLoughlin Bros., New York, ca. 1872. 9", $200–$250.* Right: *Ku Klux Klan bronze belt buckle, ca. 1920, $200–$250.*

Lincoln cased daguerreotype and wooden parade axe, ca. 1860, $2,500–$3,000.

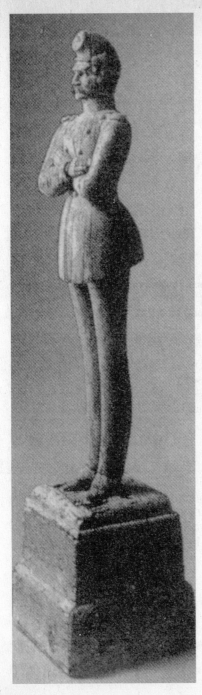

Left: *Life-size carved wooden figure of Captain Jinks, mythical hero of the popular Civil War-era ditty "Captain Jinks of the Horse Marines." Carved by Samuel Robb, New York, ca. 1879. Sold to a private collector at the 1994 Philadelphia Antiques Show for $125,000. (Photo courtesy of David Stansbury)* Above: *Cast-iron sewing bird, 5", in the shape of a Zouave soldier. Red, white, blue, and green paint, with hinged tension weight, $950. (Photo courtesy of Rex Stark)* Below: *Tasseled window curtain cord, with metal thread, from Abraham Lincoln's library in his Springfield home. From the H.W. Fay collection, this sold for $900 at Riba Auctions in October 1985, $1,000–$1,100.*

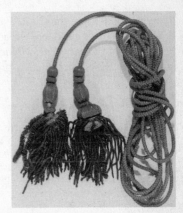

PAINTINGS, CARTOONS, AND OTHER ART MEDIA

CALLIGRAPHY

"Henry Clay National Currency, Revenue, Protection." 1850s. Pen and ink, red brown 15" drawing of Clay holding the Constitution. $650–700
(Gen. Winfield Scott Hancock) "In Memoriam." 1886. Large pen and ink calligraphy by William Errickson. Eagle with banner, 16-stanza poem with paeons of praise—"Hercules modeled in stone," "His genius saved Gettysburg," etc. . . . .
. . . . $1200–1400
"Gen. Hancock—In Memoriam. 1886." Pen and ink eagle with banner by William Errickson, 16-stanza poem of flowery praise. "His genius saved Gettysburg field." $1200–1300
Gen. Winfield Scott. Ca. 1860s. Pen and ink equestrian scene. Matching eagle and star designs on saddle blanket and canteen. $650–700

CARTOONS

Many cartoons from the Civil War era were published as individual prints as well as "poster cartoons," in addition to appearing in *Judge, Leslies Illus., Harper's Weekly, Puck, Punch, Vanity Fair,* and other leading periodicals. Many were also issued as prints by N. Currier and Currier & Ives.

Lincoln Related

"An Heir to the Throne/Or the Next Republican Candidate." 1860. Attributed to Louis Maurer, Currier & Ives, NY (2776). One of many racist, anti-Abe cartoons. Lincoln is introduced by *Tribune's* Horace Greeley as representing all the virtues of black Republicanism. Grotesque fig. of black was copied from P.T. Barnum's "What Is It? Museum," adv. from *Leslies Illustrated*; attacks Lincoln's contention that "black man was a person with certain inalienable rights." (M) . . . .
. . . . $300–350

"Dividing the National Map." Rickey, Mallory & Co., 1860. Large map of U.S. being torn by sectional issues by candidates Lincoln, John Breckinridge, John Bell, and Stephen Douglas. Litho., 13^{11}/$_{16}$" × 19^{1}/$_{4}$". *$700–800*

"Honest Abe Taking Them on the Half Shell." Attributed to Louis Maurer, 1860. Currier & Ives, NY. Lincoln samples oyster shells holding pro-slavery opponents Stephen Douglas (moderate) in one hand, John C. Breckinridge (far right) in other. Handcolored litho, 18" × 13^{3}/$_{8}$". *$350–400*

"I Knew Him, Horatio, a Fellow of Infinite Jest." By J.H. Howard; pub. by Thomas Strong, NY, 1864. From Shakespeare's *Hamlet*. Cartoon of opponent George McClellan, as Prince of Denmark, holding head of Lincoln; Irish gravedigger in background; litho, 13^{7}/$_{8}$" × 10^{1}/$_{4}$". *$400–450*

"Lincoln and Butler as Don Quixote and Sancho Panza." By Adalbert Volck, Baltimore, 1863. South considered Butler a traitor for fighting with the Union. Etching, 6^{1}/$_{2}$" × 7^{1}/$_{2}$". *$350–400*

"Lincoln's Arrival in Washington—Flight of Abraham." Baltimore newspaper cartoon, March 1861, of cat meowing as Lincoln peers anxiously from freight train box car following secret arrival in Washington for inagural (Secret Service had used precaution after learning of assassination plot). *$300–350*

"Lincoln as a Monkey." David H. Strother (attrib.), 1863. Long-tailed monkey with Lincoln head on chair issuing Emancipation Proclamation to little man. Pencil on paper, 8^{13}/$_{16}$" × 5^{1}/$_{4}$". *$125–150*

"Lincoln's Two Difficulties." *Punch*, Aug. 23, 1862. "What? No money! No Men!" Lincoln in guise as Uncle Sam stands between a tax collector and a soldier, apparently reflecting opinion of British upper class. *$100–125*

"You'll Excuse Me Gen. Butler, But as I Can't Send You Everywhere, I'll Have to Cut You to Pieces." Thomas Nast (attrib.). Shows Lincoln wielding sword before seated Gen. Butler. Original, pencil on paper, 5^{7}/$_{8}$" × 6^{11}/$_{16}$". *$1200–1300*

"Long Lincoln a Little Longer." *Harper's Weekly*, Nov. 28, 1864; following overwhelming victory at polls.................................... *$100–125*

"Man of Peace or War." 1861. Thomas Nast's two-panel view of Lincoln's inaugural speech. *New York Illustrated News*. Depicts Lincoln in robes and wearing laurel wreath as "Peace." Opposite panel labeled "War," shows him in armor and wielding sword with one foot on Uncle Sam's chest. *$75–100*

"(The) Nigger in the Woodpile." Attrib. to Louis Maurer; pub. by Currier & Ives, NY (4464), 1860. Lincoln sits atop rail fence "Republican Platform" enclosing black man. Horace Greeley assures voter that Republican ticket "has no connection with the Abolition party." (M) *$250–300*

"Mrs. North and Her Attorney." *Punch*, Sept. 24, 1864. Lady (representing the North) in mourning veil tells dejected Lincoln that if he cannot effect peace, she "will put the case into other hands." *$75–100*

"(The) Overdue Bill." *Punch*, 1861. Lincoln sits on high stool looking glum as Union soldier presents him copy of promise to subdue the South in 90 days. . *$75–85*

"(The) Political Quadrille/Music by Dred Scott." Unknown NY pub., 1860. Lampoons all the political parties; Dred Scott fiddles as Lincoln dances with black lady; Bell with Indian; Breckinbride with Buchanan, Douglas with Irishman. Litho, 13^{3}/$_{4}$" × 17^{5}/$_{8}$". *$300–350*

"(The) Rail Candidate." Attrib. to Louis Maurer; 1860; Currier & Ives, NY (5052). Lincoln rides uneasily on split rail symbolizing Republican platform ("It is the hardest stick I ever straddled") as borne by black slave and Horace Greeley. Litho, 16^{1}/$_{2}$" × 11^{3}/$_{4}$" (M)...................................... *$300–350*

"Satan Tempting Booth to the Murder of the President." 1865. J.L. Magee, Philadelphia. Booth holds fatal pistol while Devil looks over his shoulder and Lincoln sits in theater box in background; litho, $10^1/2$" × $8^3/4$" $250–300

"(The) True Issue or That's What's the Matter." Currier & Ives, NY (6236). 1864 campaign. Gen. McClellan, Lincoln, and Jeff Davis pulling on all sides of map of U.S. and tearing it. (S) $200–225

"Virginia Paw-sing." Anonymous, pub. in Richmond, 1861. Uncle Abe tries to catch mice symbolizing seceding states. Decapitated rat at right stands for the Union, a "dead issue." Litho, $8^1/2$" × 14". $200–250

"Vulcan in the Sulks." Ca. 1862. John Tenniel cartoon in *Punch*. Lincoln (as a scrawny Mars) in suit of armor with sword and shield. $65–75

"Writing the Emancipation Proclamation." By Adalbert Volck, Baltimore, ca. 1864. Vitriolic cartoon showing Lincoln writing at desk; Liberty with baboon's head; vulture drapery tie-back; pen is dipped in Devil's ink stand; framed picture above of John Brown with halo. Volk, a Copperhead, published "War Sketches" under pseudonym "V. Blada." Etching, $6^1/4$" × $4^7/8$". $100–150

Other Politically Related

"Chester Allen Arthur." By Gillam, *Puck*, 1881. Arthur as an overdressed dandy, standing in front of U.S. Capitol. $65–75

"Our National Bird." "As It Appeared When Handed to James Buchanan/March 4, 1857/The Identical Bird as it appeared A.D. 1861." Michael Angelo Woolf, 1861. Full-winged eagle vs. droopy looking plucked eagle. Litho, $7^5/8$" × 13". . . . $75–100

"Out of a Situation." *Vanity Fair*, April 1860. James (identified here as "Biddy Buchanan," dressed as woman) is told by Miss Liberty, "we shan't need your services after March" because of his "waffling" on slavery issue. $65–75

(Clay) "Where's My Thunder?" Ca. 1850s. Unknown. Clay accuses Daniel Webster of stealing his Fugitive Slave Act; 8" × 10", b&w. $75–100

(Stephen A. Douglas) "Soliciting a Vote." 1856. Unknown. Douglas, Daniel Webster, Sam Houston, and Winfield Scott surround a hapless citizen, making promises and seeking his vote; 8" × 10", b&w. $75–100

Freemont's Last Expedition. 1856. He rides abolition nag with head of Greeley, led by Deward. Border ruffian decries Abolition Soup and Wooly Head Stew at White House. $275–300

Ante-Bellum/Grant—"Carpetbag Rule." Anonymous, 1880. Lady representing "Sold South" is loaded down by huge carpetbag, with U.S. Grant atop in Napoleon hat; bag marked "Carpet Bag and Bayonet Rule"; flanked by Union soldiers with bayonets. $125–150

(Grant) "1859 St. Louis." Anonymous. U.S. Grant is satirized for his pre–Civil War occupation driving wagon as peddler of firewood. $85–100

(Grant) "A Giant among Pigmies/A Pigmy among Giants." Anonymous. *Puchinello*, April 2, 1870. Contrasting frames of Grant's image upon assuming presidency and then a year later, after he had made a number of questionable cabinet appointments. $65–75

"Grant." By Gillam. *Puck*, 1881. Grant introduces his discredited cabinet members to new president, Chester A. Arthur (another ex-Union Gen.). $45–55

"(The) Peace Policy of Our Noble President." Anonymous, *Harper's Weekly*, 1874. A sodden Grant, in the arms of Indian squaw. (Reference to his drinking and his humane policy toward Indians.) $75–85

(Grant) "Stone Walls Do Not a Prison Make." Thomas Nast, *Harper's Weekly*, Aug. 8, 1874. Huge image of Boss Tweed outgrowing his prison cell, following conviction during Grant's corrupt administration...................... *$45–55*

(Grant) "(The) Third Term Panic." Thomas Nast. Nov. 7, 1874. Symbols include Rep. elephant, fox as Dem. party; donkey disguised as lion (representing Grant's intention to run for 3rd term); and ostrich burying head in sand. Wood engraving, 11" × 15^{15}/$_{16}$".. *$35–45*

(Benjamin Harrison) "(The) Smallest Specimen Yet." Frederick Burr Opper, *Puck*, Feb. 9, 1890. Uncle Sam examines tiny Benjamin Harrison, wearing famous beaver hat, under microscope. *$25–35*

"Harrison vs. Cleveland." By Hamilton, *Judge*, Oct. 13, 1888. Three cartoon boxes for each candidate are columned-off to contrast Harrison as Civil War hero and Protectionist; Cleveland as slacker and saloon loafer. *$75–100*

(A. Johnson) "(The) Reconstruction Dose." Anonymous. Gen. Phillip Sheridan administers physic of Reconstruction as "Naughty Andy" (Johnson) kicks his shin. Miss Columbia tells Andy to behave and not interfere................ *$100–125*

"Andrew Johnson." Thomas Nast, ca. 1876. Nast caricature of Johnson as King Andy, wearing crown, confronting donkey scarecrow wearing laurel leaves (representing Grant's so-called Caesarism). Pastel on paper, 5^{11}/$_{12}$" × 40^{1}/$_{2}$"..... *$700–800*

(Johnson) "Andy's Trip to the West." Petroleum V. Nashby, 1866. Series of cartoons lampooning Andrew Johnson's disastrous campaign tour through the East and Midwest. The first frame shows Johnson speaking to not a soul at whistle stop while the crowd clamors for Grant (who accompanied him).

Another depicts Johnson being pulled on a goose float (reference to his humble beginnings as a tailor; a flatiron is know as a tailor's goose).

He is supported by Sec. Seward. Nasby nastily depicts Johnson as being drunk on his feet and held up by Seward.

He hears from Maine. Nasby shows in three frames Johnson's progressively sourpuss features, following a cool reception in Maine. Then he hears from Pennsylvania, Indiana, and Ohio; then he hears from New York............ *$125–150*

(Johnson and Seward) "My Policy in 1868." Unknown. Johnson and Seward ride smashed-up fire pumper. Johnson sits drinking atop wreckage; Seward eyes a duck. Subtitle is "The Dead Duck Still Lives"; 12" × 18", b&w............. *$150–175*

(McClellan) "Little Mac . . . Dig Your Own Grave." 1864, unknown. McClellan tries to dig into White House. Miss Liberty tells him he's unworthy, betrayed Union, aided C.S.A. Depicts skeletons of Union soldiers; 13" × 17", b&w...... *$175–200*

(Winfield Scott) "A Bad Egg/Fuss and Feathers." By P. Smith, N. Currier, 1852 (342). Gen. Winfield Scott depicted as a chicken hatched from "Free Soil" egg. Proslavery faction feared Whigs Scott and Franklin Pierce were influenced by abolitionist William Seward. *$200–225*

Slavery/Military Related

(Ante-Bellum) "Ex-C.S.A." By Thomas Nast, ca. 1870. Bearded C.S.A. veteran with hands in pockets, looking sullen in defeat. Original.............. *$600–700*

"Anti-Radical/Blacks." Ca. 1866. "Radical Love For the Soldier." Ante-bellum 3" × 4" card showing sleezy paymaster giving extra bounty of $300 to black soldiers, while refusing to pay $100 to white soldier amputee. "I'm sorry, but Congress has made no appropriation for you." Reverse, Ohio congressional race, Delano vs. Morgan. *$250–300*

"Bankruptcy." *Punch*, June 7, 1862. Union combatant in flag costume fights with knife-wielding Rebel over precipice marked "Bankruptcy.". $35–45

"John Brown Exhibiting His Hangman." G. Guerner, 1865. Brown as vengeful figure, points finger at Jefferson Davis in cage suspended above heads of emancipated slaves. Litho, 16³⁄₈" × 12¹⁄₄". $125–150

(Jeff Davis) "Ho for the Fort Monroe/The Steamer Bread & Butter Cow-an." "Andy, Seward and Wells. Colored Population Voted on the 8th./Niggers Vote Today." 1861. Jeff Davis; anti-black sentiment featuring blacks and whip-cracking slave owner; 7" × 4" card. $100–125

"Jeff Davis after Surrender April 13, 1861/After the Fall of Fort Sumter, 1863." David Claypool Johnson, ca. 1863. Mechanical card cartoon. Mechanical 3-cent postcards, event shown below title changes to one in which Davis smiles at first when tag is pulled; the other produces frown with pull of tag.. . . . . . $200–250

(Jeff Davis) Untitled. Anonymous, ca. 1870. Allegorical depiction of Jefferson Davis sulking in doorway as Negro politician Hiram R. Revels occupies his seat in Congress. $75–100

"En Amerique." Signed Cham. Frenchman in tails looking at fighters in mud representing North and South says, "Ah! Devil! I'm beginning to get mixed up in all this" (caption in French). Litho, 10³⁄₄" × 14³⁄₁₆". $200–300

"Grant Turning Lee's Flank." *Harper's Weekly*, 1863. Grant picks up Lee's coattails and gives him smack on backside with handful of switches. $125–150

"(The) Massacre at New Orleans." Thomas Nast, 1867. Oil on canvas cartoon. One of 33 "Grand Historical Paintings" by Nast exhibited at Dodsworth Hall, NYC. Depicts riot in which radicals take over state from A. Johnson Republicans. Thirty-seven blacks and three white sympathizers were killed. Johnson (shown here as the culprit) peeks from shelter and wears king's crown. Oil on canvas, 7'10" × 11'6¹⁄₂". . . . . *Value Indeterminate*

"New Confederate Cruiser." J. Cameron, Currier & Ives (4413), 1863. Dem. party in Greeley's hat on high seas; coat serves as sail. $200–250

"N.Y. Fire Brigade Zouaves 1865." French print of inebriated Zouave soldier with bottle in hand, leaning against wall on which appears a Temperance broadside. Fireman recruits volunteers in background; 12" × 16", b&w. $250–300

"Of Course You'll Dine with Me." Anonymous, 1867. Ex-Rebel cavalryman Wade Hampton, still in cavalry boots, spurs, ostrich plumed hat, and cat-o-nine tails in pocket, assuming post-war role as politician—shakes hand with Negro, seeking his support at polls. $125–150

"(The) Reconstruction Policy of Congress as Illus. in California." Anonymous, 1867. Uncle Sam watches as California Rep. Gubernatorial nominee. George Gorham does juggling act with support of Negro, Chinaman, and Indian to gain election. Gorham's nomination raised such a ruckus that they replaced him with Caleb Fay, who subsequently lost to Dem. H.H. Haight. $75–100

(Slavery) "Cutting His Old Associates." *Harper's Weekly*, Jan. 17, 1863. Black boy struts past barnyard animals saying "I ain't one of you no mo. I'se a man, I is." $75–100

(Slavery) "Forcing Slavery Down the Throat of a Free-Soiler." Anonymous, 1856. Bearded "Free Soiler" shouts "Murder" as candidates Stephen Douglas, Franklin Pierce, James Buchanan, and Lewis Cass attempt to jam black slave down his throat. Litho, 12" × 15³⁄₄". $100–125

"(The) Smelling Committee." John Cameron, 1868. Impeachment manager bigwigs including John Logan, Ben Butler, Thaddeus Stevens, who failed by one vote to oust President Johnson, circle "dead horse." Johnson, standing by ram with head of political boss, Thurlow Reed, points out that impeachment is dead and decaying. Litho, 8½" × 14½".. $75–85

Untitled. Thomas Nast, ca. 1870. Ex-Union Gen. Carl Schurz carrying two giant carpetbags—"... one in front filled with others' faults; The one behind him, filled with his own faults, he never sees."................................ $75–100

"Young Texas in Repose." E. Jones, 1852. Texas appears as evil-looking cowboy with gun and whip sitting on back of shackled black slave. Texas was deemed a particularly depraved slave-holding state. Litho, 14¹/₁₆" × 9¹³/₁₆"......... $75–100

PAINTINGS

"Battle Between the Confederate Ram *Merrimac* and the *Cumberland* off Hampton Roads, Virginia. 1862. Monogramed and dated by artist Alexander Charles Stuart. Watercolor and tooling on paper, 16" × 28¾" in period frame. (A) Skinner, June '94, $1200–1500?............................... $2000–3000

"Camp Scenes and Sketches of the ALI, South Boston." Ca. 1860s; by Frank Park. Thirty-four original watercolors and eight pencil sketches, 4¼" × 6" with leather covers. Includes "Antietam Plains"; "Civility House on Bull Run Road"; "Ft. Delaware"; "Light Infantry Regiment."..................... $2500–3000

"(The) Color Sergeant." 1885. Watercolor gouache on brown paper; signed Rufus Fairchild Zogbaum; 5½" w. × 8¾" h. (D) 1991, $2500............. $2500–3000

"Connecticut Eagle and Flags." Oil on canvas; inscribed F. Mennacher, 1861. Eagle atop U.S. shield with crossed furled flags, the Connecticut state flag and Union flag. Brilliant multicolors....................................... $750–800

"Gen't George A. Custer." 1862. By "A.A. Frain, Artist," which appears on painted ribbon below portrait. Oil, ½-length portrait of Custer inside shield. Eagle atop red, white, and blue flags, 24" × 34½" multicolored. Artist was with Co. O. 15th Michigan Volunteers and includes his discharge.......... $20,000–22,000

"General William Enoch." Ca. 1863. Oil on canvas of Union (Ohio) Civil War, unsigned. (A) $750.. $600–700

"General John Geary at Gettsyburg." 1867. Oil. Signed by J.M. Boundy. Equestrian image with Geary holding cap high, 56" × 72", framed....... $6000–6500

"The General's Rescue." Ca. 1862. Framed oil on canvas; dramatic scene of wounded general being rescued by another general and his men. Unsigned. Very dark tones, 24¾" × 29¾", some surface crazing. (A) '89, $900...... $1000–1500

"Gettysburg." Ca. 1862. Battlefield scene; brush and ink watercolor by F.H. Schell (1834–1909), a former Frank Leslie staff artist; 14" × 18"....... $15,000–15,200

"General U.S. Grant." Late 1860s. Oil of Grant on horseback; black with various gray tones; signed by Gilbert Gaul (1855–1919), member of National Academy; 22" × 32".. $4000–5000

Abraham Lincoln. Ca. 1870. Oil painting. Waist-up portrait attrib. to Xanthus Russell Smith, 9" × 11". (D) $625............................... $625–650

"(The) Lincoln Family." Oil painting. By John Chester Buttre after a Francis B. Carpenter oil painting on canvas, pub. by Buttre, NY, 1867. Family seated around dining room table, 36¾" × 27".............................. $1000–1200

"Death of Gen. Joseph Mansfield at Antietam." Ca. 1860s. The bearded Gen. lies mortally wounded under tree, after having led his division against the Rebels at Suffolk, VII, VA. Framed oil painting on canvas. Relined; some craquelure...... .... $3500–4000

"Military Prison—Little Rock, Arkansas." Ca. 1863. Watercolor; 2¾" × 5" drawing with buildings, soldiers, and prisoners working. Inscribed "A.J. Freeman, Prisoner of War, Private U.S.A." on reverse...................... *$400–450*

"Naval Prison at Kittery, Maine." Ca. late 1850s. Watercolor; bold colors in naive folk art style, 19" × 28", walnut frame.................... *$1200–1500*

"Our Country Has Lost Its Father." Ca. 1865. Watercolor; monument with Lincoln portrait, eagle, shield, two slave children; red, white, blue, and black........
.... *$600–650*

"Sherman's March to the Sea." Ca. 1912. Copy by E. Denehy of F.A.O. Darley's original. Oil; 34½" × 52½". Depicts men burning buildings and tearing up railroad tracks. (A) '89, $450... *$500–600*

"Siege of Vicksburg." 1862. Oil on drumhead. Primitive image by unknown artist. Union soldiers in foreground, with Gen. Grant viewing battle through telescope. C.S.A. flag on bluff; gunboats in river. Provenance: Newbury, MA, Chapter of Soc. of Cincinnati Deaccession............................. *$350–400*

"Skeletal Union Drummer." Ca. 1864. Unknown. Oil on canvas. Skeleton in Union uniform beats drum as fire and smoke curls around him. Lower left reads "U.S.A." Lower right has satanic invocation "666." Possibly C.S.A. origin; 8" × 12".. *$2500–3000*

"Union Soldier." Ca. 1893. Watercolor. Signed by Baker. Union soldier in uniform. Framed. Excellent condition. (A) '89, $140.................. *$125–150*

"Union Soldiers in Log Cabin." 1862. Gilt-framed oil on canvas. Four soldiers encamped in log cabin. Muskets are stacked and bayonet is being used as candle holder. Canteens and tinware at fireplace; 13" × 16". Stark FP Cat., '94, $600. ....
.... *$500–600*

MISCELLANEOUS ART MEDIA

"Bachelder's Drawings, Sketching, and Notes of the Gettysburg Campaign." Sketchbooks (2). Ca. 1863. John Badger Bachelder watercolor, ink, and graphite on paper in various sizes but avg. 10" × 12". Includes "Pickett's Charge"; "Harrisburg"; "Fair Oaks"; "Gen. Meade's Headquarters"; "Residence of Robert E. Lee." Most pages detached from binding. Provenance. (A) Skinner, Oct. '92, $9500.....
.... *$9000–10,000*

Note: John B. Bachelder served in the 3rd Massachusetts Vol. Artillery, Company A, beginning in Dec. 1862. He was mustered out in Sept. 1865 as an artificer. Many of his personal effects from his Massachusetts descendants were auctioned over a span by Skinner Americana Auctions. See also Swords, Letters, and Photographs in each of their corresponding chapters.

"Confederate Cavalryman." 1860s. Artist unknown. Graphite, charcoal, chalk drawing, 17½" × 21½". Colored chalk on paper. Stain at left margin. (A) Skinner, Oct. '92, $300.. *300–350*

"Kensaw (sic) Mt." Late 1860s. U.S., primitive mixed media on wood depicting famous battle. Fine Quality/Good Condition. (A) $935.............. *$1100–1200*

"Lincoln, Cabinet Members, Generals." Ink drawing: cameos superimposed over Emancipation Proclamation, U.S. dated 1863; calligraphy/ink by C.T. Ames, Syracuse, NY; 37" × 28". Better Quality/Fine Condition. (A) $1430....... *$1200–3000*

Prior Abraham Lincoln. 1870s. Reverse-on-glass bust portrait, Mathew Prior....
.... *$1300–1500*

"Gen. George C. McClellan." 1862. Charcoal drawing signed and dated by "Katherine M. Baker, 1862." *$1000–1200*

"(Gen.) George C. McClellan." 1862. Signed charcoal drawing by Katherine M. Baker (1838–?), a listed American artist; 29" × 19". *$850–1000*

"Pine Bluff, Ark." 1864. "13 Ill. Cav. Comp. C," 7½" × 10" matted pencil drawing of camp, soldiers, tents, horses. Unsigned. Some age-toning. (A) '89, $380 ....
.... *$400–500*

Souvenir cartoon, "Jeff. Davis going to War." This is something of a novelty card, which when turned upside-down displays the caption "Jeff. returning from War" and the picture resembles a donkey. 1861, by S.C. Upham, Philadelphia, $300–$400. (The Kit Barry Collection)

Left: *Reverse-on-glass bust portrait of Abraham Lincoln, ca. 1870s, by Mathew Prior, $1,300–$1,500.* Right: *Cartoon, from* Harper's Weekly, *"The Re-United States," $35–$45.*

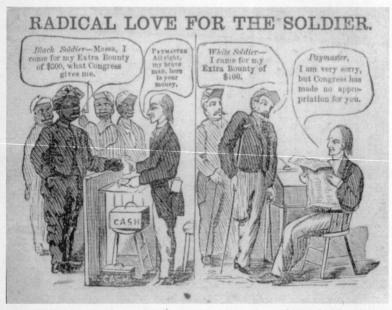

Ante-bellum cartoon, "Radical Love for the Soldier," $300–$350. (Photo courtesy of Rex Stark)

Left: *Cartoon, Lincoln, "You'll excuse me Gen. Butler, but as I can't send you everywhere, I'll have to cut you to pieces." Attributed to Thomas Nast. Original, pencil on paper, $1,200–$1,300.* Right: *Cartoon on Henry Clay's speech in defense of slavery, $250–$300.*

Watercolor, "Kensaw Mt." [sic.], late 1860s, U.S. Primitive mixed-media on wood depicting the famous battle. Fine quality. From the Larry Schafle collection, sold for $935 at auction in 1993, $1,100–$1,200.

Cartoon cards, three of a set of twelve by Louis Prange, Boston, 1865,
$250–$300 each.

PHOTOGRAPHY

ALBUMENS

Albumens (egg whites) served as a binder with silver salts. Their combined use was first published in France in 1847. In the United States, John A. Whipple and William and Frederic Langerheims succeeded in making finely detailed glass negatives with these substances. This photographic process was popular until the 1870s.

Annapolis Views. 1861, 6½" × 8½". Includes Hager's Class of '61; "Spardeck" U.S.S. *Santee*; "Gundeck"; "Gunnery model oom"; "Practice Ships" *Dale, Saratoga, Macedonian, Constitution.* Strong rich tones. (A) Riba, March '89, $800.. . . . . . . *$900–1000*

Antietam Bridge. Ca. 1862. M. Brady attrib. Taken from several hundred yards away, framed by trees and showing reflections in the stream. Also includes two albumens of "Bell Plain" with soldiers standing next to fortification; three images in all. (A) Swann, NYC, Oct. '94. . . . . *$700–800*

Army Relief Fair. (Sanitary Fair, forerunner to Red Cross.) 1864. Group of 140 mounted images with descriptions on verso; pub. by Churchill & Dennison. (A) Riba, Oct. '87, $800. . . . . *$850–900*

John Wilkes Booth. Ca., 1863; photographer unknown. Two-third view seated; hand on hip; the other holding a delicately carved cane. *$750–850*

Brady's Incidents of the War. 1861. "Ft. Richardson, Va., Camp, 1st Conn. Artillery, Col. R.O. Taylor." Mounted with printed credit; left corner stained; missing small edge piece. (A) Riba, Oct. '85, $100. . . . . *$200–250*

(C.S.A.) Gen. Pierre Beauregard. 1868. Signed and dated on recto. Minor retouching. (A) Riba, Oct. '92, $650. . . . . *$700–750*

(C.S.A.) Mosby's Rangers. 1862. Shows five men sitting on pattern rug—Sgt. A.G. Babcock, W.W. Gosden, Lt. W. Ben Palmer, John M. Munson, Sgt. Thomas Booker. Photographer: Anderson Studio, Richmond, VA. 10" × 13" oval in original frame. Light soil spots in background. (A) Riba, Oct. '85, $1300. . *$1400–1500*

Camp View, Men at Tent. Ca. 1862. "Douglas Goraline" stamped in corner. Three Union infantrymen grouped in front of open tent as if for inspection, 7½" × 5½". Excellent. *$450–500*

Charleston Cadets Guarding Yankee Prisoners. 1861 by George Cook. Guards in various casual positions look down from high wall to prisoners in courtyard below. *$2000–3000*

Chattanooga Valley from Lookout Mt. 1860s. George N. Bernard. On original

two-toned mount, titled, with Bernard credit; 10" × 14". (A) Swann, NYC, Oct.'94.
. . . . *$700–800*

City of Savannah, Ga., No. 2. 1864. George N. Bernard (No. 50 Dover), 10" × 14". Overall aging; minor spots. (A) $200. . . . . *$300–400*

Civil War Views (2). 1862. "No. 151 Upper Wharf Belle Plain"; "No. 274 Arsenal Yard, Washington, D.C." Both 15" × 10½". Some spotting and upper right damage on Arsenal Yard image. (A) Riba, '95, $275. . . . . *$300–350*

Curtis, Bonita, Sumner Corps. 1822–66. Wood & Gibson/Gardner/O'Sullivan (sig. on mount). Print with arched top shows seven men in dress uniforms with tassled caps; three carry sabres in scabbards, 7" × 9". Seven other albumens with views incl. "Blandford Church, Petersburg, Va."; "Gateway Cemetery at Gettysburg"; "Gen. Meade at Battle of Gettysburg." (A) Swann, NYC, Oct. '94. . . . . *$1000–2000*

"D" Company, 31st Mass. Vols. and Regimental Officers. Total of 101. Matted in gilt edge oval openings. (A) Riba, March '94, $1045. . . . . *$850–$1000*

"D" Company 31st Mass. Vols. 1862. Total of 101 images of Regt. officers and men in gilt edge oval mat. (A) Riba, '94, $950. . . . . *$1000–1100*

Jefferson Davis Surrounded by His Generals. 1862. Mounted oval of Davis with fan-out of 24 gem-sized albumen photos of C.S.A. Gen. staff. Similar to Lee version, but with a number of different images. (A) Riba, '94, $1500. . . . *$1400–1500*

Col. Dickinson and Major Ludlow, Fairfax. 1863. Pencil notation mount; two officers are seated in camp chairs in front of tent; pair of black soldiers also shown. Recto credit: A. Gardner, Washington; 6¾" × 3¾". Dark areas in plate. Fine, with rich tones. (A) Riba, March '83, d.n.s. (est. $1000–1500). *$750–800*

Duke de Charles, Count de Paris and Officers of the English Guard. Ca. 1862. Image by Alexander Gardner. Casual outdoor scene outside tent as men loll around table lined with liquor bottles, 8½" × 22". (A) $160. . . . . *$300–400*

Ft. Richardson, Va. 1861. Mathew Brady. On "Brady's Incidents of the War" mount. Letterpress caption on recto, 10" × 14½". (A) Swann, NYC, Oct.'94. . . . . . *$800–900*

Ft. Slemmer (Near Washington). 1862. On "Brady's Incidents" mount. Troops marching in front of battlement with U.S. flag flying above, 10" × 14". (A) Swann, NYC, Oct. '94. . . . . *$800–900*

Fortification—Heights of Centreville. 1862. On "Brady's Incidents of the War" mount. Titled, numbered, and with photographer's credit on recto. (A) Swann, NYC, Oct.'94. . . . . *$500–600*

Friends of Freedom. 1862. Composite of 51 prominent abolitionists. Entered according to Act of Congress by George W. Rose. Images incl. John Brown, Wendell Phillips, John Fremont, Horace Greeley, William Cullen Bryant, William Lloyd Garrison. Slight yellowing; mount soiled. (A) Riba, March '94, $500. . . . . *$600–700*

Alexander Gardner Group. "Ruins of Stone Bridge"; "Bull Run"; "Quaker Guns"; "Dutch Gap Canal"; Lodge No. 5 for Invalid Soldiers." Ca. 1862. Five prints, 3" × 4" images, mounted (three from Gardner's sketch book). (A) Riba, Oct. '85, $280. . . . . *$400–500*

Alexander Gardner Group—The Conspirators. 1865. With the exception of J.W. Booth, who perished in ambush during his capture, the following images were taken by Gardner in April 1865, presumably aboard the ironclad monitors *Montauk* and *Saugus*, where Lincoln conspirators were held awaiting trail by military tribunal. (1) Samuel Arnold, waist-up shot, seated. (2) George Atzerodt, waist-up semiprofile. (3) Lewis Payne, waist-up wearing sweater, seated and manacled. (4) Edward Spangler, seated semiprofile and wearing jacket, felt hat. . . . . *$2000–3000 (set of four)*

Gen. U.S. Grant. 1868. Photographer T.R. Burnham, Washington, D.C. Grant in uniform, 4" × 6". A mounted albumen oval with typed note dating it as 1868, shortly after Grant won the presidency. Thirteen other images, mostly cabinets, by misc. photographers. (A) $300. . . . . *$500–600*

Gen. U.S. Grant. 1872. Waist-up pose of Grant in uniform by M.F. Savage. Only two or three prints were made from neg. before it was broken. Minor corner damage on top and bottom right. *$500–600*

Gen. U.S. Grant U.S.A. 1868. Imperial sized image by T.R. Burnham, Boston and Washington, D.C.; 19½" × 16" plus margins. *$1000–1200*

U.S. Grant. 1862. Oval, 18" × 15". Signed "Photo by Gurney." (A) Riba, Feb.'86, $800. . . . . *$1000–1200*

U.S. Grant. 1868. Uncut sheet, 28 small albumen oval Grant bust images; in uniform, ¾" × 1". Two sides trimmed. (A) Riba, March '93, $750. . . . . *$800–850*

Gen. Halleck's Headquarters, Corinth, Miss. 1862. From the effects of Maj. D.C. Gamble, whose patriotic imprint is on recto. Plantation house with tents. Three holes in upper mount. Lower corner missing. Rich contrast. *$500–600*

Gen. Winfield Scott Hancock. Six separate poses, incl. three in 19½" × 8" size; a profile study and a seated example. Mounted in quarto leather portfolio, scuffed cover, gilt embossed, "W.S. Hancock." (A) Riba, July '91, $800. . . . . . *$900–1000*

Hanging Bodies of Lincoln Conspirators, Washington D.C. July 7, 1865. One of seven exposures of preparations for the hangings taken by Alexander Gardner inside prison walls at Arsenal. Shows condemned prisoners Mrs. Surrat, Payne, Herold, and Atzerodt. *$1200–1300*

Hanging of Lincoln Conspirators at Ft. McNair, Washington, D.C. 1865. Minor wrinkling, surface abrasion. (A) Riba, Jan. '91, $3000. . . . . *$3000–4000*

John F. Hartranft and Staff Responsible for Securing the Lincoln Conspirators at the Arsenal. April 1865, by Alexander Gardner. Pictured left to right: Capt. R.A. Watts, Lt.Col. George W. Fredrick, Lt. Col. William H.H. McCall, Lt. D.H. Geissinger, Gen. Hartranft, unknown, Col. L.A. Dodd, Capt. Christian Rath. Cracked plate in upper left corner. *$1500–2000*

> *Note:* Even though it was not possible to reproduce these Gardner images by halftone in the popular press, the above series appears to be the first photographic picture story of an event *as it happened.*

R.E. Lee Surrounded by Confederate Generals. 1862. Lee mounted oval in center encircled by 24 gem-sized albumens of his Gens., incl. Jackson, Jeb Stuart, Pierre Beauregard. Mounted on album page. (A) Riba, '94, $2000. . . . *$2000–2100*

Robert E. Lee. Ca. 1869. Seated in civilian attire, verso ink signature of "General Read, U.S.A." *$350–400*

Robert E. Lee/Arlington Va. 1865. Brady & Co. Oval portrait; seated pose. Photographer's copyright and credit. Notation in ink "Gen. Robt. E. Lee/ Arlington," 8¼" × 6⅛". (A) Swann, NYC, Oct.'94. . . . . *$4000–5000*

A. Lincoln. Ca. 1862. Large mounted oval portrait; recto credit "James E. McClees, Philadelphia" (Ostendorf, 55); minor yellowing, retouching. (A) Riba, July '93, $300. . . . . *$250–300*

A. Lincoln Mounted Oval Half Fig. 1861. C.S. German, National Gallery, Springfield, IL, imprint. Lincoln's first photo with full beard, taken June 13, 1861. Some light, age staining in mat area. (A) Riba, Oct. '86, $1600. . . . . *$2000–2200*

Abram (sic) Lincoln, Gen. McClellan and Suite. (A) Skinners, Apr. 94, $2500. . . . . *$2500–2700*

Abraham Lincoln. 1880s. G.B. Ayres blindstamp at lower right corner, framed, 8¼" × 6¼". Spotting, touch-up. (A) Riba, Jan '91, $650. . . . . *$650–700*

Abraham Lincoln Reading to Tad. 1864. Taken at Brady Washington Gallery by Anthony Berger, 5¼" × 3¾", some foxing, age tone. (A) Riba, Jan. '91, $650.....
.... *$750–800*

Lincoln and Gen. McClellan Confer under Tent at Antietam. 1862, by Alexander Gardner. Light coloring in flag area on desk. (A) Riba, Oct. '85, $850........
.... *$1000–1100*

Lincoln and Pinkerton at Antietam. 1862. Alexander Gardner. Maj. Pinkerton and Gen. John McClernand flank a top-hatted Pres. Lincoln, in front of tent. (A) Riba, Oct '85, $1400... *$1500–1700*

Lincoln (Beardless Tousled Hair Pose). 1857. Taken in Chicago by Alexander Hessler. Dark tones, some soiling in margins, 8¾" × 6½". (A) Riba, Feb. '87, $800.. *$1200–1500*

Lincoln $5 Bill Image. 1864. Anthony Berger, image of Lincoln seated in Brady chair, but at different angle than below. Basis for $5 bill. Robert Lincoln called it the most satisfactory likeness of his father. REF: Ostendorf, 92. (A) Swann, NYC, Oct. '94... *$5000–6000*

Lincoln in the Brady Chair. 1863. Full-length seated fig. of Lincoln by Alexander Gardner; a vignetted version. Lincoln's facsimile sig., Gardner's credit, and © data on recto; 17½" × 13¼" in period frame. (A) Swann, NYC, Oct. '94 ....
.... *$2000–3000*

Lincoln—Oval Portrait from Orig. Painting. 1870s. Anonymous. Half-fig. portrait, 7⅜" × 5⅜", in ornate period frame. (A) Swann, NYC, Oct.'94........
.... *$1000–1500*

Lincoln with Union High Command at Antietam. Oct. 2, 1862. Attrib. to Gardner. Lincoln stands at command post with Gens. McClellan, A.A. Humphreys, L.M. Hunt, Fitz J. Porter. Light touches in leaves and on Lincoln's coat; 6½" × 8". (A) Riba, Oct. '85, $600. .... *$800–900*

Medical Photos from Surgeon General's Office, Army Medical Museum. Ca. 1862. By order of George A. Otis, A.M.M. curator. Eleven photos incl. soldiers with wounds and recovery; bones damaged by gunshot and sword wounds; 8½" × 7". Printed case history on reverse. (A) Riba, Oct. '87, $300........... *$300–400*

Our Mess at Antietam. 1862. Mounted image by Alexander Gardner. Six soldiers in tents. M.B. Brady pub.; 7" × 9", slight stain in margin. (A) $176..... *$200–300*

Pig Roast, Anacostia Farm, Apr. 14, 1888. Attendees (penned in ink) incl. ex–Civil War Gens. Sheridan and Benjamin Butler, Oliver Green, Beverly Robertson (C.S.A.), N.H. Anderson. Framed, scattered yellowing. (A) Riba, July '93, $170... *$200–250*

(The) Potter House. 1864 or 1865. Photographer George Bernard. View of bombed out Southern mansion. From Bernard's *Photographic Views of the Sherman Campaign*; 10" × 14".................................... *$400–500*

Quarles' Mill. 1864. O'Sullivan/Timothy/Gardner/Alexander. On "Incidents of War" mount, with title, date, and photographer's credits on recto. View of waterfall and log constructed mill. (A) Swann, NYC, Oct. '94.................. *$500–600*

Maj. Gen. Philip Henry Sheridan. 1865. (1) Bust photo signed in ink by Sheridan. Verso: Photographer's label "Hoag & Quick" and revenue stamp. (2) Clipped signature. (A) Riba, July '93, $1600............................ *$1500–1700*

Sherman and His Generals. 1865. By M. Brady, on Brady & Co. mount. Gens. Sherman, O.O. Howard, J.A. Logan, W.B. Hazen, Jeff C. Davis, H.W. Slocum, J.A. Mower, and F.P. Blair. Image of Blair was affixed later as he was not present when group portrait was taken; 14" × 17". (A) Swann, NYC, Oct. '94. ..... *$2000–2500*

Sherman and His Generals. 1865. Same as above without Gen. Blair's attached photo inset into image. His name is imprinted on mount, however. . . . .
. . . . *$1000–2000*

John Surrat, Co-Conspirator in Lincoln Assassination. 1865. M. Brady photo, 8$^{1}/_{2}$" × 7$^{3}/_{4}$" plus 2$^{1}/_{4}$" border mount. Minor age tones and light spots. (A) Riba, Oct. '92, $1700. . . . . *$2000–2500*

(Union) Gen. George Henry Thoman. "The rock of Chicamauga," second in command of Army of the Ohio; commanded XIV Corps at Chickamauga. Some light margin soiling; 8$^{1}/_{2}$" × 6$^{1}/_{2}$". (A) Riba, Oct '88, $250. . . . . *$300–350*

(Union) Agawam Sidewheeler Gunboat at Four Mile Creek, Maine. Bombarded Rebel batteries at Howlett's Bluff, VA; attack on Fisher; 4$^{1}/_{2}$" × 7$^{3}/_{4}$", minor soiling, yellowing. (A) $175. . . . . *$200–250*

(Union) Camp Scenes (3). 1863. (1) Noncoms. of Co. G. 1st Conn. Artillery—large group at table in mess tent, 6$^{1}/_{4}$" × 8$^{1}/_{4}$". (2) Outdoor camp scene with seven men, one with rifle; oval, 7$^{1}/_{4}$" × 5$^{1}/_{4}$". (3) Outdoor encampment with regiment grouped near tents, 5$^{1}/_{4}$" × 7$^{1}/_{2}$", light soiling. (A) Riba, July '93, $450. . . . . *$450–500*

(Union) (2) Dress Inspection or Parade Ready. Ca. 1862. Second image of officers posed in front of Admin. building, pair is 10" × 13". Some stains, soiling. (A) Riba, Oct. '85, $250. . . . . *$250–300*

(Union) Officers of the *Peresuyet.* 1863. Photo of officers aboard Russian frigate visiting NYC. While not directly Civil War, an important photo of the period. Imperial-sized sepia image by Mathew Brady. (A) Riba, May '86, $380.
. . . . *$350–400*

Union 6th Corp Staff Officers. 1863–64. Officers at leisure in camp chairs in front of tent. Most wear round pork pie–type hats. Identified in verso under image; 8" × 10". *$200–225*

(Union) Gen. Alexander S. Webb's Headquarters and Others. 1860s. By Andrew J. Russell. Six views incl. "Wounded at Spotsylvania," "Looking Down James River," "Bridge on Washington Aqueduct," "Magazine Wharf," etc. 9$^{3}/_{4}$" × 14" and smaller. Clipped printed captions attached to mount recto. (A) Swann, NYC, Oct. '94. . . . . *$1800–2000*

George N. Bernard

The following five lots comprise a photographic record of Gen. William T. Sherman's Southern Campaign by George N. Bernard, Charleston, SC, a Brady associate. Included are some of the more desirable images from Bernard's classic photo album, all on original mounts.

City of Atlanta, Ga., No. 1. Ca. 1864, from George N. Bernard's classic album (No. 45. Dover). Panoramic view of city showing destroyed railroad roundhouse, 10" × 14", minor soil spots. (A) $480. . . . . *$500–600*

City of Atlanta, Ga., No. 2. Ca. 1864, Bernard (No. 46 Dover). Small stains and minor spots, 10" × 14". (A) $500. . . . . *$600–700*

City of Columbia (SC) from the Capitol. 1864, Bernard (No. 53 Dover). Minor margin soiling, light aging overall, 10" × 14". (A) $250 . . . . *$300–400*

City of Nashville from the Capitol. 1864, Bernard (No. 3 Dover). Minor spots and light aging, 10" × 14". (A) $200. . . . . *$300–$350*

Pass in the Raccoon Ranger Whiteside, No. 1. 1864. Bernard (No. 6 Dover). (A) $200. . . . . *$300–350*

ALBUMS

Bernard's Photographic Views of Sherman's Campaign. Pub. 1866. Folio album with 61 mounted albumen photos from negs. taken in major battles (Antietam, Chattanooga, Campaign of Atlanta) by George Bernard, Official Photo. of Military Div. of the Mississippi. Sold at time for $100. (A) Riba, Oct.'85, $5000. . . . *$6000–8000*

M. Brady CDV Portraits. Late 1860s. Brady portraits (191) incl. Lincoln, Buchanan, Pierce, Jefferson Davis; near-mint and bearing M. Brady's monogram on cover, New York. (A) April '78, $2200. . . . . *$3000–5000*

Civil War CDVs. Early 1860s. Forty-six images incl. Grant, W. Scott, Lincoln, Doubleday (Brady), Col. Garfield, Gen. Bayard, Gen. C.P. Stone and daughter. (A) Riba, March '89, $800 . . . . *$900–1000*

Columbia College 1861. Fifty-two images of students and faculty by Julius Brill. Incl. oval portrait of Prof. McCullough, Chairman of Columbia's Chemistry Dept., who became a famous turncoat at the onset of the war, fled to Richmond, and headed the C.S.A, Chemical Bureau. *$550–650*

Compiled by Rep. Nehemiah Perry, N.J. Ca. 1863. Two albums made up of 390 CDVs, incl. rare Lincoln, A. Johnson, leading Union officers, senators, representatives. Nearly half were signed by subject. (A) 1975, $2800. . . . . *$3000 4000*

Confiscated C.S.A. Photos and Correspondence (Collection). Early 1860s. From estate of Charles Hall, an engraver who served in Union Co. that captured this material. Incl. eight ⅙ plate ambros of Confederate soldiers; five ⅙ plate and ⅑ plate of war scenes, 18 letters with Civil War dates. (A) Riba, Jan '91, $11,000. . . *$11,000–12,000*

Charles Green Album of 24 Naval Images. 1862–67. Incl. CDVs on U.S.S. *Jamestown*, U.S. Steam Sloop *Powhatten*, *New Ironsides* (destroyed by fire in 1866). Also includes naval officers Charles Green, Com. Charles Wilkes. (A) Riba, '94, $1300. . . . . *$1300–1400*

Howlett's Bluff, VA. Attack on Fisher, $4\frac{1}{2}'' \times 7\frac{3}{4}''$. Minor soiling, yellowing. *$200–250*

Lincoln, Buchanan, Harriet Beecher Stowe. 1860s. Sixty-six CDVs featuring Civil War dignitaries, plus European writers, artists. (A) London, '78, $270. . . . . *$500–600*

Capt. William F. Martins, U.S. 1862–63. Compiled while confined in infamous Libby Prison; handdrawn calligraphy; autographs of 200 officers, rank, home state. (A) $4500. . . . . *$5000–5500*

Members of Wartime Congress. 1860–70. CDV portraits of 33 members of U.S. Congress. (A) April '77, $300. . . . . *$400–500*

Presidential Portraits. 1870. Made up of 1120 CDVs, incl. 18 U.S. presidents; 84 Union officers; 66 C.S.A. officers; 130 Union statesmen, authors; 11 C.S.A. statesmen. (A) New York, 1977, d.n.s. at $6000 reserve price. *$6000–8000*

Soldier's Pocket Album. Ca. 1860s. Twelve pp./twelve mos., pages stamped "E. & H.T.A." (Anthony Bros. Studio); six tintypes of Union soldiers; $1 \times \frac{3}{4}''$ albumen of Lincoln in brass mat (Ostendorf, 0-79; Meserve M-58). *$75–100*

(Union) Non-Com Staff. 1860s. Twelve CDVs. Members of 10th NY Cavalry, each identified. Vet. Surgeon, Hosp. Steward, Chief Bugler, etc. All in rich tones. (A) Riba, Oct. '88, $300. . . . . *$350–400*

(Union and C.S.A.) Civil War Gens., Statesmen. 1860–65. Images incl. Gens. Grant, Banks, Hancock, Q.A. Gilmore, Sprague, C. Cushing, A.P. Hill (by Brady), Maj. Gen. McClellan and staff, Gilmore, Butler, a Fredericks photo of Lincoln (Ostendorf 55), Jefferson Davis. (A) Riba, Oct '88, $1200. . . . . *$1500–2000*

Union Gens. and High Ranking Officials. Forty-eight images of CDVs. (A) $750.
. . . . *$800–1000*

(Union) Naval Officers and Gens. 1862–65. Fifty CDVs incl. Adms.: John Dahlgren, David Farragut, William B. Cushing, Rowan; Gens.: Abner Doubleday, W.T. Sherman, U.S. Grant, P. Sheridan, Winfield Scott Hancock, George G. Meade; also E.M. Stanton, Sec. of War, Edward Everett, orator, statesman; lone C.S.A. image signed W.A. Harris. Most with verso credits of E. and H.T. Anthony from Brady negs., and with affixed revenue stamps. Cabinet cards (14) incl. family portraits; a Civil War surgeon; Michigan Sen. Jacob M. Howard, who favored treatment for South. (A) Riba, July '93, $1500. . . . . *$1500–2000*

AMBROTYPES

An ambrotype is a positive photograph on glass, backed by black color, making negative appear as positive. It was a popular process (advertised as imperishable) patented by James A. Cutting in 1854. Surface appears far less reflective than daguerreotypes. Process lost out in popularity to paper-print images after only three years (1858).

Armory Square Hospital for Union Army Veterans, Washington, D.C. 1865. M. Brady. Wounded soldiers sit on beds in open hospital ward bedecked with patriotic decorations (Fourth of July). *$200–250*

Battle of Antietam, Maryland. 1862. M. Brady. Silhouetted observer on McClellan's headquarters at Pry Mansion overlooks smoke-filled battleground; Union horse artillery at left; infantry on right. Reputedly the only actual battle picture of the war. *$900–1100*

D.W.C. Arnold, Pvt. in Union Army Near Harpers Ferry, Virginia. 1861. M. Brady. Pvt. Arnold cradling his musket, stands beside cannon from Capt. Cochran's unit. *$1200–1500*

Chester Allen Arthur. Ca. 1880s. M. Brady. Chester Arthur, our 21st president, was Quartermaster Gen. of State of New York during Civil War. Arthur, in hat, stands next to canoe holding flycasting rod. *$400–500*

Artilleryman (Seated) with Saber. One of two ambros, ca. 1863, $\frac{1}{6}$ plate. Minor abrasion near mat opening. Geometric leather case. Also $\frac{1}{4}$ plate "Capt. with 1850 Staff and Field Sword." Thermoplastic patriotic case. REF: *Union and Constitution*, Krainik, 271. (A) Riba, Oct. '92, $320. . . . . *$350–400*

Clara Barton. Late 1860s. Two-third fig. of a smiling Barton seated in chair next to table holding large, elaborate clock. Right arm rests on table; left hand holds pair of gloves. *$2500–3000*

William Black, Drummer Boy. 1862. M. Brady. Black at 12, seated on crate. He was reputedly the youngest soldier wounded in the war. *$1500–2000*

Black Union Soldier in Uniform Cooking Beans at West Point, Virginia. Undated. Mule teams in background. *$500–600*

Bloodiest Day of the War. 1862. M. Brady. Confederate dead strewn along Hagerstown Pike, Battle of Antietam, Sept. 17, 1862. . . . . *$1100–1200*

Belle Boyd, Confederate Spy. Ca. 1862. Mathew Brady, Washington, D.C. . . . . .
. . . . *$600–700*

Mathew Brady, Photographer. 1861. Brady Studio photo. Full-standing profile, wearing pork-pie hat; taken after Brady's return from 1st Battle of Bull Run. . . . . . .
. . . . *$900–1200*

Brady's "What's-It" Wagon. 1864. Two photographers, believed to be David Woodbury (left) and E. Guy Foxx (right) sit on ground next to buckboard, while black man holds reins of horses. A wooden box marked "Brady" can be seen at front of buckboard. . . . . *$450–$500*

Kady Brownell—Lady Infantryman. 1862. Kady Brownell joined her husband in a Rhode Island regt. She reportedly saved a number of men from her unit from being killed by friendly fire at New Bern (Gen. Burnside's expedition in No. Carolina). Later, she was wounded at Manassas. *$600–700*

C.S.A. Trooper. Ca. 1861. ⅙ plate. Knee-up standing pose, with pistol tucked in belt. Pencil notation, "Henry M. Swann to his cousin Julia Swann . . . 1861." Signed by Rees, Richmond, VA, photographer. In embossed leather case. (A) Riba, Oct. '92, $1200. . . . . *$1200–1300*

C.S.A. Soldiers in Front of Barracks. Ca. 1862. Ruby-glass image of nine enlisted men at camp, possibly at Port Royal. In geometric thermoplastic case. (A) Riba, June '93, $700. . . . . *$600–700*

C.S.A. Soldier with Colt Automatic. 1862. ⅙ plate. (A) $935. . . . . *$750–800*

C.S.A. Soldier with Austrian Rifle. Ca. 1863. On ruby glass; shows ammo pouch, cap box, cross belt. Lith tarnish at mat opening; minor scratches. Embossed leather case. (A) Riba, Oct. '92, $450. . . . . *$500–600*

Camp Sprague, 1st R.I. Regiment. 1861. From Brady's "Incidents of the War" mount with letterpress caption on mount recto. (A) Swann, NYC, Oct. '94. . . . . *$900–1000*

Catawba **Ironclad.** 1865. Two bearded men (possibly designers or engineers) seated before large framed image on pedestal of Union ironclad *Catawba*. Verso stamp, Hoag & Quicks, Cincinnati. *$250–300*

Chess Game between Two Union Officers as Visiting Families Look On. 1864. M. Brady. While officers play at table in front of tent, several ladies and a small boy look on. Another young officer stands at tent entrance with hand on pole. Young black stands stolidly at right. *$450–500*

Confederate Dead at Marye's Heights, Fredericksburg, Va. 1863. M. Brady. Many bodies lying face up behind stone wall, where only minutes earlier Sedgwick's 6th Maine Volunteers had broken through the lines. *$750–800*

Cooks at a Camp. M. Brady, Washington, D.C. Over 100 cooks in aprons stand in front of long tables facing the camera. *$350–400*

Cooks at Large Union Mess Hall. Ca. 1862. M. Brady. *$150–200*

Courduroy (Log) Road at 6th N.Y. Artillery Camp Kitchen at Brandy Station, Virginia. 1864. M. Brady. One man wields ax to cut more logs. Cook with large pan stands outside door of log building. Three others, including a black soldier, stand by with hands in pockets. *$250–275*

George Armstrong Custer. Late 1860s. M. Brady Studio. Seated with legs splayed wide; gloved hands in lap; campaign hat pushed back at rakish angle. *$5000–6000*

"D" Company 31st Mass Vols. and Regimental Officers. Ca. 1863. "J.M. Aiken photographer, Ware, Mass." Large 24" × 32" mat with individual images of 106 members of regiment, behind gilt-trimmed oval cut-out. Light overall soiling. (A) Riba, June '87, $200. . . . . *$250–300*

Adm. John A. Dahlgren. Ca. 1863. M. Brady, Washington, D.C. Dahlgren, looking grim, stands in three-quarter view before cannon; one hand is on hilt of saber in sheath. Dahlgren is noted as "The Father of American Naval Ordnance.". *$900–1000*

Desolation of War—The Ruins of Galligo Mills, Richmond, Virginia. 1865. M. Brady. Charred, burned out buildings and rubble, masterfully done in light and shadow. *$650–750*

"Dictator" Seacoast Mortar on Flatcar in Front of Petersburg, Va. 1864. Timothy O'Sullivan or David Knox—M. Brady Collection. The 8.5 ton "Dictator" was capable of propelling 200-pound missiles into the air during siege operations. Eight federal cannoneers gather around mortar mount.................... *$300–350*

Charles R. Douglas, Pvt., 54th Mass. Inf. 1863. Photographer anonymous. Douglas, along with brother Louis (see following entry), is a son of black abolitionist Frederick Douglas. The Pvt. stands with arms folded next to a wooden stair railing; he wears kepi and tunic, with leather boots. *$300–400*

Frederick Douglass, Abolitionist. Ca. 1860s. Head and shoulders pose of Douglass in suit, vest, and bow tie................................... *$300–350*

Louis H. Douglas, Sgt. of 54th Mass. Inf. 1863. Young black soldier stands with arms folded, against draped background. His kepi lies on table next to him. ....
.... *$300–400*

Elisha Ellis, Pvt. with 4th Maine. 1862. Two-thirds standing view of Ellis with musket and bayonet. Ellis was a prisoner at Libby Prison following Battle of Bull Run. Later released and fought as a Lt. at Gettysburg. Image has flowered background and in ornate gilt frame. Andrews & Andrews, Belfast, ME. (A) Oct. '94. .
.... *$400–500*

Encampment of Army of the Potomac at Cumberland Landing on Pamunkey River. 1862. James Gibson/Brady Collection. Six troopers sit on hill with backs to camera, looking down on rows of tents, as far as the eye can see. *$450–550*

Federal Balloon Corps Airship *Intrepid*. 1862. M. Brady. Balloon Corpsmen inflate *Intrepid* prior to observation flight behind enemy lines. Corps was organized by Prof. Thadeus Lowe.. *$700–800*

1st Battle of Bull Run. 1861. Combat scene with Union cannoneers line in front and cavalry behind them ready to attack Rebel positions. One of the first photographs of the armies in combat. *$1200–1500*

1st U.S. Veteran Volunteer Infantry/F. Street, Washington D.C. 1865. M. Brady Studio. Panoramic view of unit leading huge parade........... *$850–1000*

(The) 1st Conn. Artillery, Federal Battery No.1. May 1962. M. Brady. McClellan's fortifications in front of Yorktown, VA, during Peninsular Campaign. Soldiers patrolling behind cannon ramparts. *$450–500*

Lt. Edward A. Flint Holding Reins of His Horse, Headquarters, Petersburg, Va. 1864. M. Brady... *$600–650*

Ft. Totten Near Rock Creek Church, Washington, D.C. 1861. M. Brady. View from battlements manned by cannoneers and riflemen in enclosed fortress........
.... *$800–1000*

Gen. James A. Garfield. 1870? M. Brady. Garfield in partial profile, seated with young daughter at his knee................................. *$1200–1400*

Georgia Light Artillery Officer. 1865. ¹/₄ plate of R.N. Reed, Tiller's Co., Light Artillery, GA, with rifle, cap box. Wears GA oval State Seal belt. Incl. Reed's signed Oath of Allegiance, 12, Aug. 1865." In floral leather case. REF: Albaugh, *More Confederate Faces*, fig. 271; Turner, *Even More Confederate Faces*, p. 66. (A) Riba, Oct. '92, $1900. .... *$2000–2500*

Georgia Trooper. 1861. ¹/₆ plate. Subject with pistols, bowie knife, bayonet, and captured Yankee battle flag. Embossed leather case. REF: Albaugh, *Confederate Faces*, fig. 329. (A) Riba, Oct. '92, $850. .... *$900–1000*

Grand Review of the Armies—Union Victory Celebration, Washington, D.C. 1865. Cavalry unit leads parade while nation's Capitol looms in background......
.... *$600–700*

Gen. U.S. Grant at Coldwater, Va., Headquarters. 1864. By Alexander Gardner with M. Brady signature. (A) $12,000. . . . . *$10,000–12,000*

Gen. U.S. Grant Seated at Table with Bible. 1870s. Brady Studio. Other books and large vase on table. Grant seated with legs crossed. Hanging globed oil lamps overhead. *$5000–6000*

Gen. U.S. Grant at Headquarters during Wilderness Campaign. 1864. M. Brady. Grant with one arm bent at waist, leaning against tree. Field chair and tent in background. *$2000–2500*

> *Note:* In a 1986 sale at Riba Auctions, an example of the above ambro, cata-logued as original and signed by Grant, sold at $850. It was, however, yellowed and in need of restoration.

Grapevile Bridge at Chickahominy Creek, Va. 1862. M. Brady. Union engineers and workers on bridge with shovels and pick completing construction, prior to the Seven Days Campaign in 1862. . . . . *$650–750*

Rose O'Neal Greenhow "The Wild Rose." Ca. 1860s. ⅛ plate. U.S. outdoor view of famed Confederate spy (subject of ABC movie); in floral leather case, slight re-pair. (A) $2500. . . . . *$2600–2800*

Guns and Munitions of McClellan's Army of the Potomac. 1862. M. Brady. Scene of cannon balls, cannons at Ship Point near Lamar Wharf after fall of York-town, VA, May 1862. . . . . *$900–1000*

Gen. Rutherford B. Hayes. 1870s. M. Brady Studio; wearing suit, with hand tucked in jacket. Another coat lies sprawled on chair. Holds pair of gloves in right hand. Stands next to table with book atop. *$1500–2000*

Huntress and the Falcon. Ca. 1863. ⅙ plate. C.S.A. waist-up image on ruby glass of Tennessee trooper holding pistol across chest; cap box. Thermoplastic case. Cor-ner chips. REF: Rinhart, p. 44. (A) Riba, Oct. '92, $850. . . . . *$900–1000*

Indian Private. 1862. Unidentified Indian, one of over 3,000 who fought with the Union. Holds revolver across chest with one hand; other holds hilt of sword in sheath. *$400–500*

Itinerant Embalmer at Battlefield. Undated. M. Brady. Morbid shot of corpse on table being embalmed. *$125–150*

Gen. Thomas Stonewall Jackson. 1871. Circulated for purpose of raising money for a monument to Jackson. Handtinted. *$200–225*

Andrew Johnson. 1865. Imperial-sized image by Alexander Gardner. Printed by Phillip & Solomens, Washington, D.C. (A) $300. . . . . *$600–700*

Frederick West Lander. Ca. 1860. Signed and inscribed imperial-sized photo; im-print below photo "M. Brady." Western explorer and Civil War Brig. Gen. Lander from MA, wearing buckskins in prairie setting. Handcolored. Attrib. to western artist Albert Bierstadt's copy as his penciled signature appears on verso. Overall age tones. (A) Riba, June '87, $800. . . . . *$1500–2000*

Robert E. Lee. Ca. 1869. M. Brady Studio, Washington, D.C. Full-figure pose; Lee with hat in hand standing in front of door. *$4500–6000*

Robert E. Lee at Home in Richmond. 1865. M. Brady photographed a somber Lee and his son, George Washington Custis Lee, plus a friend, Col. Walker Taylor, at his home in Richmond, VA. The photo shows Lee seated in uniform, hat in lap, flanked by his son and Taylor standing in partial profile, each with an arm on the back of Lee's chair. Taken several days after surrender at Appomattox Court House. *$700–800*

Gen. R.E. Lee on Horseback. Miley, Lexington, VA. 15¾" × 19¼". Minor age-toning. (A) Riba, Oct. '85, $300. . . . . *$450–500*

Lincoln (Seated). Preston Butler, Springfield, IL. 1860. One of series for artist John Henry Brown in painting life portrait as model for campaign engraving...... .... *$450–500*

A. Lincoln and Son Tad. 1862. Alexander Gardner, Washington, D.C. In rare imperial size (17" × 13"). From estate of photographer Henry Warren. Surface stain near Tad's arm. Margin tears not affecting image. (A) Riba, June '85, $3800. .... *$4000–5000*

A. Lincoln. 1860. Attrib. to H.H. Cole, Peoria, IL. 1½" × 1" oval in ornate brass frame. Excellent. (A) Riba, Oct. '85, $700......................... *$800–900*

Lincoln's Funeral Procession Down Pennsylvania Avenue in Washington, D.C. 1865. M. Brady. Large part of infantry unit standing at parade rest...... *$750–850*

Mary Todd Lincoln. 1861. M. Brady, Washington, D.C.. Mary Todd is seated; a large garland of flowers is in her hair. She also wears a corsage; holds small bouquet in lap with white-gloved hands. Taken shortly before her husband's first inauguration. *$1000–1200*

Mail Wagon of 2nd Army Corps, Brandy Station, Va. 1864. M. Brady. Horse-drawn Mail Wagon with "2nd. Corps" painted on side. One man driving; three standing next to wagon with mail sacks.......................... *$200–250*

Marines in Full Dress Uniform, with Weapons. ⅑ plate, outdoor view. REF: *Civil War Collector's Encyclopedia*, p. 316, for same group at same site. (A) Riba, Oct. '88, $600... *$700–750*

U.S.S. *Monitor* **Crew Cooking on Deck.** 1862. M. Brady. Men gather around cooking pots. One man seated smokes pipe. Man standing guard at turret. Photographed on the James River in Virginia on July 9, 1862, just months after first battle with the *Merrimac*...................................... *$1200–1400*

Father Thomas H. Mooney Performs Sunday Mass for 69th NY Inf. Regt. 1863. M. Brady. Father reads from scriptures before large wood cross outside tent. *$200–250*

N.H. Volunteers Trooper. 1861. One of two ambros. Identified as Miles Hodgen. Standing, with rifle, fixed bayonet, holding kepi with NH emblem over heart. Gold touches to cross-belt and buckle. Also standing soldier with rifle, bayonet, cap box. Light oval tarnish. Each in geometric leather cases. (A) Riba, Oct. '91, $220...... .... *$250–300*

New York State Militiaman in Grey Uniform. 1861. Brady, Washington, D.C. Full-standing; wearing knapsack; rifle with fixed bayonet on shoulder... *$450–500*

96th Pennsylvania Infantry Regulars at Camp Northumberland. 1861. M. Brady. Unit drills in front of huge campsite lined with tents. Ambulance wagon appears at far left.. *$750–950*

Seated C.S.A. Captain. Ca. 1862. "Rees" (a Richmond, VA, photo) signed in emulsion. In floral leather case. REF: Albaugh, *Confederate Faces*, fig. 422. (A) Riba, Oct. '92, $700... *$800–900*

2nd U.S. Colored Light Artillery, Dept. of the Cumberland, Battery A. Ca. 1863. Anonymous. Oval view of five black artillerymen loading cannon. Tents and trooper with flag in background. *$500–600*

Servants of Prince de Joinville Doing Chores at Camp Winfield Scott, near Yorktown, Va. 1862. James Gibson/Brady Collection. *$250–300*

William Tecumseh Sherman. 1864. M. Brady Studios. Bareheaded (his campaign hat on table) and seated; Sherman has right hand inside tunic........ *$2000–3000*

Signal Station, Washington, D.C. 1865. M. Brady. Nine Union soldiers in uniform pose at Central Station, including one holding lantern on pole. *$450–550*

Small Child Dressed in Zouave Outfit Waving Flag. 1863. Also has small toy rifle on shoulder. (A) Riba, June '85, $140. . . . . *$250–300*

Soldiers of the Army of the Potomac in Trenches Before Petersburg, Va. 1864. M. Brady. Large group of troopers face directly into camera. Two officers stand atop knoll in profile. *$900–1000*

Southern Refugee Family Evacuate War Area. Ca. 1861. M. Brady. Mules pulling wagon loaded with possessions of a bombed out Southern family. Two small lads sit atop piled-up furniture in wagon and woman wearing hood stands beside it. *$450–500*

(Fort) Stevens, Washington, D.C. (Colored) Privates and Non-Com Officers. Ca. 1863. Anonymous. In front of barracks, 24 troopers line up at parade rest with muskets; a Cpl. wields sabre. *$350–400*

31st Pennsylvania Infantry at Fort Slocum Campsite, near Washington, D.C. 1862. M. Brady. Young officer with wife and three small children outside tent. Woman holds large laundry basket. Man has large saw in hand. *$250–300*

12th New York Battery Outside Petersburg, Va. 1884. M. Brady. The photographer himself, in straw hat, stands next to one of the cannons. Photo taken on June 20, 1864, only two days before the Rebels captured the entire Battery. *$1200–1400*

(Union) Gen. Ambrose Burnside. 1860. ⅙ plate, two-thirds view in leather wall frame. Better Quality/Good Condition. (A) $660. *$500–700*

(Union) Col. (later Gen.) Ambrose Burnside, "Welcome Home" with 1st Rhode Island Volunteers, Camp Sprague. 1861. M. Brady. Burnside sits capless with arms folded in front of tree; flanked by eight of his men, three seated, five standing. *$700–800*

Union Cavalry Sgt. with Horse. 1862. ½ plate, full-standing view with horse. Wears kepi with letter "A"; Sibley tents and another soldier in background; floral leather case. (A) $1000. . . . . *$1200–2000*

Union Privates. 1862. ⅙ plate. Standing, holding rifle, knife, pistol in belt. Also ⅑ plate tintype of seated soldier. Small scratches. (A) Riba, May '86, $80. . . . .
. . . . *$1000–1100*

Union Soldiers, Standing. Ca. 1862. One of two ambros. With fixed bayonet, gold touches to cross-belt and buckle; cap box, etc. Soldier standing with New Hampshire Vols. Kepi; ⅙ plate. (A) $250 pair. *$200–250*

Union Soldier. 1863. Knee-up portrait of soldier in front of U.S. flag. Leather case split at spine. Moderate emulsion scratches on print. *$75–100*

Virginia Militia Trooper (Seated), U.S. 1861. ⅙ plate, wearing sash, sword, pistol, etc. In embossed leather case. (A) $385. . . . . *$350–500*

Virginia State House, Capitol of the Confederacy. 1865. A number of soldiers and dignitaries stand on the porch (Brady himself stands fifth from the right) and on the sidewalk below. *$600–700*

Bishop Richard Whalen. 1857. Head of western Virginia Catholic diocese, who turned away mob trying to place U.S. flag atop his church. Whalen was a supporter of States Rights and No Faith in Black Republicanism. Minor age spots. (A) Riba, Oct. '86, $250. . . . . *$250–300*

Woman and Daughter (Civilian). Ca. 1862. ⅙ plate. Pair is seated between large draped U.S. flag. Handcolored with gold stars and red stripes. Also, a tintype full-length pose of woman holding a U.S. flag and "Liberty" hat. (A) Riba, Oct. '88, $130. . . . . *$150–200*

Wounded Union Troops at Gaines Mill, Savage Station after Battle of Fair Oaks, Va. 1862. Wounded scattered out under trees. Tents, small hospital building in background. From the James Gibson/M. Brady Collection. *$550–650*

Wounded Zouave with Musket in Lap at Deserted Camp. 1865. M. Brady. Black Union soldier in cape tends to Zouave, seated with eyes closed and one arm in sling *$500–600*

Zouave Corporal. 1865. One of two ambros. ¹/₆ plate. Wearing elaborate, brocaded jacket; three rev. stamps, dated 1865. Thermoplastic case. Also ¹/₉ plate of Soldier Holding Bugle; gilt touches to instrument, buttons, collar, and kepi. Patriot case, housed in leather. REF: Rinhart, plate 68, *The Fighting Eagle.* (A) Riba, March '89, $280 . . . . *$400–500*

Zouave in Cap with Fez Holding Pistol. Ca. 1863. ¹/₆ plate. Two-thirds standing fig. holding pistol across chest; cap box, scabbard. Light touches to uniform and cheeks. Floral leather case. (A) Riba, Oct. '92, $320 . . . . *$350–400*

Classic Civil War Ambrotypes

Classic Civil War images appearing in *The Pioneering Image/Celebrating 150 Years of American Photography* by Jerald Maddox, published by Universe in 1990, rank high on an advanced collector's wish list. Those chosen here represent definite and essentially documentary intent, but are equally fascinating as carefully composed artistic statements.

"Council of War" Massaponax Church, Virginia. May 21, 1864. Timothy O'Sullivan used stop-action in a series of three images of Grant that suggest a passing of time. Grant seated between two trees; meeting with his staff; leaning over Gen. Meade's shoulder. Undoubtedly the photographer had more than one camera at ready and anticipated certain events *$1200–1300*

A Harvest of Death, Gettysburg. July, 1863. From Gardner's *Photographic Sketchbook of the War.* Bloated bodies scattered across the field in the July sun—a passionate anti-war statement on the realities of war. Ambro, but also made and sold as a stereograph *$750–850*

General Meade's Headquarters Near Brady Station. April 12, 1864. A.J. Russell, Brady Studio. Long cadre of men is strung out across the oval image, with tents and trees in background *$800–850*

Wounded Soldiers at Fredericksburg, Virginia. May 19, 20, 1864. Mathew Brady & Co. "A sympton of a more generalized urge to document and record an historic event." *$650–700*

CABINET CARDS

Cabinet cards were introduced in 1867 primarily as mass-produced celebrity portraits. They were the most important of the photography formats to follow the cartes-de-visites (CDV), although they measure somewhat larger—5¹/₄" × 4" on 6¹/₂" × 4¹/₄" mount.

Clara Barton. 1889. Fine studio bust photo of "Angel of the Battlefield"; auction lot included signed thank-you letter on Red Cross stationery; also studio photo of Carrie Nation. (A) Riba, Oct. '85, $600 . . . . *$600–700*

Mathew B. Brady as Subject. 1861. One in profile wearing spectacles; other young Brady, full-length, wearing straw hat. Seven others depict Civil War–era personalities. (A) Riba, July '91, $1500 . . . . *$1500–2000*

Buffalo, New York, Welcomes Grand Army of the Republic. 1870s. Gala street scene with large cut-out letters of G.A.R. several stories tall. Pictures of Lincoln and Grant appear on large red, white, and blue shields.. . . . . *$75–85*

Frederick Douglas. Ca. 1893. Signed by famous black abolitionist; photo by C.M. Bell, Washington, D.C.; bust view of young Douglas; few light age spots. (A) Riba, Oct. '85, $380. . . . . *$400–450*

Drummer Boy in Civil War Uniform. 1860s. Posed in tent, painted backdrop. Photographer unknown. *$50–60*

James Garfield, Profile Pose. Ca. 1870. Signed "J.A. Garfield." Slightly faded. (A) Riba, Feb. '90, $1600. . . . . *$1500–1600*

Gen. U.S. Grant and Family at Mt. McGregor. 1885. Barrett, NYC.. . . . *$25–35*

Julia Ward Howe. 1898. Signed in lower margin, plus A.M.S. of famous lyrics *Battle Hymn of the Republic.* Howe was a noted abolitionist in 1850s. (A) Riba, Oct. '86, $750. . . . . *$650–750*

Robert E. Lee. 1870s. Lee seated in chair in civilian dress. "Brady, Washington D.C." stamp and ink signature "Gen. Read, U.S.A." on verso. Minor spotting, trim on lower mount. (A) Riba, '94, $320. . . . . *$400–500*

A. Lincoln. 1860. Bust portrait of beardless Lincoln signed by Alexander Hessler, "Taken in Springfield, Ill by me." Ex-Fay Collection. (A) Riba, May '86, $500.. . . . . *$650–700*

Mementos from 26th Ohio V.V.I. Army Corps. 1870. Mulligan, Columbus, OH. *$10–15*

Lt. Col. J.C. Paine. 57th NY Vols., U.S. Signal Corps. 1865. Wilkes Barre, PA. Signed by A. Johnson (stamp). Shown in uniform wearing medals. Lot incl. folio chromolith of shield listing Signal Corps. battle engagements; also six medals from Paine estate. (A) Riba, Oct. '85, $400.. . . . . *$400–500*

(Union) William Rhodes in Union Uniform. 1861. Died at home a year later. Copied from photo. *$35–45*

Harriet Beecher Stowe. Ca. late 1895. Signed and inscribed by Stowe on verso, "Written for Frank Leonard." (A) Riba, Feb. '87, $1400. . . . . *$1200–1500*

Harriet Beecher Stowe. Ca. 1874. Seated half-length portrait of Stowe. Also one-quarter-length studio portrait of Henry Ward Beecher, abolitionist, 1875. Both by Napoleon Sarony, NYC. (A) $150. . . . . *$150–200*

(Union) Gen. Mathew Henry Avery. 1865. Seated pose. Album on adjacent table. Sepiatone. *$35–45*

(Union) Gen. Ambrose E. Burnside. Jeremiah Gurney, NYC. *$45–55*

(Union) Gen. Vaurlette in Uniform. 1863. Levin Handy, Washington, D.C. (M. Brady's nephew and apprentice). *$50–60*

Union Gen. Lew Wallace. 1880. Wallace later gained fame for his novel *Ben Hur.* *$75–100*

CARTES-DE-VISITES

Cartes-de-visites (French-visiting cards) involves an inexpensive process of paper portraiture, patented by Andre Adolphe Disderi, a French portrait photographer, in 1854. A leading U.S. exponent of CDVs was Napoleon Saroney, successor to M. Brady in the late 1860s. CDVs are created by taking multiple exposures in one sitting using a sliding plate holder in a camera equipped with four lenses and a vertical and horizontal septum. This made possible a full-length view of any figure in a more natural and relaxed position, and allowed many duplications of an identical pose.

To help raise funds for the war, the government charged a small tax on all CDVs and stereocards. Federal Revenue stamps were affixed on recto from Sept. 1, 1864–Aug. 1, 1866, helping to date their sale during that period.

Note: All entries in this section are alphabetized by surname of personage or most important identifying word in entry, irrespective of any initial parenthetical entries.

(Union) Brig. Gen. Christopher C. Andrews. Ca. 1862. Photo: De Vall's, Bluff, AK; ³/₄-length. *$200-250*

(Union) Col. Benjamin Baker, 43rd NY Infantry. Ca. 1860s. Photo: Clark, Troy, NY. *$100–125*

(Union) Lt. John Baker. Ca. 1862. Photo: Bowdoin & Taylor, Alexandria, VA. Seated in uniform. *$55–65*

(Union) Lt. Col. George Baldey, 65th (3rd Colored Volunteers). Ca. 1863. Photo: C.D. Wakely, Denver, CT. *$350–400*

(C.S.A.) Gen. Pierre Beauregard. 1868. Albumen photo signed, dated on recto beneath portrait; remounted; some retouching. (A) $715. . . . . *$750–800*

(C.S.A.) Brig. Gen. Bernard Elliot Bee in Uniform. 1861. Photo stamp "Collir" on recto. Signed by Bee below image. Credited as immortalizing Gen. Thomas A. Jackson with his "Stonewall" allusion; killed at 1st Bull Run. (A) Riba, Nov. '91, $750. . . . . *$800–900*

(Union) Capt. Charles F. Blood, Co. "A" 50th New York National Guard Inf. 1864. Head and shoulders in civilian dress. Photo: Beardsley Bros., Ithaca, NY; worn mount corners. *$50–75*

John Wilkes Booth. 1865. Pub. by M. O'Brien, Chicago. "John Wilkes Booth Himself" imprint on verso. REF: No. 5 in Gutman. *$100–125*

John Wilkes Booth. 1865. Sepia photo by S.T. Blessing, New Orleans. "Your Affectionate J.W. Boo . . ." concluding letters missing. Minor wear. (A) Riba, Nov. '91, $2800. . . . . *$3000–4000*

John W. Booth (2). 1865. Two views—one of Booth in fancy carved chair; the other with cane. (A) Riba, July '94. . . . . *$250–300*

(Union) Pvt. Woodson Bryant, Company "F", 27th Indiana Infantry. 1862. Waist-up view; in fatigue coat, slouch hat. Print with surface abrasion; minor foxing on mount. Cancelled 2¢ proprietary revenue stamp, in ink. *$125–150*

(Union) Col. Horace Capron, 14th Ill. Cavalry. Ca. 1862. Head and shoulders profile. Photo: S.M. Fassett, Chicago, IL. Green imprint on reverse. Mount trimmed top, bottom; minor foxing, print and mount. *$135–150*

(C.S.A.) Edward P. Chapin. (Officer, rank not identified.) May 1863. (Killed at Port Hudson, LA.) Full-length standing as field grade officer; wears sword belt, sash; cavalry saber at side; slouch hat with plume. Photo: G.A. Douglas & Co., Buffalo, NY. Some print spotting. *$200–225*

(Union) Brig. Gen. George H. Chapman, 2nd and 3rd Cavalry Corps, Potomac. 1864. Three-quarter-length seated in side chair. Photo: M. Brady, Washington, D.C. Few fading spots on subject. *$150–175*

Kate Sprague Chase, Daughter of Salmon Chase. 1862. Studio portrait by M. Brady; pub. by Anthony. Kate Chase was toast of Washington. Abraham Lincoln openly flirted with her, driving his wife Mary Todd to jealous outbursts. *$150–200*

C.S.A. Generals. Ca. 1863. Includes signed Beauregard by Sarony; Jeff Davis (with cut sig.); Stonewall Jackson (3), one by Bradshaw, IL.; G. Pillow; Jeb Stuart by Brisbors, Chicago; others. (A) Riba, Oct. '85, $450. . . . . *$500–600*

(C.S.A.) Lt. Col. Francis L. Cramer, 1st Alabama Cavalry. Ca. 1862. Signed by Cramer, with note from his captor, (Union) Brig. Gen. Jno. M. Corse, regarding searching out Gen. Jno. B. Hood's forces. *$350–400*

Civil War Generals, also Lincoln (by Brady). 1860s. Incl. Gen. Abner Doubleday, Grant, Scott, Clark, Meredith, Thomsan—many with Alexander and Brady imprints; total of 58 cards. (A) Riba, Oct. '85, $480.. . . . . *$550–600*

Civil War Officers, Incl. Union Gen. Sherman. 1860s. 178 views. (A) $700. . . . . *$600–700*

(Union) Gen. Thomas L. Crittenden. Ca. 1863. Veteran of Shiloh, Stones River, Chicamauga skirmishes. Later served in 17th Infantry in Dakota Territory Badlands Campaign. *$100–150*

Gov. Andrew G. Curtin, Pennsylvania. 1863. Gov. during Civil War; loyalty and special treatment of military earned him the title "The Soldier's Friend"; three-quarter length, seated; photo: M. Brady, Washington, D.C. Mount and print have pinprick (on Gov.'s leg). *$50–75*

Capt. Geo. Armstrong Custer. 1860s (original photo). This is print made in late 1880s following Little Big Horn battle. *$100–125*

(Union) Col. George B. Damon, 10th Vermont Inf. Signed in ink 1865. Led advance on picket lines at (No. Carolina's) Ft. Fisher and Ft. Welch; photo: R.A. Louis, NYC; mount trimmed; minor foxing in sky area. *$350–375*

(Union) Lt. W.L. Denniston. 1862. M. Brady. Full pose, wearing sash. *$75–100*

Stephen A. Douglas. Nov. 6, 1857. ALS, with two photos with Anthony imprint. Incl. signed Douglas paycheck, plus Douglas invitation to attend U.S. Sen. elect's Levee at Springfield, IL, State House, 1846. (A) Riba, Oct. '85, $350. . . *$350–400*

((Union) Col. Thomas H. Dunham, 11th Mass Inf. Ca 1862. Full-length standing, 2nd Lt. insignia, minor spotting. *$50–75*

(Union) Col. Isaac Dyer, 15th Maine Inf. Ca. 1862. Full standing; sword (possibly Model 180 Field and Staff) drags at side to floor; slouch hat rests on column. Photo: G.H. Loomios, Boston; minor surface abrasion, foxing; mount is foxed. *$200–225*

(Union) 1st Lt. Caleb Ensign, 1st Michigan Eng. and Mech. 1865. Head and shoulders view. Photo: Whitney & Paradise, NYC. Imprint in salmon color with full border. *$150–175*

David Glasgow Farragut. Ca. 1861. "Bogardus, NY" verso credit. Brown, dampstained. (A) Riba, July '94. . . . . *$400–500*

Adm. David Farragut Seated with Capt. Drayton. Also View of Pair on Deck of *The Hartford* in Mobile Bay. 1864. Signed on verso by both men. (A) $550. . . . . *$500–600*

(Union) Pvt. Suel T. Fisk, Company "M", 1st NY Veteran Cav. 1864. Full standing; wears 12-button uniform jacket, boots; narrow brimmed slouch hat on table. Worn upper edge of mount. *$100–125*

Adm. Foote and Other Civil War Notables. 1860s. Photos: Brady, Anthony, Sarony, Gutekunst, Gardner, and others—all with imprint on mount recto or verso. Total of 20. Incl. Grant, Henry Ward Beecher, Edwin Booth, Benjamin Butler, Horace Greeley, Gen. W. Scott. (A) Swann, NYC, Oct. '94. . . . . *$800–900*

(Union) Lt. Col. John Foster, 175th NY Inf. 1862. Brevet Brig. Gen. U.S. Vols. Three-quarter length standing; wears sash and sword belt. Born: New Hampshire; grad:

USMA; served under Anderson at Ft. Sumter; with Corps of Eng. constructed forts along NJ coast. Photo: R.A. Lewis, NYC. Mount corners clipped, worn. . . . *$100–125*

Barbara Fritchie, Civil War Heroine. 1864. Photo: Brady Studio, Washington, D.C. "For the Great National Fair" (to raise money for veterans and their families). Recto and verso Fritchie poem by Henry Wadsworth Longfellow. Trimmed corners. (A) Riba, March '93, $110. . . . . *$125–150*

Alexander Gardner. Ca. 1863. Bearded fig. of Gardner seated in ornate chair, $3^1/2$" × $2^1/4$". Reputedly the only photograph of this noted Civil War photographer. *$750–1000*

Alexander Gardner and James Gardner (Noted Battleground Photographers). 1863. Two images framed together. REF: Katz, 53. . . . . *$1800–1900*

Alexander Gardner in Buckskins. Ca. 1861. Brady, Washington D.C. Recto, unpublished, upper right corner creased. *$1800–1900*

(C.S.A.) Gen. John B. Gordon. Later became leading educator. Ca. 1862. Head view as Col.; inscribed "Gordon of Georgia." Minor abrasions; minor scuffing on top edge. Stamped on reverse: "David O'Reilly Collection/819"; photo: Tanner & Van Ness, Lynchberg, VA. *$500–600*

Grant (2) Incl. Other Union Officers and Men. 1860s. 68 images by T.J. Merrot, J.H. Van Stavoren, T.M. Schleier, T.S. Saltsman, plus Morse of Nashville; A.J. Fox, T.L. Rivers of St. Louis; R.J. Booth of Columbia, SC; L.J. Moberly of Chillicothe; Brady, Anthony, Gurney of Washington and NY. Incl. portraits of Sherman, Sheridan, Thomas McGrath; plus five images of officer with one eye. (A) Swann, NYC, Oct. '94. . . . . *$2000–3000*

Gen. U.S. Grant. 1864. Anthony/Brady imprint. Grant in uniform, seated. Inscribed under image: "U.S. Grant, Lt. Gen. U.S.A." Some light age spots. (A) Riba, $650. . . . . *$700–800*

Gen. U.S. Grant. 1868. Campaign images, sheet of 12, probably for insertion in shell pins. Bust portrait, 3" × 3" overall. (A) $250. . . . . *$300–350*

Gen. U.S. Grant. 1891. Twenty-three different Grant poses in CDV cabinet cards, including CDV by Anthony (Brady negative); other Bradys, plus M.P. Rice image. (A) Riba, Oct. '85, $800. . . . . *$900–1000*

Grant—18th President—As Two-Star Gen. 1878. Signed in photo by Grant. Unknown photog. (A) Riba, $650. . . . . *$900–1000*

Charles Green, Comdr. of U.S.S. *Jamestown*. Twenty-four images with verso or page mount notations; incl. photos of U.S.S. *Jamestown*, Sept. 1862; U.S. *Powhattan* and *New Ironsides*; also other naval officers.. . . . . *$1200–1500*

(Union) Lt. Col. James D. Greene, Mass. 6th U.S. Inf. 1861. Commanded Regt. in Maine; head and shoulders view in civilian dress; inscribed on reverse. Photo: unknown. Print somewhat muddy. *$100–125*

(Union) Brig. Gen. John F. Hartranft. 1864. Fought and received Medal of Honor in 1886 at Bull Run; later Gov. of Pennsylvania. Propietary rev. stamp cancelled, B.H. *$350–400*

(Union) Brig. Gen. Joseph Hayes, 18th Mass. 1864. Chest view; inscribed in ink, reverse "near Petersburg, Va." In 1865 became Comm. of Supplies in seceded states; introduced Amer. system of hydraulic mining to Colombia in 1887. Henry Ulke, Washington, D.C. *$600–650*

(Union) Maj. Gen. Francis J. Herron, 1st Iowa, with Gen. William Vandever, 9th Iowa. (The latter later became a Rep. Cong. from IA.) Ca. 1862. Photo: J. Sidney Brown, St. Louis, MO. Also an unidentified Maj. Herron was awarded Medal of Honor for Pea Ridge. Prints and mount tear near center right edge. . . . *$350–400*

Maj. Gen. Thomas Hooker. 1862. Issued as an adv. medium for Mrs. Allen's Photo Albums. *$50–60*

Maj. Gen. Charles E. Hovey, 33rd Ill. (Later 1st Brig. 2nd Div. East AR) 1862. Leading educ.—started 1st Illinois Normal College in 1857. Two-thirds-length standing. Ins: "Gen. Hovey—Ill." Photo: G.H. McConnell, St. Louis. Mount trimmed at bottom. *$125–150*

(C.S.A.) Gen. Stonewall Jackson. 1861. Photo: E. and H.T. Anthony, Washington, D.C. *$750–800*

Brig. Gen. August V. Kautz, Ohio 1st Div. 1864. German-born; U.S.M.A. grad.; later member of military comm. that tried Lincoln's assassins; also an Indian fighter. Slight spots in sky; mount corners worn. *$350–400*

Col. Daniel J. Keily, 2nd La. Vav. 6, 7th. 1864. Born: Ireland. Chief of Staff to Gen. James Shields. Full-length seated with kepi on lap, wearing sword belt with Model 1860 staff sword; three mil. medals. Col. Charles W. Drew of 76th U.S. Colored Troops (at left); wears double-breasted sack coat and white trousers; also unident. man. Photo: Theo. Lilienthal Gallery, New Orleans. Some trimming on mount. *$250–300*

(Union) Brig. Gen. Thomas L. Kane, 13th Penn. Reserves. 1960. Upper ⅓ view as Lt. Col.; made Gen. in 1861; an ardent Free-Soiler, he became active agent of the Underground Railroad prior to Civil War. Print mounted on thin stock. . . *$300–350*

Ku Klux Klan Member Wearing Robe. Ca. 1878. Photographer unknown. *$75–100*

(Union) Brig. Gen. Joseph F. Knipe, Led Penn. 1st Div., XII, Potomac. 1863. Full standing; wearing sash, sword belt, slouch hat. Later became Supt. of Fed. Penit. at Ft. Leavenworth. Chemical spot in sky on print; mount corners worn. Photo: Morse Gallery, Nashville, TN. *$250–275*

(C.S.A.) Maj. Gen. Fitzhugh Lee. 1862. Commanded cavalry brigade at South Mountain, Antietam; Dumfries and Occoquan raids in 1862. Later became Gov. of Virginia. E. and H.T. Anthony, Pub. Sporatic yellowing; corners clipped. . . *$150–175*

Gen. Robert E. Lee. 1865. Signed; photo: M. Brady; with 1922 letter explaining how Lee happened to sign it. *$8000–9000*

Note: Lee-signed CDVs at auction are not uncommon and often run in the $2000 range; the above specimen was endowed with a bold clear signature and sharp tones. It brought $8250 at a Brian Riba Auction in 1992.

(C.S.A.) Maj. Gen. G.W.C. Lee and Col. Walter Taylor after Appomattox. 1865. M. Brady neg. Taylor holds hat. *$500–600*

Bust Views, A. Lincoln. Two separate poses in uncut sheet of 12. 1864. Photo: Anthony Berger of Brady Gallery. Used for presidential shell badges in 1864 presidential race, 4" × 2", image size ⅝" × ½". Minor fold line and minor abrasions. (A) Riba, Feb. '86, $1000. . . . . *$1200–1300*

Abraham Lincoln. 1862. Version credited to M. Brady; Lincoln seated near table with inkwell (REF: Ostendorf, 49c); also cabinet card close-up of Lincoln seated (REF: Ostendorf, 92). (A) Riba, March '93, $600. . . . . *$700–800*

Abraham Lincoln. Ca. 1861. Half-fig. image on C.D. Frederick's mount, with Frederick's credit on recto; his New Haven, Havana, and Paris studios printed on mount verso. REF: Ostendorf, p. 93. . . . . *$700–900*

Abraham Lincoln. Ca. 1861. Seated full fig. in partial profile; Brady/Anthony credit and detailed notations on verso. *$1100–1200*

Abraham Lincoln. 1862. By Alexander Gardner. (A) $825. . . . . *$850–900*

Abraham Lincoln. 1863. By Alexander Gardner, framed with tinsel-work mat; minor spotting in image. (A) Riba, May '86, $750. . . . . *$800–850*

Abraham Lincoln. 1861. By Alexander Gardner. Seated at table with inkwell, top hat. Posed at Brady Gallery. Verso credit pub. by Anthony from Brady neg. REF: Ostendorf, 51. (A) Riba, Jan. '91, $300. . . . . *$350–400*

Mary Todd Lincoln. 1861. By M. Brady, Washington, D.C.; Mrs. Lincoln posed seated wearing flowered dress. Verso with Brady logo; minor soiling, age tone. REF: Ostendorf, p. 298. (A) Riba, July '91, $500. . . . . *$550–600*

Abraham and Mary Todd Lincoln (Pair). Ca. 1863. M. Brady imprint. (REF: Ostendorf, 0–86; Lorent, No. 57) Mary Lincoln (REF: Ostendorf, p. 298). (A) Riba, Feb. '87, $300. . . . . *$400–450*

Mary Todd Lincoln (3). 1862–63. (1) Semiprofile, holding fan; backmark Anthony Bros. from Brady neg.; (2) wearing mourning attire after son Willie's death in 1862 (REF: Ostendorf, p. 301); (3) Ca. 1863, vignette (REF: Ostendorf, p. 301).. . . . . *$75–100*

Lincoln, Seated. 1860s. Attrib. to Lewis Walker. (A) $450. . . . . *$500–650*

Note: Price range given is true if actually a Walker CDV.

Abraham Lincoln—Funeral Related (4). 1865. Lincoln's casket next to Tad's; tomb entrance; survey party at tomb site; unidentified building. Photo: J.Q.A. Tesize, Springfield, IL. Some aging, light fold line. (A) Riba, Oct. '85, $380. . . . . *$400–500*

Abraham Lincoln—Horse with Funeral Blanket. 1865. Rev. Gen. Brown (a black caretaker for the Lincolns) with horse "Old Bob." Photo: ins. "F.W. Ingmire, City Gallery, Springfield, Ill." (A) Riba, Oct. '85, $300 . . . . *$300–400*

Lincoln and Civil War Generals. Collection of small images. Incl. Grant, Lee, Sheridan, Logan, Winfield Scott; 22 items incl. several non-military. . . . *$650–750*

Lincoln and Sons (2). Ca. 1864. Lincoln and Tad look at album of Brady photos (REF: Ostendorf, '93); Robert Todd in second CDV with cancelled verso stamp (REF: Ostendorf, p. 302). Minor soiling, yellowing on both. (A) Riba, March '93, $320. . . . . *$350–400*

Mary Todd Lincoln (2). 1863. (1) Mrs. Lincoln in mourning after death of son Willie. (2) Standing portrait. (REF: Ostendorf, p. 301). Pirated version, no photo imprint. (A) Riba, Oct. '92, $200. . . . . *$150–200*

Lincoln Related (16). Ca. 1862. Subjects include: Lincoln's elkhorn chair (Brady); Lincoln's rocker; Mrs. Stephen Douglas (Fredericks); Lincoln, the last portrait (A. Gardner); Mary Todd Lincoln (Brady, 1862), Willie Lincoln (Brady). (A) Riba, Oct. '85, $800. . . . . *$500–600*

(C.S.A.) Gen. James Longstreet. 1862. Head and shoulders view. Comanded over half of Lee's infantry following the Peninsular Campaign. Late in supporting Pope at 2nd Bull Run, he delayed too long the second day at Gettysburg, but fought ably at Antietam and Fredericksburg. Print is of poor quality. *$50–75*

Pvt. William Mann, Company "H", 57th Indiana Inf. Ca. 1862. Full fig.; wounded, Missionary Ridge, 1863; Altoona 1864; Photo: J. Perry Elliott's City Gallery of Art, Indianapolis, IN; defect in upper mount; right corner turned, creased. *$175–200*

George B. McClellan and Winfield Scott. 1862. Photo: R.W. Addis, Washington, D.C. Signed in image by McClellan as Maj. Gen. Minor age spots. Scott photo by C.D. Fredricks, NY, and signed by subject on recto, "To Mrs. Saml. Sloan." Small haze spot on shoulder. (A) $250. . . . . *$300–350*

(Union) Gen. George Gordon Meade. 1862. E. Anthony from Brady neg. . *$500–600*

(Union) Brig. Gen. James Nagle. 1862. Three-quarter length seated. Organized the 48th Pennsylvania. Fought at Crampton's Gap, South Mountain, Antietam. Photo: T.C. Bowen, Pottsville, PA. Slight print foxing; mount trimmed. . . *$75–100*

100 lb. Gun Aboard Confederate Gunboat *Teazer.* 1862. M. Brady's Album Gallery 482. Cannon on ship's deck with sailor. *$100–125*

Timothy O'Sullivan. Ca. 1862. Seated portrait in partial profile, with hands crossed and holding large hat. O'Sullivan is noted for some of the war's most gruesome battle scenes, i.e., "Harvest of Death." Only known image of O'Sullivan. *$850–1000*

Lewis Paine, Alias Wood, Alias Hall—Lincoln Co-conspirator. 1865. Arrested as an associate of J.W. Booth. Entered acc. to Act of Congress by Alexander Gardner. Rev. stamp, plus Gardner stamp dated Aug. 7, 1865, one month after execution. Few minor spots. (A) Riba, June '89, $600. *$700–750*

Charles W. Partridge, of 29th Mass. Vols. CDVs plus viewer. Other views of family and friends; wood box viewer, patd. 1865; leather hinges; two rollers. (A) $300. . . . . *$400–450*

(Union) Col. John S. Platner, 1st NY Vet. Cav. 1863. Later Brevet Gen. U.S. Vols. Bust view. In the vignette is a shield-shaped badge. *$35–50*

(Union) Capt. Leander A. Poor, U.S. Vols. (Mass.). 1864. Bust view; photo: Moses Piffit, New Orleans; 2-cents orange bank check; rev. stamp canceled in ink with "X". *$100–125*

(Union) Brig. Gen. Jesse Reno. 1861. Killed at South Mountain in 1862. Part of the Barbara Fritchie legend. Reno, NV, named after him. *$750–850*

Edmund Ruffin. 1860. Photo: Quimby & Co., Charleston, SC. Seated figure with rifle held between legs. Hat in lap. Ruffin is credited as firing first shot from Morris Island against Ft. Sumter. An ardent secessionist, he killed himself when North won the war. Lower margin slightly trimmed. (A) Riba, Oct. '88, $180. . . . . . *$200–250*

(Union) Gen. William T. Sherman. 1862. Bust pose; revenue tax stamp and studio imprint of Alexander Gardner, Washington, D.C. *$500–600*

Gen. William T. Sherman and Other Civil War Officers and Soldiers. 1860s. 21 images represented by E. and H.T. Anthony, Fredericks, Barr & Young, Washburn, et al. Most with photographers credits; four with rev. stamps. Several soldiers are identified by hand. (A) Swann, NYC, Oct. '94. . . . . *$700–800*

Comdr. Albert W. Smith, Comdr. of Gunboat *Winona.* Ca. 1862. Three-quarter-length right-facing studio portrait by Brady, Washington, D.C. Signed "A.N. Smith" on recto. *$600–700*

Lt. Algernon E. Smith as Aide de Camp 111 NY Vols. 1862. Smith later was killed at Little Big Horn with Custer. *$500–600*

Adm. Joseph Smith, Asst. to Sec. of Navy Gideon Welles. Ca. 1862. Three-quarter-length portrait by Brady, Washington, D.C. Signed on recto "Jos. Smith." *$50–75*

Southwest View of Battery #1. 1862. M. Brady's Album Gallery 36. Cannon in fortification. *$75–100*

Stage Stars of Civil War Era. Ca. 1865. Includes John W. Booth's amour, Helen Western (dated the day Lincoln was shot, and found on Booth's body), Maggie Mitchell, George Carsy, Helen Wise (autographed); six items. (A) Riba, May '86, $180. . . . . *$200–225*

(C.S.A.) Alexander Stephens, Vice President of the Confederacy. 1861. Pub. by E. & H.T. Anthony, Washington, D.C. from Brady neg. *$1000–1200*

Union Gen. Alfred Sully, 1st Minnesota. 1862. Photo: G.W. Gurnsey, Sioux City, IA. *$100–125*

(Collection) 38th Mass. Regiment and Union Military Leaders. Ca. 1863. Forty members engaged in battles in Louisiana (Baton Rouge), Fort Bisland, etc. *$1000–1200*

(C.S.A.) Gen. Jeff Thompson. 1862. Photo: E. & H.T. Anthony, Washington, D.C. Missouri Guard Comr. Thompson seated in Brig. Gen. uniform. . . . *$500–600*

(Union) 1st Lt. Elisha C. Tower. 1862. Three-quarter length seated; wears sash, sword belt, cradles sword (a la Peterson's 64 Infantry Officers), sword with cross Quillons. Photo: R.C. Watkins. Print has some chemical spots. *$100–125*

Trent Affair Cartoon. 1861. E. Anthony, NY, engraving; depicts capture of two Confederates on British ship in neutral territory, which almost draws Lincoln into a war with England. (D) $650. . . . . *$750–750*

Union Martyrs. Ca. 1862. Original workup by M. Brady, which was then reduced to CDV size. Seventeen images incl. Berry, Birney, Hayes, P. Kearney, J. Sedgewick, Wadsworth, and others killed in battle; 22" × 17"; excellent condition. (A) Riba, Oct. '85, $300. . . . . *$400–450*

Vermont Volunteers. 1864–65. Vermont photographers incl. C.L. Howe, Brattleboro; O.A. Tafts, Middlebury; J. Caden, Brandon. Thirty-four images, 26 of which are signed. Incl. image of Capt. Goodrick's black boy. Includes several letters and an obituary of Lt. Edward B. Parker. (A) $350. . . . . *$400–500*

Dr. Mary Walker. 1864. M. Brady Studio. Dr. Walker was an ardent feminist and military surgeon. Pictured in black dress wearing the Medal of Honor, and holding book at table next to large ornate clock. She was first woman Asst. Surgeon, U.S. Army, and the first of her gender to win the award.. . . . . *$2000–2500*

(Union) 2nd Lt. Richard Waters, Company "E", 21st Penn. Cav. 1864. Full standing, in frock coat cap, sword belt, sash, scabbard with strap attached. Killed at Bethesda Church, VA, June 1864. . . . . *$300–325*

(Union) Gen. Edward Augustus Wild. 1863. Photo: J.W. Black, Boston. Led all-Negro regiment. Fought at Bull Run, Petersburg seige. Lost arm in battle. Headed Georgia Freedman's Bureau in 1866. . . . . *$750–800*

(Union) Young Negro Soldier with Jacket, Kepi. Photographer unknown. *$650–700*

DAGUERREOTYPES

Invented by Louis Mandé Daguerre in 1839, dags, as they're commonly known, enjoyed great popularity from 1843–55. An estimated 30 million were run off in assembly-line fashion between 1840 and 1860 in the United States alone. Dags are shiny, very precise images produced on silver-coated copper plates sensitized with iodine, and then developed by exposure to mercury vapor.

Charles Calistus Burleigh. Ca. 1840s. ½ plate; full-faced, seated pose of full-bearded abolitionist holding rolled document. Oxidation around mat. (A) Riba, June '87, $4500. . . . . *$4500–5000*

John C. Calhoun. Ca. 1849. Brady Studio. Oval half-fig. pose. Calhoun was V.P. from 1824–32. As a Sen. from SC, he promoted his theory of nullification, i.e., "a state has the right to declare null and void and to set aside any Federal law that violates the compact of Union which was voluntarily accepted by the state." This signaled the first hint of secession by the South. *$850–1000*

Gen. Charles W. Dimmock and Brothers. Ca. 1862. ½-plate view of three brothers seated: John, Charles, and Elijah. Charles, a U.S.M.A. graduate, died fighting for the Union at Richmond in 1863. (A) Riba, Oct. '86, $190. . . . . *$250–300*

Maj. Gen. Ethan Allen Hitchcock. Head of Union Volunteers in Washington, D.C. ½-plate. (A) $1760. . . . . *$1500–2000*

Erastus Hopkins. Early 1850s. Full plate. Member of Free Soil Party; abolitionist. (A) Riba, May '86, $4800. . . . . *$4000–5000*

Judge John McLean, Free Soil Presidential Candidate. 1848. Half-plate; McLean, opposing extension of slavery, gave dissenting opinion in Dred Scott case. (A) $3000. . . . . *$3500–4000*

Naval Engineer. Ca. 1860. ½-plate full-length image of uniformed engineer casually leaning against stuffed floral chair. (A) Riba, Oct. '92, $750. . . . . . . *$700–800*

1st Lt. James Monroe Ruggles. 1861. ⅙ plate; ½ view of officer in Illinois militia uniform with saber. (A) Ostreicher Mail, May '94, $1100. . . . . *$1000–1200*

(Union) Sculpture of Gen. Gouverneur Kemble Warren. 1862. ½ plate; bust fig. Photo: E. White blindstamp on plate. Abrasion, oxidation (upper 25%). (A) Riba, May '86, $700. . . . . *$500–600*

Two Sailors. 1860s. Sailors in uniform, seated. One has hand on the other's leg. Some discoloration to mat. In fine Union case. (A) Riba, June '85, $500. . . . .
. . . . *$600–700*

(Union) Gen. John Ellis Wool. 1860s. ½ plate. Hero of Bueno Vista in Mexican War; Commanded Dept. of East at outbreak of Civil War. Photo: E. White blindstamp in plate. Oxidation in upper ¼ of image. (A) Riba, May '86, $2000. . . . .
. . . . *$2000–2500*

(Union) Gen. John Ellis Wool. 1860s. ½ plate. Waist-up pose; similar to above, but crisper image. Push-button case. (A) Riba, June '89, $4000. . . . . . *$4500–6000*

SALT PRINTS

Salt prints on paper were introduced in 1839 by William Henry Fox Talbot in London, just a few weeks following the debut of daguerreotypes. For two decades, the two processes were locked in a heated race, with paper prints eventually winning out.

John Bell and Edward Everett. 1860. Constitutional Union presidential slate. Bell's portrait signed "Jno. Bell, Tenn."; 5" × 7" in oval mount. (A) $150. . . . .
. . . . *$200–250*

John Breckinridge and Joe Lane. 1860. Southern Dem. pres. slate in 1860, 5" × 7" oval mount. (A) $400. . . . . *$500–600*

Stephen A. Douglas and Herschel Johnson (paired). 1860. Oval, 7" × 5", framed; light discoloration in background of Johnson. (A) Riba, Oct. '85, $600. . . .
. . . . *$800–900*

A. Lincoln. 1859. Photo: S.M. Fassett, Chicago. Beardless Lincoln, oval, 7" × 5". Neg. destroyed in Great Chicago Fire (REF: Meserve, No. 8). Small rub area. (A) Riba, Oct. '85, $3800. . . . . *$4000–5000*

A. Lincoln. 1860. Campaign photo; beardless; imprint on verso; S.M. Fassett; 1¾" × 1½" oval in brass frame. (A) Riba, Oct. '85, $280. . . . . *$300–350*

A. Lincoln. Ca. 1858. Photo by Roderick Cole, Springfield, IL. Beardless bust image in oval mount, framed (REF: Meserve, 14; Ostendorf, 14). Sepiatone. (A) Riba, $500. . . . . *$650–700*

A. Lincoln, Beardless. May 1860. Photo: William Church, Springfield, IL. Upon request of Marcus Ward, a day after being nominated for presidency (REF: Ostendorf, 21). (A) Riba, June '85, $2000. . . . . *$2500–3000*

A. Lincoln and H. Hamlin. 1860. Jugate photo; Fassett photo of Lincoln; 1¼" ×

1" oval in brass frame. Age darkening in background. (A) Riba, Oct. '85, $900. .
.... *$1000–1100*

STEREOGRAPHS

These double-picture photographs give the illusion of depth when viewed through a stereoscope. Discovered by Sir Charles Wheatstone before the invention of photography, they were seldom practiced until displayed at the Great Exposition of the World Industry in London, 1851. Stereographs were popular up through the 1870s, and experienced a revival in 1887 up through the turn of the century, and again in the early 1930s.

(Union) Arago Steamer. Ca. 1863. By Taylor, Hartford, CT; view of gun deck. . .
.... *$50–75*

Army Blacksmith and Forge—Antietam. 1862. Anthony's War View Negatives, No. 587, War Photograph & Exhib. Co. *$50–75*

Artifacts from Gettysburg Battlefield. 1870s. Includes swords, holsters, flags. . .
.... *$25–35*

Bringing in the Wounded. 1862. No. 721 by Taylor & Huntington.. . . . . *$35–50*

John Burns—Old Hero of Gettysburg. No. 2401. Burns was 70-year-old combatant who fought with 7th Wisconsin, the 150th Pennsylvania and Iron Brigade over three days fighting at Gettysburg. Cabinet size. War Photo Co. *$35–50*

Church Built by Engineers at Poplar Grove Near Petersburg, Va. 1863. No. 3339. Anthony War Views. From Brady neg.. . . . . *$25–35*

Dead Soldiers in the Trenches. Ca. 1880s. Reprint issue of *War for the Union* series by War Publications & Exhib. Co., Taylor & Huntington. *$10–15*

Eight-Inch Mortars, Brooklyn Navy Yard. 1870s. By Webster & Albee. Cream mounts. *$15–25*

Execution of a Negro Soldier Named Johnson at Hollow Square. 1863. No. 993, Anthony's War Views. *$35–50*

Ft. Sumter View Showing Debris, Shot Shell and Broken Gun. 1870. No. 3049, E. & H.T. Anthony & Co. *$15–25*

Alexander Gardner (as subject). With photographic van in background and corpses in front. 1863. "Photographic Incidents of the War, No. 268" verso label. (REF: Katz, p. 65.) View near Emmitsville Road at Gettysburg. Light fading, soiling. (A) Riba, '94, $850. . . . . *$800–900*

Alexander Gardner and Timothy H. O'Sullivan on Road Near Gettysburg. 1863. Recto, Gardner credit. (REF: Katz, *Witness to an Era*, p. 64.) (A) Riba, $700.
.... *$700–800*

Alexander Gardner. Three views from "Photographic Incidents of the War." 1864. "Looking Toward Spotsylvania Court House from Beverly House, Gen. (Gouverneur K.) Warren's Headquarters"; "Rear View of Winter Quarters of Tel. & Phot. Depts. Attached to Headquarters, Army Potomac"; "General (Marsena R.) Patrick's Quarters." Negs. by Timothy O'Sullivan. Printed by E. Anthony, NYC. (A) $75. . . . . *$125–150*

Gen. Grant at City Point, NY. Ca. 1854. Seven views all by E. Anthony, NYC. "Gunboat on the James River"; "View of Ft. Sumter"; "Great Siege Train at Yorktown, VA."; "Ruins of Fredericksburg"; "Southern Soldiers Dead in Fort Damnation"; "Maj. Gen. Ord at Davis Mansion." (A) $210. . . . . *$200–250*

Gen. Heintzleman and Staff. 1865. "Photographic History, The War for the Union," No. 2304. Casual group pose of M. Brady and possibly his wife Julia. Minor soiling. (A) Riba, March '83, $150. . . . . *$100–125*

Gen. Robert E. Lee. Only one known and hasn't been on the market since the 1970s.. . . . . *Value Indeterminate*

Lincoln at Antietam. 1862. Photo: Alexander Gardner. Lincoln in front of tent flanked by Gens. McClellan and McClernand. George A. Custer stands apart at far right. Each image 3" × 3". *$1000–1500*

Lincoln "Flat Top." 1862. So called because Lincoln's hair stands straight up, a la Don King. Possibly one of a kind. . . . . *Value Indeterminate*

Lincoln. 1880s. Knees-up standing view of Lincoln in partial profile with left arm behind back. By Taylor & Huntington, Hartford, CT. Orange mount. No. 1312 in "Photographic War History." Long text in recto. Copy of an original stereo. Brady plate from 1864. . . . . *$200–250*

Lincoln's Funeral. 1865. Lot of 17 views. Photographers incl. Anthony, Townsend Mohr, Hall. Scenes of funeral procession, tomb, casket viewing. (A) Riba, June '87, $1000. . . . . *$1200–1500*

Lincoln Seated. 1865. From "Prominent Portraits" series, No. 2969, pub. by E. & H.T. Anthony & Co.; yellow-backed. *$300–350*

Portrait of Abraham Lincoln. By E & H.T. Anthony & Co., "Prominent Portraits, No. 2969." Verso has tax stamp and dealer's label from Springfield, IL. (A) $1650. . . . . *$1200–1500*

(Lincoln) Old Abe, the Live Wisconsin War Eagle. 1860. No. 1059, by H.H. Bennett. Yellow mount. *$50–60*

Lt. Winfield Scott at West Point. 1856. Handcolored glass version by Langenheim Bros., Philadelphia. (A) $375. . . . . *$400–500*

Slaves Picking Cotton. 1860s. By J.N. Wilson, Savannah, GA. *$10–15*

Three Soldiers. 1860s. Unknown photographer. Three Union soldiers standing, leaning against tree. One in middle is reading letter from home. *$50–75*

The War for the Union, 1861–65. Probably pub. by Taylor & Huntington. On orange and cream-colored mounts. Seven cards incl. "President Lincoln and Gen. McClellan in Gen.'s Tent"; "Gen. George Stoneham and Staff, Near Fair Oaks, 1862" (No. 436); "Gen John A. Dix" (No. 1546); "Where Gen. McPherson was Killed" (No. 3649); "Gen. Wright, Comdr. of the Bloody 6th Corps," imperial dome top. Also standing soldier image by Aucgmoody, Roundout, NY; "Camp of the 10th Mass. Regt. Near Washington" (No. 2421), by Anthony from Brady neg.. . . . . *$400–500*

(The) Wounded Soldier—John Rogers Statuary Grouping. 1880s. Pub. by several companies. Recreations of "From the Celebrated Rogers Statuettes." Shows barefooted black slave holding up wounded soldier. *$10–15*

TINTYPES

Tintypes were invented in 1856 by Hamilton Smith, an Ohio chemistry professor. They remained popular well into the twentieth century. The image was created on a metal plate exposed in the camera, but the metal was iron (not tin, as name implies) or copper, and a black japan varnish was applied. The quality was inferior to dags and ambros, and the process was used widely for inexpensive portraits. They are readily identified by their darker surface tones and thin iron plates.

C.S.A. Soldier with Pistol. Ca. 1862. ¹/₆ plate. Holds pistol across chest, bowie knife in scabbard at belt. (REF: Albaugh, *Confederate Faces*, fig. 109) Leather embossed case. Light halo effect around fig. (A) Riba, July '83, $1000... *$1000–1100*

C.S.A. Soldier, Sword at Side. 1862. Full-length standing; on label under coverglass, "Wearn & His Artists. Columbia, S.C."; Leather case. (A) Riba, Oct. '92, $380... *$400–450*

Jefferson Davis. Ca. 1863. Small bust image affixed to CDV mount. . *$1000–1200*

Jefferson Davis. 1861. Oval bust image affixed to CDV mount. 1⁷/₈" × 13³/₄". (A) Riba, '94, $1200. .... *$1000–1200*

(2) Dr. Samuel T. Davis of Penn. 77th Vols. Ca. 1862. ¹/₄ plates. (1) Davis reclining on Pulpit Rock with two other vols.; (2) Davis with sword, eagle, belt buckle; both housed in same geometric case. Also incl. ¹/₆ plate ambro of Davis holding cane, plus typed biographical chronology. (A) Riba, Oct. '92, $1200. . *$1200–1300*

U.S. Grant. 1863. 2¹/₄" × 3¹/₂" in brass frame; image has several wrinkles. William Grace adv. on recto has wear. (A) Rex Stark, June '91, $300. .... *$250–300*

Hannibal Hamlin. 1860. Whole plate. Rep. V.P. running mate with Lincoln in 1860 campaign. Incl. ALS from Jan. 2, 1872, 8 vo. 1¹/₂ p. (A) $200. .... *$300–$350*

A. Lincoln Gem Size. 1861. Photo: C.S. German, Springfield, IL. Reversed, retouched tintype. First known photo of a bearded Lincoln. (REF: Variant-0-41, Ostendorf, p. 277) (A) $170. .... *$200–250*

Lincoln Portrait. 1863. 2¹/₄" × 3¹/₂" imprinted mount; ad paper recto for William Grace, Portland. Few tiny marks. (Match to Grant above.) (A) Rex Stark, June '91, $900... *$800–900*

Marksman Assumes Texas-style Sharpshooting Position. Ca. 1870, ¹/₆ plate. Marksman in position with 4570 Springfield model. Leather wall frame. (A) Riba, Oct. '92, $320... *$300–350*

(2) Thomas O'Connell, Pvt. 106th Penn. Inf. Ca. 1862. Standing pose with musket, ammo pouch. Cannon, flag backdrop. Minor tarnish. Also a ²/₃ standing view. Taken in Williamsport, PA. Original form included by Nat'l. Copying Co. of subject Michael Tipton. Minor emulsion crazing. (A) Riba, Oct. '92, $220. ...... *$250–300*

Maj. Gen. Thomas A. Smyth, 1st Delaware Inf. Brigade, Hay's Div. Hancock's 11 Corps at Gettysburg. 1866. Shot by sniper at Farmville, VA, in April 1865, the last U.S. Gen. to die in the war................................. *$150–200*

(3) "Three Tough Guys of Co. H, 2nd NY Heavy Art." Ca. 1862; ¹/₄ plate notation on verso label. Uncased; ¹/₉ plate of two seated men, one in uniform, Co. G. 6th Mass. Vol. Photo: John C. Carr, St. Charles, MO; also ¹/₆ plate ambro of two soldiers holding hands; some soiling of emulsion crazing on ambro. (A) Riba, March '94, $500. .... *$450–500*

Union NCOs (Plus 2 Ambros). Early 1860s. ¹/₆ plate full-standing portrait of a Pvt. in thermo case; painted background; ¹/₉ plate ambro, waist-up of Cpl.; ¹/₉ plate ambro of Pvt. (A) Riba, March '93, $220.......................... *$225–250*

(2) Union Officers. Early 1860s. Waist-up seated officer, C.L. Ely, with pencil notation; second of unidentified officer holding sword. Light soiling. (A) Riba, March '93, $500... *$500–550*

(2) Union Soldiers. 1863. Possibly NY Reg. Two handtinted images: ¹/₄ plate of full-standing soldier, arms crossed, some surface abrasion; ¹/₆ plate ambro, seated soldier in overcoat. Both lightly tinted and in leather cases. (A) Riba, March '93, $300... *$350–400*

(2) Union Soldiers. ¹/₉ plate plus ambro. 1862. Seated soldiers, each cradling rifle; wearing cross belt. Ambro tarnished at mat opening. (A) Riba, March '83, $200...
.... *$150–200*

Union Soldier. 1860s. Whole plate, 10" × 7" colored image—standing soldier holding kepi, hand on sword in scabbard; American flags, cannon tents, and two guards in background. Some surface spotting. (A) Riba, March '93, $450. ....
.... *$450–500*

Union Soldier (Possibly Negro) Seated with Wife and Child. Ca. 1865. On verso brass preserver: "John McTarsngy, Civil War, died 1864, 1443 Andersonville, Ga." Lotted with ²/₃ view standing soldier, John Huett (identified on verso). Both in leather cases. (A) Riba, Oct. '92, $275. .... *$300–400*

Union Soldier Standing at Parade Rest. Ca. 1863. In black frame with gilt touches. Few light scratches. *$150–175*

Union Soldier Standing at Parade Rest. Ca. 1863. Bearded fig. carrying rifle with bayonet; painted background of campground. Oval frame............ *$150–175*

Union Soldiers, Pvt. and Lt. Ca. 1863. Pvt. is seated with Lt. who holds 1850 foot officer's sword and wears eagle belt. Possibly brothers? Horiz. format. In embossed leather case. *$300–400*

Virginia Militiamen. Ca. 1862. ¹/₆ plate; pair seated, one with rifle, bowie knife. Minor tarnishing at mat opening. Embossed leather case. (A) Riba, July '93, $200.
.... *$150–200*

Col. Wright, Capt. Sturtevant, 1st Lt. Howard, 14th NH Vols. 1865. Officers Hospital, Annapolis, MD; affixed rev. stamps; light crazing; minor bend. (A) Riba, July '93, $350. .... *$350–400*

Young Union Recruit. 1860–70. Trouper poses at attention behind studio-painted false campsite background. Included with 20 other tintypes, incl. portrait of three sailors lounging on the river and civilian sports scenes. (A) Swann, NYC, Oct. '94.
.... *$500–600*

Zouave Close-up Standing. 1863. ¹/₄ plate. With rifle, fixed bayonet, sword, cap box. Touch-up to fez tassle and uniform buttons. Minor surface abrasions. Floral leather case. (A) Riba, Oct. '92, $700............................ *$750–800*

MISCELLANEOUS

Glass Negatives. Cartoon glass plate negatives of Thomas Nast, 1860s–80s. Brady Studio. Used for CDV-size photos. Approx. 55—probably the complete archives of Nast cartoons commissioned by Brady. In original M. Brady wooden box. (A) Riba, Feb. '86, $1300. .... *$1500–2000*

Glass Negatives. Confederate military leaders. Set of 45 original M. Brady wet plate glass negatives. (A) $990. .... *$900–1000*

Glass Lantern Slides. The Great Battles of the Civil War. Ca. 1870s. Complete set of three wooden boxes containing 132 slides housed in wooden frame plus 46 standard-type slides. *$300–400*

Photograph. A. Lincoln. 1858. Waist-up view of beardless Lincoln by Christopher S. German, Springfield, IL. *$200–250*

Photograph. Photographs of Abraham Lincoln, first proofs. 1910. Seventy-one page-mounted photos by Frederick Hill Meserve, with paper wraps. Pencil notations, corrections in his hand. Eventually privately printed. (A) Riba, May '86, $300..... *$350–500*

Photograph. Union Cadet. Ca. 1862. Young man in uniform, handcolored with

U.S. flag backdrop; "H.W. Ladd . . . NYC" imprint, 9" × 6½" image in gold frame. (A) Riba, Oct. '85, $170. . . . . *$250–300*

Platinum Print. Lincoln's Sec. of War Edwin M. Stanton. 1892. Pub. by M.P. Rice from orig. Gardner neg. (REF: Katz, p. 147) (A) Riba, '94, $1000. . . . . . . *$900–1000*

Silverprint. A. Lincoln. Ca. 1890s. "© G. B. Ayres." Beardless, head and torso pose; from Hessler's earlier original neg.; 8¾" × 7". (REF: Ostendorf, p. 26) (A) Riba, July '93, $1000. . . . . *$1100–1200*

Silverprint. Joseph Wheeler, Chief of Confederate Cavalry of the Army of Miss. 1861. Ny Anson, NYC (blind stamp and Anson label on recto). Oval of Wheeler as 1st Lt. U.S. Dragoons, Cavalry Guard; 7½" × 5½". (A) Riba, Oct. '88, $750. . . . .
. . . . *$900–1000*

8th Co., Second Infantry Sharpshooters. ⅙ plate tintype, from the Hank Ford collection, $500–$600.

Left: *Confederate soldier from Georgia, with Bowie knife and pistol.*
¹/₆ plate tintype. Photos of armed military men command higher prices
than an unarmed pose. From the Doug Jordan collection, $700–$800.
Right: *James Totten, Army officer and chief of artillery. ¹/₂ plate*
daguerreotype. Totten had a diverse military career, including service on
the Western frontier, rarely illustrated in other reference books. (Doug
Jordan collection), $4,000–$5,000.

Left: *Confederate soldier from Texas, with pistol. ¹/₆ plate ambrotype. The*
pose with a weapon increases the value. If the soldier were identified, the
value would double. (Doug Jordan collection), $500–$750. Right: *Union*
recruit, armed with Springfield musket. ¹/₆ plate ambrotype. (Doug Jordan
collection), $200–$300.

Left: *Union amputee with cutout corps badge. CDV. Identified as Winters, 4th New York artillery, $400–$500. (Photo courtesy of Rex Stark)* Right: *General Burnside beside a horse, from a print or painting. ¹/₆ plate ambrotype, $150–$200. (Photo courtesy of Rex Stark)*

Left: *Lt. General U.S. Grant. Albumen. Photographed by F. Gutekunst, with Grant's signature below the image area, $900–$1,000.* Right: *One of a handful of known daguerreotypes of Lincoln. Sold for $17,600 at Winter Gallery in 1984, $20,000–$22,000. (Photo courtesy of Winter Gallery)*

Left: *Framed ambrotype taken by Mathew Brady of Gen. Sherman, $800–$900.* Right: *Union fifer, ¹/₂ plate ambrotype, $2,300–$2,500.*

Tintype of recruits in a tent by Alexander Gardner, $400–$500. (Photo courtesy of Riba Auctions)

CDV of General Sherman and his staff on the morning of the battle for Atlanta, $500–$550. (Photo courtesy of Rex Stark)

Large albumen of the Officers of St. Andrew's Society, Washington, DC. The photo was taken by Alexander Gardner and includes notable Civil War photographers David Knox, John Reekie, and Gardner himself. Sold for $2,000 at Riba Auctions in 1994, $2,000–$2,500.

Left: *Union drummer, ¹/₄ plate tintype, with ornate gutta percha frame of the period. Hank Ford collection, $1,800–$2,000.* Right: *Zouave drummer boy, ¹/₂ plate ambrotype, $750–$800. (Photo courtesy of Riba Auctions)*

Alexander Gardner albumen of Col. Dickinson and Maj. Ludlow, Fairfax, VA, 1863, $800–$900.

Rare CDVs by F.W. Ingmir include (clockwise) *Lincoln's tomb, dog, home, and horse. Value indeterminate. From the Hank Ford collection.*

Classic photo of the Shiloh battlefield by Alexander Gardner, $400–$500.

Famous tousled-hair pose of Lincoln by Alexander Hesler. Mounted albumen, $900–$1,000.

U.S. Grant at field headquarters. A stereograph by Alexander Gardner of a photo by E. Antony, NY, $200–225.

SHEET MUSIC

POLITICAL CAMPAIGN RELATED

Note: Listings in the sheet music chapter are arranged alphabetically by title or subject of the song. Therefore, music relating to U.S. Grant will be found with the "G" listings, Lincoln with the "L" listings, etc.

"President Arthur's Grand March." 1881. Published by O'Shea Bros. Bust portrait of Chester Allen Arthur. For Arthur's innaugural following moving up from v.p. after Garfield was assassinated.................................. $25–35

"Bell & Everett Schottisch." 1860. Composed by Francis H. Brown, published by Firth and Co., NY. Cameo sketches of Bell, Everett, and eagle with cannon and shield... $35–50

"Blaine & Logan Songster." 1884. Lithograph of Lincoln and Garfield in oval against large banner, Washington and Grant are illustrated at top in small rosettes, Republican candidates Blaine and Logan portraits within small shields. $50–75

"Blaine & Logan Victory March." 1884, Republican slate; by Jas. J. Freeman. Advertisement giveaway by R.H. Macy & Co., NY; jugate portraits of Blain & Logan. "(The) Great Unknown Candidate." .... : $35–45

"J.C. Breckinbridge." 1860. Published by A.C. Peters, Cincinnatti; political campaign song... $50–75

"Buchanan's Union Grand March." 1856. Published by Nathan Richardson, Boston; lithograph of Buchanan bust flanked by U.S. flags............. $75–100

"Buck's Private Confession Publically Revealed." 1856. Words: anon; Music: "Lucy Song" from *Songs Old & New* (1882); accuses 15th president James Buchanan of selling out to the South. $100–125

Butler's Grand March." 1884. Arranged for Piano Forte; anon. Lithograph of Greenback presidential candidate Gen. Benjamin Butler holding plumed hat, standing next to horse. $50–75

(Clay) "Prize Song—The Whig Chief." 1884. Boston Clay Club No. 1. Shows Clay's birthplace, Ashland, and White House. Red, gold, green, blue, and yellow. $125–150

(Clay) "Confederacy March." 1860. By Alfred F. Toulmin of Patapsco Institute. Published by George Willig, Baltimore; dedicated to Jefferson Davis, C.S.A. Presidential Inaugural.........................:....................... $50–75

"Douglas Grand March." 1860. Democratic campaign song; Geo. L. Walker, Philadelphia. Photo of "Hon. Stephen A. Douglas." $50–75

"Garfield & Arthur Campaign Songbook." 1880. Published by Republican Congressional Committee, Washington, D.C. Jugate of Garfield and Arthur with shield *$20–25*

"Garfield's Grand March." 1880. Published by Carl Renbort. Bust portrait of Garfield. *$35–45*

"Hail Brave Garfield." 1880. Republican campaign song. Black and white bust portrait with blue cover. Publisher unknown. *$25–35*

(Grant) "A Smoking His Cigar." 1868 campaign. Words by Ason O'Fagun, music by J.P. Webster. Picture of General Grant with cigar. *$50–75*

(Grant) "A Song for the Times." 1864. Words and music by Dan D. Emmett for Bryant's Minstrels; published by Wm. Pond & Co., NY. Lithograph of bust portrait of Grant with stylized initials "U.S.G." Emmett was premature in celebrating Grant's nomination—it went again to Lincoln. *$35–50*

(Grant) "For Grant & Colfax We Will Vote." 1868. Jugate portraits of Grant and Colfax. *$50–60*

"Grant Is the Man." 1872. By Harry Birch. Bust sketch of Grant. *$35–45*

"Gen. Grant's Quick Step." 1868. Campaign song by Edward Mack; published by Lee & Walker, Philadelphia. Lithograph by T. Sinclair, Philadelphia, of Grant bust portrait. *$50–75*

(Grant) "Good-By Andy!" 1868. Sung to air "Jim Crack Corn." Cruel farewell song following Andrew Johnson's defeat by Grant; published in Grant Companion Songster. *$35–50*

"Grant & Colfax Spread-Eagle." 1868. Published by Beadle & Co., NY. Lithograph on cover of politico waving his arms at rally. *$50–75*

"Grant & Colfax March." 1868. Anon. Published by John Church, Cincinnati. Portraits of winning Republican slate of U.S. Grant and Scuylar Colfax. . . . *$25–35*

(Grant) "We'll Vote for Grant Again." 1872. Oval bust portrait of Grant in laurel leaf border. Browntone on buff. List of Grant's Civil War victories at sides. *$40–50*

"(To the Friends of) Greeley & Brown." 1872. Published by J.L. Peters, NY. Lithograph portraits of Greenback candidates topped by eagle and crossed flags. *$35–50*

"(Gen.) Hancock's Campaign March." 1880. By Le Baron; Grand March Winner. Published by Oliver Ditson, Boston. Bust of Gen. Hancock in Union uniform. *$35–50*

"Hancock & English Songster." 1880. Published by Democratic Committee. *$20–30*

"Vice President Andrew Johnson Grand March." 1864. Published by J. Church, Cincinnati. *$35–40*

"Honest Old Abe Song & Chorus." 1860. Song, chorus, words by D. Wentworth Esq., Music by A/Wide Awake. Published by Blodgett & Bradford, Buffalo, NY. Bust sketch of beardless Lincoln. Two colors. *$75–100*

"Hurrah for General Grant!" 1868. Words by Luke Collin; music by J.P. Webster. Published by Root & Cady, Chicago. Lithograph of panoramic view of Republic Convention, Crosby's Opera House, Chicago, where Grant was nominated by acclamation. *$25–35*

"Horace Greeley's Grand March." 1872. Music for Piano Forte by Chas. Glover. Published by Wm. A. Pond, NY. Bust portrait of Greeley. Black and white. . . . .

"The Banner of Hancock & English." Bust litho of Gen. Winfield Scott Hancock, commander of the Union's II Corps at Gettysburg. *$35–50*

"When Hancock Takes the Chair." 1880. "A Rousing Campaign Song and

Chorus." Words and music by Thos. P. Westendorf. Published by Arthur P. Schmidt, Boston. Bust profile of Winfield Scott Hancock. *$35–50*

"Harrison's Grand March." 1888. Bust portrait of Republican Presidential candidate. Black and white. *$25–35*

"Gov. Rutherford B. Hayes Grand March." 1876. Bust portrait of Hayes. Black and white. *$35–50*

"Hurrah for Hayes & Honest Ways." 1876. Republican campaign song. Lithograph portrait of Rutherford B. Hayes as a Union Gen.. . . . . *$35–45*

"Johnson's Grand Union March." 1865. Republican campaign song. Three quarters view of Andrew Johnson. *$35–50*

"Impeachment Song." 1868. Words and music by L.A. Dochez. Publisher unknown. Song supports A. Johnson in Senate impeachment trial. *$50–75*

"Inauguration Grand March." 1860. Published by Oliver Ditson, Boston. Oval lithograph showing Lincoln (using same plate as "Wigwam Grand March" (see below, but adding beard).. . . . . *$50–60*

"Johnny Fill Up the Bowl." 1864. By A.W. Auner, song publisher and printer, Philadelphia. Anti-Lincoln drinking song berating him for hardships of drawn-out war in second campaign for presidency; probably by Copperheads (Northern Democrats who opposed Union Policy). Lithograph of small eagle in flight. . *$75–100*

"Lincoln Grand March." 1860. Composed and published by F.W. Rauch, Cincinnati. Three-quarters line sketch of beardless Lincoln. *$135–150*

"Lincoln Quick Step." 1860. Inaugural Ball tune published by Lee & Walker, Philadelphia. Large oval lithograph of bearded Lincoln, vignettes of Lincoln as railsplitter; tug boat on Mississippi; tools etc.. . . . . *$50–75*

"Funeral March." 1865. Music by Major General J.C. Barnard, "Played at the obsequities of the late President of the U.S., by the U.S. Marine Band." Published by Wm. A. Pond & Co., NY. *$25–35*

(Lincoln) "Farewell Father, Friend & Guardian." 1865. Words by L.M. Dawn, music by George F. Root.. . . . . *$25–35*

(Lincoln) "Rest Spirit Rest." 1865. Bust litho of Lincoln. *$40–50*

"President Abraham Lincoln's Quick Step." 1864. Published by J. Church, Cincinnati. Bust portrait of Lincoln.. . . . . *$500–600.*

"President Lincoln's Funeral March." 1865. Words and music by T.M. Brown.
. . . . *$25–35*

"President's Emancipation March." 1862. Dedicated to Lincoln; composed for piano by Geo. E. Fawcett. Published by Root & Cady, Chicago. *$25–35*

"President Lincoln's Funeral March." 1865. By T.M. Brown, published by Endres & Compton, St. Louis. Lithograph oval portrait of Lincoln surrounded by grieving deity, furled flag. *$25–35*

(Lincoln) "The President's March." 1868. Composed and dedicated to U.S. Grant by Federico Gennari, published by John F. Ellis, Washington, D.C. Threequarters illustration of Grant in uniform.. . . . . *$25–35*

(Lincoln) "Republican Campaign Songbook." 1860. Published by American Publishing House, Cincinnati. Black and white portrait of Lincoln on title page. 48 pages. *$100–125*

(Lincoln) "Old Abe Polka." 1864. Sheet music composed for piano and published by B. Leidersdorf & Co., Milwaukee, "Old Abe" Tobaccos as advertising promotion. Lithograph shows bust of Lincoln, slavery scene, Lincoln splitting logs, and illustration of products.. . . . . *$50–75*

"McClellan's Grand March." Democratic campaign song, composed by E. Mack, published by Lee & Walker, Philadelphia. Color lithograph of McClellan with hand in tunic standing next to his horse............................ *$40–60*

"McClellan's Grand March." 1864. Variation of above with bust portrait of McClellan. Multicolor... *$50–75*

"McClellan for President." 1864. Broadside published by Charles Magnus, NY, with black and white lithograph of same pose as above, air: "Pompey Moore" by John C. Cross. *$35–45*

(McClellan) "Hail Glorious Banner of Our Land." 1861. By Mrs. Mary Farrell Moore; music by Chas. Warren. Published by Lee & Briner; Cincinnati. Full-color lithograph of Miss Liberty hoisting U.S. Flag and view of ships in harbor. *$35–45*

"McClellan Conservative Union Mass Convention." Dated August 1864. "Minute Guard Flag Raising/Songs for the People." Nine songs printed on broadside sheet, including "McClellan"; "Hurray for McClellan"; "McClellan's Due"; "We Will Follow Him Forever"; and "Battle of Antietam." Issued for mass meeting in Chicago... *$200–300*

"Mack's Grand Centennial March." 1876. By E.W. Foster; published by John F. Perry, Boston. Dedicated to "The Great Unknown Candidate" Rutherford B. Hayes, Republican nominee... *$35–45*

(McClellan) "Parade March of the Great Potomic Army." 1861. Campaign song by Gen. L. Blenker; composed by Chas. Fradel. Published by C. Breusing; NY. Full-color lithograph by Sherman & Hart, NY, of bust image of Gen. McClellan flanked by men in uniform, a Zouave and infantryman. *$50–60*

"Plumed Knight & Black Eagle Campaign Song Folio." 1884. Republican slate of Blaine & Logan... *$45–65*

"Roll Along Roll Along/Shout the Campaign Battle Song." 1876. For Republican slate of Hayes and Wheeler. Oxen pull Hayes wagon to the Whitehouse. Published by Oliver Ditson, Boston. *$100–125*

"Wigwam Grand March." 1860. Published by Oliver Ditson Co., Boston. Oval line sketch of Lincoln. *$50–75*

"Ye Tailor Man." 1866. Words and music by E. W. Foster. Published by Lyon & Healy Clark, Chicago. Inscribed to "The Dead Dog in the Whitehouse." The snide reference is to Andrew Johnson's humble beginnings as a tailor; small figures of Uncle Sam and scissors form letters in title. *$35–50*

"Semour & Blair's Union Campaign March." 1868. Published by Lyon & Healy Chicago. Jugate portraits encircled by draped flags, cornucopias, winged eagle, and hands clasped above word "Union." *$25–35*

MILITARY LEADERS AND BATTLES

"Adieu March of U.S. Ship North Carolina." Dedicated to Capt. R.W. Meade. *$40–50*

"All quiet along the Potomic To-night." 1864. Poem by Lamar Fontaine (Northerner Ethel Lynn Beers claimed authorship and charged piracy), music by John H. Hewett. Lithographed and published by Geo. Dunn & Co., Richmond, Va........ *$25–35*

"(The) American Star!" 1860. Words by T. J. Donnelly, "music by Anthony Rieff, J." Published by A. Kohler, San Francisco. Color litho of eagle with talons holding sheaf of weapons; furled U.S. flags in b.g. *$25–35*

"A Requiem." 1860; In memory of E.E. Elsworth & his Zouaves; composed by

Geo. Wm. Warren. A news sheet printed in *Harper's Weekly*, June 8, 1861. Lithograph of Elsworth surrounded by cameos of Zouave battle scenes. *$35–50*

"Gen. Bank's Grand March." 1863. Half image of Gen. Nathaniel Prentiss Banks seated with saber. Banks led a decisive Red River campaign in '63. . . . . . . *$40–50*

"Battle Cry of Freedom." 1861. By George Frederick Root (a.k.a. "Rally Around the Flag Boys"). Published by Root & Cady, Chicago. Written in response to Lincoln's second call for troops. *$100–125*

"Battle Hymn of the Republic." 1862. Adopted to "Glory Hallelujah," written by Mrs. Dr. S.G. Howe for *Atlantic Monthly*. Published by Oliver Ditson & Co., Boston. *$35–50*

"(The) Battle of New Orleans" 1862. Anon. Published by Lee & Walker, Philadelphia. Vibrant chromolith of battle in Gulf with Adm. Farragut firing at blockading squadron. *$50–75*

"(The) Blue's Quick Step." 1862. By John Holiday, dedicated to Capt. James Hunt and Light Infantry Co. Winslow Blues. Published in Washington D.C. Full-color lithograph of regiment at camp site in full dress review. *$50–75*

"(The) Bonnie Blue Flag." 1861. (1st Ed.) dedicated to Gen. Albert Pike; by Harry McCarthy, "The Arkansas Comedian." Published by A.J. Blackmar & Bros., New Orleans. Lithograph of crossed flags. *$35–50*

"Bonnie Blue Flag" 1862. Broadside with Northern words, by Johnson Song Publishers, Philadelphia. Copied by permission of S.T. Gordon, Publishers, NY. All type in filigreed border. *$30–45*

"The Bonnie Blue Flag." 1862. Version published by H. J. Wehman, NY, with Southern slant and chorus refrain, "Hurrah for Southern rights." Type enclosed in elaborate border. *$35–45*

"Gen. Buell's Grand Quick Step." 1861. Gen. Don Carlos Buells, a hero of battle of Shiloh. Full figure standing. *$40–50*

"Capture of Richmond & Petersburg." 1864. Battle scene with corps badges at top. Terrific lyrics. Red, white, and blue. *$100–150*

"Beauregard's Charleston Quickstep." (To the Hero of Shiloh & Charleston) 1861. Composed by L. Schreiner. Published by J.C. Schreiner & Son, Macon, GA. Lithograph bust of Beauregard with crossed swords and laurels. *$35–45*

"(The) Carpet Bagger." Late 1860s. Words by T.E. Garrett, music by Alfred von Rochow. Published by Balmer & Weber, St. Louis. McLean lithograph of Uncle Sam carrying carpet bag labeled "Reconstruction." Comic tune sung by Billy Emerson satirizing plundering tactics of the North, dedicated to Benjamin Butler. . . . . .
. . . . *$45–65*

"Close His Eyes! His Work Is Done (A Dirge for a Soldier)." 1862. Words by Geo. H. Boker, music by Asa B. Hutchinson. Sung at Hutchinson Family concerts. Published by Oliver, Ditson & Co., Boston. *$25–45*

"(The) Conquered Banner." 1865. Poem by Moina; music by LaMache. Published by A.E. Blackmar, New Orleans. Lithograph by Feusier & Turnberg, New Orleans, of battered C.S.A. flag draped over damaged cannon. *$50–75*

"Contraband Waltz." 1862; (2nd Edition) Also includes "Skedaddle Grand March." Published by Henry Tolman, Boston. Tiny black figures serve as notes on sheet music. *$35–50*

"How Do You Like It Jefferson D?" 1864. Words and music by Amos Patton. Published by Oliver Ditson, Boston. Lithograph of black Union soldier thumbing nose at Jefferson Davis disguised as the Devil. *$75–100*

"Jeff Davis/A Traitor Who Ruined the South." 1862. Bust portrait of Davis and

Breckinridge. Picture of the Devil looking over circular map inset of seceding states. 5½" x 7" multicolor song sheet. *$100–125*

"Jefferson Davis Confederacy March." 1861. Large lithograph bust portrait of Davis, with facsimile signature. Music by Alfred F. Toulmin of Patapsco Institute. Published by Geo. Willig, Baltimore. *$75–85*

(Jefferson Davis) "Jeff's Double Quick." Published for Western Sanitary Fairs. Black and white sepia cartoon of Davis in female attire. His wife says, "It's only my mother." *$75–85*

(Jefferson Davis) "The Last Ditch Polka." 1865. By D'Accacia. Published by Oliver Ditson, Boston. Vicious caricature of rat in cage with head of Jefferson Davis; eagle atop cage. Davis was imprisoned at Fortress Monroe for two years following the war. *$75–100*

(Jefferson Davis) "The Sour Apple Tree." 1864. By J.W. Turner. (a.k.a. "Jeff Davis' Last Ditch" ballad) Published by Oliver Ditson, Boston. Satirical cartoon based on story that Jeff Davis was captured in Georgia wearing one of his wife's shawls and coats. Shows bag of gold, Bowie knife, and noose suspended from tree. *$75–100*

"Dear Mother I've Come Home to Die." 1864. Song and chorus by E. Bowers; music by Henry Tucker. Published by Firth, Son & Co., NY. *$25–35*

"Dirge." 1863. Sung at consecration of Soldiers' Cemetery, Gettysburg. Composed and arranged by Alfred Delaney, published by Lee & Walker, Philadelphia. *$20–25*

"Dixie for the Union." 1861. Words by Francis J. Crosby. Northern adaptation of Emmett tune with word changes that include "Go Meet Those Southern Traitors." *$60–75*

"Dixie's Land." 1861. Broadside variant of Emmett's text (see above). Lithograph of minstrel show walk-around. *$25–35*

"Dixie Unionized." 1861. Melody by Dan. D. Emmett. Dedicated to Cassius Clay's "Washington Guards." By A.W. Muzzy. *$35–50*

"A Tribute to the Memory of the Late Ellsworth." 1861. Published by Lee & Walker, Philadelphia. Full-color lithograph by Currier and Ives of Col. Elmer Ellsworth (shown trampling on flag), a personal friend of the Lincolns who was shot by a civilian in Alexandria, VA, while hauling down C.S.A. flag. The rebel was shot by Ellsworth's aide. *$125–135*

"Ellsworth's Zouaves & National Lancers Greeting Grand March." 1861. Composed by Adolph Baumbach. Published by Root & Cady, Chicago. Dedicated to Capt. Lucius Slade, National Lancers, Boston." Color lithograph by E. Mendel, Chicago, of four Zouaves in full dress uniform. *$75–100*

"Elegy—Gen. Boomer Who Fell at the Seige of Vicksburg." 1863. Bust portrait in elaborate floral border with laurel wreath above head. Black, white, and sepia lithograph with lavender printing. *$50–60*

"Emmett's Inimitable Plantation Songs." Arranged and sung by Bryant's Minstrals. *$25–35*

"Admiral Faragut's Grand March." 1862. ½ image of Faragut with ship in background. *$40–45*

"Farewell to The Star Spangled Banner." 1861. Dedicated to Army and Navy of C.S.A. Published by J.W. Davies & Sons, Richmond, VA. Lithograph by E. Crehen of stylized type. *$25–35*

"(The) Fatherhood of God and Brotherhood of Man." Late 1860s. Written and published by John W. Hutchinson. An idealistic Northerner's vision of post-war America. *$25–35*

"Fort Sumter Quick Step." 1861. Words and music by George Frederick Root. Published by Wm. Berge, NY. Dedicated to Maj. Robt. Anderson. Lithograph of furled flags, portrait of Anderson, eagle with arrows in talons, and Ft. Sumter scene. *$50–75*

"Gen. Fremont's March." 1861. Lincoln put Fremont in command of Western Dept. in St. Louis. Fremont is pictured on horseback. *$40–50*

"Gen. Gilmore's Grand March." 1860. Half figure portrait of Brig. Gen. John Quincy Gilmore, who commanded X Corps. of Dept. of South in 63–64. . . *$40–50*

"Gen. Stonewall Jackson." 1862. Stonewall's Death and Requiem published by A.E. Blackmar, NY. Portrait of Jackson draped by Confederate flags. *$35–45*

"God Save The South." 1861. Written and composed by Earnest Halphin. Published by Miller & Beecham, Baltimore. Lithograph of crossed C.S.A. flags with 11 stars representing final number of states in Confederacy. *$35–45*

"Gymnast Zouaves Quick Step." 1861. Lee & Walker, publishers. "Zouaves Battle March" (Wm. Dressler, publisher) U.S., full-color; Good Quality/Fair Condition; minor tears taped:(2) $121 (A) *$100–150*

"Grafted Into the Army." 1863. Words and music by Henry C. Work. Published by Root & Cady, Chicago. Lithograph of malapropish mom holding up her son's pants; vignette below it pictures grown son as sentry in Confederate army. *$50–75*

"Grafted Into the Army." 1863. Single-sheet broadside. Johnson & Co. Song Publishers, Philadelphia. Lithograph of eagle in flight. *$40–50*

Note: Lyrics above were inspired by Congress enacting first national draft law in 1863 permitting draftees to purchase exemption by hiring substitute for $300.

"Gen. Halleck's Grand March." 1862. Large oval bust portrait of Gen. Henry W. "Old Brains" Halleck, Union Chief of Staff. *$40–50*

"Gen. Hartranft's Quick Step/51st Penna. Volunteers." 1862. Oval bust portrait. *$50–60*

"Gen. Hooker's Grand March." 1863. Seated portrait of Gen. Jos. Hooker holding saber. *$50–60*

"Hymn to Liberty/Gen. Burnside, Roanoke & Newbern." 1860. Bust portrait of Burnside. *$35–45*

"How Are You Conscript?" 1863. Words and music by Frank Wilder. Published by Henry Talman, Boston. H.F. Greene, Engraver. *$35–50*

"How Are You Exempt?" 1863. Words and music by Frank Wilder. Published by G.D. Russell, Boston. Lithograph of Union soldier asking civilian how he got out of the war. *$35–50*

"How Are You Green-Backs." 1862. By Dan Bryant & Bryant's Minstrels, also by Mrs. John Wood. Words by E. Bowers, arranged by Chas. Glover. Wm. A. Pond, publisher, NY. Lithograph of ten dollar bills with picture of Dan Bryant rather than treasury secretary Salmon P. Chase. *$45–55*

"How Are You? John Morgan/ Comic Song." 1864. Sequel to "Here's Your Mule." Published by C.D. Benson, Nashville. Song about Confederate raider John Morgan's capture and imprisonment in 1863; he escaped to fight again another day. *$50–60*

"Hymn to Liberty." 1862. Dedicated to Burnside, Roanoke and Newbern. Bust portrait of Burnside. *$35–40*

"I Wish I Was in Dixie." 1860. Music by M.D. Peters Esq., music by J.C. Vierick. Published by P.P. Werlein, New Orleans (pirated from the edition below). . . . *$35–45*

"I Wish I Was in Dixie's Land." 1860. Written for Bryants Minstrel by Dan D. Emmett, arranged from Piano Forte by W.L. Hobbs, NY. *$35–45*

"I Wish I Was in Dixie's Land." Variation of Emmett's music above, with words by J. Newcomb and W.H. Peters. Arranged by J.C. Viereck. Published in New Orleans.. *$45–50*

"I Wish I Was in Dixie's Land." Variation of above with rondo and piano forte by Jean Manns. *$25–35*

"In Memory of the Confederate Dead." 1866. Published by Jeles Meininger, Louisville. Pictures fallen Generals Stonewall Jackson (center) John H. Morgan, Albert Sidney Johnston, Leonidis Polk, Jeb Stuart, Hill, and Jas. E. Rains, with names of 34 others in surrounding ribbon.......................... *$60–70*

"Stonewall Jackson." 1863. Oval portrait of Jackson surrounded by furled Confederate flags. Music By Jules Meininger......................... *$125–150*

"Stonewall Jackson's Last Words." 1866. Dedicated to Mary Jackson, the general's wife. Music by Jules C. Meininger. Published by McCarrell & Meininger, Louisville. Lithograph of Jackson with troops crossing river into trees..... *$50–60*

(Stonewall Jackson) "My Wife & Child Song." 1866. Poetry by the late, lamented hero Gen. Stonewall Jackson.* Music by F.W. Rozier. Published by Geo. Dunn & Co., Charleston, S.C. Elaborate script with small cameo of Jackson bust flanked by deities... *$35–50*

"Jullien's American Quadrille" 1860. By S.C. Jollie, NY. Published by Jullien & Co., San Francisco. Full-color lithograph of title overlay on full flying U.S. flag. ... *$35–45*

"Julien's California Imagine." 1853. Same as above, except for image—a color litho of large warrior eagle with thunderbolts in talons and unique convex red, white, and blue shield covering breast. *$35–45*

"Kingdom Coming." 1860s. Song and chorus by Henry C. Worl. Published by Root & Cady, Chicago. Lithograph of soldier marching within large stylized "K" in Kingdom.. *$35–45*

"(The) Knitting Song." 1864. Words and music anon. From *Beadles Dime Song Book*, with refrain, "Knit, Knit" about women knitting socks and mittens for brave Northern troops.. *$35–50*

"Ku Klux Klismet March." 1910. Music by Mary Gue. Published by Walter Andrell Riggs. Arranged by Riggs, Aransas Pass, Texas. Red on white illustration of hooded Klansman on horseback. Another Klansman stands holding fiery cross.
.... *$20–25*

"Ladies' Repository/1864." 1864. Carlton F. Porter, NY. Full-color lithograph of Miss Liberty holding flag banner along coastline, trampling on the chains of slavery.. *$75–100*

"(Gen.) Robert E. Lee." 1865. Includes "The Sword of Robert E. Lee" by Armand, "Funeral March" by E. Mack, "Quick March" by Chas. Young, "God Bless Robert Lee." Song and chorus by W.S. Hays. Published by J.L. Peters & Co., St. Louis. Lithograph of Lee bust portrait surrounded by draped Confederate flags. *$50–60*

"Light Guard Polka & Schottisch." 1862. Composed by Frank Staab, dedicated to Capt. Wyman and Chicago Light Guard. Published by Geo. P. Reed & Co., Boston. Colorful elaborate border; full-color lithograph of three guardsmen in full dress and wearing sabers.................................... *$35–50*

"Lorena." 1865. Anon. Love ballad. Published by H.M. Higgins, Chicago. Full-color lithograph by Ehrgott, Forbrigger & Co., Cincinnati. Three vignettes, the center one featuring a young gentleman flanked by one of a man obviously proposing to a young lady, the other of a man with arms around lady pointing to a church.......... *$25–35*

---

*Poetry actually written by Henry Rootes Jackson, another Rebel General.

"(March of those) Louisiana Banditti/of whom Sheridan is Not afraid." 1867. By Chas. Young, A.E. Blackmar, New Orleans. Caricature of Sheridan in civilian clothes charging with an umbrella. (Sheridan with military administrator for Louisiana and Texas under Reconstruction Act.) *$100–125*

"Louisville Citizen Guards March Quick Step." 1862. Published by D.P. Faulds & Co., Louisville, KY. Full-color; "Daguerreotyped by Webster & Bros.," Louisville. Two guards stand at parade rest, tents in background. *$50–60*

"Marching Through Georgia (Song & Chorus)." 1865. Words and music by Henry Clay Work. Published by Root & Cady, Chicago. Commemorating Gen. Sherman's capture of Atlanta in September, 1864. . . . . *$30–50*

"Marching Through Georgia." 1865. Broadside of the above, published by Johnson & Cartlitch, Philadelphia. *$35–40*

"Maryland Guard Gallop." 1861. Published by Miller & Beacham, Baltimore. Lithograph by A. Hoen & Co., Baltimore, of members of the 53rd Maryland Guard standing in front of battlement. *$50–60*

"Maryland, My Maryland." 1861. Written by James Ryder Randall, music adapted by C.E. (from German tune, "O Tannenbaum"). Published by Miller & Beacham, Baltimore. Lithograph of Maryland state coat of arms. *$35–45*

"Maryland, My Maryland." 1861. A Union parody by Septimus Winner. Published by Lee & Walker, Philadelphia. Elaborate type. *$25–35*

"Maryland, My Maryland." 1861. Broadside rather than song sheet, this is another Northern parody sung to "My Normandy," from *Illustrated Ballads* litho'd and printed by Charles Magnus, NY. Illustration of old man whispering in ear of Southern belle. *$25–35*

"McClellan's Farewell to the Army of the Potomic." 1864. By Magnus, Washington D.C. General McClellan beside horse. *$50–60*

"Gen. Meade's Grand March." 1862. Half figure, profile portrait Gen. Geo. Meade in large oval. *$50–60*

"(The) Merry Little Soldiers." 1862. Confederate broadside. John Hopkins, Printer (no city given). Woodcut of horse and ships. *$75–100*

"Milwaukee Light Guard." 1862. Capt. J.C. Starkweather. Full-color lithograph of four members of guard in full dress uniform, with tents in background. *$75–100*

"Monitor Grand March." 1862. Composed by E. Mack. Published by Lee & Walker, Philadelphia. Chromolith of Monitor and Merrimac engaged in battle. . . .
. . . . *$100–125*

"Mother, I've Come Home to Die." 1864. Words by E. Bowers, music by Henry Tucker. Published Charles Magnus, NY, with copyright by Firth & Son, Co., NY; (2nd. version). Lithograph of corpse of soldier swathed in U.S. flag being borne by angels. *$25–35*

"Music for the Union." 1862. Large furled U.S. Flag. Liberty Hat on pike appears above the letter "M" in elaborate red, white, and blue type as title. Published by A.C. Peterss & Bro., Cincinnati. *$35–45*

"National Jubilee." 1865; words by Carlos Wilcox; music by Konrad Treur. . . . .
. . . . *$25–35*

"Nation's Jubilee." 1865. Anon. Lithograph with vignettes of an angel, families greeting returnees at train station, and men voting at polls. Tune was published at the first postwar July 4th celebration. *$25–35*

"No Surrender Song." Music by C.C. Mera. Lithographed and published by Geo. Dunn & Co., Columbia, S.C. Small vignettes of Reb leader fighting off Union forces and battle of Monitor and Merrimac. *$100–125*

"(The) Old Contraband." 1862. Words by John Lieber, music by Rudolph Mittig. Published by W.R. Smith, Philadelphia. Lithograph of black man with walking stick, carries knapsack over shoulder. *$75–100*

"O, I'm a Good Old Rebel." 1887. Credited to Maj. Innes Randolph, a Virginia lawyer. Resistance song is dedicated to radical Republican, Thaddeus Stevens, author of vengeful Reconstruction methods. *$75–100*

"Old Abe—The Battle Eagle." 1861. Song and chorus by L.M. Bates, music by T. Martin Towne. Inscribed to 8th Wisconsin Reg. Published by H.N. Homestead, Milwaukee. Color lithograph of beloved mascot of the Wisconsin regiment, who perches on a special stand against backdrop of U.S. shield. *$100–125*

"(The) Old Union Wagon." 1861. Dedicated to 37th Indiana Regiment, "Our Brave Soldier Boys," by John Hogarth Luzier. Set to 1850s tune, "Wait for the Wagon." Published by J. Church Jr., Cincinnati. Lithograph of Lincoln holding reins of Union wagon filled with people representing "Constitution." *$75–100*

"On Picket Duty." 1864. Anon. Lithograph rendering by Fabronius of John Rogers' statuette by that name. Published by C.D. Russel, Co., Boston. . . . *$35–45*

"On to the Charge." 1860s. By John Hewitt. Dedicated in memory of Maj. John Ringgold of the U.S. Light Artillery. Full-color lithograph of Ringgold's grave marked with U.S. flag, discarded cannon, kepi hat and cross; small vingnette of Maj. being carried by his men. *$100–125*

"Our Country and Flag." 1864. "A National Song & Chorus." Words and music by Richard Culver. Published by Lee & Walker, Philadelphia. Chromolith panorama of troops in battle with nation's capitol in background; Ft. Sumpter afire in oval vignette. *$75–100*

"Our Generals." 1866. Published by Jeles Meininger, Louisville. Portraits of C.S.A. leaders, Lee (in center), with surrounding ovals of Jackson, Price, Beauregard, Longstreet, Johnston, Hill, Hardee, and Bragg. *$70–80*

"Our Generals Grand March." 1862. Anon. Published by Horace Waters, NY. Chromolith by Crow, Thomas & Co., NY, of Gen.'s McClellan, Scott, Mansfield, Burnside, and others (all identified) parade by on horseback. *$75–100*

"Our Generals Quick Step." Published by Horace Waters, NY. Multicolor cover of over 25 (all identified) Union generals passing in review on horseback. (D.) $200
. . . . *$175–200*

"Our National Confederate Anthem." 1862. Words by Ernest Halpin, composed and published by C.T. De Coeniel, Richmond, VA. Lithograph of kneeling Rebel with sword and waving flag which bears words, "God Save The South.". . *$75–100*

"(The) Palmetto State Song." 1860. By Geo. Robinson. "Dedicated to Signers of Ordinance of Secession." Published by Henry Siegling, Charleston, S.C. Large oval lithograph of Secession Convention scene. *$100–125*

"Peace." 1865. Music by Charles Moulton. Published by Scharfenberg & Luis, NY. Large type interlaced with palm branches; lithograph of woman in field listening. "Tis the voices of thousands (of returning veterans) as they come." . . . *$35–50*

"Gen. Pickett's Celebrated Charge/The Battle of Gettysburg." 1862. By a Chicago publisher. Bust portrait which list below of major battles that Pickett served in. *$65–75*

"Gen. Pope's Grand March." 1862. Large oval bust portrait of Gen. John Pope.
. . . . *$50–60*

"Rally Around the Flag Boys." 1861. Broadside. Alternate title to George F. Root's "Battle Cry of Freedom," with different words by James T. Field and music by Wm. B. Bradbury, Boston. *$40–50*

"Rally Around the Flag Boys." 1861. Same as above. Song sheet with full-color lithograph of title entwined around furled U.S. flag. *$35–50*

"Raw Recruits." 1862. Published by Firth, Pond & Co. Illustration of five humorous black gentlemen in Civil War uniforms. (A.) Paul Dias, Hanson, Mass. Oct. '94–$160. . . . . *$150–175*

"Reconstruction! Grand March." 1868. By Charles Young. Published by J.L. Peters, NY. Two vignettes: Lithograph by P.S. Dural & Sons, Philadelphia, "As it Should Be," depicting a host of angels playing musical instruments; "As It Is!" devils, witches, and other ogres playing music.. . . . . *$40–45*

"Red, White and Blue." 1861. Broadside printed in German. Lithograph of Liberty with crossed flags and shield. Published for benefit of German troops—largest ethnic group in Union army. *$30–35*

"Richmond Has Fallen." 1865. Song and chorus by J.W. Turner. Published by Oliver Ditson, Boston. Lithograph of stylized type with a snake forming the "R" and encircling cameo of burning city; face at the snake's tail is said to represent Jeff Davis. *$45–50*

"Riding a Raid." 1862. By John Randolph, Richmond, VA. Lithograph by E. Crehen of legendary Confederate Gen. "Jeb" Stuart on horseback wearing peacock plume in hat. *$40–45*

"Rising of the People." 1865. A.k.a. "The Drum Tap rattles Through the Land." Words by N.P. Beers, music by M. Colburn. Published by Firth, Pond & Co., NY, Major & Klapp, NY. Chromolith of family greeting returning Union hero. . . . .
. . . . *$35–50*

"Rosencrans Military Schottisch." 1862. Half figure profile pose of Gen. Wm. Starke Rosencrans with hand inside coat. *$50–60*

"Secession Grand March." 1860. Composed by J.R. Boulcott. Published by Bromberg & Son, New Orleans. Lithograph of bales of cotton with names of seceding states, tobacco leaves, rum cask. *$50–60*

Gen. Sedgwick's Grand Funeral March. 1864. Gen. John Sedgwick, who commanded 6th Corps, was killed at Spotsylvania. Bust portrait in large ornate frame.
. . . . *$40–50*

"(Gen.) W.F. Sherman' & Boys in Blue." Large stylized title with bust portrait of Sherman.. . . . . *$50–75*

"W.F. Sherman's Grand March." Composed by J. Val Hamm. Published by Oliver Ditson & Co., Boston. Three quarter bust lithograph of Gen. Sherman. . . . .
. . . . *$50–75*

"Sherman's March to the Sea." 1864. Profile bust portrait of Gen. Sherman against multicolor background of large eagle and crossed flags. *$60–75*

"Short Rations." 1864. Written by "Ye Tragic," "Ye Comic" (John Alcee Augustin, who served in Confederate Army of Tenn.). Published by Blackmar & Bro., Augusta, GA. Lithograph of horse at feedbag saying "Not Satisfied." *$75–100*

"Sinking of the Pirate Alabama." 1864. "New Patriotic & Comic Song." Pair of small furled flags. Rest is type. Describes sinking of Alabama by USS *Kearsarge* off the coast of Cherbourg, France. *$75–100*

"Skedaddle."* 1864. "To the Col. of the Stuyvesant Guards," by Geo. Danskin. Published by Oliver Ditson & Co., Boston. Various letters of the word bear imaginative caricatures of faces. *$75–100*

---

*Name is of Southern origin; derisive term for slaves who take flight in panic, run away.

SLAVERY/ABOLITIONIST RELATED

"John Brown." 1861. Music arranged by C. B. Marsh. Published by C.S. Hall, Charlestown, MA. Rare 2nd broadside with lithograph of small eagle and shield at top. *$75–100*

"Colored Volunteer." 1862. Ballad broadside by A.W. Auner, Philadelphia, Song Publisher. Words by Tom Craig. Refers to John Fremont's unilateral Emancipation Proclamation issued in Missouri in 1861. . . . . *$50–60*

"Eva to Her Pappa." 1853. As sung by Little Cordelia Howard in Broadway musical *Uncle Tom's Cabin*. Words and music by Geo. C. Howard (her father) and dedicated to her mother. *$45–50*

"Desponding Negro." 1792. London. Circular vignette of slave being tossed overboard from ship. Song relates of rescuer, and the slave begging for money. One of the earliest antislavery pieces. (A.) Stark '89. $350. . . . . *$350–400*

"The Fugitive's Song." 1850s. Dedicated to Frederick Douglass, a graduate from the "Peculiar Institution." Depicts a young beardless Douglass with knapsack being pursued by slave owners in far background. Goes on to laud Douglass for efforts in behalf of "his brothers in bonds and to the fugitives from slavery." "By their friend Jesse Hutchinson Junr.") of the famed Hutchinson Family Singing group from NH)
. . . . *$75–85*

"(The) Fugitives Song (I'll Be Free! I'll Be Free!)." 1850. Words by Jesse Hutchinson Jr., music by J.M. White. A variant of above. Abolitionist's song inspired by life of Frederick Douglass. *$50–75*

"Get Off the Track." 1843. Words by Jesse Hutchinson Jr., music from "Old Dan Tucker" by Daniel Decatur Emmett. The Hutchinson Family toured for years in behalf of abolition causes, song compares move toward slavery to steam locomotive.
. . . . *$125–150*

"The Grave of the Slave." 1831. Words by Sarah Forten, music by Francis Johnson. *$50–75*

"Little Eva; Uncle Tom's Guardian Angel." 1852. By Mrs. Harriet Beecher Stowe, poetry by John Greenleaf Whittier, music by Manuel Emilio. Published by John Jewitt & Co., Boston. Lithograph of Uncle Tom talking to Little Eva. . . . . . .
. . . . *$75–85*

"Poor Oppressed." 1862. A.ka. "Contraband Schottissch.") By C.D. Benson, Nashville, Tenn. Lithograph of fashionably dressed black lady with parasol. . . . . .
. . . . *$25–35*

"Charles Sumner Funeral March." 1874. Published by Lee & Walker, Philadelphia. Lithograph by Sinclair & Sons, Philadelphia. Bust portrait of Sumner, one of the staunchest abolitionists. *$30–35*

"(The) Veto Gallop!" 1867. Composed by "Make Peace." Published by McCarrell & Meininger, Louisville, Bennett, Donadson & Elmes, Cincinnati. Andrew Johnson on horseback trampling "Dead duck" adversaries: (Thaddeus Stevens, John W. Forney, Benj. Wade; abolitionists Wendell Phillips, Frederick Douglass). . . . .
. . . . *$75–100*

"Wake Nicodemus." 1861 Words and music by Henry Clay Worl. Published by Root & Cady, Chicago. Lithograph of slave Nicodemus peering from large knothole in tree trunk. *$50–75*

"(The) Soldier's Goodbye." 1863. Music by Christian Beyer. Published by Shepard Cottier & Co., Buffalo. Lithograph of Union soldier bidding tearful farewell to sweetheart as parents sit mournfully by. *$25–30*

"The Soldier's Return." 1864. By T. Van Berg. Published by Endres & Compton,

St. Louis. Color lithograph by Major and Klapp, NY. Joyous scene of returning Union soldier being embraced by his children and wife.................. *$20–25*

"(The) Song of Contrabands/O Let My People Go." 1862. Words and music by Rev. L.C. Lockwood; arranged by Thos. Baker. Published by Horace Waters, NY. Lithograph of patriotic shields in each corner of cover. *$25–35*

"Song/Thousand Years." 1863. Words and music by Henry C. Work. Published by Root & Cady, Chicago. Full-color lithograph of U.S. flag predicting future by showing 46 stars studding the canton. *$25–35*

"The South." 1862. Broadside. Parody on "Scots Wha Ha'e," etc. Lithograph of circular seal showing Reb in camp. *$75–100*

"Southern Constellation." 1864. Words by Robt. F. Carlin, Surgeon, 5th Confederate Regt., C.S.A. Published by Schreiner & Sons, Macon, GA. Color lithograph of Miss Liberty in armor, with sword and C.S.A. flag, bale of cotton and elaborate boxes next to her, plantation in background...................... *$75–100*

"(Das) Star Spangled Banner." 1862. German language broadside of national anthem as advertising promotion for Maonus Ornamental & Glorious Union Packet. Lithograph of Liberty carrying U.S. flag.................................. *$25–35*

"Star Spangled Banner." 1860. Arranged for piano by Chas. Voss. Published by G. Andre. Color lithograph of Union soldier steadying mast of furled U.S. flag; camp is in background.. *$35–50*

"Star Spangled Cross & Pure Field of White." 1862. By Subaltern. Published by Dunn, Richmond, VA. Red, white, and blue C.S.A. flag at upper third of cover....
.... *$50–75*

"Tell Mother I Die Happy." 1863. Broadside by Charles Magnus, NY, words by C.A. Vosburgh, music by Jabez Burns. Published by S.T. Gordon, NY. Lithograph of Lt. Crosby, killed at Salem Heights, dying in arms of angel; mother (at right) is on knees praying. *$35–50*

"Tis Finished." 1865. (a.k.a. "Sing Hallelujah.") Words and music by Henry C. Work. Publisher unknown....................................... *$25–35*

"Tolling Bell Approaching Mt. Vernon." 1865. Dedicated to the late Hon. Edw. Everett (orator who delivered the speech preceding Lincoln's at Gettysburg). Delineation for the piano by Chas. Grobe. Published by Lee & Walker, Philadelphia....
.... *$20–25*

"Traitor, Spare that Flag." 1861. By Rev. J.P. Lundy, adapted from "Woodman Spare That Tree." Full-color broadside by Chas. Magnus, NY. Small vignettes of sailor and Miss Liberty, large anchor, ship in background seal of New York....... *$75–100*

"Tramp! Tramp! Tramp! The Prisoners Hope." 1864. Words and music by Geo F. Root. Published by Root & Cady. Lithograph by Copcutt, Williams Co. of vignettes of battle scenes... *$35–50*

"Tramp! Tramp! Tramp! The Prisoners Hope." 1864. Broadside distributed by Horace Partridge, Boston; ornately scrolled border. *$25–35*

"Uncle Sam's Farm." 1860s. Broadside. To tune of "Walk in de Parlor and hear de Banjo Play." Andrews Printers, NY. Extolling the "Yankee Nation." *$50–60*

"Union War Gallop." 1861. Published S. Brainard Co., Composed by Wm. Dressler. Illustration of Miss Liberty in chariot with four horses.......... *$50–60*

"United States Battle March/In Memory of Col. Ellsworth." 1861. Full standing figure of Ellsworth in Zouave uniform. *$60–75*

"The United States Zouave Cadets." 1862. Published by Root & Cady, Chicago. Full-color lithograph of four Zouaves in full dress and at parade rest with muskets. . *$50–75*

"(The) Vacant Chair." 1861. Music by C.F. Root. Published by Davies & Sons,

Richmond, VA. Litho of young lady standing behind vacant chair, photo of her sweetheart Confederate soldier is on mantle.......................... *$35–50*

"Vicksburg Schottisch." 1862. By E.C. Eaton. Pub. by Woodruff & Diserens, NY. Chromolith by Henry Eno, NY, of Vicksburg harbor with two paddle-wheelers. ..
.... *$50–75*

"Virginia Marseillaise." 1862. "French Legion." C.S.A. officer carrying large Rebel flag. Published by Dunn, Richmond, VA...................... *$75–100*

"Volunteer Flag Song." 1861. Adopted as Camp Chorus by Michigan Regiments. By D. Bethune Duffield, translated and published by Chas. Swinscoe, Detroit. Chromolith of large gold eagle with banner in beak.................... *$50–75*

"Wait Love Until the War Is Over." 1863. Music adapted by T.M. Todd. Published by Lee & Walker, Philadelphia. Lithograph of Union soldier strolling with his young lady in garden.. *$35–50*

"Wanted/A Substitute." 1863. Published by Oliver Ditson, Boston. Lithograph bust of sad man "I'm Drafted," and bust of happy man "I ain't.".......... *$35–50*

"We Are Coming Father Abraham/3,000 More." 1862. Words by John Sloan Gibbons, music by Stephen C. Foster. Published by S.T. Gordon, NY. *$35–50*

"We'll Go Down Ourselves." 1862. By Henry Work. Published by Root & Cady, Chicago. Lithograph by Baker of militant, dissatisfied women beating up on men (they wanted to fight in the war)................................. *$50–75*

"We're Coming Fodder Abraham/We're Coming in a Horn." 1863. "Comic Song by an Intelligent Contraband" play on words, as contraband referred to any escaped slave. By C.T. Beauman. Published by Tripp & Gragg, Louisville, KY. Lithograph of black soldiers marching into giant powder horn. *$100–125*

"When Johnny Comes Marching Home." 1863. Music introduced in "Soldier's Return March" by Gilmore's Band. Words and music by Louis Lambert. Published by Henry Tolman & Co., Boston. Cover design of type encased in a shield of stars, small illustration of military caisson.............................. *$35–50*

"When Johnny Comes Marching Home." 1864. Broadside by Johnson Song Publisher, Philadelphia. Lithograph of oriental fantasy with turbaned men in howdahs riding elephants... *$75–100*

"When the Boys Come Home." 1865. Words and music by Charles Carrol Sawyer. Published by Chas. Magnus, NY. Lithograph of victory parade as Union troops march to cheers of crowd................................. *$50–75*

"When the Cruel War is Over." (a.k.a. "Weeping Sad & Lonely.") Words by Charles C. Sawyer, music by Henry Tucker. Published by Geo. Dunn & Co., Columbia, SC. Popular tune by both sides. *$35–50*

"When the Cruel War is Over." Same as above, a Northern version where it was popularly a broadside. Distributed by Horace Partridge, Boston. *$40–60*

"(The) White House Chair." 1856. Words and music by Stephen Collins Foster.
.... *$35–50*

"Who Shall Rule This American Nation?" 1867. Words and music by Henry Clay Work. Reconstruction song. *$35–50*

"(The) Wide-Awake Quick Step." 1860. Dedicated to Capt. Owen Moore. Written by Wm. Weed. Published by D.H. Andrews, Albany, NY. Full-color lithograph of kepi and cape with lantern in hand; vignettes of flags, eagle, U.S. Capitol, White House... *$75–100*

"Yes, I Would the War Was Over." 1864. by Septimus Winner, as sequel or answer to "When This Cruel War is Over" (see above). Published by Beadle's Dime Song Book... *$35–45*

"(The) Young America Schottisch." 1855. Composed by Francis H. Brown. Published by Firth, Pond & Co., NY. Full-color lithograph of Miss Mary Leeds of New York hoisting U.S. flag. *$50–75*

"Zouave Grand Parade March/Duett (sic) for Four Hands." 1862. Composed by S.D.S. Published by Lee & Walker, Philadelphia. Full-color A. Whatley lithograph of two Zouaves—one blowing bugle, the other advancing with musket and bayonet. *$75–100*

Left to right: *"Stonewall Jackson's Death and Requiem March,"* $150–$200; *"Virginia Marseillaise,"* $75–$100; *"Star Spangled Cross and The Pure Field of White,"* $65–$75. (Photo courtesy of Rex Stark)

Left: *Temperance/abolitionist singing group from New Hampshire, the Hutchinson Family, issued* "The Fugitive's Song" *in honor of Frederick Douglass, ca. 1850,* $250–$300. Right: *"Eva to Her Papa." Sheet music from the Broadway musical version of* Uncle Tom's Cabin. *Pictured is Cordelia Howard as Eva, who made her debut at four and was the most popular of the many young actresses to play the part,* $250–$300.

Left: *An advertisement announcing the publication of "God Save the South" as the new CSA national anthem in 1862, $150–$200.* Right: *"Star Spangled Banner" published by Chas. Voss, with multicolor Union camp scene, $175–$200.*

Stamps, Postal Covers, Letter Sheets, and Postal Stationery

Covers

Col. Robert Anderson, The Hero of Fort Sumter. Black on buff. Portrait of Anderson, the Union Commander at Ft. Sumter. *$12–15*

"Gov. John Andrew/ True to the Union." Bust Portrait in shield. Eagle above with legend. Browntone on buff. Abolition leader who built up the Mass. State Militia as war governor. *$10–15*

John Bell, Traitor. 1860 Campaign. Red, white, and blue, Bell bust portrait. Anti-Constitution Party. "Traitor" is overprinted. *$50–65*

John C. Breckinridge, Traitor: 1860. Red, white, and blue. Bust portrait. Southern Democratic Party. "Traitor" is overprinted. *$50–65*

James Buchanan "Judas" 1856 Campaign. Bust portrait. 5 lines across cover of vitriolic anti-Buchanan sentiment. *$50–75*

"Jefferson Davis/Flag" ca. 1861 small oval bust of Davis in black against red, white, and blue C.S.A. flag. *$20–25*

Jefferson Davis with Lincoln's Arm Reaching Out to Choke Him. ca. 1861. Black on white. Davis wears multi-feather cockade hat. *$20–25*

"Jeff Davis & Gen. Winfield Scott Playing Chess." 1861. "Caption: "Jeff Davis Checkmated." Black on white cartoon. *$20–25*

"Jeff Davis on the Last Platform of the Confeder-ass-y." ca. 1861. Black transfer running full vertical on the cover of Davis hanging from noose. *$45–50*

Jeff Davis, Pres/ Alexr. H. Stevens, Vice Pres. ca. 1861; black script against red, white, and blue C.S.A. flag. *$50–65*

Jefferson Davis Facsimile Signature. 1861. Large black lithograph bust portrait of Davis on bright yellow cover. *$50–60*

Uncle Jeff Davis' Patriotic Quilt 1861. Red, white, and blue. Blue flag with 11 white stars. *$75–100*

Jefferson Davis. 1861. "Southern Rights & Southern Institutions." Bust of Davis. Red, white, and blue. *$100–125*

"Don't Tread On Us." ca. 1861; snake coiled around crossed C.S.A. flags; sepia, red, white, and blue. *$25–35*

Stephen A. Douglas. 1860. Campaign. "Stand By the Flag," Red, white, and blue. *$50–75*

Stephen A. Douglas 1860. Bust portrait in black and white facsimile signature.. . . . . *$20–25*

Douglas–Johnson Crossed Flags and Quotation. 1860. Eagle at top. Legend inside shield. *$25–35*

Stephen A. Douglas Memorial. 1861. "Our Country Mourns Him." B&w bust portrait. Black border. Douglas died in 1861 of typhoid fever after rallying behind Lincoln following the firing on Fort Sumter. *$15–20*

Eagle with U.S. Flag ca. 1860s; sepiatone eagle with wings fully extended with red, white, and blue flag; type in brown:"Division by armed force is treason"-Andrew Jackson. *$35–45*

Elephant with U.S. Flag in Trunk ca. 1861; "What if a hungry rat crossed the path of an elephant? Squelch it by heaven. Squelch it"; red-white-blue on buff stock. *$35–50*

Set "For the Union" 1860s series by Charles Mangus, Washington, D.C. Each comes in different color with coat of arms of Union particular state, plus slogan. Minnesota's for example is *"Death to the Traitors,"* Utah's *"The Union Forever,"* Delaware *Our Union/God's Greatest Blessing on Earth;"* California *"The Union at all Hazards."* 25 different States in set. . . . . *$400–450 (the Set) $15–18 each.*

John C. Fremont. 1856. Campaign. Portrait; scene of Indian battle in West. B&w. *$50–75*

John C. Fremont. 1856. Campaign. Bust portrait. Test praises him as leader. *$50–75*

U.S. Grant for President. 1868. B&w. Bust portrait; Grant quote. *$25–35*

Hayes-Wheeler Jugate. 1876. Black on white cover with crossed U.S. flags beneath portraits. *$30–35*

"I'll Float Again Over Sumter" ca. 1860; words in banner over full color U.S. flag. *$15–20*

Lincoln with Crossed Flags ca. 1861; b&w bust of Lincoln; crossed red, white, and blue flags; "They can afford to do a wrong. I cannot." *$20–25*

Lincoln, small engraved bust portrait in upper right corner; verse by Philadelphia printer, R. Magee reads: "What though it be a homely face? It masks a soul that never quails. . . ." *$20–25*

Lincoln Bust Above Shield. 1860. Campaign. Red, white and blue. *$50–65*

Lincoln and Crossed Flags. 1860. Bust portrait. "The Union Must and Shall Be Preserved." Beardless bust of Lincoln. Red, white, and blue. *$75–85*

Lincoln and Jeff. Davis. "Champion Prize Envelopes—Lincoln & Davis in Five Rounds." ca. 1861-'62. Complete set of five. Cartoon imagery of Lincoln and Davis as sparring partners with Uncle Sam and Lady Liberty as observers. *$375–400*

(Lincoln) Star of the North Comet of 1861. Classic red, white, and blue cover of comet with head of Lincoln streaking across sky. *$85–85*

(McClellan) "A General of the C.S.A. Preparing to Meet Gen. McClellan." Caricature of C.S.A. officer in rather ridiculous regalia multi-plumed hat, etc.). Off at opposite end of envelope is small image of same C.S.A. general running for his life with caption, "After he met him!" Black on buff stock. (Possible color variations.) *$25–35*

Miss Liberty and Union Flag over globe. ca. 1860s; light blue on white. . *$15–20*

"Music by the Contrabands" 1862, black and white envelope with woodcut of three black musicians; by S.C. Upham, stationers, Philadelphia. *$45–55*

"(The) New Quaker Bonnet" dated 1861; bonnet with red, white, and blue full color bonnet. *$20–25*

"Our Compromise." 1862. Union banner with smoking cannon. Red, white, and blue on buff. *$12–15*

The Country's In Danger. That's what's the trouble. Uncle Sam in large beaver hat with feathers holding rifle with bayonet. Copperhead snake is at his feet, obviously shot. Red, white, and blue on white. *$20–25*

Pig carrying U.S. Flag on Saddle ca. 1860s; illustration of pig in blue with red saddle; red, white, and blue Union flag mounted; "Whole Or Moms? *$20–25*

"Secession" 1861; black and white litho of black woman carrying knapsack and fleeing with her small boy. *$12–15*

"Horatio Seymour, For President/Gen. Francis Blair for V.P." 1868. Bust portrait. Blair was Democratic Governor of N.Y. when the draft riots occurred. Black & gold. *$20–25*

"Shoot the first Man that attempts to pull down the American Flag" ca. 1862; cannon firing with U.S. Flag flying; sepia, red, white, and blue on buff stock. Same image in brown, red, and blue, with other legends. *$20–25*

Uncle Same (pushing man off battleship) ca. 1862; cartoon, browntone on buff of Uncle Sam using U.S. flag to prod man (symbolizing the South?) into the harbor, being pursued by alligator. *$25–30*

"Union" ca. 1860s; "Union" appears in gold sunburst above eagle and furled flag, full color. *$15–20*

Union Cavalryman ca. 1862; rider on horseback with fort in background topped by red, white, and blue U.S. flag. *$15–20*

"Gen. John Wool" 1861. Bust portrait of septagenarian general who led his Union troops in fighting off the Rebels at Fort Monroe. Purple on buff. *$10–12*

LETTERSHEETS

"Camp Hicks, Frederick, Maryland." January 28, 1862. B&w lithograph by L.N. Rosenthal, Philadelphia. Illustration of Camp Hicks when still in its early primitive stages, with large stand of trees. Letter is written by John B. Jenks, 12th. Regt., Mass Vols. from camp to his brother, describing the layouts of the tents in camp. .
. . . . *$50–75*

Grant-Colfax Campaign Note Paper. 1868. Matching cover, but with more ornate border around bust portraits. Black on white. . . . . *$50–75 (pair)*

"Miss Liberty with Flags." 1860s, red, white and blue Liberty holds U.S. Shield with bust portrait of George Washington. *$20–25*

Lincoln and Hamlin. 1860. Postal cover used. Jugate portraits in stylized shield. Letterhead of same motif. $100(A). *$75–100*

"Maj. Gen. George B. McClellan" 1860; full length portrait of McClellan in uniform. *$15–20*

"The Presidents of the U.S." 1860; b&w small oval cameos of all U.S. presidents from Washington through Lincoln, topped by eagle and furled flags. *$15–20*

POSTAGE STAMPS

Stamps Issued During Civil War Era.

Stamps, 1861 First Designs. Perf. 12

Three cents, brown and red, Washington bust profile.........................
.... Used *Not listed* Unused .fine *$700*

Ten cents, apple green. Washington bust. .... Used *$280* Unused *Not listed.*

Stamps 1861–1862 Second Designs.

One cent, blue. Franklin bust profile.................. Used *$12* Unused $120

One cent, dark blue. Franklin bust profile............... Used *$27* Unused *$150*

Three cent, pink, Washington bust profile. ...... Used *$300* Unused *$1900 (avg.)*

Three cent, rose pink. Washington................ Used *$46* Unused *$270* (fine)

Three cent, rose .... Used *$1.90* Unused *$65* (fine)

Three cent, lake......................... Used *Not listed* Unused *$1000* (avg.)

Five cent, buff........................ Used *$380* (fine) Unused *$2600* (avg.)

Ten cent, yellow green........................ Used *$28* Unused *$230* (fine)

Twelve cent, black............................ Used *$52* Unused *$480* (fine)

Twenty-four cent, red, lilac......................... Used *$80* Unused *$600*

Twenty-four cent, steel blue. Washington......... Used *$280* Unused *Not listed*

Twenty-four cent, violet...................... Used *$500* Unused *Not listed*

Thirty cent, orange. Franklin profile. .... Used *$62* Unused *$465* (fine)

Ninety cent, blue. Washington................ Used *$230* Unused *$1200* (fine)

1861–1866 New Values or New Colors

Two cent, black. Washington................... Used *$24* Unused *$160* (fine)

Three cent, scarlet. Washington bust profile. .... Used *$1800* Unused *$4000* (fine)

Five cent, red brown. Jefferson. .... Used *$220* Unused *$1270* (fine)

Five cent brown............................. Used *$50* Unused *$350* (fine)

Fifteen cent, black. Lincoln. .... Used *$65* Unused *$525* (fine)

Twenty-four cent, lilac Washington.............. Used *$50* Unused *$275* (fine)

Commemorative Issues

William H. Seward. Alaska–Yukon Issue 1909. Two cent carmine. Portrait of Lincoln's secretary of state who arranged purchase of Alaska. . Used *$2* Unused *$8*

Admirals Farragut and Porter. Army & Navy Issue. 1936–1937. Three cent. Purple. Oval portraits of Adm. David Farragut and Commodore David Porter. Steam sloop *Hartford* is in background. .... Used *.16* Unused *.17*

Generals Grant, Sheridan and Sherman. Army & Navy Issue. 1936–1937. Three cent. Purple. Oval images of the three Union generals with laurel branches below. Used *.16* Unused *.17*

Clara Barton, Founder of the American Red Cross. 1948. Three cent. Rose pink. Bust oval portrait of Barton, famed Civil War nurse. Large Red Cross logo in red at right. . . . . Used *.17* Unused *.25*

Washington and Lee University, 1749–1949. 1948–1950. Three cent. Purple. Bust portraits of George Washington and Robert E. Lee; University in background. . . . . Used *.17* Unused *.25*

First Nation Encampment of the G.A.R. 1945–50. Three cent. Carmine. Bust portrait of grizzled G.A.R. vet.; young Union trooper in kepi in background. . . . . Used *.17* Unused *.25*

First Reunion United Confederate Veterans. 1950–1952. Three cent. Slate gray, white. Small hourglass, top left. Bust portrait of UCF veteran with young Reb in kepi in background. . . . . Used *.17* Unused *.25*

"Civil War Centennial, Fort Sumter 1861–1961. Four cent. Union artillery-man manning big cannon at Fort. Dark green half silhoutte image. . . . . Used *.15* Unused *.30*

"Civil War Centennial, 1861–1961 Shiloh" Four cent, black on peach of infantry-man firing from rock. . . . . Used *.15* Unused *.25*

Civil War Centennial, Gettysburg 1863–1963. Five cent. Dark image on light blue, gray of Reb and Yankee fighting with rifled bayonets at close quarters. . . . . Used *.15* Unused *.25*

Civil War Centennial, Battle of the Wilderness, 1964. Five cent. Dark red and black. Silhouetted artillerymen loading cannon . . . . Used *.16* Unused *.25*

Civil War Centennial, Appomattox, 1865. Five cent, black on blue/pink. "With Malice Toward None." Lone silhouetted soldier with stacked rifles. . . . . Used *.20* Unused *.40*

Stone Mountain Memorial. 1970. Six cent. Gray, black Mammoth memorial carv-ing begun by sculptor Gutzin Borglum at Stone Mountain near Atlanta, Ga. Deep relief carving of Generals Robert E. Lee, Stonewall Jackson, and C.S.A. president Jefferson Davis. . . . . Used *.20* Unused *.25*

Harriet Tubman. 1978. Thirteen cent. Multicolor of famous abolitionist who helped over 300 slaves escape via the Underground Railroad. From Black Heritage series. . . . . Used *.20* Unused *.40*

Dr. Mary Walker, Army Surgeon/Medal Of Honor. 1982. 20 cent. Multicolor, bust oval portrait of Walker, who for three years was a Union Army nurse. First woman Assistant Surgeon General in 1864. . . . . Used *.15* Unused *.60*

Sylvanus Thayer. 1985. Nine cent. Black, green. Bust portrait of Union officer and "Father of U.S. Military Academy." . . . . Used *.15* Unused *.25*

Julia Ward Howe. 1985. Fourteen cent. Red on white, half silhouetted bust por-trait of Howe, leading abolitionist and suffragette who wrote "Battle Hymn of the Republic." . . . . Used *.15* Unused *.45*

Belva Ann Lockwood. 1985. Seventeen cent. Aqua on white (from same series as the Howe stamp). Bust portrait of feminist leader who ran for president on Equal Rights Party slate. . . . . Used *.15* Unused *.40*

Soujourner Truth. 1986. Twenty-two cent. Multicolor. Bust figure, small inset of noted black abolitionist and suffragette at lecture platform. From Black Heritage series. . . . . Used *.15* Unused *.65*

Ida B. Wells. 1989. Twenty-five cent. Multicolor, bust portrait with small figures in background. Wells was a crusading black journalist who launched anti-lynching campaign in the 1880s. From Black Heritage series. . . . . Used *.15* Unused *.65*

ABRAHAM LINCOLN COMMEMORATIVES AND GENERAL ISSUES

Note: There are numerous color, paper, size, and watermark variations in the early regular issues with drastic differences in value. For closer scrutiny, consult *The Official 1995 Blackbook Price Guide to U.S. Postage Stamps*, House of Collectibles, N.Y.

Lincoln Oval Bust Portrait. General Issue 1869. Fifteen cents. Black . . . . Used .*$40* Unused $65

Variations of this specimen include several different grills at $240 used, 400 unused; a 1875 reissue at $3100 used and $2100 unused. (all rate fine.)

Lincoln Mourning Stamp. 1861–1866. Fifteen cent. Black. Oval bust portrait issued a year after Lincoln's assassination. . . . . Used *$40* Unused *$65*

Lincoln Profile Bust 1869–1890 General Issue. Six cent. Carmine. . . . . Used *$6*. Unused *$11*

Same as above in National Banknote Grilled example $250 used, $1500 unused, rated fine.

Also from the above series—a seven-cent denomination picturing Lincoln's Secretary of War Edwin Stanton in vermillion is valued at $28 used and $50 unused and $230 used & 1100, unused as National Banknote grilled example. An 1882 Regular Issue Garfield five cent yellow and brown stamp rates $4.50 used and $110 unused, rated fine. Same as above in National Bank Note Co. Grilled version: $250 used, $850 unused, rated fine.

Lincoln Oval Portrait from 1869–1890 General Issue. Ninety cent. Carmine and black. . . . . Used *$700* Unused *$1100*

Lincoln Portrait, 1892–1898. Four cent. Dark brown. Bust portrait, in oval. A single and a double line watermark variation exist, but are in same general price range. . . . . Used *$1.85* Unused *$3.00*

Other Civil War notables appearing in the 1892–98 Series are a five cent chocolate Grant ($2.50 & $4.00) Garfield six cent dull brown ($10 & $16) and eight cent Gen. Sherman, violet brown ($7 & $11).

Note: The challenge is to find any specimen in this series in fine unused blocks of four, where value escalates to $500 and up.

Lincoln from Picture Gallery Series 1902–1903. Five cent. Blue. Oval portrait of Lincoln flanked by deities. . . . . Used .*75* Unused *$1.10*

Lincoln Memorial Issue Profile Bust from 1903–1913 Series. Two cent. Issued in 1909 to commemorate 100th anniversary of Lincoln's birth. Carmine. Head of statue from Lincoln Memorial in Washington, D.C. . . . . Used *$1.50* Unused *$2.10*

Same as above, imperforates $10 and $17; Same as above on B.G. paper: $125 & 180.

Lincoln from 1908–1921. Three cent. Bust portrait; part of a series of 27 different bust portraits in 178 varieties, counting nuances in watermark, perforations, and printing.

Note: Civil War Generals Grant, 8 cent Olive Green $5 and $42. Garfield, 6 cent Red Orange $20 and $30. Hayes, 11 cent blue $1.10 and $2. McKinley, 7 cent black $6 and $8 also appear in the 1902–1921 General Issue.

Lincoln in 1938 Series. Sixteen cent. Black, bust profile image. One of 32 values with all but three honoring presidents. Interesting in that up through McKinley the denominations correspond to sequence as presidents. . . . . Used .*50* Unused .*60*

75th Anniversary of the 13th Amendment to the Constitution. 1943. Three cent. Deep violet. Lincoln "Emancipation" statue. Lincoln at podium with slave at his feet. . . . . Used .*16* Unused .*20*

China Issue. Of the People. By the People. For the People. Lincoln and Chiang Kai-shek. 1942. Five cent. Bright blue. Map of China in background, dates 1937–1942 inside sun symbol. . . . . Used *.30* Unused *.35*

Lincoln Torso Statue with Gettysburg Address Quote. 1948. Three cent. Cobalt and light blue. Large peace branch at bottom. . . . . Used *.16* Unused *.20*

Lincoln Bust Portrait. 1953–55. Four cent. Bust profile. Red, violet. Reissued through 1954–65 in rotary press coils. Used *.17* Unused *.25*

Lincoln Torso Portrait. 1958–59. One cent. Green, black, white. Beardless (1860) portrait. Facsimile signature at top. . . . . Used *.17* Unused *.25*

Lincoln Bust Portrait. 1958–59. Three cent. Rust brown. . . . Used *.17* Unused *.25*

Lincoln-Douglas Debates, 1858–1958 1958–59. Four cent. Sepia. Lincoln at platform with Steven Douglas in background. Huge crowd in foreground. . . . .
. . . . Used *.17* Unused *.25*

Lincoln Memorial Statue, Washington D.C. 1958–59. Four cents. Deep Blue. . .
. . . . Used *.17* Unused *.25*

Lincoln Bust Profile Portrait 1965–66. Four cents. Black . . Used *.17* Unused *.25*

(Lincoln) A Nation of Readers. 1984. Twenty cent. Brown and maroon. Famous Brady photograph of Lincoln and son Tad on lap reading book. . . . .
. . . . Used *.17* Unused *.60*

(Lincoln) National Archives, "What is Past is Prologue, 1934–1984. Twenty cent. Black, tan, white, and red; profile black silhouette of top-hatted Lincoln and silhouette of white Washington. . . . . Used *.17* Unused *.60*

Abraham Lincoln, Ameripex Series II. 1986. Twenty-two cent. Brown and black, with facsimile signature in red at top. Bust portrait. . . . . Used *.15* Unused *.50*

(Lincoln) World Stamp Expo '89. Twenty-five cent. Carmine and black with reproduction of 1869 issue; Lincoln bust on carmine, black, and white stamp. . . . .
. . . . Used *.15* Unused *.50*

Cover: "Flag Officers of the U.S. Navy," depicting Goldsborough, DuPont, and Foote in full-color cameos, published by Chas. Mangus, $35–$50.

Multicolor cover "Movement of the Army from Washington to Richmond," published by Chas. Mangus, $50–$75.

The cover "Secession" depicts a black slave woman with a small boy in flight, black on buff, $10–$15.

STAR OF THE NORTH, OR THE COMET OF 1861.

"Star of the North, or the Comet of 1861" shows Lincoln's head as a streaking comet. Colors are red, blue, and white, $75–$100.

Shoot the first Man that attempts to pull down the American Flag.

This patriotic cover exhorts, "Shoot the first Man that attempts to pull down the American Flag," browntone, red, and blue on buff envelope, $25–$35.

Lettersheet, "Presidents of our Great Republic," with oval cameos of presidents from Washington to Lincoln. Published by Chas. Mangus, black and white, $35–$50.

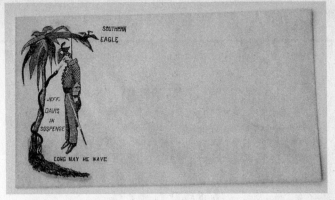

Cover, with drawing of Jefferson Davis hanging from a tree as a snake slithers up the trunk, ready to strike. With the words, "Southern Eagle," "Jeff. Davis in Suspense," and "Long may he wave." Multicolor, $50–$75.

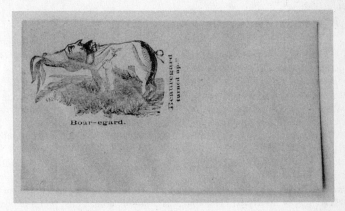

Satirical cover with the words, "Boar-egard" and "Beauregard turned up." Drawing is an illusion whereby the general is transformed into a boar when viewed horizontally. Black on buff: $50–$75.

STATUES, STATUETTES, PLAQUES, AND OTHER FIGURALS

PLAQUES

"Gov. John Andrew of Mass." 1867. Andrew was an ardent abolitionist. Organized the 6th Mass. State Militia, the first troops to reach Washington after Lincoln's summons for volunteers. Marked "RSSS 1867," 8½" h. *$100–125*

"Ambrose E. Burnside." 1862. Bronze relief bust mounted to circular bronze tray in walnut frame. Metal tag below bust reads "Miller Metallist, Providence, R.I." Bust measures 14" × 9". Possibly by Frank Simmons, a Maine artist commissioned by Miller to execute group of portraits of Gens. and members of Lincoln's cabinet. (A) Riba, June '87, $1300. . . . . *$1500–1700*

"Gen. Ben Butler." Gilt bas relief bust of Butler. By Ames Sword Co. Match for Blaine and Logan, 4" × 5½". *$100–125*

"James Garfield." Probably 1901. Memorial piece honoring Lincoln, Garfield, and McKinley as "Martyred Presidents." High relief bronze bust portraits of each against red leather background. *$125–150*

"James Garfield." Ca. 1881. Bas relief wall hanging. Brass, 29" × 23" rect. Ribbon at bottom reads "God Reigns and the Govt. of Washington Still Lives." Memorial piece. Stamped "Ploto Relievo Co., NY." (A) $165. . . . . *$175–200*

"Grant and Colfax." 1868. Framed metal (bronze) plaque with high relief profile busts, "In God We Trust/The Union Must and Shall be Preserved/The People's Choice For President and Vice-Pres." Upper corners—busts of Washington and Lincoln. By Morris Engr. Co., Patterson, NJ, 13" × 12" plus walnut frame. . . . . . .
. . . . *$1200–1400*

"Gen. Grant." Painted full-color bust portrait on zinc plaque; very ornate gilt and black scrollwork, top and bottom; 21" × 28"; depth of 3" at center. *$800–1000*

"Grant and Wilson." 1872. Norris Engr. & Pub. Co., Patterson, NJ. "Nominated at Phila. June 6, 1872" etched into steel engraved plate with dimensional bust oval bronze portraits of Grant and Wilson and two smaller cartouches of Washington and Lincoln above. Walnut frame. *$1600–1700*

"Gen. U.S. Grant." 1870s. 5" × 3" raised bust profile, right facing, in bronze against shield-shaped walnut plaque. Unsigned. *$200-225*

"U.S. Grant." 1860s. Heavy bronze 7" × 7½" plaque with bust in high relief. "Patriot & Soldier" above bust. Fits into design portion of Grant square 9½" clear large tray (REF: Hake, p. 3007) *$100–125*

(Grant) "Let Us Have Peace." Horseshoe-shaped with Grant high relief bust in center. Gilt cast iron. Slogan embossed. *$65–85*

"Robert E. Lee." Ca. 1870. Weller Pottery. Bas relief bust right-facing profile of Lee in uniform with three stars on lapel, 4½" dia. *$125–135*

"A. Lincoln." 1860s. Heavy domed high relief brass plaque of Lincoln and slave in chains with arms upraised against globe background; multicolor painted, 9" dia. *$350–400*

"A. Lincoln/1809–1865." 1907. Bronze waist-high profile desk plaque by Y.D. Brenner. Mounted on green marble. (A) Riba, Feb. '86, $400. . . . . *$450–500*

"A. Lincoln." 1865. Memorial bust bas relief. Shell brass in circular shadow frame. Original label on verso: "Wydman & Co., Cincinnati, Ohio, June 12, 1865." *$200–250*

"John Logan." Gilt relief bust of Logan. By Ames Sword Co. Match for Blaine and Butler. *$100–125*

"Gen. George B. McClellan." 1865. Walnut-framed brass bas relief plaque; pub. and for sale by J.H. Williams, NY. F.O. Darley pat. 1865; J.Q.A. Ward, sculptor. McClellan on horseback. Campaign related. (A) $380. . . . . *$400–450*

"Gen. George McClellan." 1864. Stand-up figural shelf plaque in brass of bareheaded McClellan on horseback in high relief. "F.O. Darley"; J.Q.A. Ward, sculptor; 10½" × 9½". *$100–125*

Statues

"Henry Ward Beecher." 1850s. By Robinson & Ledbetter; parian bust, 13" tall. Noted abolitionist. *$400–500*

"Gen. Ambrose Burnside." Ca. 1860s. Bronze relief bust mounted to circular bronze tray/walnut frame; U.S.; tag marked "W. Miller/Metalist/Prov. R.I."; 29" dia.; possibly work of Frank Simmons, a Maine artist commissioned by Miller to do Civil War heroes series. Some abrasion, restoration on frame. (A) $660. . *$650–750*

"Lewis Cass." 1860. Soft paste parian pedestal bust of Cass, a strong Unionist and Sec. of State under Buchanan. Resigned over Buchanan's failure to reinforce the Charleston forts in spite of threat of war. *$400–500*

"Henry Clay." 1850s. Soft paste parian pedestal bust of Clay. *$450–500*

"Gen. Custer." 1880s. Shoulder-up painted plaster statue with flesh tones and Union uniform. Name in relief at base. (A) Riba, June '88, $200. . . . . . . *$250–300*

"Gen. George Armstrong Custer." 1971. Bronze bust (one of 10); 11" h. Wears floppy Union hat with two stars. *$1000–2000*

"John Fremont." 1856. Soft paste parian bust pedestal image. Probably a campaign item. *$500–600*

"James Garfield." Ca. 1881. Attrib. to Ott & Brewer, Trenton, NJ. Parian porcelain, molded. Circular pedestal base. Base separately shaped and applied, 13" h. Possibly a memorial item. *$3500–5000*

"Gen. U.S. Grant." 1885 by Bernard Dreyfuss, NYC. Portrait bust on pedestal of

Gen. in uniform, "National Favorite," 17½" × 11½", dark orange paint. (Possibly an adv. trade figure.) (A) $220. .... *$200–250*

"U.S. Grant." Ca. 1868. Signed "Hadley, Sc." with the mark of Royal Worcester; parian bust 15½" h. (A) Riba, Oct. '86, $1000. .... *$1200–1400*

"Col. E. Burd Grubb." 1868. Unknown sculptor. Carved marble bust, 29" h., of Union officer Edw. Grubb. Grubb was later a Brig. Gen. who was a hero in battle of Harrisburg, MS; served as U.S. ambassador to Spain. *$4000–5000*

"Robert E. Lee." Ca. 1870. Unknown maker. Carved marble, 4½" h. Name incised on front of base. *$125–150*

"A. Lincoln." 1864. Stamped "William Miller & Co., Metallists, Providence, R.I." "Pat. applied for" above neck. Gilt, high relief bust profile mounted on oval copper tray with walnut frame. Miller was commissioned to do Lincoln and other Civil War heroes for series "National Bronze Picture Gallery." Only four examples are known. *$4000–5000*

"A. Lincoln." 1860s. Life-size plaster bust of beardless Lincoln in Roman toga. Inscribed on back "Lincoln From Life" by L.W. Volk. Metal plaque on base "Presented by the Hennecke Studios, Milwaukee, Wis." *$1500–1600*

"A. Lincoln/Constitutional Freedom." 1860. Hard-paste parian bust pedestal fig. of beardless Lincoln in buttoned coat and bow tie. *$800–900*

"Abraham Lincoln." 1908. Bronze bust pedestal image. By George E. Bissell, SC. Plaque at base reads "The Eleventh Congress to the Commandery of New York Military Order Loyal Legion, U.S., April 14–15, 1908." Dark patina. ....
.... *$12,000–14,000*

"Abraham Lincoln." 1861–65. Bronze bust pedestal image. Cast at Gorham Foundry by George Bissel, 16" h. (A) Riba/Mobley, Oct. '86, $8500. .... *$10,000–12,000*

"Abraham Lincoln" (Beardless). 1860. Bronzed plaster bust pedestal image. "Modeled from life by Leonard W. Volk, Chicago, 1860. © Alvas Studios." With marble base, 13" h., darkened patina. (A) Riba, Oct. '88, $650. .... *$700–800*

"Abraham Lincoln." 1909. Boston Sculpture Co., Melrose, MA. White plaster bust 32" h. × 23". Plaque on front of base reads "French Club 1923." (A) Riba, Nov. '87, $350. .... *$350–400*

"George McClellan." 1864. Bronze pedestal bust, 12½" h. on marble base. Stark FP Cat., Nov. '90, $1000. .... *$1000–1200*

"Negro Slave Boy." Ca. 1870s. Wood-carved fig. of black boy with chains around waist and arms extended, possibly to hold card tray; 14" h. with 4½" × 7" base. Black finish with traces of gilt on base. Two fingers broken. (A) Riba, Oct. '85, $250. .... *$300–400*

"Charles Sumner." 1860s. Robinson & Ledbetter, England. Nicely detailed parian bust of Sumner in toga. "Take care of my civil rights bill" marked on verso. (A) Riba '86, $500. .... *$600–700*

STATUETTES

"Army and Navy." 1880s. Two statuettes. Pair of pot metal Union figs. 13" h.; one "Army," one "Navy"; dark patina, very much like bronze. Fine except Navy fig.'s gun strap clip is chipped off. (A) $350. .... *$450–500*

"Henry Ward Beecher." 1887. Statuette John Rogers. Painted plaster, 24" h. Memorial tribute to famed abolitionist. *$450–500*

"Henry Ward Beecher." 1887. Statuette. Pedestal bust variant of preceding with

eagle and shield at base. Only known example is privately owned. . . . .
. . . . *Value Indeterminate*

"(The) Bushwhacker/The Wife's Appeal for Peace." 1865. Statuette grouping. 22¹/₂" h. John Rogers. Northern buyers gave grouping a cool reception because they thought he was humanizing the bushwacker (name given for Rebel guerilla) by showing him with young child, arms around neck, and hugging his wife. Withdrawn two years later. *$500–600*

"(The) Campfire/Making Friends with the Cook." 1862. Statuette grouping. 12" h. Painted plaster. Negro cook, standing next to large kettle, gives soldier a taste of soup. *$300–400*

"Camp Life/The Card Players." 1862. Statuette grouping. 12" h. Painted plaster. Two soldiers playing cards, using a drum as table. Several are known in parianware. . . . . *$300–400 (Plaster)*
. . . . *$700–800 (Parianware)*

"Challenging the Union Vote." 1869. Statuette grouping. John Rogers. Painted plaster, 22" h. Two men and woman, an old Unionist, and an ex-Rebel at desk checking the voting registry. Discontinued early. *$600–700*

"(The) Council of War." Ca. 1873. Statuette group. By John Rogers. Lincoln, Gen. Grant, and Sec. of War Stanton; Lincoln is seated and poring over maps. Several variations are known. *$300–400*

"(The) Fugitive's Story." 1869. Statuette grouping. John Rogers. 22" painted plaster. Abolitionists John G. Whittier, H.W. Beecher, William Lloyd Garrison listening to female slave holding sleeping baby. *$700–800*

"James Garfield." 1871. Statuette. Plaster bust memorial figure produced following his assasination; 12" h. *$50–75*

"Gen. U.S. Grant." 1885. Statuette. Bronze bust of Grant in uniform; © by K. Gearhardt, No. 87; 8¹/₂" × 7". Cast in Hartford, CT. *$500–600*

"U.S. Grant." Ca. 1876. Statuette. Glass, white opaque with frosted finish. A. Gillinder, Philadelphia; 5¹/₂" h. *$350–400*

"U.S. Grant." Statuette. Gillinder. Same as above, but in clear glass with frosted finish. *$300–350*

"U.S. Grant." Ca. 1870. Statuette. Hard paste (smooth finish) parian bust of Grant in uniform with name incised at base, 7" h. *$125–150*

"(The) Home Guard. Midnight at the Border." 1865. Statuette grouping. John Rogers. Painted plaster, 23" h. Two soldiers' wives wait apprehensively for news from the war front. *$250–300*

"A. Lincoln." Ca. 1863. Statuette. Standing figure of Lincoln wearing cloak, holding pen and "Emancipation" scroll. Metal (not white metal, but heavier); 22" h. . . *$250–300*

"Abraham Lincoln." Ca. 1876. Statuette. Designed by P.J. Jacobus for Gillinder & Sons, Philadelphia; acid finish milk glass with hollow base; 6¹/₄" h. (Other versions are solid and bear "U.S. Centennial" inscription.) *$450–500*

"Abraham Lincoln." Statuette. Same as above but in clear glass. *$375–400*

"Mail Day." 1863. Statuette. John Rogers, 16" h. Single fig. of homesick Union soldier reading letter from home. Described by art critic Charles De Kay of *N.Y. Times* as best of Rogers' Civil War entries. *$450–550*

"William McKinley." Statuette. Ca. 1896. Mfg. by Canton Glass Co.; white opaque glass; 5¹/₄" h. *$150–200*

"Gen. George B. McClellan." 1860s. Statuette. Bronze bust McClellan on bronze pedestal and black marble base, 12¹/₂" h. overall. Stark FP Cat., Nov. '90, $1000.. .
. . . . *$1000–1100*

"On Picket Duty." Ca. 1873. Statuette grouping. By John Rogers; plaster statuette of three soldiers on sentry duty................................... *$300–400*

"(The) Picket Guard." 1862. Statuette grouping. John Rogers, 12" h., painted plaster. Three soldiers, Pvt. on left has goatee. Soldier in center wears a Zouave officer's cap with veil and has mustache. A later variant (1865–66) has the two clean-shaven and the center fig. hatless. *$400–500*

"Returned Volunteer. How the Fort Was Taken." 1864. Statuette grouping. John Rogers. Painted plaster, 20" h. Soldier describes war story to blacksmith (working at anvil) as small girl listens (possibly the veteran's father and daughter). Several variants.. *$350–450*

"(The) Sharpshooter." 1862. Statuette grouping. John Rogers, 12" h., painted plaster. Two sharpshooters from Col. Hiram Berdan's famed 1st U.S. unit are skulking behind a wall and hoisting a stuffed dummy fig. in uniform to draw fire and pick off Rebels. Discontinued due to lack of popularity (considered too gruesome). Only three examples known. *$1200–1400*

"(The) Slave Auction." 1859–60. Statuette grouping. John Rogers. Painted plaster, 13½" h. Three figures; black slave family on the auction block. One of Rogers' earliest issues. *$700–800*

"Soldier and Sailor—U.S." 1860s. Statuettes. Individual matching pot metal figs. in pot metal, 8" h. (A) $390.................................... *$350–500*

"Charles Sumner." 1876. Statuette. Gillinder, Philadelphia. Bust fig. Glass, white opaque with frosted finish, 5¹⁄₂₃" h. Sumner, an ardent abolitionist, is depicted in Roman toga. *$200–250*

"Charles Sumner." 1876. Statuette. Gillander. Same as above but with clear glass and frosted finish................................... *$225–275*

"Taking the Oath and Drawing Rations." 1866. Statuette grouping. John Rogers, 23" h. Two figures. Found in parianware, creamware (of Staffordshire type), but copies and not of Rogers origin............................... *$450–550*

"The Town Pump." 1862. Statuette group. 13" h., plaster. Union soldier and young lady meet at the Town Pump. Several versions. One variant has the soldier carrying a canteen on his hip.................................. *$300–400*

"Uncle Ned's School." 1886. Statuette group. John Rogers group parlor statue, 20" h. painted plaster, buff finish. Three blacks. Uncle Ned is seated with one leg draped atop cabinet, helping young girl (standing) and young boy at his feet with school lessons. Commentary on Negro Freedman's determination to educate himself. (A) Riba, Oct. 85, $380.................................. *$400–500*

"Union Infantryman." 1886. Statuette. Plaster, 7½" h., by "C. Pizzano, Sc., Topsfield, Mass." Possibly a replication of a full-sized statue.............. *$75–100*

"Union Refugees." 1864. Statuette group. John Rogers, 22" h. in spelter (zinc/bronze) or painted plaster. Union infantryman has arm around wife and child. Two or three versions are known.................. *$400–500 (Painted Plaster)*
.... *$700–800 (Spelter)*

"(The) Vigilence Committee." 1861. Statuette. John Rogers, 12" h. Two Southern rednecks are preparing to lynch a black slave and have placed a noose around his neck. A tarpot is in background. This grouping was reportedly considered too incendiary and it may possibly have been withdrawn soon after it was patented. . . *$700–800*

"Votes for Women." Ca. 1870s. Statuette. Porcelain figural of black suffragette (believed to depict Sojourner Truth), 7½" h., full color. (A) $490....... *$500–650*

"(The) Wounded Scout/A Friend from the Swamp." 1864. Statuette. John Rogers, 23" h. Plaster grouping based on photograph by J.F. Aitken. Badly wounded Union soldier leans on black runaway slave for support. A copperhead snake at slave's feet is coiled to strike. (Lincoln was said to have highly praised this example.) *$500–600*

"Wounded to the Rear, One More Shot." 1865. Statuette. John Rogers, 23¹/₂" h. Two wounded soldiers—one seated, bandaging his leg wound; the other standing with arm in sling, a rifle resting against his chest. *$400–500*

MISCELLANEOUS

Mask. "A. Lincoln." 1865. Life mask of bronze painted plaster, attrib. to sculptor Clark Mills. Impression made only two months before assassination. . . . *$700–800*

Mask. "A. Lincoln." 1896. Life mask, bronzed plaster of beardless Lincoln by Leonard Volk. Inscribed "M.A. 1896." (A) $650. *$650–700*

Mask and Hands. "A. Lincoln." 1860. By Leonard W. Volk. Life mask and plaster casts of hands. Mask painted white. Minor chipping and paint loss on hand. (A) Riba, $450. . . . . *$500–600*

Trivet. "C.S.A., Richmond, Va." 1922. Confederate Vererans emcampment commemorative. Cast iron in spade shape with heart-shaped handle. *$125–150*

Trivet. U.S. Grant. Horseshoe-shaped with Grant high relief bust in center. Gilt cast iron. Slogan embossed. *$65–85*

Trivet. "Benjamin Harrison." Bust portrait inside horseshoe in cast iron with old paint, 5" × 4¹/₂". Cleveland match. *$35–50*

Windmill Weight. *Monitor* Ironclad." Ca. 1918. Baker Mfg. Co, Evansville, WI. Three dimensional, 78-lb. cast iron; concrete-filled counterbalance weight for windmill; 28¹/₃" warship has "M" cast in middle of port side. *$900–1000*

John Rogers statuette, "The Council of War," ca. 1873, depicting Lincoln, General Grant, and Secretary of War Stanton, $300–$400.

Left: *Life-size plaster bust of beardless Lincoln in roman toga, inscribed on the back "Lincoln from Life," by L.W. Volk, Alva Studios, ca. 1860s, $700–$800.* Right: *Bronze pedestal bust, ca. 1861–1865. Cast at Gorham Foundry by George Bissel, $10,000–$12,000.*

Left: *Bronze pedestal bust of George McClellan on marble base, ca. 1864, $1,000–$1,200. (Photo courtesy of Rex Stark)* Right: *A two-page insert from an 1866 John Rogers catalog featuring "Taking the Oath and Drawing Rations." The original Rogers statue was originally priced at $15 and is now valued at $400–$450.*

Left: *A John Rogers plaster pedestal bust of Lincoln, $500–$600.* Center: *John Rogers statuette titled "Wounded to the Rear, One More Shot," 1865, $400–$500.* Right: *Plaster statuette of a Union infantryman, 7 1/2" high, 1886 by "C. Pizzano, Sc., Topsfield, Mass," $75–$100.*

Left: *Plaque, "Robert E. Lee," ca. 1870, Weller Pottery. A bas-relief bust of Lee as a three-star general, $125–$135. (Photo courtesy of Rex Stark)* Right: *Plaster statue of General Custer, painted in flesh tones and wearing a Union uniform, ca. 1880s, $250–$300.*

Left: *Parian bust of U.S. Grant, signed "Hadley, Sc" mark of Royal Worcester, ca. 1868, $1,200–$1,400.* Right: *Parian bust of Charles Sumner in a toga by Robinson & Ledbetter, England, ca. 1860s, $600–$700.*

TEXTILES

BANDANNAS

C.S.A. "Our Heroes and Our Flags." 1862. B&w standing figures of Stonewall Jackson, P. Beauregard, Robert E. Lee. At corners surrounding figs. are four different official flags of the Confederacy, 18" × 18".................. *$2500–3000*

Jefferson Davis and His Generals. 1861–65. Pub. by E. Anthony, NY. Silk, 35" × 33". Davis medallion portrait in center with eight bust portraits of C.S.A. fanned out at corners and sides. Incl. Stonewall Jackson and R.E. Lee (both beardless), Beauregard, et al. Bordered by fern and cotton plant design. Black images on purple background (also found in blue). Collins 317................. *$1300–1500*

"G.A.R." Date unknown. Silk bandanna, 20" sq. G.A.R. symbol with eagle, flag, and star in center. Symbol encircled by 38 stars. Bordered with blue/white corps badges. Few minor spots....................................... *$75–100*

Gen. James A. Garfield–Gen. Chester A. Arthur. 1880. Jugate portraits with winged eagle above and below. Elaborately scrolled border. Brilliant red.........
.... *$200–250*

Gen. James A. Garfield–Gen. Chester A. Arthur. 1880. Jugate portraits with winged eagle above. Canal scene and shipping scene below. Paired U.S. flags in each corner. Red, white, blue, and black.......................... *$500–600*

Grand National Republican Banner. 1880. Oval jugate portraits of Garfield–Arthur enclosed in laurel border. Large winged eagle atop with legend in beak. "E Pluribus Unum" appears across shield, b&w, glazed cotton. Collins 498......... *$600–700*

Grant Campaign Bandanna. 1872. 14" × 16", chocolate brown and white on red background. Bust portrait in large scrolled circle. Crossed flags below; border of cannons and flags. Unlisted.................................... *$800–850*

U.S. Grant Lt. Gen/"I Propose to Fight it Out on This Line." 1868. 26" × 21¾" cotton. Bust portrait in circle; names of battles interwoven with leaves, branches; U.S. shields and eagle. Brown-tone portrait on white background against orange background. Collins 352...................................... *$900–1000*

U.S. Grant and George Washington "Philadelphia 1876 Centennial Exposition." Brown, orange, white, and sepia. Cameos of Washington and Grant. Vignettes of Main Building, Art Gallery, Agriculture Hall.............. *$200–225*

"Hancock–English." Match to previous Garfield–Arthur bandanna that showed canal and shipping scene below portraits........................ *$600–650*

Hancock–English Campaign Bandanna. 1880. Jugate portraits; "In Union is

Strength." Red, white, and black. Vignettes in each corner; shields top, bottom; 21" × 19"... *$300–350*

Hancock–English Campaign Bandanna. 1880. Bright red cotton; jugate oval portraits; floral border. No slogan. Pair of U.S. shields. Collins 483........ *$250–300*

"Our Next President/Maj. Gen. Winfield Scott Hancock." 1880. White on dark blue. Portrait from George Perrine engraving. Border of stars. Collins 481. Garfield match with slogan "The Peoples Choice." Collins 480. .... *$700–800*

"Andrew Johnson, President." 1864. Brown and white bust portrait in oval surrounded by flags, deities, cannons, and stacked pyramids of cannon balls. Vignette of Battle of Richmond under portrait. Oval portraits of Gens. Meade, Sherman, Sheridan, and Grant in each corner. Intertwining legend on border lists pivotal battles. Engraved by J.C. Buttre. Red background with brown, white motif. Collins 329... *$2000–2500*

"KN/1776." Ca. 1854. "Know Nothing" inscription with "1776" in beige, overprinted on brown, "KN" centered in large starburst. Surrounded by smaller stars with names of original 13 colonies. Eagle with flag in each corner; shields on borders. Red, beige, and brown; 28" × 32¼". Collins 242. .... *$450–500*

Know Nothing Party "Constitution and Law." 1856. Depicts workers and all types of citizens (one holding large furled U.S. flag), including George Washington—all looking up to Capitol building (labeled "Liberty," border of foliage, classical design). Cotton, black on white; 10½" × 12½". Stamped "Boston Chemical Printing Co." (REF: Collins, *Threads of History*, 254)................ *$450–500*

Lincoln Campaign Bandanna. 1864. Cotton. Bust portrait by Brady based on J.C. Buttre engraving. Eagle and shield borders; clasped hands encircled by stars in each corner. Red, white, blue, and brown. Collins 327; Hake AL 3026..... *$3500–4000*

"Abraham Lincoln. Late President of the United States." 1866. Silk bandanna, 32" × 30". Multicolor, including purple and yellow. Cartouches of a beardless Lincoln in center, plus eight of his Gens. fanned out and completely encircling his portrait; 12 additional bust portraits (three in each corner) surround spread wing eagles; four battle-scene vignettes. Minor discoloration. Unlisted in Collins. (A) Skinner, March '93, $1200. .... *$1200–1300*

Lincoln with Gens. Fremont, McClellan, Sigel, and Halleck. 21" × 19½". Lincoln in center with four other browntone portraits in exact size as CDVs. Bright blue background. Collins 326............................... *$6000–6500*

Lincoln and Washington. Conjoined bust portraits. Legend—"The Father of His Country/The Savior of His Country," with winged eagle above; sprig of laurel below; flag in each corner; Weger Lupsig engraving. Hake AL 3024; Collins 273.... .... *$2500–3000*

George McClellan. 1864. Center bust portrait of McClellan with laurel leaf surround. Slightly smaller cameos (same design) of 20 Union Gens. and Adms., incl. Grant, Burnside, Farragut, Pope, Foote, Buell, McDowell, DuPont, Hooker, etc. Vignettes of cannons, drums, swords, bugles, gauntlets, shield and flags below and in four corners. Red background with brown, white motif, 29" × 25½". Hake GM 3008; Collins 329. .... *$450–500*

Uncle Tom's Cabin. Ca. 1870. Brown and white linen 19½" × 16½". Over a dozen vignettes portraying scenes from Harriet Beecher Stowe classic... *$200–225*

BANNERS

Abolitionist Banner. Ca. 1850s. Poem—"I am an Abolitionist, I glory in the Name. By Slavery's Minions Hissed. . . ." 42" × 54" multicolor woven fabric and fringe border. Painted black lettering on heavy glazed muslin. Rev. inscription covers dedication of hall—"Virtue's Shrine." Minor staining. Stark FP Cat., Oct. '85, $1000.. *$1200–1400*

(Buchanan and Breckinridge) "Buck and Breck/Democracy and Slavery." 1856. Fringed cotton, 46" × 37" on wooden rod. Brown, black, blue, red. Classic cartoon banner depicting black slave in chains and overalls riding ram, with "Border Ruffians" legend running between ram's legs. Latter reference is to Southerners who crossed border into Kansas and voted illegally for slavery. Collins 244. .....
.... *$5000 plus*

(Freemont) "Hollis–Freemont Club/The Star of Freedom Has Risen. God Speed the Right!" 1856. Hollis, NH. 38" × 42" b&w on orig. wood poles with acorn finials... *$750–800*

"Hurrah for Garfield and Arthur." 1880. Handpainted rooster in green, brown, yellow and orange by noted carriage maker Edwin Burgun; 43¼" × 66¼" cotton. Collins 465. .... *$6000–7000*

(Garfield) "Our Choice–Garfield Arthur." 1880. Jugate silk banner, 26" × 36". Black, white with white stars reversed out of blue border. Swallow-tail shape.....
.... *$250–300*

G.A.R. "Welcome G.A.R." 1880s. Oilcloth banner in red, white, blue, and gold. Shows familiar eagle and star symbol, 28" × 48". *$75–100*

U.S. Grant (Untitled). 1868. Three-quarters view of Grant. B&w, 14" × 22" silk banner. Unlisted in Collins. *$275–300*

(Andrew Johnson) "Stand Firm. Our Union as It Was." 1865. Linen banner, 39½" × 49½" with handpainted bust portraits of George Washington and Andrew Johnson; branches, leaves in green; filligree in rust red and blue; tinted faces. Collins 337. .... *$7000–8000*

(K.K.K.) "Grand Dragon's Band, Klan No. 41, of Ohio." Possibly 1920. 30" × 40" silk banner with braided metallic border, fringed tassels. Ornate dragon in shield; red and black. Oak bar at top with brass rings; gilt brass eagle finial atop 8' parade standard. *$375–400*

(K.K.K.) "Muncie Junior Ku Klux Klan." 1920s. Satin and felt purple banner with yellow and blue cut-out letters. Large cross at center in double circle, 16" × 36" satin banner with gold metallic fringe and tassels. Mounted vertically on 4' standard. *$275–300*

(W.K.K.K.) "Non Silber Sed Anthar." 1920. Women's Ku Klux Klan of York, PA. Standing woman in white robe holding torch, shield with red insignia. Green, red, white, black; 29" × 54" satin swallow-tail vertical banner with silver fringe. Collins 1036. .... *$400–500*

Lincoln (Untitled). Ca. 1870. 36" × 48" cotton banner in black, white. Printed by Jos. Rhein, Detroit.. *$400–450*

(Lincoln) "Cambridge Ward 1. Republican Principles. The Nations Only Hope." 1860. Unusual two-sided 36" banner; red/white cotton on obverse black on brown oilcloth on reverse with legend "The Army & Navy are in the Hands of the Enemy—Our cause in the Hearts of the People." Reverse has some splits and small chips, minor water stain at right edge. Stark, Nov. '90, $500.......... *$500–600*

(Lincoln) "Disloyal Men Shall Not Govern Us! October Frosts Will Kill the Copperheads." 1860. Pro-Lincoln, anti-Southern Dems. Black lettering on natural cotton, 36" × 44". *$2800–3000*

(Lincoln) "Illinois, The Home of Lincoln and Grant." 1864. Swallow-tail horiz. banner with blue stripes enclosing legend in red. Collins 325. . . . . *$800–900*

(Lincoln) "Welcome G.A.R." 1870s. Encampment, 22" × 29". Black, white with red border. Bust of Lincoln. See Logan and McClellan matches below.. . *$350–400*

(Gen. Logan) "Welcome G.A.R." 1880s. 21" × 28" cotton banner in black white, orange; with bust portrait of Gen. Logan. *$275–300*

(Gen. McClellan) "Welcome G.A.R." 1870s. Black, white with red border. Bust profile. McClellan still had political ambitions at the time, running for Gov. of New Jersey. *$600–650*

(Gen. Philip) "Sheridan." 1880. Bust portrait and name in black on oilcloth, swallow-tail banner; blue border with white star reverse; similar to Blaine, Logan, and Garfield examples. Sheridan was a Rep. hopeful in 1880. Collins, p. 223. . . . . *$150–200*

Gen. William T. Sherman. 1884. Bust portrait of favorite son candidate at 1884 Rep. convention. Sherman is decked out in uniform with large sash across shoulder. Star border of white reversed out of blue. Blue, white, black swallow-tail bottom, 23¼" × 34". Set of matching portrait banners are said to exist for Lincoln, Garfield, Grant, Sheridan, Hancock, Lee, and Davis. Collins 508. . . . . *$2500–3000*

FLAG BANNERS

For President John Bell/For Vice-President Edward Everett. 1860. Portrait of Bell surrounded by oval ring of stars, running horiz. in blue field. Legend over stripes. Collins 304. . . . . *$4000–5000*

    Lincoln match to above. Collins 305. . . . . *$6000–7000*

Clay–Frelinghuysen and Markle Protective Tarriff. Political flag. 1844. Red, white, blue cotton banner with bust portrait of Clay, one of the first and most outspoken abolitionists. *$2000–2500*

"Don't Tread on Me." 1864. Red coiled copperhead snake. Red, mustard, yellow, and black; 24" × 18". Copperheads were group of Northern Dems. who opposed Union's war policy and favored a negotiated peace. Collins 324. . . . . . . *$5000–6000*

For President, Stephen A. Douglas/Vice-President, Herschel, V. Johnson. 1860. Bust portrait of Douglas with stars forming shield outline in blue field. Names overprinted in blue on stripes; 13" × 8", red, white, blue, and black. Hake 3004; Collins 306. . . . . *$5000–6000*

John Fremont. 1856. Bust b&w portrait of Fremont superimposed on upper right corner. Large single white star in blue field. Unlisted. *$1700–1800*

Garfield and Arthur. 1880. Rep. slate legend appears between stripes; 39 stars in blue field. Red, white, blue on cotton muslin. *$700–800*

For President, U.S. Grant/for Vice-President, Schuyler Colfax. 1872. Polished cotton with 36 stars (32 in circle and one at each corner in blue field). Words overprinted on stars and stripes. Unlisted in Collins *Threads of History*. (A) March '94, $6000. . . . . *$6000–7000*

Grant. 1872. Smaller oval bust portrait of Grant than in "Grant–Colfax" following. No legend. Hake UG 3003. . . . . *$3000–3500*

Grant. 1868. Red, white, blue with black oval bust of Grant as Lt. Gen. in center of

37 stars. Field of stars on right vs. usual left.; 17" × 27". (A) Tom French Mail, Nov. 1990, $5000. . . . . *$5000–5200*

Grant–Colfax. 1872. Polished cotton with 36 stars (32 in circle and one at each corner in blue field). Small oval bust portrait of Grant. Hake UG 3004; Collins 345. . . . . *$3500–4000*

Hancock and English. 1880. Legend naming Dem. slate appears within stripes. Field of 38 stars. Red, white, blue. Cotton muslin. *$600–700*

For President, Lincoln/Vice-President, Hannibal Hamlin. 1860. Rep. political. Lincoln's beardless bust portrait with 11 stars in random pattern out of blue field; "Wide Awake" appears above head. Candidates' names overprinted on red and white stripes; 17¼" × 11". Light age stain. Collins 300; Hake LI 3102. (A) Winters, March '84, $7500. . . . . *$8000–9000*

For President, Lincoln/Vice-President, Hannibal Hamlin. 1860. Rep. political. Lincoln's beardless upper third portrait encircled by 30 stars; four larger stars in each corner of blue field; 18" × 11¼". Hake AL3013; Collins 303. . . . . . *$10,000–11,000*

Lincoln and Hamlin. 1860. Blue on white legend with rail fence design above. Parade banner size (52¼" × 35"). Collins 312. . . . . *$4000–5000*

Note: At least three other variations of the beardless banner are known from the 1860 race. See Collins 299, 301, 302. Each would readily command a comparable price to above specimens.

For President, Lincoln/Vice-President, Andrew Johnson. 1864. One large star surrounded by 32 smaller stars in blue field. Candidates' names overprinted on red and white stripes. Hake AL 3014; Collins 331. . . . . *$4500–5500*

Lincoln and Johnson. 1864. Thirty-five stars in blue field. Candidates' names overprinted in huge letters; 8¼" × 6". Hake AL 3015; Collins 333. . . *$4000–5000*

Lincoln and Johnson. 1864. Stars in blue field spell out "FREE." Candidate's names undulate (as opposed to being in straight line) across red, white, and blue stripes; 17" × 12". Collins 334. . . . . *$5000–6000*

"Abraham Lincoln, 1809–1865, Noble Son, Patriot Heart, the Union Forever." 1865. Memorial flag. Watercolor on old paper; handmade; stars in star shape on blue field. Large lettering on stripes; 7⅞" × 9⅞". Minor age browning. (A) Riba, March '94, $380. . . . . *$400–500*

McClellan and Pendleton. 1864. Stars in double circles in blue field. Black overprint of legend on red and white stripes. Hake GM3004. . . . . *$2500–3000*

Horatio Seymour. 1868. 13" × 8" cotton. Red, white, blue, black, green. In overstamp of facsimile of $5 currency, in black and green, legend relates to people demanding equal payment of bonds in greenbacks and equal taxation. Seymour's portrait appears in lower right corner of currency. Statue of Freedom at left. Collins 343. . . . . *$2000–3000*

FLAGS

Army of Northern Va. Battle Flag. Ca. 1861. Removed from Georgia State House and no longer can be flown at the Citadel. (A) Conestoga, Manheim, PA, July '94, $73,700. . . . . *Value Indeterminate*

Note: Bought by historic commission currently developing museum site in Dinwiddie, VA.

Arkansas State Flag. 1860. Used in Rep. Natl. Convention by Arkansas delegation; 19½" × 17" in period frame. Some wear on lettering; a tiny rust spot. (A) Harmer Rooke (Absentee), Oct. '94, $900. . . . . *$900–1000*

C.S.A. "Stainless Banner" or "Whiteman's Flag." Ca. 1863. Handstitched silk, 27" × 42"; with oversized canton, 18" × 28". A hoist of glazed cotton. Stark FP Cat. '90, $2800. . . . . *$2500–2600*

C.S.A. "Battle Flag." From the estate of Joseph H. Hurxthal. Reputed to have been flown at Appomatox Courthouse at the peace signing; 15 stars in a circle, in blue field, with three wide stripes, red and white. All handsewn. Bad stains. (A) Riba, Feb.'87, $1000. . . . . *$1500–2000*

C.S.A. Cavalry Guidon. Handstitched homespun wool swallow-tail end. White stripe top; red below. Eleven stars on light blue field. Unusual four-point stars; 10" × 26". *$2000–2200*

C.S.A. First National Pattern Flag. Woolen with 11 applied stars. Period identification sewn to bottom of red stripes: "Captured from a Confederate battery near Acquia Creek by the Navy in a night assault—Moore." Three ties on hoist. Bright, vibrant colors. (A) Conestoga, July '94, $20,000. . . . . *$20,000–22,000*

C.S.A. Veteran's Flag. Ca. 1860s. In design of fourth issue of C.V.A. flag, March–April 1865. "U.C.V./A.N.V." (Army of Northern Va.) overprinted in black. White background; red, white, blue canton; red vertical strip at end; 18" × 35" printed muslin. Light staining on white field. *$500–600*

(C.S.A. Veteran's Flag) "Old Banner of Seccession 1865–1861." Ca. 1865. Red homespun wool; white border with nine handsewn white stars. *$1100–1200*

Confederate "Bible Flag." Thirteen stars and three stripes. Silk stars, handsewn (usually by children and used to be kept in a bible or carried by a soldier). . *$500–600*

Brig. Gen. George Armstrong Custer's Cavalry Battle Flag. Ca. 1862. Described by Dr. Lawrence Frost, a neighbor of the Custers, who had this entry in his collection, "as a swallowtail guiden of homespun wool with crossed sabers in white, mounted on a field of white and faded red." Battlegrounds "Boonsboro. Falling Water" are stitched at left. Believed to be Custer's very first battle flag. It was presented to Dr. Frost by Col. Brice C.W. Custer and Col. Charles Custer in 1955. (A) Riba, July '93, $4000. . . . . *$4500–5000*

G.A.R. Encampment Flag. Chicago, Aug. 1900. 16" × 24" silk flag with corps badges surrounding border. Red, white, and blue. *$175–200*

(K.K.K.) "By This Sign Conquer." 1920s. 18" × 11¼" cotton flag with large red cross in field of white plus legend in blue painted on fabric. *$100–125*

(K.K.K.) Headquarters Regiment Ohio Cavaliers. 1920s. Multicolored silk, 52" × 67"; royal blue background. Yellow fringe. Embroidered design of hooded rider and horse holding aloft a burning cross. Two-sided. *$500–550*

(Lincoln) "In electing me to the Presidency of the U.S. . . ." ". . .the people have mainly looked forward to good govt. and a just administration of the law. . . ." 1861. Quote from Lincoln speech overprinted on four rows of stripes; 8" × 12" silk flag; red, white, blue. *$1000–1100*

Lincoln Funeral Flags (2). Union jack with gold fringe; 36 stars. Used from Oct. 31, 1864–March 1, 1867. Framed. (A) Harmer Rooke (Absentee), Oct. '94, $1200. . . . . *$1200–1300*

108th N.Y.S.V. (New York Volunteers). Ca. 1863. Silk-fringed (on three sides) flag with ornate lettering enclosed in painted furled oval. Moderate soiling, plus a few tears. Framed. (A) Riba, March '94, $1000. . . . . *$1200–1500*

34-Star Union Flag. 1860s. Handstitched wool. Bright colors. Huge, 6' × 12'. A few small holes and wear spots. Stark FP Cat., Nov. '90, $650. . . . . *$600–650*

36-Star Flag (for Admission of Nevada). Oct. 1864. Small, 8½" × 11". Slight wear. Original flag stick. Stark FP Cat., $250. . . . . *$200–250*

36-Star Convention Flag. 1864 or 1868. Arkansas overprint in black over one of lower white stripes; 11" × 17". On original stick.....................*$200–225*

Union Flag. Handsewn with 34 stars; the names "Kellog" and "Buckmaster" are inked in on border; 4½' × 7'. Fine Civil War–period example. (A) Riba, Oct. 85, $350..*$450–500*

United Confederate Veteran's Flag. 1865. In design of fourth-issue C.S.A.; overprinted in black UCV-ANV (Army of Northern Virginia). Red, white, blue canton; white background, red vertical strip at end; 18" × 35" printed muslin. ....
....*$550–600*

Valley Post No. 156 (Nebraska) G.A.R. 1889. Wool flag by group founded by Civil War vets who moved from Indiana to Nebraska. Oversize lettering overprinted in black over stripes; 42 stars. *$500–600*

Vermont Militia Regt. No. 27 Flag. 44" × 60", all silk, royal blue with 26 white stars. Multicolored painted eagle against white circle background in center. (A) $3000..*$2500–3000*

Vermont Regt. No. 26. 1850s. Center has eagle with shield, arrows, and olive branch. Eagle holds legend "E. Pluribus Unum" and head is turned toward arrows (war position). Encircled by 26 stars. Silk. Rather tattered. (A) Riba, March '89, $550..*$600–650*

Virginia State Flag (Fragment). Oil on canvas. Framed 50" × 50". Flag is raised slightly in spots from mounting. (A) Conestoga, $2900.............*$3000–4000*

NEEDLEWORK

"Annexation of Texas." 3" swath of needlework of black slave with arm in chains begging for freedom. *$250–300*

(Anti-Slavery) "Happy Are We in the Land of Liberty." 1870s. Needlework silk-backed bookmark. Depicts ex-slaves dancing in red, white, and blue........
....*$175–200*

"Anything But a Slave Holder." 1850s. Needlework potholder. A man and woman black slave dancers, 6", multicolor. Found in Columbia, PA, a point on the underground railroad...*$400–450*

Booth, Lincoln, and Johnson. Wool yarn needlework; red, gray, brown, blue. 1868. Done in Washington insane asylum (obviously by inmate). Long inscription pleads for Pres. Johnson to pray, make known the secret of Lincoln's death, and inspire people with the love of John W. Booth. "Jesus pity the people and inspire Dr. C. Nichols, Dr. W. Godding and Mr. Johnson . . . to help in his desires." .....
....*$1500–1700*

Henry Clay. Ca. 1844. After noted painting by John Neagle. Clay standing portrait with anvil, plow, cattle, ship in background. Furled flag in right foreground; 30" × 33", multicolor. Collins 158. ....*$2500–2750*

Henry Clay, "That Same Old Coon." 1850s. Embroidery showing raccoon holding flag with Clay's initials. Slogan appears above and below animal. Multicolor on white background; 2" × 3¼"..*$325–350*

U.S. Grant, "Let Us Have Peace." 1885. Framed high relief sculpted. Silk background. "Grant" stitched on funeral bier, angel, North and South shaking hands over body, ancient gods mourning. Brilliant colors. Collins 561......*$1100–1200*

"Women of Ku Klux Klan." Embroidered pillow case, 16", white with red stitching. *$75–100*

PENNANTS

Grant and Wilson. 1872. Red, white, blue glazed cotton swallow-tail horiz. pennant. Border of 38 white stars out of blue rev. Made by American Flag Co., NY. . .
. . . . *$400–450*

"K.K.K." Date unknown. Felt pennant; 24", black yellow with large monogram of Ku Klux Klan. *$50–60*

"K.K.K." Date unknown. Felt pennant; 24". Large burning cross in white shield background. Pink, white; letters 3" h. *$60–75*

"K.K.K." (One monogram in each corner.) "We are Here Today, Tomorrow and Forever." 1920s. 10" × 23" cotton felt. White reversed out of black hooded Klansman, holding fiery cross, on rearing white steed. Red border at left. Collins 1031. .
. . . . *$85–95*

RIBBONS

Political

John Bell. 1860. Pair of oval bust front-facing black transfer on white images of Bell in slightly different poses. Hake 3001. . . . . *$2000–2500*

John Bell. 1860. Upper ½ black transfer figure of Bell. Facsimile signature below. Hake 3002. . . . . *$1000–1500*

"John C. Breckinridge." 1860. Brady torso portrait in b&w with facsimile sig, 7" × 2½". *$600–700*

John C. Breckinridge. 1860. Upper ½ black transfer figure of Breckinridge. Match to Bell above. Hake JCB 3003. . . . . *$1000–1200*

"Breckinridge & Lane." 1860. Brady torso portrait in black transfer with facsimile sig. Hake JCB 3002. . . . . *$1500–2000*

Buchanan and Breckinridge. "Democratic Mass Meeting, Providence, Sept. 3, 1856./We keep Step to the Music of the Union." Small figures of two candidates stand atop Dem. platform, embracing U.S. flag; sunburst of stars with legend "The Union/It Must Be Preserved." Eagle with shield. Hake JHB 3015; Warner 62. . . . . . . *$550–600*

(Clay) Lynn Ward IV. "The Locos Go For Polk, Texas & Slavery. We go for Clay, Union & Liberty." 1844. Bust portrait of Clay. Slogan clearly draws line between pro-slavery Locos and abolitionist Clay. HC 11. . . . . *$300–350*

"The Right Man in the Right Place/Jeff. Davis/Our First President." 1861. Red, white, and blue ribbon resembles miniature flag of Confederacy. Mounted within, a silk rosette holds sepia paper bust photograph of Davis. *$600–650*

(Stephen A. Douglas) "Douglas & Johnson/The Union Now and Forever." 1860. Black bust photo on white ribbon. Hake SD 3005. . . . . *$1500–2000*

"Douglas Committee." 1860. Black transfer bust portrait of Douglas on pale blue.
. . . . *$500–525*

(Stephen A. Douglas) "Our Union Now and Forever." 1860. U.S. flag running vertically, red, white, blue. Hake SD 3006. . . . . *$200–250*

(Stephen A. Douglas) "Popular Sovereignty/Progress." 1860. "Douglas & Johnson, Janesville (Wisconsin) National Dem. Club." B&w. Two men at top with flags. *$300–350*

(Stephen A. Douglas) Upper-Third Figure of Douglas, Front Facing. 1860. Black transfer image. No legend. Hake SD 3007. . . . . *$1000–1100*

(Stephen A. Douglas) Upper-Third Figure of Douglas, Slight Left Facing. 1860. Black transfer image; facsimile signature. Hake SD 3008. . . . . *$1000–1100*

Freemont and Dayton, "Free Soil, Free Men, Free Speech, and Free Kansas." 1856. Black on pale blue. Bust portrait of Fremont at top. "Galva" appears in large type at bottom. *$200–250*

Freemont and Dayton, "Free Soil, Free Men, Free Speech, and Free Press." 1856. Fremont (labeled "The Pathfinder") on horseback doffing his hat. Black transfer on white, pink, or blue. Note pink is lightly more scarce than the two other color variations. Hake JF 3006. . . . . *$150–200*

"Freemont and Dayton." 1856. A.k.a. "Black Republican" ribbon. Running fugitive slave with knapsack past windswept tree; skull and crossbones above names. Black transfer on white. Classic anti-Freemont; implied that Reps. might inspire slave insurrections. Black on yellow. Warner 66. . . . . *$2000–3000*

"Freemont and Dayton" 1856. Laurel-encircled portraits of Rep. candidates (one of the few images of Dayton) in black transfer on white. Facsimile sigs. Hake 3008. . . . . *$950–1000*

(Freemont) "John and Jessie." 1856. 2" × 6"; Freemont with wife pictured—the first political ribbon to feature a spouse. Black transfer on pale green. . . . *$800–825*

For President/Gen. J.A. Garfield. 1880. Sepia bust photo tipped on silver and blue ribbon.. . . . . *$150–175*

"Garfield–Arthur." 1880. Large oval portraits of both candidates in filigree border, b&w, 2³/₄" × 9". *$450–500*

"Garfield–Arthur." 1880. Large oval paper portraits of both candidates in silver border; large shield topped by eagle. Red, white, blue, woven silk, burgundy background. . . . .

"Garfield Cadets." 1880. Black on white jugate portraits in patriotic shield motif. "Our Dads Vote Right & We Will By and By." *$250–300*

(Garfield) "Cayahuga County Colored Delegation Solid for Garfield and Arthur." 1880. Red, white, and blue ribbon with swallowtail; shield of U.S. at top. *$350–400*

(Garfield) 329/"Busted by Gar—"Field. Chinese coulee with one finger upraised, pointing at "329." During the campaign Garfield was embroiled in notorious Credit Mobilier scandal. Allegedly, $329 was the proceeds from stock he received illegally from a colleague, Oakes Ames. The number appears frequently in anti-Garfield pieces. The coulee cartoon is based on Dem. allegations that Garfield intended to flood the country with cheap Chinese labor. *$750–800*

(Garfield) "Tell It to the Boys Again! Why Don't You Head (sic) Us Somebody?" 1880. Another anti-Garfield ribbon. Runs horiz. in b&w with cartoon of Garfield and English aboard riverboat with the numbers "329" on a low bridge, which appears to be knocking Garfield and English into the drink. Upriver along the bank, black man drives a team of mules labeled "lies, theft," etc.. . . . . *$800–900*

Garfield Veteran's Corps., Allegheny Co., Pa. 1880. Albumen sepia bust portrait tipped on to gold blue ribbon. *$100–125*

(Garfield) "Where Are Ye, Morey-arity." 1880. Large body with "Smiling All Over" on shirt front. With multi heads, obviously representing voters, all with wide grins.. . . . . *$800–900*

Grant–California, "We'll Fight it Out on This Line." 1866. Yellow black, all type. *$125–150*

Grant–Colfax. 1878. Reddish brown background. Red, white, blue, and black. Conjoined bust images with eagle above. Also available in blue background. . . . . . .
. . . . *$800–850*

Grant–Colfax. 1878. "We Vote to Sustain the Union." Oval jugate portraits. Few water marks. (A) $700. . . . . *$700–800*

Lt. Gen. Grant Inaugural. 1869. "Richmond." Woven by T. Stevens; Grant oval portrait enclosed by laurel fronds. Eagle and shield; pair of flags at bottom; multicolor; 10" × 2¼". *$200–250*

Harrison–Morton. 1888. Red, white, and blue. Jugate portraits in black; 3" × 5" mini-flag. *$200–225*

For President Abraham Lincoln—For Vice-President Andrew Johnson. 1864. Bust of beardless Lincoln, portrait in black on pink. *$1900–2000*

(Lincoln) "He Set the Millions Free." 1865. Rated about the finest memorial ribbon. Gilt bust and lettering on nine lines, 9½". *$200–250*

(Lincoln) "Honest Old Abe" for President/For Vice-President Hannibal Hamlin. The People's Candidate. One Strength Increasing Daily!" 1860. Beardless Lincoln bust portrait. Elephant carrying banner at bottom, may be this symbol's first appearance on a Rep. political item. *$950–1000*

"A. Lincoln." 1860. Mathew Brady Cooper Union beardless pose of Lincoln; black transfer on white. One of Brady's set of four images from 1860 race. Douglas, Bell, and Breckinridge matches; 7" × 2⅝". *$2000–2200*

"Lincoln, Hamlin and Curtin." 1860. Pennsylvania coat-tail for Andrew Curtin with anti-expansion of slavery quote above by Henry Clay. Bust portrait of beardless Lincoln. Curtin made the nominating speech for Lincoln at the Rep. Natl. convention. *$500–550*

"Lincoln and Hamlin/Union and Victory." 1860. Beardless bust image, b&w, 7" × 2". *$900–1000*

(Lincoln/Hartranft) Central Hartranft Campaign Club (Pennsylvania Gubernatorial). 1872. Lincoln Association. Red, white, blue, and black. Oval bust portraits of Lincoln and Hartranft. Ex-Union Gen. John Hartranft was Provost Marshall at Lincoln conspiracy trial. Rep. Gov. from 1872–78. . . . . *$600–700*

Lincoln Inaugural Ribbon. 1861. Ornate multicolor, large wide ribbon woven in Basle, Switzerland. Torso portrait of beardless Lincoln surrounded by brightly hued garlands; eagle and shield above. *$600–650*

Lincoln Inaugural Ribbon. 1865. Small portrait inside shield, eagle motif in center. "Kansas Union Club," gold on aqua. *$350–400*

Lincoln–Johnson Peace Commissioners. 1864. Black on deep pink. Also depicts peace commissioners incl. Adm. Farragut. *$950–1000*

"The Late Lamented President Lincoln." Memorial ribbon by T. Stevens; multicolor. Bust oval portrait with border of stars. Eagle with banner at top; pair of U.S. flags, bottom. *$200–225*

Abraham Lincoln/The Martyr President. 1865. B&w oval portrait, U.S. flag on top half of globe, 5" × 2". *$350–400*

Lincoln Memorial Ribbon, "With Charity to All." **1776–1865.** Dated 1866. Also Swiss-made (see above) and extra large (5" × 10"). Lincoln bust in large bordered oval, eagle above, with weeping Columbia below, her face buried in U.S. flag. Red, white, and blue shield; green branches and leaves. Perhaps the pick of Lincoln memorial ribbons. *$300–325*

(Lincoln/Hamlin) "Republican Candidates." 1860. Conjoined oval portraits. "The People's Choice." Black transfer on white. Hake 3029. . . . . *$3500–4000*

Abraham Lincoln/The "Rail Splitter" of 1830/For President of U.S./1861. Inaugural ribbon. Black on white bust portrait. A variant of above shows a bust portrait from a Samuel Fassett photograph........................... *$800–900*

(Lincoln) "Republican Candidates/For President Abe Lincoln of Illinois/For Vice-Pres. H. Hamlin of Maine. 1860. Large all-seeing eye symbol of Wide Awakes, crossed campaign torches, and oval bust portrait flanked by two small caped figures in Wide Awake parade garb. Sketch appeared in Osborn Oldroyd's *The Political Revolution of 1860s.* Of such rarity it's rated: .. *Value Indeterminate*

(Lincoln) "Republican Wide Awakes/For President/Abe Lincoln of Illinois." 1860. Torso beardless image in black on white ribbon, 8" × 1⅛"..... *$1700–1900*

"Seneca (New York) Wide Awakes/Lincoln and Hamlin!" Rebus type. With large "all-seeing eye." *$800–900*

(Lincoln) "Shawnee Wide Awakes/Lincoln and Hamlin." 1860. Probably from Kansas. Silk with fancy woven floral design. *$900–1000*

Lincoln Shield-Shaped Ribbon. 1862. Bust portrait of Lincoln with olive sprays surround; large bow atop. Multicolored, no text................... *$1800–2000*

(Lincoln) Union Forever. 1864. Lists slate of Lincoln–Johnson with U.S. Grant, William T. Sherman, and Philip H. Sheridan as Peace Commissioners. Bust portrait in rect. border of beardless Lincoln. Browntone on buff. *$5000–5500*

(Lincoln) "The Union Must and Shall be Preserved." 1860. Bust portrait of beardless Lincoln. Lists Lincoln and Hamlin as Rep. slate. "Free Soil, Free Homesteads and Free Territories" appears above smoking cannon and Union flag. "Protection to American Industry."............................... *$1500–1750*

McClellan and Pendleton. 1864. Black transfer bust image of McClellan in uniform, in oval between candidates' names. Hake GM 3010. .... *$2500–3000*

McClellan and Pendleton. 1864. Large all-capital letters of candidates' names running sideways in black over white. Hake GM 3011. .... *$400–450*

McClellan Old Guard. 1864. Paper ribbon, 3½" × 11", black on white... *$600–625*

Horatio Semour, Candidate for the Presidency. Gen. Frank P. Blair. 1868. Jugate portraits. T. Stevens Coventry woven ribbon; black, blue, purple and white.. *$375–400*

Semour and Blair—5th Ward. White Boys in Blue/Captain. 1868. Red, blue with black transfer bust portrait in oval wreath border................ *$850–900*

"The Union Constitution and the Flag/Must & Shall be Upheld." 1861. Large cannon with waving U.S. flag; stacked cannonballs.................. *$500–600*

"Union is Prosperity." 1861–63. Vignette of Miss Columbia holding a waving national flag... *$500–600*

(Union) "The Constitution/For the Union/We Pledge Our All." Vignette of waving flag; sprinkling of stars; sheaf of paper representing Constitution; clasped hands above: "1776," below: "1861." *$450–500*

(Martin Van Buren) "Free Soil/Free Men/Our Country Forever/No More Extension of Slavery." 1846. U.S. flag with oval portrait of Van Buren. Black on light blue. Warner 28...................................... *$1500–2000*

"Gen. James B. Weaver/Anti-Monopoly/No North, No South. 1892. People's Party candidate. Ex-Union Gen................................. *$600–650*

Veterans, Patriots, Klan Reunions, and Encampments

Alabama Div. United Confederate Veterans. 1895. Red, white, black, and gold fringe; 3" × 7½" *$65–75*

Camp Magruder, Texas. United Confederate Veterans, Galveston, TX. Red, white, blue, and black. Furled C.S.A. flag. *$50–65*

Camp Winchester, Va. Undated. Seal of Virginia; gilt tassles. Gold on purple. Encampment or Reunion. *$75–85*

Cumberland Assoc. Navy Vets., New Bedford, Mass. 1892. Baltimore and Washington Encampment. Gold, red. *$15–20*

Fifth Reunion 29th Anniversary 15th N.Y. Vols. Cavalry. Aug. 10 & 11, 1892. Legend appears in continuous scroll down to large "15" overprinted by crossed sabers and epaulets. Black on rust. *$45–55*

G.A.R. Maj. Howe Post 47, Haverhil, Mass. Undated. Red ribbon with gilt emblem of a shoe. On girl brass clasp marked "G.A.R." *$15–20*

"G.A.R. Root Post #151, Syracuse, NY. Ribbon commemorates Lt. Col. Augustus Root, a Union soldier killed by C.S.A. fire the day before Lee surrendered. The Syracuse post was named for him. Red, white, and blue with gild lettering, eagle, and G.A.R. symbol. *$35–45*

"G.A.R. National Encampment, Dept. of New Hampshire." 1923. Dedication of statue. Large image of statue of Union soldier, standing, on pedestal. Black, original. *$25–30*

Grant G.A.R. Post No. 327, Dept. of New York. 1892. Washington, D.C., Reunion. Multicolored woven silk with seated view of Gen. Grant; facsimile signature; large ornate GAR lettering. *$150–175*

Grant Ohio Volunteers 120th Regt. 27th Annual Reunion. 1895. Blue, gold silk, 7". Grant image on canteen, inscribed "Unconditional Surrender." *$85–100*

Hampshire Camp No. 445, Romney, W. Va. U.C.V. Reunion; C.S.A. flag in circle. Double-sided, white celluloid clasp depicting clasped hands. *$75–85*

Joint Assembly of Union and Confederate Fifth Va. Regiment. 1883. Black on cream, 3" × 9½". *$65–75*

Kearsarge **Assoc. Naval Vets.** 1893. Boston. Reunion; blue, white. *$20–25*

Kearsarge **Assoc. Naval Vets/1861 to 1865.** Boston. Blue, white. Brass clasp, "K.A.N.V." The *Kearsarge* was the Union dreadnaught that sank the C.S.A. *Alabama* in June 1864. . . . . *$20–25*

Ku Klux Klan Reunion, Scottsdale, Pa., Sept. 1924. 1¼" celluloid pinback of mounted Klansman with burning cross; slogan "Chirping for Scottsdale . . . find duplicate and get prize." Small celluloid cricket attached. "Scottsdale, Pa." on red, white, blue ribbon. *$100–125*

New Bedford G.A.R. 26th Encampment, Washington, D.C. 1892. Blue, white. Illus. of large war frigate in full sail. *$20–25*

"New Hampshire Prisoners of War Assn." Survivors of Andersonville, Libby, Salisbury, Belle Isle. Undated. Black on white. *$80–90*

23rd Ohio Vol. Infantry. "Antietam" Battle Reunion. 1878. Willoughby, OH. Red, white, and blue. *$15–20*

Reunion of Hagoods Brigade, South Carolina. 1898. Red, white, blue, and black. Confederate flag at top; portrait of Brig. Gen. Johnson Hagood who led his brigade at Wilderness and Weldon Railroad; later served as Gov. of So. Carolina. Ornate brass hanger. *$85–100*

(Rhode Island) 39th Reunion of R.I. 1st Cavalry, Fields Point, Rhode Island. 1908. Gold on pale yellow. *$10–15*

Gen. Sheridan "Camp Terry" Connecticut National Guard Encampment. 1888. "We Drank from the Same Canteen." Cardboard photo of Gen. Sheridan on small gilt tin canteen looped from bar over silk ribbon. Figural winged eagle atop bar. Similar encampment ribbons exist for Logan. *$85–100*

Miscellaneous

Candy Container. Ku Klux Klan. Date unknown. 10"; red, white, blue, black cloth over cardboard figural Klansman wearing black hood and holding fiery cross; hinged lid on base. *$500–550*

Flag Relic. U.S. Grant. Framed flag relic with inscription at lower right: "Presented to U.S. Grant as Capt. Grant by Govt. of U.S. on June 15, 1861, when made Col. of 21st. Reg. of Ill. Vols." Flag badly tattered. (A) Mail Auction, Stark, 1993, $600. . . . . *$600–700*

Handkerchief. Garfield and Arthur. 1880. Jugate transfer oval portraits with eagle atop, holding draped flags. Streamer above with "Our Candidates.". *$100–125*

Hankerchief. Harrison and Reid. 1888. Black transfer jugate portraits in lower right corner of linen handkerchief. *$75–100*

Handkerchief. Ku Klux Klan. Early 20th century. Appliqued "K.K.K." in red in one corner. *$50–75*

Quilt. James Garfield quilt. 1880. Made of cotton yard goods with red, white, blue. Portrait of Garfield is widely circulated image by Pach Bros. Quilt is 78" × 82" and features approx. 90 portraits and anchor and shield patches interspersed. Top fine; work at extreme edges and some bleeding of color. REF: Collins, *Threads of History*, 470. (A) Stark FP Cat., Summer '93, $1200.. . . . . *$1100–1400*

Rug. Lincoln, Robert E. Lee, and George Washington Sesquicentennial Exposition Wool Persian Carpet. 1926. Oriental rug 10' × 13'. Oval of Washington bust appears in center flanked by standing Indian and Pilgrim; Lincoln (top left); Lee top right (flaning furled U.S. flags). Oval vignettes of Statue of Liberty (lower left) and Capitol Bldg. (lower right). *$2000–2500*

Silk Purse. Varina Davis (wife of Jefferson Davis) purse. Black silk, approx. 8" h. with red, white, and blue needlework design of C.S.A. shield, battle flag, and stars and bars flag. Also elaborate monogram "D." Sold in 1984 as part of estate of direct descendant, with provenance.. . . . . *$600–650*

Tapestry. James Garfield. 1880. Woven tapestry 16" × 28". Beige, brown. Portrait in laurel wreath. Eagle, palm tree, and cattails. *$200–225*

Tapestry. Gens. Robert E. Lee and Stonewall Jackson/The Last Meeting. *1904*. Black on white silk woven jacquard. The two C.S.A. Gens. meet on horseback; several aides in background. Made for the 1904 St. Louis Exposition, 5¹³/₈" × 8³/₄". Collins 876. . . . . *$350–400*

Tapestry. Winfield Scott. Brown, blue, green, white; 16" × 22". Scott on white steed; rows of soldiers behind him. *$650–700*

Violin Cover. U.S. Grant. 1868. Quilted textile with bust image of Gen. Grant (same portrait used in campaign flags). Black transfer; red trim. Shaped to fit inside lid of violin case. Collins 346, 347. . . . . *$700–750*

Watch Fob. Ku Klux Klan. Date unknown. Beaded fob; approx. 4"; red, white, blue with crossed flags and K.K.K. monogram.. *$100–125*

Yard Goods. Civil War cannon and U.S. flag pattern. Ca. 1860s. Close plain-weave bleached cotton in red, white, blue, brown. Flag at full mast outlined in purple; cannon in lavender outline. Swath, 8" × 2". Collins 316. . . . . *$300–350*

Yard Goods. "James A. Garfield for President/Chester A. Arthur for Vice President. 1880. Roller print in red, white, and blue colors with oval cameos of candidates framed by laurel wreaths. Based on photo of Garfield by Fassett. emgraved by Rice & Sons, Philadelphia, and pub. by J.C. McCurdy, Philadelphia. Arthur photo by Saroney, engraved by J.C. Butrie; 50" × 22". *$500–600*

Yard Goods. "U.S. Grant. First in War. First in Peace." 1868. Brown, red, white. Bust portraits of Grant repeated between mil. drum and dove motifs. "Let us have Peace/U.S. Grant" under portrait. 11" × 5¹/₂". *$325–350*

Lincoln-Hamlin 1860 campaign banner, $10,000–$11,000.

Hayes-Wheeler swallowtail campaign banner, $1,500–$2,000.

Left: *Cotton banner, "Hurrah for Garfield and Arthur," 1880, green, brown, yellow, and orange, $2,000–$2,500.* Right: *Appliquéd bookmark, "Tune thy [harp] to peace," with note that it had been bought at the U.S. Sanitary Fair (forerunner to the Red Cross) in Philadelphia in 1864. From the Kit Barry collection, $250–$300.*

Left: *CDV of a Union veteran with 50th Anniversary Gettysburg Encampment ribbon and badge, $300–$500. (Photo courtesy of Skinner Auctions)* Right: *Ohio Lincoln banner, ca. 1860, $1,500–$2,000.*

Left: *Silk ribbon with Lincoln portrait and "Freedom" and "Protection,"
signed by Lincoln, ca. 1860, $1,100–$1,200.* Top right: *This tiny 13-star
souvenir flag, woven by Horstman, was worn as a lapel pin. Pins such as
these were usually worn by Sanitary Fair volunteers. From the Kit Barry
collection, $75–$100.* Bottom right: *Appliquéd silk ribbon, with the
notation "Badges like this were worn by loyal ladies of Philadelphia
during the Rebellion." From the Kit Barry collection, $350–$400.*

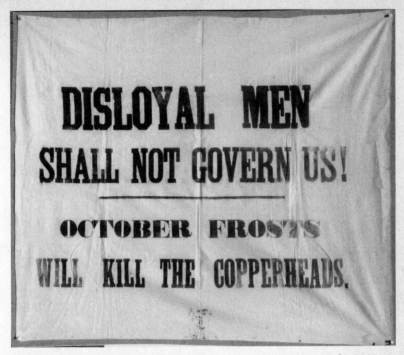

Rare pro-Lincoln banner from the 1860 campaign, 36" × 44", $2,700.
(Photo courtesy of Rex Stark)

Left: *A badly tattered battle flag of the 26th Vermont Regiment,*
multicolor, with state seal, $1,200–$1,500. Right: *From the Bond*
collection, this CSA Army of Northern Virginia battle flag broke auction
records when it sold for $67,000. (Photo courtesy of Conestoga Auctions)

Grant and Colfax campaign banner, 1868, in red, blue, and black,
$2,000–$2,500.

Left: *Ribbon, ca. 1861, $500–$600;* Right: *Pro-Union ribbon, $550–$650.*

Felt pennant, 50th anniversary of the Battle of Gettysburg, depicts General Meade's headquarters, $160. (Photo courtesy of Mark Cisco)

TIMEPIECES

CLOCKS

"Henry Clay." 1850s. Reverse painting on glass of bust portrait of Clay. Seth Thomas mantle clock. *$600–650*

Winfield Scott Hancock. 1880. Reverse painting on glass of Gen. Hancock on horseback. Seth Thomas mantle type; wooden case with arched top and turned spires at each end. *$1100–1200*

"Abraham Lincoln Mantle Clock." Ca. 1870. French works, unmarked. Metal with porcelain face. Figural of Lincoln, seated, with stack of books at feet. Clock is supported by four figural turtles in each corner as feet. (A) Riba, Feb. '86, $2000. .
. . . . *$2500–3000*

"Abraham Lincoln 8-Day Mantle Clock and Deities Set." Ca. 1880. French. L. Merti et. Cie. Lincoln seated in chair with "Proclamation of Emancipation" engraved in document in Lincoln's lap. Bell strike pendulum movement. Cast metal, 17½" h. × 17" w. Unattached to clock—statues of female deities, possibly representing war and peace, are 25" h. *$3000–3500*

McKinley Gingerbread Clock. 1898. Wood. Chestnut stained. From series honoring Spanish American War heroes, which includes Dewey and Scley, both of whom, as did McKinley, served in Civil War as well. Pressed wood bust image of McKinley. *$450–500*

McKinley, "Protection and Prosperity." 1896. Unknown maker. Cast-iron mantle clock in black finish. Bust of McKinley at top; symbols of commerce (boat, train) in deep relief at sides. Clock dial in shape of coin that reads "Sound Money." Embossed shields above face. *$1200–1400*

"Presidential Shelf Clock." Ca. 1872. Seth Thomas works and chime. Chip-wood case with glass windows enclosing CDVs of presidents, from Washington to Grant; 41" × 21" with weights. *$1200–1300*

WATCHES

Gen. G.T. Beauregard Pocket Chronograph. 1861. Made by L.B. Tuchman, Birmingham, England. Engraved, "G.T. Beauregard, May 7, 1861." With three stars. Large 18-size sterling presentation watch awarded by Beauregard. Gilt ¾ plate, key winding movement. Signed and numbered white enamel dial with roman chapters. Inside rear cover engraved: "I award to Jones for Courage, Brig. Gen.

G.T.B." (probably given to David R. Jones, a C.S.A. officer, for carrying out terms of surrender to Anderson at Ft. Sumter). Inside dust cover, "Presented to W. Sloan by Frank James, July 1888." *$5000–6000*

Lincoln Anglo-Swiss Silver Key Wind Pocket Watch. 1860s. M. Tobias, Liverpool. Relief silver shell medallion of Lincoln surmounting diamond pattern design. Runs but lacks key. Stark FP Cat., Oct. '94, $1250. .... *$1100–1200*

"McKinley–Roosevelt." 1892. Ingersol stem wind pocket watch with jugate portraits of candidates on dial.................................... *$450–500*

Relief Carved Civil War Corps Watch Fob. Ca. 1862. (Actual unit unidentified.) 7" mother-of-pearl fob with carved corps badges, including heart, diamond, anchor, shield, star. Stark FP Cat., Oct. '93, $225......................... *$200–225*

Union Soldiers Pocket Watch. Ca. 1862. T.F. Cooper, London. Handi(?) II 1704, Lever 17 jewels. Silver watch with silver chain holding watch key. Face with painted illustration of soldiers holding flag, camp tents in background, 2" dia. Drawstring leather pouch. (A) Riba, March '93, $1600............. *$1600–1700*

Left: *Seth Thomas mantle clock, reverse painting on glass of General Winfield Scott, ca. 1856, $1,200–$1,500.* Right: *Seth Thomas shelf clock with CDVs of presidents from Washington to Grant inset in case, ca. 1872, $1,200–$1,300.*

Mantle clock, eight-day, featuring seated figure of Lincoln, ca. 1880, L. Merti et Cie, $3,000–$3,500.

Pocket watch, with illustration of Union soldiers, ca. 1862, T.F. Cooper, London, $1,600–$1,700.

TOBACCO-RELATED
MEMORABILIA

ASHTRAYS

McKinley Silver Bug. 1896. Thin silver freeform ashtray with raised fluted edge and deep relief silver bug at center impaled by actual brass (gold colored) spike. *$200–250*

CIGAR BOXES

James Blaine and John Logan. 1884. Double-cover with inserted portrait cards to cover undersides. *$200–250*
"Harrison and Reid." 1892; jugate bust portraits; names in large type on lid. *$65–75*
Hobson's Peerless Cigars. Embossed multilabel inside lid with image of Union Gen. Edward H. Hobson, a hero at Shiloh and one time commander of Burnside's cavalry. *$35–50*
"Presidential Contest." 1868 Campaign, 19" x 9" wood box; Schumaker & Ettinger litho on paper on inside cover depicts candidates on high wheel bicycles including Gens. Grant and Sherman. *$500–650*
"The Three Heroes." Multicolor label on inside lid; oval portraits of Gens. Winfield Scott Hancock, Grant (center), and McClellan. *$175–200*

CIGAR CASES

"Henry Clay/The American Statesman. Candidate for 1844." Hand-painted leather case. Name in scroll under bust portrait, eagle, shield and stars. "The American Statesman" with poem for Clay. Rich mustard brown, 5" x 2⅞", Hake 3019. Stark FPC, Dec. '94, $3150. . . . . *$2000–3000*
U.S. Grant. Color ¾-length portrait on leather; Grant in uniform; 6" high. *$300–400*

U.S. Grant. Color, upper-third portrait on leather; Grant in uniform; 7". Hake GR 3012. . . . . *$900–1000*

CIGAR CUTTERS

"Ku Klux Klan." Date unknown. Silver plate cigar cutter with embossed mounted Klansman, emblems, slogans. *$125–135*

CIGAR HOLDERS

U.S. Grant Presentation Cheroot Holder in Case. Ca. 1880. 5" meerschaum carved with figural horse. Wide gold band inscribed "To General U.S. Grant from Col. J.H. Grover." Stark FPC, Dec. '93, $2750. . . . . *$2200–2500*

CIGAR LABELS

Gen. Custer Cigars. Ca. 1875. 4¼" multicolor litho oval bust portrait of a young Custer. *$125–135*

"Gettysburg Commanders." Multiembossed label with bust portrait of Gen. Meade, flanked by Gettysburg military monuments; furled flag and cannon below. *$25–30*

"Gen. U.S. Grant." 1873–76. Fulta Fabrica Tabacos Segar Manufactory, Vuelta-Abajo, Havana. 6½" x 4½". Bust portrait. B&w on pink stock. *$100–125*

"Honest Old Abe." 1873–76. Fulta Fabrica Tabacos Segar Manufactory. Vuelta-Abajo, Havana. 6½" x 4½". Beardless bust portrait. B&w on pink stock. (A) Riba, July '93, $130. . . . . *$125–150*

"Gen. J.A. Logan." 1873–76. Fulta Fabrica Tabacos Segar Manufactory. Vuelta-Abajo, Havana. 6½" x 4½". Beardless bust portrait. B&w on pink stock. *$100–125*

"Our Chieftan." Ca. 1870s. Louis E. Neuman & Co., NY. Multicolor. Large Roman scimitars and laurel surround bust portrait of Ulysses S. Grant. *$25–35*

Booker T. Washington 6-Cent Perfecto. Early 1900s. By Penn State Cigar Corp. Multicolor bust portrait of late 19th-century black educator—mint proof. *$150–175*

CIGAR LIGHTERS

"Young Patriot." Figural counter-top lighter, 1860s, white metal painted gold on marble base; young lad holds American flag. Gas-fed flame comes from top of flag pole; 14". Good Quality/Good Condition. (A) $360 . . . . *$350–400*

CIGARETTE TINS

"Dandy Fifth Cigarettes." Salmon & Gluckstein. Tin container has waist-up color illustration in circle of a 5th Maryland regimental officer in red uniform with furled flags in background. Multicolor. *$150–200*

MATCHBOX HOLDERS

Benjamin Butler. Ca. 1874; lightly glazed bisque with high relief outward facing busts of Butler on all four sides; Kepi military cap lid handle; inscribed "Contraband of War/Set Them to Work" (Butler's response when asked what to do with freed slaves). 5" h. *$300–350*
U.S. Grant. Ca. 1870s. Cast-iron figural of Grant in military cap; match to Greeley. *$275–300*
U.S. Grant. Cast-metal, bas relief bust of Grant flanked by cannons and stacks of cannonballs; black finish; 6" h. *$200–225*
Horace Greeley. Ca. 1872; cast-iron figural of Greeley bust; he wears Quaker hat; 6" h.; natural or black finish. . . . . *$150–200.*
Benjamin Harrison. Cast iron with bas relief oval profile; matchbox holder below has sunburst motif; 7" h. Cleveland match. *$450–550*

MATCHSAFES

U.S. Flag. 1860s; embossed silver. *$150–175*
U.S. Grant. Double-sided bust figural in brass; hollow hinged match to McKinley and Harrison examples; 3½" h. *$450–550*
Benjamin Harrison. Bust figural in brass; match to Grant and McKinley. *$350–450*
Gen. John A. Logan Memorial. 1886. Legend and circular bust portrait of Logan engraved in white metal. 3" × 1¾" h. *$125–150*
William McKinley. Bust figural in brass; match to the Grant and Harrison matchsafes above, 3½" h. *$300–450*

PIPES

"Henry Clay." Ca. 1844. Bust of Clay at face of 2½" h., 1" dia. white clay pipe bowl. Name and filigree pattern embossed. Long curved stem, black. *$250–300*
"C.S.A." (Alabama Volunteer Corps). Carved meerschaum, with "A.V.C." on bowl; signed Hafner. Ca. 1865. . . . . *$700–800*
Jefferson Davis. Redware figural with curved stem. *$350–450*
U.S. Grant. 1880. Curved pipe with figural bust image of Grant; black with brown brier; malacca stem. *$300–400*
Winfield Scott Hancock. 1880. Burnished mustard-colored clay presidential figural rebus pipe (hand+rooster=Hand-cock). *$650–750*
Benjamin Harrison. 1888. Campaign clay pipe; white with embossed bust of candidate on bowl; opposite has spread eagle and shield (there's a Cleveland match). *$200–275*

Hayes–Wheeler Campaign Pipes. 1876. Black wooden pipes with jugate albumen photos of the Rep. candidates. Black knobbed stems. *$250–275*

Lincoln. Ca. 1909. French made; commemorating 100th anniversary of Lincoln's birth; bearded figure crowned with laurel wreath. *$200–250*

Lincoln. Date unknown. Carved meerschaum bowl, figural bust of bearded Lincoln. Curved black stem. Rex Stark FPC, Dec. '94, $450. . . . . *$400–450*

George B. McClellan. Figural brass bust of defeated 1864 Dem. candidate; curved stem. *$1000–1100*

William McKinley. 1896. White carved ceramic bowl of McKinley with cocked hat, á la Napoleon. *$250–300*

William McKinley. 1896. Redware figural bust head McKinley bowl. . . *$100–125*

"President Franklin Pierce." 1850. Figural clay pipe bowl. Legend embossed on stem. *$175–200*

Slaves. Figural grouping; bearded man, woman, children, Meerchaum pipe; yellow patina. *$750–800*

Two Slaves Attacked by Dogs. 1850s. Carved white meerschaum of two slaves— a man and woman being pursued by dogs. Nicely detailed with amber patina. Original case marked "F.J. Kaldenburg, Manufacturers, NYC." 7¹/₂" × 3". Stem probably replaced. (A) Riba, Nov. '87, $650 . . . . *$750–800*

South Carolina Confederate Pipe. 1862. Handcarved burl maple. "C.S.A." in eagle and shield design. Carved shields. "Major Emmett Seibels–7 S.C." with 11 stars. 2¹/₄" × 3". Seibels fought at 1st Battle of Bull Run. Photocopies of his military records and letters included. *$800–900*

Tilden–Hendrix Campaign Pipes. Democratic match to Hayes–Wheeler pipe. *$250–275*

Union Solder. Ca. 1870. Carved wooden head figural of bearded man in Kepie cap, mounted on baleen holder; finial missing from bottom of holder. . . . *$200–300*

"Yorktown, Virginia." 1862. C.S.A. carved burl with large relief letters on 5" l. bowl, with spikelike projection at base. *$350–400*

SNUFFBOXES

"American Eagle and Flags." Ca. 1862. Carved beef-bone box decorated with eagle holding a flag in each talon; two birds on branch. "John" incised above bird. . . . .

Henry Clay, Martin Van Buren, Andrew Jackson and Daniel Webster. 1844. Papier-mâché. Approx. 2¹/₂" grouping of foursome; bust portraits in black transfer; deep yellow (almost tan) on deep orange background. Names appear along border. *$800–900*

Henry Clay. 1844. Clay seated at desk with document in hand. Hake 3011. 3³/₄" dia. Multicolored. At least three variants are known. *$700–800*

Henry Clay. 1844. Papier-mâché. Handpainted bust portrait in square with orange border. Legend at top with eagle, shield, and sheaf of four arrows at each side, legend below. *$700–800*

Jefferson Davis. 1861. 2¹/₂" dia. gutta-percha snuffbox with relief molded beading and round gilt sheel bust portrait of Davis under glass inset in lid. Previously unknown. *$1800–2000*

U.S. Grant. Ca. 1870s. Embossed bust portrait "Grant," tin; 1¹/₂" dia. . . . *$150–175*

U.S. Grant. 1868. Tin snuffbox, oval, with bust image of Gen. Grant. . . *$800–900*

U.S. Grant and Schuyler Colfax. Gutta-percha with embossed portraits of 1868 Rep. candidates. 3½" dia. Hake UG 3009. . . . . *$1000–1500*

Gen. Stonewall Jackson. Engraved horn snuffbox with caricature of Jackson that changes to donkey when turned. "Jackson's Best Reversed/Invert Me for better or worse—Ass or human. Take your choice." *$1200–1300*

Seymour and Blair. 1868. Circular gutta-percha snuffbox with raised jugate portraits of Dem. slate. Dates 1869–1873 (the dates of term of office, had they won). Encircled by raised chain of stars and filigree. *$350–400*

Slavery, "Traite de Negroes." 1850s. French. Gilt brass, leather bottom, 16 interlocking flaps. Embossed scene of slave trade. Black man being whipped and woman with child. *$800–850*

"A Union Forever." Ca. 1861. Rectangular snuffbox with gold eagle with arrows and streamer, "E Pluribus Unum." Slogans: "No East, No North, No South, No West" in each respective corner; 2½" × 3½". *$450–500*

TOBACCO POUCHES

Soldier's Comfort Smoking Tobacco. Ca. 1861. Muslin pouch with drawstring. .
. . . . *$200–300*

TOBACCO TINS

Hancock vs. Garfield. Tin box by Century Tobacco. V-P candidates with revolving disc in center that turns to reveal portrait of favorite candidates. Bust portraits of English and Arthur also appear in window. Black on blue. 4". *$850–1200*

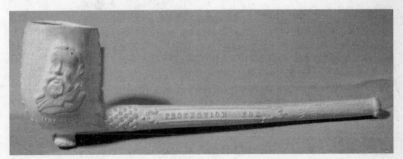

Clay pipe with bas relief bust of Benjamin Harrison on bowl. Carving of eagle and shield is on the opposite side of the bowl, $250–$275.

Cigar box, "Presidential Contest." Large wood box featuring Grant, Sherman, Hendricks, Tilden, and Byard, all riding high-wheeler bicycles, $500–$600.

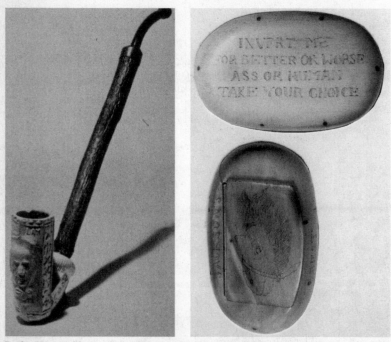

Left: *Henry Clay pipe with bas relief carving on the front of the ceramic bowl and stars on both sides, long curving wood stem, $750–$800.* Right: *Stonewall Jackson snuff box, $1,200–$1,300.*

*Meerschaum pipe,
with deep relief
figure of slave
family, $750–$800.
(Photo courtesy
of Rex Stark)*

*Union cigars,
c. 1900,
O. L. Schwenke
Lithographer, NY,
$100–$125.*

*"Our Defender"
cigars, c. 1890s,
O. L. Schwenke
Lithographer, NY,
$100–$125. (Photo
courtesy of Kit
Barry)*

Toys and Games

Banks

Heading a fascinating array of Civil War–related still and mechanical banks is the Jerome Secore "Freedman's Bank" from 1879. The bank, which has an intricate clockwork mechanism, features metal-figured black Freedman in cloth costume depositing coin in wooden desk, then thumbing his nose and wiggling his fingers. Only a few of these rare banks exist. Should a specimen surface at auction, it is speculated to bring at least a half million dollars.

Mechanical

"Artillery Bank." Bronze-plated. Ptd. 1892. Designed by Peter Adams and John Shepard. Made by Shepard Hardware. Missing trap. (A) Bertoia, Oct. '94, $160. . .
. . . . *$250–300*

"Artillery Bank, Confederate." Ca. 1900. Shepard Hardware Co. Designed by Peter Adams. Multicolor painted cast iron. Artilleryman in gray mufti. Hammer pulls back on cannon as coin is fired into tower. Paper caps can be used. Repainted fig. (A) Bertoia, Oct. '94, $400. . . . . *$700–800*

"Artillery Bank, Union." Ca. 1900. Shepard Hardware Co. Same as above with color changes in uniform from gray to blue. Repaired foot. (A) Bertoia, Oct. '94, $725. . . . . *$600–700*

Freedman's Bureau. Ca. 1882. Jerome Secor. 5¼" h. Painted wood "trick drawer" bank; reddish brown with gold stenciled lettering. Play on words denoting notorious Bureau set up in post–Civil War. "Now you see it. Now you don't" on front. Three drawers, but only top one slides open to accept coin. . . . .

"Octangular Fort." (Originally sold as "Ft. Sumter Bank.") Maker unknown, U.S. 1890s; cast iron with small cannon aimed at Fort commemorates first shot fired in Civil War. (A) Bertoia, Oct. '94, $5000. . . . . *$4000–5000*

Stump Speaker. Ptd. 1886. Shepard Hardware. Black smiling figure in top hat, deposits coin in satchel. "Bank" and "Stump Speaker" embossed on front and side. Red platform; painted brown, green, yellow, red. Rather unflattering caricature of the emerging black politician of ante-bellum years. *$2000–2500*

Still

Gen. Benjamin Butler Frog Bank. 1884. J.&E. Stevens. 6¹/₂" h. Caricature of Butler as frog (yellow body; green arms and legs) holding handful of greenbacks. "For the masses" and "Bonds & Yachts for Me" embossed on arms. Butler ran as Greenback Party candidate in 1884.. . . . . *$1200–1500*

U.S. Grant Bust Bank. 1950s. Banthrico. Dark brown matte finish, 5¹/₂" h. Facsimile signature. Match to Lee bank below *$25–35*

U.S. Grant Bust Safe Bank. 1903. J.M. Harper (English), cast metal. Brown finish, 5⁵/₈" h. Semidimensional bust fig. atop miniature safe. *$700–800*

> *Note:* The "Boss Tweed" (Tammany Tiger) still bank ($1500–2000); the "Trust" still bank by J.&E. Stevens ($1200–1500); the "Tammany" or "Fat Man" mech. bank by J.&E. Stevens ($500–650) are all satirical allusions to U.S. Grant's graft-plagued administration.

Robert E. Lee Bust Bank. 1950s. Banthrico. 5³/₈" h. Bronze finish. Facsimile signature. Commemorative bank of zinc/aluminum. (Often issued with imprint of a financial institution.). *$25–35*

Abraham Lincoln Bust. 1920s. A.C. Rehberger. Bust fig. 4¹³/₁₆" h. Bronze-finished lead bank with key locked trap. *$25–35*

Abraham Lincoln Bust. 1920s. A.C. Rehberger. Bust fig. in lead with bronze finish. Facsimile sig., 5" h.. . . . . *$25–35*

Abraham Lincoln Bust on Pedestal. Ca. 1920. 7¹/₄" h. White metal with silver finish. Key locked trap. Facsimile signature. *$50–60*

"Gen. Philip Sheridan on Prancing Horse." 1910–25. Arcade. 6" h. on base. Gilt finish. *$200–250*

GAMES

"Battlecry." Milton Bradley, 1962. Civil War strategy board game; large box version. (D) $35. . . . . *$25–50*

"Battle of Gettysburg Wood Table Top Game." 1880s. Full-color litho on box; pictures bird's eye view of battle. *$350–400*

"Civil War." Parker Bros., 1961. 19" × 9" box. (D) $32.. . . . . *$25–35*

"(The) Commanders of Our Forces." E.C. Eastman, Concord, NH; ca. 1860s. B&w card game with 80 cards naming famous battles, Gens.; shows Gen. with saber on horseback leading army with *Monitor* and *Merrimac* at right. . . *$100–125*

"(The) Draft Enforced." M. Salom, 1863. Reading card game with humorous retorts as Prov. Marshall tries to draft recruits into the Army. *$250–300*

"(The) Drummer Boy Game." Parker Bros., 1890. 9" × 15" box; board, four markers; lead players from rank of drummer boy up to Col.; board shows Civil War soldiers in formation; box cover shows drummer boy with bandaged head. . . . *$125–150*

"Game of Strategy." McLoughlin Bros., 1891. Boxed board game; backgammon-type board with checkers; box illus.—Union Gen. leading troops in battle. Multicolored. Good Quality/Average Condition. (D) $150. . . . . *$200–250*

"General Grant at Camp." W.S. Reed Toy Co., 1870s. Illus.. on box of Gen. Grant on horseback with tent in background. *$150–200*

"Great American War Game." J.H. Hunter, 1899. 25¹/₂" × 12" box; over 2' long cover illus. foldout of Civil War battle scene, with attacking Union armies; 22 metal soldiers and two wood cannons; steel balls. Multicolored. (A) $800. . . . *$1000–1200*

"Lee vs. Meade in Battle of Gettysburg." Gamut of Games, 1974. Box 21" × 10"; military strategy game. (D) $50................................. *$35–50*

"(The) Little Drummer." J. Ottmann Lith. Co. 13" × 13" box; card game; four wood markers, spinner; illus. suggests Civil War scene............... *$100–125*

"Naval Engagement." McLoughlin Bros., 1870. Separate board and pieces, 5½" × 9" box, board opens as book with multicolored illus. of Civil War soldiers, cannon, ships in bay. *$75–100*

"New Military Game." G.W. Fisher, Rochester, NY; 1859. With handcolored cards. *$450–500*

"Poor Old Soldier and His Dog." Richard Pease, Albany, NY; 1860s. Card game with handcolored card and instruction sheet; lotted with "(Game of) Uncle Tom and Little Eva"; V.S. Parkhurst, Providence, R.I.; handcolored cards. Most of label gone on "Soldier" game. (A) $880. .... *$900–1000*

"(The) Rebel." Ideal, 1961. 19" × 9" board game, based on post–Civil War adventure TV series on ABC starring Nick Adams (1959–60). (D) $75......... *$50–75*

"Skirmish at Harpers Ferry." McLoughlin Bros., 1891. Build-up board with parts tray; set of b&w pieces; cover shows lineup of cannons being fired....... *$500–600*

MILITARY MINIATURES

"C.S.A. Artillery Gun Team." Alymer; 1970s. 60 mm scale. Includes gunners, flag bearer, cannon, and wooden base............................. *$200–225*

"C.S.A. Cavalry" (3). Alymer; 1970s. 60 mm scale. Mounted at walk bearing carbines at the ready; flag bearer with C.S.A. standard; orig. box.......... *$100–125*

"C.S.A. Horse-drawn Artillery Gun Team." Alymer, 1970s. Six-horse team; three mounted gunners, three seated on limber chest; 12-pounder Napoleon Gun; orig. box. *$200–250*

"C.S.A. Horse-drawn Artillery Gun Team." Alymer, 1970s. 33 mm scale. Marching with rifles at shoulder arms; officer and flag bearer with C.S.A. flag; orig. box... *$100–125*

Gens. Grant and Lee on Horseback. Mignot, 1970s. In orig. boxes. (A) Skinner, July '91, $200. .... *$250–3000*

"Union Army Horse-drawn Artillery Gun Team." Alymer, 1970s. Three mounted gunners, three seated on limber chest; 12-pounder Napoleon Gun; orig. box... *$200–250*

"Union Cavalry Mounted at Walk." Alymer, 1970s. Unit with carbines at the ready; standard bearer with U.S. flag; orig. box. *$100–125*

"Camp on the Potomac." Haffner, 1880s. Civil War encampment display set (part of series); German; 33 mm flat tinplate soldiers, flags, pop-up cloth tents with wood box, full-color litho of camp on lid; approx. 150 pieces. (A) $1210. . . *$1500–2000*

"Confederate Cavalry." William Britains (English) 2055, ca. 1960s. Mounted at the trot, with carbines; officer bears sword; in orig. box.............. *$150–200*

"Union Artillery Gun with Gunners." William Britains (English) 2057, ca. 1960s. Orig. box. *$100–125*

"Confederate Cavalry and Infantry." William Britains (English) 2068, 1960s. Includes four mounted troopers with carbines and officer bearing sword; infantry in action firing and at the ready; includes bugler, standard bearer holding C.S.A. battle flag; officer firing pistol; with orig. box. *$375–400*

"Union Cavalry and Infantry." William Britains (English) 2069, ca. 1960s. Pair of mounted troopers with carbines, trumpeter; officer with sword; infantry in action, with standard bearer holding U.S. flag; plus bugler; in orig. box.... *$225–250*

"Confederate Infantry Assaulting with Fixed Bayonets." C.B.G. Mignot (French), ca. 1950s. Standard bearer carries C.S.A. flag; officer bears sword; set in orig. box. *$200–225*

TOYS

Educational Myrioptican, "Rebellion Story of Civil War." 1880. Color litho paper on wood, scenes unfurl by turning knobs. Better Quality/Fine Condition. (D) $650... *$500–700*

"Ft. Sumter Target Toy." W.S. Reed, 1870s. Cannons, litho paper on wood standup soldiers (probably not orig. with toy); 17" w. (A) $2420. .... *$2000–2500*

"Gettysburg Gun." Realistic wooden gun stamped "Gettysburg, July 1,2,3, 1863"; 10½" l. *$75–100*

"Historical Panorama of Rebellion." Milton Bradley, 1880s. Full-color reel of scenes of Civil War from Ft. Sumter to Burning of Atlanta. (A) $475.... *$500–550*

Historiscope, "Panorama of American History of America #1." Milton Bradley, 1880s. Handcolored reel with Civil War images. (A) $385. .... *$350–400*

"Panorama." Currier & Ives (label inside box), early 1870s. Handcolored Civil War scenes on two wooden rollers with knobs for turning in pasteboard viewing box (back missing). (A) $660. .... *$500–600*

"Zouave Alphabet Block Set." © 1908. McLoughlin Bros. 8" × 13"; nine litho on wood blocks of Zouaves and other soldiers on faces; ABC's on sides; lid shows Zouave on horseback, multicolored; lotted with (ca. 1898, by unknown maker) construction set of slotted wood hexagons, decorated on face with Zouaves with letters on reverse; pieces interlock with circular discs; includes patent papers; lid missing aprons. (A) $175. .... *$200–225*

MISCELLANEOUS

Militaria Diorama. Collis' Volunteers of the 114th Pennsylvania Volunteer Infantry. 1960. Two Union soldiers in Zouave uniforms; another wears kepi; the fourth fig., a bandsman with drum, wears plumed felt hat. (Collis, a snative of Ireland, was awarded the Medal of Honor for heroism at Fredericksburg.).......... *$600–650*

MAGIC GEN. GRANT.

The above cut represents an entirely new and very attractive toy called "Magic Gen. Grant." It is composed of a wooden cup 3 inches in diameter, and 1¼ inches in height, finished in assorted colors, each containing a perfect lithograph of Gen. Grant in Military Costume, with movable head, arms and legs. They are very sensitive to the touch, and the slightest jar sets them in motion.

They are covered by an oval glass held in place by a wooden ring.

Sample sent to any address by mail, POST PAID, on receipt of 25 cents in currency or postage stamps or 1 dozen by express for $1.75. Special price to Jobbers on application.

MANUFACTURED ONLY BY

A. A. Davis,   -   Nashua, N. H.

Left: *Bank, frog-bodied General Benjamin Butler non-mechanical bank, $5,000.* Right: *A.A. Davis catalog item shows a "magical" jiggling General Grant priced at $0.25. The toy itself would be worth $700–$800 today, though the flyer itself is highly collectible. ($50–$75)*

Civil War–era cast-iron toy match cannon (left) and toy firecracker cannon (right) replicas, ca. 1870, $200–$250 each.

Board games: (top) *"Game of Strategy,"* by McLoughlin Bros, ca. 1891, a backgammon-type game, $500–$600; (bottom) *"The Great American War Game,"* by J.H. Hunter, 1890s, $800–$900. Both from the Herb Siegel collection. (Photo courtesy of Noel Barrett Auctions)

Japanese lithographed tin windup toy, *"General Lee on Traveler,"* ca. 1930s, $400–$500.

Clockwork "walkers," produced by Ives Hotchkiss (from left to right):
Chinaman, $7,000; General Butler, $4,000; "Smoking General Grant,"
$25,000; Uncle Tom (aka "Old Black Joe"), with original box, $21,000.
(Photo courtesy of Tom Anderson auction at Barrett's, 1991)

G. Calgani Sand toy,
"Lincoln Hurdy-Gurdy,"
ca. 1862, showing Lincoln
with music box and
Secretary of the Navy
Gideon Wells as a
monkey, $5,000–$6,000.

Left: *This Stadden diorama depicts the 114th Pennsylvania Volunteer Infantry, Collis's Zouaves: $450–$500.* Right: *Gen. Butler "Walker," $5,000–$6,000.*

Left: *"Fort Sumter Target Game," by W.S. Reed, lithographed paper on wood, ca. 1870s, $2,000–$2,500.* Right: *"Stump Speaker" mechanical bank, ca. 1880s. Satirical ante-bellum portrayal of an emerging black politician, $2,000–$3,000.*

UNIFORMS

CLOTHING AND ACCESSORIES

Belt. Union cartridge belt for Spencer rifle. With "U.S." brass buckle, bayonet, and scabbard; covered cartridge holders throughout belt. Early tag attached (experimental?). (A) Dias, Oct. '94, $3000. . . . . *$3000–3500*

Belt. Union Cavalry sabre belt with officer's belt plate. Mfgr. by E. Gaylord, Chicopee, MA. Inspector's mark in oval stamp. "A.D. Laidley, Sub Inspector. U.S. Ord. Dept." (A) Dias, Oct. '94, $500. . . . . *$500–600*

Belt. Union leather belt with buckle. Brass "U.S." buckle and sword hangers. (A) Dias, Oct. '94, $350. . . . . *$300–350*

Belt. Child's Civil War belt. Authentic cut-down version studded with various military buttons and oval belt plate with initial "D." (A) Dias, Oct. '94, $400. . . . . . *$400–450*

Belt. Model 1851 Dragoon saber belt. Complete, excellent condition. (A) Dias, Nov. '94, $190. . . . . *$175–200*

Belt Buckle. Confederate lion head belt buckle. 1863. Brass. Imported from England. (A) Dias, Oct. '94, $170. . . . . *$175–200*

Belt Buckle. Ohio Volunteer Militia buckle. Brass with bullet lodged ²/₃ through front. Supposedly the buckle saved owner's life. Relic found near Lookout Mt. battlefield, along with C.S.A. buckle, several bullets. (A) Riba, Oct. '85, $1000. . . . . . *$800–850*

Belt Buckle with Strap. Confederate lion head belt buckle. 1863. On partial leather strap. Brass. Imported from England. (A) Dias, Oct. '94, $375. . . *$350–400*

Belt Plate. C.S.A. (probably) belt plate. Approx. 2⅞" × 1¾" with soldered hooks. Similar to Fig. 293 in *Plates and Buckles of the Civil War Military* by Kerksis. (A) Dias, Nov. '94, $650. . . . . *$600–650*

Belt Plate. 7th Regiment, NY, cross belt plate. (A) Dias, Oct. '94, $90. . . *$75–100*

Belt Plate. State of New York militia belt plate. Pressed brass. (A) Dias, Oct. '94, $30. . . . . *$30–50*

Belt Plate. Union belt plate. Brass with U.S. insignia. (A) Dias, Oct. '94, $125. . . . . *$125–135*

Belt Plate. Union belt plate. Small size oval brass "U.S." (A) Dias, Nov. '94, $225. . . . . *$200–225*

Belt Plate. Union belt plate. NY 8th. Brass plate with insignia. (A) Dias, Oct. '94, $55. . . . . *$75–100*

Belt Plates (2). Brass belt plates. One buckle has embossed "31" insignia; the other the letter "I." (A) Dias, Oct. '91, $165. . . . . *$150–175*

Belt Plates (3). Eagle cross belt plates. (A) Dias, Nov. '94, $75. . . . . *$75–100*

Belt Plates (2). 31st NY Regiment brass belt plates. Marked "31." (A) Dias, Nov. '94, $70. . . . . *$50–75*

Blouses. Militia officer's dress blouses. Ca. 1850s and 1860s. Belonging to Lt. William Feaning II of Hingham, MA. Dark blue wool, short waist, split tail with inside pockets, standup collars. Also includes military appointments, draft notice, exemption papers (having paid the requisite $300). Correspondence from Army friend telling of "Old Abe's reelection and how the 'Rebs' would not believe it." (A) Riba, May '86, $500. . . . . *$600–700*

Boots. Confederate cavalryman's boots. Horseshoe heels. Spur inset holes. Marked "J.K. Smith/100 Rounds." English-made. (A) Dias, Oct. '94, $350. . . . . . *$350–400*

Buttons (6). Miscellaneous Confederate buttons. Five are So. Carolina with palmetto tree emblem; the other "C.S.A." (A) Dias, Oct. '94, $100. . . . . *$100–125*

Buttons (3). Union 1st Infantry buttons. With embossed bugle insignia and number "1." (A) Dias, Oct. '94, $55. . . . . *$50–75*

Buttons (13). Assorted State Militia buttons. Includes Ohio, Massachusetts, Connecticut. (A) Dias, Nov. '94, $90. . . . . *$75–100*

Buttons. Card of 16 miscellaneous military buttons including Civil War C.S.A. So. Carolina button, Massachusetts Vol. Militia, State of Maine, etc. (A) Dias, Nov. '94, $175. . . . . *$150–175*

Cap Ornaments (8). Various Union regimental ornaments. Eight different regimental numbers and letters in a japanned tin regalia box mfgr. by M.C. Lilley, Columbus, OH. (A) Dias, Oct. '94, $275. . . . . *$250–300*

Carpet Bag. Federal carpet bag, ca. 1865. Bottom leather marked in ink, "1865, G.H. N.Y." Side leather inserts show wear; otherwise, very fine. (A) Dias, Nov. '94, $95. . . . . *$100–$125*

Epaulets. Pair of Union artillery officer's epaulets. 1860. Included with pair of eagle head insert spurs signed "Shelton." In orig. tin regalia box, dated 1860. (A) Dias, Oct. '94, $1200. . . . . *$1200–1300*

Epaulets. Pair of Union officer's silverplated epaulets. (A) Dias, Nov. '94, $85. . . .

Forage Cap. Union cavalryman's forage cap. From 8th Cavalry with maker's label inside: "Lewis J. & Isaac Phillips, NY." Fair condition. Intact with cap buckle, crossed sabers insignia, etc. (A) Dias, Oct. '94, $1200.. . . . . *$1200–1300*

Frock Coat. Brig. Gen. frock coat. Owner unidentified. Blue wool coat with dark blue velvet trim on collar, cuffs. Single vent in rear with two inner pockets. Brass buttons are Louisiana seal buttons made in Waterbury, CT. Shoulder shows epaulettes; large gold star in blue field. Label in collar identifies maker as L. Godchaux of New Orleans. Velvet is worn; one button missing; epaulettes are in good condition. (A) Riba, May '96, $450. . . . . *$650–750*

Frock Coat. Co. A, New Hampshire Cpl. dress frock coat. Ca. 1862. Nine buttons, brass with eagle insignia. Two blue stripes and star on sleeve. Name inside upper sleeve lining is "Luke Nolton Jr." The Dublin, NH, soldier was killed at the 2nd Battle of Manassas, on Sept. 1, 1862. . . . . *$2000–2500*

Hat. Officer's Hardee hat, 5th Cavalry. Ca. 1853. Crossed sabers and "C Company" with feather plume, hat cord, and eagle side emblem. Loose inner hatband. (A) Dias, Nov. '94, $2100. . . . . *$2000–2200*

Hat. Officer's Hardee hat, 8th Artillery Co. G. Ca. 1862. With plume, eagle insignia, red artillery cord. Badly damaged. (A) Dias, Oct. '94, $1000. . *$1200–1500*

Hat Cords (3). Cords for officer's Hardee hats. Two are Infantry; one is Cavalry. (A) Dias, Oct. '94, $135. . . . . *$125–135*

Hat Cords (3). Cords for officer's Hardee hats. One is Cavalry; one is Artillery; one is Infantry. (A) Dias, Nov. '94, $50. . . . . *$50–75*

Hat Cords (2). Hardee hat cords. A sword knot and a post–Civil War hatband. (A) Dias, Nov. '94, $120. . . . . *$100–125*

Haversack. Massachusetts Militia Post haversack. White cotton. Excellent condition. (A) Dias, Oct. '94, $225. . . . . *$225–250*

Insignias (Cloth). Stencilled cotton naval rating insignias. Seven examples incl. two Master-at-Arms (star over eagle and anchor); three Quartermaster (helm); two Boatswains (anchor). All in unused condition. (A) Dias, Nov. '94, $90. . . *$75–100*

Jacket. Confederate artillery jacket from Virginia. Property of Pvt. Jno. G. Winston of Pegram's Battalion, who was stationed with "Free Negro Battery" in Richmond. Greenish gray wool, with red collar and cuffs. Lined with red wool; has seven Virginia buttons marked "Mitchell & Taylor, Rich. Va." Two buttons missing; minor moth holes and edge roughness. Incl. is J.G. Winston's discharge papers. (A) Riba-Mobley, Oct. '86, $5000. . . . . *$6000–7000*

Jacket. Artilleryman's shell jacket. No buttons. Has belt pillows. Braid at collar. Slight seam split and moth damage. (A) Dias, Oct. '94, $800. . . . . *$800–1000*

Jacket. Artilleryman's shell jacket. Blue, full buttons, but not artillery. Belt pillows on back of jacket. "F.H. Shafer, Insp., Cin." stamped in sleeve lining. Minor moth damage and two mouse chews. (A) Dias, Nov. '94, $1150. . . . . *$1100–1200*

Kepi. Berdun's sharpshooter's kepi. Probably 1st or 2nd New Hampshire companies. "U.S. Sharpshooters." Bright, unfaded green wool with gutta percha buttons. Excellent inside with minor wear on inside sweatband. In good condition overall. (A) Dias, Nov. '94, $6500. . . . . *$6000–7000*

Knapsack. Union issue knapsack. Leather soft pack knapsack with shoulder straps. (A) Dias, Oct. '94, $150. . . . . *$150–200*

Knapsack. Union oilcloth knapsack. Has wool liner. Rated excellent. (A) Dias, Nov. '94, $300. . . . . *$300–325*

Knapsack. Union knapsack. Black oilcloth, complete. (A) Nov. '94, $200. *$200–225*

Pillbox. "James Buchanan." 1856. 1$\frac{1}{2}$" embossed brass pillbox with embossed bust portrait. "Buchanan." "Prepared by G. Arnaud, Cachon & Cardamom Aromatise." Stark FP Cat., Dec. '93, $1200. . . . . *$1100–1200*

Purse. James Buchanan. 1856. French. Oval bust ambro of 15th pres. with brass flange. Leather with metal clasps. *$850–900*

Purse. Garfield–Arthur 20th Inaugural souvenir drawstring purse. 1880. Washington, D.C. Red, white, and blue silk. Bust portrait of Garfield *$225–250*

Sash. Union artillery officer's sash. Fine condition. (A) Dias, Oct. '94, $400. . . . . *$350–400*

Sash. Union artillery officer's sash. Rated excellent condition. (A) Dias, Nov. '94, $350. . . . . *$300–350*

Sash. Gold cavalry officer's dress sash. 12" l. with tassels; a few tears in belt; excellent condition. (A) Dias, Nov. '94, $350. . . . . *$300–350*

Shako. Light artillery shako. With brass infantry cap badge; blue pompom. Mfgr. by W.C. Dare, Philadelphia. Shows considerable wear. (A) Dias, Oct. '94, $750. . . . . *$750–900*

Shako. Infantry shako. Ca. 1862. Leather cap styled after French Chasseur. Brass insignia plate; red, white, blue metal cockade; white pompom. Full liner and chin straps. Presented by Gen. McClellan as drill prize to members of the four best drilled regiments of Army of the Potomac. REF: *Time-Life,* "Echoes of Glory/The Union," p. 149. (A) Dias, Oct. '94, $325. . . . . *$325–350*

Shako. National Guard shako. Ca. 1863. With pompom and Pennsylvania buttons; 1st Regiment P.N.C. (A) Dias, Nov. '94, $375. . . . . *$350–400*

Shoulder Scales. Pair non-commissioned staff brass shoulder scales. Excellent condition. (A) Dias, Nov. '94, $125. . . . . *$125–150*

Shoulder Scales. Pair of Pvt./Cpl. shoulder scales. Brass; complete with original lock attachment. (A) Dias, Oct. '94, $175. . . . . *$200–225*

Shoulder Scales. Pair of brass shoulder U.S. 5th Cavalry scales, George Armstrong Custer. Worn by then Lt. Custer with Army of the Potomac, 1861. Ex-collection of Dr. Lawrence Frost.. . . . . *$8000–9000*

Sling. Cavalryman's carbine sling. Leather, stamped "G. 4th. Cav. No. 26." Sling swivel stamped "O.B. North Co., New Haven, Ct." (A) Dias, Nov. '94, $1300. . . .
. . . . *$1200–1300*

Sling. Militia drummer's sling. White leather with name "Joe England" printed in ink on inside of sling. (A) Dias, Nov. '94, $100. *$100–125*

Uniform. 79th New York City Highlanders Militia Battalion Uniform. 1860s. Four-piece uniform: blue jacket with red facings, one white chevron; blue cap with red and blue checking; plaid kilt and sporran, missing brass piece. A few tears and moth holes. (A) Riba, July '91, $1100. . . . . *$1200–1300*

Uniform. Union Civil War tunic, with pants, corps hat with emblem. U.S., 1860s. (A) $2800 (tunic); $4300 (pants); $1550 (hat). . . . . *$9000–9500 (complete)*

Uniform—C.S.A. Contraband. Equipment and clothing captured from a Kentucky Home Guard officer (573). Taken from Lt. J.W. Jennings, 27th Kentucky Col. Infantry at Wildcap Gap, in Autumn, 1862. Incl. jean cloth double-breasted frock coat with black velvet turned down collar; ten block I buttons attached. Ten 1/2" overall horn-handled double-edged dirk; Remington New Model Navy Revolver with holster. Leather belt with rectangular C.S.A. plate sweated over sword belt plate. Brass and tortoise snuff box. Also incl. correspondence. (A) '94, $7250 (almost 10× high estimate).. . . . . *$6000–7000*

Valise. Union artilleryman's valise. "U.S. Watervliet Arsenal" marked on both ends; with L.T. Prime inspector's stamp. Lined with orig. denim. All straps intact. REF: *Civil War Collector's Encyclopedia*, Lord, p. 124. (A) Dias, Oct. '94, $750. . .
. . . . *$750–800*

Miscellaneous Civil War Keepsakes

Housewife or Sewing Kit. Leather sewing kit. Interior pockets and pincushion ends. Near new condition. (A) Dias, Nov. '94, $135. . . . . *$100–125*

Nutmeg Grater. Gen. John Sedgwick engraved silver nutmeg grater. Monogram "J.S." on cover. Superior quality, no hallmark. 1½" × 2½". On small chain. Gen. Sedgwick was killed in battle subsequent to Battle of the Wilderness, 1864. (A) Riba, Oct. '85, $700. . . . . *$750–800*

Uniform. Union Civil War tunic, with pants, corps hat with emblem. U.S., 1860s. (A) $2800 (tunic); $4300 (pants); $1550 (hat).

Tunic: *$2500–3000*

Pants: *$4000–4500*

Hat: *$1000–2000*

Saddle. Confederate leather saddle captured from Pvt. with Mosby's Raiders, 1864. Good quality/good condition. (A) $440. . . . . *$350–400*

Drummer boy's jacket with star buttons at collar, worn by David Allerton, Jr., who became a drummer with a New York regiment at age twelve, $750–$800. (Photo courtesy of Riba Auctions)

Left to right: *Artillery man's blue woolen shell jacket, $1,200–$1,300; post Civil War artillery man's five-button wool blouse, State of New York, $125–$150. (Photo courtesy of Paul Dias Auctions)*

Left to right: *Berdan's Sharpshooter's wool kepi, either 1st or 2nd New Hampshire, bright green with gutta percha buttons, $6,500–$7,000; 1853 U.S. Cavalry Hardee hat of the 5th Cavalry, C company, $2,100–$2,200. (Photo courtesy of Paul Dias Auctions)*

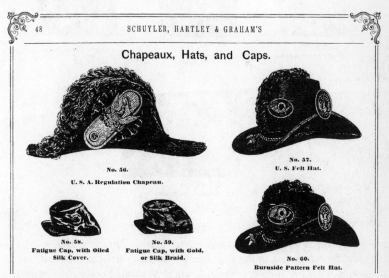

Schuyler, Hartley & Graham military uniform catalog page showing various headwear. The actual items are: Chapeaus (top left), $2,500–$3,000, if accompanied by branch of service and eagle insignia; the Hardee or Jeff Davis felt hat (top right), $2,000–$2,500; the enlisted man's kepi or fatigue cap, with bound edges (bottom left), $350–$550; and the Burnside felt hat, which is priced similar to the Hardee.

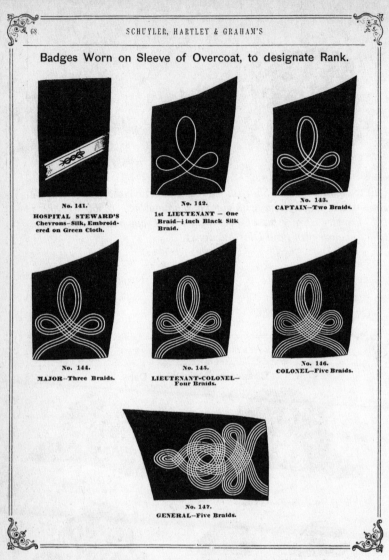

Badges Worn on Sleeve of Overcoat, to designate Rank.

No. 141.
HOSPITAL STEWARD'S
Chevrons–Silk, Embroid-
ered on Green Cloth.

No. 142.
1st LIEUTENANT — One
Braid–¼ inch Black Silk
Braid.

No. 143.
CAPTAIN–Two Braids.

No. 144.
MAJOR–Three Braids.

No. 145.
LIEUTENANT-COLONEL–
Four Braids.

No. 146.
COLONEL–Five Braids.

No. 147.
GENERAL–Five Braids.

Schuyler, Hartley & Graham catalog page showing officers' sleeve insignia denoting rank in the U.S. Army: (top row) *hospital steward, 1st lieutenant, captain;* (center) *major, lieutenant colonel, colonel;* (bottom) *general.*

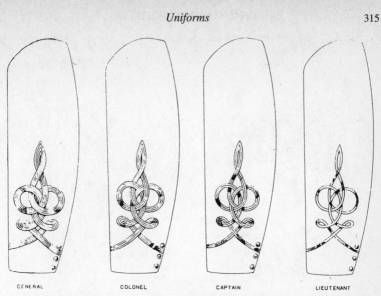

Officers' sleeve insignia denoting rank in Confederate Army and Marines:
(left to right) *general, colonel, captain, lieutenant.*

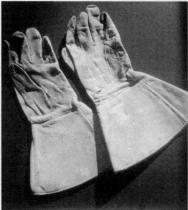

Left: *Enlisted man's frock coat from the New Hampshire Volunteers, worn by Luke Knowlton of Dublin, NH (killed at Manassas), $2,000–$2,200.*
Right: *Tan leather gauntlets worn by a New Hampshire Volunteers officer, $500–$600.*

Left: *Military bandsman's carpetbag, ca. 1860s, belonged to T.K. Jones Band, 11th Mane Infantry, $450–$500. (Photo courtesy of Rex Stark Auctions)* Right: *Pair of artillery officer's epaulets, with eagle-head inset spurs, signed "Sheldon," in original tin regalia box, $1,200–$1,300. (Photo courtesy of Paul Dias Auctions)*

WEAPONS

All numbers in parentheses that follow titles refer to listings in: William A. Bond and William Albaugh, *A Photographic Supplement of Confederate Swords,* 1963.

EDGED WEAPONS

Bayonets

Boyle, Gamble & MacFee Bowie Bayonet. (333) Fine brass unit hilt with firm name inscribed in reverse guard. Stamped "12." Unfullered blade is 13³/₄". Has minor pitting, nicks. Ex-Flayerman Collection. REF: *The American Bayonet*, Albert Hardin, 1962, illustrated. Correspondence incl. (A) '94, $11,000. . *$11,000–13,000*

Boyle, Gamble & MacFee Saber Bayonet and Scabbard. (389) Brass eagle head hilt stamped "55." 21" fullered blade. Muzzle ring bent; spring and button missing. Minus extreme tip on blade. Brass-mounted scabbard has missing tip. (A) '94, $1250. . . . . *$1300–1400*

Cook & Brother Bayonet and Scabbard. (335) Brass hilt stamped "20" on cross guard with triangular mortise. 22" fullered blade. Tin mounted scabbard with frog stud and tip missing. REF: Albaugh, *Supplement to Confederate Swords*, p. 60. Ex-Albaugh Collection. (A) '94, $1500. . . . . *$1600–1700*

Fayetteville Saber Bayonet and Scabbard. (420) Std. brass hilt; 21" fullered blade. Heavily pitted, muzzle ring battered and release button off, but spring is intact. M 1855 brass-mounted scabbard. (A) '94, $1100. . . . . *$1200–1300*

Georgia Armory Saber Bayonet and Scabbard with Frog. (401) 21¹/₂" fullered blade with obverse marked "Ga. Armory 1862." Iron hilt; checkered wood grips, one side cracked. Iron-mounted leather scabbard marked "77" above throat and "4901" on reverse. Tarred leather frog. REF. Albaugh, p. 205. Ex-Albaugh Collection. (A) $5250. . . . . *$5500–6000*

Cutlesses

Brass Hilted C.S.N. Cutless. (339) Cast-brass grip with C.S.N. on obverse pommel. Reverse marked with fouled anchor. 21" double-edged unfullered blade. Number of flaws. (A) '94, $1500. . . . . *$1600–1700*

Cook & Brother Naval Cutless and Scabbard. (334) Cast-brass grip; firm name

stamped on interior guard, 20½" unfullered blade. Minor dings. Brass-mounted leather scabbard; badly flaked and weak. REF: Albaugh, p. 60. (A) '94, $3300.....
.... *$3500–3600*

English Mole Naval C.S.N. Cutless with Scabbard. (337) Brass two-branch guard and leather grips, 19½" double-edged fullered blade stamped "Courtney and Tennent, Charleston, SC" on reverse ricasso. Brass-mounted leather scabbard with minor flaking. (A) '94, $2000................................. *$2000–2100*

English Mole Naval C.S.N. Cutless with Scabbard. (336) Same as above, but brass lacquered, blade cleaned. Scabbard has flaking. (A) '94, $2500........ *$2400–2500*

English P 58 Naval C.S.A. Cutless Bayonet with Scabbard. (341) Steel cup hilt with leather grips. Slightly bent muzzle ring. Knights head proof on German blade. Black leather scabbard; steel mounts with blockage at tip. (A) '94, $300. . . *$300–400*

Union Car Works Cutless. (393) Turned wood grip. Iron "S"-shaped cross guard. 18" wasp-waisted double-edged blade. Some nicks. (A) '94, $800...... *$700–800*

Unmarked Brass Hilted C.S.A. Cutless. (392) Hilt and guard with dark patina; hilt cast to accept D guard; 21" double-edged unfullered blade. Very dark. REF: Albaugh, p. 105. Ex-Albaugh Collection. (A) '94, $900.............. *$900–1000*

Knives and Spear Points

"Arkansas Toothpick" C.S.A. Bowie Knife. Stag handled. (A) Jim Julia, March '94, $950... *$900–1100*

Booth, Sheffield Hollow Silver-Handled Dirk. (358) To "Col. T.N. Waul, May 17, 1852" etched on blade. Ornate silver grip. 7¼" double-edged blade marked "H.C. Booth, Silver Steel, Sheffield" on obverse ricasso. Some pitting. Ex-Slaston Collection with correspondence. Amon Carter Museum Frontier Guns Exhibit, 1963. (A) '94, $2400.. *$2000–2400*

Bowie Knife with Scabbard. (450) Solid...................... *$1100–1200*

D-Guard Bowie Knife with Iron Guard. (374) Wrought-iron guard with ears on both side of wood grip. High curved quillon, 13½" flat unfullered blade; pitted with tip missing. (A) '94, $1000.................................... *$900–1000*

D-Guard Bowie with Sheath. Bone handle. (A) Julia, March '94, $1750........
.... *$1700–$1800*

D-Guard Bowie Knife with Sheet Zinc Scabbard. (352) Wood grip with "BEO" carved reverse. Two-branch guard; 15½" bowie blade with 7" false edge; 2¼" w. at hilt. Scabbard scratched with "BEO" approx. 2" below throat. "Captured by Liet. J.H. Clinton 9th. Regt. CV at Pass, Cristian Miss., April 4th., 1862" neatly inscribed. Zinc scabbard is riveted to leather interior; belt loop on reverse. Throat beginning to separate. Flayderman tag gives Medicus Collection provenance. Incl. file of Clinton's 9th Connecticut data. (A) '94, $24,000............. *$25,000–26,000*

D-Guard Knife with Leather Sheath and Frog. (354) Wood handle; lightweight. D-guard with pronounced curved quillon; 15" spear-point blade. Leather sheath with lead rivets and two-strap frog (weak in spots). REF: Albaugh, p. 128. Ex-Albaugh Collection. (A) $2200................................. *$2000–2200*

D-Guard Spear-Point C.S.A. Side Knife. (369) Wood grip. Narrow delicate D-guard with quillon; 13½" spear-point blades made from file. Label on obverse states "Picked up on Battlefield of Baton Rouge." (A) '94, $2600..... *$2600–2700*

D-Guard Spear-Point Side Knife. (375) Wood grip. Wider D-guard than above, with quillon; 15" spear-point blade from file; 2¼" w. Number of nicks and gouges. (A) '94, $1100... *$900–1000*

C. Heinz Spear-Point Side Knife with Sheath. (364) Rosewood grip. German silver guard (separating on one side); 8" spear-point blade. Leather-covered sheath. REF: Albaugh, p. 98. Ex-Jackson Collection. (A) '94, $6000 . . . . *$6000–6500*

Kentucky Side Knife with Tin-Mounted Leather Sheath. (367) Wood grip and diamond-shaped cross guard, fine. 11³/₄" spear-point blade, from file. Leather sheath with tin throat, toe, with multiple pin punches. Ex-Jackson Collection. (A) '94, $3400. . . . . *$3300–3400*

Knife Made from Confederate States Armory Cavalry Saber. (355) Brass pommel and guard marked XXIII; 60% leather; wire wrap; 9³/₄" blade altered to bowie configuration. (A) '94, $950. . . . . *$800–900*

W.J. McElroy Knife. (361) Firm name and "Macon Ga." marked on ricasso. Good condition brass pommel cap, with slightly bent brass guard. Spiral incised wood grip with open age crack; 11³/₄" double-edged spear-point blade. REF: Albaugh. Ex-Shemerluk, Jackson Colonials. (A) '94, $12,500. . . . . *$13,000–13,500*

Rodgers Sheffield Ivory-Handled Bowie with Sheath. (362) Ivory plaque. Obverse with incised vine decor; reverse: "CS" and eagle, "Co. K 41st Virginia." 14¹/₂" blade marked "Joseph Rodgers & Sons, Cutlers to their Majesties." Sheath masked with electrical tape. German silver-mounted sheath. Ex-Jackson Collection. Incl. correspondence, questionable. (A) '94, $1700. . . . . *$1500–1600*

Side Knife and Leather Sheath from Shiloh Battleground Relic. (370) Wood pistol grip with scalloped iron cross guard; 12¹/₂" bowie blade fashioned from file. Leather sheath with belt loop on reverse. Flaking at tip. Old label reads "Picked up on the field at Shiloh, Apr. 8th., 1862." (A) '94, $1700. . . . . *$1800–2000*

Side Knife with Antler Grip and Star-Embossed Tin-Mounted Leather Sheath. (366) Attrib. to Thomas Dallas. Antler grip with minor age crack. Iron cross guard; 9¹/₄" bowie blade. Leather scabbard has tin throat embossed with five-pointed star. Tin toe and tin connecting rails. Minus belt loop. Ex-Shemerluk, Jackson Colonials. (A) '94, $11,000. . . . . *$10,000–11,000*

Side Knife with Tin-Mounted Leather Sheath. (394) Nut holds wood grip to tang; iron cross guard is diamond-shaped; 13" spear-point blade. Missing tip on leather scabbard's tin throat. REF: Albaugh, p. 175. Ex-Albaugh Collection. (A) '94, $2400. . . . *$2000–2200*

Spear-Point Knife with Sheath. (359) Four-sided wood grip. (New, June 28, 1862) Carved. Brass-mounted grip with pewter ferrule; 5" spear-point blade. Tin-mounted leather sheath. All very good. (A) '94, $900. . . . . *$900–1000*

Spear-Point Side Knife with Tin Sheath. (410) Attrib. to Green County, VA. Octagonal wood grip. Iron pommel cap and S-shaped guard; 13¹/₂" spear-point blade. Several minor nicks. Belt loop on tin sheath is creased, dented. REF: Albaugh (affirms knife was made in Wolftown, Green County, VA, and possibly issued to Green County Rough & Readies). (A) '94, $3600. . . . . *$3500–3600*

Pikes

Bridal Pike. (395) With 13" spear point; 4" hook; 80" staff, 90% red paint on staff. Sticker identifies as being from Albaugh Collection. (A) '94, $800. . . . . . *$750–800*

Clover Leaf Pike. 10" spear point; 6¹/₂" guard, 72" staff, 90% red paint. (A) '94, $850. . . . . *$850–900*

Georgia Pike. (452) 12" spear point, 11 stars over "CSA." Iron ferrule and 80" staff. Spear point bent. (A) '94, $2600. . . . . *$2500–2600*

Georgia Pike with Full Shaft. Lacking C.S.A. decoration as above. Iron band; cataloged as excellent. (A) Oct. '94, $700. . . . . *$800–900*

Retractable Pike. (453) With 15" spear point. Closed 72", black paint (most on iron furniture). (A) '94, $800. . . . . *$800–850*

Winan Pike Blade and Part of Staff. (388) Iron 14½" spear-point blade. Some pitting, missing extreme point, iron ferrule. 6" wooden staff. (Souvenir of the Baltimore Riots on April 19 in 1861 when Pennsylvania and Massachusetts militia were attacked by secessionists.) REF: Albaugh, p. 192. (A) '94, $600. . . . . *$600–700*

Swords and Sabers

All scabbards are assumed correctly matched with edged weapons unless indicated. In most cases, condition ratings are provided for those items appearing at auction. Edged weapons appear alphabetically by manufacturer or generic title.

SABERS

Officer's Light Cavalry Saber (Union) Model 1840. Mfgr. N.P. Ames, Cabotville. Many pre–Civil War weapons found their way into wartime service. (A) Oct. '94, $175. . . . . *$250–300*

College Hill Arsenal C.S.A. Cavalry Saber with Scabbard. (327) Brass hilt with case "CSA"; 80% leather. Iron back strap, capstan rivet. Blade and brass-mounted scabbard with Flayderman tag giving "Medicus Collection" provenance. (A) '94, $6000. . . . . *$5000–6000*

Confederate States Armory C.S.A. Cavalry Saber with Scabbard. (332) "X" and "VIII" on face of guard on brass hilt. 20% left of leather wrap. Federal replacement scabbard. (A) '94, $1400. . . . . *$900–1000*

Conning C.S.A. Cavalry Saber with Scabbard. (379) Brass hilt numbered 18 and 49. Pommel cap, numbered 18. Rewrapped; guard's outer branch repaired. Blade stamped "James Conning, Mobile" on reverse. All-iron scabbard has drag missing. (A) '94, $3000. . . . . *$2500–3000*

English P.53 Enfield C.S.A. Cavalry Saber with Scabbard (319) Iron hilt; leather grips, 34½" blade stamped "Isaac & Co." on reverse. All-metal scabbard with minor dents and extensive coat of rust. (A) '84, $800. . . . . *$700–800*

English P.53 Enfield C.S.A. Cavalry Saber. (318) Iron hilt; leather grips; 35½" blade stamped "Mole" on reverse. All-metal scabbard. A little rough. (A) '94, $800. . . . . *$700–800*

Glaze/Palmetto Armory Model 1840 C.S.A. Cavalry Saber with Scabbard. (322) Briss hilt with all leather, wire. Blade stamped "Columbia, S.C." on reverse ricasso. All-metal scabbard. (A) '94, $2750. . . . . *$2500–3000*

Thomas Griswold & Co. C.S.A. Artillery Sabre with Scabbard. (396) Brass hilt; 75% leather; wire missing; blade missing tip. Stamped "New Orleans." Ex-Albaugh Collection. (A) '94, $3500. . . . . *$4000–5000*

Thomas Griswold & Co. C.S.A. Cavalry Sabre. (329) Blade stamped "T.G. & Co.: N.O." on reverse. All-leather brass hilt. Wire wrap with leather sword knot, All brass scabbard. (A) $8000. . . . . *$7500–8000*

Thomas Leech, C.S.A. Saber, Memphis Novelty Works. (324) Brass hilt with firm stamped in. 20% leather wrap; full-length blade dark. Brass-mounted metal scabbard, minus drag, throat. (A) '94, $2750. *$3000–3500*

Model 1840 Union Artillery Saber with Scabbard. Ames Mfgr. Co., Chicopee, MA. Marked "U.S. 1864" with inspector's initials. (A) Oct. '94, $475. . . . . *$500–600*

Model 1840 Union Cavalry Saber with Scabbard. Engraved "The Sword of Henry Ware Hall. 1st. Lt. and Adjt. 51st. Illinois Vols., returned by C.S.A. officers in recognition of his gallantry." (413) Hall fell leading the charge at Kennesaw Mountain, GA, June 27, 1864. Some old lacquer/varnish. (A) $4750........ *$4500–5000*

Model 1860 C.S.A. Cavalry Saber with Scabbard. (351) Dated 1862. Providence Tool Co. Flayderman tag gives Medicus Collection provenance. Very good, with dirty scabbard. (A) '94, $700. .... *$700–800*

Nashville Plow Works C.S.A. Saber. (326) Brass hilt with Nashville name and C.S.A. cast in guard. Rewrapped. Correct brass-mounted scabbard. Shallow dent at throat. (A) '94, $5600. .... *$5500–6000*

Sharp & Hamilton C.S.A. Cavalry Saber. (325). Brass hilt, iron back strap. All leather and wire wrap; blade stamped with above name on obverse ricasso. "Nashville, Tenn." on reverse ricasso. Brass-mounted metal scabbard. (A) '94, $10,500. .... *$11,000–12,000*

Unmarked C.S.A. Artillery Saber with Scabbard. (409) Brass hilt. 95% leather wrap. Iron wire. 30½" curved blade. Metal scabbard with heavy brass ring mounts. REF: Albaugh, p. 98. Ex-Albaugh Collection. (A) '94, $6250. .... *$6000–6500*

Unmarked C.S.A. Cavalry Saber with Scabbard. (321) Brass hilt. 100% canvas wrap. Iron wire, unfullered blade; brass-mounted metal scabbard. REF: Albaugh, p. 193. Ex-Albaugh Collection. (A) '94, $3750. .... *$3500–3700*

Unmarked C.S.A. Cavalry Saber with Scabbard/Sword Knot. (323) Brass hilt; 60% leather wrap; iron wire. Knuckle bow scratched. "Capt. John A. Steele, 11 Alabama." Scabbard with brass mounts; traces of red lacquer. Rings possibly replaced. (A) '94, $5600.. *$5000–6000*

U.S. Model 1860 C.S.A. Light Cavalry Saber. Brass French-style hilt with leather-wrapped grip. Curved 34½" single-edged blade marked "U.S./1864/A.G.M.; C. Roby/W. Chelmsford, Mass." Iron scabbard with 2-ring suspension. . . *$250–300*

Virginia Manufactury C.S.A. Artillery Saber. (408) Iron hilt; 90% leather wrap, wire, 35" curved blade. "4 Va. Regt." on reverse. REF. Albaugh, p. 172. (A) '94, $1750... *$1400–1500*

Virginia Manufactury C.S.A. Saber with Scabbard, 2nd Model. (328) Iron hilt. 90% leather wrap and wire. 35" curved blade stamped "3 Va. Regt" on reverse. Iron scabbard with tear drop stud; 40% black japanning. (A) '94, $3700. . . *$3000–3500*

Wooley & Deaton Sword Cutlers Rooster Head Saber with Scabbard. (330) Firm name marked on hilt with "Birmingham." Finely sculpted rooster devouring alligator that serves as guard and quillon. Blade has "Texas" followed by star etched on obverse and is possibly not orig. to hilt. Hilt retains 25% gilt. Scabbard in two pieces with missing leather. Ex-Goddard, Albaugh, Jackson Collections. Incl. correspondence. (A) '94, $1600. .... *$1400–1500*

SWORDS

Boyle & Gamble C.S.A. Staff and Field Officer's Sword. (295) Guard stamped 17". 70% leather on grip; 29" etched blade; small CSA on reverse, 3" from hilt. Flayderman tag with Medicus Collection i.d. (A) '94, $4000. .... *$4000–4500*

Boyle & Gamble C.S.A. Foot Officer's Sword. (312) 29" etched blade. Block CSA on reverse; flag and foliate pattern on obverse. Brass-mounted leather scabbard; minor flaking. (A) '94, $5250. .... *$4500–5000*

Boyle & Gamble C.S.A. Foot Officer's Sword with Scabbard. (297) 30" etched blade with block C.S.A. and mfg. name on reverse. Scabbard has considerable flaking. (A) '94, $4000. .... *$3800–4000*

Terminology of the Sword and Scabbard

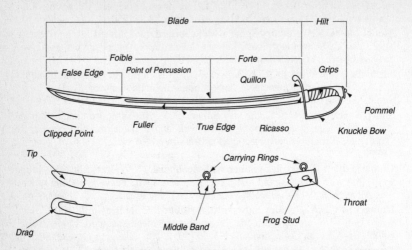

Boyle & Gamble C.S.A. Foot Officer's Sword with Scabbard. (403) 28" etched blade. Flag and foliate decoration on obverse. Cross cannon and foliate on reverse. Last 4" of blade replaced. Scabbard is Federal replacement. (A) '94, $1550.......
.... *$2000–3000*

Boyle, Gamble & Macfee C.S.A. Foot Officer's Sword. (415) "CSA" in old English script behind quillion on guard. Rewrapped; 31" light plain blade; dark, pitted. Good brass. (A) '94, $1200.................................... *$1200–1300*

Boyle, Gamble & Macfee C.S.A. Foot Officer's Sword. (303) 29½" heavy plain blade; dark, all wire and wrap. (A) '94, $900...................... *$900–1000*

Boyle & Gamble C.S.A. Presentation Officer's Sword with Scabbard. (298) "Etched by W.T. Edge, Richmond" with intricate foliate pattern and "CSA" on shield. Vine entwined "Presented to Capt. J.S. Michard by Co. E., Aug. 1863." 15% gilt on metal surfaces. (A) '94, $24,000. .... *$20,000–22,000*

College Hill Arsenal C.S.A. Foot Officer's Sword with Scabbard. (305) Full hilt. Rewrapped; 30" etched blade with shield and foliate design on obverse; flag, U.S.A. foliate on reverse. Scabbard missing toe. (A) '94, $5000...... *$4500–5000*

College Hill Arsenal C.S.A. Foot Officer's Sword with Scabbard. (404) Plain guard variant. Rough cast hilt; 31" etched blade. Obverse: Crossed cannon; trophies and foliate pattern. Reverse: CSA and trophies. Federal Model 1950 Staff and Field mounted steel scabbard. REF: Albaugh, pp. 36, 37 (illus.). (A) '94, $6000. ....
.... *$5000–6000*

College Hill Arsenal C.S.A. Foot Officer's Sword. (411) Floral guard variant. Rewrapped 28½" etched blade. Weak, obscured by pitting. REF: Albaugh, p. 35 (illus.). (A) '94, $1500. .... *$1500–1600*

Confederate States Armory C.S.A. Foot Officer's Sword with Scabbard. (306) "CSA" in guard. LIII matching. Rewrapped; 31¼" plain blade, missing extreme tip. Repair to scabbard between ring mounts. (A) '94, $4600. .... *$500–550*

Confederate States Armory C.S.A. Foot Officer's Sword with Scabbard. (419) 29½" plain blade, pitted; good hilt and wrap. Incorrect foreign scabbard. (A) '94, $4750... *$5000–5500*

Conning C.S.A. Staff and Field Officer's Sword, No. 187. (308) Tang peened to tighten blade. Orig. wrap; replaced wire; 33¹/₂" plain blade. (A) '94, $4750. . . . . . .
. . . . *$5000–5500*

A.H. Dewitt C.S.A. Foot Officer's Sword with Scabbard. (616) Cast "CS" on pommel variant. Rewrapped; 31" plain blade. Brass-mounted leather scabbard with two leather repairs. REF: Albaugh, addendum p. 22 (illus.). (A) '94, $5000. . . . . . .
. . . . *$5000–5500*

Douglas C.S.A. Staff and Field Officer's Sword. (296) "CS" and star cast in guard. Plain pommel. Rewrapped. Unmarked 30" plain blade, dark. (A) '94, $3250.
. . . . *$3000–3500*

English Mole C.S.N. Regulation Sword. (618) 10% gilt on dolphin-head hilt. Wire and wrap intact; 30¹/₂" etched blade stamped "Courtney & Tennent, Charleston, S.C." on reverse ricasso. (A) '94, $5000. . . . . *$4500–5000*

C.S.A. Foot Artillery Short Sword. (391) French pattern. Brass hilt with ribbed lacquered grip; 19" double-edged unfullered blade. Numerous flaws. (A) '94, $500.
. . . . *$400–450*

C.S.A. Foot Artillery Short Sword with Scabbard. Maker unknown. (340) "CS" and star cast in hilt. Poorly cast hilt; 18¹/₂" double-edged fullered blade. Leather scabbard with missing throat, toe; several tears. (A) '94, $1250. . . . . . *$1100–1200*

C.S.A. Foot Artillery Sword. Maker unknown. (338) Cast hilt; good patina. "C" and "S" cast in either quillon; 18¹/₂" double-edged fullered blade (incorrect for this sword). Flayderman tag shows Medicus Collection provenance. (A) '94, $1100. . . .
. . . . *$1000–1100*

C.S.A. Foot Officer's Sword. Maker unknown. (302) Wide 30¹/₂" etched blade. Block "CS" letters separated by pelican feeding young, flanked by C.S. battle flag and Louisiana State flag. Reverse has trophies and foliate decoration; 60% leather wrap on grip. Wire good. (A) '94, $6500. . . . . *$6000–6500*

C.S.A. Foot Officer's Sword and Conning Scabbard, Unmarked. (576) 30¹/₂" plain blade, wire repl. Brass-mounted leather scabbard, top mount engraved "F.M. Jones" on obverse; "Made by James Conning, Mobile" on reverse. Numbered 226. Toe missing. (A) '94, $3500. . . . . *$2500–3000*

French Model 1822 C.S.A. Foot Officer's Sword. (416) By Devisme, Paris. 75% gilt on brass hilt. "CS" incised on pommel. Horn grip lacks wire; 30" etched blade with reverse "Conf. States of America, Aide Toi et Dieu L'Aidera. Presented to Col. John B. McEwen (44th Tenn. Vols.) from his friends in Franklin." Research records included. Ex-George Wray Collection. (A) '94, $3500. . . . . . . *$3500–4000*

French Model 1850 C.S.A. Foot Officer's Sword. Presented to "William Mahone Feb. 2nd 1864" engraved on guard. Brass hilt with ribbon holder. Horn lacks grip wire, 29¹/₂" plain blade. All-metal scabbard with general pitting. Incl. provenance from Gen. Mahone descendent. Ex-John Heflin Collection. (A) '94, $2500. . . . . . .
. . . . *$2000–2500*

Thomas Griswold & Co. C.S.A. Staff and Field Officer's Sword with Scabbard. Script "CS" cast in guard; 29¹/₂" plain blade, stamped with firm name on reverse ricasso. Good wrap, hilt. Incorrect scabbard minus mounts. (A) '94, $4500. . .
. . . . *$5000–5500*

Thomas Griswold & Co. C.S.A. Foot Officer's Sword with Scabbard. (304) 29" plain blade marked with firm name on reverse ricasso. Polished wood handle, wire intact. Scabbard replaced by regulation Federal model. (A) '94, $2750. . . . *$3000–3500*

L. Haiman C.S.A. Presentation Staff and Field Officer's Sword with Scabbard. (612) Hilt with traces of gilt. "CSA" in silver letters in counter guard; 30" etched blade. Obverse lower panel: "J.S. Napier Jr. Alabama, July 1861", "CSA" in middle panel; foliate in top panel "L. Haiman & Bro., mfg., Columbus, Ga." in center panel. Brass-mounted metal scabbard has poorly repaired drag. REF: Hartzler, *Confederate Presentation and Inscribed Swords and Revolvers,* pp. 212–13. (A) $15,000. . . . . *$15,000–16,000*

L. Haiman C.S.A. Presentation Staff and Field Officer's Sword with Scabbard. (309) Hilt has sizable traces of gilt. "CS" incised in counter guard; 30½" etched blade. Lower obverse panel. "Deo Viridice" within wreath. Firm name in center panel; foliate design in top panel. Soldier in frock coat in lower reverse panel. Center: "L.L. Gray" above "CSA." Stand of trophies on top panel. Brass-mounted metal scabbard with dented toe mount. REF: Hartzler, pp. 170–71. (A) '94, $21,000. . . . . . . *$18,000–20,000*

L. Haiman C.S.A. Foot Officer's Sword and Scabbard. (380) 30" plain blade marked "F.M. Thomson" on obverse; "L. Haiman & Bro." on reverse. Scattered pitting; wire missing from grip. Brass-mounted leather scabbard; toe and rings replaced. REF: Hartzler, pp. 239–40. (A) $6500. . . . . *$7000–8000*

E.J. Johnson C.S.A. Foot Artillery Short Sword with Scabbard. (387) Brass hilt with ribbed grip. Firm name with "Macon, Ga." stamped in guard's edge; 19" double-edged fullered wasp-waisted blade. Scabbard with belt loop. (A) '94, $3250. . . . . . *$3200–3300*

Kraft, Goldsmith & Kraft C.S.A. Sword with Scabbard. (406) Brass hilt with cast "CS" in guard. 80% leather; etched blade has "CS" on reverse, plus crossed cannons, stand of arms on obverse. 11" of blade replaced. English P.53 Enfield all-metal scabbard. (A) '94, $3500. . . . . *$4000–4500*

Leech & Rigdon C.S.A. Staff and Field Officer's Sword with Scabbard. (402) Rewrapped grip; 29½" plain blade. Top mount of Boyle & Gamble scabbard scratched "RLR, 44th Regt. N.C. Vols. (2nd Lt. Robert L. Rice, Company A, 44th N.C. Infantry)." Weak scabbard with five reinforcing repairs. REF: Albaugh, p. 124. (A) '94, $5250. . . . . *$5500–6000*

Leech & Rigdon C.S.A. Staff and Field Officer's Sword with Scabbard. (574) Rewrapped grip; 28½" etched bright blade. Obverse: blank presentation panel with foliate; reverse foliate design. Brass-mounted metal scabbard with traces of gilt. (A) '94, $13,000 . . . . *$12000–13,000*

Leech & Rigdon C.S.A. Staff and Field Officer's Sword with Scabbard. Attrib. to Col. Miles Dillard, 9th Texas Inf. Rgt. 29½" plain blade; light pitting. Wood grip without wrap on wire; brass cleaned. (Attached obit. of Dillard dated 1911.) (A) '94, $2000. . . . . *$2000–2500*

Leech & Rigdon C.S.A. Field Officer's Sword with Scabbard. (311) "CS" cast within foliate guard decoration. Blade tightened but wrap looks orig.; 31½" etched blade with "Leech & Rigdon" marking. Obverse ricasso: blank presentation panel; reverse: large "CS" in panel amid foliate decoration. (A) '94, $9000. . . . *$9000–10000*

1860 Light Cavalry Sword with Scabbard. Mfgr. by Henry Boker, Solingen. (A) Oct. '94, $325. . . . . *$350–400*

Maine 10th Company 12th Maine Volunteers Presentation Saber (Union). To "1st Lt. D.S. Harriman (of named Co.) Feb. 16, 1865." Ivory handle with carved bas relief of eagle and shield. "E. Pluribus Unum" on obverse. By Clauberg Solingen, Germany. Superb condition. (A) Manion Mail Auction, '94, $11,000. . . . . *$10,000–12,000*

W.J. McElroy C.S.A. Foot Officer's Sword with Scabbard. (314) Rewrapped 29½" etched blade. "W.J. McElroy, Macon, Geo." in panel; "CS" on obverse; foliate decoration on reverse. Boyle & Gamble brass-mounted leather scabbard. Tape wrapping between lower ring mount and tip. (A) '94, $5500. . . . . *$5000–6000*

NCO C.S.A. Sword with Scabbard. (418) "CSA" cast in turned-down guard. Knuckle bow with stamped "C"; unmarked 28" blade. Brass-mounted all-metal

scabbard. REF: Albaugh, p. 191. Ex-Rawls/Albaugh Collections. (A) '94, $1500...
.... *$1200–1400*

Captured C.S.A. Presentation Foot Officer's Sword with Scabbard. (405) 50% gilt on hilt, leather wrap and wire. Painted legend, "Captured Confederate Sword by Lt. Mark Tomilson, New Haven Regt." 30" etched blade. Foliate decoration on obverse; panel with "CS" and foliate on reverse. "E.R. Armistead" in Old Eng. script and crossed cannon. Brass-mounted scabbard with some repairs. Middle and mount toe don't match throat. REF: Albaugh, p. 186. (A) '94, $6000. . . . . *$5000–6000*

U.S. Medical Staff Officer's Sword (Union). 1860 pattern. Gilt bronze hilt with American eagle on grip. Shield-shaped langet marked "M.S." in silver. Straight 20" double-edged blade; etched American eagle and "Medical Staff." Marked "Ames/Mfg. Co., Chicopee/Mass." Gilt metal scabbard with three-ring suspension and belt hooks..
.... *$300–400*

Non-Military Swords

Knights Templar Sword. Presentation sword to Gen. George C. Meade. Ca. 1860s. Extensive symbolism on figural guard and scabbard. Bone grip. Gilt-edged blade with knight, jousting scene, vines, and large etched ribbon cartouche with inscription. Made by Horstmann. Stark FP Cat., July '94, $1500. . . . . . . *$1350–1500*

K.K.K. Sword. Mounted Klansman with burning cross. Date unknown. Image embossed on small cross-guard shield; reverse has "KKK." Knight's head with plume at end of hilt, 32" Presentation sword. *$200–225*

Short Sword, Political. (W.H.) "Harrison and Reform." Ca. 1840s. Pre–Civil War, but only true political sword known; 13¹/₈" overall. Bone grip, silver guard pommel and scabbard. Stark FP Cat., July '94, $1850. *$1700–1800*

REVOLVERS AND RIFLES

Confederate Handguns

This section covers Civil War–era handguns of Southern manufacture and military use only. REF: C.C. Holloway, *Texas Gun Lore;* Albaugh, Benet and Simmons, *Confederate Hand Guns;* Gary, *Confederate Revolvers; Texas Gun Collector Magazine;* Hartzler, *Confederate Presentation and Inscribed Swords and Revolvers.*

Augusta Machine Works Revolver. Six-stop cylinder. (605) All metal smooth and untouched, 10% blue on barrel. REF: *Confederate Guns*, Albaugh, Benet, and Simmons, p. 8. Pictured in *Confederate Revolvers*, Gary, pp. 46–49. (A) '94, $25,000 .
.... *$24,000–25,000*

Cofer Revolver. 1861. 36-cal. percussion. Six-shot cylinder; 7¹/₈" octagonal barrel marked "T.W. Cofer's Patent, Portsmouth, VA." Brass frame and square trigger guard. Colt-type loading lever.. . . . . *$22,000–24,000*

Cofer Percussion Model Revolver. (48) Same model as above. REF: Albaugh, p. 148. Ex-Harry H. Brooks Collection. Sold at William H. Bond Collection Sale at Conestoga Auction, Manheim, PA, for record price of $75,000, as did the Columbus Revolver following; the Dance Revolver, also listed following, reached $32,500.

Columbus Revolver. (66) 36-cal. percussion. Six-shot cylinder, 7¹/₂" round barrel with "Columbus Fire Arms Manuf., Col. Georgia" markings. Front sight. Octago-

nal breech. Brass trigger guard; handle strap. REF: Albaugh, p. 11; Gary, p. 51. . . .
. . . . *$12,000–14,000*

Dance Navy Revolver. 1863–64. By Dance Brothers—David, James, and George—Galveston, TX. 44-cal. percussion. Six-shot cylinder, 7³/₈" half octagonal barrel. Iron frame. *$5500–5700*

Dance Revolver. 1863–64. By Dance Bros. 44 cal. percussion. Six-shot cylinder, 8" round or octagonal barrel. Iron frame. Brass backstrap, trigger guard, and blade front sight. *$6000–6200*

Fayetteville Model 1855 Pistol, Carbine. (279) 1861–63. Mfgr. by Fayetteville, NC Armory. 58-cal. single-shot, 12" barrel. Shoulder stock is detachable. "Fayetteville" with winged eagle over "C.S.A." marked on lockplate. *$3300–3500*

Griswold & Grier Revolver. A.k.a. "Brass-frame Confederate Colt." 1862–64. Griswald & Gunnison, Griswoldville, GA. 36-cal. percussion. Six-shot cylinder, 7¹/₂" round barrel. (Later models featured octagonal breech.) Brass frame. Squared trigger guard. *$4200–4500*

Griswold & Grier Revolver, 1st Model. (62) Description similar to above. Rated as very good, with a few trigger guard screws replaced. (A) '94, $7000 . . . *$7000–8000*

Griswold & Grier Revolver, 2nd Model. (49) Condition good, with minor grip chip; loading lever and replaced wedged screws. REF: Albaugh, p. 36. (A) '94, $9000. . . . . *$9000–10,000*

Griswold & Gunnison Army Model. Contemporary. Navy Arms, Ridgefield, NJ, *reproduction*, "Reb Model" (see "Yank" counterpart under Union listing). 36 and 44 cals., 7¹/₄" round barrel; 13" overall. Brass frame, trigger guard, and backstrap. Original G&G model was made from 1862–64. . . . . *$100–125*

LeMat Army Model Revolver. Contemporary. Navy Arms, Ridgefield, NJ, *reproduction* model of 44-cal. nine-shot LeMat issue, ptd. in 1856. 65-cal. single-shot lower barrel converts it to a ten-shot double-barreled firearm. Wt. 3 lb., 7 oz. Checkered pistol grip. Popular model with C.S.A. officers. *$425–450*

Leech & Rigdon Revolver. 1862–63. By C.H. Rigdon & Thomas Leech, Greensboro, GA. (63) 36-cal. percussion. Six-shot cylinder, 7¹/₂" barrel marked "Leech & Rigdon." Brass front sight, trigger guard, and handle strap. Rated very good. REF: Albaugh, p. 53. (A) '94, $16,000. . . . . *$12,000–15,000*

Richmond Pistol. Ca. 1861. Richmond Armory. 54-cal. single shot, 10" round barrel. Swivel ramrod. Butt plate and band in brass. "C.S. Richmond, Va." marked on lockplate. *$3200–3400*

Rigdon & Ainsley Revolver. 1864–65. 36-cal. percussion. Six-shot cylinder, 7¹/₂" round barrel marked "Augusta, GA. C.S.A." plus serial no., 12 cylinder stops; brass trigger guard, handle strap, and front sight. Trigger guard rounded but slightly squared, similar to Rigdon & Leech model above. *$4300–4500*

Rigdon Ansley & Co. Revolver. Same as above with backstrap scratched "Co. A. Capt. Thos. Griffith, 1st Md. Cav." and 80% old refinish. REF: Hartzer, pp. 171–72; also Albaugh, p. 54. (A) '94, $13,500. . . . . *$12,000–13,000*

Schneider & Glassick Revolver. Ca. 1863 (54) Mfgr. by William Schneider and Frederick Glassick. 36-cal. percussion. Six-shot cylinder, 7¹/₂" barrel stamped with firm name and "Memphis, Tenn." Front sight, trigger guard, and backstrap are all brass. *$4600–5000*

Schneider & Glassick Revolver. Same as above but with barrel stamped "C.S.A." Cylinder has safety slots between nipples, as opposed to safety pins. This model is totally *unlike* the three known accepted brass frame models of S.&G. Ex-Herman Stumpf, Harry Brooks, Jackson Collections. REF: Albaugh, pp. 25, 187. (A) '94, $5500. . . . . *$5000–6000*

Sherrard & Taylor Dragoon Revolver with Holster. 1862–63. (610) 44 cal. with 5¹/₂" barrel. Firm name inscribéd on barrel lug. Cylinder not orig.; possibly from a Colt Dragoon. Replaced wedge; rear sight missing. Otherwise rated excellent. Pictured in *Texas Gun Lore* by C.C. Holloway, p. 22. . . . .

Sherrard & Taylor Revolver. 1862–63. Mfgr. by Jos. Sherrard & Pleasant Taylor, Lancaster, TX. 44-cal. percussion. Six-shot cylinder, 7¹/₂" octagonal barrel. Almost identical to the Colt model. *$11,000–12,000*

Spiller & Burr Revolver. 1862–64. Mfgr. by Edw. Spiller of Baltimore, MD, and David Burr of Richmond, VA, both in Atlanta and the C.S. Armory at Macon, GA. 36-cal percussion. Six-shot cylinder, 7¹/₂" octagonal barrel stamped with firm name; later models "C.S." only. Brass frame. This model based on Colt Navy design, but Spiller & Burr failed to meet contract demands because of shortage of steel in production. An example in good condition brought $12,000 at William Bond Collection Sale, Conestoga Auctions, Manheim, PA, in July '94. . . . . *$4600–5000*

Sutherland Pistol. Ca. 1862. Mfgr. by Samuel Sutherland, Richmond, VA. 60-cal. percussion, 6¹/₂" octagonal barrel. Firm name inscribed on lockplate. . *$1200–1400*

George H. Todd Navy Revolver. (613) 36 cal. Marked "George H. Todd, Austin" on top of barrel lug and on right of frame. REF: Albaugh, p. 197. Ex-Holloway, Lingnau Collections. (A) '94, $6000. . . . . *$6000–7000*

Tranter Double Trigger Revolver. English. (68) 44 cal. "Tranter's Patent Hyde & Goodrich Agents for the United States South" engraved on top of frame. Traces of blue; checkered grips. Good and complete. (A) '94, $4000. . . . . *$3500–4000*

Tranter Double Trigger Revolver. English (566) 44 cal. "Co. E., 45th ALA INF" on left side barrel; "A.J. Bethune" on right grip (questionable). Pictured in Hartzler, pp. 137–38. (A) '94, $1000. . . . . *$950–1100*

H. Trotter Deringer. (52) 1860–61. Made by H. Trotter of Cameron, TX, for Capt. Chas. Buckholts, Co. E, 4th Regiment, Texas Mounted Volunteers. One of a pair. 36-cal. 8" overall, with 4¹/₄" part octagon, part round barrel. Two silver bands at breech. Silver-mounted with back action lock, marked with firm name. Very good, 90% finish. Ex-Harry Brooks Collection. $5000. . . . . *$5000–6000*

L.E. Tucker, Navy Revolver. 1864. (53) 36 cal. "Wailtherford, Lt. Com. Co. 1 Lt. CSA G 173" lightly inscribed on cylinder. "L.E. Tucker" within rectangle, clearly etched at top of barrel. Rated exceptional. Incl. photo of Lt. Tucker; also brass mold orig. purchased with model. Cancelled check to Tucker from Republic Natl. Bank, Dallas. Also notorized letter transferring ownership to Harry N. Brooks. Pictured in Albaugh, p. 203; shown at Amon Carter Frontier Guns. Exhib. in Jan. '64, $45,000. . . . . *$30,000–40,000*

Webley Wedge Frame Revolver with Holster. Ca. 1862. English. (72) About 44 cal. Attrib: Col. John Spring Smith, who served on Gen. Edmund Pettus' staff, C.S.A. Good leather holster; dark patina; light pitting on gun metal. (A) '94, $2600. . . . . *$2500–3000*

U.S. Military (Union) Handguns

Adams Army Revolver. Ptd. 1854 in England by Robt. Adams (probably London Armoury Co.) .44 cal., five-shot. Sliding safety. Solid frame. Small quantity found their way in service by Union militia. *$2200–2400*

Allen & Wheelock Army Revolver. Ptd. 1857, 44 cal. Six-shot cylinder, 7¹/₂" part octagonal barrel; 13¹/₄" overall. Wt. 2 lbs. Brass front sight. V-notch at center hammer functions as rear sight. *$2300–2500*

Allen & Wheelock Navy Revolver. Ptd. 1857. 36-cal., 8" octagonal barrel; 13½" overall. Wt. 2 lbs. Cylinder engraved with animal vignette. German silver blade front sight; V-notch near sight grooved in frame. Side hammer and rear guard are casehardened. *$1100–1200*

Beals Patent Revolver. Ptd. 1858 by Fordyce Beals, an E. Remington & Sons inventor. Remington was the mfgr. of 44-cal. single action. Six-shot cylinder, 8" octagonal barrel; 13¾" overall. Wt. 2 lbs., 14 oz. Brass front sight; grooved in frame rear sight. Union Navy purchased this model plus a 36-cal. version from Remington. *$2500–2700*

Butterfield Percussion Army Revolver. (13) 41 cal., 13¾" overall. Inspector's cartouche on right grip. Brass frame, backstrap with good patina. Grayed cylinder, hammer, barrel. Both grips replaced. (A) '94, $3500 . . . . *$3000–4000*

Butterfield U.S. Army Revolver. Ptd. 1855 by Jesse Butterfield, Philadelphia. Rated as 36 cal. Five-shot chamber, 7" barrel; 14" overall. A limited number of this model was used early on in the war, but Union later cancelled contract. *$3500–3600*

Colt Holster Model No. 5 Paterson Revolver with Belt, Holster. 1862–64. (287) Incl. service record of owner, Capt. William M. Lowe, a Texas Ranger in Mexican War and C.S.A. Capt. of Company E., 11th Missouri Infantry Regt. 7½" barrel with rear sight added 1" from breech. "Patent Arms Mg." on breech. Orig. leather belt with brass D-shaped buckle; iron tongue and leather holster. Incl. extensive service records, plus letters and bill of sale from descendant confirming selling revolver to L.C. Jackson. Orig. with exception of sights. (A) '94, $70,000. . *Value Indeterminate*

Colt "M" 1851 Navy Percussion Rifle. 36 cal.; frame marked "Colts Patent/U.S." Butt strap marked "U.S.N." (274) "A" carved on right side of grip. Has scratch at bottom; chamber probably blown; minor pitting; dark patina. (A) '94, $1400. . . . . *$1100–1300*

Colt "M" 1860 Army Revolver. (14) 44 cal. Missing dove tail for rear sight cut an inch ahead of cylinder. Refinished grips; minor cylinder pitting. (A) '94, $850. . . . . *$800–900*

Colt Second Model Dragoon Revolver. (506) An excavated relic. Frozen solid with 60% grips remaining. "May Victory Crown Our Banner" on backstrap; butt engr. "R.D. Beck." (Beck served as Sgt. with Co. D, 1st Cherokee Mounted Volunteers; later, 2nd Lt. Co. F, 2nd Cherokee Mounted Vols.). Relic was found near Stilwater, OK. Incl. provenance by William Albaugh and Jackson Arms. (A) '94, $5700. . . . . *$5500–6000*

Colt Third Model Dragoon Percussion Revolver with Attachable Shoulder Stock. Ca. 1860. (45) 44 cal., 7½" barrel marked "Address Saml. Colt, New York"; frame inscribed "Colt's Patent/U.S." stock has WAT inspector's cartouche on reverse of yoke. Dark patina on all metal parts. Barrel lug and cylinder have taken beating, but are smoothed out and browned. Stock has been sanded. (A) '94, $11,500. . . . . *$11,000–12,000*

Colt Single Action Army Revolver. (291) 45 cal., 7½" barrel; two-line ptd. dates on frame marked "U.S." Considerable blue on metal; grips have 60% varnish; lack inspector's cartouche. Pictured in *Firearms in the Custer Battle,* Parsons and DuMont, p. 15. Ex-John S. Dumont Collection. (A) '94, $9250. . . . . . . *$9500–10,250*

Freeman Percussion Army Revolver. (15) 44 cal.; 12½" overall. 40% blue on frame; cylinder $90%. Rest of metal gray, smooth. Grips good. (A) $1900. . . . . *$1800–2000*

Joslyn Army Revolver. Ptd. 1858 by Benjamin Joslyn of Joslyn Firearms, Stonington, CT. 44 cal. Five-shot cylinder, 8" octagonal barrel; 14⅜" overall. Wt. 3 lbs. Side hammer. *$2000–2200*

Lefaucheux Army Pinfire Revolver. Based on 1854 pat. by gunmaker Eugene

Lefaucheux, France. Mfgr. in France and Belgium. 44-cal (12 mm) single action. Metallic cartridge shell with small pin affixed at right angle to length, so shell could only be loaded one way. This model, plus a smaller cal. naval model of same design, were used briefly in the war. *$600–700*

Massachusetts Arms Co. Adams Ptd. Percussion Navy Revolver. (275) 36 cal.; 11½" overall. Has WAT & JT inspector's cartouche. Traces of blue on frame, barrel. Rest brown. Some pitting on cylinder. Good grips. (A) '94, $1300. .... *$1200–1400*

Merwin Hulbert & Co. Army Revolver, Early Model. (31) 44–40 cal., 8½" overall; bird's head butt. Minor traces of blue; most metal smooth, gray; good grips. (A) '94, $850. .... *$900–1000*

Moore Rimfire Cartridge Revolver. (104) 32 rimfire cal.; 5" barrel; 9¾" overall. Marked "D. Moore Patent Sept. 18, 1860." Backstrap engraved "E.A. Patterson/Co. C/108th. Regt. NYSV." Silver-plated engraved frame. Backstrap and trigger guard, 80% finish. (A) '94, $3700. .... *$3800–4000*

Navy Arms 1851 Navy "Yank" Revolver. 1958. Mfgr. by Navy Arms Co., Inc., Ridgefield, NJ. 36 or 44 cal. Six-shot, 7½" octagonal barrel, 14" overall. Wt. 2 lbs., 9 oz. Steel frame. Cylinder roll etched with naval battle vignette. Brass trigger guard and backstrap. Orig. mfgr. by Colt in mid-1850s. Popular *reproduction* model frequently used in Civil War re-enactments. *$100–125*

Perrin Army Revolver. Ca. 1860. French mfgr. 44-cal. double-action; six-shot cylinder. Saw limited use in war. *$900–1000*

Pettingill Army Revolver. 1856 ptd. 44 cal. double-action. Six-shot cylinder, 7½" blued barrel; 14" overall. Wt. 3 lbs. Brass cone sight. Hammerless. Grooved in frame near sight. Blued or brown frame. *$2000–2200*

Prescott Single Action Navy Revolver. (281) 38 rimfire cal., 7½" octagonal barrel. Barrel is 60% blue; good grips. Unsilvered brass frame, trigger guard. (A) '94, $700. .... *$700–900*

Raphael Revolver. Ca. 1858. French. 41-cal. double-action centerfire. Six-shot cylinder, 5½" barrel. *$900–1000*

Remington Army Revolver. Ptd. 1858. 44-cal. paper cartridge. Six-shot cylinder, 8" barrel; 13¾" overall. Wt. (approx.) 2¾" lbs. Over 125,000 of this model were issued to Union troops, second only to Colt in Civil War use. *$1800–2000*

Remington Navy Revolver. Ptd. 1858. Most specs. same as Army model, except: 36 cal. paper cartridge, plus 7½" barrel; 5000 issued to U.S. Navy.... *$2000–2200*

Rogers & Spencer Percussion Revolver. Ca. 1864. (20) 44 cal. Six-shot cylinder, 7" barrel, 13⅜" overall. Based on Freeman Model design. *$1700–1800*

Savage Navy Revolver. Ptd. 1856 and mfgr. at Savage Armory, Middletown, CT. 36 cal.; two triggers: rear ring trigger revolves cylinder and cocks hammer; the front one to fire; 14¼" overall. *$2500–2700*

Savage–North Percussion Navy Revolver. (21) 36 cal; 14¼" overall. Naval inspector's marks. Anchor stamped on top flat of barrel. Mottled gray cylinder has "P/J.R.G."; refinished grips. (A) '94, $2000. .... *$2000–2500*

Smith & Wesson No. 2 Army Revolver. (33) 32 rimfire cal., 5" barrel; 9½" overall. "Capt. G. Hunter, 7th Ill. Regt." engraved on barrel. Minor pitting around cylinder; replaced side plate; wood left grip has small piece splintered off. (A) '94, $1500. .... *$1600–1700*

Starr Revolvers. Ca. 1861. Single-action, 44 cal., six-shot, 8" barrel; 14" overall. Wt. 3 lbs. *Also* made in double-action 36- and 44-cal. model with 6" barrel. Starr Revolvers played a significant role in the Union Militia: 48,000 were issued between 1861 and war's end. *$950–1000*

U.S. Model 1855 Percussion Pistol-Carbine. "1856" marked on lock. (44) 58 cal., batch No. 12 matching. Rated as fair. (A) '94, $2700. . . . . *$2500–2800*

U.S. Model 1862 Signal Pistol with Holster. (41) 6½" overall. Brass butt stamp marked "U.S. Army Signal/Pistol/1862/AJM." "S.H. Condict & Co. Newark, N.J." stamped on holster. Dark patina on all-brass frame. Blue traces on most metal. Scuffed, flaking holster with missing tab loop. (A) '94, $1800. . . . . . . *$1800–2000*

Whitney Navy Revolver. Ca. 1861. Mfgr. under sponsorship of Eli Whitney, Jr., CT. 36 cal. Six-shot cylinder, 7½" octagonal rifle barrel with V-notch rear sight. Iron frame. Widely copied by C.S.A. armories and produced with brass frame. *$1200–1400*

RIFLES
CONFEDERATE AND UNION MILITARY RIFLES
Carbines

Burnside Third Model Carbine. (218) SN 671. 80% bright blue on right side of receiver, lever and brown barrel. Left side of gun's metal shows fine pitting. (A) '94, $2400. . . . . *$2300–2600*

Burnside Third Model Saddle Ring Carbine. 58 cal; 21" barrel with excellent bore. Lockplate marked "Burnside Rifle Co./Providence, R.I." Barrel marked "Bast Steel 1862." "Burnside Pat./March 25th, 1856" stamped on top of frame. (A) Dias, Nov. '94, $975. . . . . *$950–1050*

Burnside Fourth Model Carbine. (217) SN 24170. Butt stock on obverse scratched "J.H. Lewis Co. B. 4". Replaced hammer, barrel band, and breech block screw; 3" slivers replaced over and under lock. (A) '94, $600. . . . . *$600–800*

Colt Model 1855 Revolving Carbine. SN 878. 56 cal. Five-shot with 21" barrel. Forestock marked "US" on receiver tang. Brass blade front sight. Butt stock repaired at wrist. Trigger guard tang is cracked. (A) '94, $2700. . . . . *$2700–2900*

C.S.&P. Rising-Breech Carbine. 54 percussion, 21" barrel. Identified as C.S.&P. *$10,000–12,000*

Dickson, Nelson & Co. Carbine. Percussion. 58 cal. 24" barrel; 40" overall. On lockplate, "Dickson, Nelson & Company, Ala., 1864." Swivel ramrod. Fixed rear sight. Brass mountings. *$4800–5000*

Gallagher Saddle Ring Carbine. "Gallagher's Pat./July 17, 1860." 50 cal. breech loader. Lockplate marked "Manufactured by Richardson & Overman/Phila." Also marked patch box in butt stock; very good bore. Dias, Nov. '94, $900. . . . . *$900–1000*

Gwyn & Campbell Type 1 Saddle Ring Carbine. 52-cal. percussion single-shot, falling block action. No. 4569, referred to as Grapevine Model; frame marked "Union Rifle." Fine bore. (A) Dias, Nov. '94, $1650. . . . . *$1600–1700*

Joslyn Cartridge Carbine, Model 1862. (247) SN 1696. Condition good; several screws damaged; hammer screw replaced; front band spring broken. (A) '94, $750. . . . . *$800–900*

Joslyn Cartridge Carbine, Model 1864. (246) SN 11618. Condition very good. Minor dents; good stock with inspector's cartouche. (A) '94, $850. . . . . . *$900–1000*

LeMat Carbine. Percussion. Twin-barrel revolving carbine. Nine-shot cylinder, 42 cal., 20" barrel (38½" overall) part round, part octagonal. French-made, but designed and patented by Dr. LeMat, New Orleans. *$15,000–16,000*

Model 1855 Springfield Carbine. (220) Lock dated 1855. Replacements of rear sight, tang screw, ramrod, and swivel. Dark patina on metal; repaired swivel. (A) '94, $2600. . . . . *$2500–2700*

Morse Breechloading Carbine. Hinged breech action. 50 cal., 20" round barrel. Brass frame, mountings. Serial numbers found under frame. Otherwise unmarked. *$8800–9000*

Murray Cavalry Carbine. Percussion. 58 cal., 23" barrel. "J.P.Murray, Columbus, Ga." markings. *$9000–9300*

Murray Carbine Musketoon. Percussion. 58 cal; 24" round barrel. Iron sling swivels and ramrod; brass mountings. Lockplate with firm name as above. Breech inscribed "Ala 1864"; "F.C.H." Walnut stock. *$9200–9500*

Palmer Bolt Action Carbine. 1865. Condition very good. Pair of deep stock dents at wrist and under lock; missing sling ring; minor barrel pitting. (A) '94, $1300. . . . . *$1300–1400*

"P" Breechloading Carbine. Bronze-lined breech block, spiral grooved for firm seating of cartridge. 52 cal.; 22¹/₂" round barrel. Breech block marked "P." *$8000–8200*

"P" Rifled Carbine (a.k.a. Hodgkins Carbine). Percussion lock. 58 cal., 22" round barrel. Brass forearm tip; all other mountings are iron. "P.C.S.A." on barrel; "C44" on inside of lock. Sling ring mounted behind trigger guard bow. Walnut stock. *$6000–6200*

Richmond Carbine. Percussion lock. 58 cal., 25" barrel with two bands. Three sling swivels. "C.S." appears on bronze buttplate; "C.S." and year marked on barrel. "C.S. Richmond, Va" and year on lockplate. *$5000–5200*

Robinson-Sharps Carbine. Percussion breechloader. 52 cal., 22" barrel. "S.C. Robinson Arms Mfg. Co., Richmond, Va" plus year on lockplate. Also marked on barrel. *$2500–2800*

Sharps & Hankins Model 1862 Army-Type Saddle Ring Carbine. 52 rimfire cal. Frame marked "Sharp & Hankins, Philada." on right. "Sharps/Patent/1859" on left. One of 500 manufactured. Good bore. (A) Dias, Nov. '94, $600. . . . . *$600–700*

Sharps & Hankins Model 1862 Navy Carbine. Full leather barrel covering. Excellent bore, 52 rimfire cal. (A) Dias, Nov. '94, $850. . . . . *$850–900*

Sharps & Hankins Navy Carbine. (251) Rated very good with 95% leather covering; nice wood on stock (A) '94, $1000. . . . . *$1200–1400*

Sharps & Hankins Short Cavalry Carbine. (252) SN 4316. 19" barrel with saddle ring. Rated good, minor pitting on frame; dark patina on barrel. (A) '94, $750. . . . . *$800–900*

Sharps Model 1852 Carbine. (231) Brass patch box with "AS, SN 3487" engraved. Rated very good; smooth brass; light barrel pitting; overall brown patina; replaced sling ring. (A) '94, $1800. . . . . *$2000–2500*

Sharps NM 1863 Carbine. (230) SN C-878. Jurry rigged of spare parts (uninspected). A few damaged screws, otherwise very good. (A) '94, $2000. . . . . *$2000–3000*

Smith Percussion Saddle Ring Carbine. Breechloader. Frame marked "Address/Poulney & Trimble/Baltimore, U.S.A., Smiths Patent June 23rd. 1857." "Mfgr. Mass. Arms Co./Chicopee Falls." Good bore. Initials "J.W.M." carved in butt. (A) Dias, Nov. '94, $700. . . . . *$700–800*

Spencer Model 1860 Carbine. (138) SN 32473. Springfield modification. Stabler cutoff added plus arsenal refinish. Rated very good, 60% case colors on frame; barrel with 95% blue. ESA inspector's cartouche. (A) '94, $2500. . . . . *$2600–2800*

Spencer Model 1865 Carbine. (260) SN 16607. Stabler cutoff. Metal surfaces have dark patina; minor corrosion on lever and receiver; wood is fine. Rated good. (A) '94, $750. . . . . *$800–1000*

Tallassee-Enfield Pattern Carbine. Percussion muzzleloader. 58 cal. 25" round barrel with brass clamping bands. Brass trigger guard and buttplate. "S.C. Tallassee, Ala" on lockplate. Date marked behind hammer.. . . . . *$20,000–22,000*

Tarpley Carbine. Percussion breechloader. 52 cal., 23" round barrel. Brass breech; iron buttplate. *$42,000–45,000*

Muskets

Cook & Brother Musketoon. Percussion 58 cal., 21" barrel; 36½" overall. Swivel ramrod with large button head. Markings same as above. *$9500–10,000*

Flintlock Militia Musket. (178) Possibly British. 69 cal. with 42¼" barrel inscribed "106 VA. Regt., Alexandria" (VA). Early banana lock with iron pan. Crude bayonet with No. "17". Some pitting around touch hole; repaired frizzen. (A) '94, $2000. . . . . *$2000–2200*

Model 1863 Lindsay Double Rifle Musket. (195) Excellent. With hardened grease. (A) '94, $3700. . . . . *$3700–3900*

Model 1863 Springfield Rifle Musket. (638) Type II. Lock dated "1864." Bolster pitted. Inspector's cartouche defaced on stock. Replacement ramrod. (A) '94, $900. . . . . *$900–1000*

Model 1861 S. Norris & W.T. Clement Contract Musket for Mass. Lock dated 1863, as is short-barreled version. (A) Dias, Nov. '94, $325. . . . . *$350–400*

Morse Breechloading Altered Musket. Metallic, self-primed cartridge action. 69 cal., 40½" barrel with lug for bayonet. "U.S." and winged eagle; "Springfield 1839" marked on lockplate. *$7000–7100*

Richmond Navy Musketoon. Percussion lock. 62 cal., 30" round barrel. "C.S. Richmond, Va." plus year on lockplate. *$5000–5200*

Richmond Rifled Musket. Percussion lock. 58 cal., 40" round barrel with three bands. Very similar to U.S. Model 1855. Brass buttplate. "C.S. Richmond, Va." plus year at rear of lockplate. Year also marked on barrel. Walnut stock. . . . *$3700–4000*

Special Model 1861 Rifle Musket. (183) "Colt's Pt. F.A. Mfg. Co." marked on lock. Lock and barrel with "1862" date; surcharged "NJ" on barrel and stock. With socket bayonet. Light pitting on lock and bolster area; dark patina overall. (A) '94, $900. . . . . *$900–1000*

Todd Rifled Musket. Percussion. 58 cal. 40" round barrel. Lockplate inscribed "Geo. H. Todd, Montgomery, Ala." Walnut stock. *$12,000–14,000*

U.S. Model 1863, Type II. 52 cal., 40" round barrel stamped "V/P" and eagle head at breech. Two-leaf rear sight. Lockplate stamped "U.S./Springfield" and federal eagle, the date "1864" to rear of hammer. Slip ring socket bayonet stamped "US/F" (Flayderman 9A-341). *$400–500*

U.S. Springfield Robert's Model 1861/63 Rifle Musket Conversion. 58 rimfire cal. Missing rear sight leaves, fair bore; marked Roberts. Limited production. Pat. June 11, 1867. (A) Dias, Nov. '94, $450. . . . . *$400–500*

Whitney Rifled Musket. Similar to U.S. Model 1855, but no markings except "E. Whitney, New Haven" on lockplate. Brass buttplate. *$2800–3000*

Rifles

Ashville Rifle. Caplock side plate. 58 cal. 32⅝" barrel with bayonet lug; 48⅝" overall. Fixed sights. Buttplate, stock tip, and trigger guard in brass. Barrel bands, iron. "Ashville, N.C." incised on lockplate. *$9000–10,000*

Austrian Rifle. Caplock. 54 cal., 37¼" barrel; 53" overall. "Austrian Rifle, Tyler, Tex. 54 cal." stamped in rear of hammer. Other examples known with "C.S." and year of mfg. marking. Iron mountings. Two bands; sling swivels attached to trigger guard and band. *$3300–3400*

Baker Rifle. Converted from flintlock to percussion. 52 cal. 36" barrel; 51" overall. Lug for bayonet. "North Carolina" etched on barrel with date on tang. Lockplate marked "U.S." on buttplate tang. *$8500–9000*

Cook & Brother Artillery Rifle. Percussion lock 58 cal., 24" barrel; 40" overall. Brass mountings throughout. "Cook & Brother, Athens, Ga." marking. Serial no. on buttplate. "Athens, date, proved" on barrel. Black walnut stock. . . . .
. . . . *$7000–7500*

Cook & Brother Infantry Rifle. Percussion lock. 58 cal. Barrel 49". Iron ramrod with brass cup-shaped end. Stock is cherry. Markings same as above artillery rifle.
. . . . *$9600–11,000*

Davis & Bozeman Rifle. Percussion. 58 cal., 33" barrel; 48" overall. Brass mountings. "Ala. 1864" on barrel. "D&B Ala. 1864" on lockplate. *$4500–4600*

Dickson, Nelson & Co. Rifle. Percussion. 58 cal., 33" barrel; 49" overall. Two-leaf rear sight. Brass furniture. Firm name plus "C.S." in front of hammer; behind hammer, date plus "Ala. (may also be marked on barrel). Walnut or cherry stock. . . . . . .
. . . . *$10,000–11,000*

1861 U.S. Percussion Rifle Musket with Bayonet. 58 cal. Made by contract with S. Norris & W.T. Clement for State of Massachusetts. Lock marked "S.N. & W.T.C. for Mass." Eagle over "U.S." Dated 1863. Missing rear sight; chip in front of lock on stock. (A) Oct. '94, $625. . . . . *$600–700*

Fayetteville Rifle. Percussion. 58 cal., 33" barrel; 49" overall. "V.P." with eagle's head plus year on barrel breech; "C.S." on buttplate tang. Lockplate marked with "Fayetteville" with spread eagle over "C.S.A." Assembled from tools and parts taken by Rebels at Harpers Ferry. *$6000–6200*

Georgia Armory Rifle. Percussion. 58 cal., 33" barrel; 49" overall. Some examples fitted with saber-bayonet lug. Lockplate marked "Ga. Armory" plus year (behind hammer). Brass furniture. *$5000–5200*

Greene Breechloading Single-Shot Percussion Underhammer Bolt Action Rifle. 53 cal. Made by A.H. Waters, Milbury, MS. Tang marked "Greene's Patent/Nov. 17, 1857." Bore rated fair. (A) Dias, Nov. '94, $600. . . . . . . *$600–700*

Lamb Rifle. Caplock, plain lockplate. 58 cal., 33" barrel, which is part octagonal, part round. "H.C. Lamb & Co., N.C." stamped on yellow stock. Serial no. appears on breech, inside hammer and occasionally on stock. *$11,000–12,000*

"M" Rifle. Percussion, caplock. 58 cal., 39" barrel. British proofmarks. Inscribed "L.S.M." on lower tang; "1862" on lockplate in front of hammer; "M" and full-winged eagle at rear of hammer. *$7500–8000*

Mendenhall, Jones & Gardner Rifle. Percussion. 58 cal., 33" barrel. Sword-type bayonet lug. Iron buttplate and ramrod. Brass mountings. "M.J. & G., N.C." appears on lockplate, in front of hammer; "C.S. 1863" behind hammer. . . . .
. . . . *$10,500–11,000*

Model 1861 Two-Band Artillery Rifle. (182) 32" barrel with muzzle turned to accept socket bayonet. Barrel and socket surcharged "NJ." Lock marked "Savage R.F.A. Co." Lock and barrel stamped with "1863" date. Good condition; grease covered. (A) '94, $700. . . . . *$899–1000*

Murray Rifle. Percussion. 58 cal., 32³/₄" barrel (same markings as preceding Mendenhall rifle)... *$9000–9200*

Murray Sharpshooter's Rifle. 50 cal., 29" heavy octagonal barrel. Iron sling swivels and ramrod; brass mountings. Firm name and "Ala 1864" inscribed as with Murray Carbine... *$10,000–11,000*

Peabody 45–70-Cal. Single-Shot Rifle. "Peabody's Pat. July 22, 1862" marked on receiver. Made by Providence Tool Co. Has "CT" markings on buttplate. Good bore. (A) Dias, Nov. '94, $475.................................... *$450–500*

Pulaski Rifle. Percussion lock. 58 cal., 32¹/₄" barrel. Brass mountings. Inscribed "Pulaski, T.C.S.A. 61." Walnut stock........................... *$3000–3200*

Sturdivant Rifle. Percussion. 54 cal., 32" barrel. Mountings all brass. Serial no. is only identification... *$2000–2200*

Tanner Rifle. Percussion. 54 cal., 33" round barrel. Model similar to the Mississippi Rifle. Marked by serial no. only........................... *$3800–4000*

Texas-Enfield Rifle. Percussion. 57 cal., 23" round barrel with bayonet lug. Brass mountings. Two-leafed rear sight. "Texas Rifle, Tyler, Cal 57" marked on lockplate. "C.S." appears on barrel and buttplate. *$20,000–22,000*

Wallis Rifle. Percussion lock. 61 cal., 33" round barrel. Model is very similar to Mississippi Rifle, but without bayonet lug and patch box. *$1000–1100*

Whitney-Enfield Mississippi Rifle. Percussion lock. 61-cal., 33" round barrel with bayonet lug. Iron buttplate; brass trigger guard. Almost a clone to Enfield Model 1858. "E. Whitney" marked on lockplate......................... *$900–1000*

Wytheville-Hall Rifle. Like the Fayetteville Rifle, this model is found in numerous variations as it, too, was assembled from parts the Rebels captured at Harpers Ferry. One-piece brass casting served to convert breechloader to muzzleloader. ....
.... *$2500–2700*

C.S.A. AND UNION RIFLES

Miller Alteration Rifle. Dated 1863. "Parker Snow & Co." marked on lock. 32" round barrel with two bands. Stock cracked in lock area on both sides. Good. (A) '94, $450... *$500–600*

Model 1842 Percussion Rifle Musket. Marked "Harpers Ferry 1844" on lock. "J.W. Sattenwhite, 6th Missouri, Vicksburg, Port Hudson" crudely scratched in stock. Missing sling swivel at trigger guard; barrel shortened to 38¹/₂" (a common practice with muskets confiscated by Rebels). (A) Oct. '94, $1400........
.... *$1500–1600*

Sharps Model 1863 BL Percussion Military Rifle. Introduced in 1863 by Christian Sharps, Hartford, CT. 52-cal. Linen. Rifle-length barrel with flat brass barrel band. Marked "New Model 1863" inscribed on barrel. Made with full musket stock.
.... *$1700–1800*

Sharps Model 1869 Breechloading Military Rifle. Introduced in 1869. Modified for the 50–70 Govt. centerfire cartridge. *$1200–1400*

Sharps & Hankins Model 1861 Navy Rifle. 1959. Ptd. by Christian Sharps & William Hankins, Philadelphia. 52-cal. rimfire breechloader, 32¹/₂" round barrel; 47¹/₂" overall. Wt. 8¹/₂ lbs. Lug for saber bayonet. Saw limited service from 1861–62. Walnut stock..................................... *$1200–1400*

Springfield Percussion Rifle Musket, 1861 Model with Bayonet. 58 cal. Lock dated 1862. Union issue. (A) Oct. '94, $750......................... *$700–800*

LEVER-ACTION REPEATING RIFLE

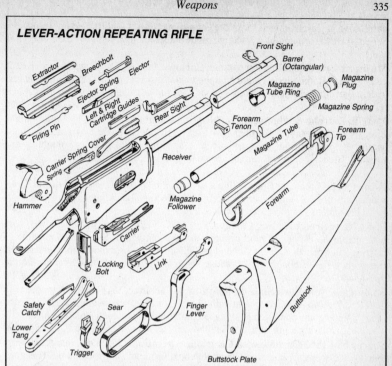

U.S. MILITARY (UNION) SINGLE-SHOT BREECHLOADING CARBINES

Burnside Breechloading Carbine. 1856, ptd. 54 cal. George P. Foster was primary maker. Used first metallic shell cartridge designed for a military weapon. Tapered end open to allow igniting powder charge by percussion cap.......... *$2800–3000*

Cosmopolitan Breechloading Carbine. 50 cal. Mfgr. in Hamilton, OH. A.k.a. "Union." Issued in three models. Lengthy hammer spans entire breechlock.......
.... *$1200–1400*

Gallagher Breechloading Bolt Action. 54 cal. Ptd. 1860. Mfgr. Richardson & Overman. Specimen modified to rimfire. Barrel tilted up to load like shotgun; cartridge linen-covered.. *$1300–1500*

Gibbs Breechloading Carbine. 1863. 52 cal.; uses paper cartridges. Ptd. to W.F. Brooks, NY, in 1862. Barrel slides forward and tilts at breech to load. ....
.... *$3200–3400*

J.D. Greene's Breechloading Carbine. Ptd. 1854. 53 cal. Barrel revolves a quarter turn by pulling forward on trigger to clear the receiver. Sleeve and barrel revolve to right to load cartridge. Uses Maynard primer................... *$4200–4500*

Joslyn Model 1855 Breechloading Carbine. Ptd. 1855. 54 cal. A.H. Waters, Millbury, CT, mfgr. for B.F. Joslyn. This was first of Joslyn systems; the rest comprised cartridge arms. Strap on small of the stock lifts up, revealing breech when ring on top of butt is released. *$3300–3500*

Joslyn Model 1864 Carbine. 52 cal. rimfire. Single-shot breechloader, 22" round

barrel (avg.). Casehardened lockplate. Iron mountings. Used by Federal troops under contract toward end of war. Some models also fell into hands of the Rebels.. . .
. . . . *$1000–1100*

Maynard Breechloading Percussion Carbine. Ptd. by Dr. Edward Maynard in 1859. 50 cal. Initial models were equipped with Maynard primer. Uses metallic cartridge. Barrel tilts up, loads like shotgun. Base of cartridge fills space between barrel and breech. *$1800–2000*

Merrill, Latrobe & Thomas Breechloading Carbine. Ptd. 1856 by Remington at Ilion, NY. Has Maynard primer. To load, cartridge is pushed in place by hand against action of spring. To open breech, strap along top of stock is brought up and forward. Breech comprises circular piece of metal with hole through it. . . . .
. . . . *$15,000–16,000*

Palmer Breechloading Bolt-Action Carbine. Ptd. 1863. 50 cal. First metallic cartridge (rimfire) bolt gun to see service in U.S. Sectional locking screw of bolt similar to breechlocks of modern cannons.. . . . . *$1900–2000*

Perry Navy Breechloading Carbine. Ptd. 1855. 54 cal. Mfgr. in Newark, NJ. Arm with magazine primer (a tube inserted through buttplate). Spring action same as cartridge in Spencer models. Second model of Perry's breech action. (First model was named the "Rebel Perry" because some of the first carbines filtered into the South early in the war.) *$4300–4500*

Remington New York State Rolling Block Carbine. (254) Contract model with "3rd R.C." comb stamped in oval with Signal Corps branch insignia over "22" over "118." Very good condition with case colors under hardened grease; barrel 90% blue. Only missing sling ring. (A) $850. . . . . *$800–1000*

Sharps NM 1863 Carbine with Cartridge Alteration. (258) DFC inspector's cartouche on obverse of butt stock. No patch box. Original six-groove bore. Has arsenal refinish. Rated near mint. (A) '94, $2200. . . . . *$2000–2500*

Smith Breechloading Carbine. 52 cal. Lever on top tang is released by pushing catch in front of trigger. Barrel thus drops like shotgun. Originally, cartridge was encased in rubber shell. Later altered to take metallic cartridge.. . . . . . *$1800–2000*

Starr Breechloading Carbine. Ptd. 1858 by E.T. Starr, Yonkers, NY. 54 cal. Used extensively by Union from 1861–65.. . . . . *$1000–1100*

Starr Cartridge Carbine. (276) SN 33913. Iron buttplate and barrel band. Rated good. Dark patina; wood good. (A) '94, $800. . . . . *$800–1000*

Starr Percussion Carbine. Ca. 1860. (242) SN 12654. Issued to "1st. Arkansas Cavalry" marked on breech. Rated good with scattered pitting on all metal; wood very sound; tang screw missing. (A) '94, $1850.. . . . . *$1900–2000*

Symmes Breechloading Carbine. 1858 ptd. 54 cal. An early experimental model that was soon phased out as Govt. issue. Maynard magazine primer. Breechlock rotates upward.. . . . . *$25,000–27,000*

U.S. Schroeder Carbine. Ptd. 1856. 53 cal. Needle gun (a long firing pin) penetrates powder charge, igniting the fulminate at the base of the bullet in advance of the cartridge. Sliding-forward barrel with eagle and "U.S." appearing on tang.. . . . .
. . . . *$12,000–14,000*

Warner Breechloading Carbine. Ptd. 1864. 50 cal. Rimfire carbine with breechblock that swings to right (like the Joslyn). Extractor, with handle that projects at bottom of stock in front of trigger guard, was worked by hand. Because extra step was required to eject shell, it proved unpopular with Union troops. . . . *$2200–2300*

Wesson Carbine. Ptd. 1859 by Frank Wesson, later a founder of Smith & Wesson. 44-cal. breechloader. Barrel tilts up and front trigger releases catch that holds it. All-metal rimfire cartridge. *$700–800*

Knives: (left to right) *B-guard Bowie knife with zinc scabbard, $2,400; D-guard Bowie knife with massive Ire guard, $1,000; CSA Armory D-guard cutlass and scabbard, $2,800; D-guard knife with leather sheath, $2,200; side knife and sheath from Shiloh, $2,700. All from the William Bond collection. Prices reflect auction sales. (Photo courtesy of Conestoga Auctions)*

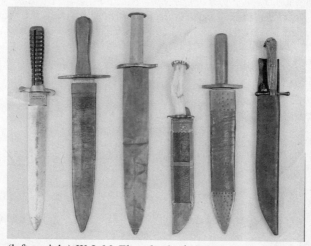

Knives: (left to right) *W.J. McElroy knife, $12,500; large side knife with leather sheath, $2,400; spear-point side knife with tin sheath, $3,600; side knife with antler grip, $11,000; Kentucky side knife with tin sheath, $3,400; side knife with stag-antler grip and leather sheath, $850. All from the William Bond collection. Prices reflect auction sales. (Photo courtesy of Conestoga Auctions)*

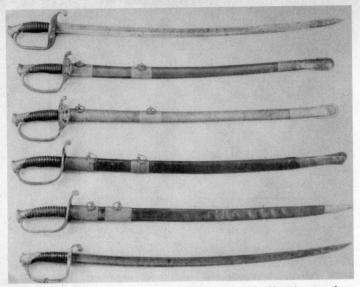

CSA swords: (top to bottom) *Conning staff and field officer's sword,*
$4,750; L. Haiman presentation staff and field officer's sword with
scabbard, 30", $15,000; L. Haiman sword with 30¹/₂" etched blade,
$21,000; Haiman foot officer's sword, $6,500; unmarked foot officer's
sword, $3,500; French foot officer's presentation sword, Devisme, Paris,
$3,500. From the William Bond collection. (Photo courtesy of Conestoga
Auctions)

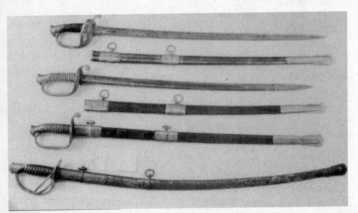

Union swords: (top to bottom) *M-1850 staff and field officer's sword with*
scabbard (below), *$1,000; Presentation M-1850 foot officer's sword*
with scabbard (below), *$1,800; M-1850 foot officer's sword with scabbard,*
by H. Folsum, $600; M-1860 cavalry saber with scabbard, $700. From the
William Bond collection. (Photo courtesy of Conestoga Auctions)

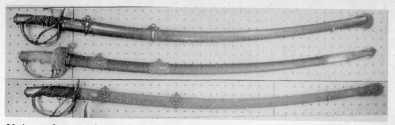

Union sabers and swords: (top to bottom) *Ames cavalry saber with scabbard, $525; Schuyler, Hartley, and Graham artillery field officer's sword with scabbard, blade marked "W. Clauberg, Solingen," $950; M-1860 cavalry saber, $240. (Photo courtesy of Paul Dias Auctions)*

Sword: Foot soldier's sword and scabbard. Belonged to Elisha W. Ellis Monroe of Maine, marked "Ames Mfg. Co.," $1,650; Russian leather sword belt with accouterments, $850. (Photo courtesy of Mark Cisco)

Artillery officer's short sword (Hank Ford collection), $600–$650.

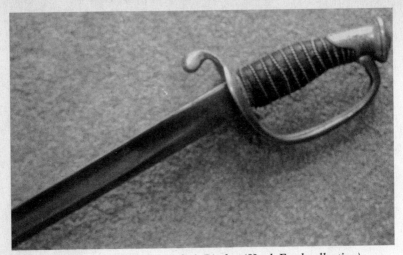

CSA foot officer's sword by Leach & Rigden (Hank Ford collection),
$2,000–$2,500.

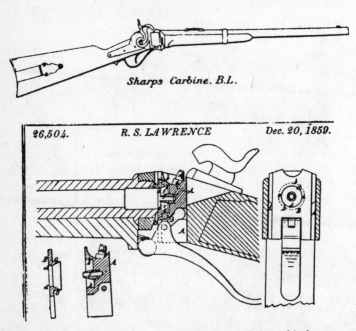

Illustration of Sharps carbine, model 1859. Though issued in large
numbers to Union forces, Sharps carbines captured by CSA troops today
consistently run in the $2,000–$3,000 range.

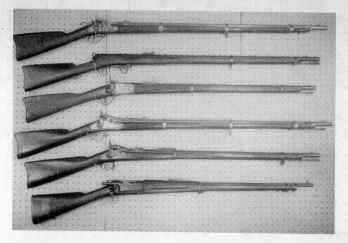

Top to bottom: *U.S. Springfield model 1861–63 .58 calibre rimfire musket, $450–$500; Greene breech-loading .53 calibre single shot percussion rifle by A.H. Waters, patented 1857, $600–$700; Austrian Lorenz .69 calibre percussion musket, with cruciform bayonet, $1,600–$1,700; U.S. Springfield 2nd Allin conversion model 1866 rifle, $400–$500; U.S. Springfield post–Civil War trapdoor rifle, $400–$450; U.S. Springfield model 1898, not priced. (Photo courtesy of Paul Dias Auctions)*

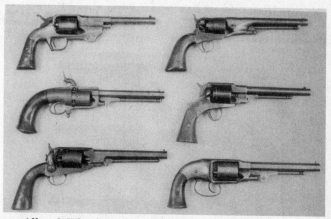

Top row: *Allen & Wheelock .44 calibre percussion Army revolver, $700; Colt model 1860 .44 calibre Army revolver, $850.* Center row: *Butterfield .41 calibre percussion Army revolver, $3,500; Freeman .44 calibre percussion Army revolver, $1,800.* Bottom row: *Joslyn .44 calibre percussion Army revolver, $2,200; Pettingill .44 calibre percussion Army revolver, $1,150.*

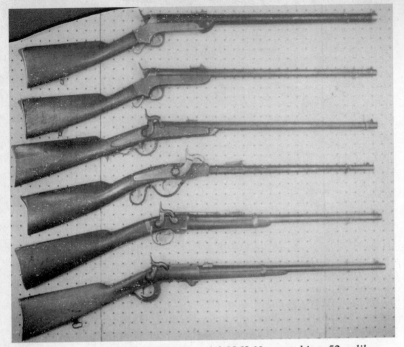

Top to bottom: *Sharps & Hankins model 1862 Navy carbine .52 calibre rimfire, $450–$500; Sharps & Hankins model 1862 Army saddle-ring single-shot rimfire carbine, .52 calibre rimfire, one of only 500 manufactured, $600– $700; Gallagher saddle-ring .50 calibre breech-loading carbine, $900–$1,000; Smith percussion saddle-ring breech-loading carbine, produced in 1857, $1857, $700–$800; Burnside saddle-ring carbine, 3rd Model .58 calibre, missing saddle-ring, $1,000–$1,500. (Photo courtesy of Paul Dias Auctions)*

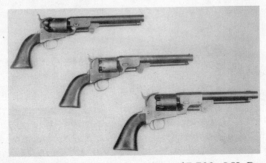

Top to bottom: *Columbus Firearms revolver, $7,700; J.H. Dance & Bros. .36 calibre Navy revolver, $3,750; J.H. Dance & Bros. .44 calibre Army revolver, $32,250.*

Top to bottom: *Spenser model 1865 saddle-ring carbine, .50 calibre: $750–$850; Remmington 1863 percussion contract rifle (Zouave rifle), .58 calibre, with original bayonet and saber, $2,300–$2,500; model 1861 percussion rifle musket (missing rear sight), made under contract by S. Norris and W.T. Clement for the state of Massachusetts, $650–$700; Springfield model 1861 percussion rifle musket, with bayonet, $800–$900; Colt model 1861 special musket, barrel marked "V" over "P" over eagle head, $1,900–$2,000; British Enfield percussion rifle musket, .58 calibre, lock marked and dated 1862, $850–$900; pre–Civil War U.S. percussion musket, model 1842, .69 calibre, marked "Harper's Ferry," with the name of a Vicksburg rifleman carved into the stock, $1,400–$1,500.*

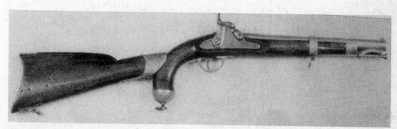

Fayetteville model 1855 .58 calibre pistol carbine, assembled by CSA troops from parts captured at Harper's Ferry, $4,250.

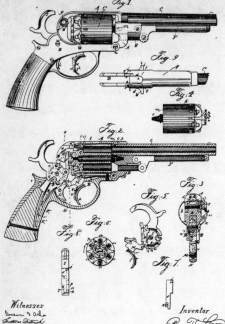

Illustration showing Starr's initial production revolver in 1861. This .36 calibre is a hybrid double and single action handgun. The curved section of the barrel frame near the hinge immediately sets it apart from the .36 calibre and .44 calibre large frame models issued soon after. The original revolver today commands $950–$1,000.

Illustration showing a stand of three Justice rifles. The rifles had two bands and sword bayonets, and were designed by Phillip Justice of Philadelphia in 1861, intended for use by Pennsylvania volunteers. The rifles were later rejected by the government because of inferior workmanship. Only a few of this scarce issue remain and command a high price today.

BIBLIOGRAPHY

Civil War. Bruce Catton. Illus., 320 pp., pap. 1985. American Heritage Library.

Civil War. Taylor Downing and Maggie Millman. Illus., 192 pp., pap. 1992. Coll & Brown, Trafalgar.

Civil War. Michael Golay. Ed. by John Bowman. America at War Ser., illus., 192 pp., YA, gr. 6–12. 1992. Facts on File.

Civil War. Vol. 2. Shelby Foote. 1963. Random House.

Civil War. Vol. 3. Shelby Foote. 1974. Random House.

Civil War. Vol. VI. Shelby Foote. 1958. Random House.

Civil War. Hazel Jansen. History of Iowa Ser., illus., 63 pp., orig., pap. text ed. 1988. Green Valley Area.

Civil War. Ed. by Raymond F. Locke. Great Adventures of History Ser. Mankind Pub.

Civil War. Lucan. Loeb Classical Library: No. 220. HUP.

Civil War. Lucan. Ed. and tr. by Susan H. Braund. World's Classics Ser., illus., 384 pp., pap. 1992. HUP.

Civil War. Carter Smith. American Historical Images on File Collection, illus., 320 pp. 1988. Facts on File.

Civil War. Geoffrey C. Ward. Pap. 1994. Random House.

Civil War. Eric Weiner. Facts America Ser., illus., 64 pp., gr. 2–6. 1993. Smithmark.

Civil War: An Aerial Portrait. Brian C. Pohanka. 144 pp. 1990. Thomasson-Grant.

Civil War: The Best of American Heritage. Stephen W. Sears. 1991. Houghton Mifflin.

Civil War: The Best of American Heritage. Ed. by Stephen W. Sears. American Heritage Library. 256 pp., pap. 1993. Houghton Mifflin.

Civil War: An Illustrated History. Geoffrey C. Ward and Ric Burns. Illus., 448 pp., pap. 1992. Knopf.

Civil War: A Narrative. 3 vols. Shelby Foote. Illus., set, pap. 1986. Random House.

Civil War: A Photographic History. Stan Schindler. Illus. 1991. Random House Value.

Civil War: A Second American Revolution? Ed. by William E. Purish. American Problem Studies, 158 pp., gr. 11–12, pap. text ed. 1978. Krieger.

Civil War: Tennessee: Battles and Leaders. Thomas L. Connelly. Tennessee Three Star Ser. Illus., 114 pp., lib. bdg., pap. 1979. U. of Tennessee Pr.

Civil War: The Town of Prattsville and the Neighboring Greene, Delaware, and Schoharie County Area. Gerald E. Sutch. xxvi, 15 pp., pap. 1987. Hope Farm.

Civil War Album. Tom Robotham. 1992. Smithmark.

Civil War Almanac. Ed. by John S. Bowman. Illus., 400 pp., pap. 1987.

Civil War Almanac. Ed. by John S. Bowman. 400 pp., pap. 1986. Newspaper ent.

Civil War! America Becomes One Nation. James I. Robertson, Jr. Illus., 192 pp., gr. 5–9. 1992. Knopf Bks. Yng. Read.

Civil War and the American System: America's Battle with Britain, 1860–1876. 2nd ed. Allen Salisbury. Ed. by Nancy B. Spannaus. 500 pp., pap. 1992. Exec. Intel. Rev.

Civil War: American Tragedy. Alden R. Carter. First Bks., illus., 64 pp., gr. 5–8, pap. 1993. Watts.

Civil War in the American West. Alvin M. Josephy, Jr. Illus., 464 pp. 1991. Knopf.

Civil War in the American West. Alvin M. Josephy, Jr. Pap. 1993. Random House.

Civil War and America's Wit. William Gibson and James Murfin. Illus., 432 pp. 1992.

Civil War Angel. Cary Lavetta. 128 pp., orig., pap. 1987. Memory Ln. Bks.

Civil War Autographs and Manuscripts, Prices Current: A Guide to Autographs and Manuscripts of the War Between the States. Rev. ed. Ronald R. Seagrave. Illus., 420 pp., pap. 1994. Sergeant Kirk.

Civil War Battlefield Guide. Conservationist Fund Staff. Ed. by Frances H. Kennedy. Illus., 320 pp., pap. 1990. Houghton Mifflin.

Civil War Battlefields. Bill Harris. Pap. Random House.

Civil War Battles. Curt Johnson and Mark McLaughlin. Illus., 1977. Random House.

Civil War Battles in the West. 2nd ed. Ed. by LeRoy H. Fischer. Illus., 112 pp., pap. 1981. Sunflower U. Press.

Civil War Battles in Winchester and Frederick County, Virginia, 1861–1865. Pap. 1988. Winchester-Frederick Cty. Hist. Soc.

Civil War Book of Lists. Ed. by Combined Bks. Staff. 240 pp., pap. 1994. Stackpole.

Civil War Books: A Critical Bibliography. 2 Vols. Ed. by Allan Nevins, et al. Repr. of 1967 ed. 1984. Broadfoot.

Civil War Books: A Priced Checklist with Advice. 3rd ed. Tom Broadfoot. Compiled by Janet Hewett and Julia Nichols. 573 pp. 1990. Broadfoot.

Civil War on the Border. 2 Vols. Wiley Britton. Illus., repr. of 1899 ed., text ed. 1990. KS Heritage Pr.

Civil War Breech Loading Rifles: A Survey of the Innovative Infantry Arms of the American Civil War. John D. McAulay. Illus., 144 pp., pap. 1987. A. Mowbray.

Civil War in Buchanan and Wise Counties: Bushwacker's Paradise. Jeffrey C. Weaver. Virginia Civil War Battles and Leaders Ser. Illus., 323 pp. 1994. H.E. Howard.

Civil War in Cabell County, West Virginia. Joe Geiger. Pap., pictorial hist., 1991.

Civil War Campaign Medal. John M. Carroll. 1976. Amereon Ltd.

Civil War Chief of Sharpshooters, Hiram Berdan, Military Commander and Firearms Inventor. Roy M. Marcol. Illus., 342 pp. 1992. Northwood Heritage Pr.

Civil War Cinema: A Pictorial History of Hollywood and the War between the States. John M. Cassidy. Pap. 1986.

Civil War Collector's Encyclopedia. Vol. V. Marjorie F. Lord. 230 pp., lib. bdg. 1989. Lord Americana.

Civil War Collector's Encyclopedia. Vol. 3. Francis A. Lord. Illus., 210 pp. 1979. Lord Americana.

Civil War Collector's Encyclopedia. Vol. 4. Francis A. Lord. Illus. 1984. Lord Americana.

Civil War Coloring Book. Peter Copeland. Illus., YA, gr. 7–10, pap. 1990. Dover.

Civil War Command and Strategy: The Process of Victory and Defeat. Archer Jones. 256 pp., text ed. 1992. Free Pr.

Civil War Commanders. Dean S. Thomas. Illus., 72 pp., pap. 1986. Thomas Publications.

Civil War Cookbook. William C. Davis. Illus., 96 pp. 1993. Courage Bks.

Civil War Cooking: The Housekeeper's Encyclopedia. E.F. Haskell. Ed. by R.L. Shep. Orig. title: *Housekeeper's Encyclopedia.* Illus., 464 pp., pap. 1992. R.L. Shep.

Civil War Correspondence of Judge Thomas Goldsborough Odell. Ed. by Donald O. Virdin. xvi, 133 pp., orig., pap., text ed. 1992. Heritage Pk.

Civil War Diaries of Col. Theodore B. Gates, Twentieth New York State Militia. Ed. by Seward R. Osborne. Illus., 197 pp. 1992. Longstreet House.

Civil War Diary of Anne S. Frobel. Intros. by Mary H. Lancaster. 320 pp., pap. 1992. EPM Pubns.

Civil War Diary of Charles A. Leuschner. Ed. by Charles D. Spurlin. 128 pp. 1992. Sunbelt Media.

Civil War Diary of Cyrus Pringle: Record of Quaker Conscience. Cyrus Pringle. Orig. title: *Record of Quaker Conscience.* Orig., pap. 1962. Pendle Hill.

Civil War Diary of Nelson Stauffer. Nelson Stauffer. Ed. by Norman E. Tanis. American Classics Facsimile Ser.: Pt. IV. Pap. 1976. CSUN.

Civil War Diary of a Plymouth Pilgrim: The Journals of Charles Mosher, 85th N.Y. Volunteers. Ed. by Wayne Mahood. Illus. 1993. Longstreet House.

Civil War Diary of Sarah Morgan. Sarah Morgan. Ed. by Charles East. 688 pp. 1991. U. of Georgia Pr.

Civil War Dictionary. Mark M. Boatner, III. Vintage Civil War Library. 1008 pp., pap. 1991. Random House.

Civil War Era Etiquette. Martine's Handbook and Vulgarisms in Conversation. Ed. by R.L. Shep. Illus., 236 pp., pap. 1988. R.L. Shep.

Civil War Etchings. Edwin Forbes. Illus., 96 pp., pap. 1994. Dover.

Civil War Extra: From the Pages of the Charleston Mercury and the New York Times. New ed. *Charleston Mercury* staff and the *New York Times* staff. Ed. by Eugene P. Moehring and Arleen Keylin. 310 pp. 1975. Ayer.

Civil War Eyewitnesses: An Annotated Bibliography of Books and Articles, 1955–1986. Garold L.Cole. 359 pp., text ed. 1988. U. of South Carolina Pr.

Civil War Flags. Whitney Smith. Gr. 1–9. 1992. Bellerophon Bks.

Civil War: Fort Sumter to Appomatox. William J. Bradley. Illus., 224 pp. 1990. Random House.

Civil War Geneology. 64 pp., pap. 1988. Genealog Sources.

Civil War Geneology. Ed. by Jane Hedlin. 80 pp., pap. 1991. AFRA.

Civil War Generals: Categorical Listings and a Biological Directory. Compiled by James Spencer. 344 pp. 1986. Greenwood.

Civil War Ghost Stories and Legends. Nancy Roberts. Illus., 192 pp. text ed., pap. 1992. U. of South Carolina Pr.

Civil War Ghosts. Ed. by Mulin H. Greenberg, et al. 216 pp., pap. 1991. August House.

Civil War Heroes. Jill Canon and Alan Archmbault. Illus., 48 pp., orig., gr. 7, pap. 1988. Bellerophon Bks.

Civil War Heroines. Jill Canon. Illus. orig., gr. 7 up, pap. 1989. Bellerophon Bks.

Civil War Journal of Billy Davis: From Hopewell, Indiana, to Port Republic, Virginia. Ed. by Richard S. Skidmore. Illus., 184 pp., orig., pap. 1989. Nuggel IN.

Civil War Justice: Union Army Executions under Lincoln. Robert I. Alotta. Illus., 245 pp. 1989. White Mane Pub.

Civil War in Kentucky. 2nd ed. Lowell H. Harrison. Illus., 144 pp., repr. of 1975 ed. 1987. U. Pr. of Kentucky.

Civil War Ladies: Fashions and Needle-Arts of the Early 1860s. Ed. by R.L. Shep. Illus., 236 pp., pap. 1988. R.L. Shep.

Civil War to the Last Frontier, 1850–1880. William L. Katz. History of Multi Cultural America Ser. Illus., 96 pp., gr. 7–8. 1992. Raintree Steck-V.

Civil War Letters of Charles Barber, Private, 104th New York Volunteer Infantry. Raymond G. Barber and Gary E. Swinson. 256 pp., pap. 1991. G.E. Swinson.

Civil War Letters of Colonel Hans Christian Heg. Hans C. Heg. Ed. by Theodore C. Blegen. Pap. Bks. Demand.

Civil War Letters of Cpl. John H. Strathern: Eighth Pennsylvania Reserve Volunteer Corps. Marlene C. Bumbela. 146 pp., pap. 1994. Clossen Pr.

Civil War Letters and Diary of Joshua Winters. Ed. by Elizabeth Swiger. Pap. 1975. McClain.

Civil War Letters of George Washington Whitman. George Whitman. Ed. by Jerome M. Loving. Pap. 49. 30 Bks. Demand.

Civil War Letters of Private Henry Kaufman (1862–1865), The Harmony

Boys Are All Well. Ed. by David McCordick. Illus., 124 pp., lib. bdg. 1991. E. Mellen.

Civil War Letters of the Tenure Family of Rockland County. Larry H. Whiteaker and W. Calvin Dickinson. Illus., 110 pp., pap. 1990. Rockland County Hist.

Civil War in Louisiana. John D. Winters. 534 pp., pap. 1979. Louisiana State U. Pr.

Civil War in the Making, 1815–1860. Avery O. Craven. Walter Lynwood Fleming Lectures. xiv, 116 pp., pap., text ed. 1968. Louisiana State U. Pr.

Civil War Manuscripts. Civil War Ser. 1991. Revisionist Pr.

Civil War Manuscripts: A Guide to Collections in the Manuscripts Division of the Library of Congress. 391 pp. 1986. Lib. Congress.

Civil War Maps: Annotated List. Lib. Bdg. 1991. Gordon Pr.

Civil War Maps: An Annotated List of Maps and Atlases in the Library of Congress. 2nd ed. Compiled by Richard W. Stephenson. 410 pp. 1989. Lib. Congress.

Civil War Maps: An Annotated List of Maps and Atlases in the Library of Congress. 2nd ed. Compiled by Richard W. Stephenson. Illus., 418 pp. 1989. USGPO.

Civil War Maps: An Annotated Lists of Maps and Atlases in Map Collections of Library of Congress. United States Library of Congress Map Division Staff. Compiled by Richard W. Stephenson. Repr. of 1961 ed. 1979. Greenwood.

Civil War Maps: A Graphic Index to the Atlas to Accompany the Official Records of the Union and Confederate Armies. Ed. by N.S. Reilly, et al. Illus., 68 pp., pap. 1987. Newberry.

Civil War Medicine. Robert E. Denney. 422 pp. 1994. Sterling.

Civil War Memoirs. Philip Sheridan. Intro. by Paul A. Hutton. Civil War Ser. 352 pp., pap., text ed. 1991. Bantam.

Civil War Memoirs of Captain William J. Seymour: Reminiscences by a Louisiana Tiger. Ed. by Terry L. Jones. Illus., 184 pp. 1991. Louisiana U. Pr.

Civil War Memoirs: Grant and Sherman. 2 Vols. Library of America. Illus., boxed set. 1990. Library of America.

Civil War Memoirs of Two Rebel Sisters. William Wintz. Pap., pictorial hist. 1992.

Civil War Memories of Elizabeth Bacon Custer: Reconstructed from Her Notes and Diaries. Ed. by Arlene Reynolds. 1994. U. of Texas Pr.

Civil War in the Midlands, 1642–1651. Roy E. Sherwood. Illus., 250 pp. text ed., pap. 1992. A. Sutton Pub.

Civil War Military Machine: Weapons and Tactics of the Union and Confederate Armed Forces. Tony Gibbons and Ian Drury. Illus., 192 pp. 1993. Smithmark.

Civil War and Miscellaneous Papers. Papers of the Military Historical Society of Massachusetts, Vol. 14. 457 pp. 1990. Repr. of 1918 ed. Broadfoot.

Civil War in Missouri as Seen from the Capital City. Dino Brugioni. 200 pp., orig., pap. 1986. Summers Pub.

Civil War and National Park Wit. William Gibson and James Murfin. Illus., 432 pp. 1992. Interp. Mktg. Prods.

Civil War and New York City. Ernest McKay. New York State Bks. Illus., 380 pp., text ed., pap. 1991. Syracuse U. Pr.

Civil War Newspaper Maps: A Cartobibliography of the Northern Daily Press. Compiled by David Bosse. Bibliographics and Indexes in Military Studies, No. 5. 1993. Greenwood.

Civil War Newspaper Maps: A Historical Atlas. David Bosse. Illus., 160 pp. 1993. Johns Hopkins.

Civil War in North Carolina. John G. Barrett. xi, 484 pp. 1963. U. of North Carolina Pr.

Civil War Nurse: The Diary and Letters of Hannah Ropes. John R. Brumgart. Pap. 1992. U. of Tennessee Pr.

Civil War: Opposing Viewpoints. Ed. by William Dudley. American History Ser. Illus., 312 pp., lib. bdg., pap., text ed. 1994.

Civil War in the Ozarks. Phillip W. Steele and Steve Cottrell. Illus., 112 pp., pap. 1943. Pelican.

Civil War Paper Soldiers in Full Color. A.G. Smith. Pap. 1985. Dover.

Civil War Papers of George B. McClellan: Selected Correspondence 1860–1865. George B. McClellan. Ed. by Stephen W. Sears. 669 pp., pap. 1992. Da Capo.

Civil War Papers Vol. 2: Commandery of the State of Massachusetts. Military Order of the Loyal Legion of the United States Ser.: Vol. 53. 631 pp., repr. of 1900 ed. 1993. Broadfoot.

Civil War Parks: The Story Behind the Scenery. William C. Davis. Illus., 64 pp., orig., pap. 1984. KC Pubns.

Civil War Party System: The Case of Massachusetts, 1848–1876. Dale Baum. xviii, 289 pp. 1984. U. of North Carolina Pr.

Civil War Pictures. D.L. Corbitt and Elizabeth W. Wilborn. Illus., xiii, 55 pp. pap. 1985. NC Archives.

Civil War Pistols. John D. McAulay. Illus., pap. 1992. Mowbray.

Civil War Postcard Book. Illus., 64 pp., orig, pap. 1991. Ballantine.

Civil War Prisons. Ed. by William B. Hesseltine. 123 pp., pap. 1972. Kent St. U. Pr.

Civil War Prisons: A Study in War Psychology. William B. Hesseltine. History—United States Ser. 290 pp., repr. of 1930 ed., lib. bdg. 1992. Rprt Serv.

Civil War Prisons and Escapes: A Day-by-Day Chronicle. Robert E. Denney. Illus., 424 pp. 1993. Sterling.

Civil War Quiz Book. John Malone. Quill Quiz Bk. Illus., 224 pp., pap. 1992. Morrow.

Civil War Quiz and Fact Book. Rod Gragg. Illus., 224 pp., pap. 1985. HarpC.

Civil War Quiz and Fact Book. Rod Gragg. 1993. Promontory Pr.

Civil War Reader. Richard B. Harwell. 1994. Smithmark.

Civil War and Readjustment in Kentucky. Ellis M. Coulter. 1926. Peter Smith.

Civil War and Readjustment in Kentucky. Ellis M. Coulter. History—United States Ser. 468 pp., repr. of 1926 ed., lib. bdg. 1992. Rprt Serv.

Civil War and Reconstruction. Joe H. Kirchberger. Eyewitness History Ser. Illus., 400 pp. 1990. Facts on File.

Civil War and Reconstruction. 2nd. rev. ed. James G. Randall and David H. Donald. 866 pp., pap., text ed. 1969. Heath.

Civil War and Reconstruction in Alabama. Walter L. Fleming. Illus., repr. of 1911 ed. 1978.

Civil War and Reconstruction in Alabama. Walter L. Fleming. BCL1 —United States Local History Ser., 815 pp., repr. of 1905 ed., lib. bdg. 1991. Rprt Serv.

Civil War and Reconstruction, 1850–1877. Ed. by I.A. Newby. Literature of History Ser., orig., pap., text ed. 1971. Irvington.

Civil War and Reconstruction Era, 1861–1877. Ed. by Kenneth Kusmer. Black Community and Urban Development in America Ser., Vol. 3. 444 pp., repr. 1991. Garland.

Civil War Records of Jefferson County, Alabama. Compiled by Marilyn D. Barefield and Chriss H. Doss. 1993. Birm. Pub. Lib.

Civil War Reenactments. Stephen W. Sylvia and Michael J. O'Donnell. Illus., 132 pp., orig., pap. 1985. Moss Pubns., VA.

Civil War Remembered. Carl Lowe. 1991. M. Friedman Pub. Grp. Inc.

Civil War Reminiscences of Major Silas T. Grisamore C.S.A. Ed. by Arthur W. Bergeron, Jr. 240 pp. 1993. Louisiana St. U. Pr.

Civil War in Ripley County Missouri. Dorothy Ponder. Ed. by Prospect News Staff. Illus., 102 pp., orig., pap. 1992. Ponder Bks.

Civil War Round Table: Fifty Years of Scholarship and Fellowship. Barbara Hughett. Illus., xviii, 206 pp. 1990. Civil War RT.

Civil War at Sea. 3 Vols. Virgil C. Jones. Illus., repr. of 1960 ed. Set: Vol. I, "The Blockaders," 483 pp., Vol. II, "The River War," 490 pp., Vol. III, "The Final Effort," 456 pp. 1990. Broadfoot.

Civil War Secret. Lisa Banim. Mysteries in Time Ser. Illus., 80 pp., gr. 4–6. 1994. Silver Moon.

Civil War Secret Agent. Steve Perry. Time Machine Ser.: No. 5. Orig., pap. 1984. Bantam.

Civil War Short Stories of Ambrose Bierce. Ambrose Bierce. Ed. by Ernest J. Hopkins. 139 pp., pap. 1988. U. of Nebraska Pr.

Civil War Sites. Tom Weil. U.S.A. Guides Ser. Illus., 200 pp., orig., pap. 1994. Hippocrene Bks.

Civil War Sites in Virginia: A Tour Guide. James I. Robertson, Jr. Illus., 108 pp., pap. 1982. U. Pr. of Virginia.

Civil War Sketches and Incidents: Papers Read by Companions of the Commandery of the State of Nebraska. Military Order of the Loyal Legion of the United States Ser.: Vol. 25. 277 pp., repr. of 1902 ed. 1992. Broadfoot.

Civil War: Slavery and the Crisis of Union. 2nd ed. Laurel R. Singleton. Public Issues Ser. Illus., 68 pp., pap. 1989. Soc. Sci. Ed.

Civil War Soldiers. Reid Mitchell. Pap. 1989. S&S Trade.

Civil War Soldiers. Catherine Reef. African-American Soldiers Ser. Illus., 80 pp., gr. 4–7. 1993. TFC Bks, NY.

Civil War Soldiers at Atlanta. Soldier Ser. 48 pp., gr. 5–6. 1991. Capstone Pr.

Civil War Soldiers Coloring Book. Alan Archambault. Illus., gr. 4–7, pap. 1985. Bellerophon Bks.

Civil War Soldier's Diary. Peter W. Funk, NY, Vol. 150. Margaret Herrick. 54 pp., pap. 1991. Kinship Rhinebeck.

Civil War in Song and Story. 2 Vols. Frank Moore. Set, lib. bdg. 1980. Gordon Pr.

Civil War Source Book. Philip Katcher. Source Book Ser. Illus., 320 pp. 1992. Facts on File.

Civil War Sourcebook: A Traveler's Guide. Chuck Lawliss. Illus., 320 pp. 1991. Crown Pub. Group.

Civil War Spoken Here: A Dictionary of Mispronounced People, Places and Things of the 1860s. Robert D. Quigley. 216 pp., pap., CW Hist. 1993.

Civil War Stories. Ambrose Bierce. 128 pp., orig., pap. 1994. Dover.

Civil War Stories of Harold Frederic. Harold Frederic. Ed. by Thomas F. O'Donnell. New York Classic Ser. 360 pp. Syracuse U. Pr.

Civil War: Strange and Fascinating Facts. Burke Davis. 1988. Random House.

Civil War Sutler Tokens and Cardboard Scrip. David Schenkman. Illus., 103 pp. 1983. Jade House Pubns.

Civil War as They Knew It. Pierce G. Fredericks. (Aeonian Pr.), Amereon Ltd.

Civil War Through the Camera. Henry W. Elson and Matthew B. Brady. Ayer.

Civil War Times in St. Augustine. Ed. by Jacqueline K. Fretwell. Illus., 122 pp., pap. 1988. Florida Classics.

Civil War Treasury. B.A. Botkin. 1988. Bk. Sales Inc.

Civil War Treasury. Albert A. Nofi. 208 pp. 1994. World Pubns.

Civil War Treasury: Being a Miscellany of Arms and Artillery Facts and Figures, Legends and Lore, Etc. Albert A. Nofti. Illus., 432 pp. 1992. Stackpole.

Civil War Treasury of Tales. Ed. by B.A. Botkin. (Aeonian Pr.), Amereon Ltd.

Civil War Times: 30-Year Comprehensive Index, April 1959–February 1989. Lee W. Merideth. 228 pp., orig., pap. 1990. Hist Indexes.

Civil War Treasury of Tales, Legends and Folklore. B.A. Botkin. 1981. Promontory Pr.

Civil War Trivia and Fact Book. Webb Garrison. Illus., 240 pp., orig., pap. 1992. Rutledge Hill Pr.

Civil War Veterans Organization, Reunions and Badges. Turner E. Kirkland. 1991. Pioneer Pr.

Civil War Veterans of Winnebago Co., WI, Vol. I:A-H. David A. Langkau. 378 pp., orig., pap., text ed. 1994. Heritage Bks.

Civil War in West Virginia: A Pictorial History. Rev. ed. Stan B. Cohen. Illus., 160 pp., orig., pap., text ed. 1982. Pictorial Hist.

Civil War in West Virginia: A Story of the Industrial Conflict in the Coal Mines. Winthrup D. Lane. American Labor Ser. Repr. of 1921 ed. Ayer.

Civil War on the Western Border, 1854–1865. Jay Monaghan. viii, 454 pp., pap. 1984. Bison Books. U. of Nebraska Pr.

Civil War in the Western Territories: Arizona, Colorado, New Mexico, and Utah. Ray C. Colton. Illus., 240 pp., orig., pap. 1984. U. of Oklahoma Pr.

GLOSSARY OF CIVIL WAR TERMINOLOGY

Accouterments: Items of equipment other than weapons or apparel carried by a military man (i.e. cap, belt, cartridge boxes, plates, canteens, etc.).

Aiguillette: Ornamental cord and tassel worn on the uniform. Often in different colors (i.e. red for red dress uniform of Union light infantry).

Ambrotype, Ferrotype, C.D.V., Dag., Tintype: See Photography section of listings.

Arme Blanche: Fancy term for the sword, often used in reference to other blades (i.e. the bayonet). See Edged Weapons in Weapons section.

Armies: At least 16 Union and 23 C.S.A. "operational organizations" that were officially or unofficially known as an army.

Banquette: Small elevation or mound of earth below crest of parapet to enable shorter riflemen to fire over it easily.

"Bleeding Kansas": Term applied to violence-plagued territory of Kansas where a five-year border war ensued after enactment of the Kansas/Nebraska Bill in 1854, leaving slavery question up to popular sovereignty. Opened up Kansas to incursions by both pro- and anti-slave factions. Major skirmishes continued until 1858, but disorder reigned until the war's advent.

Brevet Rank: Honorary title conferred for meritorious action in wartime, but lacking authority, precedence, or pay of real or full rank. In 1863, an act breveted 1,700 regular army and volunteers to rank of Maj. Gen. or Brig. Gen. Abuse brought quick end to system in U.S. Army.

Bricole: Artilleryman's leather harness for dragging guns, when horses were unavailable. Approximately 18' long.

Bridoon: Snaffle and rein of a military bridle, acting independently of bit. See Cavalry in Ammunition and Miscellaneous Field Equipment section.

Bullseye Canteen: The M-1958 U.S. canteen with nine concentric rings pressed into each side for added strength.

Bummers: Foragers for Army of Tennessee on Sherman's March through Georgia.

Camp Gear: Paraphernalia that armies took with them into the field—a camp cot, field desk, etc.

Carpetbaggers (a.k.a. *skalawags)*: Northerners who swarmed South during Reconstruction, known to gain positions in state and local governments for financial gain. So called because of popular luggage they carried.

Chapeau de Bras: See Headwear Types.

Cockade: Rosette or knot of ribbon worn on military cap or coat.

Columbiad (a.k.a. *Confederate Rodman*): Special type of Howitzer cannon, the bore equidistant throughout; often used for throwing solid shot. Known to shoot 64 lb. shell up to 2½ miles, with a 10-lb. charge.

Contrabands: Slang term coined by Benjamin Butler, when three slaves of a Virginia owner in May 1861 sought refuge at Ft. Monroe. When the slave owner demanded their return, Butler referred to them as "contrabands of war." Doctrine phased out with passage of Confiscation Acts (the first in August 1861).

Copperheads: Northern Democrats (chiefly from Ohio, Illinois, and Indiana) who opposed Union's war policy and favored negotiated peace. Lincoln exercised extraordinary executive powers in supressing them.

Corps Badges: Metal badges of the 22 Union corps, which fetch strong pieces. Cloth corps badges not sewn on kepis or blouses are of questionable value because it is difficult to authenticate them.

Crow's Feet (a.k.a. *caltrop)*: Iron pointed stars or stout nails placed with sharp points up, and strewn before enemy cavalry to slow their advance—a static, non-explosive booby trap.

Dahlgren: Standard artillery piece similar to the Columbiad. Invented by Adm. John A. Dahlgren and used primarily in the Union Navy.

Department: The basic territorial organization which usually gave its name to the field army operating within its boundaries.

Dispatch Case: Leather, sealskin, or oil cloth case with shoulder straps; used by army, navy, and marines on both sides to carry documents to the front lines.

Ditty-box: Usually of sandalwood with hinged gutta-percha cover; originally collar boxes but used to carry small items in the war.

Dog Tags (or identification discs): First used in the Civil War. Many were crude, handmade, or scratched in by the individual; others were stamped with "War of 1861," "Against Slavery," and other inscriptions. Here's a case where dug discs fetch higher prices than "as new" tags; a C.S.A. dug relic may bring $200–$300.

Draft Riots: Incited in August '62, as Lincoln called on states for 300,000 militia to serve nine months and ordered state governors to draft men if quota not filled by volunteers. Riots ensued in Wisconsin and Indiana, and threats of rioting in Pennsylvania. Secretary of War Stanton postponed the draft. The Enrollment Act of March 1863 precipitated the three-day New York City draft riots in July. When drawing for draft lottery began, a mob of over 50,000 burned and pillaged, killing more than a dozen people (most victims Negro.) Federal troops were summoned and over 1,000 people were killed or wounded. The draft was postponed until August. Other draft riots erupted in Boston; Rutland, VT; Portsmouth, NH; and Wooster, Ohio.

Dragoon: A mounted infantryman; a soldier using his horse to hie to the battlefield, but dismounts to fight. The cavalry in the Civil War was used primarily as mounted infantry—one of the few exceptions being Battle of Brandy Station, VA, the first and largest cavalry combat in the war.

Dred Scott Decision: Scott, a Negro slave, was taken by his master from St. Louis to Rock Island, IL, where slavery was forbidden by the Ordinance of 1787, and later to the Wisconsin territory where Missouri Compromise forbade slavery. When Scott tried to sue to gain his freedom in 1846, the Supreme Court ruled that slaves were not U.S. citizens and therefore not entitled due process. This decision was bitterly attacked by the North and further widened sectional hostility.

Epaulettes: Required shoulder decoration for all officers; stiff gold braid, with regiment number and insignia of rank worn on strap.

Fascines: Thin branches or saplings bundled and used to line sides of trenches.

Feathers: Black ostrich feathers adorned left side of cavalry officer's hats: three for field officers, two for company officers, one for enlisted men. See Uniforms section.

Fit and Finish: Term used to describe overall firearm worksmanship. See Weapons section.

Flags

Colors—a flag normally carried by a dismounted unit.

Camp Colors—flags 18" square used to mark color line, points of wheeling, etc. Union-white for infantry; red for artillery with regiment numbers mounted on 8' standards.

Garrison Flag—national color, 36' in fly and 20' in hoist.

Footwear:

Bootee—ankle-high laced shoe or boot (a.k.a. *Jefferson Boot*).

Brogans—ankle-high bootees laced in front.

Gaiters—lower leg coverings made of cotton or leather.

Guidon—Small silk flag or pennant carried by military units.

Wellingtons—ankle-length boots without laces in front.

Fougasse: Charges of gunpowder deposited at the bottom of a dug pit or shaft, designed to explode like a mine when the enemy passed over.

Freedman's Bureau: Emergency bureau established by Lincoln in 1865 as part of War Dept. to aid newly freed slaves obtain land and become self-sufficient. Rife with graft and double-dealing, the bureau soon became highly unpopular, particularly in the South.

Frog: A loop fastened to a strap, scabbard, or weapon to attach something else. A braid loop fastener for a cape or overcoat; a.k.a. *throg.*

Fullered: Iron that is grooved or spread. See Edged Weapons in Weapons section.

Furniture: Mountings or trappings that embellish the weapon.

Gauntlets: Regimental officer's gloves with wide flared cuffs beyond the wrist. In white or buff, usually with elaborate designs on cuffs.

Hardtack: Hard bread or biscuit of plain flour and water issued as rations. Often very hard and wormy, it was not a favorite among the troops. A concoction called *panda*, crumbled hardtack and water or whiskey, was administered to weak patients in hospital.

Havelock: Simple covering of white linen for the cap with cape to protect neck from sun. Named after a heroic English general in the 1857 Indian campaign.

Haversack: A leather carrying device to carry cartridges safely to the guns.

Headwear Types: The variety of quirky, often rag-tag Civil War headwear exemplified below confirms that many Union as well as C.S.A. units paid little attention to conformity, formality, or military regulations.

Burnside Hat—regular U.S. Army officer's dress hat, made with lower crown.

Chapeau de Bras—dress or cocked hat, worn chiefly by naval officers; could be folded and tucked under arm.

Jeff Davis Hat—a regulation Union hat that was hot, heavy, and uncomfortable; many troops "lost" them. The famous Iron Brigade (19th Indiana and parts of 2nd, 6th, and 7th Wisconsin), however, wore black versions throughout war as trademark; units became known as "Black Hat Brigade."

Fez—Brimless oriental headdress worn by Zouaves.

Forage Cap—floppy version of the 1851 shake similar to the French kepi, usually for fatigue (barracks duty.) A modern term for headwear was *Bummer's Cap*.

Hardee Hat—dress felt hat (another variation of the slouch hat) so called because a future C.S.A. Gen. William J. Hardee served on board that chose the style. Most soldiers disliked the hat's stiffness and recessed the crown or otherwise modified it.

Kepi—French origin; soft cloth forage cap. Civil War issue can be distinguished from later G.A.R. or reenactment replicas (with latter two, place your hand back from brim to the cloth top, and note that the front goes almost straight up as opposed to the pronounced slant with Civil War–era kepi).

McClellan Cap—low, soft, true copy of the kepi, preferred by Union officers to standard issue forage cap.

Sennit Hat—broad-brimmed hat usually of straw which could be waterproofed and worn as foul weather gear. The 16th NY Infantry wore them on the Peninsula in 1862.

Shako—favorite headgear since Napoleonic wars, favored by volunteer militia in 1862. Stiff cylindrical leather cap with short visor styled after the chasseur; usually featured brass insignia plate, metal cockade, and pompom.

Sicilian Cap—visorless cap and a bag ending with a tassel, worn by C.S.A. volunteers in 1861.

Slouch Hat—wide brimmed felt hat with brim usually turned down and the more rumpled, the better. Not much of a good luck talisman as both Gens. John Sedgwick and Thomas G. Stevenson were killed by enemy fire while wearing them. Federal regulations directed infantrymen to loop up right side of hat brim (usually secured with stamped brass eagle pin) while cavalrymen looped up the left.

Whipple Hat—light blue felt hat named after J.F. Whipple who produced it in 1861; brim runs two-thirds the way around the crown; leather visor in front. Worn by NY, NH troops; also U.S. sharpshooters. C.S.A. called it the *Excelsior Hat.*

Housewife: Sewing kit for needles, thread, and thimble carried in the field.

Knights of the Golden Circle (a.k.a. *Sons of Liberty*)**:** Secret order in the North of Southern sympathizers who favored the extension of slavery. Later became Peace Democrats who disapproved of the war.

Ku Klux Klan: Secret society founded shortly after war's end to reassert white supremacy by means of terrorism. C.S.A. Gen. Nathan B. Forest was said to be First Grand Wizard. An illiterate misspelling of the Greek word *Kuklos* (meaning ring or circle). The Klan saw a revival in Georgia, Ohio, Indiana in 1915 and exists to this day.

Mantlet: Protective metal shield used to protect from musket fire, often used by engineer troops or riflemen during an attack on fortification.

Martingale: Strap of harness that connects girth to nose band to keep horse from throwing back head. See Cavalry in Ammunition and Miscellaneous Field Equipment section.

Maynard Primer: Primer tape invention by a dentist by that name, used to increase rate of fire of percussion rifles.

Minié Ball: Pronounced minié rather than mínnie and not a ball but a conical lead projectile designed by French Army Capt. Claude Minié to be fired from a muzzle-loading rifle. When shot, expanding gas entered hollow base, forcing its outer side into the riffling of barrel. Introduced in 1849, it was quickly adopted by U.S. military. It greatly improved accuracy and rate of small arms fire.

Pioneers: Soldiers detailed from various companies to mend roads, erect defenses, and remove obstacles for convoys.

Plastron: Piece or swatch of cloth usually shield-shaped, worn on the front of a shirt or coat, often of a facing color.

Polka: Form of jacket slit at both sides, usually cut with slight flare and falling some 6" below waist line.

Pompoms (used interchangeably with *plume*)**:** A feather, horsehair, or worsted standing hat decoration worn from brim to above crown. Color coded red for artillery, light blue for infantry, yellow for cavalry.

Rattle Alarms: Wooden rattles with ratchets used to summon Naval crewmen to duty in times of emergency.

Roundabout: Waist-length jacket.

Shoulder Scales: Stamped brass ornaments theoretically used to ward off saber blows from cavalrymen, but their effectiveness is doubtful; saw limited use in combat.

Sons of Confederate Veterans: Founded in 1896 to preserve and defend the history and principles of the Old South.

Stock: Regulation tight-fitting leather strap worn around enlistee's neck. Many troops declined to wear them.

Surcingle: Blue web girth that binds blanket, saddle, or pack to horse's body. See Cavalry in Ammunition and Miscellaneous Field Equipment section.

Sutlers: Civilian suppliers to regiments who often took considerable risk in visiting combat areas to peddle various needful goods, i.e., shaving and sewing kits, polishes, tobacco. When troops were short of money, they were also known to provide chits or IOUs; also loaned money at fair rate of interest.

Talma: A long cape or cloak; in the Civil War, especially applied to overcoat worn by mounted troops.

Vedette: Sentry riding horseback.

V.P. (Viewed and Proved): Initials struck on barrel of Union weapons such as the prolific Springfield Model 1861, to verify its having passed government ordnance inspection. Usually accompanied by eagle head acceptance mark with stock stamped with inspector's initials.

Vulcanite: Not a space alien but a hard rubber material used for uniform buttons, cups, pipes, soap containers, and other Civil War–era impedimenta. Also called *ebonite*. Often confused with gutta-percha, a type of hardened rubber used in talmas (a long cap or cloak.)

Zouave (Zoo av'): Elaborately uniformed member of a Union unit patterned after French infantry group once composed of Algerian recruits.

AUCTION HOUSES

ABSENTEE, MAIL AUCTION, AND FIXED PRICE CATALOG HOUSES

Al Anderson, P.O. Box 644, Troy, OH 45373. (513) 339-0850. Political memorabilia with emphasis on badges, pinbacks.

Tom French, 1840 41st Ave., #102-128, Capitola, CA 95010. (408) 426-9096. Political, patriotic memorabilia.

David Frent, P.O. Box 455, Oakhurst, NJ 07755. (908) 922-0768 or (908) 922-2753. Political memorabilia, badges, pinbacks, and heavy emphasis on ribbons.

Hake's Americana & Collectibles, P.O. Box 1444, York, PA 17405. (717) 848-1333. Emphasis on political but also includes Civil War–related material.

Harmer Rooke Galleries, Absentee Auctions. 32 East 57th St., 11th Floor, New York, NY 10022. (212) 751-1900. Photographica, Civil War and Lincoln memorabilia, classical antiquities, American Indian art, numismatics, advertising antiques, and medical antiques.

Historicana, Robert W. Coup, 1632 Robert Rd., Lancaster, PA 18601. (717) 291-1037. Political and patriotic entries.

Jefferson Rarities Collection, 2400 Jefferson Highway, 6th Floor, Jefferson, LA 70121. 1-800-877-8847. Fixed price catalog of manuscripts, autographs, and books.

Manion's International Auction House, Inc., Box 12214, Kansas City, KA 66112. (913) 299-6692. Militaria, including weaponry, medals, uniforms, ephemera, and documents.

Political Gallery, Thomas D. Slater, 1326 88th St., Indianapolis, IN 46260. (317) 257-0863. Political memorabilia, advertising some Civil War–related entries.

Rex Stark, 49 Wethersfield Rd., Bellingham, MA 02109. (607) 966-0994. Has gravitated from mail auctions to fixed price catalog recently. Always a varied array of Civil War material, political, and general memorabilia.

Periodic Lists

The following parties issue periodic lists in their respective specialties:

William Bopp, Washington Square, P.O. Box 33, Walpole, NH 03608. Early tin and paper toys.

Civil War Images, Henry Deeks, P.O. Box 2260, Acton, MA 01720. (508) 263-1861. Civil War photography.

Doug Jordan, Box 20194, St. Petersburg, FL 33742. Dags, ambrotypes, and other early photography.

Cordelia and Tom Platt, 66 Witherspoon St., #1600, Princeton, NJ 08452. (609) 921-0856. Autographs.

Profiles in History, Joseph M. Maddalena, 345 North Maple Drive, Suite 202, Beverly Hills, CA 90210. 1-800-942-8856. Autographs.

Sheet Music Center, Box 367, Port Washington, NY 11050. 1-800-JASS-MAN. Sheet music.

Don Troiani, P.O. Box 660, Southbury, CT 06488. (203) 262-6500. Civil War uniforms, weaponry.

University Archives, 600 Summer St., Stamford, CT 06901. 1-800-237-5692. Autographs.

Live Auction Houses

Andrews & Andrews (Dan and Elsie Andrews), Belfast, ME 04915. (207) 338-1386. General antiques with some Civil War material.

Auction Gallery of Paul J. Dias, Inc., 30 East Washington St., Rt. 58, Hanson, MA. (617) 447-9057. Military weaponry, uniforms, and accessories; ephemera.

Noel Barrett Antiques & Auctions, P.O. Box 1001, Carversville, PA 18913. (215) 297-5109.

Bill Bertoia Auctions, 2413 Madison Ave., Vineland, NJ 08360. (609) 692-1881. Toys, banks, games.

Butterfield & Butterfield, 220 San Bruno Ave., San Francisco, CA 94103 or 7601 Sunset Blvd., Los Angeles, CA 90046.

Christie's East, 219 East 67th St., New York, NY 10021. (212) 570-4141. Vintage advertising, toys, Americana.

Conestoga Auction Co., Inc., P.O. Box 1, Manheim, PA 17545. (717) 898-7284. General antiques, but often holds firearms auctions.

J.C. Divine Gallery, Milford, NH 03055. (603) 673-4967. Weaponry and Civil War regalia.

Eldred's Auctions, East Dennis, MA 02641. General antiques, but covers ephemera, weaponry, and Civil War on occasion.

William "Pete" Harvey Auctions, 1270 Rt. 28 A, P.O. Box 280, Calumet, MA 02534. (508) 540-0660. Weaponry, uniforms, accessories.

William J. Jenack Auctioneers, 37 Elkay Drive, Chester, NY 10918. (914) 469-9095. Periodic military and ephemera auctions.

James D. Julia, Inc., P.O. Box 830, Fairfield, ME 04937. (207) 453-7125. Vintage advertising, toys, firearms, and Americana.

Henry Kurtz Auction, New York, NY. Militaria (lead soldiers and other miniatures).

Rick Opfer Auctioneering, Inc., 1919 Greenspring Drive, Timonium, MD 21093. (301) 252-5035. Vintage advertising, toys, black memorabilia, Americana.

Skinner Auctions, Inc., Rt. 117, Bolton, MA 01740. (617) 779-5528. General line of antiques, but frequently offers toys, advertising, and Americana.

Sotheby's, 1334 York Ave. at 72nd St., New York, NY 10021. (212) 606-7000. Toys, Americana.

Swann Galleries, Inc., 104 East 245 St., New York, NY 10010. (212) 254-4710. Photography, posters, ephemera with frequent Civil War examples.

CIVIL WAR COLLECTIONS AND LIBRARIES

Many resources with extensive Civil War collections exist among the nation's libraries, historical societies, and museums. Most welcome serious students, authors, and collectors seeking specialized information. Some will loan materials to your local library, and your librarian can help you arrange a loan. A letter outlining the information you seek should bring a prompt response. The following comprise the major resourses available:

ALABAMA

Birmingham Public Library, 2020 7th Ave. North, Birmingham, AL 35203. Collection includes 15,000 books, documents, etc.

Mobile Public Library, 701 Government St., Mobile, AL 36602. Personal papers and documents of Daniel Geary, C.S.A. Director of Mobile Defenses, 1861.

Museum of City of Mobile Reference Library, 355 Government St., Mobile, AL 36602. C.S.A. collection.

Troy State University Library, Troy, AL 36081. Includes John H. Dent papers, 1851–92; 25 volumes, manuscripts, etc. of the noted planter, plantation owner.

ARIZONA

Northern Arizona University Special Collection Library, P.O. Box 6022, Flagstaff, AZ 86011. Joe Strachan collection; letters in German by Capt. Carl Costmann, 3rd Iowa Infantry.

CALIFORNIA

California Institute of Technology Memorial Library, 1201 East California Blvd., Pasadena, CA 91125. 3,000 volumes of Civil War material, including the Morley and Amos G. Throop letters and papers.

Claremont College Honnoid Library, 9th and Dartmouth Sts, Claremont, CA 91711. Extensive Civil War material in 70,000-volume library.

Lincoln Memorial Shrine, A.K. Smiley Public Library, 125 West Vine St., Redlands, CA 92373. One of the largest Lincoln memorabilia collections, including 3,000 pamphlets, campaign badges, prints, stamps, and medals.

Occidental College Library, 1600 Campus Rd., Los Angeles, CA 90041. Maps, manuscripts, and photographs (uncataloged).

San Diego State University Malcolm A. Love Library, 5300 Campanile Drive, San Diego, CA 92182. Maps, diaries, manuscripts, and artifacts from the Civil War period.

Stanford University Libraries, Stanford, CA 94305. Collection includes papers of Gens. William R. Schafter and Frederick Steele.

University of California, San Diego Central Library, La Jolla, CA 92093. Manuscript collection; family correspondence from war.

University of California, Santa Barbara Library, Santa Barbara, CA 93106. 31,000 volumes, including the William Wyles Collection of Americana.

CONNECTICUT

Museum of Connecticut History, Southbury, CT. Curator Don Troiani. Manuscripts and artifacts, including military uniforms.

Trinity College Library, 300 Summit St., Hartford, CT 06106.

DELAWARE

Hagley Museum and Library, P.O. Box 3630, Greenville, DE 19807. Interesting patent papers; papers of Adm. Samuel Francis du Pont and Gen. Henry du Pont.

DISTRICT OF COLUMBIA

American National Red Cross, National Headquarters Library, 17th and D St., N.W., D.C. 20006. Clara Barton Memorial Collection. Material relating to women's role in the war and to the Sanitary Commission, forerunner to the American Red Cross.

Ford Theater National Historic Site, 511 10th St. N.W., Washington, D.C. Museum in basement contains many Lincoln artifacts relating to his career.

Georgetown University Library, 37th and O Sts., N.W., D.C. 20057. Correspondence of various Civil War military figures and politicians.

Library of Congress, Washington, D.C. 20540. Papers of Gen. William T. Sherman; Mathew Brady and staff photos; massive Civil War print and broadside collection.

National Archives of the United States. Washington, D.C. A nationwide network of presidential libraries, reg. archive offices and federal record centers. Inexhaustible (3¼ billion entries) compendium of incomparable documents including the Bill of Rights, the Constitution, Declaration of Independence, and the Emancipation Proclamation; over 5 million photographs; Gen. Lee's 1865 signed amnesty oath; land grant as bounty to A. Lincoln as a captain after the Blackhawk War.

National Museum of American History, Washington, D.C. 20540. Including the Isadore Warshaw collection of business Americana (numerous advertising posters, flyers, etc., relating to the Civil War).

GEORGIA

Carnegie Library, 607 Broad St., Rome, GA 30161. Collection of Civil War–related material includes 450 volumes and maps.

Emory University Robert W. Woodruff Library, Atlanta, GA 30322. 16,000 volumes, manuscripts, maps, pictures.

Georgia Southern College Library, Statesboro, GA 30458. Spencer Wallace Cone papers.

ILLINOIS

Chicago Historical Society Library, Clark St., Chicago IL 60614. Manuscripts, maps, and 150,000 volumes. Meserve American (27 volumes) with 8,000 Civil War photographs.

Chicago Public Library, 78 East Washington St., Chicago, IL 60602. 7,000 volumes. Anti-slavery pamphlets, large collection of regimental histories; Grant, Sherman, and Breckinridge manuscripts; letters, diaries, photographs. C.S.A. battle plan for Shiloh. Arms, equipment, uniforms. G.A.R. Hall and Memorial Association of Illinois collection.

Galesburg Public Library, 40 East Simmons St., Galesburg, IL 61401. Major Lincoln concentration; Illinois regimental histories.

Illinois State Historical Society Library, Old State Capitol, Springfield, IL 62706. 16,000 volumes; manuscripts, maps, and photographs.

Illinois State University Miller Library, Normal, IL 61761. Harold K. Sage Lincoln collection (approximately 1,200 volumes and 1,500 pamphlets, newspaper clippings, and correspondence).

Knox College Library, Galesburg, IL 61401. Collection of approximately 15,000 volumes.

Lincoln's Tomb Historic Site, Oak Ridge Cemetery, Springfield, IL. Lincoln family resting place with numerous photos and artifacts. For information as to above and other Lincoln sites in Springfield, phone 1-800-545-7300.

McLean County Historical Society Library and Museum, 201 East Grove, Bloomington, IL 61701. 3,000 volumes, maps, manuscripts, and photographs. Military heritage of Illinois, including the 33rd and 94th Regiments, 3rd Volunteer Infantry.

Newbury Library, 60 West Walton St. Chicago, IL 60610.

INDIANA

Butler University Irwin Library, 4600 Sunset Ave., Indianapolis, IN 46208. Charles W. Moore Lincoln collection.

Indiana University Lily Library, 7th St., Bloomington, IN 47405. 160,000 volumes, including manuscripts, maps, and photographs.

Louis A. Warren Lincoln Library and Museum, Ft. Wayne, IN. Significant Lincoln photgraphy collection.

Morrison-Reeves Library, 80 North 6th St., Richmond, IN 47374. Extensive collection on the Civil War and Lincoln.

Willard Library, 21 First Ave., Evansville, IN 47710. 500 volumes, including battle accounts, biographies of generals, memoirs, letters, biographies and diaries.

IOWA

State Historical Society of Iowa Library, 402 Iowa Ave., Iowa City, IA 52240. Iowa regimental histories, diaries, etc.

KENTUCKY

Abraham Lincoln Birthplace National Historic Site, Rt. 1, Hodgenville, KY 42748. Reconstructed Kentucky log cabin furnished with Lincoln artifacts.

LOUISIANA

Louisiana State University Troy H. Middleton Library, Baton Rouge, LA 70803. Warren Jones Lincoln Collection.

Tulane University Howard-Tilton Memorial Library, 7001 Freret St., New Orleans, LA 70118. Diaries, letters of Louisiana soldiers. Including papers of C.S.A. Gens. R.E. Lee, P.G.T. Beauregard, T.J. Jackson, A.S. Johnson, and J.H. Stubbs.

MAINE

Boudoin College Library, Brunswick, ME 04011. Military papers including Chamberlain and Fessenden family, Oliver Otis, Hubbard family and McArthur family papers.

Maine Historical Society Library, 485 Congress St., Portland, ME 14101. Extensive collection on Maine regiments.

MARYLAND

Antietam National Battlefield Site Library, P.O. Box 158, Sharpsburg, MD 21782. Mongographs in regiments and troopers.

Hood College Josephy Henry Apple Library, Rosemont Ave., Frederick, MD 21701. Irving M. Landauer Civil War collection.

Salisbury State College Blackwell Library, Salisbury, MD 21801.

MASSACHUSETTS

American Antiquarian Society, 185 Salisbury St., Worcester, MA 01609. Thousands of items of ephemera, much of it Civil War related; 2 million newspapers; vast ephemeral printing collection of the society's founder Isiah Thomas.

Boston University Muger Memorial Library, 771 Commonwealth Ave., Boston 02215. Includes Paul Richards collection; also Martin Luther King papers.

Concord Free Public Library, 129 Main St., Concord, MA 01741. Manuscripts, maps, photographs.

Harvard University Widener Library, Cambridge, MA 02138.

Lynn Public Library, 5 North Common St., Lynn, MA 01902. Papers, books relating to Massachusetts regiments.

Memorial Hall Library, Elm St., Andover, MA 01810. Includes Charles Barry's original drawings of Lincoln ca. 1860.

State Library of Massachusetts, 341 State House, Boston, MA 02133. Extensive collection on New England's participation in Civil War.

MICHIGAN

Andrews University James White Library, Berrian Springs, MI 49104. Courville Civil War collection; some 350 entries including weaponry, accessories, etc.

Monroe County Library System, 3700 Custer Rd., Monroe, MI 48161.

University of Michigan William L. Clements Library, Ann Arbor, MI 48109. Vast collection of Civil War related material.

MISSISSIPPI

University of Southern Mississippi William D. McCain Graduate Library, P.O. Box 5148, Southern Station, MS 39406. Ernest A. Walen collection on history of the C.S.A., including over 600 Confederate imprints; various manuscripts and collections.

MISSOURI

Central Missouri State University Ward Edwards Library, Warrensburg, MO 64093. Extensive border state material.

MONTANA

Eastern Montana State College Library, 1500 North 30th St., Billings, MT 59101. G.A. Custer's personal and military papers; complete 7th Cavalry records, numerous Civil War papers (from the Custer Battlefield National Monument collection).

NEW HAMPSHIRE

New Hampshire Historical Society Manuscripts Library, 30 Park St., Concord, NH 03301. Military record of New Hampshire regiments.

NEW JERSEY

Princeton University Library, Nassau St., Princeton, NJ 08540. James Perkins Walker collection, including Civil War papers.

NEW YORK

Buffalo and Erie Historical Society, 25 Nottingham Ct., Buffalo, NY 14216. Major Civil War military history collection.
Columbia University Libraries, 801 Butler Library, 535 W. 114th St., New York, NY 10027. Historian Allan Nevins papers (40,000 items); Sydney H. Gray papers (20,000 items); Peter A. Alexander papers (7,500).
Fenton Historical Society Library, 67 Washington, Jamestown, NY 14701. Includes muster rolls, history of New York state regiments, letters, diaries, etc.
New York Historical Society Library, 170 Central Park West, New

York, NY 10024. Extensive ephemera holdings including Bella C. Landauer collection of ephemera.

New York Public Library, Fifth Ave. and 42nd St., New York, NY 10016. 25,000 volumes.

St. John Fisher College Library, Rochester, NY 14627. Over 1,000 volumes, including papers, records of G.A.R.

St. Lawrence University Owen D. Young Library, Canton, NY 13617. Correspondence from numerous Union volunteers, 1861–64. Papers of Union spy Pryce Lewis.

Union League Club Library, 38 East 37th St., New York, NY 10018. 30,000 volumes.

United States Military Academy Library, West Point, NY. Extensive battle accounts (USMA accounted for almost 37 percent of C.S.A.'s 425 generals; 40 percent of Union's 583 generals).

University Club Library, 1 West 54th St., New York City, NY 10016. Includes Southern Society collection of papers, memorabilia on C.SA. and reconstruction.

University of Rochester Rush Rhees Library, Rochester, NY 14627. 150,000 items relating to Secretary of State William Henry Seward, 1825–1872.

NORTH CAROLINA

Duke University William R. Perkins Library, Durham, NC 27706. Papers of Gens. Robert E. Lee and P.G.T. Beauregard, C.S.A. government, and Jefferson Davis; thousands of Union and C.S.A. letters and diaries.

University of North Carolina, Chapel Hill Wilson Library, Chapel Hill, NC 28514. Wilmer Collection of Civil War novels (over 825 from 1861 to present) with related bibliographical material.

OHIO

Ohio Historical Society, Archives Library Division, 1982 Velma Ave., Columbus, OH 43211. Regimental histories and Ohio narratives.

Ohio University Vernon R. Alden Library, Athens, OH 45701. Brown family papers cover activities of 36th Ohio and 4th West Virginia Regiments; also Kentucky campaign.

Public Library of Cincinnati and Hamilton County, 800 Vine St., Cincinnati, OH 45202. Collection focuses on Ohio military unit histories.

Western Reserve Historical Society Library, 10825 East Blvd., Cleveland, OH 44106. William P. Palmer Civil War collection.

Wilmington College Watson Library, P.O. Box 1227, Wilmington, OH 45177. Collection focus on Ohio Quakers and their role during the Civil War.

PENNSYLVANIA

Adams County Historical Society, Gettysburg, PA 17325. Extensive collection of manuscripts, maps, and photographs.

Gettysburg College Musselman Library, Gettysburg, PA 17325. Documents and artifacts from area battlegrounds.

Gettysburg National Military Park, Gettysburg, PA 17325. Vast collection of 18,000 photographs, other campaign and Battle of Gettysburg material.

Military Order of the Loyal Legion of the U.S. War Library and Museum, 1805 Pine St., Philadelphia, PA 19103. 10,000-volume Civil War collection.

Union League of Philadelphia Library, 140 South Broad St., Philadelphia, PA 19102. Significant Civil War collection including Secretary of War Edwin Stanton's papers, with fascinating commentary on Lincoln's assassination.

University of Pittsburgh Hillman Library, Pittsburgh, PA 15260. 10,000 volumes, including the collections of John Hay, the McClellan-Lincoln collection (partial, see Brown University John Hay Library, below), Eli H. Canfield, Elmer Ellsworth, Rush C. Hawkins, William Corliss, and Augustus Woodbury.

U.S. Army Military Institute, Carlisle Barracks, Carlisle, PA 17013. Large Civil War collection of personal letters, diaries, and memoirs of Union and C.S.A. military men.

RHODE ISLAND

Brown University John Hay Library, 20 Prospect St., Providence, RI 02912. Houses the McClellan-Lincoln collection, one of the most esteemed Lincoln holdings, acquired for Brown by John D. Rockefeller. Comprises some 15,000 volumes and much related material. Significant broadsides, including Carrier Addresses.

Providence Public Library, 150 Empire St., Providence, R.I. 02903. Harris collection of slavery and Civil War regimental histories, accounts of war by women, and writings of abolitionists.

SOUTH CAROLINA

College of Charleston Library, Charleston, S.C. 29401. Wartime records from Bank of Charleston; personal letters, papers of area families and individuals.

South Carolina Historical Society Library, 100 Meeting St., Charleston, SC 29401. 50,000 volumes relating to the state's pivotal role in secession and the war itself.

University of South Carolina Library, Columbia, SC 29208. Reputedly the South's richest collection; strong in regimental histories of both Union and C.S.A.

TENNESSEE

Lincoln Memorial University Carnegie Library, Harrogate, TE 37752. Abraham Lincoln Center for Lincoln Studies was established here. One of the country's largest Lincoln and Civil War collections. Including material from National Civil War Council Center regarding military surgery and medicine; also Center for Study of Military Music, with 7,000 sheet music entries dating from the War of 1812.

Memphis Pink Palace Museum Library, 3050 Central Ave., Memphis, TE 3811. Numerous books on loan from Shiloh Military Trail and other sources.

Public Library of Nashville and Davidson County, 8th Ave., North at Union St., Nashville, TE 37203.

University of Tennessee Chattanooga Library, Chattanooga, TE 37401. 3,500 volume Civil War collection; emphasis on the C.S.A. standpoint, just as Wilder collection takes Northern stance.

TEXAS

Rice University Fondren Library, 6100 South Main St., P.O. Box 2179, Huntsville, TX. Several Civil War collections of military records, diaries, letters.

Sam Houston State University Library, P.O. Box 2179, Huntsville, TX 77340. Porter Confederate collection rich in lore of Texas' role in the Civil War.

University of Texas Libraries, P.O. Box P, Austin, TX 78713. Littlefield collection of research materials is strong on ante-bellum Southern history.

VIRGINIA

George C. Marshall Research Foundation and Library, Drawer 920, Lexington, VA 24450. Civil War code material from the famed William Friedman collection.

Petersburg National Battlefield Library, 601 Court Street, Petersburg, VA 23804. Detailed accounts of siege of Petersburg, one of war's bloodiest battles.

Portsmouth Public Library, 601 Court St., Portsmouth, VA 23704. Emphasis in Tidewater and Lower Tidewater naval history.

University of Virginia Alderman Library, Charlottesville, VA 22901. Some 1,500 collections concentrated here with special focus on the Army of Northern Virginia and campaigns and battles in the state. Papers of Gens. R.E. Lee, J.E.B. Stuart, Jubal Early, William Smith, Eppa Hunton, John S. Mosby, John D. Imboden, Henry A. Wise, and others.

Virginia State Library, 12th and Capital Streets, Richmond, VA 23319. Includes extensive collection of photographic and printed images.

Washington and Lee University Library, Lexington, VA 24450. Over 25,000 volumes and 10,000 manuscripts detail life of R.E. Lee, Virginia, and the Civil War. Includes 8,000 glass-plate photographs by Miley.

WISCONSIN

State Historical Society of Wisconsin Archives, 816 State St., Madison, WI 53706. Regimental papers and other material relating to states participation in the Civil War.

University of Wisconsin Memorial Library, 728 State St., Madison, WI 53706. Very unusual and scarce collection of the military brass band that marched with Gen. William T. Sherman's army.

University of Wisconsin Milwaukee Library, 3203 North Denver St., Milwaukee, WI 53201. Allen M. Slichter collection gives C.S.A. spin to war.

CURRENT CIVIL WAR PERIODICALS

Led by *Civil War Times Illustrated*, the largest circulation monthly publication with 160,000 readers, Civil War coverage is intense, exciting, and replete with offerings of vintage artifacts; also replications of goods plus services of interest to reenactors as well as scholars and collectors.

America's Civil War. Leesburg, VA.

(The) Artilleryman. Published quarterly by Cutter & Locke, Inc., 4 Water St., P.O. Box C, Arlington, MA 02174.

Blue & Gray Magazine. Pub. monthly by Blue & Gray Enterprises, Inc., P.O. Box 28685, Columbus, OH 43228.

Camp Chase Gazette. Published 10 times a year. 3984 Cincinnati-Zanesville Rd., N.E., Lancaster, OH 43130.

Civil War Book Exchange & Collector's Newspaper. Published 6 times a year. Cutter & Locke, Inc., 4 Water St., P.O. Box C, Arlington, MA 02174.

Civil War Magazine. Published bi-monthly by the Civil War Society. Country Publishers, Inc., 133 East Main St., P.O. Box 798, Berryville, VA 22611.

Civil War News. Newspaper published 9 times a year. P.O. Box C, Arlington, MA 02174.

Civil War Times Illustrated. Published monthly by Cowles Magazines, 2245 Kohn Rd, P.O. Box 8200, Harrisburg, PA 17105-8200.

Confederate Veteran. Published bi-monthly by the Sons of Confederate Veterans. Non-members may also subscribe. P.O. Box 820169, Houston, TX 77282-0169.

(The) Courier. Another collector publication. P.O. Box 1863, Williamsville, NY 14221.

Grave Matters. Newsletter for necrolithographers and those in quest of Civil War burial grounds. Steve Davis, 1163 Warrenhall Lane, Atlanta, GA 30319.

Journal of Confederate History. Published quarterly (book length). Guild Bindery Press, P.O. Box 2071, Lakeway Station, Paris, TN 37752-0901.

Lincoln Herald. Published quarterly (since early 1900s) by The Lincoln Memorial University Press, Harrogate, TN 37752-0901.

North South Trader's Civil War. Published monthly. 918 Caroline St., Fredericksburg, VA 22401.

Southern Partisan. Review published quarterly. Recently founded Southern Heritage Society; membership dues also include quarterly newsletter championing cause of keeping C.S.A. flags flying.

Union Times. Published 8 times a year by UADF, 7214 Laurel Hill Rd., Orlando, FL 32818. Covers upcoming Civil War commemorative events and reenactments.

COLLECTOR'S GENERAL AND SPECIALTY PUBLICATIONS

Antique Toy World. P.O. Box 34509, Chicago, IL 60634. Monthly. Devoted to entire world of toys, games, and banks.

Antiques & the Arts Weekly (Newtown Bee). Newtown, CT 06470. Weekly tabloid newspaper; covers major shows, auctions, museum collections, including black and Civil War related.

Antiques Review. Published monthly; tabloid newspaper. 12 East Stafford, Worthington, OH 43085. General antiques, but includes toys, Americana, and Civil War related articles.

Guide to Buyers, Sellers & Traders of Black Collectibles. CGL Box 158472, Nashville, TE 37215. Monthly newsletter.

Keynoter. Published tri-annually. Official American Political Items Collector pub. For membership form, write P.O. Box 340339, San Antonio, TX 78234.

Major Civil War–Related Organizations

Armies of Tennessee, CSA and USA, Mickey M. Walker, Commanding General, P.O. Box 91, Rosedale, IN 47874.

Association for the Preservation of Civil War Sites, Inc. (APCWS), Gary W. Gallagher, President, P.O. Box 1862, Fredericksburg, VA 22402.

Children of the Confederacy, P.O. Box 4868, Richmond, VA 23220.

Civil War Press Corps, Lt. Col. Joseph Malcolm, P.O. Box 856, Colonial Heights, VA 23834.

Civil War Round Table Association, Jerry L. Russell, National Chairman, P.O. Box 7388, Little Rock, AR 72217.

Civil War Token Society, Cynthia Grellman, Secretary, P.O. Box 3412, Lake Mary, FL 32746.

Confederate Historical Institute, P.O. Box 7388, Little Rock, AR 72217.

Confederate Memorial Literary Society, The Museum of the Confederacy, 1201 East Clay St., Richmond, VA 23221.

Daughters of Union Veterans, Vivian Getz, Treasurer, 503 South Walnut St., Springfield, IL 62704.

Hood's Texas Brigade Association, Col. Harold B. Simpson, Director, Hill College History Complex, P.O. Box 619, Hillsboro, TX 76645.

Institute of Civil War Studies, International Institute for Advanced Studies, Suite 403, 8000 Bonhomme St., Clayton, MO 63105.

Jefferson Davis Association, Frank E. Vandine, President, P.O. Box 1892, Rice University, Houston, TX 77251.

Ladies of the GAR, Elizabeth B. Koch, 204 East Sellers Ave., Ridley Park, PA 19078.

Military Order of the Loyal Legion, William A. Hamann III, Recorder-in-Chief, 1805 Pine St., Philadelphia, PA 19103.

Military Order of the Stars and Bars, William D. McCain, Adjutant General, Box 5164, Southern Station, Hattiesburg, MS 39406.

Military Order of the Zouave Legion, B.F. Scalley, Acting Adjutant General, 513 Greynolds Circle, Lantana, FL 33462.

National Lincoln–Civil War Council, Edgar G. Archer, Director, P.O. Box 533, Harrogate, TN 37752.

National Society of Andersonville, Helen H. Harden, Secretary, P.O. Box 65, Andersonville, GA 31711.

National Woman's Relief Corps, Florence Rodgers, Treasurer, 629 South 7th St., Springfield, IL 62703.

Robert E. Lee Memorial Association, Lt. Gen. John F. Wall, Stratford Hall Plantation, Stratford, VA 22558.

Sam Davis Memorial Association, Katherine Walkup, Regent, P.O. Box 1, Smyrna, TN 37167.

Sons of Confederate Veterans, Adjutant-in-Chief, Southern Station, P.O. Box 5164, Hattiesburg, MS 39401.

Sons of Sherman's March, Stan Schirmacher, Director, 1725 Farmer Ave., Tempe, AZ 85281.

Sons of Union Veterans, Frank Miller Heacock, Suite 614, 200 Washington St., Wilmington, DE 19801.

Ulysses S. Grant Association, Ralph G. Newman, President, Morris Library, Southern Illinois University, Carbondale, IL 62901.

United Daughters of the Confederacy, Mrs. Donald R. Perkey, P.O. Box 4868, Richmond, VA 23220.